THE RED ORCHESTRA

WITNESSES TO WAR

LIVING THROUGH THE BLITZ
Tom Harrisson

INTO THE VALLEY
John Hersey

MOLLIE & OTHER WAR PIECES
A. J. Liebling

THIS IS LONDON
Edward R. Murrow
edited by Elmer Davis

ORWELL: THE WAR COMMENTARIES
edited by W. J. West

THE RED ORCHESTRA
Gilles Perrault

THE RED ORCHESTRA

GILLES PERRAULT

*TRANSLATED
BY*

PETER WILES

SCHOCKEN BOOKS / NEW YORK

English translation copyright © 1969 by Simon and Schuster, Inc.

All rights reserved under International and Pan-American
Copyright Conventions. Published in the United States
by Schocken Books Inc., New York. Distributed by
Pantheon Books, a division of Random House, Inc., New York.

Originally published in French as *L'Orchestre Rouge* by
Librairie Arthème Fayard, Paris in 1967. Copyright ©
1967 by Librairie Arthème Fayard. This translation
originally published by Simon and Schuster, Inc. in 1969.

Perrault, Gilles.
[Orchestre rouge. English]
The red orchestra/Gilles Perrault.
p. cm.—(Witnesses to war)
Translation of: L'orchestre rouge.
Reprint. Originally published: New York:
Simon and Schuster, 1969.
ISBN 0-8052-0952-2
1. Trepper, Léopold, 1904–   . 2. World War, 1939–1945—Secret
service—Soviet Union.   3. Spies—Soviet Union—Biography.
I. Title. II. Series.
D810.S8T653   1989
940.54'8647—dc20
89-42657

Manufactured in the United States of America
Display Typography by Eric Baker Design/Susie Oberhelman
First Paperback Edition

FOR MY PARENTS,
GEORGES AND GERMAINE PEYROLES,
WHO PLAYED IN ANOTHER ORCHESTRA.

CONTENTS

Prelude

Walter Schmidt took off his earphones, scraped back his chair and tried to ease some life into his limbs. He felt tired and depressed. The signs of another June day had begun to appear above the horizon, but in the East Prussian summer the hours of darkness are soon counted. He looked at his watch. Three-thirty. His shift did not end until six, and meanwhile he had nothing whatever to do except stay tuned to the Norwegian Resistance. Strictly routine. The transmitter, tucked away in the mountains, was fed and operated by a small group of partisans. Night after night, at three forty-eight precisely, they made contact with London and relayed a message consisting of ten or a dozen coded groups. Schmidt knew that a team of German experts had been sent to Norway with orders to track down the secret station. Easier said than done: the mountains had a screening effect and made the signals hard to pinpoint. Attempts had been made to solve the problem from above, by installing direction finders in a small spotter plane. But as soon as the Fieseler Storch flew over the fjords, the transmitter went off the air. The crew would continue to hunt so long as their fuel lasted, then fly home empty-handed.

But they'd catch them in the end; they always did. And did it really matter? Schmidt was unable to work up much feeling about the Norwegian underground. The Norwegians were transmitting to London, and London was doomed. There seemed little point to recording all these messages and trying to break the code, when the originals would soon be readily obtainable from a London office. The Führer may have called off the invasion of Britain, but he was merely biding his time. The old lion was being kept as a tidbit, to be consumed at leisure after the Russian bear had been hacked to pieces. Four days earlier, on June 22, 1941, German Panzer divisions had swarmed across the River Bug and flattened the Soviet frontier guards beneath their metal caterpillars. Since then, the High Command had been very sparing with details of the operations. This was a good sign. The same reticence had been displayed in May, 1940, at the start of the Battle of France—what was the point of supplying the fleeing,

9

disorganized French generals with valuable information? And now the Russian generals were in the same predicament, with no way of knowing exactly where the front lay. Why should the Wehrmacht tell them? In a few days, when the fighting was nearly over, Radio Berlin would put out a special communiqué, preceded as usual by the triumphant blare of trumpets, to announce the destruction of the Red Army. But Walter Schmidt would not join the victory parade below the walls of the Kremlin. He would still be here in Kranz, doggedly keeping track of the inconsequential messages of a phantom transmitter.

The Kranz monitoring station was within a few hundred yards of the Baltic. Schmidt stared despondently at the dunes above the beach. No gulls flying this morning—they had retreated inland. Their absence meant there would almost certainly be a storm before the new day was over, but Schmidt did not know how to read the signs. He was from the Bavarian mountains. The bleakness of these Prussian wastes sapped his spirits; he felt more depressed than ever. He returned to his bench, put on the earphones, tuned the receiver to 15, 465 kilocycles, the frequency employed by the Norwegian Resistance, and lethargically awaited the call-signal which would come speeding through the ether at three forty-eight precisely.

———◆———

The three paragraphs above are more or less pure invention. I do not know the identity of the German radio operator responsible for tuning in to the Norwegian transmitter on the night of June 25– 26, 1941. I have no information concerning his frame of mind. Nor am I familiar with the migratory urges, local or intercontinental, of Prussian seagulls; a storm may have been brewing over Kranz on June 26, 1941, but that is pure speculation.

Thus, although I have elected to show the radio operator at Kranz a Bavarian consumed with disappointment at his inability to join in the sweeping advance on the eastern front, I might equally well have depicted him as a fat sluggard thanking his lucky stars for being spared the choking dust of the Russian roads, or even as a fanatical Nazi waiting, stern-jawed, for those Norwegian Schwein- hunde *to transmit their message. The fact is that if I were to confine myself to the few authenticated items of information available, I should be restricted to writing as follows:*

The monitoring station at Kranz had orders to intercept secret transmissions. On the night of June 25–26, 1941, one of the operators tuned in at the usual time to the frequency used by a Norwegian transmitter. But the call sign he picked up was not the one usually put out by the Norwegians; indeed, it was quite unknown to him: "KLK from PTX . . . KLK from PTX . . . KLK from PTX . . ." The call sign was followed by a message made up of several cipher groups. The operator reported his discovery and listed the frequency employed.

These quiet beginnings heralded a campaign which was to become a nightmare to Reichsführer Himmler and Admiral Canaris, the heads of Germany's two secret services, and which eventually prompted Adolf Hitler to declare, on May 17, 1942, "The Bolsheviks are our superiors in only one field—espionage." And at that time the Führer had been given little more than a glimpse into the stunning achievements of the Red Orchestra.

PART I

THE NETWORK

1. The Schooling of a Leader

In the jargon of the German secret services, the head of a spy network was a *Kapellmeister*, a *chef d'orchestre*—an orchestra leader who directed and coordinated the playing of his instrumentalists.

The hero of this story, Leopold Trepper, is a Polish Jew born in Neumarkt, near Zakopane, on February 23, 1904. His father, a traveling salesman, wore himself out in his efforts to provide for his wife and ten children. He died when young Leopold was nearly twelve. The boy proved unusually bright, and his family decided that no sacrifice was too great to give him a good start in life. At that time Poland was still in the grip of strong anti-Semitic traditions and subject to a military dictatorship; it was bled white by war and economic upheavals. These adverse conditions lengthened the odds against the Treppers. It was rather as if the survivors on the raft of the *Medusa* had donated their meager rations to one of their number, to give him strength to clamber to the top of the mast.

After completing his schooling in Lvov, Leopold went on to study history and literature at the University of Krakow. He was then eighteen, and the future began to look hopeful. He contrived to keep body and soul together with the help of a small scholarship and the unstinting sacrifices of his family. His tutors thought well of him. A year later Poland was hit by an economic crisis, and the university student began his long fight against hunger. Inevitably it ended in defeat.

In 1924 he gave up his studies and became in turn a mason and a locksmith. But the crisis worsened, disrupting the lives even of artisans. The young man came slipping down his mast until he was flat on the ground, indeed, below it—down in the mines of Katowice. After two years he emerged, to work as a laborer in a Dombrova foundry. He was still hungry. The whole of Dombrova was hungry. Maddened by their poverty, the workers rose; but their rebellion was swiftly crushed by the Polish lancers. Trepper was found to be one of the ringleaders. He was arrested and thrown into jail. He was then twenty-two years old, and his hunger was as intense as ever.

A photograph of the secret Communist cell to which he belonged has survived undetected despite the stringent searches of the prewar Polish police and later of the Gestapo. It shows ten or a dozen very young men with shaven heads and set, remote expressions. They are all alike; a shared passion dwells within them, and the strain under which they are living gives their features a uniform harshness. They are at once wild and hopeless. If clad in flying suits rather than these skimpy jackets, they could easily pass for a squadron of Japanese suicide pilots. Trepper himself is easily identifiable from the photograph. Even when age and suffering would have undermined the granite firmness of his face, he would still be recognized by those pale-gray eyes, whose implacability could change to a surprising tenderness.

Trepper spent eight months in the jails of the Pilsudski dictatorship. The methods of interrogation used on members of the outlawed Communist Party were even more savage than those later practiced by the Gestapo, the most common being the medieval water torture. Eventually Trepper was released without even the formalities of a legal trial. He set out for Warsaw. He took nothing from the town of Dombrova except the first four letters of its name; for the next ten years his alias was Domb. Subsequently he became known as the "Big Chief," both to his own men and to the members of the Gestapo.

There were no jobs available in Warsaw for a man who had taken part in the Dombrova uprising. He applied for an immigration visa for France, but this was refused; the French authorities were in no hurry to import an industrial agitator. Trepper was well aware, however, that he could not go on living in Poland; there he had no future except to die of starvation.

His last hope lay in the "Hechalutz" organization. He sought admission, was enrolled and managed to slip out of Poland at last. Hechalutz was a Zionist body financed by wealthy American Jews. Its aim was to promote immigration to the Promised Land. Palestine was still under British mandate, and the British were remarkably successful at keeping out the tragic throng, who were to perish in the gas ovens of Auschwitz, only a few years later—admittedly, a fate which the territory's administrators could not have foreseen. Hechalutz was responsible for picking the small, privileged band of immigrants officially allowed into the country each year. With a typically

American regard for future returns, the organization's backers sought to fight Communism even as they furthered the Zionist cause. Preference was therefore given to candidates who appeared to be easy prey for the Party's recruiting agents. With his frustrated ambitions, unhappy past and uncertain future, Leopold Trepper fulfilled every requirement. He was given a sum of money and put aboard a train which took him by way of Vienna and Trieste to the port of Brindisi, where he took ship for Palestine. He was then twenty-four and quite unaware that hunger had followed him out of Poland.

It accosted him like a stanch old friend almost as soon as he stepped ashore at Haifa. After a spell of stone-breaking on the roads, he became an agricultural worker in a kibbutz. The most congenial job to come his way in Palestine was an apprenticeship in an electrical engineering works. It definitely looked as though the Trepper family sacrifices had all been in vain, for what hope was there now of Leopold's ever reaching the top of the mast? But certain reports indicate that in 1929 he became a member of the Central Committee of the Palestinian Communist Party—which, if true, would mean that it was the backers of Hechalutz who had wasted their dollars.

Be that as it may, the Unity group was unquestionably his handiwork. Communist-inspired, it sought to unite Jews and Arabs against the British administration. Trepper and his associates were rounded up and jailed in 1930. Forewarned of a plan to deport them to Cyprus, Trepper called a hunger strike. It was not taken seriously at first, but the strikers persevered. The London newspapers began to speak out, and questions were asked in the Commons. Britain's High Commissioner in Palestine decided to release these inconvenient prisoners. Since they were too weak to walk, they were placed on stretchers and set down outside the prison gates.

A few weeks later, Trepper effected an illegal entry into France. For a time he was a dishwasher in a Marseilles restaurant; then he proceeded to Paris, where he became a housepainter. This was destined to be the last of the long series of implausible trades carried on by Leopold Trepper. He had now discovered his true vocation. The man who was subsequently to achieve fame as the "Big Chief" was beginning his apprenticeship.

<hr />

In those days the Soviet Union had a spy network operating in France which was amazingly simple in conception as well as admirably effective. It was based on the *rabcors* system, involving the use of "worker-correspondents." The idea derived from Lenin himself. The revolution had driven the majority of experienced Russian journalists into exile, as they belonged to the bourgeoisie; and since there was a shortage of trained professionals to replace them, amateurs had been asked to come forward. Ordinary workers in factories and collective farms set themselves up as press correspondents and flooded the Soviet newspapers with articles discussing local problems and denouncing traitors and saboteurs. The police took full advantage of the scheme; so did the Russian secret service, after the decision to apply the same system abroad.

By 1929 there were three thousand *rabcors* in France, some of them employed in state arsenals or in factories where war materials were manufactured. The ostensible purpose of their contributions to the Communist press was to denounce the poor working conditions to which they were subjected, but they could hardly do so without supplying bits and pieces of information about the work itself. The more revealing articles were never published. They were passed to the Soviet embassy in Paris, which forwarded them to Moscow. If a given *rabcor* seemed well informed on a subject of really worthwhile interest, an agent would call and question him until a complete picture had been built up.

This highly profitable organization functioned with undisturbed efficiency for three whole years. In February, 1932, a denunciation was laid before the French police. Despite this lucky break, it took the superintendent in charge of the case—a man with the disquieting name of Faux-Pas-Bidet—more than six months to dismantle the network. His reports are unsparing in their praise of the spies he was endeavoring to track down. Their leader, in particular, was remarkably adept at giving his pursuers the slip and emerging unscathed from their traps; he seemed to have drawn up a list of every house in Paris with a double exit. The police, however exasperated, felt a real admiration for their quarry and nicknamed him Fantômas.* When at last they caught him, they discovered that he was a Polish Jew who had come to France by way of Palestine. He was twenty-eight years old and his name was Isaiah Bir. His deputy was twenty-seven; like Bir, a Polish Jew who had entered the country after a brief spell in Palestine. His name was Alter Ström.

Their professional technique amazed the French police. It wasn't

---

* Fantômas is the hero of a long line of thrillers by Marcel Allain.—TRANSLATOR

Fantômas they were interrogating, but the perfect embodiment of the "man in the street." Bir lived in a cheap hotel and never received any mail or any visitors. Most of the time, he kept in touch with his group through a young woman who was generally presumed to be his mistress. A drab system, but effective: the network was subdivided into such watertight compartments that most of the agents escaped arrest. Among them was Leopold Trepper, who had been a childhood friend of Alter Ström. Working under Fantômas had been a highly educational experience for Trepper. When the Gestapo were after him, a few years later, it would have paid them to refer to the dossier compiled by Charles Faux-Pas-Bidet; but apparently they never did. They imagined they were thoroughly conversant with Leopold Trepper's activities, yet they remained blind to his existence as Leiba Domb.

Trepper was twenty-eight when he escaped the police haul by hurriedly boarding a train. As soon as he reached Berlin he made contact with the Soviet embassy. After a few days' delay he was instructed to travel to Moscow by a certain train. When it arrived, he was to remain in his compartment after the other passengers got out: someone would come and collect him. Trepper complied with all this. He had no idea of the future they had in mind for him, but he must have been hoping that some new mission would come his way within a short time. In fact, he waited for four years. Despite his turbulent past and his fund of varied experiences, and despite his activities under the direction of Fantômas, he was regarded in Moscow as no more than a promising apprentice.

And so, in 1932, eight years after leaving the University of Krakow, Trepper went back to school.

— ✦ —

So much for the early life of the Big Chief. In my account, I have jumped from place to place and year to year, as if Poland and Palestine, Paris and Moscow, were mere steppingstones across a narrow stream.

But it is easier to summarize twenty years of a man's existence than to give a full and accurate account of a single quarter of an hour within that span. Take, for instance, the memorable occasion when Trepper met Georgie de Winter. It happened in Brussels, in 1939. Georgie was the daughter of a tall, lanky, strikingly handsome American, a cross between Gary Cooper and Cary Grant, who was a set designer at Paramount Studios in Hollywood and was trying to make his way as an actor. After returning to Belgium with her mother, Georgie led the life of a young girl of good family, and studied classical dancing. She was twenty years old and very beautiful. Photographs show how radiant she was, with her sparkling eyes, graceful bearing and perfect figure. Twenty years later, when the survivors came to tell their story they made Georgie sound like a cool, serene oasis unexpectedly encountered during a long and horrible journey.

Trepper was thirty-five at the time. He was not exactly handsome. The intriguing, powerfully wrought head and features were an asset; so were the wavy blond hair and those expressive eyes. But he was thickset and only of middling height. His appeal lay elsewhere, in a personal magnetism stemming from a mixture of ferocity and gentleness. Bill Hoorickx, an artist, calls him "a really big, commanding figure, with the strength and vitality of a bull." "He made you feel he was always living under pressure," adds Monsieur Mignon, printer. But Madame Queyrie, an officeworker, brings out the other side of his nature: "His heart was in the right place. He was the kindest of men." And Claude Spaak, a writer, takes the same view: "He displayed an infinite humanity." Trepper possessed an inner strength that soothed and allayed fears; in his presence everything became simple. He would have made an excellent father-confessor.

———◆———

They met one day when Georgie went into a shop to buy some pastries. As she was paying the bill, she happened to drop her gloves. Trepper rushed forward and retrieved them for her. Disarmed by his eagerness, intrigued by the way he talked, she agreed to see him again. A few months later, when Brussels was occupied by the Wehrmacht, she was out walking with a woman friend. A German officer went by on the other side of the street, and she saw him drop his gloves. A man sped along the pavement, picked them up and handed them to the German. The man was Trepper; Georgie decided he must have a mania for picking up gloves. She did not approach him, for he had forbidden her to do so when either of them was in company. But all this was still in the future. . . .

They met. To Georgie, of course, Trepper seemed no more than he claimed to be—a man with a good head for business. How could she possibly guess that her agreeably portly friend had helped foment an uprising in Poland, toiled as a stone breaker in Palestine and been the secret accomplice of Fantômas? There was nothing to indicate that he had come from Moscow, or to suggest what he had been up to in the Soviet capital.

What, in fact, *had* he been up to?

From 1932 until 1934, he had studied at Prodrovsky University. In 1935 he had contributed a column on the arts to *Truth*, a newspaper for Russian Jews. But he had also been a student at the Red Army Academy, where General Orlov taught espionage. In 1937 his friend Ström, Fantômas's former deputy, returned from France after completing his prison sentence. He threw doubts on the accepted version of the events which had led to the network's destruction. Previously, guilt had been attributed without question to a man called Riquier, who worked on the editorial staff of *L'Humanité*. Ström expressed strong doubts on this score, however, and he proposed that Trepper be sent to Paris to bring the full truth to light. In 1937, five years after his flight, Trepper returned to France with a forged passport made out in the name of Sommer. Pretending to be a relative of Ström, he began by conferring with the two principal lawyers who had served at the trial—Ferrucci, and André Philip, the well-known Socialist leader. Then he embarked on an investigation in depth. After a few months he decided that Riquier was definitely innocent. His conclusion was important, for it cleared the French Communist Party of harboring an informer. But Trepper did even better than that: he unmasked the real traitor, who turned out to be a Dutch Jew, former head of a Soviet spy ring in the United States. The man had been picked up by the F.B.I. and had agreed to switch loyalties, continuing to feed the Americans with information even after Moscow had transferred him to France. The denunciation of Fantômas's network had come to the Sûreté from the F.B.I. Trepper returned to Moscow to make his report, this time using a Luxembourg passport bearing the name Majeris. He informed his superiors that documentary evidence was being assembled in Paris which would establish the truth beyond all doubt. Five months later he went back to France and collected a thick bundle of papers—photostats of the letters which had passed between the Dutch-born traitor and the American military attaché in Paris.

The "businessman" whom Georgie was to meet in a Brussels pastry shop had come to Belgium to set up a new network. And this time he would be in charge as the "Big Chief."

They met and found each other attractive. This would seem to point to a happy beginning, counterbalancing the horror that would surround the end of their relationship. But Georgie, for all her charm, was five months pregnant by a lover who had decamped. And Trepper, for all his kindliness, was betraying Luba, his companion through the bad times. He had met Luba in Palestine, where she had been active in the Unity group. She and Trepper were the same age, both of them Jewish, both of them Poles. Like his, her formative years in Poland had been discolored by poverty and the struggle against oppression. In the days when he was still imagining that he could hoist himself to the top of the mast, she was working in a chocolate factory, studying at night, hoping to become a school-teacher. She was a Communist militant and belonged to a cell run by a youth named Botvin. At about that time a Polish informer was wreaking havoc within the outlawed Party. After two unsuccessful attempts on his life by other groups, the Jewish cell operating under Botvin decided to square accounts with him, and he was duly disposed of. Luba then fled to Palestine, where she worked with Trepper. She was arrested while taking part in an illegal Communist demonstration and was sentenced to prison; she would have been deported had she not gone through the motions of marrying a Palestinian citizen. Finally, anxious to join Trepper in France, she passed herself off as the wife of a Syrian Arab, so that she might share his passport.

Clearly, when a relationship has been forged in circumstances like these, there can be no question of the usual bourgeois comedy of infidelity. It was not long before Trepper brought the two women together. He was secretive in all things, apparently, except affairs of the heart. But again I am rushing ahead of events; at this point Trepper is still picking up Georgie's gloves, while Luba and her two children await his return to their luxurious apartment. The elder boy had been born in Paris in 1931, but his parents, having entered the country illegally, had been unable to register his birth. The younger was born in Moscow in 1936. The child who will later play a part in this story, however, was not Luba and Trepper's, but the male infant growing to life in Georgie's womb.

2. The Foreign Excellent Trench Coat Company

Michael Dzumaga, a Canadian citizen born in Winnipeg on August 2, 1914, had enlisted in one of the International Brigades set up to fight Franco. He landed in Spain as bearer of passport Number 43671, issued in 1937. This passport was taken away from him as soon as he arrived. What happened to Dzumaga afterward I cannot say. He may be alive or he may be dead; but if he ever went back to Canada, it was certainly without his passport. This, appropriately doctored and now bearing the name Mikler, was in the possession of the Big Chief. Dzumaga's experience was a common one: nearly all Anglo-Saxons who joined the International Brigades found themselves deprived of their papers for the greater benefit of Soviet Intelligence.

The Big Chief, now alias Adam Mikler, came to Brussels in the autumn of 1938. He at once made contact with a Jewish businessman, Leo Grossvogel, whom he had met in Palestine. Grossvogel came of a line of prosperous burghers who had been in Strasbourg for several generations. After a short, romantic stay in Palestine, he had returned to the world of business. From Brussels he ran a business called "Le Roi du Caoutchouc" ("The Raincoat King"); it had many branches and specialized in all lines of rainwear. An ardent Communist, he fell in unreservedly with the projects that Trepper outlined to him. Trepper had ten thousand dollars at his disposal. His idea was to invest it in an export business which would serve as a cover for the network's activities. A new company was floated and given an unidiomatic English name, "Foreign Excellent Trench Coat Company"—another rainwear concern. The management was entrusted to a plump, jovial Belgian in his late fifties or early sixties, a *bon vivant* with a white mustache and ruddy cheeks: Jules Jaspar. This was a master stroke. The Jaspar family was one of the country's outstanding bourgeois dynasties. Jules's brother had been prime minister; one of the streets in the capital was named after him. Jules himself had long served as Belgian consul in Indochina, and later in Scandinavia.* Armed with such a figurehead, the firm was above suspicion. Nat-

---

* His nephew was, until recently, Belgian ambassador in Paris.

urally he had no inkling of the dark secrets lurking beneath his trench coats.

The Big Chief spent most of 1939 setting up the new network and giving it a trial run. By the time the Second World War broke out, he was ready and waiting.

By a strange coincidence, the first mission assigned by Moscow to the Soviet agent Trepper bore a marked similarity to the mission entrusted by Berlin to the German agent Leverkuehn.

———◆———

In March, 1940, Paul Leverkuehn of the Abwehr was given the highly unusual and colorful job of exploring an unknown region. Assignments in the twentieth century are generally more prosaic, even when secret. The area in question was traversed by the ancient Silk Road, once followed by Marco Polo. If there was an ounce of romance in him, Leverkuehn must have considered himself a lucky man.

The last shots in the Polish campaign had been fired six months earlier, and all was quiet in Europe now, except for the fighting around Lake Ladoga, where the Finns and Russians were locked in battle. The French and German armies sat and stared at each other across the Rhine—for this was the period of the Phony War. Leverkuehn's colleagues were keeping a watchful eye on the disposition of French forces and doing their best to pinpoint the forts in the Maginot Line. Their counterparts in the Deuxième Bureau were keeping a watchful eye on the disposition of the German forces and doing their best to pinpoint the forts in the Siegfried Line. There was no apparent reason why the Phony War should become any less boring in the foreseeable future. Leverkuehn packed his bags and set out for Tabriz, in Iran, where his "official" duties were to be those of German consul. The only serviceable map that he took with him was a world map, on the scale of one-to-a-million, on which the area which he had been sent to explore appeared as the white space denoting an "unknown region."

In March, 1940, the Russo-German Pact was at its zenith. Hitler and Stalin had teamed up to destroy Poland; now they were business partners. Huge quantities of Russian grain were being transported to Germany in place of the usual imports, halted by the British naval blockade. But even more important than Russian wheat and Russian phosphates and Russian cotton was Russian petroleum. This was the lifeblood of the Blitzkrieg, which played so large a part in the thinking of Germany's war leaders. To dissuade Stalin from cutting the precious link that reached from the Caucasus to the Panzer divisions of the Wehrmacht, Hitler agreed to sacrifices which seem almost unbelievable when we recall that he had already decided that he would eventually wage war on Russia. In return for supplying oil, Stalin received artillery, fighter and bomber aircraft, and a prodigious quantity of machine tools. On March 30 the Führer declared that deliveries of war material to Russia were to be given priority even over orders placed by the German army itself; he handed over the heavy cruiser *Lützow;* he even talked of selling Stalin the plans of the battleship *Bismarck,* which was to be the biggest in the world. For the sake of getting the fuel, Hitler was parting with weapons in the full knowledge that they would soon be turned against him. History offers few examples of so massive a forced sale.

The Russian oil was stored at Baku. The French General Weygand was in Syria with a force reputed to consist of a hundred and fifty thousand French troops. The distance from Syria to Baku is about six hundred miles, as the crow flies. The problem: if Weygand decided to launch a daring raid on Baku in the hope of destroying the wells, would he find the one traversable road through the Kara Dag mountains which alone would enable him to reach his objective?

The area which he had to reconnoiter was not entirely unknown to Leverkuehn. In 1915 he had taken part in the Schenber-Richter expedition to Persia, Syria and the Caucasus; in fact, he was the last surviving member—hence his selection for this second scouting mission. But a quarter of a century had gone by since his previous visit, and he knew nothing of the great works accomplished by the Shah of Persia (now Iran), Riza Pahlavi.

Taking only a chauffeur and an interpreter with him, he drove deep into the desert. He discovered very quickly that the track leading across the Kara Dag range could certainly be used by lightly equipped mountain troops. Continuing southward along the Silk Road, he examined the shores of Lake Urmia and pressed on as far as Saqqiz, where he was considerably demoralized by the sight of a magnificent concrete bridge. During a break in the journey, his driver and interpreter took a stroll and came upon a spectacle which dis-

tressed them even more: hanging from a gallows were the bodies of
two Kurdish highwaymen. Leverkuehn's companions refused to go
any farther. He tried to reason with them, pointing out that the eyes
of the German High Command were upon them; but they were not
to be swayed. So the party returned to Tabriz, and there Leverkuehn
learned that a car had been attacked within a few miles of the gallows;
one passenger was dead and two others wounded. The assailants had
been caught and had revealed that the true purpose of their mission
had been to kill the German consul. Leverkuehn blessed the cowardice of his companions and drew up his report for Berlin. It must have
made a considerable impression there, for its final conclusion was that
if Weygand were to launch a few divisions against Baku, they would
not meet any major obstacle, either geographical or human.

While Leverkuehn was studying the problem at first hand, the
Big Chief had been trying to work out the answer from a distance
of several thousand miles. For Stalin, like Hitler, was in fear of losing
his oil—*their* oil. It was General Weygand who, in 1920, had stemmed
the onrush of the resurgent Red Army before the walls of Warsaw.
His anti-Communist sentiments were notorious. If there was any
chance of a successful attack on Baku, he would not hesitate.

Trepper was able to set the Soviet leader's mind at rest. No
doubt Daladier, as Prime Minister of France, had asked the General
Staff to look into the possibility of destroying the Russian oil. But,
although an attack by land-based forces may have seemed entirely
feasible to Leverkuehn, no such step was ever contemplated by
General Gamelin, commander in chief of the French army. Instead,
he asked London to organize a combined naval operation which would
send a Franco-British task force all the way across the Black Sea.
This could be done only if Turkey agreed to jeopardize her neutral-
ity by opening the Dardanelles. The military chiefs asked the diplomats to do their utmost to persuade the Ankara government. When
the German Wehrmacht entered Paris a few months later, a complete
record of these abortive negotiations fell into their hands.

If the Big Chief's findings prompted relief in Moscow, any alarm
which Leverkuehn's may have occasioned in Berlin was short-lived.
Three weeks after his report arrived, German troops invaded Denmark and Norway. This sudden speeding-up of the war made an
attack on Baku unlikely. Stalin was taken completely by surprise.
For months he had been expecting an expeditionary force to land in
Scandinavia, but he had been sure it would be Anglo-French. And

he had calculated that its mission would be to march into Finland and do battle with the Red Army.

Stalin, of course, was soon to give even clearer evidence of his blindness: he was so neurotically obsessed with fear and hatred of far-off Britain that he altogether failed to notice the threatening buildup of German forces on his own borders. But in this present case he was convinced he was right, and his conviction was bolstered by the reports of his intelligence service.

It must be recalled that in the winter of 1940 the fate of Finland was very close to the hearts of the French and British peoples. If they found it hard to work up much feeling for the soldiers playing cards in the subterranean fastnesses of the Maginot Line, they were stirred by the exploits of the Finnish ski troops. These daunting, silent figures, enveloped in their white coveralls that made them invisible against the snow, were holding the Red Army pinned down in the northern forests. They fought with the valor of David, and Russia was inevitably seen as a monstrous Goliath. On the international stage, Stalin was cast, in the role that he would soon be handing on to his talented understudy, Mussolini—that of the villain administering the stab in the back. He had finished off Poland when she was already overpowered by Hitler, just as Mussolini would shortly strike at France in her hour of helplessness. Two months later, Stalin attacked Finland. He was expected to dispose of her in one bite, but to the general excitement and satisfaction, Finland refused to be gobbled up.

It is doubtful whether public opinion in the Allied countries held Germany in as much detestation as Russia at this stage. But it was in political and military circles, traditionally anti-Communist, that feelings ran really high. Allied generals were clearly tempted to forget the avowed enemy, Germany, whom they had within shooting distance, and "give the Russians their come-uppance." In February, 1940, General Weygand wrote to Gamelin: "I consider it essential to put 'Paid' to the Soviet Union in Finland and elsewhere." On becoming Prime Minister, Paul Reynaud informed the French war cabinet of his eagerness to act against Russia "either in northern Europe or in the Black Sea, south of the Caucasus." Gamelin recorded: "Nearly all members of the cabinet gave the impression that they cheerfully agreed to this war."

The Allies set about raising an expeditionary force of fifty-seven thousand specially equipped troops. Finland's Marshal Mannerheim confirms in his memoirs that he received an assurance from General Ironside, Chief of the British General Staff, that a first contingent of fifteen thousand men would be ready to move by the end of March. When the month was only two days old, Norway and Sweden turned down the Allies' application for right of passage. On March 8, Daladier informed Mannerheim that if Finland asked officially for Allied aid the expeditionary force would force its way across Scandinavia. Mannerheim was old enough and wise enough to decline the offer. During the Polish campaign he had watched a hundred and ten Allied divisions sitting idle, even though Hitler, active in the east had left only a buffer force of twenty-three divisions between the Rhine and Berlin. And all through the present winter of 1939–40 he had been keeping watch on the static Phony War. The Finnish Marshal had no faith in the Allies' fighting spirit; he doubted whether they had any real appetite for doing battle on the shores of Lake Ladoga, when they showed such perfect passivity on the banks of the Rhine. By the middle of March he was advising his government to negotiate an armistice with the Russians.

History had come close to dealing some very strange hands indeed. Think what would have happened if the Allies *had* clashed with Russia, either in the far South (Baku) or in the far North (Finland). Within a year, like it or not, they would have found themselves partners with Hitler against Stalin in Eastern Europe, even while they grappled with the Führer on the western front. Anything could have sprung from such confusion, including the defeat of the civilized world.

————◆————

These plans for an Allied intervention at Baku or in Finland sound flimsy today, and soon they will have lost all interest for everyone but the scholar enamored of the might-have-beens of history. But at that time, every piece of intelligence relating to them was unquestionably of vital importance to the Kremlin. For years Stalin had been proclaiming his grim warning: "The Second World War has already begun." But his political vision suffered from a pronounced imbalance; Berlin, Rome or Tokyo might cause him disquiet, but the focal point of his suspicions never shifted from London.

We have no direct knowledge of the reports sent in by the

Big Chief, but judging by his later work they must have been precise, well substantiated and thorough. If ever they emerge from the archives of the Kremlin, the world may be in a better position to understand why the intrigues of Mr. Neville Chamberlain should for a long while have appeared more daunting to Stalin than the intentions of the German Führer.

Indeed, at this point in the winter of 1939–40, Moscow was entirely ignorant of the nature of those intentions. The Gestapo had swept away the German Communist Party and put the Soviet spy networks out of action. Now that he had signed his pact with Hitler, Stalin was eager to stand by its terms: he forbade the setting-up of a new spy system. The chiefs of Soviet Intelligence knew that to disobey this order might well cost them their lives. They did disobey it, but only in a wary and limited fashion, contenting themselves with laying the foundations for future enterprises. Germany to them was such an "unknown region" that it might almost have been left blank on the map, like the area which Paul Leverkuehn had set out to explore.

Britain, on the other hand, was duly "ringed" by the Big Chief's network. Trepper had taken up residence in Brussels for legal and geographical reasons: Belgian law was exceptionally easygoing on spies, punishing their activities only if these were directed against the country's own interests. His mission was to invade the British Isles, using Belgium as a springboard. Nothing could be more characteristic of the meticulousness with which Soviet Intelligence always proceeds. When the German Abwehr tried to get at Britain's secrets, it was content to parachute a few luckless agents into the Home Counties, where they were very soon caught and hanged. The Russians, on the other hand, began by enmeshing their adversary in a vast net. Trepper spent the whole of 1939 weaving a spider's web around seven major seaports trading with Britain: Oslo, Stockholm, Copenhagen, Hamburg, Wilhelmshaven, Ostend and Boulogne. In most of them he set up branches of the Foreign Excellent Trench Coat Company, staffing them with his agents. The contacts which Jules Jaspar had established during his days in the consular service made operations in Scandinavia especially straightforward and smooth.

Thus, Germany was "clean," and the activities of the Big Chief's network were directed against Britain. The pattern of Soviet espionage in the west was curiously akin to those "impregnable" coastal bases, like Singapore, which in a year or so were to fall so easily to attacks from the interior—all their heavy guns were pointing out to sea. The Führer had already made up his mind to launch three million men against Russia, yet every one of the Big Chief's batteries, from Boulogne to Oslo, was trained on London.

Things could scarcely have got off to a worse start.

————◆————

On May 10, 1940, the Wehrmacht struck westward.

To the younger Nazis, the ease with which they swept through France came as no surprise—the Führer had promised them it would happen. But to Franz Fortner, a veteran of Verdun and other nightmares, there was something miraculous about it. As a lieutenant in the Panzerkorps, Fortner now covered as much ground in a single hour as he had once covered in six months. Instead of splashing about in foul-smelling trenches, he was bowling along macadamized roads and sunning his old scars through the open turret of his tank. War might follow war, but no two of them were alike, and this one was a big improvement on the last.

Fortner played his part in the big breakthrough and then in the dash to the Channel ports. On the outskirts of Dunkirk he was raised to captain and given command of a Panzer company. The roads were cluttered with prisoners, and as his tanks rumbled along they overtook long lines of refugees, whose creaking carts had to be thrust aside. Amid this tragic human tide was a civilian car which, for once, had no mattress lashed to its roof and no bird cage protruding from its open trunk. Clearly, the people in it were not refugees. Moreover, instead of fleeing, it was following the battle, slipping between the armored columns, prowling round the field H.Q., moving up to the front line with a fuel convoy, dodging both the Stuka machine guns and the Allied artillery. If Fortner saw the car, did he give it a second thought? He was just a soldier on active service, and problems of security did not directly concern him—not at this stage. Besides, when they stopped the car and checked the occupants' papers, German military police expressed immediate satisfaction and waved the vehicle on. The driver, Durov, was Bulgarian consul in Brussels: the respect due to his diplomatic status was intensified by the knowledge that his country was engaged in a political flirtation with Germany. Next to him sat Grossvogel; on the back seat, the Big Chief.

The car broke down between Knokke-le-Zoute and Brussels, as

it was driving alongside a column of SS. The colonel in charge was most obliging. He at once placed a car at the consul's disposal and had a young lieutenant transfer all the luggage from one vehicle to the other. It is easy to imagine the serene, approving eye with which Trepper watched the SS lieutenant carefully handling the valise containing his radio transmitter.

Durov, it seems, did not belong to the network. He was a friend of Grossvogel. More accurately, Grossvogel had a business relationship with a Bulgarian named Petrov, and the latter had introduced him to Durov. A few days after the invasion of Belgium, Grossvogel told Durov that he was desperately worried about trade. The Ostend branch of Le Roi du Caoutchouc had been destroyed by a German bomb, and he was anxious to know what had become of his other shops. Durov offered to take him on a tour of the firm's branches. Officially, the consul would be making the journey to ascertain the fate of Bulgarian nationals in the fighting zone. It takes a rather unusual human being to expose himself to the perils of battle on so illusory a pretext. . . .

The tour began on May 19, 1940, at the height of the Belgian campaign. The Big Chief, who had burnt his Canadian passport by this time, was afforded a ringside view of the Germans' exploitation of their breakthrough at Sedan, and then of the battle of Abbeville. He sped toward Dunkirk with Fortner's Panzer company and was an eyewitness to the fall of the town. In his pocket was a notebook crammed with facts and figures. He took a particular interest in the Wehrmacht's method of bringing up reinforcements, in the part played by the Stukas, and in the tactics used by the Panzers to knock out the enemy's antitank defenses. As soon as the trio had completed their tour, the Big Chief sent an eighty-page report to Moscow, giving a detailed account of the new strategy which Hitler had devised and carried out: the Blitzkrieg.

This report, like all its predecessors, was delivered via the Soviet embassy. Thanks to the diplomatic pouch, it was not yet necessary for Trepper to send his messages over the air; but he sensed that the radio would soon be his only link with Moscow—which was why he had risked his life retrieving the transmitter from its hiding place in a villa at Knokke.

Even as Molotov congratulated Hitler on the "splendid success achieved by the Wehrmacht," the Big Chief was getting ready for the Russo-German war that lay ahead; on his own initiative, he was pivoting his batteries around by a hundred and eighty degrees. They would no longer be trained on England, but on Germany.

———◆———

After the fall of France it was decided that the German army should be rejuvenated. All middle-aged officers were withdrawn from the front-line units. Franz Fortner, then forty-seven, had to say goodbye to his tanks and move to the Abwehr, which sent him to Belgium on counterespionage duties. The prescribed enemy was, of course, the British Intelligence Service; Fortner had been appointd to help safeguard the secrets of Operation Sea Lion, the code name given the projected invasion of Britain. But in the summer of 1940 he received a strange telegram from Berlin informing him that a Soviet mission, about thirty strong, had arrived in Brussels. True, Russia was supposed to be a friendly power, but all the same . . . Duly alerted, Fortner kept a vigilant eye on the members of the mission; but there was no sign of any suspicious activity, and when they left he was able to send a reassuring report to Berlin.

A few weeks later, another group of visitors arrived in Belgium. They were a hand-picked party, and their applications for visas had been thoroughly investigated, so the Abwehr did not feel in any way troubled by their presence. The team was made up of diplomats and senior officers from pro-German neutral countries like Hungary, Bulgaria, Spain and Rumania. The Germans were intent on wooing them; it was hoped that a demonstration of the Wehrmacht's invincibility would persuade them to join forces with the winning side. The visitors looked on in wonderment as they were shown over the sites of recent battles. German staff officers shepherded them everywhere, maps in hand, photographs at the ready, analyzing the victorious campaign in the calm tones of able technicians. To insure that every detail would be clear beyond doubt, each member of the group received a complementary dossier of events. Among those present was the Bulgarian consul, and sticking close to him wherever he went was a companion who remained as quiet and unobtrusive as a last-minute guest should always aim to be. It was the Big Chief.

3. Some South Americans in Brussels

September, 1965. Guillaume "Bill" Hoorickx, a Belgian artist, received me in his Paris studio on the Avenue Émile-Zola. Of medium height, very slim, with dark, alert eyes, he had the general appearance of a man in his early fifties. He was sixty-six years old and had suffered prolonged interrogation by the Gestapo, followed by imprisonment in Mauthausen concentration camp. He loathed talking about the past. His latest works hung on the studio walls, abstract paintings of remarkable beauty. On one of them was superimposed the sentence, "If I am not myself, who will be?"

Hoorickx says: "The military collapse in 1940 had driven me as far south as Tarbes, in the Hautes-Pyrénées. There I was employed in the arsenal. When the Germans arrived, we sabotaged the whole place. I had no experience of that kind of thing, of course, but the French showed me how, and we did a beautiful job of it. I think that's one of my most satisfying memories.

"Afterward I went back to Brussels and went to visit my wife. She and I had separated, but we remained good friends until the very end; I often went to see her. On one of those visits, before the war, I had met a Uruguayan named Carlos Alamo. He was extremely handsome and likable, and I soon realized that, although he might look like a tango dancer, there was far more to him than that. We had had lunch together two or three times.

"Anyway, when I got back from Tarbes, I went to find out how my wife was. She was living with Alamo. They told me that they had taken cover in Ostend during the general exodus from Brussels. Alamo ran a shop there. Selling raincoats, if I remember rightly.

"This has nothing to do with your story, but I may as well tell you about it. When I was repatriated in 1945, I found my wife suffering from cancer. 'I'm going to die,' she said, 'but I knew you'd come back, and I made up my mind to wait for you. Let's drink a bottle of champagne together.' We drank that bottle; and two days later my wife was dead.

"But to return to what I was saying: I met Carlos Alamo again. And at about the same time I made the acquaintance of a man called

Rauch, a Czechoslovakian. I can't remember where I bumped into him. In a bar, perhaps; or maybe at the St. James Club. Rauch was about fifty, tall and very dignified—the complete stockbroker. He was the Czech agent of a Belgian munitions firm. He, Alamo and I took to going out together.

"Rauch lost no time in sounding out my political opinions. When he was quite sure that I was anti-Nazi, he disclosed that he was working for the British Intelligence Service, and he asked me to help him. Naturally, I said I would. Rauch explained that his information was conveyed to London via Alamo, who had access to a transmitter. I was present during several transmissions. They took place in a villa at the corner of the Avenue de Longchamp (or Avenue Winston-Churchill, as it is known today) and some street whose name escapes me. Inside there was a radio operator and one or two women whom I can hardly remember.

"It so happens that I speak perfect English. The kind they spoke at the villa was far from perfect. This detail worried me, and I mentioned it to Rauch. His answer was that they were not English, but American. 'And a good thing too,' he said, 'for America is neutral, and it's far safer for us to work with Americans.'

"It's true that Alamo claimed to be of American origin and said his mother was still living in New York, but I found all this hard to believe. One day, as we were saying goodbye, he told me he was going to the Uruguayan consulate. I followed him. He headed for the consulate, all right, but at the last moment, instead of going in, he crossed the street and went off. I told myself that he was definitely not American, and apparently not Uruguayan either, and that the whole business was growing very mysterious. What I found hardest of all to understand was why Rauch should want to lie to me.

"Naturally, I let them have all the information that came my way. It didn't amount to much as a rule, but I did my best.

"At about that time—it must have been in the autumn of 1940— I used to go quite often to see my brother-in-law, who was a dried-fruit importer in Antwerp. His business had been requisitioned, together with all its stock. Two or three times a week he had to deliver a truckload of dried fruit to Antwerp airport, which by then, of course, had been taken over by the Luftwaffe. One day I asked him to let me drive the truck. After depositing my load, I went to the canteen and got into conversation with some Germans. 'What the devil are you going to do with all that dried fruit?' I asked. 'It's for England,' they said. I asked them what they meant. 'We're getting ready for the invasion,' they said. 'Once it starts, our pilots will be in the air every hour of the day. They won't have time to hang around here for meals, so they'll take along a supply of dried fruit.' I reported this conversation to Rauch.

"On another visit to Antwerp, I saw a single, unescorted British aircraft appear from out of the blue. I remember it was a magnificent day. The plane dived down over General Motors, loosed a stick of bombs and flew off. One of the bombs fell on the body-building shops and set fire to the paint supplies; within minutes, the whole factory was ablaze. That same day, I attended a demonstration in the main square of the city: lines of women were parading behind a black flag. I asked what the black flag was for. I was told that it had always been a symbol of famine and that the women were protesting against the shipment of potato supplies to Germany.

"I returned to Brussels in the afternoon and related these two episodes to Rauch and Alamo. As it happened, they were in the middle of preparing a transmission, so they were able to incorporate these pieces of information. Afterward we had dinner and talked of this and that. At about midnight we tuned in on the overseas service of Radio Moscow, as we often did. That night there were two announcers, a man and a woman, taking turns reading the news. I can't remember whether it was the woman who read the item about the British plane, and the man who described the demonstration, or vice versa; either way, it gave me quite a shock! I stared at Alamo and Rauch. They looked embarrassed. Then Alamo got up and turned off the radio. 'Listen,' he said to me, 'if ever you open your mouth, it'll be the last thing you do!' And his tone was as threatening as his words.

"Next day I went to see Rauch and demanded to know what was going on. 'Look,' he said, 'I really am in British Intelligence, and I'm keeping these Russians under surveillance. Be careful. We're risking our necks, you and I. This bunch is even more dangerous than the Germans!'

"This, of course, was before Hitler's attack on the Soviet Union; the Russo-German Pact was still in force.

"I felt awfully embarrassed to hear that Carlos Alamo was Russian. A few days earlier, he had complained of not knowing anyone and asked me to introduce him to a woman. So I arranged a foursome for dinner: Alamo, myself and two Russian girls, Princess Sherbatov and a friend of hers, who's now my wife. I saw Alamo jump when he heard the Princess' name, but I wasn't paying much attention. Afterward he tried to make a play for her, but his approach was terribly clumsy, almost crude. To make things worse, his table manners were awful, really disastrous, and the two women sat tearing him to pieces—in Russian, of course. Anna, my wife, admitted to me later that they called him all the names under the sun. Then, when I found out that poor Alamo was Russian and had understood every word, I was very sorry for him. . . ."

◆

December, 1965. I arrived in Brussels at 11 P.M. and decided to try my luck despite the late hour; I might as well find out at once whether I had made the journey for nothing. It was Margarete Barcza herself who answered the telephone; she agreed to see me. When I asked her what time of day would suit her best, she replied: "Why not now? I always go to bed very late. Or very early—depending on how you look at it." That night I sat listening to her until 4 A.M.

In 1940 she was twenty-eight years old. Tall, blond, well-built and inclined to be showy in her dress, she did not pass unnoticed, even by the Gestapo. Her beautiful eyes have withstood the passage of time and the serious illnesses which have beset her. She speaks in a light, animated voice with a distinct Brussels accent.

Margarete Barcza says: "My first husband, Ernest Barcza, was seventeen years older than I. We lived in Czechoslovakia, where my family originally came from, and it was there my son René was born in 1932—I was just twenty. Life ran very smoothly and pleasantly for us. My family had made a lot of money exporting hops. I had started out as a millionaire's daughter, now I was a millionaire's wife, and I saw no reason for things ever to change. But when the Munich agreements were signed and the Germans annexed the Sudetenland, we had to move to Prague. A year later we left there just before Hitler's troops arrived, and fled to Belgium. I forgot to tell you we were Jews.

"In Brussels, we went to live at 106 Avenue Émile-de-Béco. My husband and I had an apartment on the sixth floor, and my parents were on the fifth. Obviously, things were no longer as they had been, and our chief entertainment was playing bridge with our neighbor who lived across the landing, a very nice man in the Belgian civil service.

"On March 15, 1940, my husband went to bed as usual after his card game, and he died during the night; a heart attack carried him off within a few hours. A month and a half later, Belgium was invaded. There were air raids and we had to go down to the cellar. It was there I got to know the tenant from the fourth floor. He was a Uruguayan student named Vincent Sierra. No one could call him handsome: he was shorter than I, with blond hair and thick, fleshy lips. But he was so thoughtful and considerate—madly charming. He dressed divinely, and not only did he have plenty of money but he knew how to spend it, which is rare. To cut a long story short, we fell head over heels in love, so much so that I refused to flee to France with my parents.

"We moved into a magnificent apartment in the Avenue Slegers. There were twenty-seven rooms, including seven bedrooms. We turned one room into a gymnasium, and every morning a masseur used to come after we did our exercises. We had a country house too. It was a good life again. We went out almost every evening and did plenty of dancing. Vincent was a marvelous dancer, and the two of us won many contests. I especially remember our first New Year's Eve together. We spent the night at the Naumur Casino, and it was absolutely marvelous.

"In March 1941, Vincent decided to give up his studies and go into business. He set up an import-export concern called Simexco. The hardest thing was to find the number of stockholders required by law. We approached a number of Belgian friends. I remember going to see our old neighbor in the Avenue Émile-de-Béco, Monsieur Seghers. I asked him to come into business with us in much the same way as one would ask someone to make up a foursome at bridge; he agreed.

"Incidentally, this import-export business came as a complete godsend to Monsieur Rauch. He was an old friend of my family; we had known him in Czechoslovakia and met him again in Brussels. The war was preventing him from doing his usual work—I've forgotten what it was. Anyway, he was hard up. I'd introduced him to Vincent, who gave him some translations to do. Now he brought him into the firm as business manager, or something of the sort.

"Vincent was a great success at business. He really threw himself into it. He was tired by the end of the day, and he used to say to me: 'It's so nice to come home to you and talk of things that don't really matter. . . . There's such wonderful peace and quiet here. . . . You don't ask questions. . . .' The fact is, he never told me a thing about his work. On one occasion, though, he left a small parcel at home and said someone would be calling for it. Eventually the bell rang, and when I opened the door I found a very, very good-looking man. He seemed quite bewildered and immediately started backing away. 'Isn't Mr. Sierra in?' he asked nervously. Then he bolted. It was funny to see such a handsome man be so timid. Later on, I learned it was Carlos Alamo, another Uruguayan.

"Only one thing marred the honeymoon: we were both insanely jealous. Early in 1941, business took Vincent to the Leipzig Fair, and afterward to Prague. It was sheer hell for me. I treated myself to diamonds and fur coats, as a way of killing time, but I lost half a dozen pounds in a few days. He had openly admitted that he was engaged, and he had even shown me a photograph of the girl. But she was in Uruguay, so I felt reasonably safe from her. I was far more worried by the thought of the girls he might meet in Brussels or on his travels. For instance, he made weekly visits to Paris, also on business, and was away for two or three days. Once I went through the pockets of one of his jackets and found the autographed photo of a cabaret dancer named Nila Cara.* You should have heard me go for him! I insisted that he stay in Paris only for a day at a time. Of course it meant that he'd be traveling two nights in a row, but that was just too bad! Another thing: he was in the habit of making business appointments in a nightclub here in Brussels, the Moulin Rouge. I used to ring him up, to make quite sure he was there. It would put him in a terrible rage!"

There is one figure common to the stories of Bill Hoorickx and Margarete Barcza: Rauch. It is only fair to admire the professional skill of this man who, doubtless abetted by good fortune, succeeded in establishing links with two members of the Red Orchestra. And likewise it seems only fair to pay our respects through him to British Intelligence and its undeniable flair for infiltrating every dark corner. These acknowledgments must be made swiftly, however, for Rauch was not destined to remain on the scene for long; the Big Chief soon steered him gently but firmly onto the sidelines.

———◆———

Robert Christen, Swiss citizen and Brussels restaurateur, close to sixty, short, thickset and self-assertive, says: "Oh, I've always

---

* An advertisement from an edition of *Paris-Soir* published at about that time reads: "Tomorrow, Friday, at 7 P.M. A cocktail party to toast friendship. Nila Cara will welcome you to the Beaulieu Bar, 168 faubourg Saint-Honoré, Balzac 4964."

worked at night, monsieur! I spent thirty years singing comic songs! Before the war I entertained at the Broadway, right here in Brussels. Saturday after Saturday I used to watch the same regular customer walk in, a Uruguayan student. He took real interest in the attractions, and we got to know each other after a while. I'd tell him about Switzerland; he'd show me snaps of his fiancée, his house in Montevideo, his car and all the rest of it. The Broadway closed down after the Germans came, for the proprietor was Jewish. I went to work at the Moulin Rouge. I'll tell you one thing, I'll never forget the French Cancan troupe at the Moulin Rouge. Every one of the girls was Jewish. They had all been in separate acts, but their male partners, who weren't Jewish, had dropped them, so they'd all banded together. At the Moulin Rouge I met my friend Sierra again. He was often there with his girl-friend, a big blonde who wasn't afraid to look at a man. One day Sierra asked me to buy some stock in an import-export business he was setting up. I told him I wasn't up to that sort of thing, but he was so insistent that in the end I gave in. Later on, I was even appointed managing director. Needless to say, I hardly ever set foot inside the door; by then I was running the Florida, where he and his friends were frequent visitors, so I had other things to occupy my mind. . . ."

◆

In Brussels: the Broadway, the Florida, the Moulin Rouge, elegant supper parties with beautiful Russian ladies, all-night visits to the best casinos, tango contests, furs and jewels.

In Paris: the Folies-Bergère, the Casino de Paris, nightclub singers and cabarets. The Big Chief and Georgie de Winter, true Parisians now, were to be seen in all the most expensive settings. They even allowed themselves to stay out after curfew, for they went home in cycle-drawn taxis, to which the Germans showed a certain indulgence. They lived in the Rue Fontaine at first, then in the Rue de Prony; they also had a small villa at Le Vésinet. Trepper insisted on living in apartments that were luxurious and especially well heated; he loved beautiful things—paintings, books with fine bindings; his suits and shirts had to be of the best quality; he adored good perfume and was continually buying different kinds for Georgie; he was crazy about Edith Piaf and bought all her records; he went only to restaurants that could offer him the very best in food and drink. Throughout that winter of 1940–41, Parisians had to endure hardships of

which this free-spending couple were blissfully unaware; the black
market kept them warm, the black market dressed them, the black
market fed them.

It may sound like Sybaris, but it was more like the dark wood
where the Sleeping Beauty lay enthralled—Trepper and his network
were only waiting for the stroke of the magic wand to bring them
to life.

4. "The Germans Will Attack Tonight"

Trepper had arrived in Paris in August, 1940, accompanied by
Georgie. Luba and her two children were safe and sound in Russia,
having been repatriated via Marseilles through the efforts of the
Soviet ambassador in Vichy. So the Big Chief was able to give all
his mind to the great confrontation that lay ahead. It was obvious
to him that the enemy was going to be Germany and her armies,
which were engulfing Europe like an evil tide. And, although Brussels had been an adequate base for an espionage war against Britain,
Paris would be a better focal point for activities against the Third
Reich. Trepper therefore set up his headquarters in the French
capital and began building an organization commensurate with his
new status. Moscow had just appointed him "Resident Director"—
in other words, head—of Soviet espionage throughout western Europe.

He had his two ablest lieutenants with him. The first of these was
Leo Grossvogel, who had been dispossessed of all his property under
the anti-Jewish laws of the Occupation. Trepper soon enjoyed the
benefit of his business acumen and powers of organization. Within a
few weeks he had put the network's finances on a sound basis and
rented a dozen flats all over Paris for use as hideouts and rendezvous;
he had recruited agents to act as "letterboxes" to ensure rapid internal
communications without breaching the various rigidly watertight
compartments. He was the architect of the entire physical complex
of the network, the man who made sure that every wheel was in
place and turning. Yet he was able to project an irreproachable social
façade: who could suspect this imposing individual, so obviously
upper class, who dressed with such extreme sobriety and loved serious

music? The cloak-and-dagger school of spying was wholly alien to his temperament. He carried on his espionage activities with the same unruffled meticulousness that he brought to the selling of raincoats; the merchandise was different, that was all. His qualities were those of a good chief of staff: tell him what end you had in mind, and he would furnish the means.

How to describe Hillel Katz? One might say without exaggeration that if Trepper had instructed him to go to Gestapo headquarters and give himself up, he would have obeyed without question. He was young, short and extremely slight in build, with glasses that took up half his face. The general opinion was that he looked a perfectly ordinary Frenchman. But in fact he was a Polish Jew, like Trepper. They had met in Palestine and had been on that notorious hunger strike together; then they had come to France, where Katz had worked as a bricklayer. In time he became the Big Chief's right-hand man. He was unfailingly cheerful and optimistic. There was no chink in his devotion, no limit to his self-denial. He was cast in the mold of all true martyrs—one of those who seem predestined to be caught, yet gladly lay down their lives on behalf of a cause. With all that, it would have been surprising if little Katz had not eventually died under the Nazi axe.

Leo Grossvogel and Hillel Katz—they formed the Jewish Old Guard of the Big Chief's Red Orchestra.

———◆———

The Belgian network was almost completely inactive. Routine radio contact was maintained with Moscow, for the conveyance of information supplied by such minor people as Hoorickx. But the real sources were not yet being tapped, and the organization as a whole was lying low. At its head were two Russians, both under the age of thirty.

Trepper, like everyone else, had an affectionate regard for Mikhail Makarov, alias Carlos Alamo. For one thing, he was a hero. As a lieutenant in the Russian air force—ground staff, not flying staff —he had been sent to Spain to serve with the Republicans. One day the Nationalists achieved a breakthrough, and there was serious danger of their mopping up the whole front from the rear. The Republican artillery called for an immediate air attack, but no pilots were available. Makarov leaped into a plane and took off. Far from possessing a license, he had no knowledge of the controls except for the smattering acquired by keeping his eyes and ears open. He located the Nationalists, bombed and strafed them, flew back to base and made a perfectly respectable landing. They carried him off the field on their shoulders in triumph. That was Makarov.

On their first meeting in Belgium, in the spring of 1939, Trepper invited him to have a drink in a café. Makarov ordered brandy. The waiter brought large balloon glasses and poured in the usual measure. But Makarov motioned to him to go on pouring. The waiter obeyed, in some bewilderment, and filled the glass right up to the brim. Makarov looked on contentedly. He could not make out why Trepper kept kicking him under the table. Finally he grew annoyed. "What are you worried about?" he exclaimed. "I can afford it!" That too was Makarov.

He bought a car. The Big Chief was strongly opposed to the idea of spies owning cars; the habit led to brushes with the law, especially in cases of accident. Makarov knew only one way to drive—with the accelerator pressed down to the floor. One day when Trepper was out with him, he lost control of the wheel and the car crashed into a tree. Trepper extricated himself from the debris and stood silently surveying the scene of the disaster. Makarov was beside himself with fury. "How can you possibly remain so calm?" he shouted. "It just isn't normal!" To which Trepper replied quietly, "What do you expect me to say, you fool?" Again, that was Makarov.

He was put in charge of the Ostend branch of the raincoat company. He did not understand the first thing about business, mixed up the accounts, seldom went to the shop, and kept complaining of being bored to death. Makarov all over!

In June, 1940, when Belgium was collapsing fast, Trepper told him to go and collect the transmitter hidden in Knokke-le-Zoute and bring it back to Brussels. But Makarov did not have time; he was in Ostend, busy making love with Madame Hoorickx. Trepper had to carry out the mission himself.

He had no choice but to report it all to Moscow. Makarov was found guilty of flagrant incompetence, and at the end of the summer he received a telegram from the head of Soviet Intelligence ordering him home. He threw himself on Trepper's mercy. "My whole career is finished!" he said. "You know what a disgrace like this means to an officer. . . ." He talked of suicide. Trepper, magnanimous as always, persuaded Moscow to give him one last chance and let him remain at his post. He felt a real affection for Mikhail Makarov; the man was a hero.

———◆———

Paradoxically—and curiously enough—no one felt any affection for Captain Gurevich, though he was the soul of conscientiousness. He had arrived in Brussels from Montevideo on July 17, 1939. His passport, Number 4649, had been issued in New York on April 17, 1936. It was made out in the name of Vincent Sierra, born on November 3, 1911, and living at 9 Calle Colón, Montevideo.

Like Makarov, Gurevich had fought in Spain in the International Brigades with the rank of captain. And, again like Makarov, he had achieved his moment of glory during the campaign against Franco. Not in the air, but under water, while going by submarine from Russia to Spain. The vessel had some engine failure and lay at the bottom of the sea for several hours. The crew gave themselves up for lost, but eventually a mechanic succeeded in repairing it. Gurevich remained cool, calm and collected throughout these long hours of stress, or so he afterward claimed. He had not originally been slated to serve in the Big Chief's organization. His instructions were to proceed to Copenhagen and set up a network there. His stay in Brussels was to have been brief, a few months at most, during which he would study commercial law and perfect his knowledge of foreign languages. But when war broke out, he was instructed to stay where he was and place his services at the disposal of the Big Chief.

The latter was well satisfied with Gurevich. Unlike Makarov-Alamo, Gurevich-Sierra succeeded in adapting himself perfectly to the social life of the Belgian capital. He kept up a cracking pace, entertaining lavishly and establishing contact after contact; he was industrious and astute. No doubt about it: Sierra was a first-class recruit.

But nobody liked him—apart from Margarete, of course, who pined whenever he was away. He was regarded as arrogant and pushing, a bluffer. Veterans of the Red Orchestra are unanimous in their disapproval: "Kent? Oh, that bastard . . ."

For although Gurevich-Sierra was to acquire the additional title of Little Chief (after succeeding the Big Chief as head of the Belgian network), he was known to everyone, even Moscow, as Kent. That particular pseudonym had been of his own choosing. It's a story in itself. Around 1929, a novel called *The Diary of a Spy* was published in Russia. The author, N. G. Smirnov, related the adventures of a British agent, Edward Kent, notable for his astuteness, ice-cold nerve and incredible audacity. Gurevich read this novel when he was a boy of eighteen, and it bowled him over. All right, now—imagine you are running an intelligence service. One day a bright young spark offers to spy for you and states that he intends to operate under the name James Bond. Your reaction, surely, is to thank him with a charitable smile and advise him to rechannel his energies into the writing of escapist fiction. The man who recruited Kent had no such reservations. Presumably the Slavic mind works in a different way.

Kent's colleagues in Brussels had no idea where the alias had come from. There was no specific reason for their general dislike of him. For instance, take Luba Trepper, who until she left for Moscow acted as link between Kent and the Big Chief. She adored Makarov, the amiable loafer, but couldn't stand the sight of the ever-industrious Kent. She was troubled by his immoderate spending and his taste for luxury; she argued that a man so strongly addicted to the good things of life would inevitably shrink from risking his neck. How could she possibly know? Trepper listened to what she had to say, but did not take it too much to heart. One day he called at Kent's large and beautifully furnished apartment in the Avenue Slegers. With tremendous pride Kent showed him his wardrobe and the forty or fifty suits that hung inside. Trepper glanced at them and nodded. "Bravo! Very impressive!" he murmured. "If I were you, I'd take a snapshot. It will make you a souvenir for later—though it may not be you who'll be looking at it." Kent did not take kindly to this remark.

Alamo and Kent: they were the Big Chief's Russian "Young Guard." He did not have the same confidence in them as in his old Jewish colleagues, who had been trained in the hard school of poverty, who could blend into their surroundings like chameleons and who knew all there was to know about underground warfare. Men like Trepper and Katz could dabble in luxury without the slightest risk of drowning in it. Alamo and Kent were a different matter. One wouldn't know what metal they were made of until they had been put to the test.

◆

The test was approaching. This was accepted as a fact in London and Washington; it was accepted in the neutral capitals, where banner headlines reported that the Wehrmacht was massed along the

River Bug, ready to strike eastward; it was accepted in Geneva, whence the Soviet Resident Director Alexander Rado sent warning after warning to his superiors at home; it was accepted in Tokyo, whence Sorge gave several weeks' notice of the date set for the German attack: June 22, 1941.

It was accepted as a fact in Paris too. Even before the beginning of May, the Big Chief had tried to alert the Kremlin to the dangerous buildup of Hitler's forces. He was in contact with a sapper in the German engineer corps, Ludwig Kainz, who had worked on the German fortifications along the Bug after the Polish campaign. In April, 1941, he was posted back to the Bug on temporary duty. He saw at once that everything had been altered during his absence and that preparations were being made for an attack. When he got back to France, he bet Trepper a case of champagne that war would break out before the end of May. He lost the wager, but insisted that the attack had only been postponed for a month while Hitler got the Italians out of trouble in Albania and Greece. Kainz was so sure of this that he was prepared to bet on it, double or nothing.

Kainz was not the Big Chief's only source of information. He was also keeping closely in touch with an amiable Austrian colonel, in charge of provisioning the Wehrmacht in France. In the spring of 1941, this man told Trepper confidentially that his work was now becoming a good deal easier; he had fewer and fewer mouths to feed, for the army of occupation was being rapidly whittled down. Where were the departing troops bound for? Trepper learned the answer from hundreds of reports he received from French railway men—they were being sent east, to Poland. Finally, in the month of June, a series of drinking bouts yielded final confirmation: he fell in with a party of senior SS officers who were celebrating their departure for Poland; they invited him to join in a toast to the imminent defeat of the Soviet Union.

Trepper warned Moscow on two separate occasions. His reports were transmitted via the Soviet military attaché in Vichy, General Susloparov. Officially, Trepper was not supposed to have any dealings with him. But it alarmed the Big Chief to see the fatal hour approaching while he was not yet equipped for battle: he desperately needed transmitters. Defying instructions, he badgered and wheedled the attaché. Susloparov, complacent old army man, reassured him, saying there was no need to hurry.

On the evening of June 21 Trepper arrived in Vichy and rushed to see Susloparov: "Here is a message of vital importance, for immediate transmission!" Susloparov asked what all the excitement was about, and Trepper revealed that the Wehrmacht was poised to attack Russia that very night. The General roared with laughter. "Why, you must be out of your mind," he said. "It's unthinkable, altogether impossible. I refuse to transmit such a telegram. You would simply be making a fool of yourself!" But Trepper was so insistent that finally the General gave in. The message was transmitted without further delay.

The Big Chief, worn out, went to a hotel room and fell asleep. Next morning he was awakened by the proprietor, who was shouting, "Monsieur! This is it! They're at war with Russia!"

Two days later, Susloparov's assistant returned from Moscow after a long and roundabout journey. Trepper, still in Vichy, asked whether his warning had been taken into account. The Russian told him: "I saw the Director [of Red Army Intelligence] the evening your telegram arrived. He assured me that it had immediately been shown to the Boss [Stalin]. The Boss was very much surprised. 'As a rule,' he said. 'Trepper * sends us worthwhile material that does credit to his political judgment. How could he fail to detect at once that this was merely a crude piece of British provocation?' "

British provocation. These words were now thoroughly familiar to the chief of Russian Intelligence. Back in April, he had sent Stalin a report from a Czech agent announcing (a) that the Skoda armament works had been instructed not to fill any more Russian orders, and (b) that the Germans were massing troops along the Soviet frontier. Stalin made a red-ink notation in the margin of the report: "This information is a piece of British provocation. Find the author of this provocation and punish him." Disguised as a Tass Agency correspondent, Major Akhmedov, head of the fourth branch of the Russian secret service, was sent post-haste to Germany to unmask the culprit; but the crushing attack launched by the Wehrmacht did not leave him time.†

---

* In fact, Stalin said "Otto," not "Trepper," for it was by the former alias that the Big Chief was officially referred to in Moscow. To Georgie he was "Eddy"; to Katz, "René"; to Spaak, "Henri." He is known to have used also the aliases "General," "Georges," "Uncle," "Bauer," "Gilbert," "Herbert," "Sommer," and others too. For the purpose of simplification, most of these have been disregarded. Otherwise readers would soon have been as baffled as the Gestapo; it would have been unreasonable to subject them to such an ordeal.
† The episode was described by Major Akhmedov himself after he had deserted from the Soviet secret service and fled to the West. (See his testimony before an investigating committee of the United States Senate in October, 1953.)

Thus, until the very moment when the shooting started, Moscow went on denying the possibility of a war reported as imminent by Geneva, Tokyo and Paris, to say nothing of London and Washington. Unquestionably, this was largely due to Stalin's anti-British fixation, brought to a neurotic pitch by reports, a year earlier, of the Allies' high-handed intentions with regard to Baku and Finland. But there seems no doubt that it was also a political miscalculation. Stalin had long ago announced his intention of leaving the capitalist nations and fascist states to fight it out among themselves; the Red Army would not go harvesting in Europe until both sides were worn out. In the spring of 1941, Stalin took the view that the wheat was not yet ripe, that Britain and Germany had not yet bled each other white, and that—whatever else might happen—Hitler would never run the risk of attacking in the east before rounding off his victory in the west.

He was wrong. We know the price his country had to pay: "an aerial Pearl Harbor," as Paul Carell called it, with thousands of aircraft destroyed on the ground; division after division driven back in disorder, encircled, wiped out, so that the road to Moscow lay open.

In Tokyo and elsewhere the cost was psychological. What could be more weakening to a spy's morale than the discovery that he has been risking his life for nothing, that his warning cries have been heard but not listened to? Klausen, Richard Sorge's radio operator, recalls one occasion when Moscow's reply had been: "We doubt the veracity of your information." "Richard was furious. That was the only time we both lost control. Richard sprang out of his chair. He strode wildly about the room, holding his head in his hands. 'It's more than I can stand!' he said. 'Why won't they believe me? How can those wretches ignore our message?' " *

But in Trepper's case, a sense of elation dominated all else, even his rancor at having been unheeded. All who had dealings with him in that historic week testify to his enthusiasm; he was radiant with happiness, literally beside himself with joy. Undoubtedly Stalin was right when he said that Trepper was not lacking in political judgment. Trepper granted that the Russo-German Pact might be necessary as a means of winning time for the Red Army. But only after an agonizing struggle had he stifled his inner feelings and listened solely to the voice of reason. It is essential to realize that Trepper

---

* Nicole Chatel and Alain Guérin, *Camarade Sorge* (Paris: Julliard, 1965), p. 87.

and his Old Guard were not exactly professionals in the business of espionage; in no way do they resemble those supermen of spy fiction, bristling with gadgets, who carry out any mission for any client; they are equally unlike the flesh-and-blood professionals of the 1960s, whose mislaid faith, whether they work for East or West, has been replaced by an obsession with the technical intricacies of their trade. Had anyone called them spies, they would have rejected the label; they regarded themselves as revolutionaries. A member of their generation, Otto Braun, was later to describe himself and his colleagues in the following terms: "We were not bureaucrats dealing in conspiracy, but romantics dealing in revolution." Trepper felt that the whole course of his career had unfolded in a single, undeviating line: industrial agitation in Dombrova, political work in Palestine, and now the search for information in western Europe. It was the selfsame battle, fought on different fronts. One may doubt the existence of such sentiments in the second half of the 1960s, but it is impossible to deny their existence, a quarter of a century ago, in the minds of the Big Chief and those who worked under him. At that time, Trepper had no hesitation in asserting that the outstanding figure of his generation, and the supreme embodiment of its attitudes, was a man by the name of André Malraux.

For the members of the Red Orchestra, June 22, 1941, marked the beginning of a relentless struggle in which every one of them was exposed to the risk of death or, through torture, of permanent self-abhorrence. Such perils seemed of little account, however, when measured against the immense relief they all felt at emerging from their previously equivocal position. Despite the official line, despite the Russo-German Pact, the men serving in Brussels and Paris had known for years that Nazi fascism was the archenemy. And in the eighteen months which had passed since the fall of Belgium and France, they had seen this truth reflected in the yellow posters bearing the names of persons to be executed; they had caught the scent of it in the charnel-house smell drifting across Europe from Poland, where the majority of them had left their families; their hearts had been awakened to what their minds had already acknowledged.

For men like these, June 22, 1941, was a day to be celebrated.

And besides, Trepper was a Jew.

When I first started my investigations, I did not consider it vital to record that A or B was Jewish; I felt the words would have as much relevance as the fact that I myself am a native of Auvergne. My only reaction was, so to speak, a technical one: it seemed to me distinctly unwise to combine the already formidable risks of being a secret agent with those of being a member of a hideously persecuted minority. As time went by, I discovered that this was a rather shortsighted view. Not long after the German attack on Russia, the Big Chief was asked why his network contained such a high proportion of Jews. He replied: "Because they have a special score to settle with the Nazis."

Himmler certainly understood this too. The men whom he detailed to "scour away this Jewish rot" (the Red Orchestra) were given written orders to employ every available means of obtaining confessions. As far as I know, this is the only occasion on which the Reichsführer dared put his signature to a document authorizing torture to the point of death. If this sounds like a gratuitous detail, one must bear in mind the quite distinctive procedures employed against the Red Orchestra, the special nature of the snares and intrigues brought into play, and the remarkable personal reactions displayed by Himmler's men—all based on the fact that the opponent was Jewish and therefore despicable, however artful he might be. A Jew was hard to catch; once caught, he was like putty. Whenever I asked former Gestapo men why they had taken the risk of releasing such and such an agent from custody, in the seemingly faint hope of his standing by his promise to betray his comrades, I would meet with a surprised stare and the words: "But, good heavens, he was a Jew!"

In short, as well as being the date of the German invasion of Russia, June 22, 1941, also marked the beginning of a richly symbolic duel to the death, fought out in the arena of Occupied Europe, between the hard-core fascists of the Gestapo, those deadly and sinister Goliaths of the Master Race, and Trepper's small band of Jews, the poor Davids of a martyred people.

5. An Elusive Transmitter

In Trepper's Red Orchestra, a soloist of prime importance was the pianist. This, of course, was the radio operator, playing on his transmitter—also known as a "music box."

The discovery by the Kranz monitoring station of the pianist using the call sign "PTX" was not regarded as a historic event in the upper echelons of the Abwehr, or even of the Funkabwehr, the offshoot establishment specializing in the detection and annihilation of secret transmitters. No sooner had the Wehrmacht plunged into Russia than Occupied Europe burst into music. So far, the authorities had failed to discover for whom these illicit symphonies were intended, but the coincidence was surely too strong to disregard; as the musicians had apparently been conjured into being by the opening of the eastern front, it seemed probable that the music lover was housed somewhere in Moscow.

A logical deduction, and a highly reassuring one. For the Germans, things had got off to a good start—or rather, they were progressing better than ever. The established pattern of success was quite unmarred. After Poland, Denmark, Norway, Holland, Belgium, Britain, France, Yugoslavia and Greece, it was now Russia's turn to run before the invader. The Führer had predicted as much: "The entire Soviet structure is rotten; one good kick at the door, and it will all come tumbling down." Once again the main problem was the handling of the flow of prisoners. Beside these triumphs, what did the existence of a few spy rings matter? The orchestras would fall silent one by one when there was no one left in Moscow to listen to them. Even now, their thin melodies were being drowned out by the blare of trumpets which heralded "special communiqués" on the German radio announcing further victories. If the testimony of his assistants is to be believed, the head of the Funkabwehr was all in favor of letting this pointless activity die a natural death.

A few days after the detection of the "PTX" transmitter, the Kranz station picked up signals from another unknown source. The specialists, working in collaboration with their colleagues at Breslau, tried hard to locate it. After several attempts they forwarded their report to Berlin, where it was received with a shrug. The experts set to work again and checked their previous calculations. According to them, there was now little room for doubt: a secret transmitter, technically similar to the first, was operating in Berlin. The Abwehr reacted to this assertion as though it had received a violent electric shock. The emergence of a few scattered boils on the body of Occupied Europe constituted no real threat and could, indeed, be dismissed as a natural development; they would be attended to in due course. But a pianist in Berlin itself, obviously playing in concert with other instrumentalists! It was as though a hideous cancer had been found at the very heart of the Nazi empire. If Russia's present-day leaders were to be told of a secret American transmitter operating within three hundred yards of the Kremlin, their alarm and astonishment could not exceed those exhibited by the German leaders when they read the Funkabwehr's report.

After all, it was common knowledge that the German Communist Party had been annihilated by the Gestapo. All that remained of the organization—in its day the most powerful in Europe—was a sprinkling of cells, cut off from the world and full of informers. Traditionally, Soviet espionage had always functioned within the framework of a large Communist superstructure; deprived of that superstructure, it was like a fish out of water which must inevitably die for lack of it. Moreover, the German authorities were convinced that Stalin's conduct in this matter had been aboveboard after the signing of the Russo-German Pact. The Gestapo had even been treated to the rare and exquisite pleasure of receiving, from the hands of the OGPU itself, several German Communists who had earlier fled to Russia. True, the idyl had lost a little of its pristine quality after a while. With or without Stalin's backing, the heads of Soviet Intelligence had sought to rebuild the semblance of an organization in Germany. But their poor attempts had been laughed to scorn in Berlin. Had there ever been a greater flop, for instance, than the attempt to implant agents by way of the Baltic countries? When those countries had passed into the Soviet sphere of influence in 1940, the five hundred thousand German nationals living and working there had been repatriated by Berlin. Several thousand of them * at once disclosed to the Gestapo that before they left they had been approached by Russian Intelligence, which had used threats and financial inducements to persuade them to spy on their own country.

---

* Fifty per cent of those repatriated, according to Heydrich, but this figure would appear to have been inflated for propaganda purposes.

In Berlin it was argued that the other side must be in desperate straits to employ so crude a method, offering so small a chance of success; and if they were reduced to this, it must be because all the standard procedures had failed.

Before launching his military attack on the Soviet Union, Hitler had ordered the compilation of a splendidly plausible dossier designed to show that Russia was really to blame for the war. It contained allegations of frontier incidents, unauthorized Russian flights over German territory, deceitful diplomatic maneuvers, and other misdeeds of a similarly damning nature. Reinhard Heydrich, chief of the Gestapo's Security Service (SD), had been given the job of drafting a report on Soviet espionage in Germany. Here again, the aim was to make it appear that the Russians had infringed the Pact so heinously that Germany had no choice but to respond with war. The Heydrich Report, Registration Number IV EL 17/41 g RS, was published in Europe by the Deutscher Ausländer Dienst. The French version may not reflect too well on their translators, but it is couched in a wonderfully artless tone not often encountered in official documents of this type:

Since the conclusion of the Pact, the Russian secret service has been working in an almost provocative way. Already unrestrained in its normal methods, it went so far as to make ample use, for its own designs, of Russia's diplomatic agencies within the Reich—headed by the Russian embassy in Berlin. When, some time ago, the then ambassador, Shkvartsev, was recalled from Berlin and replaced by Dekanozov, this substitution was the signal for an even greater intensification of snooping for political, economic and military information. In Russia, Dekanozov, an intimate of Stalin, was head of the intelligence branch of the N.K.V.D. (Russian People's Commissariat for the Interior), in which the OGPU constitutes a special espionage branch. The mission, entrusted to him by Moscow, consisted of gaining access to the armed forces of the Reich through a network of confidential agents, which he was to develop; and above all of procuring reports about the Reich's military strength and plans of operations. His faithful assistant was OGPU-member Kobulov, so-called "embassy counselor," who displayed intense activity in the field of espionage, shamelessly making use of his diplomatic immunity. The goal that Russian espionage set for itself in Germany was, quite apart from obtaining military information, to ferret out the political intentions of the Reich government and, by developing secret radio installations in numerous places in Germany, to set up warning posts capable of sending, by means of clever code language, all the news that might be important for Russia.

Thus, ever since 1940, there had been vast preparations for mobilization in the field of espionage, preparations achieved through pecuniary resources on an inconceivable scale. The German countermine service is able to intervene in time.

This strange wording raises several questions. Why, for example, saddle German counterespionage with the preposterous name "countermine service"? But the general message was plain enough: the Nazi security forces had been a hundred per cent successful in foiling the Soviet plots; they had arrested all of Moscow's agents and impounded all their transmitters. On the eve of war with Russia, Heydrich felt able to assure his Führer that Germany was as clean as a new penny; there would be no prying or snooping.

But what about the reports of the radio experts at Kranz? It was impossible to attach credence to them without shedding doubt on the accuracy of the Heydrich Report. Some members of the Abwehr were prepared to support the experts; but many refused to believe in the existence of the Berlin pianist, insisting that the equipment employed in locating him was simply not accurate enough. Consequently, both sides—believers and nonbelievers alike—were aware of an urgent need to improve the equipment, to find out for certain whether the pianist was in Berlin.

Swift developments might have followed, had it not been for the Goering gang. By 1941 the man who had lost the Battle of Britain was rapidly going to pieces. The time was not far distant when he would take to using makeup, wearing several rings on each hand, and even, whenever he had the chance, dressing up in a Roman toga. In the end, the "man of iron" became a bloated copy of Nero. Yet from 1933 until 1939 he had been the most powerful man in Germany, apart from the Führer himself. Nominally head of the Gestapo, he had lost little time in surrendering the use of this police tool to Himmler and Heydrich; but he had clung jealously to the "research institute" on which he had graciously bestowed his own name. The Hermann Goering Research Institute controlled all telecommunication, together with all radio transmission in Germany and Occupied Europe. In its possession were long-range beam detectors of an accuracy unrivaled anywhere in the world. Goering may have fallen out of favor, but control of the Institute still left him in a position of exceptional power. All attempts to wrest it from him were in vain. The SS were entitled to seek assistance from the Institute in case of need, but over-all control of its activities lay entirely with Goering. And when the Funkabwehr (which was a branch of the Wehrmacht, and therefore devoid of the dark prestige of the SS) came in search of aid, there was always one of Goering's men to slam the door in their faces.

This was annoying, but not disastrous. The German radio industry was the most advanced in the world; it was perfectly capable of turning out the desired equipment. The prime need of the Funkabwehr was for long-distance tracking devices that could determine the approximate position of any given transmitter. For instance, Kranz declared that the call sign "PTX" came from within an area defined as follows: northern Germany, Holland, Belgium, northern France. It might as well have been Patagonia. It was essential at least to locate the town before the search could begin in earnest. At that point the short-range detectors could be brought into play to pinpoint the particular building where the transmitter was installed.

The Funkabwehr got in touch with the Loewe-Opta-Radio Company, which submitted a number of very interesting schemes. The problem with short-range detectors was to make them as unobtrusive as possible, so that they would not arouse suspicion. The old-fashioned models so far employed by the police and the Funkabwehr were so bulky that they had to be housed in vans. Furthermore they called attention to themselves by the presence of a circular tube, over a yard in diameter, affixed to the roof of the vehicle. Something better had to be devised. As a first step, the detector was shrunk to the size of a suitcase. But the man operating it had to wear earphones, and this, together with the suitcase, was bound to betray his activities to anyone who happened to be on the lookout. So it was decided that the suitcase should be concealed in a slowly moving car; experiments proved encouraging. Soon afterward came another step forward: the detector was made small enough to be worn under the user's coat, attached to his belt. There was no longer any suitcase to give the game away. As for the earphones, they were replaced by an appliance which could be worn as discreetly as a hearing aid. The Funkabwehr had found the answer to their problem at last. They told Loewe-Opta-Radio to start production; now all they had to do was wait for the goods to be delivered.

As time went by, however, jubilation gave way to disappointment, and then to real annoyance. The project advanced at a snail's pace and showed no sign of being brought to a conclusion, despite sharp rebukes and warnings from the Funkabwehr. And yet the engineers in charge appeared to be full of good intentions, even if these were sometimes misplaced. They were continually reshuffling their departments to improve efficiency, but in practice these upheavals always seemed to produce a number of snags. Expert technicians were posted to the Russian front, and not until after they had gone was it realized that the work could not be completed without them. And there was a final blow: when at last the long-range direction finders were completed, they were sent to the wrong address. Half of them had been intended for the Funkabwehr, the remainder for the Goering Research Institute. In the event they were all dispatched to the Institute. There was no hope of recovering them. It was heartbreaking.

Three Red Orchestra agents were on the staff of Loewe-Opta-Radio, one of them at management level. Their immediate superior in the network was an officer at the Hermann Goering Research Institute.

Following its detection at the end of June, the transmitter that was assumed to be operating from Berlin stayed on the air for three weeks; then it fell silent, to the keen satisfaction of those who had always believed that Kranz had been mistaken. Early in August the transmissions began again and continued for about a fortnight; after that, complete silence. These stoppings and startings wholly undermined the morale of the men in charge of the Funkabwehr, whose nerves had already been taxed by Loewe-Opta-Radio's continual delays. They were in the dark, with no light to guide them except the ominous signals flashed from the set using the PTX call-sign—that is, the first transmitter picked up by Kranz. By September 7 two hundred and fifty of its messages had been monitored, and the cipher experts were busily engaged in trying to break the code. The regularity of these messages was disconcerting, of course, but in a way less disquieting than the vagaries of the second transmitter. Since they were unable to take positive steps against the capricious pianist who might (or might not) be lurking in Berlin, it was decided to track down his hard-working colleague without delay. Kranz maintained that the latter was communicating with Moscow. The rate at which he tapped out his signals, the frequencies he employed and the times of transmission, all were closely related to those favored by the musician reported to be playing in Berlin; obviously the two pianists had gone to the same school. The arrest of one might well uncover the trail of the other.

Kranz slowly tightened the net. First, Germany and France were eliminated. Then Holland. That left Belgium. It was difficult to be more precise, but the experts reckoned that the PTX transmitter must be somewhere along the coast, probably at Bruges. The local representative of the Abwehr was brought into the chase. He was Franz Fortner.

Fortner was well organized by this time. He could draw on the services of a network of informers run by two Flemings who had already worked for the German secret service during the First World War. He instructed them to mingle with "extremist" circles in Bruges and frequent the popular cafés. The telegram from Berlin had specified that the transmitter was working for Moscow. Applying common sense, a commodity which he always rated high, Fortner went searching for his quarry in the place where it was most likely to be found—among the Belgian Communists. He was convinced that his informers had only to keep their eyes and ears open and they would soon pick up the threads leading to the troublesome pianist.

———◆———

This is how the Big Chief went about things when Moscow decided to reinforce his Orchestra with Mikhail Makarov, alias Carlos Alamo. To begin with, he had to provide the new recruit with the cover afforded by Le Roi du Caoutchouc company. Makarov had about ten thousand dollars. Trepper advised him to put an advertisement in the Belgian newspapers, stating that a South American businessman was interested in buying a partnership in a thriving concern. At this same time it happened that Madame Grossvogel was badgering her husband to find someone to take over her time-consuming duties as manager of the Ostend branch. Grossvogel mentioned the matter to the Big Chief, who suggested that he look at the personal columns in the newspapers. The Belgian followed this advice, and his eye was immediately drawn to Carlos Alamo's proposition; he wrote to him, care of the newspaper. Makarov reported his offer to the Big Chief, who conceded that a partnership in a rainwear business might constitute an effective cover. The deal was concluded. Makarov took over the running of the Ostend branch.

The whole operation was straight out of the textbook. During his training in the craft of espionage, Trepper's Russian professors had doubtless told how a pair of Soviet agents had made contact in an Anglo-Saxon country. The two men joined the same golf club, but scrupulously avoided meeting on the course. One day the club president invited them both to a dinner party. They pretended not to know one another at all and waited for the president to introduce them. The advantages of the method are obvious: if the police were to arrest the agents and try to show collusion between them, they could claim to have met under the most innocuous circumstances— at a golf club dinner; if necessary, the president would confirm the story.

But the Big Chief was improving on the lesson he had learned as a student. For Makarov and Grossvogel had no idea that they were both members of the network. The Russian was convinced he had found an ideal cover in a run-of-the-mill business firm. The Belgian supposed he had been dealing with a perfectly ordinary South American who had nothing whatever to hide. Even under the most savage torture, Grossvogel and Makarov could never denounce each other, since neither knew who or what his business partner really was.

This was the network which poor Fortner was hoping to flush out by the methods described. He may already have met the Big Chief, but obviously he was still a long way from knowing him.

———◆———

Fortner's informers had nothing to show for all the time they had spent eavesdropping in the cafés of Bruges—except, of course, a substantial list of expenses. According to their reports, the local Communists had suspended all activities in the hope of being quietly forgotten; they had been stunned by the Wehrmacht's whirlwind victories in Russia, and were convinced that Moscow was about to fall. Franz Fortner passed these findings on to Berlin. He received a telegram by return, stating that the transmitter must be operating from Knokke-le-Zoute. His hirelings transferred their custom to the cafés of Knokke and consumed a good deal of drink; but at no time did they hear any of the regulars jovially inquire whether the latest transmission had been a success. Forty-eight hours later, another telegram arrived from Berlin, this time naming Gent as the target area.

Determined to fight to the last drop of liquor, the informers swooped down on the cafés of Gent. Fortner dispatched the usual negative report to Berlin, but this time his superiors refused to be swayed; in their next telegram they stated that the transmitter was definitely hidden within the precincts of Gent University. Fortner organized a full-scale police hunt, which eventually ended in one of the university laboratories, where a group of physics students stood clustered round their professor, carrying out practical experiments in short-wave-radio work. The long, heroic battle of the bistros had ended in farce and failure.

Nevertheless there was no question of shelving the affair. Fortner, provided with his own receiver, himself heard the secret transmissions going out night after night. It was, of course, impossible for him to pinpoint the signals, for he had no tracking equipment; but this detail does not seem to have caused his chiefs to lessen their demands on him. Berlin was up in arms and determined to have the pianist's hide. Fortner was inundated with irate telegrams and phone calls and stormy personal visits, all insisting on early results. The Funkabwehr no longer risked naming the particular town in which the transmitter was concealed; it was sufficient for Fortner to know that the messages were being sent from somewhere in Belgium.

But however bitter the dregs might taste in Berlin, the flow of wines and spirits brought comfort to the Abwehr's informers as they continued to explore the many and varied cafés which Belgium has to offer.

6. A Born Officer

February, 1965. I had traveled to Munich on the labyrinthine train that I hoped would lead me to Franz Fortner. My contact in the city was Colonel Giskes, former head of German counterespionage in Holland. There was no doubt whatever that he knew where Fortner lived, but would he be willing to tell me?

Today, Giskes is a hale and hearty old gentleman, whose white hair goes well with his fresh complexion; he might almost have been hewn from pink granite. He lives the quiet life of a modest pensioner, in a small house built beside a small lake in the Munich suburbs. The welcome he gave me was as friendly as could be. After showing me to a chair, he announced that Reile would be joining us, which came as a surprise. From his headquarters in the Hotel Lutétia in Paris, Colonel Reile had directed German counterespionage in Occupied France over a period of four years. In short, with Giskes of Holland and Reile of France together in this plushy drawing room, only one man was needed to make a summit conference of former princes of German counterespionage operations in the west. The absent man was the one I had come in search of: Fortner of Belgium.

But I was no longer thinking about Fortner or the Big Chief or the Red Orchestra. The mantelpiece was cluttered with the usual keepsakes, of no interest to anyone except their owner. Among them were a number of those small metal flasks whose convex shape allows them to be slipped into the hip pocket. I knew what they meant to the old gentleman: they were reminders of his triumphantly successful Operation North Pole. After capturing a radio operator sent to Holland by the British, and persuading him to change sides, Colonel Giskes had duped London so successfully that dozens of Dutch agents, parachuted into the country as reinforcements, found German reception committees waiting for them when they landed, instead of the Resistance workers they had been expecting. The flasks on the mantelpiece bore witness to this tragedy. They symbolized the two moments when a man's life had attained its height. First the joy and excitement of takeoff—for this ration of whiskey was handed to him as he boarded the plane. The man slipping the flask into his hip pocket stood at the pinnacle of his existence. Driven from his country by defeat, he was returning to lay the foundations for victory—a hand-picked champion, carefully trained for the fight ahead, a hero treated with every consideration, till the moment he entered the plane. An hour later, he touched the lowest depths of despair. He was in the hands of Giskes, who always courteously invited prisoners to drink their whiskey before confiscating their flasks. Afterward, the man had set out along the hard road which led to a dawn appointment with the firing squad, and the flask had ultimately come to rest here, on this mantelpiece in a Munich house, among the ashtrays and the family photographs.

But for these macabre trophies, it would have been hard to establish any connection between the pensioner who sat nibbling biscuits and the mastermind of Operation North Pole. With the arrival of Oscar Reile, however, all the ghosts of the past were re-awakened. He is tall and scraggy, with a strained, twisted face and eyes that avoid being met; this man who conducted so many interrogations has the dull, hesitant voice of a suspect held for questioning. Yet Colonel Reile has never been subjected to the agonies which he imposed on hundreds of members of the French Resistance. He was in the Abwehr—like Giskes, like Fortner—and after the war the Allies left the gentlemen of the Abwehr in peace, reserving their reprisals for the guttersnipes of the Gestapo. Before very long, Reile—again, like Giskes—was absorbed into the intelligence service of the new Federal Republic. By what strange process of mimicry has he come to resemble the men who, twenty-odd years ago, used to be brought to his office in the Hotel Lutétia?

A fortnight later I was in West Berlin, ringing Franz Fortner's doorbell.

———◆———

A short, stumpy figure with a huge nose, a massive neck, giant ears, a stentorian voice, and a laugh that goes right through him: Franz Fortner at seventy. He must have made a formidable impression on the people whom he used to rouse from their beds in the early hours of the morning, with the harsh cry "Gestapo!" For although officers in the Abwehr might be gentlemen rather than guttersnipes, they were not above donning the dark plumage of their Gestapo colleagues and imitating their cry: it made a more menacing impression.

I had given him prior notice of my visit, and he let it be known that he was ready to talk. Up to what point, I wondered? When he let slip the name Claude Spaak, his wife flared up, berating him for his rashness. She felt that nothing but harm could come from implicating public figures in these past events. But I was already aware that Claude Spaak, brother of the famous Belgian statesman, had worked for the Big Chief. After questioning me for a while, Fortner decided that in view of the information I had previously acquired there was no harm in telling me the rest—though he was insistent that his real name should not be mentioned in my book.* These preliminaries seemed to show that the Fortners were not willing to accept that the past was past.

Anyway, it was agreed that the discussion should continue. But

* Naturally I have respected this wish. "Fortner" is, therefore, a pseudonym.

in what language? Fortner had forgotten his French, and my German was not good enough to carry me through lengthy exchanges which were likely to be full of technical terms and in which every adjective would carry weight. I suggested that we bring in an interpreter, and I named a woman whose reliability was beyond question. Fortner refused to let her in the door; he was so concerned for his safety that he never admitted strangers. I suggested then that we hold our talks elsewhere. Fortner ruled out any hotel room in West Berlin: it would be only too easy for someone to plant a microphone. A private apartment, then? That, he insisted, would be just as risky; but had I considered the French Consulate? He felt it would provide an admirable haven. So did I, but unfortunately I was not empowered to requisition official premises.

I forget whose idea it was to try to get Fortner to come to Paris. There I should be on home ground, and if he was willing to make the trip I could guarantee that our exchanges would be safe from outside interference. His immediate response was to turn me down flat; he recalled a number of celebrated kidnapings that Soviet Intelligence had carried out on French soil. At the same time, he obviously had an itch to see Paris again. He was beginning to veer toward agreement, when his wife put her foot down; she refused to accept the hazards entailed in such an expedition.

I left West Berlin next morning, feeling more bewildered than bitter. For years, the Red Orchestra had been Fortner's quarry. It was disconcerting to find the roles so completely reversed. The reversal had a certain piquancy, and I could not help enjoying it, but it was depriving me of the benefit of Fortner's personal recollections.

On my return to France, I wrote him a letter full of outrageously lyrical language, singing the joys of Paris in the spring. Three weeks later Fortner arrived at Orly. The airport was bristling with spotless new flags: it was the twentieth anniversary of the Allied victory over Germany.

Flags confronted him everywhere throughout his two-day visit; there were ceremonies all over Paris; the city was in festive mood. These reminders of a victory which had meant his own country's defeat kept poor Fortner in a state of permanent discomfort. He took pains to make it understood that his decision to cooperate with me was motivated by loftier considerations than a good meal. How entertained the Big Chief would have been by his old adversary's verbal contortions! In 1939 he was officially on Fortner's side against us. After 1941 he was on our side against Fortner. Since 1945 we and

Fortner had been associates in the fight against the network which the Big Chief had brought into being. Secret warfare calls for great flexibility of mind, and Fortner had clearly not broken training.

That is what appeals to me about him: Franz Fortner is an amateur; he always has been. When he left the Panzers after Dunkirk, he was instructed to report to a certain address in the center of Hamburg. He walked into the building named in his posting orders and knocked on a door bearing the sign, "Abwehr Department." A voice bade him enter. He introduced himself and asked what type of work he had been assigned to. "But didn't you read the notice?" "Yes, why?" "Do you mean to say you've never heard of the Abwehr?" "Can't say I have, particularly." "I see. Well, you'll be engaged in counterespionage." "Me? But I don't know the first thing about it!" "You speak English, don't you?" "A little—" "Speak French?" "Yes, a little. But—" "Fine, we'll send you to Brussels."

◆

Before he set out, he was handed a bundle of technical literature. It was no match, of course, for the thorough and intensive training which Trepper had received at the Red Army Academy, but it was better than nothing. And the new spy catcher was cheered by what he read; basically, his new profession was a good deal like the one he had practiced before the war. In civilian life he was a magistrate; his duties were roughly equivalent to those of a French *juge d'instruction;* it was he who sanctioned the arrest of lawbreakers and subjected them to interrogation. From now on, he would be arresting and interrogating spies. Was it really as simple as that? He thought so; but he was mistaken. The work of the examining magistrate begins with the arrest of the criminal; the work of the spy catcher is to all intents and purposes finished when he slips the handcuffs on his prisoner—at least, it should be. For the examining magistrate is concerned with the arrest and confession of one man. The counterespionage officer is after a complete network. The arrest of a single spy amounts to no more than the snapping of a link, whereas the real objective is to shatter the whole chain simultaneously. To achieve this it is necessary to shadow the identified agent, keep a close watch on whom he meets and where, put him in touch with a double-agent, and make every effort to persuade him to change sides. Of course, there may come a time when he must be arrested, but only when all else has failed.

Fortner still had a long way to go. As yet, he was merely searching for his quarry in cafés along the Belgian coast. There could be no denying that he had a lot to learn. Well, he would learn it—and meanwhile, the chiefs of German Intelligence would just have to put up with the loss of time; they had only themselves to blame for appointing this well-meaning amateur to do battle with the Big Chief's trained professionals. And in the end, of course, he would win. He would not return empty-handed: in a campaign directed against a small group of isolated men, he could call on the full machinery of German repression. Eventually he was bound to get his hands on the Big Chief. What would he do with him when that moment came?

He certainly would not torture him. His legal training forbade such things. It was his privilege, his duty even, to send a spy to his death, but he would not touch a hair of his head. Quite apart from his professional background, Fortner is a man of sound principles who regards violence with horror. Today, at the age of seventy-three, he devotes much of his time to a charity working to improve the lot of prisoners and assist in their rehabilitation.

Nor, in the event, did he conduct the interrogation as though he were dealing with one of his prewar criminals. As we chatted together over luncheon, Franz Fortner would occasionally close his mind to the delicacies set before him, lean toward me and, in a deafening whisper, embark on a sentence beginning with the words, "Speaking as one officer to another"—a phrase which is invariably a little embarrassing when addressed to someone who has never risen above the rank of corporal. Fortner is an officer. He is the kind of man who accepts his epaulettes in much the same spirit as a medieval knight accepting his sword or his Crusader's tunic. When he wishes to typify a human being admirable in every way, he will say, "The man was a born officer." Trepper could officially claim the rank of general in the Red Army. To him, of course, it was just a bit of nonsense; but Fortner instinctively modified his attitude as soon as he found out.

Fortner *did* learn his job, as time went by, but he always remained a "born officer." In human terms, this was commendable. In professional terms, it invited disaster. The Big Chief had already dealt victoriously with far more daunting opponents—the merciless authorities in Poland, the tough, well-trained Britons in the Palestine Police, the French counterintelligence agents hard on the trail of Fantômas—not to speak of his own leaders, who were perhaps the most daunting of all.

When Trepper boarded the train for Moscow, after clearing up the riddle surrounding the betrayal of the Fantômas network, he must have been wondering what was in store for him at the end of the journey—whether he would be taken to the building in Znamensky Street which housed the Soviet Military Intelligence (the "Center"), or to the cellars of Lubianka prison, where Stalin's victims were discreetly slaughtered? At that same moment, dozens of regional spy chiefs were on their way back to Moscow with dread in their hearts; they were all aware that they faced the risk of execution, and they could only wonder why.

What *was* the reason? After a gap of thirty years, the truth is hard to disentangle. It all began with a wonderfully elaborate plot worked out by Reinhard Heydrich. He produced forged documents purporting to show that Marshal Tukhachevsky, chief of the Red Army, was conspiring against Stalin. He had them conveyed to Moscow by a long and roundabout route. His object, quite plainly, was to unleash a holocaust in Soviet ruling circles: if the bears could be induced to devour one another, the Nazi wolf would reap the benefit. Heydrich's plan proved successful beyond all hopes. A wave of purges broke over Russia, robbing the army of its leadership. Can all this really have been occasioned by a few documents forged in the secret laboratories of the Gestapo? That is open to doubt. Stalin probably saw through the trick, but decided to use it to rid himself of an unduly popular marshal and a turbulent general staff. It seems equally likely that Tukhachevsky really had been planning a putsch. All in all, Heydrich probably did no more than start the hearse wheels rolling.

The origins may be muddled, but the consequences were plain: Stalin instantly vented his wrath on the Red Army. Those who had formed its backbone were either packed off to Siberia or treated to a bullet through the head. According to the most reliable sources, half the total number of officers were eliminated in this way—which meant thirty or forty thousand human beings. One target for special treatment was the department of Military Intelligence. This was logical enough. If the army was plotting, where else would the hub of conspiracy be but in this branch which kept to the shadows and dealt exclusively in secret intrigue? All the senior members of the hierarchy were disposed of, and then the agents working abroad were recalled to Russia; these were the most suspect of all, for their remoteness from the central authority gave them a freedom of movement admirably suited to conspiracy.

A BORN OFFICER 65

Had Trepper's name been included in the list of those wanted for questioning, or was he returning purely and simply because he had completed his mission? We cannot tell, but it is of minor importance. The fact is that by the act of returning to Moscow he was plunging into the bloodbath and could not fail to get splashed. We know that he had been the talented protégé of Jan Berzin, chief of Military Intelligence; Berzin was executed, together with his deputy, Alexander Korin. We also know that Trepper later said: "I saw all my friends vanish one by one, and I knew my turn was bound to come. It was my posting to Brussels that saved my life."

We have no detailed account of those terrible days, but it is not hard to imagine what they were like—an atmosphere of unremitting fear. Interrogations, during which men protested their innocence without knowing what they were accused of; confrontations with comrades who came in between two policemen and serenely admitted having been traitors for the past ten years. And always the fear. The obsessive need to supply the right answer—which set of words would open the doors to salvation, which set would lead straight to the cellars? Impossible to tell. Every answer was like a bet placed at roulette, with one's life as the ultimate stake. Slimy denunciations. Fits of cowardice. "According to X's statement, you addressed certain antirevolutionary remarks to him five years ago. . . ." "X is lying! Besides, I've always suspected him of being in the pay of the Imperialists." The weakest, and the most unlucky were removed to the shadowy depths of the prison. But the others, the men who were allowed to go free—can they be said to have emerged unscathed? They had been thrust into the arena like gladiators, and it was only by taking their comrades' lives that they were able to save their own.

That much is undeniable. But the gladiators of ancient Rome had rebelled and formed themselves into an army, and for years afterward they inflicted crushing defeats on the proudest of the Imperial legions —for no other reason than that their barbaric combats had made them stronger, more supple and more ruthless than the troops pitted against them.

It was the same with Trepper. Even if he was not a victim of the purge, even if his life was not directly threatened, he had seen his superiors and brothers-in-arms slaughtered by the score. And if he had to fight for his life, then he must afterward have set out from Moscow with the blood still dripping from his wounds. That is his own business; Trepper's spiritual welfare is outside our province. Yet this season in hell brought him to a kind of perfection—emphatically not the kind sought by the man of good will or the "born officer." To arrive at it, he had needed more than the adventures of his wandering youth, or his training with Fantômas, or even his indoctrination at the Red Army Academy. He was now capable of bearing up under the terrible ordeals that lay ahead. It was Trepper who had returned to Moscow; it was the Big Chief who set out from there for Brussels.

◆

We had talked about him a good deal by the time the waiter brought the brandy. It did not occur to either of us to propose a toast to the subject of our discussions, nor was there any need: the lunch, and our brief conference in Munich, were tribute enough in themselves. At a nearby table, a gentleman with a florid complexion was taking his son to task for his general worthlessness and undependability; beyond them, two men were discussing export figures; also present, of course, were the various members of the restaurant staff, a carefully graded hierarchy. All these people knew who Sorge was, but were not even aware that the Big Chief existed. Sorge's network had been completely wiped out by the Japanese police in 1943. Western counterespionage is still trying to unravel the workings of the Red Orchestra. Like every other art, spying has its unknown men of talent; they are, needless to say, its greatest practitioners.

7. The Harassed Pianist

Late in September, 1941, while Fortner's negative findings continued to swell the Abwehr's files, further signals were picked up from the "Berlin" transmitter. It functioned as capriciously as before, alternating spells of silence with bouts of feverish activity. But this time there could be no room for doubt; the pianist was in Berlin.

The Funkabwehr was given strict orders to put an end to this scandalous situation.

It cannot be denied that the age of technology has robbed life of many of its major thrills. The chase, for instance, is no longer what it used to be: the ferocity of the boar hunt has gone for good, and nothing could be tamer than the present-day practice of riding to hounds in suburbs where little is achieved save traffic jams and a few uneasy moments as the horses lose their footing on slippery macadam roads. Yet technology has in part made up for this loss by producing an altogether engrossing version of the oldest and cruelest hunt of all: the manhunt.

The pianist plays the part of the pursued stag. Obviously he does not enjoy the same mobility as the animal, for as a rule he always transmits from the same spot. On the other hand, hidden in a large town, he is as difficult to drive from cover as the stag hidden in a thick forest. It would be foolish to hope to stumble on either by chance: the hounds must find the tracks, pick up the scent and hear the cries of the hunted animal; the radio operator's scent and cries are, of course, the sound waves which he projects into the ether.

Not only are these waves detectable, but special tracking equipment makes it easy to determine the direction of the beam. By process of cross-checking, it is therefore possible to pinpoint the position of the transmitter. Imagine that you are a German serving in the Funkabwehr with orders to silence a transmitter operating in Occupied Paris. How do you go about it? You send a team of men with a tracking device to the Place de la Concorde, say, and another to the Place Wagram; you yourself, however, do not stir from your office; the pleasures and excitements of this kind of chase are all in the mind. Your weapons are a street map of Paris and a pair of celluloid discs with graduated markings from zero to three hundred and sixty degrees, with a silk thread attached to the center of each disc. You place the discs on the street map so that the center of the first fits exactly over the Place de la Concorde, and the center of the second exactly over the Place Wagram. You are ready and waiting; now it is up to your two teams of hunters to do their work.

As soon as the pianist starts transmitting, they pick up the beam, determine its direction and pass the facts and figures back to you. If the team in the Place de la Concorde reports a bearing of eighty degrees, you take hold of the silk thread attached to the appropriate disc and hold it across the map in line with the eighty-degree mark. Let's say the thread runs straight along the Champs-Élysées, crosses the Place de l'Étoile and trails off somewhere in the direction of Neuilly. At this point, the team in the Place Wagram tells you its findings: a hundred and sixty degrees. You take the second length of thread as you did the first, and hold it in line with the hundred-sixty-degree mark. It stretches down the Avenue de Wagram and extends toward southern Paris. But the two threads intersect at the Place de l'Étoile. You know that your quarry·is lurking exactly where they meet—in other words, under the Arc de Triomphe.

Of course it isn't really as simple as that. In the first place, you need several such operations before you can confidently narrow your search to the area round the Étoile. Then again, pianists obviously do not hide in public monuments, or even in isolated houses, for these are easy to trace; they have a preference for working-class neighborhoods, with row upon row of tenements. Your pair of silk threads will quite often prove inadequate for determining the exact position of the pianist. To find him, you will have to employ the "suitcase" technique, which should detect fluctuations in the electric field in the immediate vicinity of the transmitter. If you don't happen to possess these useful instruments, or if they fail to produce results, then you will have to organize a search party, send them to the most likely group of buildings and instruct them to throw the main switches, one by one, while the transmission is in progress. For we are back in the nineteen-forties, don't forget, and the transistor has not yet been introduced; transmitters will not work unless they are plugged in. If you cut off the electricity in a given building and there is an immediate break in transmission, you can be sure that your prey is on the premises; it only remains for you to unleash your hounds.

——————◆——————

It is the degree of intelligence shown by the quarry that gives hunting its interest, and from this point of view man is no disappointment. He will make every attempt to cover his tracks. Every pianist performs on a given wavelength; the receiving station tunes in to this wavelength at the agreed times of transmission; once alerted to this procedure, his pursuers place themselves in ambush. Thus, the pianist is like the stag whose regular patterns of movement are known to the gamekeepers. But he is able to modify this pattern by varying his wavelength. The operation is a tricky one: unless there is perfect harmony and understanding between pianist and receiving station, the soloist's pyrotechnics will be self-defeating and result only in loss of contact. Here, for instance, is the transmitting routine employed by one Soviet radio operator: he used to put out his call signal on forty-three meters; Moscow would acknowledge reception on thirty-nine meters; the pianist would then transmit his message on forty-nine meters. And he would introduce an additional stratagem: when he changed from forty-three to forty-nine meters, he would put out a fresh call signal to throw the pursuers off the trail, by leading them to think that another transmitter was joining in.

Time can be gained by such tricks, but the enemy is bound to see through them in the end. For complete success, a pianist would have to multiply his acrobatics, altering his wavelengths and call-signs over and over again. This is technically possible, but due allowance must be made for human lapses. The pianist is not a robot. Working as he does under exhausting nervous strain, an overcomplicated transmitting routine might well cause him to lose his way. A more down-to-earth solution would be to transmit from a variety of addresses. But if he does this, his pursuers will stage an increasing number of roundups in the streets, and a good many pianists will be caught in the dragnet, hopelessly incriminated, by the fact that they have their transmitters with them. Conclusion: it is not the equipment that must be moved, but the operators. If the network is a wealthy one, each pianist will have several "music boxes" at his disposal. Failing this, the pianists will take turns with the instruments available, each performing on his own personal wavelength. In this case, the time factor becomes of prime importance. It is up to the pianist to sense whether a particular hideout is on the point of being blown wide open. Meanwhile the pack endeavors to reach the lair with ever greater rapidity, in the hope of surprising its quarry.

You will recall that two stationary teams were employed to deal with the transmitter concealed beneath the Arc de Triomphe. The method was slow and cumbersome: you were able to take only one bearing per transmission; afterward you had to move your equipment, wait for the next transmission and start all over again. But you are suddenly given one of the RDF (radio direction finding) vans built by the Loewe-Opta-Radio Company. This will enable you to speed things up. One of your teams continues to operate from a fixed point (in Paris, an army barracks in the Boulevard Suchet), but the other drives around the streets. The resulting mobility allows several bearings to be taken, where only one could be taken before, and you achieve your objective far more quickly. If, as you soon will, you have several vans at your disposal, you can take many bearings, which will result in even greater speed; it will take you an average of only forty minutes to locate a transmitter and raid it.

The pianists counter these moves by progressively reducing the length of their transmissions. You, meanwhile, force them to squander their precious stock of minutes and seconds; you keep them cooped up in the lair by jamming their messages so that they have to be repeated several times. The pianists then surround themselves with a string of lookouts; the latter have no difficulty in spotting your gray-topped Peugeots, but before long you disguise the vehicles as ambulances or bakery trucks. At the same time, you have your hunting ground thoroughly patrolled by police, with orders to arrest anyone hanging about the streets in a suspicious manner. Anyway, the lookouts do not bother you for long; soon the Loewe-Opta-Radio Company can supply you with a direction finder so small that it can be worn around the waist. When your vehicles are reasonably close to the transmitter, they draw up and unload a number of pedestrians, all deeply absorbed in their newspapers. This is an altogether different story from the old "suitcase" method; the ultrafine wire connecting the apparatus to the wearer's ear is practically invisible.

The final stages of the hunt are dangerous and may entail loss of life or limb. If caught in the act, the pianist may decide to shoot it out. Or his transmitter may be fitted with a booby trap. Or your men find a bottle of brandy on his table, already open and partly consumed; they help themselves and are fatally poisoned. But these are the normal risks of hunting; they provide its bitter savor. They may cost you a few men, but the final victory is yours. By the summer of 1943, the network no longer transmits from Paris, except in cases of extreme urgency; you have won full control.

———◆———

It was a silent, stealthy hunt, with no echoing horns or gaily colored habits, yet it nearly always ended like the other kind—with the killing of the game. And it was of decisive importance, too, for in the war between Resistance elements and German invader it was invariably the battle on which everything else depended. Without a transmitter, a network loses all value; it has been set up for the sole purpose of collecting information and can be effective only if it passes that information on. Yet the very instrument that justifies its existence automatically places the network in jeopardy, for it alerts the other side to its activities. Take the heads of the Abwehr: they had no idea that a Soviet spy ring was operating in Belgium, much less in Germany; it was the pianists who put them on the track. A submarine is not detectable to the naked eye when submerged, but it calls attention to itself the moment it raises its periscope. A spy ring is

like a submarine obliged to sail with its periscope permanently showing above the surface—the periscope being the aerial of its transmitter.
It was a cruel hunt, for the quarry was human. Each time one
of the Big Chief's radio operators sat down at his transmitter, the look
on his face showed the strain which the hunt was imposing on him,
the agonized suspense of feeling the trap close. He was as vulnerable
as an infantryman emerging from his trench and exposing himself
to the enemy's machine-gun fire. He knew that the pack was on his
trail; he pictured the police vans creeping closer and closer; in his
mind's eye, he saw those casual-looking pedestrians picking their way
along the pavement, with the short-range detectors concealed beneath
their coats; already he seemed to hear the shots which would soon
shatter the lock on his door. For this man, courage took the form of
staying in his chair and going on with the transmission. That must
have been harder than facing a bayonet charge.

It was a thrilling hunt, for heroism, stripped of its pomp and circumstance, here attained its highest and purest form. The time was
not far off when Moscow, turning a deaf ear to the Big Chief's entreaties—and issuing what amounted to a death sentence—would
oblige the pianist performing on the "PTX" to transmit night after
night for *five hours at a stretch*. It will at once be obvious to the
reader that the pianist in question was a man of even greater valor
than the soldier who is ordered to cover the retreat of an entire
column by standing his ground and delaying the enemy until he is
killed. Lieutenant Makarov, alias Carlos Alamo, the man who had no
taste for action unless it was dashing and flamboyant, is even more
admirable for those five hours' continuous transmission than for his
extraordinary maiden flight over the battlefields of the Spanish Civil
War.

It was a frantic hunt, for in the eyes of the pursuers the flow of
information which the pianist was passing to the enemy was like the
sight of their own blood running from a septic wound. To silence
the transmitter was to stop the hemorrhage; to make the pianist talk,
and so uncover the remainder of the network, was to kill the infectious germs.

It was a grotesque hunt at times—as witness events in Berlin during the month of October, 1941.

Things had got off to a bad start: the RDF vans manufactured
by the Loewe-Opta-Radio Company had been sent to Paris and Warsaw; none was available to the Funkabwehr when it launched its of-

fensive against the pianist operating from the heart of Berlin. Who was to blame for this appalling blunder? At the Funkabwehr they directed bitter jibes at the Hermann Goering Research Institute. Whatever the truth of the matter, they were going to have to do without vans and rely on stationary equipment. In plainer words, they were about to waste a good deal of valuable time. For the pianist was obviously a wily fox: preliminary bearings showed that he transmitted from three separate establishments. The outlook was far from cheerful.

A major problem arose concerning the style of dress which ought to be worn by the two teams operating the RDF equipment. There could be no question of leaving them in their military uniforms; that would make them too easy to spot. On the other hand, the chief of the Funkabwehr was completely opposed to the idea of their wearing mufti; that kind of thing would mean the end of discipline in the Wehrmacht and lead to the total undermining of the German armed forces. The incontrovertible argument was that a soldier in civilian clothes was prevented from showing his superior officer those outward signs of respect provided for in the regulations. The reader may well find this hard to believe, but the truth of the story is vouched for by W. F. Flicke, a former member of the Funkabwehr. In the end, a compromise was agreed upon: the two teams were to wear the paramilitary outfit of the postal services.

On the first day of the operation, the pianist glanced out of one of the windows in the house from which he was transmitting and saw a large tent down in the street, sheltering a team of post-office workers. So far, so good: the post-office authorities used tents of this kind for cable laying and repair work. It did not even unsettle him to observe that Wehrmacht trucks were being used to carry the equipment for the job; there was such a dearth of transport at present that the public services were quite likely to turn to the army for help. On the other hand, he could think of no rational explanation for the fact that the men engaged in the work were attired in post-office uniforms. He could have sworn that cable-laying teams and repair gangs usually wore overalls.

On the following day, the pianist strolled about for a while before going to the flat that served as his second hideout. At one point he came upon a large tent sheltering a team of post-office workers. He ambled past the tent and heard a man say quietly, *"Jawohl, Herr Leutnant!"*

On the third day, while sauntering in the vicinity of his third hideout, the pianist came to a halt beside another large tent sheltering another team of post-office workers. He asked one of them for a light: this particular man appeared to be standing guard. As he held the proffered flame to his cigarette, he distinctly caught the characteristic whistle of a receiver tuned to a certain wavelength.

On the fourth and subsequent days, the teams of German technicians stayed tuned in in vain. Eventually they were obliged to pack up their tents, return their uniforms to the post office and go back to their usual surroundings, there to mull over their disappointment. They had nothing to show for all their efforts. There was deep depression at every level of the Funkabwehr.

Among the opposition in the Berlin network, which German counterespionage pictured as being strongly organized and fiendishly well-directed, all was chaos and confusion. The network had been formed too quickly. The Soviet diplomats whose mania for "prying" and "snooping" was castigated in the Heydrich Report had been repatriated to Russia at the outbreak of war, in exchange for the German embassy staff in Moscow. Before leaving, they had sown a few seeds for the future, but only at the very last minute, on the run, proceeding in a rough-and-ready manner particularly ill-suited to espionage. For in the end, owing to the very nature of the activities involved, inadequate groundwork is bound to prove even more fatal to spying than to other forms of endeavor.

The intermittent silences of the Berlin transmitter were at present taken to be part of a deliberate campaign of mystification. In fact, they were due to the pianist's inexperience. By mistake, he plugged his "music box" straight into the mains; the equipment burnt out. After it was repaired, he became confused by the complicated instructions he had been given. They would have been ideal for a virtuoso, but far exceeded the capabilities of this beginner. The Russian embassy official from whom he had originally received the set had told him to change his call signal and wavelength after a certain number of effective communications, in accordance with a prearranged rhythm. As we saw earlier, this was one way of putting the Funkabwehr off the scent. By "effective communication" Moscow meant a radio contact in the course of which information was passed on. The pianist interpreted the phrase in quite a different way;

for him, *any* radio contact was an "effective communication," even
if it merely repeated an earlier message or cleared up some technical
detail. The inevitable consequence of this misunderstanding was that
Moscow stayed tuned to wavelength A while the pianist vainly put
out call signs on wavelength B. In the end, the two sides managed to
get in touch and thrash the problem out. The transmissions started up
again. In keeping with his instructions, the pianist employed a series
of six wavelengths and thirty call signs. In other words, his first six
"effective communications" were all made on different wavelengths;
for the seventh, he returned to the one he had used for the first
"effective communication," and so on. The same system governed
the use of call signs; and since changes in the latter followed a
separate time pattern, the Funkabwehr seemed doomed to permanent
bafflement. In the event, however, it was the pianist who soon became
baffled—even more so than at the start. He had been supplied with
a list of thirty call signs. But certain months of the year have thirty-
one days. To the headquarters staff in Moscow, and to all experienced
pianists, it was self-evident that no transmission was to be made on
the thirty-first day; in this way, the monthly rhythm would not be
upset. The Berlin pianist was unaware of this convention. He transmitted on the thirty-first day, reverting to the first call signal on
the list. The upshot was that when Moscow tuned in again on the
thirty-second day, they couldn't find their man—while he was vainly
putting out calls on a completely different wavelength. Contact had
been broken.

Something desperately needed to be done about it. Back in
Moscow, the Center decided that a number of experienced radio
operators should be parachuted into Germany. But these agents
would have no chance of escaping the tight German security net
unless they were first put through a vigorous course of training. Another thing: Germany was a very long way from the Russian air-
fields. It would be necessary to persuade the British to take charge
of the operation, and this called for high-level negotiations. Between
them, training and negotiations would lead to a considerable loss of
time, at a stage in the war when the German attack had lost none of
its initial momentum and was still shattering the human wall which
the Russians had erected in its path. One by one the Soviet divisions
were being driven back, encircled, annihilated; the road to Moscow
lay open. With the Red Army on the brink of disaster, the information sent back by the networks was as irreplaceable as an oxygen
tank to a patient at death's door. There could be no question of

letting the Berlin network remain unproductive while preparations were made for the "drop."

On October 10, 1941, Kent was summoned to the rescue. The text of the message Moscow transmitted to him in Brussels is worthy of note, for it presages the first appearance in this story of a figure attired in ceremonial frock coat, white gloves and shiny top hat—the German executioner. For as a result of the thoughtless transmission of these few sentences, dozens of men and women were in due course hanged or beheaded:

KLS from RTX. 1010. 1725 wds qbt.
From Director to Kent. Personal.
Report immediately Berlin three addresses indicated and determine causes failures radio links. If stoppages recur, undertake transmissions personally. Efforts three Berlin groups and transmission information vitally important. Addresses: Neuwestend, Altenburger Allee 19, third right. Coro —Charlottenburg, Fredericastrasse 26a, second left. Wolf.—Friedenau, Kaiserstrasse 18, fourth left. Bauer. Send Eulenspiegel back here. Password: Director. Report progress by October 20. New (repeat new) plan in force for three stations. qbt ar. KLS from RTX.

Three days later, on October 13, the Berlin network received the following message from the Center:

RSK from BTR. 1310.1425.54 wds qbt.
From Director to Freddy for Wolf who will pass on to Coro. Kent arriving from BRX. Responsible for reestablishing radio traffic. In event of failure or further stoppage all material to be conveyed to Kent for transmission. Held-up material to be handed to him. Attempt resume traffic on fifteenth. Center will stay tuned from 0900.

So Kent proceeded to Berlin, with orders to carry out emergency repairs. He had already established contact with the German network back in April, on the occasion of that visit to the Leipzig Fair which had so distressed poor Margarete Barcza that she had lost those half-dozen pounds. This time he met the two leaders of the spy ring in the Berlin zoo. Within a few days he had procured an extra transmitter for the pianist and had put him in touch with an elderly Communist militant who had studied radio telegraphy in Moscow before the war; the idea was that the old man would coach the pianist up to standard. After Berlin, Kent traveled to Prague. During the journey, he made contact with the wife of Rauch, the agent working for British Intelligence. We know this because he sent Maria Rauch a telegram stating that he would meet her on the platform at Graudnitz, where his train was scheduled to stop for a few minutes; he told her to look out for him near the dining car. The nature of Kent's mission to Prague is unknown, but it certainly helps to demonstrate that the Red Orchestra had musicians everywhere.

He returned to Brussels early in November, with the satisfying feeling that he had accomplished his mission. But it was not long before bad news caught up with him: the Berlin pianist had been obliged to cancel his recitals. On October 21, just after Kent's departure for Prague, the Funkabwehr had gone ahunting. The pianist was forced off the air. From now on, in compliance with Moscow's orders, all information gathered by the Berlin network had to be transmitted via Brussels. With typical thoroughness, Kent had already provided for this eventuality by establishing a string of couriers between Germany and Belgium. Naturally this would mean a lot more work for Brussels. Poor Alamo, spending more and more hours at his transmitter, was still dreaming of the great times he had had in the Spanish war.

8. Rendezvous at Stalingrad

It may be asked whether failure to transmit the intelligence garnered in Berlin would have cost the Russians much. The value of the information at stake can be assessed from the following messages:

Coro to Director. Source: Maria.
Heavy artillery from Koenigsberg bound for Moscow. Heavy coastal batteries dispatched Pillau same destination.

Coro to Director. Source: Gustav.
Material losses armored units eastern front equivalent eleven divisions.

Coro to Director. Source: Arwid.
Hitler ordered capture Odessa by September 15. Delaying actions
southern end of front seriously upsetting lineup German attack.
Information supplied by an OWK officer.

Coro to Director. Source: Moritz.
Plan II in force past three weeks. Probable objective is to reach
Archangel-Moscow-Astrakhan line by end November. All troop
movements being executed in accordance with this plan.

Coro to Director.
Tanks belonging propaganda companies delayed in Bryansk since
October 19 pending entry German troops Moscow originally
scheduled October 20.

Coro to Director. Source: OKW via Arwid.
Eastern front. Majority German divisions, sorely taxed by heavy
losses sustained, have lost their normal human potential. Fully
trained soldiers now amount to only small percentage. Reinforcements made up of soldiers with four to six months' training.

These are typical of the hundreds of messages sent. The Berlin
network was fully conversant with the Wehrmacht's invasion plans;
it knew just how the German forces were distributed, and the
strength and quality of the reserves; it was able to give advance notice
of sectors where paratroops were to be dropped; it kept Moscow
informed of the enemy's losses in men and equipment. And that was
not all. The network had precise information on Germany's output
of fuel and chemicals, and the monthly production figures of the aircraft industry. Its antennae extended to the upper echelons of the
Nazi Party and had even infiltrated the High Command, so that it
was familiar with the lines of reasoning and patterns of dispute
prevalent among the senior generals. It was able to interpret the
subtle schemes which lay behind Ribbentrop's secret diplomacy. It
kept track of Hitler's day-to-day movements.

This was the brand of vital information which now had to be
relayed via Kent's transmitter.

＊

And it was to Brussels that the Center directed its constant flow
of requests for information. Some of these were concerned with
troop movements in Belgium and Holland, or with the production

capacity of factories working for the Germans, or with the attitude of the civilian population. But most of them ranged far beyond the local scene. If the Director wanted to know more about the strength of the Swiss army, or the military potentialities of the German chemical industry, or the real extent of the Wehrmacht's losses, he invariably contacted Brussels:

Director to Kent.
Need report on Swiss army in relation to possible German invasion. Strength of army in event general mobilization. Nature of existing fortifications. Quality of munitions. Details air force, armor and artillery. Technical resources of various armed services.

Director to Kent.
Established production capacity German chemical works (poison gas). Report on preparations sabotage factories in question.

Director to Kent.
Schneider's sources seem well-informed. Ask him to ascertain total German losses to date. Break down figures by campaigns and separate branches service.

Brussels was also used as a clearinghouse for the information gathered in France by the Big Chief. This was as plentiful and many-faceted as the intelligence collected by the Berlin network, and equally accurate. No other Allied espionage system in the 1939–45 war was anywhere near as successful in laying bare German intentions. Here are a few samples:

Source: Suzanne.
Line proposed by High Command for winter quarters to be adopted by German army early November, runs Rostov–Isium–Kursk–Orel–Bryansk–Dorogobusch–Novgorod–Leningrad. Hitler has rejected this proposal and ordered sixth attack on Moscow with all available matériel. Should offensive fail, German troops in retreat will temporarily be without matériel reserves.

Source: Emile.
Two new toxic combinations discovered: 1. Nitrosylfluoride. Formula: HC_2F. 2. Kakodylisocyanide. Formula: (CH_3) 2 ASNC.

Source: Ninette.
Germans mustering craft in Bulgarian ports for operation Caucasus.

Source: Berlin.
Some military circles now rule out possibility total victory view of failure Blitzkrieg eastern front. Distinct tendency to influence Hitler toward negotiating with Britain. Influential generals OKW think war will last another thirty months and hope afterward for compromise peace.

Source: Jacques.
Germans have lost cream of their army on eastern front. Superiority Russian armor undisputed. High Command disheartened by Hitler's continual alteration strategic plans and objectives.

Source: Paulette.
German officer reports mounting tension between Italian army and Fascist Party. Serious incidents Rome and Verona. Military authorities sabotaging Party indoctrination. *Coup d'état* a possibility, though not in immediate future. Germans mustering forces between Munich and Innsbruck for possible intervention.

Source: Maria.
From a German senior officer returning from Berlin. Influential military circles skeptical outcome war eastern front. Even Goering doubts military victory. German garrisons and depots empty of troops. Speculations in Berlin concerning death of Hitler and subsequent military dictatorship.

Source: Pierre.
Total strength German army: 412 divisions, 21 currently in France, chiefly second-line divisions. Numbers continually dwindling on account of frequent withdrawals. Troops previously in south and vicinity Bordeaux along Atlantic Wall now heading east. Three divisions involved. Total strength Luftwaffe nearly a million men, including ground staff.

Source: José.
Six miles west Madrid, German monitoring station intercepting British, American and French radio communications . . . Disguised as a business firm trading under the name "Stürmer."

Spanish government informed and abetting scheme. One officer and fifteen men in mufti. Branch office in Seville. Direct teleprinter service between Madrid and Berlin, with relay stations in Bordeaux and Paris.

———————◆———————

So Brussels was more than the head of a Resistance organization covering Belgium and Holland; it was the heart of that extraordinarily complex system which had acquired the name "Red Orchestra." It pumped in the information gleaned by dozens of agents scattered all over Europe and conveyed it to the Center by the main artery of its radio link.

To the ears of Moscow, half deafened by the roar of German bombing and shelling, the voice of Brussels was the voice of hope. Fronts might be giving way, dikes bursting one by one and the dark tide washing over the land until it all but reached the walls of the Kremlin, but Brussels continued to register and pass on those tiny dissonances which belied the proud trumpetings of the German war machine: the doubts expressed by Hitler's generals, the troops' exhaustion, the wear and tear on matériel. And at the point at which the Führer was confidently bawling, "I declare today, without the slightest reservation, that our enemy in the east is overthrown and will never rise again," it was the voice of Brussels that kept Moscow from renouncing all faith in the future.

Brussels also supplied the Red Army chiefs with a good deal of tactical information, but they were so mercilessly hustled by the enemy that they had little opportunity to take advantage of it. The sheer weight of German superiority deprived Russia of any hope of withstanding the impact, even though she had been warned of what was to come. She had not yet been afforded sufficient breathing space to reorganize her defenses and turn the incoming intelligence to good account.

But at long last such a breathing space was granted, and a message from Brussels earned a place in history, instead of vanishing in the wastebasket of some field H.Q. On November 12, 1941, even as the commanders of the three German army groups on the eastern front were meeting in Orcha to complete their plans for the final onslaught on the Soviet capital, whose armored vanguard was now only fifteen miles away, the Center received the following historic communication:

Kent to Director. Source: Coro.
Plan III, directed against the Caucasus and originally scheduled for November, will be carried out in spring 1942. All troops to be in position May 1. Whole logistic effort directed to this purpose begins February 1. Deployment bases for offensive against Caucasus: Lozovatka–Balakleya–Chuguyev–Belgorod–Achtyrka–Krasnograd. Headquarters in Kharkov. Details following.

Moscow, of course, was never captured. Five days later, on November 17, 1941, the Mongolian horsemen of the 44th Division drew their sabers and charged in defense of Mussino, less than thirty miles from the Kremlin; their bloody assault marked the arrival on the battlefield of the fresh divisions drawn from Siberia. Stalin had been able to throw these fresh divisions into the breach because the head of the Tokyo spy ring, Richard Sorge, had assured him that Japan was not going to stab Russia in the back by attacking Siberia. And even while the fight for survival continued at the gates of Moscow, the Red Orchestra, by its historic message of November 12, was giving the Soviet leaders nine months' notice of the crucial battle awaiting them—at Stalingrad, on the distant Volga.

Sorge had made it possible to stave off defeat at Moscow. Now Trepper and his men were paving the way for victory at Stalingrad.

——◆——

Following their setback in Berlin, the staff of the Funkabwehr noticed that the PTX transmitter had increased its output considerably. Comparison of the numbers of messages transmitted showed that the PTX pianist had taken over the duties of his silenced colleague in the German capital. As a result of the patient quests carried out from Kranz and Breslau, the Funkabwehr was now certain that the transmitter was concealed somewhere in Brussels. The Funkabwehr lost no time in supplying Fortner with a team of experts, complete with RDF vans and a pair of short-range, suitcase-style detectors. With all this gadgetry and expertise, failure seemed impossible. This time the hunt was off to a good start.

9. The Atrébates Raid

He was still referred to as the PTX pianist, though obviously he had abandoned his original call sign long ago; by now he was employing thirty different ones and juggling with wavelengths like a born master. The Funkabwehr's technicians strove hard to keep up with his acrobatics, but on November 17 they made a discovery that would add appreciably to the complications of the hunt: there were three secret transmitters in Brussels, all—at different times—using the same call signs and the same wavelengths. In these circumstances, it was impossible to tell which of the three was the notorious PTX that had been causing trouble for so long, even though one was more active than the others.

The tracking teams arrived in Brussels on November 30, 1941. Their mood was one of despondency. It would not be easy to trace three separate transmitters using identical call signs and wavelengths; and if the pianists also had a good number of hideouts, the hunt would be uphill all the way. On the other hand, they were cheered by the fact that the transmissions took place at night, for the curfew would deny the pianists the protection of a string of carefully posted lookouts. This time there would be no need to dress up as post-office workers.

The first attempt to take bearings proved an unmitigated disaster. The lieutenant in charge could not believe his eyes when he found that his lengths of silk thread *did not intersect at any point*. There was something very wrong somewhere, and he didn't know what. As a test, they took bearings on a German transmitting station whose coordinates were previously known to them; they discovered that their equipment was "out" by several degrees. Since the vans were absolutely new, it could only be assumed that saboteurs were at work within the Loewe-Opta-Radio Company. The tracking party returned to the hunt, making due allowance for the various deflections.

It did not take long to establish that the three pianists were operating from set points—the first from the Etterbeek district of Brussels; the second from Ukkel; the third from Laeken. The Funkabwehr specialists would have preferred to operate calmly and steadily, in hopes of bagging all three transmitters at the same time; but they had to take their orders from the local Abwehr leaders, who decided on a different course. Berlin had been badgering them about the PTX transmitter for months, until it haunted every moment of their days. The wretched thing must be silenced at the earliest possible moment, or they would never have any peace. Once they had wiped out this nightmare, there would be ample opportunity to track down the other two pianists at a later date.

The technicians took the view that the PTX transmitter was almost certainly the one which had been performing most assiduously during the past few days, from somewhere in Etterbeek. A number of bearings were taken, and the pianist's lair was traced to a narrow, seedy-looking street with hardly any stores—the Rue des Atrébates.

Franz Fortner says: "Officially, I was still in charge of counter-espionage in Gent, but Berlin had ordered me to keep an eye on developments regarding the secret transmitter. When it was traced to Brussels, I moved into a magnificent apartment in the Boulevard Brand Whitlock which had been abandoned by its English owner. Incidentally, she wrote to me after the war and thanked me for leaving everything in good condition. The concierge, of course, had no idea what my line of work was; she imagined I was in the black market, and to encourage that belief I used to let her have some soap now and then.

"The arrival of the Funkabwehr team changed the position entirely. Up to that point, I had been reduced to listening to the PTX every night on my receiver, without being able to do anything about it. I was particularly impressed by the technician in charge of the 'suitcase' detector. He was a sergeant, very ambitious, very self-assured. He told me without hesitation: 'I'm going to capture that transmitter!'

"Soon the operation was in full swing. I even remember us installing equipment in a Fieseler Storch and flying over the city. We were greatly helped by that fact that the transmitter was on the air five hours a night. The Russians obviously had no suspicion of what was going on. And why should they have? They could hardly have guessed that we had such accurate equipment. The suitcase detector, in particular, was a technical marvel without equal anywhere else in the world; even the real old professionals were beside themselves with admiration when they saw it. I'm fairly certain this was the first time it had been used outside Germany.

"Anyway, our investigations led us to the Rue des Atrébates. My sergeant was convinced that the transmitter was in number 99 or 101 or 103. At my instructions, discreet inquiries were made about the occupants. Living in number 99 was a Flemish family noted for its pro-German sympathies. The tenants of number 101 were South American; according to neighbors, they worked for the German Economics Ministry. Number 103 was empty. Instinct told me the transmitter was bound to be hidden in the empty house, but we needed to make absolutely certain. At the rear of these three houses, and in the same block, was a requisitioned house in which two members of the Todt Organization lived; we discovered this from the Brussels Housing Department. I got our commanding general in Belgium to confine these two men to their quarters for a few days. We told them what was going on; they promised to keep their mouths shut and stay indoors. So we moved in with them, and for four or five nights the sergeant was able to carry out tests within a very short distance of the suspected houses. Finally he assured me that the transmissions were coming from the middle house, number 101, where the South Americans lived. It was time to take action.

"But unlike my sergeant, who—self-assured as ever—could see no reason why the two of us should not go bursting in on our own, I took the view that considerable caution was necessary. Informants had made it clear that the Communists were now much tougher to deal with; if attacked, they were determined to fight to the death. I talked the military authorities into lending me ten members of the secret police. Would ten be enough? I was not altogether sure. It so happened there was a barracks quite close to the Rue des Atrébates, in the Boulevard St.-Michel. Stationed in the barracks was a battalion of elderly territorials, all aged fifty or over, who were used for guarding railway lines, viaducts and so forth. The commanding officer gave me a chilly welcome and told me that he could do nothing for me. But one of his company commanders got excited over the project and put twenty-five men at my disposal.

"Now at last we were ready to strike. The raid was timed to take place at about 2 A.M. on the night of December 12–13, 1941."

———◆———

Bill Hoorickx says: "As time went by, I got to know Carlos Alamo better and better; we even shared a flat, on occasion. His personality appealed to me considerably, and we had endless discussions. It may surprise you that most of our talk was about metaphysics. In my early years, I had wanted to join a Protestant mission to the colonies; I even studied tropical medicine, before painting got a hold on me. But I still had a strong faith, and I thoroughly enjoyed debating religious issues with Alamo. To him, it was a revelation—for in Russia, of course, such matters are not raised. I will not claim I converted Alamo, but I did give him a greater sense of things spiritual.

"None of which alters the fact that Alamo was a man, with a man's weaknesses and appetites. I'd introduced him to a very pretty colored girl from the Netherlands Indies—Sumatra or Java. Her name was Suzanne Schmitz. He made her his mistress, and for a while she even lived with us. One day he invited us to dinner in the Rue des Atrébates. I'd been there a couple of times before and had mentioned the fact to Rauch. 'Really,' he said, 'I didn't know they also had a place in that part of town.' I wasn't unduly surprised at his ignorance: it would be wrong to say Rauch was deliberately left out of things, but he always gave me the impression of being rather withdrawn. He was a 'lone wolf.'

"I accepted Alamo's invitation, which naturally included Anya, the woman who is now my wife. But when I mentioned it to her, she said, 'Impossible. You must call it off. I promised Olga Sherbatov we would have dinner with her.' I phoned Alamo, who was extremely disappointed and tried to make us change our minds. But we couldn't let our friend Olga down. So it was arranged that Suzanne should go to dinner at the Rue des Atrébates alone on the evening of December 13."

———————◆———————

The Big Chief arrived in Brussels on December 12 and proceeded to Kent's apartment, where a room was always ready for him. It seems safe to assume that he was in an optimistic frame of mind: the Japanese had bombed Pearl Harbor five days earlier, and this extension of the war altered the outlook completely. He was carrying one of the three suitcases he always took with him on his travels. They varied in size, but all were of the highest quality and built to the same design. There was a wardrobe compartment large enough to hold two, four or six suits; also a shoe rack and a special drawer for books. Margarete had been considerably surprised when she had seen him with these suitcases, for they were exactly the same as

Kent's; she had been even more surprised to discover that Alamo owned an identical set.

She was none too fond of Trepper; he made her uneasy. Following Kent's departure for the Leipzig Fair, Trepper had shamelessly taken up residence in the Avenue Slegers and done his best to make a play for her. He stuck at it for three whole days and then decamped, saying, "I wanted to find out whether you were faithful to Vincent and whether he could rely on you." Margarete had been mistrustful of him ever since, despite all the presents he heaped on her; she was convinced that whenever he went out with Kent, he took him to the whores. This goes some way toward explaining why she had been so ready to chalk up a point against him, one day when they had all been listening to the German radio. At the end of the news bulletin, Trepper switched the radio off and instinctively began talking in German. Margarete knew the language too well not to notice his Jewish accent. "Why, he's a Jew!" she said to Kent. Kent denied it, but not very strongly.

The purpose of the Big Chief's visit to Brussels was to meet Makarov, alias Alamo, from whom he had been receiving one complaint after another—"Comrade, what am I supposed to be doing here? I don't know what you're up to, but it's 'way over my head! I'm not a complete dead loss, believe me! Give me a plane, and at least I'll be of *some* use. . . ."

The two men were due to meet in the Rue des Atrébates on the following day, December 13.

Fortner says: "On December 12, 1941, at about ten in the evening, I and my sergeant and three Abwehr officers took up our positions in the villa occupied by the two members of the Todt Organization. We had half a dozen police with us; the rest were hidden in number 97, next door to the Flemish family. The territorials, in their barracks, were standing by to seal off the street. They were armed with submachine guns, and I had told them to slip heavy woolen socks over their boots so that there'd be no suspicious noises to give the game away.

"My plan was simple: an attack with brute force. I and two of the police were to swoop on the Flemish family; an officer and another pair of police were to get into the South Americans' house; and the same for the empty house. The third Abwehr officer was to take command of the territorials when they reached the Rue des Atrébates. We had flashlights, axes, and even firemen's ladders with us, in case of a rooftop chase.

"At 2 A.M. I set up my equipment. Half an hour later it returned positive results, and I gave the signal for the attack.

"The Flemish family were startled out of their wits when I and my two companions burst in on them, and it was immediately apparent to me that the transmitter was not concealed in their house. On my right, at number 101, the Abwehr officer shouted: 'In here! It's in here!' Shots rang out. I saw the police firing at a man as he came out of the building. The territorials rushed after him.

"I hurried into number 101, where the South Americans lived. On the ground floor, a woman lay undressed and asleep on a camp bed. She was a beautiful girl of twenty-five or so, but Jewish, typically Jewish. On the first floor was the transmitter, still warm and already being examined by my sergeant. On the second floor we found another woman in bed; she was tall, rather good-looking, between twenty-five and twenty-eight, very Jewish. There were shouts of 'We've got him! We've got him!' so I went downstairs again. The fugitive had been caught trying to hide in the basement of the building opposite. He had put up a fight and been knocked about; he was bleeding. He had a South American passport, perfectly in order. As for the woman on the ground floor, she handed me a French identity card made out in the name of Sophie Poznanska. I pointed out to her that for a French national she spoke very poor French; and from then on she kept her mouth shut. The injured man adopted the same attitude; we couldn't get a word out of him. I returned to the second floor. One of the police called after me and reported that the Poznanska girl was seeking permission to go to the lavatory. I said she could go, provided that someone stood guard over her. She wouldn't hear of it.

"The woman on the second floor was named Rita Arnould. She sobbed as she told me: 'I'm glad it's all over. I never wanted to be a member of the ring; my boy friend made me join against my will.' I spoke to her in French at first, but she said, 'Look, we may as well talk German; it will make things easier.' 'Do you know German, then?' 'Of course I do—I *am* German. I was born in Frankfurt.' She was prepared to tell me all she could. I had one of the men fetch a couple of bottles of wine, so that she and I could have a little drink together.

"The plain truth was that poor Rita had never had any luck. Her father had died while she was still a child. After leaving school, she studied philosophy at Frankfurt; during this time she was a member of a Communist cell led by a certain Isidor Springer, who was her boy friend. After Hitler came to power she left Germany and moved to Brussels, meaning to continue her studies there. Instead, she met and married Arnould, a textile salesman twice her age. She turned her back on philosophy and her political activities. She would probably have lived out the rest of her days as a good housewife, if Arnould had not died in 1940, leaving her unprovided for. She then had the bad luck to meet Springer again—he too had fled to Belgium. He installed her in the Rue des Atrébates, where she did the cooking and housekeeping. The job paid well enough to enable Rita to take care of her old mother. And quite apart from that, as a Jew living in a country under German occupation the poor girl obviously couldn't afford to be too choosy.

"I have to admit my heart went out to Rita Arnould. I was convinced that she was merely a victim of circumstances and had never really been a party to the network's activities. I did what I could to make things easier for her. I confined her to a hotel room, instead of clapping her in jail. I told her mother not to worry. And several months later, when I was setting out on a mission to San Sebastian in Spain, I even offered to take Rita with me and leave her there. Her reply made my blood run cold. 'What's the use?' she said, fatalistically. 'I've talked, and Soviet Intelligence will catch up with me wherever I go.' She was shot a little while afterward.

"Ah well . . . let's get back to that first night of December 13. While we were talking together, Rita suddenly whispered: 'Keep your eyes open downstairs.' 'What for?' I asked. 'Go take a look,' she said, 'you can't miss it.' I went down and told the police to make a thorough search. One of them tapped the wall behind the camp bed; it sounded hollow! The Poznanska girl was now lying down again. I told her to get up. She refused. The police grabbed her, thrust her aside and broke down a hidden door set in the wall. Beyond the wall was a small room dimly lighted by a red bulb. I had someone change the bulb so that we could see better. And shall I tell you what we *did* see? It was a forger's paradise! It contained all the equipment needed for turning out counterfeit documents: blank passports, rubber stamps, official forms, everything! And besides this, there were rows of bottles filled with strange liquids, and glasses con-

taining crystals. Rita warned me that these were poisonous, so we
sent them to Cologne for analysis. The lab report stated that they
were ingredients for making a highly sophisticated, almost unde-
tectable form of invisible ink.

"The contents of that closet gave me one of the biggest shocks
of my life. Try to imagine how I felt when I saw printed forms, in
mint condition, which could only have come from official government sources in Berlin. I simply couldn't believe it! This implied
the existence of a really vast network, with tentacles everywhere.
And just then my sergeant came down from the first floor with some
half-burnt documents he had found beside the transmitter. They were
all written in German! I couldn't get over it. I questioned Rita, and
she said, as though it were the most natural thing in the world, 'Why
yes, of course: it was usual for the work here to be done in German.'
My brain was reeling.

"Among the other things we found in the closet were two
identity photographs no doubt intended for use on false passports.
According to Rita, one of them showed a man known as the Big
Chief; the other, the Little Chief.* The photographs were admirably
clear. As I studied them, I had the uncanny feeling I'd seen these
two characters before. Rita was unable to tell me anything whatever
about the Big Chief. On the other hand, she knew that the Little
Chief lived in or near the Boulevard Brand Whitlock, which made
him a neighbor of mine; that his mistress was a fair-haired woman who
was noticeably taller than he, and that they often went out for walks
together, taking a large dog with them. With information as precise
as this, we could count on picking up our man during the day.

"We withdrew from the Rue des Atrébates at about 6:30 A.M.,
but I left a policeman and an interpreter on duty there, with instructions to arrest anyone who walked into the trap.

"I immediately went to the chief of the Abwehr in Brussels and
told him what a successful night we had had. He was altogether delighted, of course, and at once began drafting a report for Berlin.
But what code name were we to give the network? As you know,
to us in the Abwehr a spy ring was an 'Orchestra.' We spoke, for
instance, of the 'Ardennes Orchestra,' operating in the Bastogne area.
My superior suggested 'Russian Orchestra,' but I said, 'No—"Red
Orchestra" would be better still!' "

---

* Alias Vincent Sierra, alias Kent.

We know only the alias, and not the real name, of the man who had been arrested and slightly wounded in the Atrébates raid. He called himself Camille. A Palestinian Jew, veteran of the International Brigades, he had married a Frenchwoman and settled in Paris. Trepper had met him there and packed him off to the Rue des Atrébates for training as a pianist. Camille was brave, impetuous and zealous. He died without talking.

Sophie Poznanska was the network's cipher expert. She excelled at this intricate and demanding specialty. If she betrayed her code to Fortner, it would be a terrible blow to the Red Orchestra. But Sophie Poznanska did not talk. Before long, she took her own life in the cell at St.-Gilles prison, where, on Fortner's instructions, she was being held for questioning.

Meanwhile Rita Arnould, in a warm and comfortable hotel room, was ready to tell all to German counterintelligence. At first sight, she did not seem likely to be in on the Red Orchestra's secrets; she had merely cooked the meals and made the beds.

Still, she had provided clues which seemed likely to lead to the Little Chief in a matter of hours. And it seemed reasonable to expect that a number of agents would walk straight into the trap set in the Rue des Atrébates.

The first caller claimed to be the owner of the house and said he had come for the rent. The policeman and the interpreter asked to see his papers, and put through a telephone call to the Brussels Housing Department. The man really was the owner of number 101; he was allowed to leave.

The second caller was dressed like a tramp; he stank and had not shaved for some time. There was a basket slung over his arm, with a number of rabbits moving about inside. He asked to see the lady of the house and said she was in the habit of buying from him. He was told that the lady of the house was not available. He tried to argue, but was soon kicked out.

Not long afterward, the doorbell rang for the third time. The caller was asked to step inside, and his papers were examined. These bore the name "Carlos Alamo." The policeman searched his pockets and found several messages in code. Out came the handcuffs. Carlos Alamo knew most of the members of the network, and was fully conversant with the code employed at the Rue des Atrébates.

The fourth caller was not at all easy to deal with. He inquired in a domineering tone whether anyone knew what time the garage along the street opened. Which garage? The one the Germans had requisitioned. He was ordered to step inside and show his papers. He produced a special pass issued by the Todt Organization. This clearly put the policeman and the interpreter in an embarrassing position, but they decided to hold him for the time being. The caller flew into a rage and warned that they would be in dire trouble with the military authorities if they did not telephone their superior at once. The policeman rang the Abwehr and mentioned the special pass. "Release him this minute!" shouted the officer. So they did.

Toward the end of the day, a pretty colored girl was taken into custody—Suzanne Schmitz.

◆

On the evening of December 13, Kent and Margarete accompanied Trepper to the railway station, but the trio reached the platform just in time to see the tail light of the Paris train receding into the distance. They decided to go back to the Avenue Slegers. As they approached the street, they saw that the police had set up a roadblock and that a line of cars was parked outside Kent's apartment house. He hurried to a café, telephoned his own number and heard a man's voice answer the call in German. Kent and Margarete took shelter in the home of a Belgian friend. Trepper caught the next train to Paris.

Afterward he commented that his predominant feeling was one of bafflement. For some time past he had been fearing a catastrophe in Brussels; Moscow's insistence on a nightly transmission lasting five whole hours was bound to end in disaster. Indeed, it was to lessen the danger that he had lately decided to rest the transmitter in the Avenue de Longchamps and transfer the main load to the "music box" in the Rue des Atrébates, which had had very little work prior to December. How had the Germans managed to track it down so quickly? Traditional methods of detection required more time. And if they had been betrayed, then the outlook was black indeed—for what could now be considered safe?

The raid on the Rue des Atrébates gave rise to an extraordinary amount of confusion and suspicion. Among its consequences was the spanking of an SS *Hauptsturmführer*, but we have not yet come to that choice episode.

Brussels, the very heart of the network, had been dealt a crushing blow.

10. Closing the Breach

From the first day of my researches into the Red Orchestra, I had been building up a mental picture of Georgie de Winter—"La Belle Georgie," as they all called her. She was known to have survived Ravensbrück, but had disappeared from view after returning from the camp. Some of the network's survivors thought she might be in Belgium, but had no idea where. I had given up all hope of finding this invaluable witness. I was left with the Georgie I had seen in my imagination; she seemed destined to remain no more than a graceful digression in my story.

But in July, 1965, I interviewed a veteran member of the Orchestra who was permanently bedridden as a result of the sufferings he had endured in captivity. When I mentioned Georgie's name, he smiled and handed me a wedding invitation announcing her marriage to an émigré Polish colonel. The ceremony had taken place only a short while earlier at Soulorgues, near Lasalle, in the Cévennes.

I set out for Lasalle with considerable impatience and a certain amount of anxiety (it is always perilous to put dream and reality side by side). In addition, I felt some concern about the potential consequences of my visit.

I had long since come to realize that the Red Orchestra was a kind of Loch Ness monster in the eyes of some people who are, or were, connected with intelligence operations. I am referring specifically to those ex-members of the Abwehr or Gestapo who are so eaten up with anti-Communist fears that they cannot speak or write a word about the Orchestra without instantly assuming a prophetic, doom-laden tone. Walter Schellenberg, former head of the German Foreign Intelligence Service, concludes his observations on the subject as follows: "The work on *Rote Kapelle* was to continue right up to the end of the war. The silent struggle became more and more intense, until the conflict was carried on not only in Germany and the countries occupied by her, but throughout the world." *

Paul Leverkuehn (the Abwehr agent whom we earlier saw roaming Persia in search of roads that might lead to Baku) argues

---

* *The Schellenberg Memoirs* (London: Andre Deutsch, 1956), p. 329.

that "the struggle [to destroy the Red Orchestra] was never finally concluded, and there can be no doubt that that same organization, perhaps in some cases employing the very same men, is still active today." * Flicke insists that "the Red Orchestra has certainly not spoken its last word"; † while Fortner goes further and suggests that it still has a good deal to say for itself today.

In short, they are doing their utmost to pass on the torch to their logical successors, the staffs of the Western counterintelligence agencies. At first I thought the latter were declining to accept it, not because it was held out to them by dubious hands, but because they were convinced that the flame had gone out. Then certain details led me to believe that they were not so certain of this and were therefore continuing to show an interest in anyone who had ever worked for the network. No doubt they were merely doing their duty and acting in the national interest, but I did not feel any great urge to join the gallant band of police informers.

It is pleasurable to entertain honorable scruples when one knows they are of no real import. For, in pursuing my inquiries, I made no attempt to conceal the motives that lay behind them. Whenever I came across an eyewitness of the events I proposed to describe, I would send him or her—as a visiting card and an ice-breaker—a copy of my latest book, which at one point featured the name Constantin Melnik. Upon anyone who might have reenlisted in the Red Orchestra, this name would have had much the same effect as the sound of a leper's bell. Moreover, I fired my questions with the avowed intent of writing a book, and it was clearly understood that each and every answer was liable to be published.

My impatience was about to be satisfied, and my concern could scarcely be described as oppressive. But the sense of anxiety endured —was Georgie going to prove a disappointment? Although I had never seen her face or heard her voice, I drove toward Lasalle feeling as apprehensive as a man going to meet a woman whom he had once loved and has not seen for twenty years.

———◆———

Lasalle lies sprawled along a narrow, seemingly interminable street lined with houses like dark caverns. At the far end of this cut-

---

* Paul Leverkuehn, *German Military Intelligence* (London: Weidenfeld and Nicolson, 1954), p. 183.
† W. F. Flicke, *Spionnagegruppe Rote Kapelle* (Munich: Verlag Welsermühl Wels, 1957).

throat's paradise, one returns to the corkscrew road which makes the Cévennes car rally one of the most difficult on earth. For two miles it overhangs a small valley, empty except for a few buildings big and solid as fortresses. When I reached the hamlet of Les Horts, it took half an hour to discover a bumpy track plunging down into the valley and then climbing toward the three or four houses anchored to the opposite slope. Georgie's was the next-to-last house. It was hard to envisage this secluded spot as the nerve center of an intelligence organization; and even if Georgie was only a "letter box," I was sorry for the postman.

The house was compact, with a low roof and walls strong enough to withstand a siege. Later, I was taken down to the cellar and shown an underground passage which came out somewhere on the mountainside; it had once enabled the inhabitants to escape being dragooned into the army. I knocked in vain, and was just about to give up and go away when a young woman appeared behind me, from the garden; she was dressed in slacks and a shirt. Georgie, who had been twenty years old in 1940, bore a striking resemblance to Mrs. Jacqueline Kennedy.

Georgie's husband was in Montpellier hospital, recovering from a heart attack.

Inside the house were a dog, several cats and a haunting ghost of the past. The former were banished to the garden so that we could talk at ease of the latter. After her release from the concentration camp, Georgie went to see her mother in Belgium. The Belgian security police tailed her, arrested and interrogated her. In France, the chiefs of the *Département de la Surveillance du Territoire* (D.S.T.), which is chiefly responsible for counterespionage (as well as aliens, immigration, etc.), spent a long time brooding over her case. In 1962—yes, 1962!—two carloads of D.S.T. officers drove up from Marseilles, took Georgie to the Lasalle police station and questioned her nonstop for forty-eight hours. The local people were very thrilled and entertained suspicions of some dark mystery—possibly a murder, or even several. Georgie had already suspected that her mail was being opened; now she learned that all her movements were being watched and would continue to be. It really took some believing!

She was tall and slender, with black hair which, that summer, hung down over her shoulders. Her eyes shone brilliantly. Her voice was as youthful as her bearing. Indeed, the most striking thing of all about this survivor of the Gestapo and of Ravensbrück was the almost childlike quality of her voice, clear as crystal and inclined to break on certain syllables.

◆

Georgie de Winter says: "Shortly after the outbreak of war, Eddy (the man you know as Trepper) advised me to take refuge in the United States; he even offered to pay my fare. But I didn't want to leave him, and I couldn't see any particular danger in sharing his lot—not even after the gendarme's visit. This was in Brussels in May, 1940, during the German offensive. A Belgian gendarme called at our address and asked me for information about the 'foreigner' who was living with me. At that time I had no idea what Eddy was up to, but something told me I'd better not tell the truth: I gave him a false name and a false nationality. Was this because I had unconscious suspicions? Possibly, but I swear I acted purely on impulse.

"I was overjoyed when we moved to Paris, which I adore. There we really lived a magnificent life. You can't imagine the kindness of that man, his sensitivity and attentiveness. Whenever he had to travel, he used to reserve me seats at concerts and plays for every evening he'd be away. He was always buying me things. And he adored my son Patrick, whom we had naturally taken with us. In those days, before Pearl Harbor, I used to go regularly to the United States Embassy and pick up food parcels for Patrick, distributed by the American Aid Society. The people there advised me to return to the States, and Eddy himself kept urging it, offering me a small nest egg in dollars to live on. But I loved him too dearly. I was ready to die for him. Mind you, although he was endlessly sweet to me, I sensed that he could also be quite merciless. Once he came home absolutely furious at somebody. He launched into a long tirade—just like a prosecutor making an indictment. Then all of a sudden he cooled off and said calmly, 'Very well, if that's the way it is, let him be struck down.' It was spine-chilling, I can tell you.

"He introduced me to some of his friends—he didn't have many. I was very fond of Hillel Katz, who was such good company, and Leo Grossvogel, who was simple and kind and had a passion for classical music. Eddy seemed to hold both of them in the palm of his hand. You felt that his word was law, and they would have jumped into the fire if he had ordered them to.

"But he never talked about business with me. All in all, he was very secretive. Though I'm not particularly curious, I doubt if I'd be able to act the same way today. But at the time I was only twenty and he was nearly forty, and I was very much in awe of him. And I realized immediately that I mustn't try to pin him down with questions. He was slippery as an eel. Anyway, I hadn't any real desire for facts; they didn't interest me. I was very young and carefree, we loved each other and life was marvelous.

"Being an American, once the United States came into the war I was liable to be arrested and put in an internment camp. At this point, Eddy calmly came and told me that he was working for British Intelligence, and he provided me with forged papers in the name of 'Elisabeth Thevenet.' I swallowed the story about British Intelligence. Really and truly, it didn't matter to me either way. Whether he was a spy or a raincoat salesman, my feelings for him were exactly the same.

"So life went on as before, except that I was always afraid of being picked up by the police with my false papers. One day I said to him, 'I'll get caught in the end, and I'll land in jail.' He shrugged and said, 'People like you and me, we survive anything.' He was always very cool and self-possessed. The only time I ever saw him flustered was once when we were out rowing at St.-Germain-en-Laye. Our boat nearly capsized, and I just managed to right it by clutching at the branches of a tree. Eddy was as white as a sheet, and he admitted he couldn't swim. In fact, he didn't practice any sport, which astonished me in a man who was so elegant and practically a maniac about cleanliness.

"Anyway, to return to my false papers: I very nearly *did* get arrested. It happened as I got off the Métro at St.-Michel station. There was a squad of policemen blocking the exit. I pretended I had got out at the wrong station and I went over to a subway map; of course I was hoping to get on the next train. But a sergeant spotted me. He said to one of his men, 'Get me that young lady, will you? Something tells me she hasn't got an easy conscience.' I was trembling as I took out my identity card. 'Why, what a coincidence!' he exclaimed. 'You were born up north, in Neuvilly? One of the boys over there is from Neuvilly.' He called out and a man came over to us, grinning all over his face. I was in a complete panic. Naturally he started babbling about Neuvilly people and places, and I wriggled out of it as best I could by saying I had moved away when I was a small child. After that, they let me go without any fuss. My God, I was afraid!

"At that time we were living in the Rue Fontaine, but we also had a little house at Le Vésinet. I used to go to the Place Clichy for dancing lessons every day; Eddy insisted on it, so that I'd be able to take care of myself, if I was alone, later on. I was also studying foreign languages. In the evening—almost every evening—we used to go to some restaurant and then wind up in a cabaret; he had a passion for cabaret singers. Ah, what a wonderful life we had! I can honestly say I've never been so happy."

———◆———

Yet it would be quite wrong to think of Paris as a haven of self-indulgence, far removed from the real battles being fought in Brussels and Berlin. If the Belgian capital—prior to the raid on the Rue des Atrébates—was the heart of the Red Orchestra, and the German capital its brain (a brain garnering and sorting information with the precision of an electronic computer), then the French capital was its nerve center. It was from Paris that couriers continually set out across Europe with the Big Chief's orders; and into Paris came that ceaseless flow of reports which, on transmission to Moscow, enabled the Director to keep up with the activities of every single agent.

The rare birds who enjoyed the luxuries of Occupied Paris were, of course, compounded of many elements, and it is possible to distinguish at least two main social groups: the political or economic collaborators and the upper hierarchy of the Resistance movement. They had one thing in common: they had taken sides; for them, the war was still going on. The French had been almost unanimous in declaring for an armistice, and they had been absorbed in anguished contemplation of their navels ever since. From 1940 until 1944, the great national problem was to discover if ration tickets would really be worth anything—in trains and waiting lines and offices, they talked of nothing but food. Being a defeated nation has its price. On the other hand, a person had only to reject the security implicit in the armistice, and his nutritional problems were solved. If you fought, you ate. Which was how such strange opposites came to be rubbing shoulders in the small black-market restaurants—the collaborators (they had jumped aboard the Nazi bandwagon, or rather the Nazi armored train); the Resistance leaders (they were bent on derailing it); and the flower of the German officer corps (like it or not, they were keeping the engine stoked). What gave their junketings such piquancy was that the guests were well aware that they might have to

pay the bill with their life's blood. For the officers, the final serving
of dessert might be followed by the direct hit of an Allied shell; for
the others, the fee might be the twelve bullets of a German firing
squad, or victimization in the next purge.

Thus, the senior echelons of the Resistance did not go hungry.
Rémy—and could any of its leaders have been more dedicated?—
stated in 1942 that he spent as much on food in three days as an ordinary Parisian family could afford to spend in a month. In *Playing
With Fire*, the best novel inspired by the Resistance movement, Roger
Vailland sets scene after scene in illicit bars and concealed nightclubs,
and even supplies a short guide to black-market restaurants; he comes
within an inch of awarding them stars. There was a practical reason
for all this: a man engaged in the secret war, with false documents
and no fixed address, was often debarred from obtaining his food
legally; he could hardly stroll into a government office and apply for
a ration card. There was moral justification, too: it was bad enough
risking torture and death, without going hungry too; it was just, equi-
table and salutary that the Big Chief should not be reduced to a diet
of turnips. Finally, there was a technical explanation: in some cases,
and certainly in Trepper's, the "cover" adopted by an agent imposed
a certain style of living. To this point I shall be returning later.

◆

So Paris was no rest home; it was the G.H.Q. from which the
Big Chief directed the battle. As soon as he got back from Brussels,
he set about closing the breach opened by Fortner.

The first problem was Kent. Luba Trepper had been right. He
was ideal for peacetime work, when only his freedom was at stake;
but he simply did not have it in him to place his life in jeopardy. He
was just an ordinary little man whose head had been turned by
Smirnov's book, and who was fast losing his nerve after the raid on
the Rue des Atrébates. There was nothing more contagious than
panic. Now that Kent could clearly be seen as a risk to be eliminated,
Trepper decided to bundle him off to Marseilles, in the Unoccupied
Zone. There he would find the worthy Monsieur Jaspar, former head
of the Foreign Excellent Trench Coat Company. Why shouldn't the
two of them set up a local network with an independent transmitter?
The Unoccupied Zone was well suited to such an enterprise, for
surveillance was obviously less strict in that part of France. But the
Big Chief did not pitch his hopes too high. Kent had been weighed

and found wanting. If he so wished, Marseilles could offer him a new area of activity; for the moment, it was primarily a dumping ground. As for Margarete Barcza, in Trepper's view, her influence was altogether deplorable—Kent loved her so passionately that he was even more afraid for her than for himself; she was softening him and wasting his time. Trepper offered to get her into Switzerland, where she could wait safely for the end of the war and a more propitious time for their love affair. But Kent would not hear of it; he had no intention of going to Marseilles without her. The Big Chief was obliged to give in.

Kent took pains over his departure from Brussels. He had many social contacts in the city, and a "midnight flit" would have aroused suspicions. He made a point of looking up all his acquaintances and giving a plausible excuse for his departure.

As one of them, Robert Christen, proprietor of the Florida, described it: "Late in December, 1941, he called to see me at my home and said, 'Listen, Robert, I've got to slip over the border into France. The Gestapo are on my tail.' 'The Gestapo? But why?' 'Germany has declared war on the United States, and my country is bound to fall in with the Americans. The Boches suspect as much and are preparing to round up all Uruguayans.' I said I understood and wished him luck. He asked if I would mind keeping a trunk for him till he returned. Naturally I agreed."

Paris was the first stage. Kent traveled direct, but Margarete and her son René had to steal across the border, for their identity cards were overprinted with the word "Jew." They were reunited on December 20, at the Hôtel Océanic. Kent was worried and on edge, but it would have taken more than that to keep the couple from their daily round of the Paris nightclubs, while the concierge took care of René. On December 19, Kent set out for the Unoccupied Zone, leaving Margarete and the child in Trepper's safekeeping. True to form, the latter got them tickets for the matinée at the Alhambra. Next day he had them delivered to a point somewhere along the demarcation line. The crossing proved difficult. Margarete and René marched for nine solid hours in a temperature of 5 degrees above zero; they had dogs after them and were shot at. Finally, in a state of complete exhaustion, they came to a farmhouse. Here they were picked up by a baker's truck and driven to the railway station. Margarete reached Marseilles on December 31. Madame Jaspar was not at all pleased to see this elegant creature walk into her home; but soon afterward she was taken ill, and Margarete nursed her devotedly. Madame Jaspar revised her attitude. Anyway, Kent arrived in turn, armed with new identity papers for himself and his mistress. They moved into an apartment house in the Rue de l'Abbé-de-l'Epée.

Another member of the Belgian network was in danger: Rita Arnould's lover, Isidor Springer, knewn as Romeo because he was always chasing women. The Big Chief sent him to Lyons, with instructions to lie low. Romeo was strikingly handsome, a diamond cutter from Antwerp who had fought with the International Brigades, held a commission in the Belgian army and been decorated for gallantry in 1940. Lying low would not come easily to a man with such a past; there was every likelihood of his stirring things up in Lyons.

The second problem concerned the prisoners. Would they talk? And if they did, what would they give away? The whole future of the network lay in their poor manacled hands, and Trepper was unable to proceed with the game without knowing which trumps, if any, were now falling to his opponents. He set up a special group whose sole duty was to keep him informed about the five people held in captivity—Alamo, Sophie Poznanska, Camille, Rita Arnould and Suzanne Schmitz (the latter, in fact, was soon released). They learned of the frequency and length of the interrogations, and of the psychological and physical condition in which the prisoners returned to their cells. They reported everything to Trepper: Rita's talkativeness, Alamo's and Camille's continuing silence, Sophie Poznanska's suicide. They kept watch on the Abwehr H.Q. to make sure that work there was proceeding at its normal pace; any sudden sharp increase in activity would be the sign that a prisoner had talked.

◆

The breach had been closed; now the Belgian network had to be reorganized. But Kent and Alamo were out of action, and Trepper's rightful place was in Paris; so who was to assume command in Brussels? Moscow's answer: Captain Constantin Yefremov. This, it might be thought, was a newcomer who would be parachuted into Belgium. Not at all; he had been living there for the past two years. The Big Chief had known of his existence and had met him once or twice, but the Director had been holding him in reserve. Now Yefremov suddenly appeared on the scene at the moment of need, taking Kent's place at the helm. The Center had its failings, but it must have been an undeniable pleasure to be working for such a smooth-running organization.

It had already proved its efficiency at the time of Yefremov's entry into Belgium. He arrived from Switzerland in September, 1939, bearing passport number 20268, issued in New York on June 22, 1937, and made out in the name of Eric Jernstroem, Finnish student, born in Vasa on November 3, 1911. War had just broken out when Yefremov presented himself at the frontier, and the Belgian police were fussy about details. As it happened, he had tarried in Switzerland and his passport had expired three months earlier. He was required to produce a sworn statement that he had been of good behavior during the last five years, together with a written undertaking not to settle in Belgium and the name of a Belgian guarantor. He satisfied all three requirements, but the Belgian police decided to look further, and asked the Swiss authorities for information on Yefremov. The reply was favorable enough: "No record at central registry." So, Yefremov had not aroused the suspicions of the Swiss police, renowned for their vigilance. But the Belgians, still not content, contacted the Finnish consulate in New York and inquired what, if anything, they knew about him. Reply: "Jernstroem has been living quietly in the U.S.A. since 1932 and is a loyal Finn." These reassurances, which satisfied the Belgian police, cannot but arouse our admiration, for Yefremov had never set foot in the United States. The inquiries would have been his undoing had the Center not had an agent inside the Finnish consulate in New York. And, to appreciate this fully, we must recall that, even as the Finnish agent in New York was covering up for the Soviet spy in Brussels, the Russian and Finnish armies were locked in battle around Lake Ladoga.

Yefremov was quite a handsome young man, over six feet tall, very blond, with blue eyes, a thoughtful brow and a somewhat melancholy expression; in general appearance, he matched the popular conception of a romantic poet. In fact, he was a military engineer of the third grade (in other words, a captain), specializing in chemistry. As soon as he reached Brussels, he enrolled at the Polytechnic and settled down to the life of a conscientious student. When at last the Big Chief took him out of cold storage and plunged him into the waiting cauldron, German counterintelligence had not the slightest reason to suspect him.

They met in Brussels, at the home of one of the network's agents. The Big Chief gave his new deputy full details of his new duties, allowed him a hundred thousand Belgian francs for his initial expenses, and advised him to tread warily. The network was to be put under wraps for six months. The two transmitters which had eluded Trepper's researchers were to remain silent until further notice; couriers were to move as little as possible; the various separate cogs were to operate in strict independence of one another. Yefremov was perfectly willing to accept these recommendations. He was certainly easy to deal with. A little *too* easy, perhaps. To Trepper he seemed spineless, a most unlikely successor to Alamo, who dreamed only of fighting, and to Kent, who bristled at the idea of losing his fifty suits. In contrast, Yefremov was like a rich man's son taking over the family business with an air of bored resignation.

Emphatically, the Young Guard was no match for the Old.

11. In Search of a Pianist

After the swoop on the Rue des Atrébates, Moscow was cast in the role of the passerby peering through the window of a dance hall, watching the musicians perform but unable to hear what they are playing. The information just wasn't getting through any longer.

The Berlin network was hamstrung by the amateurishness of its pianists and the close watch maintained by the Funkabwehr. In Brussels, Fortner's RDF vans were still patrolling the streets. As for Paris, the Big Chief was without a transmitter. General Susloparov, repatriated with the Soviet embassy staff, had decamped without handing over those sets for which they had so often applied.

What were they to do? The one and supreme hope lay with the French Communist Party, Theoretically, Trepper was not allowed to have any dealings with them. It was a cardinal rule of Soviet Intelligence that spy rings and local Communist Parties were to be kept strictly separate. This rule had its exceptions, just like any other. There was an existing arrangement whereby the "Resident Director" and a representative of the Party met once a year. The meeting was *always* sanctioned and planned by the Center. Trepper had been given a list of possible meeting places. If he received a picture postcard of Mont Blanc, he knew he was to meet the Party emissary at point A; a view of the Old Harbor at Marseilles meant a rendezvous at point B, and so on. As for the date, a prearranged figure was added to the date shown on the postmark. The time of meeting was invariable.

If circumstances demanded, the two sides could agree to meet at more frequent intervals—once a month, for example. But Moscow's permission had to be obtained first. It was all very complicated.

In 1941, Trepper's annual meeting with the Party was held in December. But whether before or after the attack on the Rue des Atrébates we have no means of knowing, although it is obviously so important. The meeting almost certainly took place *before* December 13; otherwise the Big Chief's problems would have been settled earlier. For it was not until February, 1942—two months after the Atrébates disaster—that Trepper, in his efforts to break his isolation, reestablished contact with the Party. It therefore seems likely that the routine meeting had been held before December 13, and that both sides had agreed to meet more frequently.

Two months gone to waste! For sixty days Moscow's most important source of information had been completely stopped. This was the inescapable concomitant of an efficient separation; speed and security do not always go together. If one is scandalized by the thought of these two wasted months, one must also accept that on another occasion Moscow sacrificed a hundred lives in the interest of speed—we have already seen how the telegram sending Kent to Berlin gave the addresses of the three local leaders, thus providing a surplus of work for the Nazi executioner.

The Party's emissary turned up at the February rendezvous holding the prearranged symbol of identification—a small-circulation newspaper. He was a very elegant figure, fairly young, dark and of medium height. He operated under the name Michel. Trepper outlined his requests. In the first place, the Party must undertake transmission of the messages which had accumulated during the past two months. This was an unusual procedure, but the gravity of the situation allowed no choice. To keep it from becoming permanent and thereby demolishing the safety curtain that divided Party and network, they would have to obtain a new transmitter for the Red Orchestra without delay.

A few days later, the Party's emissary brought Moscow's answer. As we have seen, the Director now instructed Trepper to establish contact with Yefremov and set him up as head of the Belgian network. Just this once, the emissary was prepared to allow the Orchestra to feed two or three hundred cipher groups a week into the Communist Party's transmitters; this was no great quantity, but the Party's radio traffic was already excessive. As for the new transmitter which Trepper was clamoring for, the Party's technicians would have to see to that.

At this point, Fernand Pauriol appeared on the scene. He was what one might call the virtuoso pianist of the Party, a real expert at handling "music boxes," a grand master in the art of radio liaison. We don't know how he came to achieve this distinction. He was a journalist, formerly an editor of *Rouge-Midi* and now Marseilles correspondent of *L'Humanité*. He had dark hair, regular features with an expression at once serious and open; his smile was very youthful and his eyes were warm and friendly. He handed Trepper a transmitter which he himself had made. It was not powerful enough to send messages all the way to Moscow, but it would reach London, where its signals would be picked up at the Soviet embassy and relayed to the Center. Now all Trepper had to do was to find a radio operator. This was easier than getting hold of a transmitter. Camille—whom Trepper had been planning to employ in Paris—was a prisoner; but Susloparov, though failing to supply any transmitters, had at least found him a pair of likely performers—the Sokols. Communists of Russo-Polish origin, they had put their names down at the Soviet delegation and asked to be repatriated. Occupation: radio repairmen. This sounded promising.

But the Big Chief was never a man to rush into things. Through his contact with the Party, he asked for the Sokols' background history. The inquiry led nowhere; the couple, who had entered the country from Belgium, were unknown in French Communist circles. So then, with characteristic thoroughness, he asked the Belgian Communist Party for information. The reply was favorable in the extreme: the Sokols were utterly dedicated militants who had been expelled from Belgium for their political activities. Why, then, this fanciful claim to be radio repairmen? According to the Belgians, Hersch Sokol was a physician and his wife, Myra, a Ph.D. in social science! In fact, their claim was a ruse, a white lie, which they hoped would end their existence as "displaced persons" and facilitate their return to the Soviet Union.

Hersch was born in Bialystok in 1908. It was a Russian town in those days, but in 1918 it became Polish. The Warsaw government banned instruction in the Russian language, but neglected to send any Polish teachers. All education came to a standstill. The Jewish community set up a Hebrew school, but Hersch's parents, well-to-do tradespeople, decided to send him and his brother to a German school in Frankfurt-am-Main. Hersch was so gifted and resourceful, so brimming with energy that he completed his secondary education at the age of sixteen. At this point he was still torn between medicine and a career as a musician, for he showed great talent as a pianist. In the end, medicine prevailed. He left for Geneva and spent two years there, at the medical school. Then he met a cousin who had emigrated to South Africa. The cousin invited him to join his firm; Hersch accepted. Six months at a famous school in Britain were sufficient to give him a perfect command of English. Immediately afterward, he went to Johannesburg to his cousin's clothing factory. He got on remarkably well and was sent to Paris as a buyer. He remained there for a year. Then he and the cousin quarreled. Also, he found Johannesburg, with its tense racialism, quite unbearable. Hersch went back to Geneva and then concluded his medical studies at the University of Brussels. He intended to specialize in pediatrics. It was at this time that he married Myra, a girl born in the Vilna ghetto who had capped an outstanding academic career with a doctorate in social science, also at Brussels.

In short, a brilliant pair, but aliens far from home. Hersch was unable to set up a practice, and there were no suitable openings for Myra. He was reduced to working as a traveling salesman in medical supplies; she became secretary to a Socialist member of parliament. Foreseeing this impasse, they had asked to be repatriated to Russia a whole year before the end of their studies. They were turned down on the pretext that no housing accommodation was available in Moscow. In 1935 they asked, and were refused, a second time. Barred from returning to the hearth of Socialism, they worked to further the cause where they were, and joined the Belgian Communist Party— they had already belonged to student organizations of the extreme left. Their activities were chiefly cultural. Hersch took advantage of his business travels to give an ever-increasing number of lectures on Marxism. But Belgium, like most other countries, prohibited political activity by aliens. In 1938, the Sokols were expelled, and took refuge in France.

As soon as war was declared, Hersch enlisted in the Foreign Legion. He was demobilized after the signing of the armistice. Occupied France was no place for a man who was both Jew and Communist, out of funds and out of work. He and Myra went to the Soviet delegation in Paris and lodged a third request for repatriation. This time it was a matter of life and death; so on his application form, Hersch wrote: "Occupation, radio repairman." Since Russia was short of technicians, a couple of radio repairmen might receive accommodations more easily than a doctor and a Ph.D. in social science. With this false declaration they were signing their own death warrants.

When Trepper at last went looking for the Sokols, he found only Myra; Hersch had just been taken to Pithiviers camp, where Jewish aliens were imprisoned. The Big Chief might have given up; instead, he persevered. He did so because he had recognized in Myra, and sensed in Hersch, three qualities rare enough in themselves and even rarer in combination: intelligence, courage and faith. There could be no question of allowing this couple to fall by the wayside; they were fully entitled to a share in the battle and quite capable of being turned into pianists. Myra began her apprenticeship at once. But how were they going to get Hersch out of Pithiviers?

◆

La Ferté-Choisel is one of those prettified villages in the Chevreuse valley to which successful Parisians repair every weekend, donning garments of suede and velvet, and becoming themselves part of the show. On the Wednesday of my visit in April, 1965, the streets were empty, the shutters closed, the very flowers in the gardens seemed to sense their own purposelessness. I had great difficulty in finding my way to the Spaaks' house.

It was one of the loveliest—no doubt simply because it was lived in. A gardener was engrossed in contemplation of a rose and did not look up as I approached. The lady of the house showed me into a study furnished in the English style, complete with wall-to-wall carpet. A bookcase ran along one of the walls. Facing the desk was a Magritte painting of two handsome children in a surrealist setting. A record player stood in a corner, and on a low pedestal table was a pipe rack; tins of tobacco were distributed at strategic points in the room. The broad bay window afforded a view over lawns sloping gently down toward (I felt sure) a river. The whole atmosphere of the place made me think of Baudelaire's lines, *"Là, tout n'est qu'ordre et beauté, luxe, calme et volupté."*

Claude Spaak is easy to describe to anyone who has ever seen a photograph of his brother, Paul-Henri. They are opposites in every way. Claude, the writer, is as spare and austere as Paul-Henri, the politician, is stout, rosy-cheeked and merry. The latter would have been an ideal subject for Rubens, the former seems to invite the clear lines of Bernard Buffet. He selected a pipe, filled it and sat down behind his desk. He wore a full beard terminating in a short goatee. His voice was calm and deliberate. He picked his words with care and was remarkably good at keeping his story on the move—after all, that was his profession.

Claude Spaak said: "Some Belgian friends had sent the Sokols to us for help. They had recently been expelled from Belgium on account of their Communist activities. This was before the war, of course. My wife and I belonged to a group of left-wing intellectuals, which is why our assistance was sought. For quite a while they lived right here in Choisel.

"My wife was very fond of them. For my part, I found their sectarianism a little excessive and rather oppressive; but I admired their idealism, the absolute purity of their convictions. They were a commendable couple, people of real quality. To them, the Russo-German Pact represented a real crisis of conscience.

"In the end they found rooms somewhere near the Eiffel Tower, but we continued to see quite a lot of them. One day early in 1941 Myra told us that her husband had been arrested as a Jewish alien and sent to Pithiviers camp. There was hope of getting him out, though, for Harry—we used to call him Harry—had been born in a Polish town now controlled by the Red Army. And because of the Russo-German Pact the Germans were not harming Polish Jews born in the Soviet-occupied zone.

"Myra got the Soviet delegation in Paris to certify that her husband really did belong to this category. Indeed, I believe he had by then become a Soviet citizen, for the town where he was born had been reincorporated in the Soviet Union. The next step was to convey the certification to Harry, so that he could present it to the camp authorities. Myra asked me to go to Pithiviers. I remember she made me swear on the heads of my children that I would deliver it into Harry's own hands. The delegation had warned her that a second certificate could not be issued in any circumstances. So this sheet of paper was Harry's last hope of salvation. To lose it, or let it go astray, was tantamount to sentencing him to death.

"The train I caught was packed with poor people on their way to visit prisoners. It was terrifying to see the wretched state they were in. There was not a square yard of hotel accommodation left in Pithiviers. I was forced to spend the night in a tiny room in what I

can only describe as a brothel. Next morning, about a thousand of us
—mainly women—set out for the camp, walking in procession, with a
police escort. Eventually we came to a sort of waste ground, en-
closed by a barbed-wire fence ten feet high. We all crowded in.
Facing us, beyond a fifty-yard strip of no man's land, was a second
barbed-wire cage, packed tight with about five hundred prisoners.
We've all learned a good deal since 1941, we've all read or heard the
most terrifying accounts of what went on, but you must understand
that what I saw that day came as a violent shock—it was like Dante's
inferno. The poor devils were behaving like lunatics. Messages were
being screamed back and forth, hands were helplessly reaching out
parcels, the women were sobbing and wailing. It was the kind of
scene that haunts you forever after. Police were walking up and
down between the cages, quite indifferent to what was going on.

"I managed to call one of them over and explain the situation to
him. He agreed to take the certificate to Harry. I hesitated, remembering my oath to Myra. I said, 'You realize it's his life you're holding
in your hands?' He replied, 'I give you my word of honor that I will
deliver the paper to him.' On the other hand, he refused to take a
parcel I'd brought with me. He had good reason to refuse: had he
been seen walking away with a parcel, there would have been a riot.

"I stood and waited for a half hour, and I can assure you those
thirty minutes' exposure to collective hysteria left their mark on me.
And then my policeman came back and handed me a page torn from
a notebook. On it were written these words: 'Thanks—Harry.' I felt I
had been treated to a kind of miracle."

◆

Listening to Claude Spaak, I thought of another miracle. For it
must have seemed a miracle to Alamo when Trepper stepped in and
saved him from being sent back to Moscow, where there was every
chance of his being dismissed from the service. Then in 1941, after
Atrébates, Alamo was under sentence of death in a Brussels prison.
Had he returned to Moscow, they would gladly have given him the
plane he longed for, and he would have been blasting Stukas out of
the sky. Miracles can be a mixed blessing.

It was the same with Hersch Sokol, whom Claude Spaak imagined
he had rescued, and who must have regarded himself as a saved man
when he emerged unscathed from the compound at Pithiviers. In fact,
he was exchanging the relatively easy death of the gas chambers for

the prolonged agonies of a death which would follow Gestapo tortures. Should we pity him? By now we must realize that, for most of the human beings who figure in this story, failure to do battle was a fate worse than torture and death. And Hersch Sokol was leaving Pithiviers in order to fight.

———◆———

I keep anticipating the demise of the Orchestra's musicians, which tends to obscure the fact that seven months of intense activity had claimed only one life—that of Sophie Poznanska, who died by her own hand. The head of a large French Resistance network was later to say to me, "I can at least claim the honor of running the organization which suffered the heaviest losses." Trepper would rather have prided himself on the opposite; frequent hitches are hardly the sign of a good network. And despite the blunders perpetrated in Berlin, and the Atrébates disaster, the Red Orchestra was still playing its concerto, with Hersch Sokol at the piano.

Nothing could have occasioned more intense exasperation in Berlin. The seizure of the Atrébates transmitter had been a wasted effort. All three transmitters in Brussels should have been put out of action at once, instead of giving warning to two pianists who were sure to return to work as soon as the storm had blown over. Besides, what was the point of silencing a transmitter if the organization behind it remained intact? Fortner had seen red and had pounced on the bait, instead of taking his time and planning the operation properly. He knew that 101, Rue des Atrébates was one of the Orchestra's regular haunts; why had he not set up an observation post across the street so that his men could photograph suspicious-looking callers? Why had he not tailed the couriers until they led to the people who controlled the spy ring? The total bag yielded by his operation was as follows: Rita Arnould, who babbled away gladly but knew almost nothing; Alamo and Camille, who refused to open their lips; and Poznanska, who took her own life. A mighty poor return for so much effort.

The Abwehr called in its hounds, with the firm intention of making a fresh start. Somehow the scent must be picked up again, and this time they must have more patience. Now that the game had fled, the trackers were reduced to poring over the texts of PTX messages monitored over the past several months. These messages were the despair of the Wehrmacht's code breakers, to whom they had been entrusted by the Funkabwehr. The chief clue to the secrets of a ciphered text lies in the alphabetical frequencies. If the text is in English or French, the letters *a* and *e* will obviously occur more often than *x* and *z*. A process of statistical examination will show which letters have been substituted for the most common letters of the language in question. After that, it is comparatively simple to deduce the rest. But the Red Orchestra was using a highly complicated grid code. Under this system, five thousand telegrams could be enciphered before any telltale repetitions appeared. In other words, the game was lost in advance.

But the Funkabwehr had no intention of giving up. Since the Wehrmacht threw up its hands, they would set up their own team of code breakers. They enlisted the services of an expert, Kludow,* and gave him about fifteen mathematics and philology students to whom he would teach his craft. Meanwhile, the intercepted telegrams were in Brussels. The Funkabwehr demanded their immediate return. Brussels replied blandly that they had all been burned: what was the point of keeping them, since they were undecipherable? This was an unbelievable blow, but it did not necessarily mean that all was lost, for German monitoring stations were supposed to keep copies of all recorded messages for at least three months. In considerable trepidation, the Funkabwehr dispatched an officer to the four stations which had listened in to the PTX transmitter. In Göteborg he harvested ten or a dozen messages; the remainder had been used as scrap paper. In Langenargen he was informed that all the documents had been sent to Stuttgart, where a cipher school had been established; he hastened to Stuttgart and managed to salvage a few messages. In Hanover, the pickings were meager; almost all had been destroyed. In Kranz, the officer was led down to the cellars, where huge sackfuls of telegrams were awaiting delivery to a paper mill. After several days of sorting, the officer returned to Berlin with his booty. He had saved about three hundred telegrams from oblivion—far too few to give the code breakers any hope of success.

However, Kludow was shown the documents found near the Atrébates transmitter; they had been fished out of the stove a moment or two after Camille had tried to dispose of them. Kludow studied these charred sheets and discovered that one of them was in the form of a coding grid. This was clear proof that the PTX messages had been encoded in the Rue des Atrébates. After several days of dogged

---

* Pseudonym chosen by the author.

effort, Kludow succeeded in reconstructing one of the words on the grid. By a stroke of luck it was a proper name, the name of a character in the code book used by Sophie Poznanska. (Another copy, of course, was in use at the Center, in Moscow.) Victory seemed in sight at last. For the Funkabwehr now knew that the telegrams had been encoded at the Rue des Atrébates, and that the book used for the code contained the aforesaid proper name. Conclusion: all they had to do was to recover the books left in the Rue des Atrébates and examine them carefully until they found the right one. After that, the surviving telegrams would soon offer up their secrets.

Berlin promptly telephoned to Fortner, who explained with some embarrassment that the police trap at the Rue des Atrébates had been maintained for only a few days, after which the premises had been, vacated; subsequently, two strangers had turned up with a cart and taken all the books away. Not a volume was left.

This admission scarcely improved Fortner's standing in Berlin. Still, there was always Rita Arnould. She must surely have dusted the books at times, and she might be able to remember some of the titles. Rita agreed that Sophie Poznanska used to keep quite a few books on her desk, but she could recall only five names. Four of these were on sale in Belgian or German bookshops; the vital proper name did not appear in any of them. An emissary was sent to Paris, with instructions to buy the fifth, *Le Miracle du professeur Wolmar*, by Guy de Téramond. It was the one they were after! By the beginning of June, 1942, Kludow and his team of assistants were in a position to tackle the three hundred extant messages picked up from the PTX transmitter.

The tide was beginning to turn. In Berlin, however, the mood was one of dejection rather than exultation. The men responsible for national security had not yet recovered from the shattering discovery that an enemy transmitter had been operating in Berlin itself. In addition, there were those German documents found in the Rue des Atrébates, to say nothing of Rita Arnould's bland assertion, "Why yes, of course. It was usual for the work here to be done in German." So there was a spy ring active at the very heart of the Reich, making out-and-out fools of the authorities. It was at this time the Führer admitted: "The Bolsheviks are our superiors in only one sphere: espionage."

And Schellenberg, head of German Foreign Intelligence Service, writes: "Again and again, [Hitler] demanded information about our counterespionage work. He believed the Russian Secret Service to be much more thorough and probably much more successful than the British or any other secret service. For once his intuition was to prove correct. Toward the end of 1941 he had already ordered immediate steps to be taken against the rapidly spreading Russian espionage activities in Germany and the occupied countries." *

And the detailed list of Reichsführer Himmler's telephone calls bears witness to his interminable conversations with Heydrich concerning the Red Orchestra.

To members of the Abwehr and the Gestapo, this was certainly no time for rejoicing. They shook their heads, saying to each other: "They are strong—very strong."

———◆———

Another man who played a part in this story is Ernst von Salomon, considered by many to be the greatest living German author, although he is less well-known outside Germany. He was a veteran of the *Freikorps* (he fought in the Baltic and Upper Silesia) who—after serving a five-year sentence for his part in the assassination of German Foreign Minister Walther Rathenau—wrote his famous works: *Die Geachteten, Die Kadetten, Die Stadt* and, in more recent times, *Der Fragebogen*. The Nazis kept him under observation. They even packed him off to prison from time to time, though it must be added that he generally wound up imprisoned by most other regimes. His wariness saved him from a worse fate. One of the reasons for this wariness was a girl called Ille. She was young, beautiful, scatter-brained and Jewish—the Gestapo were unaware of this last fact. Among their numerous acquaintances were a charming young couple named Harro and Libertas Schulze-Boysen. Here is what Salomon has written about them:

[Harro] invited Ille and myself to come with him to see a friend, a certain Herr Harnack, a close relative of the celebrated theologian, the late Adolf Harnack. I had met Herr Harnack and his wife at both the Russian and the American Embassies. She was an American by birth and called herself Harnack-Fish. The young couple had an assured place in diplomatic circles. The Harnacks lived near the Halle Gate, in a large, well-furnished apartment. Ille and I went there, stayed for an hour, and then left. It was a bad habit of Ille's and mine to discuss any gathering we had attended as soon as we had left, if possible the moment the door of

* *The Schellenberg Memoirs*, p. 321.

our host's apartment had closed behind us, at the latest as soon as we reached the street. On this occasion Ille began as soon as we were out of the apartment.

"I like that!" she said. "There they stand, leaning against the mantelpiece, with a cup of tea in their hand, quite casually discussing things . . . things—well, any one of the things they discussed could cost them their heads."

I said nothing. She behaved in exactly this way in our home. Ille said: "It looks all wrong to me. I feel there's something very, very wrong. And I can trust my feelings, I think." Then she said, with intensity: "Promise me this! Promise we'll never go there again! I don't want to have my head cut off just casually. I don't want it."

I said nothing and was glad Ille felt that way. If only she always thought so! She said:

"I like that! They stand about there, well-dressed, decent-looking people and they talk about 'cross channels of communication'—do you know what that means?"

I did, but I said nothing. Ille said:

"They describe Hitler and Himmler and Rosenberg and Frick as utter fools, and they tell me, me who've never even met any of them before except the Harnacks and the Schulze-Boysens, they tell me—"

Ille broke off in the middle of her sentence. Then, stirring an imaginary cup of tea, she said:

"They say to me, 'Do you know, dear lady, I have heard from an absolutely sure source, because you see I have a direct link with Zürich . . . of course we exchange our information.' . . . And then," said Ille, "he suddenly catches sight of another man and says, 'Excuse me for a moment, dear lady,' and gives the other man a yellow envelope, saying 'Strictly confidential' and winks. . . . And there I sit on the sofa and can hardly breathe. So I ask who the decent-looking old man is and who is the one he spoke to, and they tell me that one's a ministerial counselor and the other's an adjutant, and that one over there is in the SS and this one here is a diplomat . . . now tell me, can you understand it all?"

I said:

"Yes, yes, that's the way it is. Now let's be getting home." *

Harro Schulze-Boysen and Arvid Harnack were the leaders of the Berlin network. Sprinkled among the guests, that evening, were a number of their agents. The mighty security services of the Third Reich were being held at bay by these socializing lunatics with their yellow envelopes and their meaningful winks, all hamming away like villains in an old-fashioned melodrama.

---

* *The Answers of Ernst von Salomon* (New York: Putnam, 1954), pp. 301–2.

On May 22, 1942, while lunching at his G.H.Q. in Rastenburg, East Prussia, Adolf Hitler declared:

Spies nowadays are recruited from two classes of society: the so-called upper classes and the proletariat. The middle classes are too serious-minded to indulge in such activity. The most efficient way of combating espionage is to convince those who are tempted to dabble in it that, if they are caught, they will most certainly lose their lives.*

12. A Master Investigator

Franz Fortner had lost little time in releasing Suzanne Schmitz, the Indonesian girl who had blundered into the trap at the Rue des Atrébates. She was not a member of the network. A few days after her release she received the following letter from Carlos Alamo, whose spelling and sentence structure were rather insecure:

Saint-Gilles Prison
Block C, Cell 193

DEAR SUZONE,

I am sorry for the troubles I have involontrally cause you.

As the things I am suspect of seem very cirious, I ca'nt say how long the prelimary investigation will last or what the final resolt will be. However, having a clear consciance, I feel calm and almost cheerfull. Dear Susone, I would be very grateful to You if you could tell Bill, that a am ecspecting some 2–3 packets of sigarettes. The tobacco problem is most agravatting here, and it is a real harship not to smoke.

If I knew Bill's present adress, I would spare You, dear Suzone, the bother of forwarning him . . .

I send You my best wishes and, belief me, all my thuoghts are with you.

YOURS CARLOS ALAMO

P.S. It appars that to be able to write from here you must have envelops and stamps and I am reduce to beg this from you, Suzonne.

---

* *Hitler's Table Talk, 1941–1944* (London: Weidenfeld & Nicolson, 1953), p. 503.

P.P.S. I seems I can write to only one person. I have chose you among all others. Do'nt be cross. I did not want to see you when you were at the Hôtel de la Gare du Midi, because I was not shave for several days already and my apparance was not that of a Gentleman. Do not worry about my future I am a great fatalist and if some things happen to me—this because it were written in the book of my life. *God knows* what he is doing.

I would dearly like to spend an hour with you now. . . . But we see each other again, for we are optimists, are we not? For the present the Germans were quite correct in delling with me.

My cell is quite nice; pity I am all alone in it. If only I had something to read. . . . Au revoir my dear little Suzone, I have bored you enough. I send you my fond love. CARLOS

I have already remarked that Franz Fortner did not believe in torture: "For the present the Germans were quite correct in delling with me." We also know that he was rather gullible; he allowed the letter to go on its way without voicing a single objection and did not even question Suzanne about the mysterious "Bill" whom she was to "forwarn." Stranger still: when the prisoner, who was noticeably upset by his religious discussions with Bill Hoorickx, asked the latter for a Bible, Fortner was not inquisitive enough to seek out the figure who, through the agency of a ravishing Indonesian girl, supplied a known Communist agent with a work wholly alien to the beliefs and attitudes fostered by the Center.

The letter was signed "Carlos Alamo," and so were those that followed. After a long silence, however, Suzanne Schmitz received a communication signed "Mikhail Makarov-Carlos." She did not know what to make of it. But the Big Chief was afraid he understood it all too well.

His special surveillance group had tipped him off that Alamo was being taken from St.-Gilles prison to an unknown destination. A few weeks later, his agents warned him that a certain Mikhail Makarov had arrived from Berlin and been committed to St.-Gilles. Trepper, of course, was unaware of the Russian's exact identity: he merely knew his alias. He sent an urgent wire to Moscow, asking, "Who is Makarov?" Answer: "It is Alamo."

So he had talked! At the very least, he had betrayed his own identity. What else had he given away? The names of the men and women working for the Brussels ring? The code based on *Le Miracle du professeur Wolmar*, which had been used for encoding most of the information obtained in the German capital? The Big Chief probably imagined that the Gestapo had resorted to unendurable tortures. If so, he was wrong. On reaching Berlin, Alamo had been housed, fed and pampered in the home of Kriminalrat Karl Giering, a high-ranking SS official.

◆

Walter Schellenberg writes: "Himmler was asked [by Hitler] to supervise the close collaboration of my Foreign Secret Service Department with Müller's Security Department of the Gestapo, and the Abwehr of Canaris. This operation—to which we gave the code name *Rote Kapelle* [Red Orchestra]—was coordinated by Heydrich." *

This was cumbersome, like everything else in the Byzantine structure of the Nazi state, but it was a step of major importance. The value attached to the measure can be gauged from the list of people involved: Himmler, Reichsführer SS, the second most powerful man in Germany; Heydrich, head of the SD and, by extension, of police forces throughout the Reich; Müller, known as "Gestapo-Müller" because he held that organization within his savage grasp; Schellenberg, in charge of the intelligence department of the SS; and Admiral Canaris, chief of the Abwehr, the branch of the Wehrmacht which dealt with espionage and counterespionage.

Schellenberg was jealous of Müller, who loathed him but dealt tactfully with him because Heydrich appeared to back him even while threatening him on occasion, depending on whether he himself was in a strong or weak position vis-à-vis Himmler, who admired Heydrich, which meant he feared him and did not hesitate to conspire against him through Müller and Schellenberg, both of whom abominated Heydrich . . . And so on, *ad infinitum*.

But Heydrich, Müller and Schellenberg had at least one thing in common: their bitter hatred of Canaris. Their personal wranglings were as nothing compared to the holy war which they were waging against him, a war in which all the SS organizations were aligned against the army traditionalists of the Abwehr.

True, every nation has parallel rivalries among its various secret services. The American C.I.A. has clashed with the F.B.I., the French S.D.E.C.E. with the D.S.T., Britain's M.I.6 with the Special Branch,

* *The Schellenberg Memoirs*, p. 321.

and the Soviet K.G.B. with Red Army Intelligence. But the battle between the SS and the Abwehr had one distinguishing feature: it ended on the gallows. It was a duel to the death, viciously fought out through confidential files about Heydrich's grandmother Sarah, the financial indiscretions of certain Abwehr agents, and Canaris's contacts with the enemy. The outcome of the duel is well known: the Abwehr was wholly taken over by the SS in February, 1944, and its leaders were put to death. Little Admiral Canaris was hanged on the frosty morning of April 9, naked as a newborn child, with the Allied artillery rumbling in the distance. To make his agony last as long as possible, the SS used a length of fine piano wire.

As we know from Schellenberg, it was in early 1942, by direct order of an irate Führer, that these implacable foes were forced to work together. A composite group was set up under the title "Rote Kapelle Kommando," for the sole purpose of liquidating the Big Chief's organization. To Trepper, there could be no finer tribute than this unprecedented alliance of all Germany's intelligence departments against an enemy regarded as too dangerous for an uncoordinated attack. But the tribute brought exceptional perils in its wake.

Colonel Rémy writes: "Today we have a detailed knowledge of the ruthless campaign which Himmler, as overlord of the Gestapo, was continually directing against Admiral Canaris, head of the Abwehr. We benefited considerably from their rivalry." *

But the Big Chief did not benefit at all.

Rémy also remarks: "The rules of the game demanded that we be shot if caught. The Abwehr adhered rigidly to this convention, and we had no grounds for complaint. But most of its officers conducted their interrogations with perfect propriety, and I know of several examples of prosecutions and sentences enacted under their aegis which can be quoted as models of their kind. . . . It was a very different story with the Gestapo—whose inhuman methods, I am bound to admit, were more effective." †

The SS members of the Rote Kapelle Kommando were certainly capable of inhuman behavior. But, in fact, they contributed something far more daunting than any instrument of torture: experience and intelligence.

---

* Rémy, *Mémoires d'un agent secret de la France libre*, 2 vols. (Paris: France-Empire, 1959), Vol. 1, p. 327.
† Rémy, *op. cit.*, Vol. 2, p. 413.

Fortner made frequent visits to Berlin, to report on the progress of his mission. He had acquired a kind of celebrity there; colleagues used to point him out in the mess and refer to him as "the
leader of the Rote Kapelle." All good clean fun. But one day he was
summoned to headquarters and presented with the startling information that from now on he would have to collaborate with the SS.
Fortner was bowled over by this news, as any officer and gentleman
would have been. The Abwehr had always held aloof from those
black-shirted guttersnipes. Indeed, some of its members were unable to
conceal their horrified contempt even from their prisoners. They
would say to them, "I'm an official of the Abwehr, and you may be
sure that whatever happens I shall never lay a finger on you. We
simply do not believe in that sort of thing. However, you must realize
that if you persist in your silence I shall be forced to hand you over
to the Gestapo. And there, my poor friend, I leave you to imagine
what will happen if you fall into *their* hands. Either way, you are
bound to talk in the end; so wouldn't it be more sensible for us to
come to a gentlemanly understanding?" Taken all in all, this had
proved an effective and unsullying division of labor—whereas working side by side entailed the risk of getting splashed.

Fortner felt extremely despondent as he set out for his appointment with SS Hauptsturmführer Karl Giering, head of the Rote
Kapelle Kommando. On arrival, he was confronted by a very tall,
thin, cadaverous-looking man who offered his hand with a smile and
said hoarsely, "I'm a regular officer, you know, not an SS person. Is
it all right with you if we work together?"

The two men saw at once that they spoke the same language.

Giering was one of the ablest police officers in Germany—some
say the ablest of all. Each time there was an attempt on Hitler's life,
it was he who was accorded the honor of leading the investigation.
Anyone who imagines this was because of his devotion to Nazism is
very much mistaken. In Giering's eyes, Adolf Hitler was the head of
state—no more, no less. He would have been just as fanatic about
capturing the assailants of a Socialist or Communist leader. He had
the same philosophy as his faithful deputy, Willy Berg, who liked to
boast: "I was a cop under the Kaiser, and a cop under the Weimar
Republic. Now I'm a cop under Hitler, and I'll still be a cop if
Thaelmann * comes to power." When the entire German police

* Ernst Thaelmann, leader of the German Communist Party.

force had been drafted into the SS, both men had been fitted out with the black garb of Himmler's special flock and assigned their places in the hierarchy. They had taken it in their stride, permitting themselves a wry smile, perhaps, as though at some necessary masquerade, but certainly no other reaction. Long years of police work make a man immune to excessive zeal. He sees too much, knows too much and inhales too many evil smells.

Giering had accumulated some piquant information about the Nazi "supermen," and he was not taken in by any of them. He was as far removed from the gentlemen of the Abwehr, who believed in God, as from the guttersnipes of the SS, who put their faith in the devil. He believed in nothing, least of all in that animal called Man. He was a cop down to his fingertips, inhabiting a world of cold, gray offices, munching sandwiches as he skillfully adjusted his thoughts and words to the particular wavelength of each new prisoner. In general, the Abwehr respected a cornered foe, while the Gestapo itched to see his blood flow. Giering had no such feelings; he simply wanted the prisoner to "sing." He expended a good deal of intelligence in his efforts to insure that the prisoner *did* "sing," showing endless guile and an awesome temper if the situation demanded. His former colleagues insist: "He was the best." His former opponents acknowledge: "He was the most dangerous."

His right-hand man, Willy Berg, was cast in the same mold. Berg had been Ribbentrop's bodyguard on his celebrated visit to Moscow for the signing of the Russo-German Pact. Berg was short and rather plump, providing a comic contrast to the spindly Giering. They made a sardonic pair, and neither of them paid the slightest attention to "Heini" Himmler's grisly talk of expunging this "Jewish rot." They were simply a trifle bewildered by the scale of the operation to which they were now committed.

An interesting detail: Giering was living under sentence of death, and he knew it. His husky, boozer's voice was due to a cancerous growth gnawing at his throat. The two principal remedies proposed by his doctors were, somewhat surprisingly, coffee and alcohol. He imbibed a prodigious quantity of both. Whenever he appears in the course of this narrative, one should remember the brandy bottle on his desk and the coffeepot on the stove or portable heater. One might also remember the race between Giering, who might or might not succeed in destroying the Red Orchestra, and the cancer which would unquestionably succeed in destroying Giering.

Alamo was clearly the most important of the agents picked up in the Rue des Atrébates. He had told Fortner nothing. On Giering's instructions, he was transferred to Berlin. Giering could easily have had him tortured, for his Kommando included several masters of the art. He was not systematically opposed to the use of torture, but it had to be effective. He had quickly sized up his man as a diehard, a zealot who made a fetish of sacrifice and had a craving for the heroic. It would be a fatal error to allow him to die on the rack after treating his interrogators to a final, defiant rendering of "The Internationale." Far better to rub him the right way and treat him well. The two men chatted over the brandy bottle. Alamo let slip that he had fought in Spain. "In which service?" asked Giering. The question was right on target. "Why, the air force, of course!" Alamo was completely carried away as soon as the talk turned to flying. This sudden change triggered off an idea in Giering's mind. That same evening Alamo was released from his cell and put up in the interrogator's apartment. He was introduced to a tall, melancholy young man who had recently lost a leg while serving as a pilot in the Luftwaffe; it was Giering's son. They held many engrossing conversations in the days that followed, moving their hands this way and that, as pilots always do when describing their duels in the sky. It was well worth trying. But Alamo limited his effusions to aeronautics; he did not disclose either the code or the grid plan employed by the Brussels network. Realizing that his attempt had failed, Giering sent him back to St.-Gilles prison. Success or failure, however, it was obvious that a master investigator had been at work.

13. The Gestapo Picks Up the Scent

Fortner was slowly but surely learning the ropes. For the time being, he was allowed a free hand in Brussels. Giering had realized that the only hope of reopening the offensive in Belgium lay in Rita Arnould. Fortner, out of native kindness, had immediately adopted the same approach to Rita that Giering, from pure guile, was now adopting to Alamo. And the girl was more pliable than the Russian.

She had already revealed several ominous-sounding aliases—"the

Big Chief," "the Little Chief," "the Professor," and so on—as well as providing some helpful particulars. As for her lover, "Romeo" Springer, she did not know where he lived but knew that he often went to the Paris Bourse. Fortner made inquiries there, but without success; the bird had flown, leaving no trace at all. He received a useful tip-off, however; he was advised that if he was interested in Springer he should keep an eye on the woman in charge of the Bourse's typing pool. Fortner discovered that she was interpolating messages in the official correspondence, and that these messages were being relayed to a woman working at the Paris office of the Belgian Chamber of Commerce. Did this mean the network had antennae in France? Fortner made photostats of the documents, then allowed them to go on their way. The woman in the Paris office must be acting as a "letterbox." She was placed under surveillance.

He also questioned Rita about the agent who had worked in the well-stocked forger's room at the Rue des Atrébates. She was sure he was a Polish Jew, but did not know his address or his regular haunts. This did not give Fortner much to go on, but at least he was on familiar ground. It takes years for a counterfeiter to reach the top of his profession, and there is every likelihood of his attracting the attention of the police at some stage in his career. Fortner had brought several forgers to justice in his days as an examining magistrate. He made inquiries of the Belgian police and learned from its files that a certain Abraham Raichman, a Polish Jew, had been suspected, before the war, of supplying the outlawed Communist apparatus with counterfeit banknotes. The description on his record card tallied with that given by Rita. But how was Fortner to find Raichman? It was at this point that fortune smiled on him for the first time.

One of his assistants, Weigelt,* claimed to know a Belgian police inspector who was in a position to supply the Abwehr with false papers. This was well worth looking into; the Abwehr's informers needed to change identity at frequent intervals, and on the whole the Belgian police were not so docile as to be a reliable source of documents. Fortner inquired how much the service would cost; the figure quoted was a thousand francs per identity card. Fortner pulled a face at this, but Weigelt pointed out that the inspector's offer contained an additional advantage: it would establish a link with the Communist organization. So Fortner requested a meeting with the Belgian police inspector.

---

* Pseudonym chosen by the author.

The latter's name was Mathieu; his "contact" was Abraham Raichman.

◆

There was as great a difference between a Raichman and an Alamo as between Giering, for instance, and a run-of-the-mill Gestapo man.

Alamo, who held a commission in the Russian armed forces, was serving in the Red Orchestra just as a French officer will work for the Deuxième Bureau, if he happens to be assigned to it. He would have been only too willing to renounce cloak and dagger in favor of an ordinary uniform. To Raichman, on the other hand, the gray cloak of espionage was like a second skin; without it, he would feel naked and lost. He was a revolutionary militant, a professional purveyor of conspiracy, a man shaped by years of service for the Comintern.

Until the outbreak of war a Communist Party had been active in every country, fighting for its objectives at the national level. At the international level, the Comintern had coordinated these local activities to play their part in the global offensive. In short, the Comintern was the G.H.Q. of worldwide revolution. Its members, hand-picked from the ablest elements in individual parties, were tantamount to an aristocracy; they had the virtues and failings of such a body. Their downfall came with Stalin's decision to build up Russia's own might, at the sacrifice of worldwide revolution. The early Stalinist purges served, among other things, to bring the Comintern to heel.

Needless to say, there was considerable rivalry between the Soviet secret services and the networks controlled by the Comintern. The former, rigidly Stalinist, were working for Russia; the latter were serving the proletariat in every country. We must be wary of generalizations, however: Trepper was closer in temperament to men like Raichman, a Comintern agent, than to fellow Center agents like Alamo; the Big Chief cannot be glibly categorized. When Kent and Alamo arrived in Brussels, they treated him to a recital of the instructions they had received at the Center. Among other things, they were to keep away from women and stay out of bars.

"Exemplary advice," replied Trepper. "I take it, then, that you've left your private parts on ice in Moscow? No? Ah, how awkward! Well, my advice is this: if a woman attracts you, go ahead. Be careful, that's all." The Comintern flavor of this reply would not have been well received at the Center, in Znamensky Street. For the styles of the two organizations were emphatically dissimilar. Center agents saw themselves as cool, efficient technicians; in their eyes, Comintern agents who sought to perpetuate the romantic tradition were showy amateurs. Center agents dressed like businessmen; Comintern agents had a reputation for grimy fingernails and long, untidy hair.

When the war came, men employed by the Comintern went into battle under a severe handicap. They were members of an organization that had fallen from grace; many of them had been involved in ideological disputes with the Kremlin. They were made use of, but kept under close supervision. If a disaster befell them, Moscow would certainly not put itself out to help them.

Naturally, getting caught was the worst disaster of all. Yet, even here there were degrees of misfortune. In Alamo's case, for instance, it was all quite straightforward. He was a Russian officer. His country was at war with Germany, so he was fighting on her behalf. Not even the most blinkered SS man could see any objection to this. A Comintern agent, on the other hand, carried in his wake a long history of conspiracy, industrial strife and armed insurrection. He may even have served in Germany in the days before Hitler, when the country had witnessed clash after clash between the Comintern and the *Freikorps*, and later between Comintern and Nazi groups. Throughout that period there had been continual street fighting; bodies were found mutilated after death; people were always being kidnaped, tortured, assassinated; it was a time of punitive raids and mass shootings. Many scores were left unsettled, and no hatred is more intense than that which springs from the fumes of civil war. So it is easy to imagine the mental processes of a butcher working for the Rote Kapelle Kommando: a man like Alamo was a pleasing windfall. It was even more pleasing if the Soviet agent was also a Jew. But best of all was the Soviet agent who was a Jew and who had also worked in Germany for the Comintern—the mere thought of such a catch was mouthwatering. The prisoner was well aware of this, and his morale declined accordingly. It was not amusing to be welcomed in the Gestapo cellars as a special tidbit.

And Comintern agents ran a greater risk of getting caught than the others. Their long, crowded years as activists had made most of them known to one police force or another. Somewhere in a Belgian or French or Dutch office was a record card or even a complete file listing their description, their contacts and their habits. Kent and Alamo were luckier in this respect: they were men without a past.

Had it been wise of Moscow to amalgamate the Comintern

networks and the traditional national intelligence services in the aftermath of the German attack? The Russian leaders presumably had had no choice. The desperate nature of the situation demanded the use of all their resources, even those which might seem rather suspect.

Besides, generalizations always blur when the moment of truth arrives. For agents facing torture and death, there is no such thing as a Secret Service attitude or a Comintern attitude. It becomes a matter of a particular agent's inner strength or weakness. He might be worn out after too many years of clandestine activity, battered by the compromises such an existence entails, disappointed at the frustration of his hopes, sapped by ideological bickering and the fear of being purged. On the other hand, the ordeals he has lived through may have tempered him to the hardness of steel.

Here, without added comment, is an account of my visit to one of the Comintern agents who worked in concert with the Red Orchestra:

A grim barracks of an apartment house clinging to the slopes of Ménilmontant. Concrete staircase; long corridors with cement floors; plywood walls. The human hive in all its ugliness.

The three Bruns * live crowded together in a tiny apartment: one room plus kitchen. Madame Brun is a short, rather plump, but lively woman. Her husband looks distinctly older. He wears glasses and keeps his white hair plastered back; his face is waxen and deeply lined; he has a very gruff voice. Pictures of pop stars have been pinned to the walls—the handiwork of their son, a boy of about eighteen. He kindly consented to turn down the volume of the record player, whose bellowings had been clearly audible three floors below. The sudden silence was a thing to marvel at.

Brun told me he had received my letter, but had been rather perplexed by it. "Me work for the Resistance? Why, I was never in the Resistance!" I explained what I was after, and why. They all seemed flabbergasted. "Oh," said Brun, "you must be talking about the time I was dodging the draft." He had ignored the conscription papers calling him up for compulsory labor in Germany. What an uproar! He told me all about it. There was the time he hid a fellow draft dodger in a handcart and smuggled him through a German roadblock. There was the time a French cop came to arrest Brun in his own home—for he had gone in hiding right here, in this huge apartment house. He said to the cop, "All right, I'll go with you. But have you noticed that I live on the sixth floor, that there's a big stairwell, and plenty of people around?" The cop let

* Pseudonym chosen by the author.

the matter drop, doubtless picturing only too clearly what would happen to him if Brun raised the alarm at the center of this human hive. Another high point in the Brun saga was the day they bicycled out into the countryside to buy some beans; on the way back, they ran into a German roadblock. Of all the things that could have happened! Even after twenty years, they still remembered the look on the soldier's face as he questioned them and tested the weight of their sack of beans. . . .

By the look of it, my visit had been a wasted effort. But I stayed put in my chair and kept on voicing my conviction that Brun had been a member of a spy ring; I had seen his name on Gestapo documents, and some of his comrades had confirmed the fact.

And suddenly he unfroze. Could I by any chance be referring to those old messages? Ah, well, that was different. Why hadn't I said so in the first place? Well yes, it was true he used to carry messages—that much he couldn't deny. But he was unable to give me any details, any names: it had all happened so long ago. . . .

Madame Brun's eyes were nearly popping out of her head. "What! You used to carry messages!" She couldn't get over it. A husband who had made a stand against being drafted for forced labor was a husband to be proud of, but not in the same class as one who had actually fought in the Resistance. She was at once delighted and furious. "Why didn't you ever tell me?" He shrugged. "What good would it have done? Women are best kept out of things like that."

Well, at least he had now admitted to carrying messages. He used to hide them in the handlebars of his bike and proceed to a certain point along the road between Étampes and Orléans. There, he would go through the motions of relieving himself beside a ditch and place the documents in a rusty old tin can. This was the "dead letter box" technique; the advantage was that it obviated all contact between agents. According to the experts, it had not been adopted by Soviet Intelligence until after the Second World War. The experts were wrong.

"But who used to hand you these messages?" "A comrade." "He must have had a name, an alias?" "I never knew it." ("Of course not," said his son, who proudly admitted to reading a good deal of spy fiction, "your network was divided into watertight compartments." "Oh, really?" said Brun, in a simple-simon voice; but there was, I noticed, a quiet gleam in his eyes.) "And who introduced you to this man?" "Can't remember. . . . Some pals." "What did he look like?" "Don't ask me, he's gone from my mind completely." "All the same, it's remarkable: you can remember the exact expression on the face of some unknown German sentry who happened to catch you with a sack of beans, yet you don't know if the man who might have been sending you to your death was fair or dark." "That's right—funny, isn't it?" "And where did he hand you the messages?" "In a flat over at—" "Over at where?" "Over at— Do you know,

it's slipped my mind." "What were these messages about?" "I never knew
—I'm not inquisitive, you see. . . ."

If all Comintern agents were like that, Trepper must have thanked
his lucky stars for their help.

———————◆———————

Abraham Raichman was *not* like that. Although higher in rank,
he was weaker in character. He had been a member of the legendary
Pass Apparat set up by the Comintern. This was a full-scale factory
in Berlin, specializing in the production of false papers. It had a staff
of a hundred and seventy, with thirty thousand rubber stamps, machinery for printing and engraving, photographic processing equipment, et cetera. Year in, year out, two thousand passports came out
of that factory, along with thousands of other documents of all kinds.
The official annalists of counterespionage write boringly in general,
but their prose takes wing when they write of the *Pass-Apparat*—"a
performance unique in history"; "a miracle of skill, precision and
imaginativeness." Even after a quarter of a century, they still remember the Berlin "shoemakers" with emotion. In the private
jargon of Soviet Intelligence, a forger is a "shoemaker," and—
naturally enough—false papers are known as "shoes." The reason is
obvious enough: some shoemaking tools, the awl for instance, are
also employed in the counterfeiter's craft.

It cost the Gestapo a good deal of effort to liquidate the *Pass-
Apparat*, whose members then dispersed to every part of Europe.

Trepper had a high regard for Raichman the shoemaker, but
little faith in Raichman the man. The latter, he felt, was conceited,
foolhardy, and too quick to show contempt. The Orchestra could
not afford to lose the services of so accomplished a craftsman, but
they meant to keep him on a short rein. So long as the Big Chief
was in Brussels, all went well. But when he moved to Paris and introduced Raichman to his youthful successor, Kent, the shoemaker was
far from happy—"What! He's my boss? Why, he's still wet behind
the ears!"

After the Atrébates raid, Yefremov took over from Kent—another novice who fell far short of Raichman's high standards. One
day Raichman informed Yefremov that he was in touch with a Belgian
police inspector working for the Resistance. This was Inspector
Mathieu, who had said to him, "Why waste your time manufacturing

false papers, when I can fit you up with real ones?" Yefremov reported the offer to the Big Chief and asked whether they ought to accept it. Trepper replied immediately: "It is better to have poor shoes
of one's own than good shoes supplied by an outsider. Sever contact."
Yefremov was too young for his word to carry weight with Raichman. The contact was not severed.

The Abwehr in Brussels gave Mathieu the cover name "Carlos";
after all, they were working on a case positively teeming with fake
South Americans. German Intelligence were addicted to rather
ponderous jokes of this kind, and sometimes paid dearly for them.* If
the Belgian network heard that a Belgian police officer was working
for the Abwehr under the code name Carlos, then the network would
realize the hunt was on and would lose no time in unmasking Mathieu.
But as it transpired, the Abwehr had no reason to regret its little touch
of humor; not a word leaked out.

Inspector Mathieu soon showed himself to be a first-rate recruit
for the Germans. This came as no surprise to Fortner, who still sums
him up in the ritual phrase, "He was the best type of German army
officer." Physically, he was a tall, broad-shouldered specimen, as Aryan
as they come. From a moral standpoint, it depends on whether one
takes the view of his German masters, or of his victims. In the eyes
of Franz Fortner, his execution by firing squad at the end of the war
was an act of brutal injustice by the Belgian authorities. In a voice
trembling with emotion, Fortner paid this rather disconcerting
tribute to the dead man: "He was a great European." It was like
the funeral oration of some eminent world statesman.†

Be that as it may, Mathieu proved wonderfully effective. As an
experienced policeman, he knew better than to rush things by betraying curiosity. He simply stated that he was at Raichman's disposal.
He pretended not to be interested in the use that would be made of
the identity cards he was undertaking to supply. This easygoing

---

* Colonel Verneuil, who held a senior post in the underground Deuxième
Bureau, was once invited to meet an agent of whom he had no previous knowledge. The agent was to identify himself by means of the phrase, "Monsieur,
we have been waiting for you for a long time." Verneuil turned these words
over and over in his mind and decided that he did not like the sound of them.
He did not keep the appointment. The fun-loving Gestapo waited for him in
vain.
† Fortner is not necessarily correct in claiming that Mathieu was shot. Some
of the information I have received suggests that he may still be alive.

approach smoothed his path to success; there was no need for him to go to the network; the network would come to him.

The reader will recall how, before fleeing to France, Kent had left a trunk in the care of Robert Christen, the proprietor of the Florida.

Robert Christen says: "A few weeks later I had a visit from Nazarin Drailly. He was business manager of the firm which Sierra had talked me into joining. He told me he had called to pick up the trunk. 'Out of the question,' I said. 'Sierra left it in my safekeeping and its going to remain under my roof until he gets back.' Drailly looked quite put out for a while, then he said, 'Listen, you're running a very great risk. Do you know what's inside that trunk? A radio transmitter!' That was how I discovered what they had dragged me into."

At Raichman's instigation, the network found a safer hiding place for the transmitter: Mathieu's house. The inspector offered to conceal it in his garage. Raichman looked the place over and agreed. A team of experts arrived from Berlin to examine the apparatus. Wearing gloves so as not to leave fingerprints, they carefully dismantled it and then photographed it, part by part. Fortner admits that the quality of the equipment came as a complete surprise to them. Of Soviet manufacture, it was superior to German transmitters and even to those used by British agents.

When the examination was complete, the transmitter was returned to its hiding place. The Abwehr waited jubilantly for someone to call and collect it. Next time a pianist showed up in Brussels, he would be caught at once; there would be no need to resort to the complex gadgetry used by the Funkabwehr.

For the time being, however, Brussels remained silent. Hersch Sokol was still performing as the Orchestra's solo pianist.

◆

The Big Chief was afraid for him. He implored Moscow to face up to the danger of another disaster like the one at the Rue des Atrébates; he spoke out against the Center's draconian rule that the passing of information should always take precedence over the agent's safety; he demanded that Sokol's transmissions be limited to half an hour. All in vain. The Director continued to bombard the pianist with interminable lists of questions—unlike the Big Chief, who condensed his messages to the bare minimum in order to reduce the length of time spent on the air.

At least Sokol no longer had to transmit the vast quantity of information picked up by the Berlin ring. Did this mean that the aerial reinforcements promised by Moscow had arrived at long last? Yes and no. In May, 1942, Erna Eifler and Wilhelm Fellendorf were dropped over East Prussia by a Russian bomber; in the end, it had been decided to give up the idea of flying them in by way of England. Both had a wide experience of undercover activities. Erna had initially worked in Germany as a member of a *rabcor* network similar to the one which Fantômas had organized in France. Later she had served successively in Vienna, Shanghai, Holland and Britain. Fellendorf, a former officer in the International Brigades, had operated in Czechoslovakia, Belgium and Holland. They had spent the past few months in intensive training at a Soviet spy school. They would need to draw on all they had learned. Their mission was to proceed to Hamburg, where both of them had lived, and where they had reliable friends; from there, they were to make contact with the Berlin network.

The first part of the program went off without a hitch, except that they lost their radio on landing. Despite the hazards, they successfully worked their way across Germany until they reached their appointed haven. But it began to seem that they would never make contact with Berlin. The month of June found them still in Hamburg. Admittedly, the problem of communications had become less acute. Some of the messages were being radioed by the Berlin transmitters, which were still working sporadically in spite of technical difficulties and the undiminished threat of the Funkabwehr. The majority were taken by courier to Amsterdam and then relayed to Moscow on the transmitter operated by the Dutch branch of the Red Orchestra. The Brussels transmitters were to be brought back into service as soon as the immediate danger to them had passed.

In spite of this, Sokol was being grossly overworked; the Big Chief's French network had reached such proportions that several pianists should have been handling the continual flow of information. Hersch Sokol was too intelligent not to realize that his days were numbered. Stoically he remained at his desk, tapping out messages, with the telltale headphones shutting out all other noises. On June 9, 1942, after a long, patient pursuit employing every technical device at their disposal, the Gestapo broke down the door of his house in St.-Germain and dragged him away from his transmitter. Myra was captured with him.

At first they were assumed to be members of some French or-

ganization. When it emerged that they really belonged to the Red
Orchestra, Giering gave orders for them to be transferred to Berlin.
Fortner met the couple and asked Sokol how he had become a radio
operator. "I was sitting outside a café," said Sokol, "absent-mindedly
drumming my fingers on the table, when suddenly one of the other
customers smiled at me and started mimicking my actions. Then he
came over and asked if I wanted to be a radio operator, as I seemed
to have a natural gift for that line of work." Fortner was furious.
"You may be a pediatrician, but there's no need to play childish
games!" He was unable to get anything out of Sokol.

Eventually he handed the prisoner over to the professional torturers of the Rote Kapelle Kommando. In their eyes, he represented
a wholly unexpected chance to give fresh impetus to the investigations which had bogged down in Brussels. They applied the harshest
methods. Sokol would not talk. So they started on Myra. She would
not talk, either. In desperation, the Kommando resorted to its favorite
trick: they held a revolver to Hersch Sokol's temple and warned
Myra that unless she cooperated he would be slain before her eyes.
She revealed one of Trepper's aliases: "Gilbert."

That was all either of them disclosed. They *could* have given
away the Big Chief's radio code; they could also have led the Kommando to Trepper's second in command, Hillel Katz.

———◆———

Claude Spaak continues: "Shortly after Harry's [Hersch Sokol]
lucky release from Pithiviers, my wife told me, 'I've just met Myra.
We mustn't drop in on them unexpectedly any more; they're engaged
in undercover work.' She continued to see Myra from time to time,
and the latter handed her a roll of gold coins, asking if we could hide
it somewhere in the house. I agreed, of course, but I said to my wife,
'Something might happen to us or to the Sokols, and we ought at least
to know whom to give the coins to in an emergency.'" She agreed.
It was arranged with Myra that we should hand the coins over to
anyone introducing himself as 'Henri.'

"In those days we had a pied-à-terre in the Rue de Beaujolais,
opposite the Palais-Royal; Colette, the writer, lived next door to us.
And it was there, one day, that we had a visit from 'Henri'—the man
you call Trepper. He was a solid-looking character, about forty-five
or so, with a fairly marked Russian accent. He seemed thoroughly
humane, and inspired total trust; his eyes shone with goodness.

"On this particular occasion, he was very much on edge. 'Your friends have been arrested,' he told me. 'They've been transmitting from a little house in St.-Germain; their messages were picked up by the Soviet ambassador in London. Things look very black for them: they're Jews *and* Russians *and* spies.' This was rather like a doctor telling his patient, 'You have cancer and TB, and now you're developing an intestinal obstruction.'

"We were silent for a while, then I told him I'd give him the coins. But he declined. 'No, I don't need them. If I ever do, I'll send someone to collect them.'

"And he disappeared."

The two Brussels transmitters which had eluded the Funkabwehr had remained off the air, except for a few routine exchanges to keep up contact with Moscow. Following the arrest of the Sokols, the Big Chief instructed Yefremov to put one of them back into service. Six months had gone by since the raid on the Rue des Atrébates. Trepper had every reason to suppose that the danger was dying down.

14. The Code Breakers

In Berlin, Kludow (the Funkabwehr's code expert) and his students were working around the clock to decipher the surviving batch of messages picked up from the PTX transmitter. Of the three hundred in their possession, ninety-seven had been based on fragments of Téramond's *Le Miracle du professeur Wolmar*. Neither then nor later did the Funkabwehr discover that *Le Femme de trente ans*, by Honoré de Balzac, had been used for all the rest. Thus, two thirds of the treasured pile turned out to be quite useless, and the experts tackled the remainder in a mood of grim resolve.

Needless to say, the signals did not follow Téramond's story sentence by sentence. The relevant passages had been selected in accordance with a prearranged system that was entirely unknown to the Funkabwehr. So they had to find the appropriate sentence for each individual message. Sometimes luck led them straight to it;

sometimes they had to explore almost the entire book before finding it. This slow and laborious process is the accepted lot of the code breaker. But in this case the task was made more thorny than usual by the nature of the book itself. No one can claim that *Le Miracle du professeur Wolmar* is a great novel. Guy de Téramond wrote it in Arcachon in the year 1910, after previously publishing *La Force de l'amour* and *Le Mystérieux inconnu* ("a work which may safely be entrusted to any hands"). The network's decision to use it is no doubt explained by the publisher's note on the front page: "This book, issued as a free supplement for subscribers to *Le Monde illustré*, is not for sale." It had had only limited distribution and never came on to the market, and the Abwehr's special envoy to Paris had found it only after exploring the stocks of innumerable secondhand dealers.

The contents of the book must have been maddening to Kludow's scholarly band, who were obliged to learn it almost by heart. The hero, Professor Wolmar, a brilliant surgeon, hits upon a theory: "All the phenomena of abnormality are produced by adhesions to the brain matter . . . and from this he goes on to infer, with his customary boldness of vision, that if only he were to cleanse the [criminals'] brains of all the adhesions paralyzing their intelligence and will power, he could turn them into rational, level-headed, responsible human beings." After much pleading, he finally receives permission to experiment on a convicted murderer called Little Fritz, "one of those degenerate beings, one of those pieces of flotsam which are still, unbelievably, to be found at the very heart of civilization." Little Fritz's death sentence is commuted and he is sent to prison after the operation, which appears to have failed. But he escapes and becomes a kind of Superman, endowed with the most astonishing and beneficial powers. He wants to thank the professor, and decides that the best way is to send the following telegram to the Kaiser: "Unless you begin disarming by 4 A.M day after tomorrow, I shall blow up all of Germany." It was signed: "France." Guy de Téramond concludes his story with the words, "In an uncontrollable surge, the entire German nation swept away its emperor and its ministers and, responding to the powerful spirit of universal brotherhood, lost no time in seeking peace."

It was a galling experience, having to study Little Fritz's telegram to the Kaiser in the hope of fathoming the Big Chief's telegrams to the Director, but Kludow's team overcame their repugnance. By June, 1942, they were able to decipher two or three messages a day. The actual contents of the telegrams were of no great concern to them. Like all code breakers, they scrutinized words so closely that they no longer saw the underlying meaning. For them, victory lay in ferreting out the secret contained in the telegrams; it was no concern of theirs if the secret, once extracted, constituted the clearest portent of German defeat.

No, that was for the Abwehr to worry about. And the Abwehr chiefs were terrified. Flicke tells us they used to go to their offices sick with worry at the thought of the messages that Kludow handed them with such a triumphant smile. The presence of secret transmitters in Berlin was alarming enough in itself. The statements made by Rita Arnould, and the discovery of German official documents at the Rue des Atrébates, came as a painful blow. But as the telegrams were deciphered, they revealed that the disaster was far worse than anyone would have dreamed. It was simple: there was not a sector in the political, economic and military life that was not known to the Russians in every detail. The Third Reich, one of the mightiest police states of all time, lay helplessly exposed to Moscow's gaze.

In mid-June, Kranz reported that one of the Brussels transmitters was back in service. The Abwehr did not hesitate; there was no question of carrying out those slow, painstaking investigations which might finally lead to the very heart of the network: they had no time! In a few days—on June 28, 1942—the Wehrmacht's Panzer divisions would be making a decisive onslaught. "Operation Blue" promised to sweep them all the way to Stalingrad and give them control of the Caucasian oil wells. After the reverses of the winter campaign, after the rivers of German blood that had stained the Russian snow, everyone in Berlin knew that the forthcoming offensive would be absolutely decisive; the outcome of the war was about to be decided somewhere between Voronezh and Stalingrad. It was simply not possible to allow the air to be filled with messages which might disclose to Moscow the secrets of Operation Blue.

———◆———

Franz Fortner says: "Naturally, it came as a most unpleasant surprise when Berlin informed us that a transmitter was again operating in our area. No agent had ever called to pick up the set concealed in Mathieu's garage; so our trap had been a waste of time, and we had to start from scratch, just as for the Rue des Atrébates.

"The tracking teams came back to Brussels, including my old

sergeant technician in charge of the 'suitcase' detector. The Funk-abwehr spent the first few days taking the usual bearings from fixed points. It must seem unbelievable, but it's true: the transmitter was operating all night long, which obviously made our task much easier. I must confess I could never understand the Russians' attitude. Were they really so overworked? After all, an underemployed pianist is more use than a pianist locked up in jail. No, I think they simply weren't aware of the advanced techniques we were using. I can't see any other possible explanation. Not unless they were cold-bloodedly sacrificing radio operators.

"Anyway, we very soon discovered that the transmitter was somewhere in the Laeken district. Unluckily, an electric railway ran through the neighborhood. It jumbled the electric fields—or something like that—and much to his annoyance my sergeant had to admit that his 'suitcase' wouldn't work. We had to resort to a Funkabwehr van fitted with equipment powerful enough not to be jammed by the railway. It was a camouflaged military vehicle, but we hardly had to worry about spotters, because we only operated after curfew. On the other hand, there was a risk that we ourselves might be stopped and questioned, and that was something I wanted to avoid at all costs. I certainly didn't want reports leaking out that a mysterious vehicle was roaming the streets at night, that the police weren't interfering with it, and so on.

"Sure enough, it happened.

"On the very first evening, we bumped into a police patrol. We were all wearing civvies, of course, and carried 'genuine false credentials,' which we had obtained through Mathieu. The police examined our identity cards and asked what we were doing outdoors at that hour. I intimated that it was something connected with the black market. I did my best to talk them out of it, but they insisted on examining the inside of the van. I couldn't allow that; they would have seen our apparatus. I tapped my driver on the shoulder and he drove off at full tilt, scattering the policemen. We managed to shake them off, but the hunt was over for the night.

"On the second evening, another farce! There was a Luftwaffe barracks in the area. We drove past it so often that the sentries became suspicious and pounced on us! We were taken to the guard-house, and we had to show our papers and explain ourselves and telephone my superiors for confirmation. I was furious.

"These incidents wasted valuable time, but luckily the trans-mitter continued to operate five hours a night, and in the end we located the house where it was hidden—a tall building with a lumber-yard on one side and a shop on the other. According to my sergeant, the set was sure to be on one of the upper floors. It was hard for him to be more specific. Anyway, the rest was up to me.

"My first step, as in the Rue des Atrébates, was to recruit extra manpower. We couldn't allow the bird to escape, and I preferred to take too many precautions rather than too few. I was given twenty-five members of the secret police. In addition, I went back to the Luftwaffe barracks and explained what I was up to. The airmen were very young and enthusiastic; the scheme excited them, and they put themselves at my disposal. I decided to launch the attack at 3 A.M. on June 30.

"It was a marvelously clear, moonlit night, so I instructed the airmen to hide in the lumberyard until zero hour; then they were to emerge from cover and seal off the street. I and my squad of police moved into the ground-floor apartment of the house in question. We woke up the tenant, who proved to be very friendly, offering us coffee and making conversation. At three o'clock we went into action. I assigned two men to each floor and told the rest to stand by. We galloped up the stairs. Suddenly I heard a shout from the attic: 'Hurry! Hurry! It's up here!' I raced to the attic. It was divided into small compartments. I hurried to the part where a light showed, and there I found my two men—alone! I ordered them to search the other compartments, while I quickly took stock of the scene. On a small table was the transmitter, still warm. Beside it lay a bundle of documents written in German. Dozens of postcards were strewn about the room, posted from various German towns. It was enough to take one's breath away. On the floor, a jacket and a pair of boots. The pianist must have felt very safe, to put comfort before security. But how could he possibly have escaped? I glanced up and noticed the dormer window was half open. I poked my head out, intending to take a look at the roof. There was a loud shot and I ducked quickly. Someone down in the street shouted, 'Look out! He's crouching by the chimney!'

"I went downstairs with the documents. My airmen friends had moved out into the street, but were taking cover in doorways; the fugitive was shooting at them. He was clearly visible as he sprang from roof to roof. He had a revolver in each hand and was blazing away between leaps. I could sense that my boys were dying to get him, but I told them, 'Whatever you do, don't shoot! I want him alive!'

"Our man reached the last building in the block: he was cornered. But he smashed one of the dormer windows and disappeared. We heard a woman calling for help. 'What's going on?' we shouted up at her. She said a man had just raced through her bedroom and down the stairs. We sped to the house and searched every floor. No sign of him! I began to fear the worst. However, some of the airmen went down to the cellar, picked up an overturned bathtub and found him hiding underneath. They were so angry and worked up that they started beating him with the butts of their rifles. I ordered them to stop and took my prisoner to Gestapo headquarters. He seemed panic-stricken. He was a short, stocky, hard-featured man, about forty years old, terribly working-class. I must say, he didn't make a great impression on me.

"He immediately wanted to know whether I was Abwehr or Gestapo; I set his mind at rest. He spoke French, but none too well and with a heavy accent. Next he asked me to fasten his hands in front of him, instead of keeping them handcuffed behind his back. 'Oh, no,' I said, 'that's an old trick! You're just looking for a chance to jump me and hit me over the head.' He insisted that he had no such intention, but I remained suspicious. As a gesture, however, I laid my gun on the table and said, 'There, you see, I'm unarmed. You have nothing to fear.' He complained of the beating he had received, and I felt obliged to point out that it was his own fault—he ought not to have opened fire; troops never like being shot at when they can't shoot back. He calmed down, and after a while we started chatting in German; he spoke it perfectly.

"Eventually I informed him that I proposed to question him about his identity. He stared uneasily at the two policemen in my office. I ordered them out, removed his handcuffs and said, 'Go ahead. We're all alone, just the two of us, so you can speak quite openly.' Relaxing visibly, he told me that his name was Johann Wenzel and that he had been born in Danzig in 1902. A German! But he added: 'I warn you here and now, I'm not the kind of man who makes bargains. You needn't expect any disclosures or betrayals from me!' 'Now, now,' I said, 'you aren't being sensible.' But I couldn't get another word out of him. So I packed him off to St.-Gilles prison.

"If I'm to be thorough, I must tell you of our subsequent discovery about the ground-floor tenant—the man who had been so friendly and offered us coffee. It turned out that his real purpose had been to delay us as long as possible. He was a member of the network, and it was he who had housed and fed Wenzel. By the time we went back for him, of course, he was gone. His name was Schumacher.

"Following Wenzel's departure, I went to report to my superiors. They immediately telephoned the news to Berlin. Twenty minutes later, Berlin called back with intense excitement and informed us: 'You've caught one of the most prominent members of the prewar German Communist Party, one of the chiefs of the Comintern's underground apparatus.' The capture was such a major and miraculous event in their eyes that they could hardly believe it could be the same man.

"To finish up with Wenzel, I should add that the Berlin Gestapo sent for him a few days later. He was out of his mind with fear, for obviously the Gestapo had old scores to settle with him. Giering and his men set to work on him. They tortured him for six or eight weeks, then sent him back to Brussels. When I saw him again, I simply didn't recognize him. He was a broken man. He had revealed everything to them, including his code and his cover name, 'the Professor.' He was called that because he was a great specialist in radio communication and had trained many pianists in his time.* Giering informed me that the prisoner was now prepared to work for us.

"But to return to that night of June thirtieth: I got home at about 7 A.M., completely done in. I still had the documents which had been found beside the transmitter. These were messages which Wenzel was about to send, or else had just received. The messages—very long ones —were nearly all in code, of course, but two or three were in clear. Tired as I was, I was curious enough to glance at them. One of them referred to a vitally important address in Berlin which must at all costs remained concealed from us Germans. Moscow did not say 'Germans,' but 'Huns' or 'Boches,' or something of the same flavor. The other messages were enough to drive all thought of sleep from my mind. It was unbelievable!

"What I had in my hands was highly detailed information about German production of tanks and aircraft and about our losses and reverses. The *coup de grâce* was a telegram giving the fullest possible facts about the offensive in the Caucasus. Our troops had only just gone into action, they were still hundreds of miles from their objective, yet the plans for the operation were set out in their entirety, complete with statistics: how many divisions were involved, *which* divisions, and what equipment they had. It was all there. A real disaster!

"Obviously, Berlin had to be warned. We telephoned them, but

---

* Among his pupils were Alamo, Camille and Sophie Poznanska.

they refused to believe us. So I set out by car that same day and drove straight to Abwehr headquarters, in Tirpitzstrasse. I had placed the messages in a briefcase, and held this under my arm. At the main entrance the officer in charge of the guard asked me to open the briefcase; he wanted to look inside. I refused, and when he insisted I drew my revolver, pointed it at him and said, 'If you try to take this briefcase from me, I'll shoot!' This caused quite a stir, of course, and I won my point. Afterward I had to wait half an hour before I was received by the senior officer in charge of Belgian affairs. But I refused to show him my briefcase and insisted on seeing Colonel Bentivegni, senior assistant to Admiral Canaris. The colonel showed me into his office, and there I handed over the documents. After reading them, Bentivegni at once took me to see Field Marshal Keitel, Chief of the OKW. Keitel was thunderstruck by the message relating to the Caucasus campaign. He simply could not believe it.* As for the hush-hush Berlin address which the Germans must never be allowed to discover, it proved to belong to a high-ranking personage in the Luftwaffe who had many connections in ruling circles. A great scandal was in prospect. . . ."

———◆———

There had already been one great scandal in connection with Operation Blue. A few days earlier, on June 19, Major Reichel, a staff officer of the 23rd Panzer Division, had set out in a reconnaissance aircraft to make a survey of the front line. His Storch was shot down in a sector held by the Russians. Reichel had his maps with him and also a typewritten summary of the first phase of the forthcoming offensive. Divisional headquarters were so horrified by this blow that they immediately launched a local attack in the hope of recovering the Storch and its occupants. The wreck was found—empty. Reichel and the pilot had vanished, but a patrol found two bodies buried a hundred yards or so away and these were presumed to be theirs, although identification was difficult because of the condition of the bodies. There was no sign of Reichel's briefcase or maps, so they must have fallen into Russian hands.

Hitler's insuperable dread of Soviet espionage had driven him to prescribe the most rigid security measures for the spring offensive.

---

* Moscow also received extensive and accurate information about Operation Blue from the Soviet spy ring operating in Switzerland and drawing on German sources.

Instructions to local commanders were to be given orally; a strict ban had been placed on all written orders. Reichel's superiors were sentenced to several years' detention for having issued the typewritten summary, but these punitive steps did not get to the root of the problem. What was to be done? Keitel was in favor of postponing the attack. Field Marshal von Bock and General Paulus were opposed to any delay; the situation was now such that a breakthrough *must* be attempted. Hitler gave them the green light.

On the night before the attack, the troops of the 23rd Panzer Division, who had just arrived from France and bore the emblem of the Eiffel Tower, were awakened by the blare of Soviet loudspeakers. A grim warning was being directed at them: "Soldiers of the 23rd Panzer Division, the Soviet Union salutes you. Your gay days in Paris are over now. Your comrades will already have warned you of what is happening here. Soon you will find out for yourselves. . . ."

The men of the Hungarian Second Army, sheltering in their individual foxholes, were likewise roused from sleep by a voice bellowing: "Hungarians! We know you will be crossing the Oskol at dawn tomorrow. You will find nothing there to block your path. We shall counterattack whenever we wish and at the place of our choice. Then you will rue your excursion to Russia. You will curse your leaders for obeying Field Marshal Keitel and sending you here."

And the members of the 24th Panzer Division received a similar eve-of-battle warning of the fate in store for them: "Panzergrenadiers of the 24th, you will not encounter us somewhere south of Voronezh, as your leaders claim. Give up hope of encircling us there, for we will be gone. Eke out your supplies of bread, ammunition and fuel. For it is we who shall soon be encircling you. And the luckiest among you will be those who have saved a bullet to blow out their brains with."

The troops' morale may have been somewhat dented, but the High Command refused to be seriously perturbed—Reichel was to blame for these temporary difficulties. The disasters which occurred later, however, could not possibly be attributed to the single typewritten sheet which had fallen into Russian hands.

There is no need to describe the German offensive of 1942— the lightning pace at which it began, the dash toward the Caucasian oil wells, and the final assault on Stalingrad. Suffice it to say that, for the first time since the outbreak of war, the High Command saw all of its plans foiled, one after the other. When the Panzer divisions completed their pincer movement, they found nothing inside the trap. Slowly but surely, the Russians led the enemy on until, at last, the battle was fought out at a time and place of their own choosing. In his excellent book *Hitler's War on Russia*, to which I am already indebted for the account of the Reichel escapade, Paul Carell writes: "This concentration of the Russian forces left no doubt at all that Timoshenko was acquainted with Hitler's plan and was now making the correct countermoves—tying down the bulk of the German forces on the northern wing outside Voronezh, in order to gain time to detach the bulk of his own Army Group from the Oskol and Donets and pull it back over the Don. And in which direction was he withdrawing his force? Oddly enough, toward Stalingrad." *

It was as a result of Kent's historic message to Moscow on November 12, 1941, that the Red Army intended keeping the appointment at Stalingrad.

———◆———

Senior members of the Abwehr and Gestapo were as shaken by the telegram disclosing that Berlin address as the High Command had been by the revelations concerning Operation Blue. Actually, there is some question whether the address was in fact given. According to some sources, the truth may be more complex; they suggest that the message contained top-secret Luftwaffe information which could have been known to only three officials at the Air Ministry; if this was so, investigations could soon have brought the culprit to light. Fortner insists that the address *was* given. The controversy is of no great importance; all parties agree that the message led the Gestapo to its quarry. And in any case, a few days after Fortner's dramatic journey to the German capital, Kludow dealt an even more crushing blow to the Red Orchestra's Berlin network.

Kludow's code breakers had initially applied their skills to messages *transmitted* by Kent. Perhaps because he was tired of the accumulation of sickening disclosures—or simply because his mind was sharper—someone high in the Abwehr suggested that Kludow turn to the messages *received* by Kent; these might well contain hints about the composition of the networks.

On July 14, 1942, Kludow dynamited the Berlin stronghold of Soviet Intelligence by cracking that calamitous telegram which the

———

* Paul Carell, *Hitler's War on Russia* (London: Harrap, 1964).

Director had sent to Kent on October 10: "Report immediately Berlin three addresses indicated. . . ."

The Rote Kapelle Kommando unleashed its hounds without delay.

———◆———

Walter Schellenberg continues:

After Heydrich's assassination in May, 1942, Himmler had taken on the job of coordinating and supervising *Rote Kapelle*. Very soon, serious tension arose between him and Müller, which worsened to such an extent that sometimes when Müller and I were reporting to him together, Müller, many years my senior, would be sent out of the room so that Himmler could discuss matters with me alone. Müller was intelligent enough to recognize this situation, and whenever he had anything particularly difficult to bring up would ask me to do it for him. Once with an ironical smile, he said to me, "Obviously he likes your face better than my Bavarian mug."

In July, 1942, Himmler ordered both of us to appear at Supreme Headquarters in East Prussia with a full report on *Rote Kapelle*.

We had only a few hours in which to get the report ready and when we met Müller began by telling me how invaluable my reports on *Rote Kapelle* had always been to him, and how very comprehensive my knowledge of Russia's spying activities seemed to be. After a few more obvious flatteries, he asked me to take the report to Himmler for both of us. But I said that as I was responsible for only about thirty per cent of what had been achieved he might as well report on the matter himself. "No," he said, "you'll get the red carpet; I'll probably get the boot."

I was not then aware of Müller's real reasons for this request. He must already have been planning to pull out from the work against the Russian Secret Service; but I shall refer to this later.

When I arrived at Supreme Headquarters I was surprised to hear that Himmler had ordered Canaris to report to him at the same time. He had planned to discuss the matter with Hitler that evening and wanted to have us all available to answer any questions. Himmler was in a very bad mood that day. He probably realized that Müller was avoiding a discussion with him. He read the first paragraphs of the report—it was to go to Hitler—and at once began to criticize it in the most disagreeable way. It was obviously biased, he said; the credit due to the Foreign Counter-Intelligence of the Wehrmacht [Canaris's organization] and the Military Radio Counter-Intelligence were [*sic*] not fairly presented. "Are you responsible for this report or is Müller?" he asked with a malevolent sneer. I said that I was.

"That is typical of him," he said, "to belittle other people's achievements so as to put himself in the most favorable light. A thoroughly petty attitude, and you can tell him I said so."

To make things worse, he called in Canaris and asked him for details of the Abwehr's collaboration with Military Radio Security on the case. It became increasingly clear that Müller had somewhat distorted the truth in his own favor. Himmler became quite unpleasant toward me, forgetting that it was not I who was responsible for the report. In the end he realized this. "I give you the right to repeat this reprimand to Müller word for word," he said.

The Führer was so upset by this report and by the treachery it revealed, that he did not wish to speak to anyone, so neither Canaris nor I was required to report to him that evening.*

Schellenberg's account throws light on two matters of some importance. In the first place, the Gestapo was doctoring its reports. Müller asserts quite plainly that the Berlin network had been uncovered thanks to the confessions the Gestapo had wrung from Wenzel. According to Müller, Kludow would have been incapable of deciphering that crucial telegram with the addresses of October 10, 1941, if "the Professor" had not handed over his code. The claim was a crude one: Wenzel obviously had his own personal code, wholly unconnected with the Atrébates code; so how could it possibly have helped in mastering the latter? On this occasion, Müller was lying purely for the sake of prestige. But soon we shall find the Gestapo falsifying its reports in far more dramatic circumstances, and for far more sinister and compelling motives.

Also worth noting is the "upset" experienced by the Führer after reading Müller's report. It deserves bearing in mind that only a few weeks earlier—on June 7, in fact—Hitler had declared to his luncheon companions at Rastenburg:

Our Department of Justice frequently enraged me by its handling of crimes of treason. . . . Eventually I had to tell Gürtner [the Minister of Justice] of my implacable resolve to have traitors, who had been too leniently treated by the normal courts, handed over to an SS Commando and shot. . . . If you wish to wage war successfully or to lead a people successfully through a difficult period of its history, you must have no doubts whatever on one point—namely, any individual who in such times tries, either actively or passively, to exclude himself from the activities of the community, must be destroyed.†

---

* *The Schellenberg Memoirs*, pp. 321–23.
† *Hitler's Table Talk, 1941–1944*, pp. 518–19.

15. Playing the *Funkspiel*

After the high drama of his visit to Berlin, Fortner returned to his own post in Belgium. The investigation was not yet completed, but it was bound to be brought to a successful conclusion before long. In the days following the Atrébates raid, he had lost the thread and been brought to a standstill. But this time things were different; thanks to Raichman, he could return to the chase whenever he pleased. The breach effected in the Soviet spy ring was still unrepaired. Naturally, there was no question of rushing things; on the contrary, the situation called for the quiet, subtle stalking of the Big Chief's agents.

As usual, things got off to a bad start. Letters found in Wenzel's possession clearly identified his mistress, Germaine Schneider. She was promptly arrested by the Gestapo, but she insisted that her relationship with "the Professor" was entirely sentimental. The Gestapo believed her and let her go; she disappeared. Soon afterward, it emerged that Germaine Schneider, alias "Papillon" and "Odette," was another of those Comintern agents who, like Wenzel and Raichman, had been incorporated in the Red Orchestra. She was thirty-nine years old and married to a Swiss, Franz Schneider, who played a limited part in his wife's underground activities. Germaine had been living in Brussels ever since 1920. Deported as a political agitator in 1929, she had slipped back into Belgium after a short interval. Her apartment had been a natural haven for Communist leaders in transit: Maurice Thorez and Jacques Duclos had been seen there, among others. Since the outbreak of war, she had served as a courier between Belgium and Germany. Most of the secret information picked up in Berlin had been conveyed to Brussels by this vital cog which the Gestapo had so foolishly let slip through its fingers.

With both Schumacher and Germaine Schneider on the run, the network would be on the alert and would at once take measures to protect the security of its agents. True, but this in itself was Fortner's good luck. On hearing of this latest blow to his Belgian branch, the Big Chief instructed Yefremov to establish a new cover. So Yefremov approached Raichman, who raised the matter with Inspector Mathieu, who reported it to the Abwehr.

Fortner says: "There was talk of obtaining an identity card for a young student. Mathieu asked for a photograph, of course, and he showed it to me. The subject was a fine-featured, fair-haired youth with an appealingly candid expression. Mathieu promised to supply the identity card, and it was agreed that he should deliver it to the student in person. Raichman arranged for the pair to meet on July 30, between noon and one o'clock, on the bridge overhanging the Botanical Gardens—right in the heart of Brussels!

"Needless to say, I turned up as well, together with two carloads of police. We followed Mathieu at a distance, and after a few minutes saw a lanky young fellow walking toward him. The newcomer was at least six feet tall; this was our man, sure enough. He joined Mathieu in the middle of the bridge, and the Inspector handed him the identity card. Then we stepped in. He made no attempt to escape—not that he had a chance—but you should have heard his cries of indignation! I've listened to some complaints in my time, but none to rival his. He couldn't understand this unspeakable outrage. He was a subject of Finland, whose soldiers were fighting side by side with ours! And I hadn't heard the last of this! And he demanded to be allowed to call the Finnish consulate. It was deafening. In the end, I said to him, 'Listen, there's no point in making all this fuss. If you really are a Finn, you've nothing to worry about.'

"Anyway, I allowed him to telephone the consulate. He had barely put the receiver down when two Finnish officials came bursting into my office, beside themselves with rage. They shouted their heads off and wouldn't let me get a word in edgewise. 'Why, this is disgraceful! We know all about this young man. He is, as he says, a loyal Finnish subject, a law-abiding student at Brussels University!' I managed to quiet them at last by stating that we had good reason to think that 'Eric Jernstroem' was in fact a Soviet agent, that we were going to make a thorough check, and that they would naturally be informed of the outcome of the investigation."

It's a safe bet that Fortner, whatever he said later, was alarmed by the prospect of a diplomatic incident. In its report, the Gestapo pays tribute to the experts who had primed Yefremov for his mission. "His disguise was perfect in every detail, down to the last button on his underwear."

We are not told precisely what made Yefremov's cover so watertight, but the techniques of Soviet espionage are familiar enough to give us a general idea. The "student" probably hid in his pockets a telegram bearing his fictitious home address in Finland, an old, torn Finnish trolley ticket, the membership card of a Helsinki library, a prescription stamped by a Finnish pharmacy, et cetera.

An investigator's convictions might easily be shaken by all this. But if Fortner had any qualms, they were short-lived; in this particular instance, the quality of the framework—Yefremov himself—was not up to the quality of the cover.

There are three conflicting versions of his downfall:

1. According to one veteran of the Rote Kapelle Kommando, persuading Yefremov to turn traitor was the simplest of tasks. He was a Ukrainian, and therefore prone to anti-Semitism. It was pointed out to him that all his superiors were Jews, and that he would be a real fool to sacrifice himself for such riffraff; he agreed.

2. According to Fortner, Giering's team of torture experts arrived in Brussels and set to work on the prisoner. He held out for a few days, then he was broken.

3. According to another Abwehr officer, Yefremov succumbed to a more subtle maneuver. His whole family was in Russia—including his young wife, whom he adored. She was an engineer, specializing in railway engines, and she was deeply patriotic. Yefremov was told that unless he cooperated the Center would be informed that he had betrayed Wenzel—which was, of course, quite untrue. This would cost him his wife's love and esteem, and she herself would be exposed to reprisals by the Soviet authorities. Yefremov decided that love came before duty.

———

Are some men and women more vulnerable than others, when the moment of truth comes? Do they have flaws and chinks in temperament which make them easier to break down? Or is it through some basic inner frailty that they reveal so many superficial weaknesses to the interrogator? When Grossvogel's captors threatened to shoot his wife and little girl before his eyes, he replied in his bland businessman's voice, "Shoot, if you please." Sokol did not falter under the whips of Giering's men, nor in their icy water torture. True, Grossvogel and Sokol were members of the old guard. But so was Wenzel, alias "the Professor," before he donned the uniform of a Gestapo flunky.

There was no general rule. Where the Gestapo began, there humanity ended—and with it, logic. A hundred and fifty pounds of flesh bleeding under the torturer's lash is no longer quite human; it is not quite animal; it is something in process of becoming either a hero or a traitor. The final metamorphosis is unpredictable, often surprising, occasionally incomprehensible. It is not for us to judge; the right to judge belongs only to those who were once forced to step into the cage where Giering's men stood waiting with their implements. Those who did not talk deserve our admiration and also our gratitude; thanks to them we have a sense of being greater. As for the others, let their betrayed colleagues judge them if they so wish.

———◆———

Fortner says: "Yefremov admitted that he had replaced Kent as head of the Brussels network. We questioned him especially about its radio links with the outside world. It had three transmitters at its disposal. There was Wenzel's, there was the one hidden in Mathieu's garage, and there was a third, held in reserve at Ostend. Yefremov told us who the pianist was—a paymaster in the Belgian navy. We arrested this man, but he no longer had the transmitter, and he claimed he didn't know where it was. Of the three sets whose signals had been picked up by the Funkabwehr, this was the only one that escaped us, allowing for the fact that the set in Mathieu's care had never been brought into service. We had impounded the other two—the first at the Rue des Atrébates; the second in Wenzel's attic. According to Yefremov, the network had no other pianist for the Ostend transmitter—which meant that we had heard the last of the secret transmissions, and this was naturally a tremendous relief.

"Yefremov also revealed the name of his contact with the Dutch network. To be frank, we hadn't even known that such a network existed. The courier maintaining communication between Brussels and Amsterdam was a little Jew—yet another of them!—who operated under the name 'Spectacles.' I arrested him, thanks to Yefremov. He was shaking with fear and at once agreed to place himself at my disposal. I told him that he and I were going to Amsterdam, that he would be released if he behaved himself, but the slightest attempt to escape would be his finish. He promised to toe the line.

"So off I went to Holland, together with my 'Spectacles' and three police officers. The local chief of counterespionage was Colonel Giskes, of the Abwehr. I told him about Yefremov's disclosures and asked whether he knew anything. He replied, 'Yes, I know there's a Russian transmitter in my area, but I must confess I haven't had time to attend to it. I'm up to my neck in Operation North Pole.' "

This is a good moment to take stock of Colonel Giskes as he was in the days when he was building up the collection of whiskey bottles I observed on his mantelpiece twenty years later. He was engaged in what the Abwehr referred to as *Funkspiel*, or "radio game." This intricate and intellectually stimulating operation was in a sense the crowning point, the apotheosis, of the hunt for enemy pianists. Instead of slaying your captured quarry, you put it to work for you, employing it as a bait. By this means you established contact with the other side and gradually penetrated their secrets, uncovered their organization, apprehended their agents. After a few months of *Funkspiel*, Giskes' bag was impressive: fifty-three agents taken prisoner immediately on arrival from England; eighteen turncoat pianists in regular contact with London; thousands of weapons seized within moments of being dropped from British planes. And yet it was perhaps premature to talk of a triumph, even for the most successful *Funkspiel*. The snag was that you could never be certain. Had you really pulled the wool over the enemy's eyes? Was he completely taken in? True, he was still sending arms, money, even men; but secret services are not above soiling their hands—it is their job to do just that. They might be making a deliberate sacrifice, simply to lead you on.

If London questioned the renegade pianists about the Dutch coastline and the German defenses there, Giskes could deduce that the Allies were planning to land in Holland—and he would be mistaken. Then again, a *Funkspiel* required continual feeding, for if the renegade pianists were to stop sending information, suspicions would be aroused and the game brought to an end. So the messages that were sent out contained a carefully judged mixture of truth and falsehood —a little of the former, a good deal of the latter. Even so, if the other side was not taken in they could derive a good deal of benefit from the *Funkspiel*. Falsehood sometimes points the way to truth; on the basis of what someone is trying to make you believe, you can often deduce what he is seeking to conceal from you.

A third reason for maintaining the pretense of being taken in was that the *Funkspiel* was costly in time and manpower. Feigning belief was the simplest of tasks: all that you, the enemy, had to do was send the renegade pianists the usual lists of questions. But what a headache for the *Funkspiel* chief. He had to go down on his knees to one official organization after another, to obtain bits and pieces of intelligence which would sound convincing in the fake messages. The generals and civil servants did not always understand the subtleties of the *Funkspiel*, nor was it possible to enlighten them without jeopardizing the secrecy of the operation. So they balked at imparting information; they argued that far too much was being made of the project; they proclaimed, with shallow good sense, that there was no point in making agents turn renegade if you were simply going to do their work for them. Consequently, there were endless and exhausting clashes between these petulantly tight-fisted officials and the puppet master, who dreaded the prospect of running out of material for his *Funkspiel*. It is only too easy to imagine the nightmare task confronting Colonel Giskes, who had *eighteen* transmitters to feed—to say nothing of the fake crimes and acts of sabotage that had to be stage-managed, the "reception committees" to be organized every time London announced a parachute landing, and the work entailed in supervising several dozen unsuspecting agents who were deliberately left at liberty and had to be turned, without their knowledge, into responsive marionettes. With all this to attend to, how could Giskes be expected to deal with the Russian transmitter? Operation North Pole was monopolizing the time and energy of the colonel himself and every member of his staff.

He had caught fifty-three agents sent over from London. But how many German troops had been killed on the eastern front as a direct result of messages radioed by the Soviet pianist? Thanks to the English parachutists, he had impounded thirty thousand pounds of explosive gelatin, three thousand Stens, three hundred Brens, five thousand revolvers, two thousand grenades, five hundred thousand clips of ammunition, seventy-five radio transmitters and a considerable amount of money. But how many tanks, trucks and aircraft had been destroyed by the Red Army on the strength of information garnered in Berlin and relayed to Moscow via Amsterdam? In the final reckoning, was Operation North Pole really a triumph for the Abwehr, or had German counterintelligence in Holland walked straight into a trap? *

There is a fourth reason for letting oneself be party to a *Funk-*

---

* Such information as is available suggests that London soon saw through Giskes' deception, but continued to feign belief. This was not, of course, done to protect a Soviet transmitter, whose very existence was probably unknown to the British. But British Intelligence took similar advantage of their adversaries' total preoccupation with Operation North Pole; unbeknownst to Giskes, they set up a new network, which escaped detection right up to the end of the war. In addition, London almost certainly used North Pole to fox Berlin about the Allies' invasion plans. The lists of questions sent to the renegade pianists cleverly gave the impression that the second front was to be opened in Holland.

spiel. I mention it purely for the record, and without great conviction, for it does not seem to carry much weight among professionals in the intelligence business (human feelings are not their strong—or, as they would say, their weak—point). A *Funkspiel* saves lives. There can be no question of executing renegade pianists and replacing them with German experts, for every radio operator has his own individual touch, and his opposite number at the receiving station would immediately spot any change. So long as Giskes thought he was hoodwinking London, his fifty-three prisoners were safe and sound; they would not die until the *Funkspiel* was over and their usefulness was at an end.*

Operation North Pole is outside the province of this book. But as we shall soon be treated to the sight of Johann Wenzel, alias "the Professor," performing under the aegis of his German captors, it seems wise to explain how a *Funkspiel* works.

———◆———

Fortner says: "Giskes was prepared to allow me a free hand, so I moved into Gestapo headquarters and sent Spectacles out into the streets of Amsterdam. Alone, of course. Obviously, he might have taken advantage of this and bolted, but you know the old saying— nothing ventured, nothing gained. And I was relying on his fear rather than his word.

"He knew several 'letterboxes' in Amsterdam, but there was little to be gained from these. My aim was to arrest the man in charge of the network, with whom he had direct contact. So he went to the apartment where he generally met the man, but we were out of luck: he was not there, and the concierge said that he had been away for several days. Spectacles knew of another address where his superior was sometimes to be found. I sent him there posthaste, but again there was nobody. I said to myself, We've had it! Someone has seen Spectacles in my car and raised the alarm. I went to the second apartment myself and unearthed a transmitter. Well, that was better than nothing. I instructed Spectacles to go back to the first address and leave a message for his chief, requesting a meeting at five that afternoon in a café whose name I've forgotten.

"The café was very large and busy, which made it difficult to

———

* It would be unfair not to point out that Colonel Giskes made considerable efforts to save them from the firing squad. But the Gestapo's word carried more weight than his.

keep watch on—especially as I wanted to avoid using too many people, in case our man should smell danger and beat a hasty retreat. So I turned up at the rendezvous with two plainclothesmen and the Amsterdam Gestapo chief. The three of them went in and sat down, while I loitered outside on the pavement, feeling pretty apprehensive and gripping the 6.5 Mauser I always carried in my pocket.

"Spectacles arrived just before five o'clock and sat at a table where a couple were already installed. I followed him in and sat at a table nearby. A group of Dutchmen had to squeeze together to make room for me; as I told you, the place was packed—which threatened to complicate matters. Spectacles ordered some coffee, and so did I. We took our time drinking it, but no one came. I was beginning to give up hope, when suddenly Spectacles stood up to greet a very tall, powerfully built, but rather weak-faced man—a spineless giant. He sat down at Spectacles' table, and they struck up a conversation that dragged on and on for at least five minutes. Where on earth were my three colleagues? I was on tenterhooks. At long last, the two plainclothesmen arrived and tried to handcuff the giant. He struggled and shouted for help, and soon the whole café was in an uproar. I saw that serious trouble was brewing, so I slipped out quietly, to avoid being identified. Inside, all hell was breaking loose: the customers were taking the prisoner's part and threatening to lynch my men, who were unable to clear a passage to the door till they drew their revolvers. Meanwhile, a small, threatening crowd had gathered on the sidewalk, and we were about to have a full-scale riot on our hands. Believe me, there was electricity in the air. In the end, we managed to get clear and drive our man to Gestapo headquarters.

"There he refused to answer any questions. The Gestapo people started knocking him about, and since I had no authority to stop them—after all, I was merely a guest—I decided I had better leave. But I learned later that the Kommando succeeded in breaking him completely. His name was Anton Winterink. He was an ex-Comintern agent who had teamed up with the Red Orchestra. He betrayed his entire group and even agreed to collaborate in the *Funkspiel*."

There is no telling who betrayed the Hollander, Kruyt. He had been a Protestant minister, but had been converted to Communism and fled to Russia. There he volunteered for a special mission and was given the same espionage training as Wilhelm Fellendorf and Erna Eifler, the agents who had been dropped over East Prussia the previous May. Kruyt was assigned to be Yefremov's deputy. Eventually he was sent to Britain by submarine, to be trained as a parachutist. The course was a grueling one, and his companions must have marveled at this foreigner who was old enough to be their father and in many cases their grandfather—he was sixty-three. At last he was put aboard an R.A.F. bomber with another Soviet agent and dropped over Belgium on a moonless night in late July, with a carefully padded transmitter strapped to his left leg. His companion, with whom he had shared all the hardships of the past few months, had been dropped shortly before on the outskirts of The Hague. Kruyt landed without mishap, buried his parachute, and disappeared into the darkness.

Three days later someone betrayed him to the Gestapo. After savage treatment, he took advantage of his torturers' momentary inattention to swallow the cyanide capsule he had managed to keep hidden. Immediate use of the stomach pump brought him back from death. The interrogation began again, and the first question he was asked was: "Who was the parachutist dropped over The Hague?" When he still would not say a word, the German shrugged and said: "Either way, he is in our hands. He was killed when he landed on the roof of a house." For the first time, Kruyt had the look of a man sixty-three years old, exhausted by hardships, torture, and the bitter knowledge that he had been betrayed. "He was my son," he murmured. They let him attend the funeral, then stood him against a wall and shot him.

16. *Coup de Grâce* at Brussels

The Gestapo once arrested a member of the Deuxième Bureau who had been engaged in active work for the Resistance. They questioned him for hours on end, but he would not open his lips. Eventually, the German in charge of the interrogation gave up and signaled to his assistant, who withdrew with a purposeful air. A few moments later, the Frenchman heard the ominous sound of water running into a bath in the next room. "Oh, so that's the way it is," he said with a shrug. "You should have said at once that this was to be a serious discussion." And he began to talk. He talked for as long as a game of chess might last. When he had sacrificed a few pawns, in a series of gambits designed to protect his principal pieces, he sealed his lips again and was spared all further interrogation.

This man was a professional. Yefremov and Kruyt were amateurs. Nearly all the people who figure in this story were amateurs. There were no half measures for them; they either touched the peaks of heroism or plumbed the depths of treason. Once they started on the downward slope, there was no stopping them. To a professional, the words *heroism* and *disloyalty* are almost devoid of meaning; he is playing a game of chess. A chess player does not feel dishonored when he sacrifices a few pawns; all that matters is to save his king and queen. The amateur, on the other hand, is fighting for his ideals, which are as fully embodied in the most junior agent as in the head of the network. He does not evaluate the position point by point, nor does he weigh the practical consequences of his acts of weakness. His loyalty will either remain absolute or disappear altogether. So he has only to disclose a single name, and the rest will follow; he has violated his creed for all time. The amateur has farther to fall than the professional, and he will inevitably sink lower. Sickened with himself, he wallows in his own vileness. Unquestionably there is a strong element of self-punishment, and sometimes masochism, in this attitude. The amateur is the victim of his own impossibly exacting standards. Having failed to be the perfect hero, he has no choice but to become an unmitigated coward, a scum of a traitor. Such is the fatal logic in his system. It never occurs to him that he may well be only a poor devil subjected to intolerable pressure. Within a week of his arrest, Yefremov had sunk to the level of telling Giering's team: "If I were in your position, I would do such-and-such. I know them well, and I can assure you they'll walk straight into the trap. . . ."

The first essential was to keep the network from knowing that Yefremov had turned traitor. He was instructed to send a letter to Raichman, explaining that the problems created by Wenzel's arrest had obliged him to lie low, but that he would emerge from cover as soon as the dust will have settled.

The second essential was to make quick use of Yefremov to demolish the network, without giving the Big Chief time to reorganize his stricken forces. Having betrayed Spectacles, Yefremov proceeded to betray Anton Danilov. By rights Danilov should have been mentioned long ago. A Russian officer, in 1939 he had arrived in Belgium from Paris, where he had done intelligence work under the cover of the Soviet consulate. What is one to say of him? He is a rather depressing figure. Veterans of the Red Orchestra and of the Rote Kapelle Kommando are united in their contempt for him, describing him as "low," "shabby" and "a poor specimen of humanity." He was employed in a subsidiary role, as a courier; it appears that he also performed occasionally as a pianist. Poor Danilov! Later he would die on the scaffold, with nobody caring. Even in the moment of execution, he would be a totally uninspiring drudge.

Germaine Schneider was a far more interesting proposition for the Kommando: she might lead them all the way to Trepper. Yefremov dutifully asked Raichman to put him in touch with her. When this had been done, he tried to reason with her: "The network is wide open now. What's the use of denying it? You can be sure the Big Chief will worm his way out of trouble, leaving us to foot the bill. Our only hope is to cooperate with the Germans. You could be useful to them. Even your husband has something to offer."

Germaine asked for time to think it over and immediately warned the Big Chief. The latter instructed her to sever all contact with Yefremov and proceed to Lyons. She was unable to leave Belgium at once, for she did not have the proper papers, but she went to a hideout unknown to Yefremov. The Kommando were momentarily at a loss, but soon fought back, this time aiming at Germaine's Swiss husband, Franz Schneider. As he operated on the fringe of the network and did not really belong to the Orchestra, Trepper had seen no point in whisking him away. In this he was wrong, for Schneider knew a great deal. Among other things, he knew—from Germaine—that Yefremov was now working for the Kommando. And yet, strangely enough, when Raichman invited him to a meeting with Yefremov, Schneider kept the appointment. This must seem incomprehensible, and it remains one of the unexplained mysteries in the story of the Red Orchestra. Some say he kept the appointment to find out whether Yefremov *really* had gone over to the enemy. This is somewhat reminiscent of the great, the admirable, the inimitable Kovalsky, head of a Communist Resistance organization operating in France. Kovalsky caused so much anxiety by his habit of going to rendezvous without taking the slightest precaution that finally his men persuaded him to work out an elementary security system. It was decided that a briefcase lying on a window ledge would mean that the enemy was inside the apartment chosen for the rendezvous.

One day Kovalsky noticed the briefcase, made a dash for the stairs, miraculously avoided blundering into the Gestapo trap, and came down again as fast as his legs would carry him. His friends were dumbfounded. "I spotted the briefcase," he told them, "and I wanted to make quite sure there was no trouble brewing." If the great Kovalsky was capable of such behavior, why not Franz Schneider? Fictional heroes may adhere rigidly to the rules, but when dealing with real people one has to allow a measure of eccentricity.

Arrested and interrogated, Franz Schneider disclosed the name and address of a German woman who served as a link in the chain between Berlin and Brussels. He insisted, however, that he had no idea where his wife was. He suggested that the Germans ask Wenzel; Wenzel was bound to know. But Wenzel either did not know or would not tell. All trace of Germaine appeared to have been lost.

And so it might have been, but for Raichman. Not long afterward he approached Inspector Mathieu for an identity card for an agent on the run. The photograph he handed Mathieu was unmistakably that of Germaine Schneider. Mathieu undertook to supply the card and asked Raichman to arrange a meeting between him and the agent. The stage was set for a repeat performance of the scene that had cost Yefremov his freedom on the bridge overhanging the Botanical Gardens.

What was happening? Was Raichman still unaware of Yefremov's arrest? Could it really be that Franz Schneider, fully alive to Yefremov's defection, had neglected to warn Raichman when he arranged a rendezvous with Yefremov? And how about the Big Chief? Was his special surveillance group no longer informing him of events in Brussels? Or had he cold-bloodedly abandoned the survivors of the Belgian network to their fate?

Trepper knew that Yefremov had been arrested, that he had returned home three days later, explaining to his concierge that he'd had some little nuisance with the authorities—something about his papers—and that since then Yefremov had been frantically trying to reestablish links with as many of his old contacts as possible. So Trepper was certain beyond all doubt that Yefremov had gone over to the enemy. If the Big Chief did not warn Raichman, it was doubtless because he considered him highly suspect—Raichman had failed to sever contact with Mathieu when clearly ordered to do so. But then why let Franz Schneider blunder into a trap? Why let Schneider's wife,

Germaine, get tangled in the fatal web spun by Raichman and Mathieu?

The answer is that the situation had turned into a rout. Unlike the general of a defeated army, the Big Chief knew roughly where his battalions were and how deeply the enemy had penetrated; but, like the general, he was unable to pass on the orders that would re- trieve the situation—his liaison had been destroyed. This was the inherent danger of dividing the network into such watertight com- partments: it paid dividends in the early stages of an enemy attack; but if a decisive setback occurred, there was no chance of repairing the damage. Trepper had probably lost contact with the two Schneiders and with everyone else as well. He saw their perils, but could do nothing to warn them. And if the agents themselves could not see or hear, they could still sense those perils; panic took hold of them, and they reeled with loneliness and fear. Franz Schneider went to his rendezvous in the sure knowledge that the Gestapo would be waiting—anything was better than remaining in isolation with his doubts and terrors. And Germaine, cut off from the network, hunted by a Gestapo that had already caught her husband and her lover, en- trusted her future to the dubious hands of Inspector Mathieu.

But after his season of exceptional usefulness, Raichman had finally lost his cutting edge as a tool of the Kommando. Fortner and Mathieu waited in vain for Germaine Schneider to keep her appoint- ment; it was Raichman himself who turned up. Had the Big Chief succeeded in warning her after all, or had she felt some grain of suspicion? We have no means of telling. Nor had the Kommando. But it deduced that the other side had realized the truth about Mathieu —and in that case, Raichman's usefulness was at an end. So Raichman was arrested.

"He was a loathsome criminal," says Fortner, "terribly short and dark—a real Jew! He immediately offered to work for us. His servility was nauseating, and I can assure you he disgusted us all. But what could we do? We couldn't afford to be too squeamish. We needed what he had to offer."

The Gestapo report was equally damning: "Being of a supine, Jewish nature, Raichman at once betrayed his mistress, Malvina Gruber, who likewise placed herself at our disposal."

An agent who had been working for the Soviet Union since 1934 was bound to have a good many contacts. Raichman would no doubt prove as valuable under lock and key as in the days when he had been

Mathieu's unwitting partner in betrayal. Perhaps he might even lead them all the way to that Big Chief who had emerged as the Kommando's archenemy, the adversary who haunted every moment of the working day.

As for Malvina—that plump and matronly Czech citizen—she was a prize catch too. She admitted that she had crossed the Franco-Swiss border many times, carrying messages to and from the Soviet group operating in Switzerland. And no sooner was she arrested than she disclosed vital information about the Little Chief. Not content with turning down Trepper's offer to get Margarete into Switzerland after the Atrébates disaster, Kent had wanted to avoid having her travel to Paris alone with her son. So he had Malvina accompany her. Margarete had unwisely revealed that her ultimate destination was Marseilles. Now the Kommando would find it easy to lay hands on the two lovers and make them pay for their foolhardiness.

But before turning their attention to Paris and Marseilles, the authorities had to make sure that Brussels itself was scoured clean.

Fortner says: "After the victory over France in 1940, the Reich made highly attractive offers to the neutral nations, in the hope of inducing them to set up companies in the occupied territories. We needed all kinds of goods and materials, and we weren't sure at that stage how far we could rely on the cooperation of French, Belgian or Dutch businessmen. The neutrals, on the other hand, had no reason to hold back. Another advantage: they were able to offer much stronger securities than could any citizen of a defeated country.

"In Brussels, as elsewhere, these neutral firms were accorded every imaginable facility. They could telephone or telegraph all the way across Europe; their executives received the *Ausweis* [travel permits] enabling them to move about freely. Indeed, it was as if the state of war didn't exist for them.

"Naturally, we exercised a degree of caution and kept a discreet eye on them. Which was how I came to open a routine investigation into the affairs of Simexco, a firm headed by a South American businessman. Simexco was one of the largest concerns in Brussels; it did considerable business with the Wehrmacht, and its executives were continually on the move. What worried me was the extraordinary number of telegrams it exchanged with Berlin, Prague, Paris, and so on. I expressed my concern to the head of Abwehr III N, the department responsible for supervising telecommunications. He insisted there was nothing to worry about; Simexco was as genuine a company as one could hope to find, and there were no grounds whatever for taking away its privileges.

"But I still wasn't easy in my mind. I decided to go and see the senior commissariat officer in Brussels, who was ultimately responsible for all contracts entered into by the Wehrmacht. When I asked his opinion of Simexco, he cried, 'Ah, they're very good, very efficient people! If only they were all like that. Their work is beyond reproach, and in addition they're very decent to us. Of all the businessmen here, they're the only ones with whom we have any real personal contact. They're always inviting us to dinners and receptions, and I must say they treat us royally.'

"For my own part, I was rather disturbed to hear of those personal contacts. Members of the commissariat do not, as a rule, spend their time enjoying themselves with their contractors; it simply isn't done. Simexco must have had a hard job wooing them, and I wondered what their purpose had been.

"I asked the chief commissariat officer to tell me about the officials of the firm. He told me that the South American had gone to France and been replaced by a Belgian, Nazarin Drailly, but that the key figure in the company appeared to be another businessman residing in Paris. He made frequent trips to Brussels—among other things, to collect the firm's profits—and my companion had met him very often. He called him an altogether remarkable man, dynamic and sure in his touch, an unshakable supporter of the German cause. At this point I asked what he looked like. Since by now you will have realized who it was, I need hardly tell you that I broke into a cold sweat as I listened to the description. Finally I produced one of the photographs we had found at the Rue des Atrébates. 'Is that he?' I asked. And yes indeed, it was he—the Big Chief! As for the 'South American,' how could it be anyone but Kent?

"You can imagine how stunned and alarmed I felt. Times had changed since I went looking for Soviet agents in out-of-town cafés, but I didn't expect to find them in the highest German circles in Brussels! And, of course, their links with the commissariat gave them a bird's-eye view of our position. Thanks to Simexco and its contract work for the Wehrmacht, they knew everything about the size of Germany's forces in Belgium and their equipment, about the building of the Atlantic Wall (in which the company was playing an active part!), and so on, *ad infinitum*. In addition, the commissariat's duties required its members to travel extensively, mix with a wide variety of people, and have a finger in every pie. And when I thought of all the tongues that must have been loosened by Kent's generosity with wines and spirits. . . ."

Margarete Barcza says: "People can say what they like about Vincent, but he was wonderfully good at holding his liquor. Not like those feeble German officers—a few brandies and they were under the table! We used to entertain them nearly every evening. They knew they were always welcome, the food was good and the drink even better, and there were always pretty girls among the guests—I won't mention any names—who weren't, shall we say, altogether prudes. Life was one long *fiesta!*"

◆

According to some sources, Simexco was the victim of Yefremov's treachery, not of Franz Fortner's professional flair. When Trepper had handed over control to Yefremov, he told him about Simexco, but urged him to keep away; after Kent's long spell as head of the firm the situation was extremely risky. It is argued that Yefremov exposed Simexco when he gave away all his other secrets. And the Kommando's realization of what the firm was up to coincided with his betrayals. On the other hand, Fortner was already on the right track. Although the thorough search of Kent's apartment revealed no clues to his commercial activities (which reflects well on the Little Chief's professionalism), Fortner's investigations prior to the Atrébates raid had shown that the "South Americans" living at number 101 were working for the German Economics Ministry. And why should we doubt Fortner's word? He has been admirably open about his various blunders, and it would be unfair to start disbelieving him when at last he can point to a success. And in fact the two theories are not incompatible: Yefremov's denunciation may have served as conclusive evidence in an investigation which was already far advanced.

Now that Simexco *had* been exposed, what steps were to be taken?

"We made inquiries about the stockholders," Fortner told me. "They were Belgian businessmen who obviously had no idea of what they had blundered into. I called at the Simexco offices, pretending that I was a commissariat officer who wished to purchase stationery for the occupation forces. I was received by the business manager, Nazarin Drailly. Nothing in his attitude aroused the slightest suspicion; I might have been any customer calling on any trader. Anyway, he didn't have any stationery, so the discussions fell through. As we were anxious to find out more, we decided not to arrest anyone for the time being, but to tap the firm's telephones and generally keep it under surveillance. But I must tell you of the enormous surprise which was still in store for me—and, heaven knows, this investigation had already brought some big ones!

"When I first arrived in Brussels, I felt it would be a mistake to move into Abwehr headquarters; the other side would have spotted me at once. It would be better to open an office under an assumed name, where my informers could come and see me without risk. So I labeled myself 'Riepert, Imports and Exports' and rented an office at 192 Rue Royale. And do you know where Simexco's head office was? At 192 Rue Royale! They were on the same floor, right next door to me, and the dividing wall was so thin that we could hear one another! In fact, it seems obvious that they must have wired my room. Now, you remember that when I found some photos of the Big Chief and the Little Chief at the Rue des Atrébates I had the strange feeling that I had seen them before? Of course I had! I'd passed them on the stairs a dozen times! We used to meet on the landing and tip our hats to one another! I may add that after the Atrébates raid they took great care not to set foot in the Rue Royale again; otherwise I'd certainly have identified them. Wasn't that incredible, though? Absolutely incredible! If one read it in a novel, one would accuse the author of going too far."

Incredible indeed, even more incredible than Fortner supposes. For his failure to realize what lay behind Simexco was matched only by Simexco's failure to realize what lay behind "Riepert, Imports and Exports." For months Soviet espionage and German counterespionage had shared the same landing, and the truth had never dawned on either!

17. Some Second Fiddles

Emmanuel Mignon was born on November 22, 1917, in the town of Saint-Nazaire, but from the age of eighteen he has been a printer on a Paris newspaper. Today his hair is very white and very long, and his skin is fine and pale as porcelain; the astonishingly black eyebrows make a pleasing contrast with all this whiteness. His eyes are shrewd and he has all the traditional qualities of cynicism and sharpness that are attributed to Parisians and to newspaper printers.

Mignon says: "In 1941 we were already living here in the Rue de la Huchette. When we moved in, my wife and I said, 'Well, we aren't going to stay long in a dump like this, so what's the point of fixing it up?' Result: we've been here over twenty-five years, and by now we're used to it.

"It was our concierge who got me that job with Simex. She was a Communist, she knew my feelings, and she knew I was looking for work. So she thought of me when a friend of hers, Katz, asked if she knew anyone who wanted a job. No—now I remember: first she asked one of the other tenants, but office work didn't appeal to him, so I reaped the benefit. I can honestly claim to have been with Simex when the firm was born. It was part of my job to see that the cards were printed right, that the firm was properly registered, and so on. To begin with—this must have been in September, 1941—we were in the Champs-Élysées, in the building just above the Lido. There were two offices and a small reception room.

"I was interviewed first by a man named Jaspar, in his fifties or early sixties, rather stout, a typical member of the old professional classes. But he didn't stay long; soon afterward he left to take charge of a Simex branch that had been set up in Marseilles. Sierra [Kent] also left for Marseilles, and we didn't see him again. Before that, he often used to come and see us in the Champs-Élysées. He was a typical Brazilian, terrifically well-dressed, sort of a playboy—an olé-olé type, if you see what I mean—and he always had marvelous-looking girls with him. We also used to see quite a lot of Gilbert [the Big Chief], a cheery, cigar-smoking Belgian—a very nice fellow. Naturally, I found out later that he wasn't a Belgian; but take it from me, he could have fooled anyone. He had the right accent, all the right expressions, the whole thing. He wasn't an ordinary man, this Gilbert. You felt he was always under pressure. Even when he was just gossiping about this or that, he was trying to get all he could out of you. Grossvogel was on the payroll too, but we didn't see much of him at the office. He was always rushing about, supposedly scouting for business.

"After Jaspar left, Alfred Corbin became head of the firm. He was tall, with a heavy mustache, shy at first, but he thawed out once he felt at home. Very, very patriotic, Corbin was! Politically, I'd say he was in the left wing of the Radical Party."

Robert Corbin is bedridden with sciatica, which he contracted in Mauthausen concentration camp. He is tall, like his brother Alfred, with the same clear brow and thick mustache. He has all the dignity and courtesy of a British army major retired after long service in India—perhaps this manner is a relic of the days when he used to work at Creed's, in the Rue Royale, that French bastion of English style.

Robert Corbin says: "Before the war, Alfred and I used to run our own business at Giverny mill, near Mantes. We produced poultry feed. After 1940 the outlook was pretty grim, especially as I'd lost my job at Creed's, which had been impounded by the Germans. But Alfred happened to have made friends with one of his regimental colleagues of the 1940 campaign—a certain Katz. Katz suggested he take charge of an import-export concern that had just been formed. Alfred hesitated, but in the end he agreed, strictly for financial reasons. The terms he was offered were most attractive. . . ."

————

Vladimir Keller had arranged to meet me at 8 P.M. On April 24, 1965, outside 37 Rue de l'Université, which is an annex of the Finance Ministry. He turned up on time, preceded by a really huge Alsatian dog. (When I mentioned his name to the attendants on duty at the ministry, they immediately said, "Ah yes, the man with the dog.") He had just returned from taking the brute for a walk, or it might have been vice versa. Keller is very small and slender, but he has a large, craggy head big enough for a giant, astonishing on his slight, youthful body. In addition, his eyes had a certain oddness, being set at different levels. In short, there was nothing commonplace about Keller's features; but they were lit by a warm, friendly smile that shone with kindliness. Born in Russia of a Swiss father and an English mother, he spoke French with a German accent.

Keller, the Alsatian and I made our way into the ministry. The huge building, deserted for the night, looked even gloomier than usual. The corridors were poorly lighted and silent as the grave. In its eagerness to be home, the Alsatian suddenly bounded forward, pulling Keller right off balance. Keller tugged at the leash, his panting mingling with the dog's growls, but as he was too weak to rein him in, he was simply pulled after it. So, we galloped through a maze of deserted corridors till I was out of breath and had lost all sense of direction. Eventually a freight elevator carried us up to the sixth floor, where we rushed through another series of corridors, getting narrower and narrower all the time. The animal was going so fast that we could hardly manage the endless succession of doors that had to be opened and closed. Finally we stopped short at a door that looked exactly like all the rest. It was opened by Madame Keller—she could hardly have failed to hear us coming. I caught a glimpse of a bathtub. The Kellers asked me in, but the monster, which had hitherto treated me with indifference, suddenly began to bark ferociously, and came at me, slobbering and showing its fangs. I turned tail and fled, despite the shouts of the Kellers, urging me to stand my ground. Between them, they managed to grab the animal and bundle it into the next room. I staggered through the doorway and sank into a chair, too overcome even to wonder at this bizarre dwelling perched at the top of a ministry where Madame Keller was employed. The French civil service abounds with mysteries such as this; no outsider can ever hope to understand them.

Vladimir Keller says: "In 1941, I was working as a mechanic in a garage at Le Havre. But after the Germans came, I spent most of the time interpreting for them. And I didn't like that. You're Swiss, I said to myself, and the war may be no concern of yours; but you like living in France, and the Germans won't be here forever, so you'd better not mix with them, or it might be held against you. One of my friends told me of a possible job in a Paris firm called Simex. He warned me that it did a lot of trade with the Germans, but said that the profits went toward easing the hardships of French prisoners of war. No one could object to that, so I called at the Simex office in the Champs-Élysées and had an interview with Monsieur Grossvogel.

He was very German-looking—or maybe he was from Alsace—and he had the self-assurance of a successful businessman; in fact, somebody told me he was the raincoat king of Belgium, or something like that. I found him very pleasant and helpful. My friend had given me some German documents to translate, as proof of my linguistic abilities. I showed my translations to Monsieur Grossvogel; he was satisfied and hired me on the spot. That was on September 2, 1941. When I returned to the office the next day, Monsieur Grossvogel had been replaced by Monsieur Corbin—a charming man, good as they come.

"Monsieur Mignon was already on the staff. He seemed to do a bit of everything, acting as receptionist, answering the telephone, and so on.

"I saw Monsieur Katz once or twice, and Monsieur Gilbert more often. I had been told that he had his own business in Belgium. The fact is, he spoke exactly like a Belgian. Personally, I suspected him of smuggling currency between France and Belgium, but that was no concern of mine. He was a very agreeable man who always found something pleasant to say. His self-confidence was really tremendous; you felt he had deep reserves of strength. The only time I ever saw him down at the mouth was when he said to me, 'Ah Monsieur Keller, I wonder if I'll live very long. In my family, we're inclined to die young. . . .'

"There were plenty of comings and goings. The permanent staff consisted only of Monsieur Corbin, Monsieur Mignon, Mademoiselle Cointe and myself. Mademoiselle Cointe was Monsieur Corbin's private secretary. She was still quite young, but inclined to be old-maidish. And—do you know?—as soon as I joined Simex I got the impression that the most important person in the office, despite the official hierarchy, was not Monsieur Corbin but Suzanne Cointe. . . ."

———◆———

Suzanne Cointe's sister, Catherine, had agreed to meet me during her lunch hour at the Café Georges V, in the Champs-Élysées; she worked in a nearby fashion house. I had no difficulty in recognizing her from her own description: "I'll be wearing a black raincoat and beret and carrying a black briefcase." Our conversation was shrouded in these mourning colors. And yet it was a summer's day; the sun warmed the outdoor tables, and the Champs-Élysées was full of tourists. All around us sat pretty girls chattering with their boy friends and taking no notice of our discordant presence. But eventually the sight of Catherine Cointe all dressed in black and crying bitterly, while I fired questions at her and industriously wrote down the answers, drew startled looks from the adjoining tables. I began to distribute inane smiles, which were meant to indicate that I was neither a heartless sleuth nor a sadistic blackmailer. It was an uncomfortable situation. Fortunately, Catherine Cointe had no idea what was happening. She was too deeply immersed in her tragic memories.

Catherine Cointe says: "There were three of us—two girls and a boy. Our mother was Polish, and very much the *grande dame;* she brought us up very strictly. And as Papa was a general, I need hardly tell you we were reared in accordance with the best patriotic traditions. Before the war we used to live in Besançon, where he was stationed. He used to point at the fortress and say to us, 'When the Boches attack, my men and I will seal ourselves off in there and stand firm.' Whenever he said that, we were expected to ask, 'What will you do when you run out of ammunition?' And then he would say, 'We'll blow ourselves up, rather than surrender!'

"I'm telling you all this to give you some idea of the upheaval caused by Suzanne's conversion to Communism. She turned Communist under the influence of a man you must have heard of—the film director Jean-Paul Le Chanois. Of course she didn't break with us completely. We remained close, but my parents suffered terribly.

"Suzanne had studied music and was a piano teacher before the war, and also devoted a good deal of time to a choir she had formed— the 'Chorale Musicale de Paris,' a Communist organization. But after the defeat in 1940 nobody could earn a living anymore, merely by giving piano lessons. So she took a course in stenotyping and joined a firm called Simex. I have no idea how, or through whom, she got the job. She seldom talked to us about her work. But occasionally she would come out with some such remark as: 'Ah, we're going to sell them some more junk for the Atlantic Wall!' I realized from her hints that there must be something illicit about her activities. And indeed her happiness was the most significant thing. You see, Suzanne was an idealist; I'd almost call her a fanatic. She simply had to dedicate herself to some cause or other. On account of Le Chanois, it was Communism; but she might equally well have joined the Salvation Army. Fighting the Germans made her happy; it reconciled her Communist ideals with the patriotic traditions of our family. She was never so bright and cheerful as during this spell with Simex, when she was risking her life. She knew perfectly well that she was risking it, but never once did I see her look nervous or worried."

My talk with Jean-Paul Le Chanois took place in an office at the Comcico film company. He is in his late forties or early fifties, bald, with a dynamic, restless intelligence and a much keener interest in the affairs of the world than is usually found among film people.

Le Chanois says: "When I first met Suzanne, she was nineteen and I was fifteen. She was well-educated and intelligent, with a strong personality. She had once been a pupil of Cortot, but decided that she wasn't gifted enough for a concert career. This had left her with a certain lingering sadness, but she was a realist. As she had no money, she resigned herself to becoming a piano teacher.

"I was in love with her—so deeply in love that in the end she became interested in me, though I was only a kid. It was thanks to her that I escaped from my middle-class background, that 'self-satis-fied part of the community' as Victor Hugo calls it. At that time she was under the influence of Nietzsche; one of her uncles had put her on to him.

"It wasn't until after I got my degree that Suzanne and I became lovers. I broke with my family and went to live with her. It lasted two years, two years of sheer happiness, for we were perfectly attuned to each other. To me, it was like a miracle, the fulfillment of a child-hood dream. And then we split up; we were young and eager for experience—it was only to be expected. But we remained good friends.

"Strongly influenced by the Russian Revolution, I joined such things as the Théâtre Ouvrier de France and Prévert's Groupe Octobre. I introduced Suzanne into these circles. Her interest was purely philosophical at first; then it became practical and she turned completely from her earlier, Nietzschean views. It was then that she founded the People's Choir, which was her brainchild from first to last.

"In 1939 I tried to enlist, but they turned me down on account of asthma. Afterward I moved into a small flat in Square Carpeaux—three rooms under the eaves, that you reached by an open-air stair-case at the back of the building. It was very nice and attractive. Imagine my surprise when I discovered that Suzanne was living in the same building! We were overjoyed to see each other, but being neighbors had its drawbacks, for we were both in clandestine work, since Communist activities were banned during the 'Phony War.' So we decided not to meet too often. Then came the flight from Paris, which we made separately. When we returned to Square Carpeaux, the situation had altered completely. With the birth of the Resistance, the Communists were part and parcel of the nation again. This has been admirably written by Aragon, who may be said to have restored the tricolor to us.

"As soon as I got back, I set up an underground network. As for Suzanne, she told me that she was joining a business concern, but she implied that it was only a cover for something else. For security reasons, we met only rarely, especially as our concierge was an out-and-out Pétainist. Suzanne told me very little about her work at Simex. The only detail I can recall is that among the things they supplied to the Wehrmacht, were skis for the troops fighting in Russia. . . ."

———◆———

Emmanuel Mignon says: "Simex was amusing; we used to get a lot of fun out of our work. The firm dealt exclusively in black-market goods. People would turn up from all over, offering the most extraordinary merchandise, and we'd ask the Boches if they were interested. They never said no. Some of the junk we managed to unload on them was simply unbelievable. On one occasion we received some so-called Oriental rugs—several bales of them. We opened one bale, to take a quick look, and were driven back by a cloud of moths. We wrapped it up again and decided to sell the whole consignment to the Todt, just as they were. They paid up without a murmur. Yes, I should say that the Todt Organization was our chief customer. The men in charge knew perfectly well that our merchandise came from the black market, but they didn't seem to mind.

"All highly unsavory, you'll say, and so it was; it was for that very reason I went on working for Simex. My wife and I were members of the Famille Martin Resistance network. My chief instructed me to submit regular reports on all items sold to the Boches and note the names of overzealous suppliers, so that we could settle scores with them when victory came. Life is certainly peculiar—I used to hand my reports to a certain Charbonnier, who was a double agent for the Gestapo. (He was shot at the time of the Liberation.) The upshot was that my reports denouncing the firm as a nest of collaborators used to go straight to Gestapo headquarters. A pretty good joke, now that we know what Simex really was.

"Once we sold them a disused railway that someone had approached us about. They bought the rails, and the ties were sold off as firewood. Why, I even delivered a wheelbarrowful to Cointe's place in Square Carpeaux.

"We also sold them several hundred thousand oil drums. At first they were good quality, but after a while we could get only damaged ones. It was my job to supervise the repair operations. I used to roam around the repair yard chalk-marking all the holes that needed patching. Then the welders would move in and conscientiously solder them, well to the side of the holes. I may be a natural optimist, but I used to say to myself, This can't go on; it's bound to lead to trouble. But there was nothing! Not a peep! Truckloads of oil drums full of holes were dispatched to Germany, day after day, and we never had one word of complaint! The Todt would have bought the moon from us if we'd put it up for sale!

"All this used to worry Corbin. Events were moving too fast for him, and he seemed frightened by these black-market intrigues. He jammed on the brakes as hard as he could, saying it was dangerous to go too far. But Keller put his heart and soul into it, no doubt because he was working on commission. He was quite a man, Keller, but he had one maddening eccentricity: every time he telephoned the Boches, he would open conversation with a resounding 'Heil Hitler!' It used to give Cointe the shivers!

"Crazy things happened all the time. One day a poor white-haired old Jew, with the yellow star over his heart, turned up at Simex and asked for a job. Corbin could never say no to anyone; he hired him. Next morning the old man came into the office clutching an enormous typewriter and several fat books. He was an expert in the import-export field, he knew the customs regulations backwards, and he was carrying the rule books. The poor devil meant well, he was desperately anxious to make himself useful, but what earthly use were rule books to a firm which could sell moth-eaten rugs to the Todt Organization any day of the week? So he used to sit at his typewriter, with his books beside him, doing nothing from morning to night. Of course, we didn't cold-shoulder him on purpose, but what could we say? And then, one morning, he didn't turn up. We never found out what became of him. . . .

"You must think the firm was rolling in money, with all this racketeering. It wasn't, though. The wealth poured in, but there was never a penny to draw on. No sooner was the safe full than Katz or Grossvogel would pay us a flying visit and go off with the bundle— supposedly so they could go prospecting; but the funny thing was, those two never brought back any merchandise.

"Simex was full of odd things like that. For instance, correspondence with the Marseilles branch didn't go through the mails, but was delivered by a man who worked in a restaurant car on the P.L.M.* railway. He used to bring Jaspar's and Sierra's letters to the Champs-Élysées, and whenever we had letters for them I used to take them to his home address. Poor devil, he lived in a real hovel in the Rue de Meaux. Mind you, this was no more surprising than any of their other tricks; I assumed that the letters were about such rotten black-market deals that they'd better not fall into the censor's hands."

———◆———

Apart from Suzanne Cointe, whom the Big Chief called "our man at Simex," not one member of the staff suspected the firm's true role. They stumbled blindfolded into the spy ring; by the time the Big Chief untied the blindfolds, it was too late for them to back out. This may seem a dubious way of doing things, a deplorable piece of deception. But Trepper has argued: "I was careful to pick men who, I felt sure, would do what was required when the decisive moment came." Perhaps; but it must be hard to determine in advance whether a man will accept torture and death for a cause which he has espoused somewhat blindly . . .

Simex opened its offices in the autumn of 1941, just above the Lido. Twenty yards farther down the Champs-Élysées, on the same sidewalk, at the same moment, Colonel Rémy was setting up the base for his network in the Ermitage Cinema building. Here he found the same advantages afforded by the Lido building: a reassuring commercial façade, a maze of corridors which made shadowing really difficult, and above all, many exits. But Rémy, who had the Gestapo on his heels, was obliged to move his base at frequent intervals. After a good deal of peregrination, one of his deputies reported that a certain Colonel Lévy, who was a sound patriot, would be willing to rent an apartment to him.

"We got the concierge to arrange a meeting with the owner, who lived two floors up," writes Rémy. "There could be no ques-

* Paris-Lyon-Méditerranée.

tion of my concealing from him the deadly risks to which he would be exposed if we moved in."

The meeting was arranged, and he told Lévy: "My friend Prévost has outlined what I propose to do with the apartment I'm asking for. I'm going to make it the new headquarters of my network. The Germans are well aware of its existence and have already given us a number of serious blows. I have reason to believe that SS General Oberg, who has just arrived in Paris, has expressly ordered its annihilation. Our headquarters will be very active; I'll need a number of people there, to receive visitors, and so on, for I still don't have any alternative premises." *

To each his own method. Or, if you prefer, to each his own moral standard. Before passing judgment, however, one must understand exactly what was at stake. All Rémy knew about Colonel Lévy was that he had the reputation of being a good patriot; when they met, he formed a favorable impression. This doesn't seem like much to go on, but for Rémy it was enough, and he wagered the lives of his agents and the very existence of his network on Colonel Lévy's good faith. His sense of fair play demanded it. The Big Chief, on the other hand, cared nothing about fair play. He was prepared to deceive any number of Corbins and lead them blindfold to the scaffold, rather than jeopardize the security of his network by a misplaced trust.

———◆———

Thus, there was nothing whatever in common between the two organizations in the Lido building and the Ermitage Cinema. They were separated by twenty yards of sidewalk, yet it was as though they lived in different worlds. In the end, of course, the people at Simex *did* team up with Rémy's men; but at this moment they preferred to cross the Champs-Élysées to the Marbeuf Cinema, just opposite, where the Todt Organization had its headquarters.

On the other hand, there were many affinities between Simex and the French Economics Service at 101 Avenue Henri-Martin. While Simex specialized in heavy materials, the Economics Service supplied the Germans with textiles, coffee and medical items—all purchased unofficially, of course, from black-market sources. For this was the ingenious economic policy carried out by the German occupation: not content with the already enormous quantity of goods

* Rémy, *Mémoires d'un agent secret de la France libre*, Vol. 2, p. 111.

and raw materials which France had to provide under the armistice agreements, they were illicitly extracting a great deal more. Thus, the black-marketeers were finishing up the work begun by the German delegates at Vichy.

There was another similarity between Simex and the French Economics Service. The chief of the latter was a certain Monsieur Masuy, reputed to be the inventor of the modern version of the water torture, involving the use of a bathtub. Along with his commercial activities, he was in the pay of the Gestapo and the Abwehr. In the Avenue Henri-Martin, among the sacks and crates of merchandise, prisoners were tortured on behalf of the Germans—just as in the Champs-Élysées, amid bales of Oriental rugs, information was collected on behalf of the Allies.

As for the Paris officers of the Todt Organization, there was a perfectly simple reason for their shutting their eyes to the appalling quality of the goods they received from Simex. They had all, without exception, taken generous bribes—the Big Chief had bought them *all*.

18. A White-Russian Love Story

"They are everywhere, monsieur! They're overrunning the country—it's a positive invasion! The finest estates, the smartest villas —they've commandeered them all! In these parts, they are masters of all they survey."

This may sound like a patriot's *cri de coeur*, directed against the Germans in 1943. But in fact the year was 1966, and the speaker was Dr. Darquier, complaining about the "Jewish occupation" of St.-Tropez. His brother, Jean Darquier, alias de Pellepoix, had been Commissioner for Jewish Affairs during the war. His predecessor had been Xavier Vallat, a firm anti-Semite, though rather in the manner of those Dutch people who, after the early deportations, covered the walls of Amsterdam with the slogan, "Keep your dirty hands off our dirty Jews!" The Gestapo, thwarted in its plans, insisted on Vallat's replacement by a real slave driver. Jean Darquier did well enough to be sentenced to death after the Liberation. But by then he had slipped across the Pyrenees, so he was not there to hear sentence pronounced. Today he lives in Madrid, on the payroll of the Spanish Army General Staff, while his brother, entrenched upon the heights of St.-Tropez, goes on cackling like one of the geese on the Capitoline Hill, warning of the Jewish peril.

At seventy, Dr. Darquier is a wiry old man, with his white hair combed over his forehead. He is voluble and high-strung; one might even call him volcanic, for a lava of ugly words pours from his mouth, irremediably spoiling the beautiful setting: the magnificent villa, the paradisiacal garden and the view over the gulf. But it wasn't the Jews I had come to talk about; I wanted information about Anna de Maximovich.

Dr. Darquier says: "Anna? Ah, what a character! Six foot tall and weighing about 225 pounds. A phenomenon! She had straight blond hair, a round face, pale-blue eyes—and she was gay, always very gay. Not very feminine, as you can gather. But a physical strength—incredible! She never needed help in handling patients when they became agitated, and she never used a straitjacket; she just used to sit on them and wait till the fit was over. Two hundred twenty-five pounds may be an exaggeration, but certainly two hundred. A real phenomenon. Later on, I'll tell you about the rape.

"She was a neurologist and owned a nursing home at Choisy-le-Roi. In fact, that was how I came to meet her. She asked me to call at the nursing home a couple of times a week to make sure everything was in order. Establishments of that kind, you know, are very closely supervised. There is a danger of illegal restraint: families might try to rid themselves of a tiresome relative by pretending that he's mentally ill. At that time—before the war—I was chief lecturer in neurology at the Faculty of Medicine in Paris, so I was well qualified to vouch for Anna. And, in fact, her patients were harmless lunatics, people whose nerves had been shot to pieces—nothing really dramatic.

"Did you know that she and her family had escaped from Russia during the Communist Revolution? Her father had been a well-known general in the Tsarist army.* Anna often described their flight to me—how she hid behind the door of their house and waited for the Reds, ax in hand, while her father and one of the servants stole out through the garden. The general was dead when I met Anna, but her mother was still with her—and she was an extraordinary

---

* In 1914, Baron Maximovich was the first Russian general to advance into Germany at the head of his troops.

character too, straight out of Russian folklore. She was a truly matri-archal figure; her influence over her children was all-powerful. As for Anna's brother, Vasili, I've met him perhaps once or twice. He's short and dark, with a trim beard. He didn't amount to much. There was nothing Russian about him, except—well, perhaps a bit of the "mysterious Slav," if you know what I mean.

"But Anna was the living embodiment of Russia. So earthy! When she came out with those bawdy Russian jokes—ours are milk and water, by comparison!—I just didn't know where to look. Mind you, for all her crudeness, she was extremely good at her job. She might be rough and tough, but she certainly knew how to handle her patients.

"And she was an out-and-out Tsarist, you know. To her, the Tsar was really the 'Little Father of the People.' She longed to see Russia return to its old regime."

Vasili and Anna: a pair of well-born Russian émigrés ruined by Communism. Paris was swarming with them. But these two had nothing in common with the seedy mass of ex-aristocrats, driving their taxis and strumming their balalaikas, lost in nostalgia. They were second-generation émigrés who turned their back on the past and were facing the future. When their father died penniless, they were taken under the wing of Monsignor Chaptal, the man who helped so many refu-gees, of all races and nationalities, who flocked to Paris during those troubled years. Thanks to him, Vasili entered the School of Civil Engineering and later became a mining engineer, while Anna studied medicine, specializing in neurology. They had a sister; but I know nothing of her, except that she played no part in this story.

In 1936, a dozen political organizations competed for the loyal-ties of the White Russians in Paris. Most were orthodox Tsarists; others tended toward fascism or socialism; some tried to blend those two extremes. All, without exception, were eccentric and unimpor-tant. At the most conservative estimate, one out of every three of them acted as an informer, either for the French police or for the Nazi Secret Service or for Soviet Intelligence. Among these political groups was the Union of Defenders.

Quoting the testimony of one of its members, Pyotr Volodin, the historian David J. Dallin writes:

In 1936 the Union of Defenders hired a small hall in the rue Dupleix for meetings, dances, and so forth; its funds barely covered the small costs. One night a tall and rather stout well-dressed woman in her forties arrived in a fine car and told the union's members of her interest in their organization. She said she operated a sanitarium for mental patients and was in a position to help the union financially. Now the union's quarters were painted, and rugs appeared on the floors; soon a union newspaper began publication. From time to time individual members received sums of from $10 to $15. Expenses mounted; from 1937 to 1939, these were covered from the profits of the "sanitarium."

In 1939 a rumour spread among the membership that there was something "fishy" about Anna's money, and that trouble was ahead, but nobody wanted to believe the "gossip." *

In the event, the Defenders never found out whether Anna's money was fishy—and, if so, how—for on the day war was declared nearly all of them were arrested by the French police and interned in Le Vernet camp as suspicious aliens. Vasili Maximovich was hauled into the net a few months later, but Anna, vice-president of the Union of Defenders, escaped internment on professional grounds— the harmless lunatics in her mental home could not do without her.

One thing we do know of Anna—a detail unknown to the Defenders and Dr. Darquier—is that among the patients at Choisy-le-Roi during the late thirties, were men wounded while serving with the Spanish Republican Army.

———◆———

Le Vernet internment camp was in the Department of Ariège, some twenty miles from the Pyrenees and the Spanish border. It was spread out over some 125 acres fenced-in with barbed wire. After the roundups of September, 1939, it became a sort of general dumping ground for Spanish Republicans, Russian émigrés (whether Tsarist, socialist or fascist), French Communists, persons convicted under common law, and also a few hundred German refugees who had miraculously escaped the clutches of the Gestapo, and even some who had contrived to escape from Hitler's concentration camps. No one could have been more fiercely anti-Nazi than these German refugees, but this did nothing to alter the attitude of the French authorities. The latter were far too busy paving the way for victory to bother with trifles. Anyone who happened to be labeled "suspect" by the police was packed off to the camp without more ado.

* David J. Dallin, *Soviet Espionage* (New Haven, Conn.: Yale University Press, 1955), pp. 158–59.

Baron Vasili Maximovich had spent his first seventeen years among the splendors of imperial St. Petersburg, and afterward Monsignor Chaptal had softened the hardships of his life as a refugee. In becoming an engineer, he probably thought that he was starting a new and peaceful life, immune to the convulsions of history. The illusion was shattered as he stepped through the gates of Le Vernet. Inside the camp he found cold, hunger, humiliation.* He saw the unbelievable paradox of the German refugees—Hitler's most fanatical enemies imprisoned and starved by a nation at war with Hitler. He was an eyewitness of the events on that terrible day when the Gestapo, hard on the heels of the victorious Wehrmacht, arrived at Le Vernet and proceeded to sift its cargo of human flesh—and the French guards placidly handed over that cargo, while their leader, Marshal Pétain, prattled about "peace with honor."

No doubt Vasili had already learned his lesson—that, in times like the present, a man *had* to concern himself with politics; for, like it or not, politics insisted on concerning itself with him.

After the Gestapo, a committee of Germans arrived at Le Vernet with instructions to recruit workers for the Third Reich from among those prisoners who could be regarded as trustworthy. The committee was headed by Colonel Hans Kuprian. The latter needed an interpreter, so Vasili offered his services and was accepted. Better than that, he struck up a friendship with Kuprian. The colonel was an army officer of the old school and a passionate monarchist. He considered Germany to be in the hands of upstarts, and the Baron Maximovich, for his part, had been driven out of Russia by a gang of ill-mannered guttersnipes (who, moreover, had signed a pact with Hitler's gang— a case of like attracting like). The two men could not fail to get on well together. When his mission was over, Kuprian got Vasili released and arranged to meet him in Paris, where he would find for him a post worthy of his abilities.

And it was there, in the ghostly, semideserted capital, that brother and sister were reunited in August, 1940.

---◆---

Dr. Darquier says: "I was naturally called up in 1939 and assigned to an ambulance unit. I was taken prisoner but released soon

* Arthur Koestler, a veteran of Le Vernet, describes the appalling conditions existing at the camp in his book *Scum of the Earth* (New York: Macmillan, 1941).

afterward and returned to Paris in November, 1940. On my first visit to Choisy I found a troop of Germans camped in the grounds of the mental home. I strode into Anna's office and said, 'So the Boches are here?' She nearly jumped out of her skin. 'Ssh! Be quiet!' she said. Sure enough, a German nurse had entered on my heels. You know, one of those *souris grises*.' They used to install one in every hospital to keep an eye on things and report them if necessary. Anna's brother, Vasili, was present that day. And I still remember one small detail: lying on the desk was a copy of the Russian newspaper *Izvestia*."

In November, 1940, copies of *Izvestia* could certainly be found in Paris; the Russo-German Pact was still in force. But what was a militant Tsarist like Ann Maximovich doing with a Bolshevik paper? Darquier was not unduly perturbed. He may have been right. A newspaper is not a Bible. Besides, mystery of any kind is hard to reconcile with his portrait of Anna as an openhearted, outspoken, backslapping retailer of smutty jokes. Darquier refuses to budge from his conception of her; yet when we consider what we have seen of her, it is hard to know the truth. Did she remain forever the sixteen-year-old tomboy who covered her father's escape, ax in hand, as the Bolsheviks closed in on him? What about her brilliant annexation of the Union of Defenders—and on whose account? And when she had nursed those Spanish Republicans, were her motives political or purely humanitarian? Why did she read *Izvestia?* Simply because she wanted news of home? For a big, uncomplicated girl, she certainly poses a number of questions.

On the other hand, her brother Vasili—the "Mysterious Slav"—soon afterward decided on a step that was entirely devoid of ambiguity. He offered his services to the Big Chief.

This may sound straightforward, but it certainly did not seem so to Trepper. Vasili had been introduced to him by Michel, his contact with the French Communist Party. Now, if Maximovich had been a Center agent of long standing, he would scrupulously have refrained from mixing with Communist circles. It was therefore easy to deduce that he was a recent recruit, which was ample reason for being on guard. And what a background he had! Son of a baron and general, he had slipped out of Russia in the baggage train of the White Army, been welcomed to Paris by an archbishop, and grown up in the heart of an émigré society eaten up with hatred of the

Soviet regime. Vasili Maximovich would cut a strange figure among the Big Chief's flock—the Katzes, the Sokols, the Grossvogels, and other sheep who had grazed in very different pastures. Was it a wolf the enemy was trying to introduce into the fold?

Trepper sent an urgent wire to the Center, asking for instructions. The Center wired back: use Maximovich if he seemed to have possibilities, but observe extreme caution at all times. A vague but predictable reply—for indeed, who is in a better position to weigh the pros and cons than the man on the spot, the head of the local network? Moscow's contribution, especially in wartime, is confined to searching the Comintern's huge record files for a dossier on the candidate. If he has none, or if the record doesn't amount to much, then the decision is up to the head of the network. This crucial responsibility requires him to be part psychologist, part father-confessor, part fortuneteller—and very lucky besides. From the ingredients at his disposal, he has to be able to piece together a man's personality and background, his strengths and his weaknesses. But the jigsaw is incomplete, a good many pieces are missing; those he possesses are frequently contradictory—take Anna, for instance. He has to make up for the deficiencies and solve the contradictions by instinct and experience; he must sense that Inspector Mathieu's "new shoes" are a risky gift; he must divine the exceptional qualities of a man like Sokol, and foresee that Alfred Corbin will not waver when the blindfold is removed from his eyes—never forgetting that the fate of the whole network may depend on his every decision.

So, General Orlov, that specialist in the workings of Soviet Intelligence, can write that the head of a network "bears considerable similarity to the creative novelist," in that he selects characters and guides their actions. If he doesn't want the critics to attack him, the novelist must construct a logical plot and make his heroes behave in a manner compatible with the mental outlook he has given them. Unless the head of a network observes the same rules, he and his "characters" will very soon find themselves in front of a firing squad. For he "inspires and directs the feelings and actions of real people"— unlike the novelist, who is lucky enough to inhabit the world of the imagination.*

The Big Chief made a careful study of the Maximovich jigsaw and decided to go ahead. And thus, in this atmosphere of mutual sus-

---

* Alexander Orlov, Handbook of Intelligence and Guerrilla Warfare (Ann Arbor, Mich.: University of Michigan Press, 1963), p. 95.

picion and hesitation, there began a most fruitful partnership, one
that provided one of the most piquant episodes in the history of the
network. For Baron Vasili Maximovich, who was still only thirty-
nine, but whose appearance was marred by corpulence and by an
unfortunate swelling of the legs, had been chosen by fate to become
the Casanova of the Red Orchestra.

———◆———

Margarete Hoffman-Scholz was German, forty-four years old
and not very beautiful. She had spent the past quarter of a century
waiting for her Prince Charming. She came from an excellent Hannover
family. One of her uncles, Lieutenant Colonel Hartog, former commissioner of woods and forests, was in Paris, serving on the staff of
General Heinrich Stülpnagel, commandant of *Gross Paris*. Margarete's papa had asked this uncle to keep an eye on his little girl when
she was sent to Paris as a volunteer member of the Women's Auxiliary
Service. But Margarete was safe; she was secretary to Colonel Hans
Kuprian, a man of true breeding. They came from the same world.
All of which, though very delightful, could not alter the fact that she
was nearly forty-five and far from beautiful.

And then fate smiled on Margarete, in opening the gates of Le
Vernet camp to her; she was a member of Kuprian's committee. She
did not see the squalor, the suffering and the ugliness, but only Vasili
Maximovich. And she was dazzled by him. The poor fellow's legs
were elephantine, his face looked pinched with hunger, and he was
dressed like a scarecrow; but beneath the shabbiness Margarete dis-
cerned the man of noble birth. He deigned to look at her; he probably even went so far as to speak to her. This was more than enough
for the aging spinster from Hannover. By the time she left Le Vernet,
she was literally beside herself with love.

She went back to Paris with Kuprian and resumed her duties at
Staff Headquarters. Obviously her heart was not in her work, and
she must have asked herself a hundred times a day, "Will he come?"
He came as he had promised and at first showed little enthusiasm for
the proposals of the German Labor Service. Whereupon Kuprian
offered him a very fine engineering post at the Henschel factories in
Kassel. The news plunged poor Margarete into agonies of apprehension. And then a miracle happened: Vasili declined the post. In her
joy and exhilaration, Margarete never doubted for a moment that it
was simply because he wished to remain at her side. How deceived she

would have been to learn that her lover had in fact yielded to the entreaties of the Big Chief.

Trepper had explained to Maximovich that he would be more useful in Paris than in Kassel. He had said to him, "Set up an intelligence group. Mix with White Russians, the French aristocracy and prominent Catholic circles; befriend German officers; but whatever you do, avoid the French Left like the plague." In fact, Maximovich's best "cover" would be his own normal life as an expatriate Russian nobleman—just as Trepper's own situation required him to play the black-marketeer, throw his money about, and wine and dine members of the Todt Organization in all the black-market restaurants in Paris.

The romance flourished. Vasili obtained a permanent pass for the Hotel Majestic, where the Germans had their General Headquarters. He used to call for Margarete every evening. She would tell him all about her day's work. As her memory could be faulty, she readily agreed that the best and easiest plan was to give her beloved copies of the documents which passed through her hands. She obtained others from her colleagues. As a result, every top-secret report about camps in France found its way into the Big Chief's possession. When that subject was exhausted, Trepper asked Maximovich to channel the fair Margarete's energies toward another area of activity. She got herself transferred to the central billeting office for troops in France. As soon as Trepper had garnered the information he needed, Maximovich cleverly steered Margarete into a third sector: she joined the secretariat of the German ambassador, Abetz. Her industriousness soon earned her the trust of the entire embassy staff, together with access to the most confidential documents. Through her efforts, Moscow was kept informed of political deals with the Vichy government, of the feelings and attitudes of the French people, and of Germany's plans and setbacks. Was Margarete really so stupid as not to realize that she was simply betraying her own country? There is no reason to think so. Presumably love had extinguished the traditional feelings she had acquired in her childhood. As they said in the old days, who can fathom the mysteries of a woman's heart?

Among the level-headed, there were occasional expressions of concern and unease. Margarete's uncle, for instance, did not approve of her feelings for Maximovich; but his words of warning were thrown to the winds. The situation also worried some of the security officers at headquarters; they reminded Margarete that there was a war on and that she must observe the greatest discretion in her work. Margarete paid no heed. Even her mousy friends were infatuated with Vasili: he was so elegant and sensitive; he always had a bunch of flowers for Fräulein A, a box of chocolates for Fräulein B. . . . Besides, he was a baron. How could anyone dream of suspecting a baron?

The officers of the general staff certainly did not dream of it. Most of them were well born, well educated opponents of National Socialism. They whispered against a regime which waged war on the gentlemen of England yet signed a treaty of friendship with those Bolshevik vulgarians. They regarded Vasili as one of themselves, accepting his invitations, inviting him in turn and speaking openly before him. One day General von Pfeffer, a monarchist and one of the German signatories of the armistice with France, was holding forth to a carefully selected audience: Lieutenant Colonel Hartog, Dr. Seiffarth, Dr. Huetgens and a few others. The war against Russia had begun at last, and these gentlemen were delighted, but von Pfeffer insisted that the Communists would never be crushed while Germany was at war with Britain and the United States. Conclusion: she must negotiate with these latter so that the entire Wehrmacht could be thrown into battle against Russia. "Negotiate?" said Maximovich. "But what about the Führer?" "With or without the Führer," retorted Pfeffer.

Nothing could show greater trust than a remark like that.

◆

In her view of the task of the Red Orchestra, Anna Maximovich showed as much foresight and patience as a bull in a china shop. On one occasion she offered to supply the Big Chief with enough curare to poison a thousand people; this, she argued with shining eyes, was a heaven-sent opportunity to rid Paris of the entire German headquarters staff. Trepper nearly had a fit. He told her plainly that she must give up these Shakespearean dreams. He had already needed all his charm to dissuade Vasili from turning out homemade incendiary bombs; it would be madness to waste such valuable agents on such grotesque projects. Thanks to Vasili, he knew what was happening at the very heart of German headquarters. Through Anna, he was kept informed of the diplomatic maneuvers of the Vatican—she enjoyed the friendship of Monsignor Chaptal and also of the Jesuit Father Valensin, who was at the center of every intrigue. In addition, she

saw a great deal of Dr. Darquier. The latter was able to tell her what
was going on behind the scenes in Vichy, where his brother was playing the puppet.

"For the Maximoviches," Darquier assured me, "the great turning point was the German attack on Russia. Their views remained as
Tsarist as ever, but they now became bitterly anti-German—once
Holy Russia was attacked, all her children must defend her; it was as
simple as that. Their mother told them this over and over again; and,
as I said earlier, they obeyed her every whim. Mind you, in Anna's
case, this anti-German business didn't appear to go very far. There
was a German telephone cable running through the grounds of the
mental home, and it was always being cut. I knew Anna was the
culprit, and I used to say to her, 'Listen, for heaven's sake stop these
tomboy tricks or you'll end up in serious trouble.'

"As for her Mata Hari act, I must confess I didn't believe it for
one moment. It used to make me laugh, that's all. You should have
seen the mysterious airs she put on; and the way she'd hint darkly at
this or that—she was priceless! I used to say to myself, If she were
really in espionage, she wouldn't go to all this trouble to make me
think so. Sound reasoning, wouldn't you say? Do you know when
I finally realized that it wasn't just a game? Not until 1955 or 1956,
when a D.S.T. officer paid me a visit. I thought it was about my
brother again. (Every year, a couple of gendarmes come and ask
whether I have any news of my brother; in fact, I'm beginning
to get tired of it. 'He's in Spain,' I tell them, 'and he's very well.
Good night!') But it wasn't my brother this time. The policeman
wanted to know whether I had any information about a certain
Louise, who had, he said, been on Anna's staff at the mental home. I
had no recollection of the woman.

"We chatted for a while, and the police officer told me all about
Anna, whom I had completely lost track of after 1942; he told me
what she had done, what her true role had been, and so on. I was
staggered—absolutely staggered! He even showed me a page from
the D.S.T. report, containing a reference to me. At the foot of the
page the following rather splendid note appeared: 'It would seem
that Dr. Darquier did not knowingly belong to the Red Orchestra. . . .' You are right to laugh, my dear sir. They really are the limit
at the D.S.T. How can they possibly have supposed, even for a moment, that I—of all people!—could ever voluntarily work with *those*
people! In what one might call a Jewish organization! For many Jews

were involved in it, were they not? You see the absurdity of linking
me with *them?* And now that I think about it, even the name 'Maximovich' has a faintly Jewish ring, don't you feel? I wonder, I wonder
. . . Of course, you'll say that when the Tsar chose his generals he
didn't pick kikes. . . . Anyway, we'll never know; it would take a
lot of researching.

"Yes, I lost track of Anna after 1942. The mental home was
going downhill, one felt it, and in the end she sold it to the mother of
that child who got raped. Ah yes, I must tell you about that. It's a
perfect Anna story. The villain was a young German soldier, not a
day over eighteen, from the company camping in the grounds. He
got into the building and entered the room where a little insane girl
was lying in bed. He promptly began to rape her. The child
screamed, which soon brought Anna racing along the corridor. Without a moment's hesitation, without calling for help, she grabbed the
soldier by the scruff of his neck and the skin of his behind, pulled
him off (the worst had not been consummated, she assured me
later), and flung him down the stairs! The young devil bolted; he
knew when he was beaten. That evening there was a tremendous
fuss about it. The company commander came and apologized, but
Anna said that she was going to make a formal complaint to their
headquarters. The officer explained that if she did so, the boy would
be court-martialed and certainly shot. She relented. And the following day we were treated to an extraordinary spectacle: the Germans spread-eagled the boy between two trees and flogged him till
he was unconscious.

"Anyway, it was the little girl's mother who bought the place
from Anna. She turned it into an old people's home. And I never saw
or heard any more of Anna until the D.S.T. officer showed me that
incredible little note concerning myself."

This did not mean that Anna walked out and left her "harmless
lunatics." She moved them to Billeron Château, near Groize, in the
Department of Cher. Until 1940 it had been occupied by a community
of nuns; but the sisters had left in the general exodus and had never
returned. Anna had decided to rent the château, and her mother and
sister were already living there.

It is not so much a château as a "stately home." No towers or
turrets, but a spacious building distinguished by an elegant simplicity

of line, with high, thick woods all around it. There is also a horseshoe arrangement of large outbuildings. A little to one side, in its own clearing, stands a tiny chapel, an intricate little jewel in striking contrast to the simplicity of the neighboring château; perhaps the original owners had wished to reserve such artistic splendors for God alone. Leading up to the château from the main gates is a half-mile avenue of ancient trees.

The caretakers still remember Madame Maximovich. "She was a very, very great lady, quite out of the ordinary. She had lost all her estates in Russia in the Revolution, but she used to say to us: 'To anyone who knows how the country was managed in the old days, what happened in 1917 seems the most natural thing in the world. It was bound to come.' "

They also remember Vasili and his sister. Big Anna used to stride about the grounds like a drill sergeant, clad more often than not in a long purple lace dress, which made people think she belonged to some religious order. She didn't, of course, but it must have been quite a sight.

They also have a clear recollection of the patients whose nerves unwound in the sylvan calm, and of the countless visits paid by Margarete Hoffman-Scholz's colleagues and by German officers' wives who wanted to get away from Paris for a while.

Among the latter was Käthe Voelkner. But when she drove up that long, beautiful avenue on a summer's day in 1941, she wasn't in search of rest: she had come to Billeron Château to be "screened."

Käthe was a German citizen, born in Danzig on April 12, 1906, daughter of a Socialist art teacher. Her face was ordinary despite the mass of ash-blond hair, but her body was muscular and quite extraordinarily supple; she was an acrobatic dancer. She had made a series of shabby, unsuccessful European tours with her lover and manager, an Italian named Podsialdo, by whom she had two children. Eventually the little family found themselves stranded in Leningrad, without a penny. They were taken care of and Käthe was even given a chance to study. The experience made a convert of her, and it was almost certainly during this period that she joined the Soviet secret service. She left to tour Europe again, but this time carrying out a plan devised by the Center, and carefully avoided Nazi Germany. In 1937 she was ordered to Paris, and for the next two years she danced in a night club there.

After the outbreak of war in 1939, she went into hiding with her lover and children in a house in the twentieth *arrondissement;* otherwise she would have been interned as an enemy alien. She and Podsialdo turned these long, furtive months of the "Phony War" to good account by learning stenotyping. In 1940 she emerged from cover and offered her services to her victorious compatriots. She was taken on by the Labor Service, or "Sauckel Organization," whose headquarters was at the Chamber of Deputies. Podsialdo obtained only a minor post, but Käthe became secretary to the head of the Paris office, Dr. Kleefeld. She enjoyed his complete confidence—was she not a German, and had she not spent nearly a year hiding from the French police?

On his return from internment at Le Vernet, Maximovich called at the Chamber of Deputies to see what the Labor Service had to offer him. He met Käthe, chatted with her, sensed her inner feelings and formed the impression that she might make a first-class recruit. But suppose he was wrong?

He had her invited to Billeron. For a fortnight, big Anna and little Käthe walked and talked in the peaceful grounds of the château. When Käthe left, Anna said to her brother, "In my opinion, she's all right." But Vasili remained on his guard. He had come a long way since the days when he only dreamed of incendiary bombs. He saw Käthe again in Paris, and he packed her off to Billeron for another series of walks and talks with Anna. By now the leaves had turned brown, and the massive tree trunks were shrouded in mist—it was the autumn of 1941. Anna confirmed her favorable verdict, and Vasili decided that it was time to discuss Käthe with the Big Chief.

Their discussion took place after the Atrébates raid, so Trepper was very much on guard; he was afraid of an attempt to infiltrate the Orchestra. Käthe had clearly not breathed a word to Maximovich about her earlier association with Russian Intelligence; she had only shown a discreet anti-Nazism. Nor had Trepper—for reasons which will emerge—asked the Center for any information about her. Even if he had done so, a favorable reply would not have allayed his doubts: Käthe had disappeared in September, 1939, severing all contact with the Center, to reappear in Dr. Kleefeld's office in July, 1940. Had this been an admirable initiative, putting herself into position to be of service again? Or had she turned traitor and gone over to the winning side?

The Big Chief didn't balk at jumping any river if he had to; but first he always looked for a safer crossing before taking the risk. The problem of recruiting Käthe he approached very gingerly indeed. His first step was to see the girl without actually meeting her. He got Anna to invite her to a restaurant with plenty of mirrors. Trepper sat at a nearby table, scanning the mirrors to see whether a watch was being kept on her movements. There was no sign of anything suspicious. He now proceeded to stage two—meeting Käthe. A rendezvous was arranged in a Métro station, on a platform with several exits. Käthe asked what method of approach and recognition was to be used. Vasili told her not to worry about that, for the man she was to meet already knew her. Käthe, of course, was greatly startled to hear it. But the arrangement had an obvious advantage: if Käthe was an *agent provocateur*, she would be unable to lead the Gestapo to their victim—she would have to wait to be approached by Trepper, who would have time to look around. As a further precaution, he had Katz tail her all the way from her home to the Métro platform. If he saw anyone else shadowing her, he was to warn Trepper by a discreet signal. Inside the station, accomplices placed at strategic points kept their eyes open for gentlemen in long raincoats and Tyrolean hats.

The meeting passed off without a hitch; Käthe spoke of her desire to be of use. Now came stage three: she was put to the test. She was asked to supply various seals, rubber stamps and specimens of handwriting. She delivered them. After this, she was regarded as an enlisted member, and they got down to serious business. Käthe started supplying documents, but not directly to Trepper. The latter sent one of his people, Madame Giraud. With Katz keeping watch, she met Käthe in the Métro station and took delivery of Dr. Kleefeld's secret reports, concealed between the pages of newspapers. Madame Giraud was instructed to stroll about the streets for at least six hours before going home, always within sight of the faithful Katz. Then she must hold on to the documents for three days, after which they were to be delivered to the Big Chief, not by the lady, but by her husband.

This may seem a great deal of fuss and bother. But if all the network chiefs had gone about their work like this, the Nazi executioner would have claimed fewer victims.

Through Käthe, Moscow learned of the manpower problems which were thwarting Hitler's plans and of the decision to solve those problems by enslaving the people of Occupied Europe. Kleefeld knew all about it—the quotas demanded of each country, their transportation to Germany, and (invaluable, this) which industries had been singled out for priority. Before long, Moscow was fully aware of the recruiting difficulties and of the vast numbers of men who were dodging conscription by joining the *maquis*. This was important.

But Käthe did even better. She introduced into the Orchestra ranks a Frenchman employed at the Wehrmacht's Central Billeting Office, in Paris. At first sight, he did not appear to have much to offer. In fact, he was possibly the most important recruit ever acquired by the Big Chief.

———◆———

One day Vasili Maximovich told Trepper that he was in a rather tricky situation: tongues were beginning to wag. Unless his relationship with Margarete was placed on an official footing, there was going to be a scandal; any day now, rumors would begin to circulate that they were having an illicit affair. And if that should happen, Maximovich's position as an agent would be in jeopardy; he would soon be excluded from German official circles. Trepper begged him to marry the woman, but Vasili stroked his beard and pointed out that he was not yet reduced to outright surrender. He could withdraw to a second line of defense that could certainly be held for a few months—in other words, they could announce their engagement. "And, thank heaven," the Russian added, "in our circle it is out of the question for couples to sleep together between announcement and wedding."

Moscow had to be informed. The Big Chief asked for the Director's blessing, and the Director was graciously pleased to bestow it. *Gross Paris* was flooded with invitation cards stamped with the arms of the Maximovich family. The reception was elaborate—the fairest daughters of the exiled Russian aristocracy waltzed with the proudest members of the German officer corps, the champagne flowed, and the love birds received the felicitations of all the generals of the Hotel Majestic.

19. Harmony and Discord

It is time to take bearings.

This summer of 1942 saw the final downfall of Brussels and Amsterdam, but the Paris network's stronghold seemed impregnable. Ringed with lookouts, reinforced by the most rigid internal security system, it was ready to withstand the assault.

Thanks to Grossvogel, the purely technical, administrative arrangements were of a very high level. There were a dozen empty apartments or rooms available to members of the Orchestra: 13 Quai St.-Michel; 94 Rue de Varennes; 6 Rue Fortuny; 78 Avenue de Wagram, et cetera. There was also a suburban house at Le Vésinet and a villa at Verviers. The network even had a base well away from the front line—Billeron Château, where ill or exhausted agents were sent to recuperate, side by side with the wives of Junker officers. Situated within a few miles of the demarcation line, Billeron also provided agents in peril with an emergency exit to the Unoccupied Zone; local guides led them across to safety. In addition, the Orchestra had its own sources of supply—the Corbins' farm provided an abundance of eggs and poultry, while Thévenet, a cigarette manufacturer and stockholder in the Belgian branch of Simexco, continued to keep Paris well-stocked with his tobacco.

Financially, the network was flourishing. The net profits of Simex and Simexco reached 1,616,000 francs in 1941 and 1,641,000 francs in 1942, after deduction of operating costs for the Belgian, Dutch and French networks. Trepper kept a strict account of all expenditures, for—like all other Soviet network chiefs—he knew that he would have to submit his accounts to Moscow. He and his men were paid in dollars (the dollar has always been the monetary unit employed by the Center). In 1939, the Big Chief received $350 a month. This was cut to $275 when his wife and children returned to Moscow via Marseilles. Kent, Alamo and Grossvogel at first received $175 a month, then $225. But from June 22, 1941, all agents, from the biggest to the smallest, were paid a uniform wage of $100 a month; this was war and they were regarded as troops on active service. Naturally, they were allowed unlimited expenses.

At first glance, the expenses seem light. In the period from

June 1 to December 31, 1941, Brussels cost $5,650 and Paris $9,421. From January 1 to April 30, 1942, $2,414 went to the French network, and $2,042 to the Belgian network, while Kent, in Marseilles, received $810. From May 1 to September 30, 1942, the figures are given in francs: 593,000 for France; 380,000 for Belgium; 185,000 for Kent.

But these figures cover only routine expenses—agents' pay, rent money, et cetera. To gain an accurate picture of the network's finances, we must add the bribes issued to German officers, the bill for Maximovich's engagement party, the upkeep of Billeron Château, and so on. The Big Chief could afford to spend on a grand scale, for —thanks to the activities of Simex and Simexco—the money handed to the Germans came out of their own pockets. The Third Reich was subsidizing the Red Orchestra, just as a living organism will nourish the cancer which is eroding it. Indeed, it was subsidizing the Orchestra to such a degree that for a while the Center even thought of making the Big Chief the banker for all Soviet networks in the West.

Trepper kept his accounts hidden inside a large clock in the house at Verviers. At Katz's home, a collection of jam jars contained a hoard of a thousand gold dollars: their reserve against any financial crisis. And Claude Spaak still had the roll of gold coins which the Sokols had left in his safekeeping. Even if Simex and Simexco were uncovered, they would have money to go on with.

◆

The confidence which sprang from these strong foundations enable the network to get through a prodigious amount of work. As we know, Simex's role was to infiltrate the Todt Organization and obtain information about the Wehrmacht's building program in Occupied Europe. Vasili Maximovich's job was to penetrate the German High Command in Paris and report on troop movements, officers' postings, morale, intrigues against Hitler and secret deals with Vichy. Käthe Voelkner kept watch on the invader's manpower problems, while Anna collected information on Vatican politics and France's internal affairs. In Lyons, Romeo Springer was in close touch with the Belgian ex-minister, Balthazar, and with the American consul; from these he received much valuable information.

And that was not all.

The network had recruited a pair of agents in the German telephone exchange in Paris. They listened in on conversations between the French capital and Berlin and reported everything of importance straight to the Big Chief.

The Orchestra could also draw on the services of the local Comintern. This was headed by Henry Robinson, a tall, thin, forty-four-year-old Jew with dark, alert eyes. This is how the Gestapo subsequently described him in its report: "A German Jew speaking fluent German, English, Russian, French and Italian. Employs many identities, but nobody knows which is the real one. Founder of the Young Communists with his friend Humbert-Droz. French Young Communists' delegate to the Comintern in 1922. In 1923, head of the Workers' Politico-Military Party in the Rhineland during the French occupation. In 1924, technical supervisor of the Workers' Politico-Military Party for Central and Western Europe. In 1929, General Muraille's deputy for Soviet Intelligence in France. In 1930, head of the European Intelligence Service of the Red Army's Fourth Section. In 1940, head of the activist and military branch for Western Europe."

This *curriculum vitae* may be marred by inaccuracies (even if he did carry out a few missions for the Center, Robinson's allegiance remained from first to last with the Comintern), but it speaks for itself: the man was a veteran of secret warfare. Hardly older than the Big Chief, he had already been deputy to General Muraille, chief of Soviet espionage in France, three years before Trepper arrived to begin his apprenticeship under "Fantômas." Since that time, Robinson had been putting down stronger and stronger roots and broadening his contacts among the French, while Trepper had spent long periods in Russia and Belgium.

Yet it was Trepper, not Robinson, who now gave the orders. Trepper was a member of the Red Army's secret service, brought to the fore by the outbreak of hostilities. Robinson was a Comintern man, and the prestige of the Comintern had slumped; Stalin suspected it of deviationism, while to the young technocrats at the Center it seemed inefficient and antiquated. Indeed, when he instructed Trepper to join forces with the Comintern group, the Director had felt it necessary to add a good many words of warning: Robinson had been in ideological conflict with the Kremlin, he was politically unreliable; he was suspected of having acted as an informer to the French Deuxième Bureau. So he was to be used very prudently indeed.

General Susloparov organized a meeting between the two men on the eve of Operation Barbarossa. Subduing his probable bitterness, Robinson immediately placed his Belgian and French agents at the Orchestra's disposal and presented the Big Chief with his own personal network of informants. He had wormed his way into French ruling circles and had several sources at the heart of the German High Command. His agents soon began to provide Trepper with accurate reports on a wide range of subjects: General Giraud's escape and its consequences; the raid on Dieppe; the results of Allied bombing raids over France; the preparations for the Anglo-American landing in North Africa, et cetera.

The groups controlled by Vasili and Anna Maximovich, by Käthe Voelkner, by Romeo Springer and by Robinson were so many hives of industry, turning out information with clockwork regularity. To be complete, we must add the individual contacts which this or that agent happened, quite by chance, to establish with various informants. The Big Chief, for instance, derived much benefit from the confidences of a maiden lady, Mademoiselle Mayol de Lupé, whose brother was chaplain to the Legion of French Volunteers, a body fighting on the Russian front in German uniform. Monsignor Mayol de Lupé, who might have stepped straight out of the Inquisition, was the dominant spirit of this strange unit, in which mercenaries rubbed shoulders with poor misguided boys who somehow imagined themselves to be defending the honor of France, improbably draped in the Swastika. We may safely assume that his sister's conversation sometimes contained items of information obtained from the Monsignor.

Nor must we forget the considerable number of German officers whom the Big Chief had met while transacting business for Simex, or else in the course of his social evenings. All these men became regular suppliers of information—unwittingly, as a rule, but sometimes of their own volition. We have already mentioned Kainz, the Austrian engineer working for the Todt Organization, who had informed Trepper of the preparations for Barbarossa. At the time, Kainz had simply been guilty of careless talk—though he had never had any sympathy for the Nazi regime. Since then, however, he had been sent on a mission to Kiev, in the Ukraine. On September 29–30, 1941, he had seen 33,771 Jews—men, women and children—massacred in the ravine of Babiy Yar. He had seen them march toward the dunes, with their bundles on their backs, and then sit down beside the road, waiting for their turn as they listened to the remorseless rhythm of machine guns already mowing down their brothers. Thirty-three thousand seven hundred seventy-one human beings murdered in the space of forty-eight hours—the pinnacle of Nazi horror, a record never equaled, not even when the death factories of Treblinka and Auschwitz were working at maximum efficiency. Ludwig Kainz had seen all this, and he now felt much of what the poet Yevtushenko was to set down twenty years later:

> *Over Babiy Yar*
> *rustle of the wild grass.*
> *The trees look threatening, look like judges.*
> *And everything is one silent cry.*
> *Taking my hat off*
> *I feel myself slowly going grey.*
> *And I am one silent cry*
> *over the many thousands of the buried;*
> *am every old man killed here,*
> *every child killed here . . .*
> *No part of me can ever forget it.**

After the experience of Babiy Yar, Kainz was one of us.

———◆———

Moscow could afford to feel well-satisfied. Through sheer talent and industry, the Big Chief and the French network had achieved the supreme aim of any intelligence organization: it had breached the enemy's security *at the highest level.* Schulze-Boysen and his colleagues in the Berlin network had done the same—but they were Germans, and therefore had a head start. Had Trepper merely penetrated the enemy's security at a humble level (which was as much as most Allied networks ever did), the result would have been infinitely less profitable to the Kremlin—Paris was hardly the navel of the Third Reich, and the ordinary pattern of daily life in the French capital was of no direct consequence to Russia. But we know that Maximovich's reports of anti-Hitler intrigues of officers like Pfeffer were helpful in Moscow's propaganda campaign, which was intended to weaken the Wehrmacht. The Kremlin knew little about the "traditionalist" German officer or his attitude toward the regime. Now the Russians were able to draft the appeals of the "Committee for a Free Germany" (headed by Field Marshal Paulus, the vanquished commander

---

* Yevgeny Yevtushenko, *Selected Poems* (Baltimore: Penguin Books, 1962), p. 83.

at Stalingrad) in the light of Maximovich's information. Similarly, Vasili's and Anna's contacts among the Russian émigrés—and Robinson's contacts too—were invaluable at a time when the Germans were seeking to further their own ends by reviving Ukrainian nationalism, Tartar nationalism, Cossack nationalism, and so on. The exiled aristocracy in Paris knew, from their German opposite numbers, that the policy in question was utterly treacherous; the Nazis were simply trying to divide and conquer, then later enslave them. The Big Chief passed on the émigrés' confidences and reactions, and Moscow worked them into its propaganda. There is no limit to the number of examples one could quote.

Naturally, the Soviet General Staff received its share of the plunder. Apart from general information on the Wehrmacht's plans and broad strategic decisions, Russia knew immediately of each decision to transfer a division from Europe to the Russian front; the news was flashed to Moscow before the division had finished packing its bags—sometimes even before its own commander was notified.

This was a great help; but even better would be detailed descriptions of the units involved. It was here that the French Resistance really triumphed. Generally the Resistance was incapable of breaching the enemy's security at the highest level, but it made up for this by massive infiltration further down the scale. Thanks to its thousands of agents, all willing amateurs, it managed to piece together— with a bribe here and a bribe there—the intricate mosaic of the enemy's far-flung army, down to the last detail. Indeed, in 1944, it was the French Resistance, and the Resistance alone, which after the Allied landings in Normandy obtained the surrender of the most powerful fortified point along the coast—Ostek, near Cherbourg. Ostek had held out for four days, against every assault; its officers gave in only after an American, parleying under flag of truce, showed them his map, which gave an even more detailed picture of German defenses than did their own. Each individual weapon was pinpointed, complete with range and angle of fire and ammunition reserve down to the last shell or clip. It showed how many men were assigned to each blockhouse, and the name of the officer in charge . . . The sight of this map was too much for the Germans; psychological warfare succeeded where a hail of fire and steel had previously failed.

The Big Chief's specialist groups couldn't attend to these minute details; they mixed with beribboned generals, not with sergeants; nor were there enough of them to cover such a wide field. But Trep-

per, like the other heads of Resistance networks—like Rémy, like
Sainteny, like Marie-Madeleine Fourcade—had a host of part-time,
junior agents at his disposal, a whole army of makeshift spies. Francs-
Tireurs et Partisans, Communist militants, Jewish combat organizations, foreign Resistance groups—a whole anthill was secretly toiling
for the Red Orchestra. Each time a Wehrmacht truck drove into an
ambush, each time an enemy post was stormed, the German soldiers'
papers were sorted and analyzed locally, together with any documents
found on their officer; if they contained information of general interest, they were forwarded to the Big Chief. Of even greater value
were the facts gleaned by the Resistance cells assigned to "German
work"—in other words, to infiltration of the Wehrmacht. The activities of such cells were spearheaded by girl militants, with orders to
consort with German officers and men and extract as much information as they could. The task was delicate. As one report frankly ex-
presses it, "They were dealing with men who only wanted to seduce
them. The girls had to hold them off, yet at the same time win their
confidence, and one can see that the shift from the erotic to the political was not easy to achieve."

Only the best pickings of this vast crop of information were
telegraphed to the Center; it would have been physically impossible
to telegraph every item. And among these pickings were the facts
and figures relating to each unit transferred to the Russian front.
And this is how the troops of the 23rd Panzer ("Eiffel Tower")
Division came to hear those Red Army loudspeakers proclaiming that
their "gay days in Paris" were over now. One can see how terrifying
this was to the ordinary soldier just come from France to face an unknown enemy who seemed to know all about him and his comrades.
He felt exposed, from the start, to the all-seeing eye of a diabolical
foe. The self-confidence was knocked out of him, just as it was to be
knocked out of the defenders of Ostek two years later.

It can only be added that seldom in the history of espionage has
a network given such grounds for pride and satisfaction as the French
network of the Red Orchestra gave its chief in the summer of 1942.

And yet it is an established fact that the Big Chief's real struggles
and anguish began in that same season of that same year.

———◆———

In the first place, the war was going badly. Twenty-five years
later, we are able to take in triumph and disaster at a glance: We see

the German High Command launching Operation Blue, while we already have an eye on Stalingrad. But Trepper did not have this reassuringly broad view. Like everyone else, all he could see was the Wehrmacht surging toward the Caucasus, Rommel hammering the British in the desert, and the Japanese army fanning out across the Pacific.

In the second place, the perennial problem of transmissions had grown more acute than ever.

Hersch Sokol was captured on June 9; Wenzel fell into Fortner's hands at the end of the same month. Who was to take over?

Kent was a possibility. He had a transmitter, and his activities in Marseilles during the past eight months had remained undetected by the Vichy police—which was not surprising, considering the life he led.

"It was heavenly," says Margarete Barcza. "My dream had come true: he never left me. We spent our afternoons at the beach. When it was cloudy we went to the movies, as many as three a day, or we stayed home and danced, or drove to our house in the country. Now and then he went and had a drink with Monsieur Jaspar, to discuss work; but as that would make me furious, he used to get out of going. Not that it was hard to persuade him—Vincent was thoroughly fed up with the whole business. After all, we were in love, we were happy, why should we have bothered about anything else? My son René was with us, but that was no problem. Far from it—Vincent loved him as though he were his own child. Yes, it was a really heavenly life, and all we wanted was to see it last.

"Vincent had a plan to make sure it *did* last. The idea was to slip into Switzerland without telling anyone, and stay there till the war was over. He had plenty of money and a passport with a Swiss visa. But I had no papers whatever, of course. He wanted me and René to move to the Haute-Savoie, while he went straight to Switzerland to make arrangements to get us across the border. I wouldn't hear of it. The thought of being apart from him, even for a few days, was more than I could stand. So we remained peacefully in Marseilles, telling ourselves that the war would be over some day, and with luck we'd pull through. To be on the safe side, Vincent made me send René, who was almost eleven, to a local boarding school. That way, he wouldn't be left stranded if things went wrong for us.

"Trepper visited us several times and started badgering Vincent. They used to go into a room, keep their voices down, and stop talking when they heard me coming. It used to drive me mad! Once I even threw Trepper out. He was furious, because it was just before breakfast, and he couldn't bear to be done out of a meal. He lived for his food!

"Mind you, Vincent was just the same. Ah, you really would have thought he'd never had a decent meal before he came to Belgium and France! In restaurants, he'd sometimes order two or three main courses. And even that wasn't enough; when we got home, I'd have to make him a little snack! Honestly, he was an absolute glutton."

Kent was lost to the network. He invented a thousand and one reasons for not using his transmitter, and claimed it was always breaking down. In the end, Trepper had to call in some technicians attached to a local Resistance group, and they soon declared it was in perfect order. Even then, Kent balked. It was out of the question to rely on him for the network's radio communications. The Center was most indignant and kept upbraiding the Big Chief about his deputy's idleness. Trepper preferred not to show Kent the telegrams, lest they demoralize him altogether; the best he could hope of the onetime Little Chief was that he would continue wallowing in defeatism and gluttony without exposing the network to the attentions of Vichy counterintelligence.

Robinson had a transmitter, too. But he simply did not live up to his long, impressive-sounding record as a Comintern agent; he was scared stiff of the Funkabwehr's R.D.F. vans. His only advantage over Kent was that he didn't force the Big Chief to waste valuable time in vain entreaties. Robinson refused point-blank to sit down at the "piano" and no power on earth could make him do so.

This left only the Girauds.

Pierre and Lucienne Giraud, aged thirty-four and thirty-two respectively, had been recruited by their old friend Katz. At first they had acted as links between the Big Chief and Michel, his contact with the French Communist Party—and also, as we have seen, between the Big Chief and Käthe Voelkner. In the spring of 1942, while Sokol and Wenzel were still at liberty, Grossvogel installed the couple at St.-Leu-la-Forêt, near Paris, with a transmitter provided by Pauriol, the Party's radio expert, who had previously supplied Hersch Sokol's set; the Girauds were told to master the use of the equipment. In this they failed and thus were unable to establish contact with the Center when Trepper instructed them to do so after Sokol and Wenzel were captured. The Girauds returned to their liaison work, and the Big Chief was compelled to rely on the Party's transmitters again;

this was just as unsatisfactory as it had been after the Atrébates raid, for the Party's transmitters were already heavily engaged.

The Girauds were deeply troubled by their failure, and did their best to make up for it. They recruited the rare bird who really might be capable of handling the set: Valentino Toledano, a Spanish Republican who had fled to France after the retreat from Catalonia. Interned by the French authorities but later liberated, Toledano was now working as an electrician for a German transport company in Paris. Grossvogel rented a house for the trio at Le Pecq, in Seine-et-Oise. At the end of the summer, Trepper gave the green light for a new attempt. But even before it took place, the Gestapo arrived from out of the blue and made straight for the transmitter, which was buried in the garden. The Girauds fled. They were seen in Paris after the Liberation, in 1946, but soon disappeared again, leaving no address. Toledano, curiously enough, was not questioned by the Gestapo. At the end of the war he slipped over the border into Spain, where his wife soon joined him. It was, to say the least, most unusual for any veteran of the Republican Army to return to Spain only six years after Franco's victory; Valentino Toledano must surely have given substantial proof of his political conversion. We cannot swear that the Gestapo went to Le Pecq on Toledano's denunciation, but the theory sounds probable, to say the least.

What *is* certain is that, after this new blow, Trepper was once again without a transmitter. But by now he was also used to it. It was certainly not at the root of his great troubles. Nor was the collapse of the Brussels and Amsterdam networks (the rigid security system operating in Paris would limit the damage) or the inevitability of a similar collapse in Berlin (he did not know how imminent that collapse was).

No, Trepper's great troubles were rooted in Moscow itself.

———◆———

We know that the Kremlin had refused to heed the Big Chief's warnings about Operation Barbarossa. And Sorge in Japan, Rado in Switzerland, and other agents elsewhere had all suffered the same rebuff; the bitterness of being disbelieved was the daily bread of a network chief.

General Susloparov's failure to supply Trepper with transmitters had hardly been his fault; his responsibility ended as soon as he had passed Trepper's demands on to the Center, and the Center had ignored them because it did not believe there was going to be a war.

Then, when the war did come, the Director's orders acquired a vehemence as disproportionate as his earlier lethargy. Despite the Big Chief's warnings—despite his entreaties!—the network's pianists had been forced to play for hours at a stretch, and we have seen Alamo, Wenzel and Sokol in the hands of the Gestapo as a direct result. But it is always the same in wartime: commanders, snug in their head-quarters, enjoy ordering others to stand and be killed, when a slight shift to left or right could save them. The Director continued to treat his radio operators as though they were shock troops, despite the enormous risks. In fairness, it must be said that foolish demands like these are common to all the secret services in the world.

The first real wound came with that famous telegram of October 10, 1941, giving Kent the addresses of the three heads of the Berlin network. When the Big Chief heard of it he was stunned. It just isn't possible, he said to himself; they've gone mad! Three vital addresses given away in a telegram which might well be intercepted and decoded—as, indeed, it was! Why hadn't the Center dispatched a courier to Brussels with the addresses safely lodged in his memory and with a cyanide capsule—just in case. Or, if it was really so urgent, the addresses could at least have been sent in three separate messages, using three separate codes, to lessen the risk of losing all of them at once. From that day on, for all the Director's protests, the Big Chief never again disclosed to Moscow the names and addresses of his sources—a sacrilegious violation of the traditions of Soviet Intelligence. He even concealed the identities of most of his agents (which is why he preferred not to ask Moscow for information about Käthe Voelkner). Indeed, he went even further: when his own radio communications were working again, he continued to send his most vital reports via the French Communist Party's transmitters, either because those reports contained essential information or because their interception might jeopardize the existence of the network. This safety measure had a further advantage: the reports in question would be read not only by the Director, but by others as well. Trepper entrusted them to Pauriol, who passed them on to the Communist leader, Jacques Duclos. In Moscow they were taken down by personnel working for Dimitrov, head of the Comintern, and were shown to the all-powerful Central Committee, at the same time as to the Director.

After that rash telegram to Kent, however, the Big Chief was merely wary of the Center's imprudence; he did not yet actually distrust the Center itself.

Then came the Atrébates raid and the emergency security measures that followed—Kent transferred to Marseilles; agents in greatest danger of arrest moved to Lyons; the Brussels network lying low for six months. All this infuriated the Center, which came close to crying treason. Trepper was told not to panic over trifles, and to recall Kent at once. The Big Chief replied that, as the man on the spot, he was a better judge of the situation than the Director. Kent remained in Marseilles and Romeo Springer in Lyons. Next, Moscow ordered the Brussels network to start operations again, without delay, under the leadership of Yefremov. Trepper refused to budge. He had sized Yefremov up: his total contribution to the Orchestra's work had consisted of sitting on a bar stool and noting the regimental insignia of the German soldiers who happened to join him for a drink.

After Yefremov's arrest, when Trepper informed the Center, the Director replied: "We know. He radioed us that he had got into some trouble about currency. But it is all settled, and he has been released." The Big Chief didn't need to be told this, and he also knew the price Yefremov had paid for his "release": the betrayal of the network. But how to convince the Center? Trepper sent Grossvogel and Pauriol to Brussels to examine the case from every angle. They came back with categorical proof that Yefremov had turned traitor. The Big Chief wired the news to the Center. The Director wired back: "Fear is upsetting your judgment. Orders are to reestablish contact with Yefremov at once." Trepper, Grossvogel and Pauriol could do no more than smile wryly to themselves.

When Wenzel was arrested, again the Big Chief informed the Center. Reply: "You are mistaken. Wenzel is still transmitting and sending us excellent material."

Winterink, the Dutchman, was arrested. Center to Trepper: "You are out of your mind. He is still supplying us with information as good as before his alleged arrest. Keep cool!"

The Big Chief was not yet out of his mind, but he felt he soon might be. Night after night he tried to think of some explanation for those incredible messages from Moscow, forcing himself to reject the terrifying suspicion that the Center contained one or more traitors in the pay of the Germans, whose aim was to destroy the networks *from within*. But if that were so, whom could he believe or pin his hopes on? If the Center itself had been infiltrated, all was surely lost.

There was an alternative theory: perhaps the Director imagined that he, Trepper, had been caught in the roundup at the Rue des Atrébates. After all, viewed from Moscow, the dexterity with which he had emerged from the trap may well have seemed too good to be true. And if the Director believed that Trepper was in the hands of the Gestapo, then every word the Center received from him was automatically treated as a lie. But why, in that case, proclaim the fact so openly? Why not pretend to be taken in by the Germans' bluff, if only to discover their game? Besides, if the Big Chief really had sunk so low as to play for the Gestapo, he would obviously also have betrayed Yefremov, Wenzel and Winterink. The theory did not stand up to examination. Indeed, none of the theories explored by the Big Chief's inventive mind could provide a logical basis for the Center's attitude.

Only one thing was certain: Moscow was being fooled by the excellence of the information transmitted by the renegades. Trepper had grasped the mechanics of the *Funkspiel*. He had also divined its major difficulty: obtaining permission to pass enough genuine information to the enemy to make them believe in the false. The people manipulating Yefremov, Wenzel and Winterink had plainly secured this permission; Moscow was more than satisfied with their messages. Now the information transmitted by the three men before their arrest had already dealt one savage blow after another to the German Wehrmacht in Russia. To allow it to continue this way, the authors of the *Funkspiel* must be trying to achieve something of quite exceptional importance. The Big Chief might be proud of his achievements, but he found it unbelievable that the masters of the *Funkspiel* would gamble for such high stakes merely to put one Soviet network out of action. Even if that *were* their sole objective (after all, as intelligence people themselves, they knew the vital importance of their own line of work), they would never have succeeded in convincing outsiders in the Wehrmacht that the project was worth the risk entailed.

The *Funkspiel* was therefore concealing some other purpose—but what was it?

The secret lay in Brussels, where the Kommando was completing its roundup. The "counterespionage group" set up by the Big Chief had been dispersed, annihilated. In any case, it would no longer be a question of spying at prison gates and bribing warders, but of examining Giering's secret files. Trepper's anxiety was so great that he decided to risk Vasili Maximovich's future as an agent by having him inquire into the situation. Lieutenant Colonel Hartog, Vasili's fiancée's uncle, acted as liaison officer between Paris and Brussels headquarters; possibly he would know if and when the Kommando was moving to France—and, most vital of all, what its plans were. Vasili took up the challenge without flinching, although he knew the uncle disliked him. But, in the event, it was this very dislike which saved him. After a few unexplicit social calls, before he had even revealed his true purpose to Hartog, the latter's secretary—a Fräulein Kreuziger—informed Vasili that her superior would be grateful if he would henceforth deprive him of the pleasure of his conversation.

Now all the Big Chief could do was wait.

20. Roundup in Berlin

It was like a dream. No novelist would dare to invent a plot so far removed from reality as the one that caused the downfall of the Berlin network. The group was about to perish as it had lived—in freakishness and confusion.

Ever since July 14, 1942, when Kludow had cracked the telegram with the addresses of the three leaders of the Berlin network, the Gestapo had been exploiting the break. They had identified the heads of the network: Harro Schulze-Boysen, Luftwaffe officer; Arvid Harnack, *Oberregierungsrat* at the Ministry of Economic Affairs; and Adam Kuckhoff, a well-known writer, author of the play *Till Eulenspiegel* and director of Prague Films. Schulze-Boysen and Harnack were prominent members of Berlin society, rubbing shoulders with the highest-ranking members of the Nazi regime. Now they understood how the country's best-kept secrets had found their way to Moscow. Two Gestapo *Kriminaldirektoren*, Panzinger and Koppkow, took over the investigation. They outranked Giering and worked directly under the great Gestapo—Müller himself. Seasoned experts in anti-Communist warfare, they had liquidated the clandestine German Communist Party, packed its members off to the scaffold or to concentration camps, and placed informers in those few vestiges of the organization which had been deliberately allowed to survive as pointers to any future resurgence.

To their infinite surprise, the Red Orchestra—that dread specter —turned out to be easier to dismantle than a suburban Party cell. They had no internal security system; they arranged meetings over the phone and sent messages through the regular mail—any ordinary little militant was a wilier adversary than these superspies! With the Gestapo's blacklist growing longer every day, there could be no question of Panzinger and Koppkow embarking on a premature roundup. It was the whole network that would fall into their hands like an overripe peach.

On Saturday, August 29, 1942, there was a great deal of hustle and bustle at Funkabwehr headquarters. Kludow and his young team were moving to more spacious offices on the floor above. The operation was probably conducted in the spirit of an undergraduate romp. Kludow lost no time in clamping down, however; he announced that they would all work the following day—Sunday, August 30,— to make up for the time wasted. There was general consternation in the ranks, but not, perhaps, on the part of Horst Heilmann, a fervent, self-disciplined Nazi and the most industrious member of Kludow's staff. As he had arranged to go boating on the Wannsee next day, he needed to let his friends know that he'd be unable to keep the appointment. He picked up the telephone which had just been installed in Kludow's office and dialed a Berlin number. The maid answered; her employers were out. Horst left a message for them to call him back as soon as possible. He had the maid write down Kludow's number, for the telephone in his own new office was still awaiting connection.

———◆———

There are times when history seems almost to encourage phrases which a purist would reject as oversimplifications. Here it gives grounds for saying that the Nazi empire reached its apogee during the twenty-four hours of Sunday, August 30, 1942. Never had the Führer wielded power over so many lands and so many men as on this memorable day; never had Germany seemed so close to holding the world in her grasp.

It was a burning day, from every point of view.

Rommel's Afrika Korps was drawn up ready for battle, with its sights set on the Pyramids. The Desert Fox had regrouped his forces for an offensive that would capture Cairo, Alexandria, the Nile Delta

and Suez—"the greatest prize of all," as he says in his diaries. All these
targets lay, invitingly, within sixty miles of his advance positions.
The German tank crews lay sprawled under their vehicles, stifling
in the furnace heat of the Egyptian summer. They were waiting
for the twilight, which would bring coolness and, soon after, the red
flare that would be the signal for attack. They had driven thousands
of miles across an inhuman desert which turned their tanks into merciless ovens. For months they had been fighting an opponent who continually outnumbered them and was invariably better armed. They
had buried many dead comrades along the way. But tomorrow they
would sit in the Cairo bars, drinking English beer and smoking
Virginia tobacco.

Rommel was closer to the Terek river than to Rome, twice as close
to the Terek as to Berlin. And the Terek river, in the Caucasus, was
the last remaining obstacle between General von Kleist's armor and the
oil fields of Baku. The south bank bristled with the heavy guns and
automatic weapons of three Russian divisions. Kleist decided to assail
it with a single regiment. At three o'clock in the afternoon of August
30, 1942, in a temperature of 120 degrees Fahrenheit, the foot soldiers
of the 394th Panzer Infantry, from Hamburg, leaped into their assault
boats and headed for the enemy bank. The Terek at that point is a
sixth of a mile wide, with a fierce current, eddying dangerously at
times. Each Russian shell sent up a column of water, and the small
boats ran a slalom between them. The hail of machine-gun fire
knocked the crests off the waves, ricocheted against the hulls, mowing down the German troops whenever they emerged from the foam-
ing waters. Yet the infantrymen reached the shore, dug into the sand,
crawled toward the bank, formed a hedgehog and withstood the first
Soviet counterattack. By nightfall, the bridgehead was firmly enough
established for thoughts to turn to the final push which would lead
all the way to Baku. The men of the 394th had trudged a long way
since crossing the Bug, fifteen months earlier. They had fought in
the thick winter snow and floundered in the springtime mud. They
had lost count of their dead and maimed, and those who had gone
mad under the horrors of the battlefield. But tomorrow their tanks
would be refueled with gasoline drawn from the Causcasian oil wells.

On this same Sunday of August 30, Hitler was at his headquarters at Vinnitsa, in the Ukraine. It was even more stifling inside
the plain wooden hutments than in the open air. The Führer could

not stand the heat, and he was to return to his dank lair at Rastenburg, in East Prussia, shortly afterward. But on that Sunday, the
successful crossing of the Terek and the impending advance of the
Afrika Korps probably made him forget the rigors of the Ukrainian
summer. He was no doubt poring over his maps, on which was being
inscribed, in characters of fire and blood, and by his will alone, one
of the most amazing military ventures of all time; already he pictured
Kleist's spearhead units meeting up with Rommel's somewhere near
Baghdad, and then advancing together toward the Indian Ocean
where the Japanese army was awaiting them—with the SS tank crews
singing their savage refrain:

> *The worm-eaten bones of the whole wide world*
> *Tremble beneath our onslaught.*

Hitler was convinced that his dream was on the point of being
realized. Ten days earlier, the Canadians' raid on Dieppe had achieved
nothing, apart from strewing the pebbly beaches with dead bodies.
Hitler imagined he had staved off a genuine invasion attempt. In the
west, he was invulnerable for a long time to come. In the east and in
Africa, he was about to deal the decisive blow. Worldwide dominion
was almost within his grasp.

◆

In Berlin, it was less hot than in the Caucasus, the Ukraine or
Egypt. Indeed, that August 30 was simply a magnificent summer day.
Forgetting the war (they had no idea it was at its turning point),
the Berliners went peacefully to the woods surrounding their capital.
A considerable number of them, of course, were women, children
or men too old to fight; but there were also the sick, the wounded,
the exempt, officers attached to defense departments in Berlin, and
troops on leave who found themselves wondering whether all this
were not a dream.

On the Wannsee, that paradise for yachting enthusiasts, there
were fewer boats than before the war, but this only added to the
pleasure. People lay idly on the sun-warmed decks, listening to the
water lap against the side, to the soft strains of guitars and harmonicas,
and to the songs passed on from vessel to vessel; sun, water, peace—
happiness.

"But," Balzac would have written at this point, "an attentive observer would have noticed" that certain crews were freely stepping from yacht to yacht for apparently harmless reasons; that lively discussions were taking place around stoves, while the women cooked potatoes; and that a succession of boats was drawing up alongside a vessel steered by a lordly-looking, blond giant—like old-time men-of-war gathering round the flagship to receive the admiral's instructions.

How the scene would pain modern technocrats of the espionage industry! For these nautical frolics were in fact the setting chosen by Schulze-Boysen, helmsman of the "flagship," for a plenary conference. Here on the Wannsee he had brought together no fewer than *thirty* members of his network. One would refuse to believe it if the event were not set down in the Gestapo report and if a survivor, Günther Weisenborn, did not unreservedly attest to the facts.

On the evening of August 30, the troops from Hamburg dug themselves in on the south bank of the Terek. For five days they stood up to the Soviet counterattacks. Then they turned their backs on the east, pulled back across the river and began to trudge westward in a retreat that did not end until the last day of the war.

The red flare streaked across the Egyptian sky, and the grenadiers of the Afrika Korps launched yet another attack against the "Desert Rats." They were stopped in their tracks by Montgomery, who had long planned to defeat them here at El Alamein. They turned their backs on the Pyramids and embarked on the long, harsh trek which would lead this time to the barbed-wire compounds of captivity.

The weekend yachtsmen on the Wannsee tied up their vessels and returned to Berlin. For them, all the pleasures of living waned with the light of this beautiful summer day. Their suntanned necks were destined for the hangman's noose or the polished blade of the guillotine.

———◆———

At about 9 A.M. the following day, August 31, the phone on Kludow's desk rang, interrupting him in his work. According to Flicke, of the Funkabwehr, he picked up the receiver and heard these words: "Schulze-Boysen here. You wished to speak to me?"

Kludow nearly jumped out of his chair. The heads of the Abwehr had told him under seal of secrecy the real names of the people who had been unmasked through his efforts.

"Hello? I'm sorry . . . I didn't quite hear . . ."

"Schulze-Boysen. My maid has just given me your message. I was to call you as soon as possible. What can I do for you?"

"Hello? Well, er—you see . . . yes . . ."

"Hello? I'm listening . . ."

"I'm so sorry . . . As a matter of fact, may I ask whether your name is spelled with a *y* or with an *i?*"

"With a *y*. Of course. I think I must have the wrong number. You didn't call me?"

"Well—no—I don't think so . . ."

"Obviously a mistake on the part of my maid. She mixed up the number. Do forgive me."

"Not at all."

When Kludow informed his superiors that he had just been talking on the telephone to Schulze-Boysen, they assumed he must be suffering from overwork; plainly, he was hearing voices. They suggested that a spell of leave might do him good, but he stubbornly denied that it had been a hallucination. And in the end he overcame their skepticism by admitting that he had asked Schulze-Boysen how his name was spelled. Ever since Kludow had known the man's identity, the *i*-or-*y* question had been preying on his mind. He had been so dazed by surprise that the query had tumbled from his lips before he realized what he was saying.

Kludow's confession was at once convincing and catastrophic. Schulze-Boysen had presumably realized that he was being shadowed by the Gestapo, and had telephoned the Funkabwehr to see how the land lay. And in this case, Kludow's question would have confirmed his suspicion that the authorities were on to him.

When Koppkow and Panzinger were told what had happened, they complained bitterly that their investigation had been sabotaged. The web in which they had been hoping to catch the *whole* organization had now been irreparably broken. They were forced to take immediate action.

Harro Schulze-Boysen was arrested that same afternoon. Koppkow cleverly lured him out of his office at the Air Ministry—a scandal must be avoided at all costs. He was apprehended in the street, and the rumor was spread among his colleagues that he had been sent on some secret mission abroad. His wife, Libertas, was captured a few days later, on her return from a visit to Bremen. The Harnacks were arrested on September 3, at the seaside resort where they were spending their holidays.

By the end of the first week of the roundup, the teams working for Panzinger and Koppkow had packed a hundred and eighteen people into the cellars of Gestapo headquarters in the Prinz-Albrecht-strasse. Among them was Horst Heilmann, Kludow's trusted assistant, who turned out to be an active member of the Red Orchestra. For this same Schulze-Boysen who was crazy enough to hold yachting rallies on the Wannsee was at the same time capable of planting an agent inside the Abwehr—indeed, in its holy of holies, the deciphering department. It is rare indeed for a network chief to qualify for extremes of praise *and* criticism! But, as we shall see, Schulze-Boysen was a man out of the ordinary in every way.

As for Horst Heilmann, he might be young, but his political past made him an old campaigner. A veteran of the Young Communists and a Party member, he had gone over to the Nazis and quickly drawn attention to himself by his fanatical dedication to the cause; hence his selection for service in the Abwehr's radio station and afterward in the top-secret deciphering department. But one day he met Schulze-Boysen, and his ideas changed tack again, this time for good: he remained loyal to him until the day he died. He recruited another member of the coding office, Alfred Traxl, and for a whole year he supplied Schulze-Boysen with the most valuable information. Yet is it possible that he told him nothing about Kludow's team and its labors, nothing about the decoding of the fatal telegram?

There are differing views about this. Some people claim that Heilmann learned of the imminent danger to his chief while moving office on Saturday, August 29; according to this account, he telephoned Schulze-Boysen to give the alarm, rather than merely to say he would be unable to keep the appointment on the Wannsee. But in that case, would he have been content to leave a message with the maid? Surely he would have made every effort to contact Schulze-Boysen on that Saturday evening—and again on Sunday evening, after leaving work. After his day on the Wannsee, Schulze-Boysen went to the house of one of his Berlin friends, Hugo Buschmann, and stayed talking until four in the morning. According to Buschmann, he was "worn out, starved, and rather on edge." A normal reaction, if he was conscious of the slow tightening of the Gestapo net. But he asked Buschmann to arrange a meeting with a Croatian diplomat from Zagreb—which he scarcely would have done had he felt he was on the point of being taken prisoner. So Heilmann had certainly not warned him by then. Was this because he did not know of Schulze-Boysen's visit to Buschmann and was vainly waiting for him at his home address? The peril was so great that he would surely have waited until Schulze-Boysen got home, at about 4 A.M.; or if he thought Schulze-Boysen might not return home at all that night, he would surely have gone to see him at his Air Ministry office first thing next day! No, Heilmann was doubtless familiar with Kludow's progress, but he cannot have known of his decisive achievement in deciphering that Moscow telegram to Kent; the secret was still confined to the higher echelons of the Abwehr.

A hundred and eighteen arrests by the end of the first week of September, 1942! And from the first interrogations, Panzinger and Koppkow realized that the two mainstays of the entire organization were Arvid Harnack and Harro Schulze-Boysen.

21. Epitaph for Two Germans

Readers interested exclusively in the history of espionage may skip this chapter. They know the hard facts—who was involved, and what kind of information was being passed to Moscow.

But others may be drawn to the two heroes of this episode and may wonder how a nephew of the distinguished theologian Harnack and a grandnephew of Admiral von Tirpitz came to be working for Soviet Intelligence. And they may be puzzled by the motives that impelled these two men to shed rivers of their compatriots' blood. For anyone wishing to explore the real identities of the chiefs of this absurdly ill-organized but remarkably effective network, something more is needed than the dry cataloguing of facts and dates. One of the clerks at the Center would soon be transferring two record cards to the archive section—the agents "Arvid" and "Coro" had been liquidated; those had been their pseudonyms. We are no longer concerned with them as agents, but as human beings.

Physically, they present no difficulty; the photographs speak for themselves. Harro was a splendid Nordic specimen—tall and fair, with blue eyes and chiseled features. Fortner remarks bitterly of him, "And yet he seemed a German officer right down to his fingertips." As for Libertas, his wife, a written order was issued immediately

after her arrest, stating that two officials must always be present
ing her interrogations, for she was so disturbingly beautiful th
was feared she might fatally undermine the resolve of a lone examiner.
The Harnacks were more ordinary. Arvid had a placid face and the
look of a scholarly man. He seemed to be reserved, sparing of words
or gestures, and not easily moved. He and Mildred cannot often
have gone sailing on the Wannsee.

They themselves are silent forever, and the only way to form
an over-all impression of their personalities was to piece together the
glimpses supplied by those who had fought with or against them,
in the same way that the police try to build up a picture of an unknown suspect.

It was a strange quest.

———◆———

Veterans of the Abwehr and the Gestapo seldom speak of the
subject without indulging in heavy caricature. This, according to
one of them, is how Lieutenant Herbert Gollnow was enlisted in the
Red Orchestra:

"Gollnow worked for Air Intelligence; his job was liaison with
the Air Ministry, where he met Schulze-Boysen. He was a young
boy and had risen from humble origins through sheer hard work.
His father was dead. He adored his mother, who thought the world
of him.

"Gollnow's outstanding quality was ambition. He was determined
to go places, and he felt he was wasting his time in Berlin. Promotions and decorations were earned at the front, not in the corridors
of ministries. Who better than Schulze-Boysen could pull strings and
get him shipped to a fighting unit? Gollnow was dazzled that a figure
like Schulze-Boysen, with such powerful connections, should con-
descend to take an interest in him. But, of course, Schulze-Boysen
hadn't the slightest intention of getting him shipped out; Gollnow
was far too useful to him in Berlin. But he promised him the earth
and a golden future, and began by inviting him to lectures at the
Academy of Foreign Affairs. That was the first stage. Stage two
consisted in persuading Gollnow to learn a foreign language. A
good knowledge of English, for example, was indispensable for a real
career. Schulze-Boysen suggested that he advertise for a teacher in
the personal columns of the Berlin newspapers, and promised to help
him sift the replies.

"There were only two of them. The first was from an elderly schoolmaster who, reasonably enough, set forth his charges. Schulze-Boysen's advice was: 'Why not try the other—it might be a more attractive proposition.' The other 'offer' was from a woman—Mildred Harnack. Gollnow went to see her and was welcomed in the most charming manner. 'I'm an American,' she said, 'and it will give me great pleasure to chat with you in English over afternoon tea.' Gollnow, greatly awed by his surroundings and by this society lady, stammered a few words about prices. She waved the question aside and said smilingly, 'Don't even think of it! I wouldn't dream of charging you—I'm only too happy to have the chance to speak my own language.'

"Gollnow related all this to Schulze-Boysen, who clapped him on the back and exclaimed: 'Terrific! Free lessons from a pretty woman! Herbert, you're the luckiest man alive!'

"Gollnow's dominant feeling was one of unease, however, as he sat stiff and upright in the Harnacks' drawing room, tea cup in hand staring obediently at Mildred's lips as she demonstrated how to pronounce English vowel sounds. He had gone straight into the army from a modest family background, and simply did not know how to cope with the social refinements suddenly thrust upon him. One of his worst moments came when Arvid Harnack, wearing his usual stern expression, arrived unannounced halfway through a lesson. By this time, Gollnow had begun to consider it strange that Mildred should entertain him alone for hours on end without her husband objecting. He also felt that his teacher's amiability exceeded the limits of mere pedagogic concern.

"When he saw Harnack come into the drawing room, he first thought that an unpleasant scene was about to take place; then he reflected that upper-class people acted according to a very strange code indeed. For Harnack was as charming as could be, inquiring about his progress in English, and the nature of his duties in the army. Gollnow, blushing bright red, mumbled that he did not feel free to answer this second question. Harnack gave him an understanding smile and said, 'You know, I'm an *Oberregierungsrat* at the Ministry of Economics myself, so I'm quite used to keeping secrets.'

"This was sufficient to awaken a feeling of trust in Gollnow. He let it be known that he worked for the Abwehr. Slowly but surely the talk came round to the military situation, and Harnack deplored the way the fighting had bogged down on the eastern front —this was during the winter of 1941–42.

"Gollnow hastened to reassure him. 'Don't worry,' he said, 'things will soon be moving again.'

" 'I'm amazed that you should say that,' replied Harnack, 'for if an offensive were planned, I would surely know about it!'

" 'Forgive me, *Herr Oberregierungsrat*, but in this matter I may be perhaps better able to speak than you.' And Gollnow, delighted at this opportunity to show himself in an important light, revealed that a regiment of Caucasian prisoners had been persuaded to change sides and were now being trained for the infantry. They were to be parachuted into their own region, behind the Russian lines, at the start of the next offensive.

"Of course, it turned out later that the Russians had all the plans for this offensive. Mind you, staff officers turn out plans by the dozen —that's what they're there for—and most of them simply gather dust in somebody's office. But this story about Caucasians being trained in sabotage had the authentic, irrefutable touch which persuaded Moscow that the plan to attack the oil fields had now gone beyond the hypothetical stage: practical preparations were being made.

"As soon as the others learned that Gollnow was pliable, things happened very fast. In other words, Mildred slept with him. So did Libertas, Schulze-Boysen's wife. In fact, they were both Lesbians, so Gollnow was treated to some pretty titillating experiences. They had no difficulty in turning his head completely and making him forget his most rudimentary loyalties—and even his ambition. Just think of it! Two women, one of them at least—Libertas—a real dazzler, and both of them cultured aristocrats to their fingertips. And here they were, offering themselves to him—showing him pleasures he had never even dreamed of!

"Gollnow gave away all he knew. He knew plenty. At that period, the Abwehr was sending sabotage squads behind the Russian lines. Not one of them ever came back. All on account of Gollnow. And you know, until the Schulze-Boysen gang was arrested we had the greatest admiration for Soviet counterespionage, we thought it was absolutely infallible! Gollnow even slipped the Russians information about the agents we were smuggling into Britain, and our attempts to sabotage the planes flying between the U.S.A. and Portugal—all sorts of things. Believe me, he would have betrayed his own mother for the right to attend the 'fourteen-points' parties. These were surprise parties organized by the Schulze-Boysen gang. The cream of Berlin society came to them—high-ranking officers and functionaries and the aristocracy in droves. The women were not allowed to wear more than the equivalent of the fourteen points allowed as the yearly ration. You couldn't buy much material with fourteen points, so the women were more or less naked. Naturally enough, the guests at these parties soon settled down to wholesale adultery.

"But note that the women weren't alone in practicing this method of recruitment. Take those two young men in the decoding department, Heilmann and Traxl. Don't think that Schulze-Boysen got them by winning them over to his fairly hazy political doctrines—good heavens, no. He went to bed with them, and that was that! Heilmann was mad about him. He would have followed him to the gates of hell—as indeed he did. And he wasn't the only one. Harro was as successful with the men as Libertas was with the women."

Margaret Boveri says of Mildred: "With her fine blond hair, sternly brushed back at the temples, her clear, direct blue eyes with their level gaze, she embodied for me the very prototype of the American Puritan." *

Axel von Harnack, Arvid's cousin says: "Mildred had bright eyes and a luminous expression. Her features were framed by blond, sleek hair. Her warm personality made her liked wherever she went. The very least one can say about her is that she was one of nature's aristocrats. . . . Her direct, open ways went perfectly with the extreme simplicity of her clothes and her general style of living." †

Otto Meyer, ‡ an eminent civil servant in wartime Germany, says: "Schulze-Boysen a homosexual? First I've heard of it. He had so many affairs with women that I don't see how he could have had the time to sleep with men as well. As for Libertas, it's true she led a very free life. She was a strange girl, high-strung as a thoroughbred; I'd almost call her 'macabre.' Friends of mine went to some of their parties that ended in orgies. But they loved each other, make no mistake about that. Theirs was a love-match. As for the debauchery, that began toward the end of their lives, I don't know whether to ascribe it to their espionage activities, the constant fear and tension, or whether they cold-bloodedly resorted to vice to corrupt possible sources of information. Mildred was neither beautiful nor sexy, but she had a

---

* Margaret Boveri, *Treason in the Twentieth Century* (New York: G. P. Putnam's Sons, 1963), p. 256.

† Axel von Harnack, "Arvid und Mildred Harnack," *Die Gegenwart*, 31 January 1947.

‡ Pseudonym chosen by the author.

captivating intelligence, an undeniable charm. Like everyone else, she used to have affairs. But at the same time she remained very pure, very moral. Each new relationship was *le grand amour*, the one great passion of her life. Schulze-Boysen had made her completely his, and between them they were the real mainstay of the network."

Ernst von Salomon says: "Harro a pederast? I know nothing about it. It's quite possible. What of it? It's true he and Lib allowed each other complete sexual freedom, but what's so extraordinary about that? They were merely keeping up the bohemian style of living which had been so common in Berlin between the wars. You have to have lived through it to understand. In those days you couldn't even get a kick out of sleeping with your best friend's wife—it was all too easy. As for Mildred Harnack, there was a story to the effect that she had tried to approach Hitler in the hope of seducing him. He hadn't even deigned to look at her, which is why she hated him. But as for her leading a fast life, seducing young officers and all the rest of it, I don't believe it for a moment—for one thing, she was far too ugly!"

According to survivors of the network, it was standard security practice to camouflage dealings between agents of opposite sexes as amorous encounters and assignations. They are indignant at the deplorable character sketches given them by the Gestapo. They reject out of hand any allegation that might tarnish the halos of their martyred colleagues.

Otto Meyer and Ernst von Salomon are obviously right: the vicious caricatures of the Gestapo and the simon-pure pictures of their friends give equally distorted and irrelevant impressions of the men and women of the Berlin network. In short, the people concerned were neither angels nor brutes. One might have guessed as much.

———◆———

There are no disputes about Harnack. This is how he is described by Reinhold Schönbrunn, one of his old political friends:

> Fanatic, rigid, industrious, conspicuously energetic and efficient, Harnack was not precisely a likable person, not a jolly good fellow; always serious, he had little sense of humor. . . . There was something of the puritan in this man, something narrow and doctrinaire, but he was extremely devoted. His wife, Mildred, shared these traits with Arvid.*

———

* David J. Dallin, *Soviet Espionage*, p. 236.

And the sketch drawn by Axel von Harnack, Arvid's cousin, comes fairly close to Schönbrunn's description:

Arvid had an ingenious, brooding, meditative mind, was skilled in debating and always inclined to engage in it. A certain hardness was characteristic of him; moreover, he was inclined to be sarcastic, especially when debating with an inferior adversary. He was very ambitious, though his self-confidence was based on recognized achievements. . . .*

Even veterans of the Gestapo acknowledge Harnack's intelligence and sincerity. They refrain from involving him in their extravagant accounts of sexual orgies. Panzinger, who was no fool, spent long hours discussing political and economic problems with him. Even the judges who passed sentence on him paid tribute to his scholarship and his austere virtues.

This respect was initially prompted by Harnack's dry-as-dust mastery of facts and figures. He impressed people almost as much as he bored them. Even more to the point, he was never anything other than a brilliant right-hand man—as is so often the case with people of that particular brand of intelligence. Right-hand man to a man less clever, less well-balanced, less cultured than he, but endowed with an almost frightening vitality, tireless in play and in work, born to charm and excite people, a natural leader: Harro Schulze-Boysen, the guiding spirit of the Berlin network.

"He was a complete buccaneer, witty and clever, but impulsive and unrestrained, reckless, given to exploiting his friends, ambitious in the extreme, an innate and fanatical revolutionary." †

A severe but debatable portrait, its author was Alexander Kraell, president of the court which judged Schulze-Boysen and his friends. His nationality and the office he had held were bound to incline him to severity. On the other hand, one would have expected Allen Dulles to have sung Schulze-Boysen's praises; as Roosevelt's envoy to Switzerland during the war, Dulles' mission was to encourage anti-Nazi movements inside Germany. But here is what he says:

---

* Alex von Harnack, *loc. cit.*
† Evidence given on August 6, 1948, at the time of the inquiry into the Roeder Affair. (This was one of the de-Nazification inquiries undergone by all of the responsible Nazis. Note that these were conducted by the German authorities themselves and had nothing to do with the postwar trials held by the Allies.)

At first he opposed both Nazis and Communists—the former he considered too bourgeois, the latter too bureaucratic. He concocted a political farrago around the idea that there was no Left or Right, that political parties did not form a straight line but an incomplete circle, which did not quite close. The Communists and Nazis, of course, were at the unclosed ends of the circle. Schulze-Boysen decided his party would fill that gap and close the circle. He was young, blond, Nordic—a product of the German Youth movement. Always wearing a black sweater, he went around with revolutionaries, surrealists and the rag-tag and bobtail of the "lost generation." *

One is startled to find such contemptuous coldness directed at a man who contributed so amply to the defeat of Nazism, and therefore to the Allied victory. Admittedly, Dulles—future head of the C.I.A.—is what one might call an "innate and fanatical" anti-Communist. Can it be that he viewed Schulze-Boysen as just another loathsome Soviet agent?

And what has the officially authorized German Resistance to say of the Berlin network? Not a word. It ignores it. Indeed, it does better; it spurns it.

True, that particular Resistance movement was somewhat right-wing, whereas Schulze-Boysen belonged emphatically to the left. The old gentlemen conspiring with and on behalf of General Beck used to hold their meetings in aristocratic clubrooms. Unlike Schulze-Boysen, they did not go recruiting in working-class areas. They looked for salvation from the West, not from the East. And yet the gulf was not as wide as all that. After all, Count von Stauffenberg, hero of the attempt on Hitler's life, was ready to negotiate with Moscow—and in no grudging spirit—if the British and Americans turned a deaf ear to his proposals. Indeed, a few days before the assassination bid, he made contact with senior members of the underground Communist Party and tried to get them to participate.

True, the honorable gentlemen of the right-wing opposition tended to assign their activities to the loftiest metaphysical plane. They insisted, for example, that they were toiling "for the moral and religious renaissance of the German people, for the suppression of hatred and deceit, and for the rebuilding of a European community."

---

* Allen W. Dulles, *Germany's Underground* (New York: Macmillan, 1947), p. 100.

Borne up by these noble dreams, they shrank from the thought of sullying their hands with espionage—with one exception, a really notable exception, for they themselves maintain that he was the best and noblest among them and the author of their richest endeavors. The man was Colonel Oster of the Abwehr, deputy to Admiral Canaris. This *"chevalier sans peur et sans reproche"* passed German military secrets to the enemy in exactly the same manner as Schulze-Boysen. Of course, his informations were not taken seriously by the Western governments concerned. But if they had been—and this was certainly Oster's hope and intention—then his treason would have caused as much German bloodshed in the west as Schulze-Boysen's caused in the east.

Here again, it is clear that Oster and his friends were prepared to see Germany's sons mowed down by the British and French, but not by the Russians. But one might have quarreled with the line of action chosen by Schulze-Boysen without denying the purity of his intentions, the importance of his role and the courage he showed at every turn. Instead of which, he is one of the forgotten men of history, while Oster is lauded to the skies.

The memoirs of Ulrich von Hassell, one of the leaders of the German Resistance, are entitled *Of Another Germany*—in other words, a Germany not taken in by Nazism, but even fighting it. If anyone could claim citizenship in that "Other Germany," it was Schulze-Boysen. Yet in the eyes of Alexander Kraell (an adversary) and of Allen Dulles (an ally)—both of them later champions of the Bonn Federal Republic—the "Other Germany" to which he belonged was Herr Ulbricht's Germany, East Germany, where he would be today if the executioner had spared him. This explains their tacit condemnation of Harro Schulze-Boysen's activities; but it does not explain the cool reserve, even the thinly disguised contempt, with which they regard him as a human being. It is odd, to say the least, that two such different men should hold such similar attitudes.

Even more surprising is the deafening silence which nowadays surrounds Schulze-Boysen's grave. The general public cares little for high politics and its changing fashions. A traitor is a traitor, whatever his master's identity. And to this general public, Schulze-Boysen is more than likely to seem a mere spy, a mere traitor to his country. Yet the same words could be applied to Richard Sorge, and Sorge's name is legendary. People accept Sorge; they admire his achievements even if they cannot agree with him. He will never appear on the honor roll of the German Resistance, but he is widely considered "the greatest spy of all time." The world marvels at that celebrated telegram from Sorge which helped drive the Germans back from Moscow; yet no one gives a second thought to Schulze-Boysen's telegram that paved the way for victory at Stalingrad. At least Sorge's technical skill is acknowledged, but Schulze-Boysen is denied even that.

In the first place, he doesn't seem to be serious. He didn't impress people—a bourgeois with bohemian tastes. The black sweater carefully chosen to set off his handsome head of blond hair. All-night discussions in fashionable bars, surrealist poetry and—even more embarrassing—surrealist politics. No left or right, but a circle. The Communists? Too bureaucratic. The Nazis? Too bourgeois. As Ernst von Salomon has said, "he used to proclaim his intention of blowing that whole fossilized, antiquated world sky-high. He was all in favor of a national revolution, but unlike the Nazis he wanted to see it carried out by the elite and not by the common herd, whom he despised. Hitler, in his view, was merely a very vulgar person with whom it was infra dig to associate." So he placed a few firecrackers under the tired old world and then went home to bed in his artist's studio in the Altenburger Strasse. His family probably thought he was merely sowing his wild oats, and before long he would recall his position as a descendant of Admiral von Tirpitz and return to the fold, accepting all its traditions and rituals. And his family might well have been right, had it not been for that little upstart Hitler.

In the event, however, he was picked up by the SS, imprisoned in a bunker, and worked over by louts who understood nothing of the subtleties of "politics in the round." This was the real turning point for Schulze-Boysen. In the furnace heat of the bunker, soft clay hardened to a firm and compact entity—a solid mass of hate. He was never to forget his sufferings and humiliation. He was never to forgive. Salomon met him in the street at a time when his face was still swollen from his beating; he had lost half an ear. "I have put my revenge in cold storage," said Schulze-Boysen, "and now I'm allied with the people who are best at fighting that gang." Six years later, he said more or less the same thing to Hugo Buschmann: "In 1933, I was jailed by the SS—the first of several such experiences. Since then, I have had only one aim: revenge!" *

Klaus Fuchs too was brutally treated by the SS at about the

---

* Hugo Buschmann, "De la résistance au défaitisme," Les Temps modernes, 1949, Nos. 46–47, p. 266.

same time. Subsequently he left Germany, worked for the Allies in the field of atomic research, let the Russians have the secrets of the bomb, and was caught, tried, convicted. But in Fuchs's case, the longing for revenge was inspired by something more serious than a mere beating. His father was in a concentration camp; his mother committed suicide; later, one of his sisters threw herself under a train. The extent of Fuchs's sufferings cannot but command respect. What he later did had a measure of justification. Schulze-Boysen's mishap was a trifle by comparison; for him the fists of the SS guards were his first taste of reality; a rich boy who had got into a scrape. And, sure enough, his family soon got him out; they complained to Levetzow, head of the Berlin police, and he sent a squad of men around to rescue him. Schulze-Boysen emerged from the bunker mentally and physically battered, shorn of the pleasant pipe dreams of a would-be poet and amateur politician. He joined forces with the Communists— not from intellectual conviction, but because "they were the people who were best at fighting that gang." Doctrine did not interest him; in 1939, he was practically ignorant about Marx and Lenin. Nothing could have been further from the sound ideological convictions of a Sorge or a Harnack. In the last analysis, only one thing drove him: the urge to erase the pain left by those blows in the SS bunker. It sounds perilously inadequate.

———◆———

Upon this weak foundation reposed the wonderfully efficient machinery of the Berlin network. One can only marvel at the contrast between motivation and results: it is like an engine operating at full power on a thin trickle of fuel.

Hatred can blind. It can also clarify, refine, purge. With Schulze-Boysen, it instantly plucked the scales from his eyes. From then on, the gaze which he directed at the world was absolutely lucid, almost scientific. Impossible not to smile at the political hot air he spouted before 1933, difficult not to acknowledge the accuracy of the forecast he made in a letter to his father on October 11, 1938: "I predict to you today that a world war will break out in 1940–41 at latest, though probably by next spring. It will be followed by a class war in Europe. But I maintain emphatically that Austria and Czechoslovakia were the first two battles in the new war."

The day the third battle (Poland) began—and, with it, the Second World War—Harro Schulze-Boysen gave a party to celebrate his birthday. This is how Hugo Buschmann describes it:

It was attended by writers, actors, painters, a film producer, doctors, lawyers, pretty women—and it wasn't exactly a birthday they were celebrating, but the outbreak of war. What illusions those people had! They were all convinced that the end of the Third Reich was in sight; indeed, most of them thought it was imminent. . . . Only the Air Force officer, whose jaw quivered with hatred whenever the Nazis were mentioned, offered any objection; he didn't want to be a wet blanket; that little upstart, Hitler, was bound to be defeated in the end, but it wasn't going to be that easy. The speaker was Harro Schulze-Boysen. Then he went on dancing, something he was very good at. The women watched him admiringly. Eventually, he grew tired of all the uproar. He drew me into a corner and, fastening upon a remark of mine, he said: "Poland is about to go under, but that's only an interlude. It will be the signal for the armies and air forces of the West to destroy one another. . . . Those people," he went on, with a nod toward his gaily chattering guests, "overestimate the military strength of the West. In the first place, Britain still needs to arm herself. They have no air force to speak of, either in England or in France. But they have a breathing space until next spring, for key operations in Poland will take up the rest of this year. That lunatic Hitler still thinks he'll make mincemeat of Britain as soon as he has finished off Poland. He imagines he'll then be able to follow the plan of *Mein Kampf* and finally direct his war powers against the East. No, the British are bound to stand up to him. They can't wriggle out of it by making concessions. One day the odds will be equal. And when that happens, the established order of things will be upset from one end of Europe to the other, because the forces of the bourgeoisie will be worn out from fighting each other." *

The lucidity of this analysis was more than matched by Schulze-Boysen's implacability when the time came for action. He put every ounce of energy and hatred into the battle with "that gang"—although, once the war started, the term "that gang" inevitably widened to include not only the Nazis but his compatriots, his brothers, the whole German people. Not for him the ambiguities which disturbed the consciences of so many Germans opposed to Hitler. They were aghast to see the blood of friends and relatives shed in foolish attempts to further a senseless enterprise, yet at the same time they took secret pride in the exploits achieved by that bloodshed. They wanted to see Hitler crushed, but were distressed by talk of a German defeat. And such torments were not confined to Hitler's right-wing opponents, the reactionary nationalists of the Herren Club. Hugo Buschmann was a left-winger, but he recalls: "Several times when I

* H. Buschmann, *loc. cit.*, p. 264.

heard close personal friends talking airily in this fashion, people who had been politically active before 1933, I asked them, 'Do you want us to lose the war—yes or no?' Nearly always, after a moment of nervous hesitation, the answer was No." *

Some people in Germany managed to surmount these contradictions; they recognized that the end of Nazism could only be achieved on the far side of national defeat. But they did nothing to foster that defeat. They were not strong-minded enough to take hold of the dagger and stab their fellow Germans in the back. Schulze-Boysen, on the other hand, went on stabbing and stabbing until the day the Gestapo came and snatched the dagger from his hands. And without the least sign of inner anguish or conflict. Never once did his heart rebel against the cruel edicts of his mind. And he had no patience with the softhearted. He one day remarked to a lachrymose friend: "You have the overresponsive tear gland of the *petit bourgeois.*"

But his hatred really must have been white-hot, or surely even he would have wept at times! It is not as if he confined himself to transmitting facts and figures as disembodied as some general plan of campaign. One thinks of those parachutists the Abwehr used to drop behind Soviet lines, and whose names and faces Schulze-Boysen knew perfectly well. One pictures them, pale and grim as they clambered aboard their aircraft; sheep cased in steel and armed with lethal weapons, but sheep all the same, bound for the slaughter which Schulze-Boysen had prepared for them.

Perhaps this exaggerates the extent to which revenge governed his behavior; perhaps he himself exaggerated it when he roared his hatred at Salomon and Buschmann. He was certainly a man who thrived on storms—they alone used his energies to the full. In pre-1933 Berlin, he had been like a vessel becalmed on still waters. Not until the Nazi squall began to blow were his sails stretched taut at last; it took the bunker incident to give a pretext for unleashing this great store of unused vitality.

Arvid Harnack and Harro Schulze-Boysen—a pedant who had stopped asking himself questions because he knew all the answers, and a hothead burning for fulfillment and perhaps revenge as well, anxious to see his own scars mirrored in the world at large. For a year they traveled side by side along this road strewn with dead and wounded, feeling no dismay, deaf to all the groans, blind to the blood and tears

---

* Hugo Buschmann, *loc. cit.*, p. 273.

—one obedient to the call of history, the other exclusively concerned with his own small destiny.

If they are unmourned and unsaluted twenty-five years later, and if no adolescent heart ever beats the faster for reading of their exploits, it may well be because they were both somehow lacking in humanity.

Just the reverse were the members of the official German Resistance movement. They were brimming over with humanity and eaten up with doubts, scruples, crises of conscience. Goerdeler, Beck, Hassell—how preferable they all seem, with their fine, tormented souls, to robots like Harnack and Schulze-Boysen! And, for that matter praise continues to be heaped on them. Twenty or thirty books have been written about their activities—seldom in history can so many lines have been devoted to men who had so little influence on events. For the sum total of their achievements is easily arrived at: zero. As with Schulze-Boysen, there is a startling contrast between motives and results. But in their case, it is reversed: admirable motives, infinitesimal results. After years of plotting and conspiring and whispering, they finally made up their minds to kill Hitler. And they bungled it. Net result: a brief spell of deafness for the Führer, from perforated eardrums. Stauffenberg was heroic, Goerdeler expended amazing energy, Beck and Hassell demonstrated that they were perfect gentlemen; but they did not curtail the war by *a single day* or shorten by *one hour* the sufferings the Nazi regime was imposing on countless millions of human beings, including their fellow countrymen. History, which is less concerned with intentions than with deeds, will probably say that the German Resistance movement was made in the likeness of its leader, General Beck, who within hours of the unsuccessful attempt on the Führer made two unsuccessful attempts to commit suicide; General Fromm had to turn to an officer and say, "Help the old gentleman." He had failed to kill Hitler, and he could not even kill himself without assistance.

Meanwhile, the SS were busily classifying humanity according to their own strange lights—exterminating with bullets and gas what they chose to regard as the lower strata. They too were certainly not troubled by overresponsive tear glands. The very nature of these men no doubt called for opponents like Harro Schulze-Boysen and Arvid

Harnack, opponents as utilitarian and grim—but, at the same time, as effective—as a steel blade.

It would be unfair to conclude without pointing out that there is one country where Schulze-Boysen and his friends are acknowledged and commemorated—East Germany. But in the books and plays devoted to them, no mention is ever made of their secret transmitters and the hundreds of messages they wired to Moscow. Attention is focused exclusively on the network's underground political activities: it used to publish pamphlets and leaflets and a fortnightly news sheet. The survivors of the Berlin group, with the sole exception of Günther Weisenborn, all strictly observe the secrecy imposed on their intelligence work. Thus, Schulze-Boysen is scaled down to a heroic paster of billboards, and his group is reduced to a mere bunch of political agitators with little to show for their efforts. It is as though the agents of the Berlin network, already hanged on the Nazi gallows, were being strangled anew by the high priests of German Communism.

———◆———

Thus, by the late summer of 1942, German counterespionage had cleaned up Berlin as well as Brussels and Amsterdam. But far from appeasing the Nazi leaders, these successes unleashed their fury by disclosing the size and efficiency of the Soviet network. Here was an organization masterminded in Paris, garnering information in Prague, Berlin, Madrid, anywhere you cared to mention, and wiring it to Moscow on transmitters concealed in Brussels and Amsterdam. All this at a time when frontiers were supposed to be impenetrable, and when most of Europe was subject to the most severe police repression ever known. The Gestapo and the Abwehr were told, in no uncertain terms, that they must capture the man behind these operations. Hitler demanded that Himmler supply him with a day-by-day progress report. The Rote Kapelle Kommando pulled out of Brussels and Berlin, and centered all its resources in Paris, with the specific intention of tracking down the Big Chief.

It was headed by Karl Giering, that master detective. With him he brought a crack team of about twenty men, and he also had unlimited cooperation from the Paris Abwehr and Gestapo and their French auxiliaries. Here, without comment, are the replies given by

Franz Fortner, the Abwehr's liaison with the Kommando, to questions about his colleagues in the Kommando:

"*Willy Berg?*"

"*Giering's right-hand man. Fifty or thereabouts. Tiny, practically a dwarf. He was hard as nails, unscrupulous. A real butcher.*"

"*Richard Voss?*"

"*Physically, he was Berg's opposite—extremely tall and broad-shouldered, with fair hair. A butcher.*"

"*Otto Schwab?*"

"*Yes, a small man. He had a pliant, conciliatory nature. He preferred guile to force.*"

"*Ella Kempka?*"

"*Ah, the secretary. Rather a pretty blonde. She attended every one of the interrogations, without showing the slightest feeling; she had seen plenty of others in Berlin, where she worked at Gestapo headquarters.*"

"*Eric Jung?*"

"*Tall, slim, athletic-looking. He was always very pleasant to me. Far from pleasant to the prisoners, though. A butcher!*"

"*Rolf Richter?*"

"*Hard! Terribly hard! Even with women, he was merciless.*"
Et cetera, et cetera.

PART II

THE BIG CHIEF

22. The Kommando in Paris

On arriving in Paris in late summer, 1942, the Kommando moved into the headquarters of the French Sûreté in the Rue des Saussaies; it was allotted a suite of offices on the fourth floor. On the very first day Abraham Raichman, the Brussels forger, was sent out into the streets with instructions to pick up the threads leading to Trepper. The trusted repository of the Gestapo's hopes, Raichman set up house in the capital together with his mistress Malvina. He was free to come and go as he pleased. The only thing he *had* to do was meet Fortner every morning and give him a progress report. The meetings took place over breakfast at the Café Viel, in the Boulevard des Italiens.

Raichman paid a round of visits to those "letterboxes" who happened to be known to him. With each of them, he left a message asking the Big Chief to meet him at the earliest possible moment; he even named a time and place. Several hours in advance of each rendezvous, Giering would patiently spread the police net in which he hoped to catch his big fish. But Trepper never showed up.

The Kommando had another line of approach: Simone Pheter, who worked in the Paris office of the Belgian Chamber of Commerce. Thanks to Simone and her correspondent in the typing pool of the Brussels Bourse, the French and Belgian networks had been able to communicate with one another behind a seemingly foolproof official façade. The system had operated perfectly until investigations into Romeo Springer had thrown light on his recruit at the Bourse and, in turn, on her Paris correspondent. Hitherto the Kommando had been content to keep a close eye on their correspondence; but now it was time for action. A letter posted in Brussels asked Simone Pheter to organize a meeting between her chief and an agent from Belgium—this was to be Raichman. Not for a second did Simone suspect that the letter was a forgery. She told her correspondent the date and the hour of the meeting, which was to be held in a Paris restaurant. When the day came, she herself took up a position in the restaurant, realized that it was under surveillance, and simulated a violent fit of hysterics only a few seconds before her chief walked into the room. The other customers gathered round her. Her chief arrived, saw the press of people, sensed danger and stole quietly away. He was Leon Grossvogel.

Yet it would be wrong to suggest that Raichman failed to earn the pieces of silver which were slipped to him at regular intervals. The simple truth was that he knew little of the Paris network; hence his failure to penetrate it. On the other hand, he subsequently worked wonders in Lyons, which had become the new theater of operations for the surviving members of the Brussels network: Germaine Schneider, Romeo Springer and also Schumacher, the man who had offered to make coffee for Fortner at the time of Wenzel's arrest. Raichman knew them all and easily reestablished contact with them. The fact that Lyons was in the Free Zone was no longer an obstacle to the Kommando's activities; for a month earlier—in September 1942— negotiations with Vichy had opened the unoccupied part of the country to German counterespionage. Admiral Canaris himself had traveled to Paris to see that the matter was successfully concluded. Thanks to the docility of the Vichy government's envoys, two hundred and eighty Abwehr and Gestapo agents crossed the demarcation line on September 28, equipped with false papers provided by the French police. Most of them went straight to Lyons and moved into lodgings rented in advance. Their prime purpose was to trace and silence a score of transmitters sending messages to Britain from positions in and around the city. But they took advantage of this opportunity to sweep up the residue of the Brussels network—with the help of Raichman, who was promptly dispatched to the scene. As for the teams sent to Marseilles, they were hunting Kent and Margarete Barcza, who, according to Malvina, had gone to earth somewhere in the district.

But these were small fry compared to the Big Chief. What did the authorities know about him after fifteen months of investigation? They had his photograph, the one found at the Rue des Atrébates. They knew one of his aliases, Gilbert, given away by Myra Sokol. They knew, from Wenzel and Yefremov, that he was now operating from Paris. And that was all. Three transmission centers had been destroyed (Brussels, Amsterdam, Berlin), dozens of agents had been arrested, but the Red Orchestra's internal security system was so strict that not a single line led to the master spy!

Unless Simex could provide a clue.

Giering already had some knowledge of its Paris branch through the watch kept on Simexco in Brussels—the two firms exchanged a considerable business correspondence. Giering's suspicions were confirmed by a visit to the record office of the Seine District Commercial Court, where the company had been registered on October 16, 1941, and listed as Number 285,031 S. Among the shareholders was Leon Grossvogel. Giering knew from Yefremov that Grossvogel was one of the Big Chief's lieutenants.

But there could be no question of searching the entire trade register of the Seine area or requesting information from the French police; the enemy was everywhere, walls had ears! Giering and Fortner decided to make inquiries about Simex at the headquarters of the Todt Organization.

◆

Fortner says: "We decided to take every last precaution and avoid any slip, however small, which might give us away. For this time we were dealing with the Big Chief himself! Anyway, we called at the Todt Organization headquarters in the Champs-Élysées (we were wearing civvies, of course), and asked to see Hauptsturmführer Nikholai, the Gestapo's liaison officer. As a blind, we introduced ourselves as representatives of a German company in Paris on business, and anxious to obtain certain information. Oh, we couldn't afford to take any chances! For instance, how were we to know that the receptionist to whom we handed our cards wasn't one of the Big Chief's agents? And there were Frenchmen everywhere—in the waiting room, in the corridors, even in the offices themselves. Anyway it was simple: Giering and I, we distrusted everybody.

"We waited and waited. Hours went by. Giering began to lose patience. And all to no avail, for in the end the receptionist informed us that Nikholai was too busy to see anyone and we'd have to come back another time! We were rather put out.

"Next morning we returned to the Todt Organization, but this time we went prepared: Giering had in his pocket a certificate signed by General von Stülpnagel, commander in chief of *Gross Paris*, stating who we were and demanding total cooperation from all and sundry. We presented ourselves to the receptionist—still as businessmen—and he told us to wait. But Giering and I had no intention of waiting; we flared up and insisted that he inform Nikholai of our arrival without delay. He walked off and we followed him; as soon as he opened the office door, we pushed past him. Nikholai tried to shut us out, but I put my foot in the door, and that was that! He stood there, crimson-faced in his black SS uniform, bellowing insults at us, until Giering handed him the certificate. You should have seen the effect. He calmed down in a flash and became very respectful; in fact he looked scared. Giering made him stand to attention and swear that he would never breathe a word about what we were about to say to him. You should have seen his face!

"At this point I took out my photograph of Trepper and asked, 'Do you know this man?'

" 'I should say so! A marvelous character!'

"Giering and I looked at each other.

" 'What do you mean by that?'

" 'Well,' said Nikholai, 'he's a businessman with whom we've done a lot of trade during the past year. Among other things, he has supplied a good deal of material for the Atlantic Wall. He's extremely well-disposed toward us, extremely cooperative . . . I like him very much.'

" 'We'd like to meet him. Is that possible?'

" 'Nothing could be easier. His *Ausweis* for the Free Zone is due to expire in a few days, and any moment now he'll be calling me and asking me to renew it.'

"After that, we asked him a few more questions. He said the most flattering things about Simex—'a really sound firm, that one, really collaborating sincerely with the Occupation authorities'—it was like Brussels all over again. And then we left, after reminding him of his oath of secrecy. It was agreed that he'd tip us off as soon as he had made his appointment with the Big Chief.

"But do you know what that fool Nikholai did? Without even warning us or asking our advice! Instead of waiting for Trepper to contact him of his own accord, he wrote and hold him that his *Ausweis* was about to expire and asked him to call at the Todt and get it renewed. Not very subtle! Admittedly, Nikholai didn't realize we were dealing with the Big Chief; he must have thought we were on an ordinary case.

"We had no choice but to think up something else. But what? How were we to get the contact we needed without giving warning? We gave the matter a great deal of thought, and in the end we hit upon the solution: to continue the little game we had started with Nikholai. We must contact Simex, pass ourselves off as businessmen and propose them a deal. We worked out our plan with great care. We'd say we had come from Mainz to buy industrial diamonds. I need hardly tell you that at the time these were very scarce and much sought-after. A million and a half marks' worth of diamonds—it was enough to tempt anybody.

"We asked Nikholai how we should go about proposing the deal to Simex. 'Nothing simpler,' he said. 'Working for us here at Todt is a Madame Likhonin. She's on the best terms with the Simex people. You must speak to her.' To be safe, we made a few inquiries before we went and saw her. The results were reassuring; she was a fine woman, altogether admirable. The widow of the last Tsarist military attaché in Paris. A White Russian. Everyone at the Todt Organization sang her praises. In fact, her son worked there too. Really fine people. We contacted Madame Likhonin and suggested the diamonds deal to her. She was very excited about it, as you might expect, and promised to ask her connections at Simex. Giering and I pretended to be ultracautious merchants; we told her this was an enormous deal into which we were sinking all our assets, and that she must realize we were anxious for sound guarantees—in short, the contract would have to be signed by the managing director of Simex in person. She saw our point and promised to act without delay."

◆

By the autumn of 1942, Simex was no longer in the Champs-Élysées. The Lido building, that home of sharks and swindlers, was not at all to Alfred Corbin's liking. He felt it didn't "give an impression of soundness." In February, 1942, Emanuel Mignon, the company's general factotum, was told to look for new premises. That was easy; in those days, Paris was full of "To Let" signs. On February 20, Simex left its two cramped rooms at the Champs-Élysées and moved into a luxury apartment on the third floor of 89 Boulevard Haussmann, just opposite the church of St. Augustin. The second floor had been requisitioned and was occupied by a German official department.

For several months now, Alfred Corbin had known the truth about the firm of which he was nominal head; but it was not until the company moved office that Katz, Trepper's deputy, opened Mignon's eyes to Simex's real purpose and function. He suggested that Mignon join the Orchestra; but when Mignon said he already belonged to the Famille Martin network, it was decided that things

should remain as they were, since one of the golden rules of undercover work formally forbids working for two organizations at the
same time. And anyway, Emanuel Mignon's connections with Simex
soon came to an unexpected end; in September he disappeared for
reasons unrelated to our story.

"I was without news of him," says Madame Mignon, a blond,
blue-eyed Pasionaria with a strong, handsome face, spirited and precise
in her speech; "and, worse still, without money. After a week I
decided to go to see Monsieur Corbin and ask if I couldn't take over
my husband's job. He said he would have to refer the matter to his
board, but in the meantime he lent me a thousand francs to tide me
over. As a matter of fact, he never even asked me to give it back!
He was a very sweet man, really exceptionally kind. Forty-eight
hours later I received an express letter informing me that my request
had been accepted.

"That was how I came into Simex, and there I remained, for
the head of the Famille Martin network, Captain Darcy, insisted that
I continue to keep an eye on what was happening there. Naturally I
didn't know about the conversation between Katz and my husband;
nor did Darcy, apparently. I wasn't at all happy with my assignment.
Violent action was what I had been hoping for—tossing grenades at
Germans, assassinating people . . . But Darcy said I was far more
useful at Simex than with the *maquis*. And to think I used to give
all my reports to Charbonnier, that Gestapo thug! *

"Life at Simex was very pleasant and homelike. I was the first
to arrive, at about nine o'clock. A little later—at about nine-thirty—
Keller would arrive. I liked him very much. He was kind and considerate. And very learned. Mademoiselle Cointe was never there
before ten. She was dried up and sharp, with a cantankerous disposition—a spinster to her fingertips. But at least she had one thing in her
favor: her voice. It's marvelous. She used to sing all day long. Her
favorite song came from Smetana's *Bartered Bride*. Monsieur Corbin
was last to arrive at the office: he used to get in at about ten-thirty.
He often brought us food, for he had a farm, where he raised sheep
and cattle. Cigarettes, too. Thanks to him, we were never without
them.

---

* Monsieur and Madame Mignon were decorated with the Croix de Guerre
for the entire range of their activities as members of the Famille Martin network. Naturally, keeping an eye on Simex was only a very small part of their
work.

"I only saw Madame Likhonin once or twice: by the time I joined Simex, she was already out of favor. This was clear from the way Keller told me never to hand her the mail which was addressed to her, care of Boulevard Haussmann. I was to give it either to Mademoiselle Cointe or to Keller himself. But still, Madame Likhonin always made a considerable impression on people. She was a real thoroughbred, still very beautiful in spite of her age, and always perfectly elegant. My husband had told me that she was the mistress of Kessmeyer, one of the powers-that-be in the Todt Organization."

◆

Keller spoke, while his dog growled from the other side of the door: "Madame Likhonin was beautiful, but she looked her age. To me she looked like an adventuress. She was an important figure in the firm, for it was she who had brought us the Todt Organization as our clients. That was her private preserve; no one else was allowed to have a hand in deals with the Todt. Here's how the system operated—it was very simple. Brokers would turn up at the office and offer us goods of every kind. Monsieur Corbin would draw up the papers. I would translate them into German. Mademoiselle Cointe would type them out. Finally Madame Likhonin would propose them to the Todt, while I canvassed the other German organizations.

"Monsieur Gilbert often used to make things awkward for me. He would make me offer the Germans goods we didn't possess. The Germans used to get angry and demand delivery, and I had a terrible time getting out of it. At the time, I just couldn't make Monsieur Gilbert out. It amazed me that such a serious-minded man should do things like that. Afterward, of course, I realized that by offering the Germans goods he couldn't supply, he was able to get invaluable information about their needs and projects. It was the same with Monsieur Corbin. Several times he asked me to deliver messages to railway workers at the Gare de Lyon. I also used to pick up mail from a bar opposite the station; the proprietor slipped the letters inside a newspaper before handing them to me. Really, I imagined they had to do with black-market deals which called for particularly careful handling. I didn't look for any deeper explanation.

"Especially as I had nothing to complain about! My basic salary wasn't very high, but I received a five per cent commission on all purchases and sales I made. And this brought in enormous sums. We were living well. To say nothing of the food and cigarettes Monsieur

Corbin used to hand out so generously. Throughout that period, I ate only in the best black-market restaurants. No one can say we were deprived.

"One day I went to order a suit from a big tailor in the Avenue de l'Opéra. The tailor was wearing a suit made of a material I liked very much. So I ordered one made of the same cloth. But when it arrived I realized it wasn't new. It was the tailor's own suit—he had merely altered it to fit me. I told Madame Likhonin the story, and she said, 'Give me his name. I've got friends in the Gestapo. They'll attend to him.' The words made my blood run cold, and I began to look at her with a different eye.

"At this point she went for a vacation to Spa, in Belgium. She was gone for some time and several invoices were overdue, so Monsieur Corbin told me to call at the Todt Organization and ask them for payment. 'Come, now,' said the people at the Todt, 'these invoices were paid to Madame Likhonin long ago.' Monsieur Corbin was furious when he realized she had been embezzling, but when she got back, she wasn't at all put out. Far from it! She made a tremendous scene and accused me of poaching on her preserves—'The Todt is my concern and no one else's!'

"After this explosion, she called at Simex far less often. The atmosphere was no longer the same."

Fortner says: "Madame Likhonin brought us a quick reply on the diamond deal, as agreed, but it turned out to be negative. The head of Simex was unable to sign the contract. He had a serious heart condition and was undergoing treatment. It sounded fishy, but Nikholai confirmed that Trepper *did* have heart trouble and frequently convalesced at the Château des Ardennes, in Spa. We sent a team of men to the château, but there was no sign of him! 'This is quite intolerable,' we said to Madame Likhonin. 'We can't go on waiting. Are you handling the deal or not?' Next day she arrived all smiling. 'It's arranged,' she said. 'He'll travel to Brussels on such-and-such a date to sign the contract.' Yes, we had suggested Brussels as a rendezvous. It sounded reasonable enough, for the diamonds were in Antwerp. But our real reason was that we preferred to operate there; we felt at home. Paris is so big.

"Giering and I decided to arrest the Big Chief as soon as he stepped off the train at the Gare du Sud in Brussels. We sealed off every exit from the station and had a Gestapo squad with us on the platform. Even so, I admit we were very nervous as we waited for the train. We were convinced there would be trouble, and possibly shooting—the Big Chief wouldn't allow himself to be captured just like that. Even Giering was uneasy.

"The train drew in, we scanned the passengers' faces—and guess whom we saw? Madame Likhonin! Alone! What a letdown! I went over to her. 'I'm terribly sorry,' she said, 'he couldn't come. But I am fully empowered to sign the contract. If you are still prepared to make a deal, I'll get the diamonds from Antwerp tomorrow.'

"Naturally I declined the offer. And I had the woman followed. She went straight to Simexco.

"Our plan had misfired."

Keller says: "I told you about those Todt invoices so that you'll realize what a shock I had a little later on. It happened after the industrial-diamonds affair involving the Germans from Mainz. Madame Likhonin turned up unexpectedly and said to me: 'Good news. There's an officer at the Todt who has drawn up a whole list of customers for you. All you have to do is contact my son; he'll take you to the officer in question.' I couldn't believe my ears. After raging at me for poaching on her preserves, she was deliberately opening the gates to me!

"Anyway, I called at the Todt offices, in the Marbeuf Cinema. There I met young Likhonin, and he took me to see the German. On the door was a sign saying, 'Gestapo Liaison Officer.' His name was Nikholai, and he could not have been more pleasant. He had a bar in his office, and while pouring me a brandy he began to explain: 'Look here, I have some very large orders for fortifications in the prohibited zone—the Atlantic Wall. The best plan would be for you to go there yourself and get in touch personally with the authorities. For that, you need an *Ausweis*, but I can get one for you in no time at all. Do you have your papers with you?'

"I handed them to him. He examined them, gave me a funny look and said, 'Well, well . . . Swiss father, English mother, born in Russia . . .' As he filled in the application for an *Ausweis*, he told me confidentially that he was in a highly distressing situation. His family had disappeared in an air raid. Also, he had serious financial worries. He beat around the bush like this for some time before he finally asked me—wearing a distinctly awkward expression—whether it wouldn't be possible for the head of Simex to help him out for a while.

It was rather embarrassing. 'Look,' I replied, 'I've no idea, but I can always ask him.' 'Splendid!' he said. 'And for my part, I'll let you know as soon as your *Ausweis* is in order.'

"A few days after this interview, a party of uniformed German soldiers turned up at Simex. It was I who attended to them. They explained that we had previously supplied them with some machines, and they wanted to obtain certain spare parts for repairs. This was a dumbfounding request, as you can imagine! Our job was to offer the Germans goods brought in by shady middlemen who had filched them from heaven knows here. After-sales service was the very last thing we could provide! Anyway, I wriggled out of it as best as I could by saying that we would try, but I couldn't promise anything. Whereupon one of the soldiers said to me, 'Excuse me, but I have a raging toothache. May I telephone my dentist for an appointment?' I showed him the telephone, and he dialed a number and really did talk about a toothache. At the time, it didn't arouse my suspicion. Today, I wonder whether it wasn't a trick to make sure that our line was being properly tapped, or something of the kind.

"Naturally, I informed Monsieur Corbin of what Nikholai had said to me, but I don't know how things turned out. Monsieur Corbin was a changed man by then. He seemed tense, on edge, eaten up with worry. Often he would stare at the big wall map in his office and say to me, 'Oh, Keller, what wouldn't I give to be in some quiet little backwater miles and miles from here!' It was also at this period that he talked about giving me a raise. 'Keller,' he said, 'we'd like to see you earn a decent living.' I was staggered! I'd never been so well off in all my life! I suppose they'd made up their minds to implicate me."

In that fall of 1942, following hard upon Raichman's attempts at betrayal, upon the invitation to renew an *Ausweis*, and upon the abortive industrial diamonds deal, the affair of the loan to Nikholai was the fourth trap set for the Big Chief. Giering and Fortner were hoping that he would leap at this opportunity to bribe the Gestapo's representative at the Todt Organization. But in the event it was Corbin who dealt with the Hauptsturmführer and provided him with forty thousand francs. Nikholai signed an I.O.U. So now Trepper was in a position to blackmail him. Perhaps the Big Chief would make a personal approach at last—this was Giering and Fortner's one remaining hope. If it failed to materialize, if the Big Chief refused to swallow the bait, they were determined to sever contact with Simex and Simexco. Their patience was exhausted.

There was one thing they did not know (Giering died without learning the truth, and Fortner will learn it only when he reads these lines): Maria Likhonin had betrayed them. When they had first approached her, she had gone to the Big Chief, crying bitterly, and made her confession: "The Germans are making me work against you, they want me to give you away." Trepper took the news with good-natured restraint. "There, there," he said, patting her on the shoulder, "things aren't as bad as all that."

◆

Things *were* bad, and well he knew it. The vise was closing on his commercial cover. For the past eighteen months, Simex and Simexco had enabled him to penetrate the most exclusive German circles and to cross, almost at will, the frontiers guarded by the Gestapo; they had made him probably the wealthiest spy in the history of espionage. But now it was time to close up shop. His personal safety was not at stake, nor the safety of his Old Guard. Trepper, Katz and Grossvogel no longer called at the company offices. Corbin and his staff did not know where they were hiding. And Trepper had devised an extraordinary vanishing trick for himself, to make him disappear before the Gestapo's very eyes like a rabbit spirited away by a conjurer. But what about Suzanne Cointe, who had been working for the Orchestra from the outset? What about Jules Jaspar and Alfred Corbin, who had been hoodwinked into joining the network, but who had not wavered—despite the prospect of the scaffold—when Trepper had removed their blindfolds? What about Keller, who imagined he was working for a charitable institution whose profits went to help lighten the load of French prisoners? What about Juliette Mignon, the Famille Martin agent?

Trepper had long been planning a strategic withdrawal for his Marseilles branch. Jaspar and Kent were to slip across to North Africa and set up a new office in Algiers. Subsequently, members of the Paris staff would be able to join this advance party and stay out of harm's way. With this in mind, Jaspar had already obtained a visa for Algiers the preceding June 15, and held satisfactory negotiations with Chataigneau, Governor General of Algeria; but the project dragged on and on without ever reaching fruition. Kent was doing all he could to slow things down; because of his feelings for Margarete, he did not want to leave Marseilles.

On November 8, 1942, the American troops landed at Algiers,

effectively sealing off this line of retreat. The Wehrmacht invaded the Free Zone.

A week later, Kent and Margarete Barcza were arrested.

The arrest took place on November 12, 1942, at the couple's home, 85 Rue de L'Abbé-de-l'Epée. The concierge rang the doorbell at the usual time; she had come to do the chores. Margarete identified her through the peephole, turned the handle, and was knocked flying as five men burst into the apartment. They were French police. They had been waiting since dawn, hidden in the cellar of the building.

Kent remained impassive, but Margarete burst into sobs. And in fact the police seemed to show more interest in her than in him. "It's her, it's the spy," they shouted. They searched the house and found some weird-looking diagrams in a drawer. The discovery made them whoop with joy. "Here's all the evidence we need!" they cried. "Plans of fortifications!" Between sobs, Margarete explained that the diagrams were in fact knitting patterns she had cut out of a fashion magazine.

The two prisoners were taken to the police station at the Gare St.-Charles. There they were stripped and searched. The woman searching Margarete found a chestnut in a coat. ("I adore chestnuts; they're so smooth and cool. I'd picked this one up at Spa, in September, 1940, when we were so happy. I had put it in my pocket without thinking. You can imagine how sad I felt, seeing it again in these circumstances.") The woman gingerly trapped the chestnut in a pair of tweezers, and called for help. "Be careful! There's bound to be an explosive inside!" The entire police station was up in the air. The chestnut was carefully wrapped and forwarded to an unknown destination—probably some municipal laboratory.

Kent and Margarete spent their first night of detention lying on the cold concrete floor of the St.-Charles police station. Next day, November 13, they were handed over to the Gestapo.

Although it was the French police who carried out the arrest, they were acting on information supplied by the Gestapo. For weeks past, vehicles disguised as ambulances and bakery trucks had been scouring the streets of Marseilles for the Little Chief and his mistress. The German team was headed by SS Sturmbannführer Boemelburg. Like Giering, he had a vast experience of criminal investigation; indeed, he was a prominent member of the prewar equivalent of Interpol. Boemelburg had nothing solid to go on except the photograph of Kent that had been found at the Rue des Atrébates. But from information gleaned in Brussels he knew that Margarete dressed strikingly enough to arouse attention ("In those days I used to love going about in a top hat.") and that Kent was conspicuous for his truly phenomenal appetite. Waiters were bound to remember such a customer, and it could be only a question of time before Kent's gluttony proved his undoing. Among the items found in his apartment were fifty pairs of shoes and five thousand cigars. When questioned about his motives for hoarding all these things, Kent replied: "Who knows if one will still be able to buy them tomorrow?" Obviously, after his austere early years at the heart of the Communist world, the flowing riches of capitalism had gone to his head. And it seemed likely that his days of self-indulgence were now gone forever.

In the late afternoon of November 13, Kent and Margarete left Marseilles in a pair of Gestapo cars. Boemelburg was with Kent, and one of his lieutenants with Margarete; the other seats in the two vehicles were filled by half a dozen French police officers. They were heavily armed, for Boemelburg was afraid the network might stage an ambush to free the prisoners; and although the German army had moved into the Free Zone several days ago, it had yet to establish full control. Throughout the journey, therefore, the French police kept their revolvers and submachine guns trained on the edges of the road, ready to open fire. Despite Boemelburg's efforts to engage them in conversation (he had a perfect command of French, slang included), they remained obstinately silent, as though all this had nothing to do with them.

The party spent the night in a requisitioned hotel in Lyons. Kent and Margarete were locked in the same room, but their clothes were taken away to eliminate all risk of escape. Kent remained very calm. Margarete kept on firing questions at him, but all he would say was, "Don't worry! Above all, don't worry!" According to Margarete, she still imagined that they owed these happenings to Kent's Uruguayan nationality. The French police had accused her of being a spy, and no one knew better than she that the charge was untrue; why should it have been any more true of Kent?

The convoy reached Paris in late afternoon of the following day. The prisoners were incarcerated in the Rue des Saussaies. They were again allowed to share a room; but this time they were placed in charge of a guard, who recited poems to Margarete all night long.

On the morning of the third day, the cars set out for Brussels. The police from Marseilles had been replaced by German guards. Kent and Margarete were driven straight to the prison stronghold at Breendonck. Life had been a bed of roses for Margarete Barcza since the day she was born, and when she heard the heavy iron gates bang shut on them she suddenly became hysterical. Her heart seemed to give way. Later, as she regained consciousness, she heard a doctor say, "If you put her in prison, she won't survive for long."

Once again they were placed in the same cell, but during the day they were under constant surveillance by two guards, who were relieved every two hours; at night, a Gestapo man slept in the cell. They were allowed to talk to each other, but their conversations were inconsequential. Kent remained completely unruffled. He was subjected to a few interrogations, but no brutality was employed.

A few days later, they were taken to the Brussels headquarters of the Gestapo, in the Avenue Louise. Here, they were ordered into a large black Mercedes. The right-hand rear door was sealed from outside by a thick rope wrapped around the handle and stretching from bumper to bumper; it was impossible to open. Kent was instructed to sit next to this door. Margarete sat in the middle, with a Gestapo man on her left. Up front, beside the driver, another Gestapo man sat turned around so he could keep his submachine gun trained on the prisoners. He remained in this uncomfortable position throughout the journey. The Mercedes was full of parcels that members of the Brussels Gestapo were sending home to their families. Except for the driver and the guard with the submachine gun, all the passengers had piles of presents on their knees.

They did not arrive in Berlin until after dusk. The first stop was Gestapo headquarters in Prinz-Albrechtstrasse. Kent was taken away and locked in a basement cell. Sleeping within a few yards of him were Harro Schulze-Boysen and Arvid Harnack, whom he had met at the Berlin zoo a year earlier, when he had been sent to help them reorganize their transmitting system. Then the Mercedes drove Margarete to the Alexanderplatz prison. She was locked in an empty cell. She had another fit of hysterics, but the guards were unmoved. Finally she lay down on her straw mattress. Her face was bathed in tears, her body shaking spasmodically, involuntarily seeking the warmth of Kent's flank against her own. She still could not understand why the world had suddenly become so horrible. It was as if all her happiness had been laid waste by a terrifying bolt from the blue.

23. Disaster in Paris

At about nine-thirty on the morning of November 18, 1942, Keller received a telephone call from Nikholai: "Your *Ausweis* for the prohibited area is ready. Will you come and pick it up?" He went immediately to the Todt Organization. Nikholai welcomed him with open arms and thanked him warmly for helping him raise a loan. Keller inquired about the names and addresses of the customers whom he was to visit in the prohibited area, but his host sidestepped the question. "Don't worry, now. I'll have to get in touch with them first." He told Keller he would be coming to Simex with another customer later in the morning.

And he did arrive, with a man called Jung who said he was looking for soldering irons. Keller promised to do all he could to find some. He felt there was something distinctly odd about his visitors' behavior; they were very restless, inspecting every square foot of the room and staring hard at the various documents which lay on his desk.

At the same moment, in the adjoining room, Alfred Corbin was talking with his brother Robert. The latter knew nothing whatever about Alfred's undercover activities. He was amazed to find Alfred "tired and despondent, with a hunted look." It was the first time he had ever seen him in such a state. He did not question him, for he knew how reserved and cryptic he was about everything concerning his private life.

Alfred Corbin was afraid. The day before, November 17, he had met the Big Chief, who informed him of Kent's presumed arrest and urged him to make himself scarce. "Why should I run away?" Corbin replied. "There's nothing they can prove against me. They haven't a scrap of evidence! The only man who could compromise me is Kent. But you have absolute confidence in him, haven't you?" He had accompanied Kent to the Leipzig Fair, on that business trip which had served as cover for the initial contacts with the Berlin network. Taken aback by Trepper's silence, Corbin repeated: "You have absolute confidence in him?" Whereupon Trepper had shrugged and said, "Listen, the Gestapo is the Gestapo. You ought to get out." Corbin had refused to do so. He was a decent man who believed in the decency of others. Kent would not denounce him; it would be wrong. The Gestapo would not arrest him without evidence: it would be unjust.

But, despite it all, he still felt afraid. In a weary voice, he told his brother he was lunching with a German officer and asked if he would join them. But the prospect seemed to weigh on him, and in the end he backed out. Calling Keller, he asked him to act as host in his stead.

Keller took Nikholai and Jung to a first-rate black-market restaurant in the depths of a cellar near the Gare St.-Lazare. Starting with the hors d'oeuvres, the two Germans began to revile Switzerland, calling it, among other things, "that foul little nation of cowards and clockmakers." Keller, of course, was a Swiss citizen, and he lost his appetite. Why this outrageous attack on his country? The truth is, the examination of Keller's identification papers had aroused the darkest suspicions in Nikholai. And it's true that a Swiss father, an English mother and Russian birth are vital statistics out of the ordinary. Indeed, the members of the Kommando were inclined to wonder whether those documents were not an out-and-out forgery. Hence the present brilliantly subtle psychological maneuver: if Switzerland were insulted in Keller's presence, and he really *was* a Swiss citizen, then surely his patriotism, cut to the quick, would lead him to protest. But in fact Keller merely stared at the tablecloth, looking rather red in the face as he glumly chewed his meal. He suffered the abuse in silence: quarreling with customers was not good for business. In the end, however, the onslaught became so crude that he took his revenge by coldly leaving Nikholai to pay the bill. The goodbyes they addressed to one another were not exactly cordial. Nikholai suggested that Keller and Alfred Corbin should call at the Todt's offices next day; the time was fixed for four o'clock. The German urged Keller to be strictly punctual.

Toward the end of the afternoon, Madame Mignon opened the door of Simex to a "visitor about thirty years old, blond, shifty-eyed and nervous as anything." He began by asking to see Monsieur Gilbert; then he asked for the managing director. Madame Mignon replied that both were away at present. He hung around in the waiting room for several minutes, behaving very oddly. "You should have seen how he carried on—he almost seemed scared. He kept looking out of the window, as though he were keeping watch on the boulevard." Madame Mignon began to feel seriously worried, and as soon as he left she confided her fears in Mademoiselle Cointe. The latter tartly put her in her place and advised her not to poke her nose into things that did not concern her. This was their second clash within the space of a few hours. The day before, Suzanne Cointe had asked Madame Mignon to go to a locksmith and order a duplicate of the key to the service entrance; and this morning she had asked where the new key was. It wasn't ready. This had made Mademoiselle Cointe extremely annoyed. Madame Mignon had pointed out that she hadn't known that it was as urgent as all that, and anyway, where was the fire? At this, Suzanne Cointe had snapped at her, with her customary air of superiority, "My dear Mignon, some of the things which happen here are not for you to know about."

At six o'clock Madame Mignon left the office in the Boulevard Haussmann, still troubled by an underlying sense of disquiet. Monsieur Corbin had been away all afternoon. She was sorry she had not been able to tell him about the strange visit she had received.

That evening, Suzanne Cointe dined at home with her family in the Square Carpeaux. For some days now, her mother and sister had been surprised by her unusual edginess. "There's trouble brewing," she had told them. "The Russian woman has given us away." From this they deduced that Madame Likhonin had tipped off the Germans about Simex's unscrupulous business practices. Many a time Suzanne had said, "We're selling them junk."

As soon as the meal was over, she left the apartment, climbed the iron staircase to the top floor, and rang Jean-Paul Le Chanois's doorbell. She looked tense and grave.

"I've come to say goodbye."

"Why? Are you going away?"

"No, but there's serious trouble at Simex, and I think the worst may be about to happen. I wanted to kiss you goodbye before . . ."

They flung their arms around each other.

———◆———

At dawn next day—November 19, 1942—a thick fog fell over the Russian front, where Paulus's Sixth Army, in its extreme spearhead position, was bent on dislodging the last defenders from the last ruins of Stalingrad which were still in enemy hands. From the depths of this freezing, indissoluble mass came the many and varied sounds, muffled yet unmistakable, of an army preparing to attack.

Hitherto, every defeat sustained by the Red Orchestra had coincided with a military victory for the Axis. But today was different; the blow that the network was about to suffer would coincide with the worst disaster Hitler had ever known. (At dawn he was still asleep in his "eagle's nest" at Berchtesgaden, high in the Alps, far above the Russian fogs and the dense mist hanging over Paris.) For at first light the Red Army emerged from the gray shrouds, struck at the German front north of the Stalingrad pocket, hammered its way past the defenses and made a thirty-mile breakthrough to the rear of Paulus's army. The trap had been sprung, and the Führer refused to let Paulus fight his way out. The future of the war was now decided for good.

The strains of the Red Orchestra might become fainter and fainter, its musicians fewer and fewer. But from now on, Soviet agents who woke in cramped cells to the prospect of being hanged or shot or guillotined could at least take comfort in the distant roar of the Red Army surging toward Berlin. And they were able to think with pride of the contribution they had made to that army's recovery.

———◆———

At 10 A.M. on that November 19, the doorbell rang at the Simex office. Madame Mignon went to see who it was. She found herself confronted by the blond man who had behaved so oddly the day before. With him were a dozen men in civilian clothes.

"Is Monsieur Corbin in?"

"Ah, so you know his name today? And I see you've brought company!"

"Answer my question! We're the police."

"No need to tell me that—do you think I can't smell?"

"Really, madame, I must ask you to be quiet and go back to your own office."

The Gestapo's French auxiliaries spread out and made a hurried search of the twelve-room apartment, but the only person they found was Suzanne Cointe. Alfred Corbin and Keller had engagements elsewhere and would be away from the office all morning. Mademoiselle Cointe looked on, deathly white, as the police searched her personal belongings. Madame Mignon, who hadn't the same cause to tremble, kept up a nonstop flow of verbal abuse.

"What a rotten bunch you are! I can understand the Germans behaving the way they do, but there's no excuse for you! It makes me sick!"

"Do you think we have any choice?" they said. "Someone has to maintain law and order."

They took their two prisoners away, without even bothering to continue the search. On the stairs, Mademoiselle Cointe turned and whispered to Madame Mignon: "You were right about your blond visitor."

They were separated. Madame Mignon was taken to police head-quarters. There she remained for four days, leading the warders a dog's life and making the walls echo with continual demands, complaints and curses—so that her release, when it came, was greeted with general relief. Despite her loud hostility to the police at the time, she afterward observed of the men in charge of her: "They were very nice, really. They obviously didn't enjoy the job they had to do." One of them taught her the Morse code, which earned him a reprimand from his superior—niceness could be carried too far.

Suzanne Cointe was taken to the Rue des Saussaies.

Alfred Corbin and Vladimir Keller were walking along the Champs-Élysées in the direction of the Marbeuf Cinema. It was a quarter to four. Keller, thoroughly uneasy, said to his employer for the fourth time: "There's no getting away from it, that man Nikholai worries me. Who ever heard of a Gestapo officer handling business affairs?" Corbin, immersed in his own thoughts, murmured a few reassuring words.

The afternoon edition of *Paris-Soir* was on sale in the streets. The German shock troops were still advancing steadily through the ruins of Stalingrad. Bizerte had just been occupied by the Wehrmacht. Franco was mobilizing. Marshal Pétain was to speak later in the day about the Allied landing in North Africa. But the French public were given more telling news as well, in headlines as black as those announcing the Marshal's speech: "Early in 1943 the tobacco ration will be suspended until further notice." And spread across two columns on the front page: "Loss of North Africa will rid us principally of corpulence."

As they walked on, Keller happened to recognize a garage owner whom he had met in Le Havre. He went over to him and, practical as ever, asked whether he would be interested in buying a load of spare parts. The garage owner leaped at the offer, and a deal was concluded there and then. Keller went back to where Corbin was waiting. Once again they directed their footsteps toward the Marbeuf Cinema.

At five minutes to four, Keller came to a halt and looked at his companion.

"Look here, Monsieur Corbin, are we really going in?"

"Why yes, of course we are!"

They went into the entrance hall. As usual there were plenty of people about, including German soldiers. Keller threaded his way toward the elevator at the back of the lobby. Corbin was just behind him. He was about to open the elevator door when he heard a voice challenge him—"Herr Keller?" He glanced around. Even as he turned a pair of handcuffs slipped on to his wrists. A quarter of a century later, Vladimir Keller still marvels at the skill with which it was done. His briefcase was snatched from under his arm. It contained the payments for his latest commissions: a hundred and thirty-eight thousand francs. "In those days, it was quite a sum!"

Confronting him, pistol in hand, was Jung, part-time seeker after soldering irons and *Kriminal-Obersekretär* of the Rote Kapelle Kommando. On his left, four uniformed soldiers brandishing machine-pistols were blocking the exit to the Rue Marbeuf.

Jung hustled him and Corbin toward this exit and ordered them into a car drawn up at the curb. It drove off with savage haste. No more than ten seconds had gone by since the moment Keller had reached out to open the elevator door.

Alfred Corbin had turned extremely pale. With his head tilted backward and his eyes half closed, he murmured: "My poor little Denise is going to be left fatherless." The German sitting next to the driver turned round and said sharply, "Show a little dignity, will you? Take an example from your colleague; he, at least, knows how to behave."

Keller felt utterly bewildered. What on earth was Corbin talking about? He must be out of his mind! Keller's immediate supposition had been that the Gestapo had poked its nose into the graft that had been going on between Simex and the Todt Organization—hence their arrest. Corbin's words prompted him to think that it was more serious than he had imagined. Nikholai must have uncovered some particularly rich deal. Even so, Corbin was piling on the agony!

Eventually the car drew up outside Gestapo headquarters in the Rue des Saussaies. Jung took Keller to his office. "Sit down!" Keller obeyed, but was immediately struck across the face. "On your feet!

The good times are over for you!" The German ordered him to turn out his pockets. "First give me your *Ausweis* for the prohibited area." He examined it closely. "Ah," he said with a hint of regret, "you haven't used it."

The *Ausweis* had been a trap. The Kommando had hoped that this highly dubious Swiss national would use it to carry out secret missions in the prohibited area. Yet Jung surely must have known that it had been in Keller's possession only since the previous day.

"Where is Gilbert?"

Keller did not know. He was dealt a couple of hard slaps and several stiff punches. "Where is Gilbert?"

Keller insisted that he had no idea. Jung opened a drawer, took out a length of rope and secured the prisoner's legs with it. Then he grabbed a stick and made as if to wedge it between the bonds. This is known as the "tourniquet" torture: the interrogator turns the stick until the rope, tightened to breaking, bites deeply into the victim's flesh. Before setting to work, however, the German turned the radio on full blast. An English voice began to thunder; the set was tuned to the BBC. Keller realized that the intention was to drown his cries of pain.

"You'll be wasting your time!" he bellowed.

Jung looked thoroughly taken aback. He turned down the radio. "What? What are you saying?"

". . . I explained to him that I have a physiological peculiarity: I am sensitive to trivial aches and pains, but beyond a certain point I cease to feel anything. If someone slaps my face, I certainly feel the sting; yet I could be flogged to death without so much as a murmur. Doctors I've spoken to say the condition is very rare, but there is a scientific explanation for it. Anyway, I thought I might as well tell Jung. By the time I'd finished speaking, he looked very disconcerted; he just didn't know what to do."

In the end, the *Obersekretär* decided that he had better stick to routine. As he wedged the stick between the cords, he said to Keller, "We of the Gestapo are often accused of being inhumane, but it simply isn't true. Here at the Rue des Saussaies we don't even use the full range of torture implements the French left for us."

He began to turn the stick. The rope made deep ridges in Keller's legs. Keller stared vacantly at the ceiling while Jung—his face turning crimson and his veins standing out—did all he could to wrest a gasp from him. Finally the German got completely out of breath and gave up. He untied the rope, ordered Keller to stand up and administered a series of cuffs and punches.

"There," he said, "that's for your little joke yesterday, when you left us to pay the bill!" *

At about eight o'clock that evening, Keller and Corbin were taken outside and put into a Gestapo car. They sat side by side on the rear seat. Immediately in front of them were the driver and an escorting officer. It was a moonless night and the blackout turned the streets into dark tunnels. After a while the driver was forced to admit he had lost his way. Luckily, a pedestrian emerged from the gloom at that very moment—an elderly gentleman strolling with his hands behind his back, very dignified. The officer got out and asked him the way to Fresnes. The pedestrian glanced through the window and saw the handcuffed prisoners.

"Damned if I know and damned if I care!" he cried.

"Do you know who you're speaking to? A German officer! If you don't answer, I'll arrest you too!"

"Don't you take that tone with me! To hell with your threats!"

"The old gentleman was beside himself with rage," Keller told me. "He called the German every name under the sun. The atmosphere got so stormy that the driver got out to support his superior; it looked as if they'd come to blows. 'This is our chance!' I said to myself. For how would they catch us: you couldn't see beyond your nose! The handcuffs were no problem. Quick as a flash, I thought of Racoua, a scrap dealer at Aubervilliers who was hand-in-glove with Simex. If I knew anything about Racoua, he wouldn't turn a hair at sawing off a couple of pairs of handcuffs! I nudged Monsieur Corbin and signaled to him to slip out of the car. He shook his head; he wouldn't do it. And yet it was he I was really thinking of. On account of his remark about Denise. I thought he must really be in a serious jam, and for him it was do or die. But he was like a lump of jelly. And it wasn't as if they had tortured him. You see, for all his qualities, Monsieur Corbin simply wasn't a man of action. He wasn't cut out for that kind of work."

Outside, the quarrel died down. The irate old gentleman disappeared into the darkness, muttering to himself. The driver found his way again. When they reached Fresnes, Corbin and Keller were

---

* When I asked Keller what he thought of Jung, he reflected for a while and then said gravely, "I didn't feel he was particularly correct or honorable in his behavior."

separated and placed in solitary confinement. Their wrists were hand-cuffed behind their backs, which made sleeping difficult. But Giering was anxious not to take any risks; he was afraid they might attempt suicide.

He and Fortner had agreed to a division of labor. While Giering liquidated Simex, Fortner was in Brussels, dealing with Simexco. Never, probably, can a police swoop have called for so little effort: all Fortner had to do was step outside his office in the Rue Royale and knock on the neighboring door. There was nobody on the premises, apart from an innocuous clerk; the files were not found to contain a single compromising document; an inspection of the walls did not reveal even one concealed microphone. Fortner was convinced that they had been removed just before his search. In short, all his efforts had been to no avail. But he did have the names and addresses of all Simexco's shareholders and employees, and these could be picked up whenever he liked.

◆

Denise Corbin was expecting her father in their apartment at 15 Rue Cernuschi. She was alone: her mother was out of town, staying with relatives; she was due back next day.

Denise was studying for her *bachot* in philosophy at the Lycée Jules-Ferry. She knew nothing whatever about her father's activities. To her, Katz was simply a friend from his army days and a regular guest at the Rue Cernuschi. Trepper was simply that rather gruff figure who had called to discuss business two or three times. When she mentioned the Big Chief to me twenty-five years later, she still spoke of him as "my father's employee."

Eight o'clock came, and still no sign of Alfred Corbin. Denise decided to telephone her uncle, Robert Corbin. She told him of her concern. He questioned her: did she know any of her father's plans for the day? Well, she said, he had an appointment at the Todt Organization toward the end of the afternoon. In that case, said Robert Corbin, he must have been held up; perhaps they had invited him to dinner. Denise repeated these reassuring phrases to her mother when she telephoned from the country an hour later and was astonished at her husband's absence. "He must have been held up." There was no point in upsetting Madame Corbin; she was a woman who panicked at the slightest excuse.

Denise stayed up till midnight, studying and waiting; then sleep

got the better of her. Six hours later, the telephone wakened her with
a start. It was her uncle. Had Alfred got back all right? She went and
looked in his room. There was nobody there. The bed had not been
slept in. Robert asked his niece to meet him outside Simex at 8 A.M.

First they called at the local police station, to get official permission to enter the firm's premises. The officer in charge said he
would neither give nor withhold such permission. Robert Corbin
went off in search of a locksmith and took him to 83 Boulevard Haussmann. The door had not been sealed by the authorities. Inside, everything was in order. After a quick inspection of the offices, uncle and
niece went home.

They were worried, but not immoderately so. Simex, as they
well knew, engaged in rather odd commercial operations. Perhaps one
of them had gone wrong, which would explain why Alfred Corbin
had been so much on edge: he had smelled trouble. Denise also told
Robert Corbin about a loan which her father had referred to several
times lately. A German officer had borrowed forty thousand francs
from him, and Alfred Corbin had seemed a bit worried over it.
Presumably he had feared that he might not get his money back. But
if he was now in trouble with the Todt Organization, the loan was
bound to have a beneficial effect—one does not deal harshly with a
man who has lent one forty thousand francs.

Robert Corbin decided that the firm must have gone too far with
its black-market activities. His purpose in going through the offices
had been to suppress any incriminating documents, but he had not
come across any. He had come away empty-handed, except for the
address book he had found in his brother's desk.

Madame Corbin arrived back in town that day. Like her daughter
and brother-in-law, she hadn't the slightest suspicion that Alfred belonged to a spy ring. In spite of this, the news of his disappearance
threw her into a mad panic. Without even pausing to unpack, she
made an indiscriminate bonfire of his papers; she even destroyed the
letters which he had sent her in their courting days, as well as the
antijamming aerial which had enabled them to listen to the BBC.

The ashes were still warm when the doorbell rang. A party of
French police trooped into the flat—the same men who, with the
Gestapo, had raided the Simex offices the day before. They were most
reassuring: Alfred Corbin was being held in connection with some
trivial black-market offense; the matter would soon be cleared up.

There was no question of interfering with the freedom of Madame Corbin and her daughter; all that was asked of them was to remain indoors for a few days. With these soothing assurances, the party withdrew. But two men were left on duty in the Corbins' hallway, just beside their front door.

The Kommando was hoping that the Big Chief would come to the apartment for news, thereby blundering into the trap.

Keller and Alfred Corbin were interrogated further. Only one question was fired at them, but it was repeated a hundred times over: "*Wo ist Gilbert* (Where is Gilbert?)" They pleaded ignorance, but Giering refused to believe them. He asked Berlin to send him a torture expert. In the meantime, his men limited themselves to the brutalities of the traditional third degree. "A few blows," Alfred Corbin later recorded in his notes, "but nothing really serious." As for Keller, his small physiological peculiarity discouraged even the most determined.

After three days of fruitless waiting, the French police guard at the Corbins' were relieved by Germans attached to the Kommando, among them, Eric Jung. The two women were still allowed a considerable measure of freedom: Robert Corbin and his wife were able to visit them whenever they pleased, doing their shopping and sharing their meals. But the Germans shrewdly brought continual psychological pressure to bear on Madame Corbin. They stopped talking of black-market operations and began to talk of espionage. Naturally, they said, they were more than ready to believe in Alfred Corbin's innocence. The tragedy was that he might suffer for the real culprit, Gilbert. In wartime, justice hadn't time to be over-fussy! They were deeply sorry for Madame Corbin. Basically it was more to her interest than anyone else's that Gilbert should be found. To them, it was just another job: if they failed, it wasn't a matter of life and death. But if they didn't put their hands on Gilbert, Alfred Corbin might easily lose his skin. . . .

It was all too much for Madame Corbin. Harried by these mock-compassionate voices, she roamed the apartment, seeing continual reminders of her absent, threatened, innocent husband—he *was* innocent; she was sure of it. "If I could tell you anything, I would!" she cried. "But I know nothing! Nothing at all!"

At eleven o'clock on the morning of November 24, 1942, she remembered something seemingly insignificant. In the course of one of his visits to them, Gilbert had complained of toothache. Alfred Corbin had given him the address of the family dentist: Dr. Maleplate, 13 Rue de Rivoli, near the Hôtel de Ville. There was no reason to withhold this detail from her guards. As far as she knew, Gilbert was only a minor business associate of her husband. She was convinced that he had deliberately made use of Alfred without his ever suspecting the fact. If he *had* suspected, if he had willingly worked for Gilbert, then surely she, his wife, would have known! So why should she hesitate between Gilbert's life and her husband's?

It seems probable—indeed, certain—that a professional would have disclosed this fragment of information, just as Madame Corbin did. It was over six months since that toothache, and the Big Chief must surely have said goodbye to Maleplate long ago. The dentist's address was exactly the kind of useless pawn a skillful chess player would sacrifice to save his main pieces. There was only one chance in a thousand that its capture would enable the Gestapo to reach a checkmate.

Today Dr. Maleplate is a sturdy, hale-looking man with iron-gray hair, a florid complexion and uncommonly alert eyes. He says: "On the morning of November 24, 1942, I was working as usual at Laënnec Hospital, where I was on the staff. At about noon, someone in the office told me I was wanted on the phone. It was my dental mechanic. 'You must come at once,' he said. Naturally I wanted to know why, but all he would say was: 'I can't tell you anything, but you must come.' I immediately asked my superior for permission to leave.

"I sat in the Métro, eaten up with worry. I thought it must be my father. He was a dentist too: in those days we used to work together, here in this office. He was getting on in years, and I was afraid he might have had a heart attack or something really serious, or my dental mechanic wouldn't have wanted to hide the truth from me.

"I got to St.-Paul station at about half past twelve and found the mechanic waiting at the top of the stairs with a bunch of flowers in his hand. He was fidgeting in his hurry to get home; it was his daughter's birthday, or her saint's day. 'The Gestapo are at your office,' he said. 'They're waiting for you.' I heaved a sigh of relief and thought, Oh, is *that* all it is!

"There were two of them, in plain clothes. One was very tall, the other quite short [Giering and Fortner]. They asked me to get my appointment book and read them all my appointments for the week. I did so. They listened carefully, without showing any reaction. When I had finished, they said, 'Would you mind going through the list again?' So I recited all the names a second time, but even that wasn't enough for them. 'And again, please.' At this point I noticed that I had made a mistake. 'Ah,' I said, 'at two o'clock this afternoon I *did* have an appointment with Madame Labayle, a colleague's wife. Afterward she telephoned to say she was unable to come, so I offered her appointment to another patient. But I forgot to cross out Madame Labayle's name and substitute Monsieur Gilbert's.''

◆

Wherever his continual travels might take him, it was at Neumarkt that the Big Chief spent each November 24—in the spirit, if not in the flesh—for it was the anniversary of his father's death, and time had not detracted from the solemnity of the day.

The Gestapo's roundup of the Simex staff had inevitably added to his habitual sadness. But at least he knew he had done all he could to avert it. Alfred Corbin and Suzanne Cointe had been forewarned. If they made no attempt to avoid arrest, in Corbin's case it might be due to certain illusions; but above all, both of them knew that if they did escape, their families would be subject to enemy reprisals. Obviously the Big Chief did not know that Alfred Corbin had turned down the chance to flee from the Gestapo vehicle on the night of November 19. Had he known, he would certainly have understood Corbin's refusal: what was the point of escaping from prison if it meant throwing in his wife and daughter in his place? Racoua, the scrap dealer, might have sawed off the German handcuffs, but no one on earth could sever the ties that bound Corbin to his family.

As for Madame Mignon and Keller, they were a different story. They knew nothing. It would have been a mistake to have warned them of the danger, for that would have spoiled their innocence—an innocence that was bound to convince the Gestapo in the end.

The harvest that the Red Army was reaping on the Don may have helped to ease the Big Chief's sadness. But even this miraculous reversal of fortune could not allay all his anxiety and fear.

The Moscow Center had lost all sense of reality. Four months after the arrest of Wenzel, Yefremov and Winterink, it was still lending credence to their messages. Trepper's warnings were ignored altogether. Indeed, the Director made little attempt to conceal his suspicions of the Big Chief himself. The head of Soviet Intelligence in western Europe was accorded less trust by the Center than was Karl Giering.

It was bad enough for Moscow to be taken in by a *Funkspiel* of any kind; but we know that Trepper had been troubled for months by a mounting conviction that this particular *Funkspiel* was not an end, but a means—the springboard for an even more ambitious maneuver on the part of the Kommando.

Anna Maximovich had just been unmasked. This was serious, this was tragic, but at least it was logical. However, when her membership in the Orchestra became known she was *approached* by the Kommando; and this was perturbing and bewildering, for at first sight there was no rational justification for it. Trepper had no idea what had led to Anna's downfall. We know the truth, however: the Maximoviches had been brought to disaster as a result of a threefold discovery. First, the discovery of their records in the archives of the French police. The Abwehr had turned to them for information after Margarete Hoffman-Scholtz, in keeping with German army regulations, had sought official permission to marry Vasili, an alien national. The French Sûreté had taken note of Anna's leftist sympathies and of the fact that she had nursed wounded veterans of the Spanish Republican Army. Kludow and his team had opened a second breach when they deciphered a number of her telegrams containing the gist of several reports drafted by Ambassador Abetz; these pointed clearly enough to Margarete and, through her, to Vasili. Finally, another intercepted telegram reported the poor results of an Allied air raid on the German city of Hamm; it said: "Our trusty friend has seen the damage. It is nonexistent." Investigations by the Abwehr revealed that, after filing her request for permission to marry, Margarete had traveled to Germany and passed through Hamm; when questioned, the poor besotted girl admitted that she had passed information to her Baron.

Anyone familiar with the Kommando's methods would have expected them to pounce on the two Russians without a moment's delay. Instead of which it left Vasili in peace and dispatched an emissary to Anna. The latter was offered an amazing deal: they would turn a blind eye to her underground activities if she successfully engineered an interview between Giering and the Big Chief.

An interview!

When Anna told him of all this, Trepper instructed her to flee.

She hurried back to Billeron and slipped across the demarcation line into the Free Zone. And there she was arrested, at the same time as Kent—though the Big Chief was still unaware of this. Vasili guessed what had happened. It distressed him to be without news of his sister. He was ill, his poor legs were more swollen than ever: "If they come looking for me," he told Trepper, "I'll kill myself that minute. I'd rather go straight to the next world." The Big Chief replied: "No, no. Leave this world if you like, but take with you as many of those scum as you can."

An interview! The trap would have seemed insultingly unsophisticated if Trepper's agonized perplexity had not been intensified by the other recent developments. We know of the snares the Kommando had set for him through Nikholai, the offer to renew his *Ausweis*, and the seemingly golden opportunity to put pressure on a Gestapo officer by lending him forty thousand francs. Both had failed. The third snare—the proposed purchase of industrial diamonds by so-called manufacturers from Mainz—had also failed. Indeed, the Big Chief had rubbed it in, much to his own amusement, by telephoning Nikholai and saying: "Simex deals with anyone but the Gestapo." So there was obviously no point in persevering. Yet persevere they did. After the arrest of Corbin and his associates, even though there was no longer the slightest chance of passing himself off as a manufacturer from Mainz, Giering had Madame Likhonin suggest to Trepper that they reopen negotiations for the industrial diamonds—and reopen them not just anywhere, but in Berlin!

All this made it seem as though the Kommando were less interested in arresting the Big Chief than in establishing contact with him. But with what end in view? And to serve what maneuver?

On November 22, Trepper met Michel, the emissary from the French Communist Party. He told him of Giering's bewildering proposition and asked him to inform Moscow that he was prepared to go to Berlin if the powers-that-be considered the issue worth clarifying.

Next day, November 23, he decided to stage a strategic withdrawal pending receipt of the Center's answer. The network went into hibernation: operations were suspended, contacts severed, communications banned; everyone was to lie low until further notice. In the evening, he held one last meeting with his Old Guard, Katz and Grossvogel. With their assistance, he drafted one more telegram to the Director. It reveals his despair at being continually disbelieved:

"The situation is worsening hour by hour. Kent is probably under arrest. Simex has been liquidated. But most serious of all are your statements concerning Yefremov, Wenzel and Winterink. Clearly, the Gestapo carries more weight with you than I do." In addition, the trio wrote a long letter to Jacques Duclos, begging him to convince Moscow that the network had genuinely suffered grievous setbacks and that the pianists really had defected to the Germans. What more could they do?

It was decided that Katz and Grossvogel should set out the very next day for their respective hideouts in Marseilles and Vichy. In parting, Trepper said to both of them, "If you're unlucky enough to be caught, make every effort to find out what the Kommando is up to and why."

He had already made his own arrangements. Georgie was to remain hidden in the house at Le Vésinet. Two months earlier, he had already persuaded her to put Patrick out of harm's way. Initially he had been sent to a boarding school at St.-Germain-en-Laye, but he was so poorly cared for that they had to remove him at once. Through a friend of Georgie's, a certain Denise, they obtained the address of the Queyries, good people living in the suburbs, at Suresnes. The Queyries fussed over Patrick as though he were their own child, and he now seemed quite safe from the Kommando.

As for himself, Trepper was due to die within the next few days. The death certificate would be signed by a doctor at Royat, whom he had met while undergoing treatment, and there were plans to erect a gravestone on which Giering and his men could feast their astonished eyes.

But there was something he wanted to do before heading for the Auvergne mountains—before marking out a false trail for the Kommando to follow and taking final refuge in the Beyond. He was anxious to obtain a clean bill of health for his teeth. His appointment with Dr. Maleplate today was the last in the series. He had been so busy that he had put it off week after week.

◆

Dr. Maleplate says: "When I mentioned Gilbert's name, they didn't betray any special reaction, but one of them asked me, 'Do you know your patients well?' 'Up to a point, yes.' 'In that case I want you to go through the list again and tell us who each person is, what he does for a living, and so on. You don't happen to keep rec-

ord cards?' 'No.' 'What a pity. Well, go ahead.' So I read out all the
names again, giving a few particulars about each patient. All I knew
about Gilbert was that he had been recommended to me by the
Corbins. To me, he was just an ordinary businessman who spoke with
a Belgian accent and always arrived with a briefcase under his arm.
He was very sympathetic, no doubt about it, but showed little in-
clination to talk about himself.

"They thanked me and went away, but five or ten minutes later
they returned. This time there were three of them. Later I learned
that they had had a quick council of war in the café below. 'We're
going to arrest Gilbert,' they told me. 'Do whatever you like,' I
said, 'it's no concern of mine.' 'Oh no,' exclaimed the tall one, 'you're
not getting out of it as easily as that! You're going to cooperate,
whether you like it or not!'

"They outlined their plan to me. I was to get rid of my mechanic, open the door myself, usher Gilbert to the chair and begin the
treatment. When I saw them rush at him, I was to hurl myself back
into a corner. This was for my own safety; they were convinced
there would be trouble, and fully expected an exchange of shots. They
were already showing signs of nerves. For instance, my telephone
rang while they were explaining things to me. The tall one pulled
out his Luger and shouted: 'Who is it and what do they want?'
'Look,' I said, 'calm down. It's only one of my colleagues.' He
was telephoning to remind me that we were due to operate that evening in a private hospital in the Rue d'Alésia. I answered in mono-
syllables, confirming that I'd be there; then I hung up.

"When my mechanic arrived, I sent him up to the apartment with
my father—yes, we used to live over the office. Then the doorbell
rang a second time. It was an old lady, one of my father's patients. I
showed her into the waiting room. No, I'm wrong—it was the old
lady who arrived first, then my mechanic. In any event, two o'clock
was fast approaching and Gilbert was due at any moment. It was my
first appointment of the afternoon."

The front door opens on to a long passageway. There is only
one room on the right side of the passage, the dental mechanic's
laboratory. There are four rooms on the left: the waiting room, then
the surgery where Dr. Maleplate's father used to work, then an office
which, nowadays at least, is full of prints and other items doing hom-
age to the memory of Napoleon, and finally Maleplate's own office.

Giering posted a man in the mechanic's laboratory, to cut off the Big Chief's line of retreat. He and Fortner went to the far end of the passage and stationed themselves behind the door of Maleplate's office. It had been arranged that the latter would take Trepper in by way of the Napoleonic sanctum. The passage turns on the other side of the office, so there was no possibility of the two Germans being detected.

Outside, of course, the Kommando was lurking in full strength, together with its French auxiliaries. The whole block was surrounded.

Afterward, Trepper described how uneasy he felt as soon as he stepped inside. Something was wrong. The waiting room was empty, apart from the old lady; normally it was packed. The doctor ushered him in by way of the office, just as he usually did; but, unusually, the office door leading to the passage was closed.

"I sat him in the chair," Dr. Maleplate continued. "He was extremely relaxed. Poor devil, I said to myself, what point is there in tinkering with his tooth? This is hardly the time to cause him pain. I chatted to him and went through the motions of selecting my instruments. And he smiled at me and said, 'Things are looking up, aren't they? Did you hear the news on the radio?' I was in a cold sweat, for at that very moment I heard the jingle of handcuffs just beyond the door. Time was beginning to drag, so I placed some cotton in his mouth and began to adjust my drill; but at long last they made up their minds to get started. They came at him fast, pistols in hand. He put his hands up and said, 'I'm unarmed.' He was very pale, but perfectly calm. As for the Germans—all I can say is that *they* were the ones who were in a panic!"

Fortner confirms this: "The dentist was shaking, and Giering and I were in a terrible state of nerves. Oh there's no getting away from it, he was the calmest man in the room. He didn't turn a hair! 'Bravo!' he said to us, as Giering slipped on the handcuffs, 'You've done a good job.' I replied modestly: 'It's the result of two years' search.'"

As they were leaving Dr. Maleplate said to the prisoner, "I want you to know this was none of my doing." "Well of course not!" said Trepper. "As if I'd dream of bearing you a grudge, even for a moment!" Then came a polite discussion about the dentist's fees, but Dr. Maleplate refused to accept any payment. The Big Chief shook hands with him and departed, handcuffed between big Giering and little Fortner, between Gestapo and Abwehr.

He and Georgie had arranged to meet in Rueil at the end of the afternoon. They were supposed to be dining together at St.-Germain-en-Laye. She waited and waited, but he did not come. Time and again Trepper had told her, "I may be arrested at any moment. You must be prepared for it. When it happens, sit tight, and whatever you do, don't go looking for news."

But Georgie was so consumed with worry that she did go looking for news. She telephoned Katz. They arranged to meet at the Chien qui fume Café, in Montparnasse. Their conversation was brief and distressing. "I'm practically certain he's been caught," said Katz. "Some of the others have just been arrested. I'm on the run, too. And my wife is in the hospital, having a baby." Poor Katz was destined never to see this baby, and to Georgie he himself seemed like a child whose father has just been snatched away. He was supposed to leave for Marseilles that very evening, on the Big Chief's orders. But he didn't go. He was like a bird fascinated by a snake—he had lost the use of his reflexes and was merely waiting for the death bite.

Georgie, on the other hand, was panic-stricken by what had happened. She sent her maid, Marcelle Loukia, to ask the guards at the Cherche-Midi prison whether Trepper was being held there. She chose the Cherche-Midi because she had read in the papers, only a few days ago, that the actor Harry Baur had been thrown in there. It was a rash step, indeed an insane one given the personality of Georgie's chosen messenger. Marcelle Loukia, a forty-year-old Negro woman from Martinique, held somewhat racialist views; she held that the Germans were members of an inferior species, and she minced no words on the subject. When her first mission proved unsuccessful, Georgie had her go knocking on the doors of every prison in Paris; each time, the maid drew a blank.

Then Georgie herself scoured the capital wearing her favorite coat—"it was a plaid with the most glorious colors, a really luxurious coat, the kind one seldom saw in those days." Thus attired, she walked past the building in the Rue des Saussaies. At the time, the Kommando knew nothing whatever about the Big Chief's wife except that she owned a magnificent coat: Giering ordered a search for "the woman in the plaid coat." She might easily have gone to Alfred Corbin's and walked straight into the police trap; but luck was in Trepper's favor for once, and she called at Robert Corbin's home instead. Madame Robert Corbin confirmed that there had been a wave of arrests. Finally, Georgie proceeded to Katz's address. The concierge recognized her and cried out: "Don't go upstairs! The Gestapo are there!" She hurried away, traveled out to Suresnes, where Patrick was, and informed the Queyries that her husband had been arrested. "He'll get out of it somehow," she said. "You'll see. It's not for nothing that his friends call him a ball of fire."

24. The End of the Concert

The Big Chief talked.

"In the car," Fortner tells me, "he asked whether I was Abwehr or Gestapo. I replied that I was a German army officer. He looked relieved. Then he said, 'So far as I'm concerned, it's all over. I shall tell you certain things, but you will have to accept the fact that I'm not going to tell you everything.' Needless to say, Giering and I were stunned by this unhoped for statement—if the Big Chief agreed to collaborate, it would mean the end of Soviet espionage in the west. And so, even in our preliminary discussions, I did my best to establish human contact with him. We sat drinking coffee and smoking cigarettes as we talked about his life and his family. He chatted quite freely, and I must say I listened with unfeigned interest and sympathy. He was an admirable man, very calm and restrained. I felt I was exchanging reminiscences with an old colleague."

After the life story came the evening lecture. The members of the Kommando listened dumbfounded as Trepper treated them to a lecture on the art of espionage. First he outlined the broad principles: any network needed a rigid separation of units, the systematic use of cover names, a continual process of decentralization (so that no one agent could name more than a handful of others), and a strict separation of pianists (who are especially vulnerable) and the remainder of the network. Trepper then set forth what he regarded as standard security precautions. A good agent, he said, should never carry weapons, which would put him at the mercy of a routine police check. He should do without a car. He should live in the suburbs, where it was easier to detect if you were being shadowed than in the crowded city streets. He should not receive an immoderate amount of mail and should have his correspondents send postcards rather than letters, for no one distrusts a man who gets postcards. Documents should never be passed from hand to hand without being camouflaged (in pens, matchboxes, newspapers). Meetings between agents should preferably be timed for Sundays and holidays, when the police are less numerous and less watchful, and these meetings should be fixed for such ordinary and well-frequented places as bookshops and drugstores, and also at sports arenas, on lakes (with boating facilities) and in swimming pools—but only (and the Gestapo scrupulously recorded this word of warning in its report) at the appropriate season.

Finally Trepper described a number of technical tricks that took Fortner's breath away and made even old hands like Giering and Berg realize that they were still merely dabbling in the rudiments of counterespionage. He explained, for instance, how public telephone directories could be used for arranging rendezvous. The place being agreed in advance, they had only to set the day and the hour. An agent would go into a telephone booth, open the directory at a predetermined page and underline a word on the fourth line: this meant a meeting at four o'clock. A circle drawn round a word on the sixth line meant the sixth day of the week—that is, the following Saturday. Thanks to this system, preliminary contact between the two agents was quite unnecessary. In addition, if the agent arranging the rendezvous had any doubts about the other, he could make sure that the latter came to the telephone box unescorted and unshadowed.

After the Big Chief's lecture, the Abwehr drafted a report containing the following lines, which were intended as a retrospective justification for the slowness of the investigations: "All previous experience acquired in the west was valueless to us. It soon transpired that the Russians had been working with great professional expertise. This is why it was necessary for the Abwehr to learn the theories governing the training and planting of Soviet agents, theories hitherto unknown to its officers."

It is reasonable to infer that the "previous experience acquired in the west" had in fact been acquired at the expense of Resistance networks hastily improvised by well-meaning amateurs who knew little or nothing about the rules of espionage. The best of them—Rémy—later itemized the cost of a betrayal by only *one* of his agents: "Sixty arrests, fifty-two transportations, fourteen deaths in camps, one death in prison, two executions, two disappearances without trace —and I'm not certain that this list is complete." * And the traitor was

---

* Rémy, *Mémoires d'un agent secret* . . . , Vol. 2, p. 51.

not even an agent of prime importance! Neither Yefremov nor Raichman had been capable of doing so much damage, nor could any other
member of the Red Orchestra—Trepper excepted—for decentralization and rigid separation prevented the gangrene from spreading to
the entire organism. This is not to denigrate Rémy. His greatness lay
in the fact that he *was* an amateur, quite untutored in defensive
stratagems. Indeed, he makes the point himself: 'Where were the men
who might have taught us? Despite our numbers, we very seldom came
across experts prepared to guide and sustain us. We had no choice but
to rely on such resources as we found in the ship's hold.' *

Gallant captain of a makeshift crew, sailing without benefit of
maps or compass, but with eyes fixed on a star. A few months after
these events, Rémy learned that one of his men—arrested by the Gestapo—was seeking to reestablish contact. "I was informed that Gaspard had been released and wanted to see me. 'Released.' I was sure
of his loyalty, but I suspected an all too German trap. Gaspard was
being shadowed, that was certain. Still, there could be no question
of leaving him in the lurch. I arranged to meet him under the Eiffel
Tower at 11:45 A.M. The Champ-de-Mars was an ideal spot for a
quiet talk. It was impossible to keep someone under surveillance there
without his noticing. Besides, it was close to my base, where I had a
great deal to do." †

Two mistakes and one dangerous gamble. First mistake: arranging a rendezvous near his home. The Gestapo was familiar with this
practice, a common one among overworked network chiefs. After
persuading an agent to defect, the Germans would put him in the back
of a car and spend hours driving him around neighborhoods where he
had had his rendezvous; sooner or later he would catch sight of the
people who had been his contacts. Second mistake: choosing the
Champ-de-Mars, especially as he was aware that Gaspard might be
shadowed: how could he hope to escape from that deserted esplanade?
The magnificent gamble lay in the six words: "I was sure of his
loyalty." They occur again and again in Rémy's book, like a litany,
like a prayer. On learning of the arrest of agents whom he had earlier
invited to his home (third mistake), he reflected: "To change my
place of residence would be to question my friends' loyalty and courage. I decided to stay put." ‡ And later, in identical circumstances:
"For over a week, I didn't go home even once without telling myself

---

* *Ibid.*, Vol. 1, p. 413.
† *Ibid.*, p. 474.
‡ *Ibid.*, p. 498.

I should be arrested before the night was out. I certainly thought of moving to another flat, but did not have the heart to do so. That would be to belie the trust which I owed to those of my friends who were in prison." *

This kind of attitude would have shocked the wary minds at the Center. But as Rémy saw it, retaining confidence in his associates was no mere passive tribute, but an act of faith which could only strengthen the network; through the invisible workings of divine Providence, it would succor and reinforce agents, even while they were undergoing torture. Obviously the professionals were far ahead of Rémy in matters of technique. Yet he and his makeshift crew managed to bring the vessel into harbor despite the endless succession of gales and ground swells. They really must have possessed some asset of an entirely intangible nature. Perhaps it derived from the star, which gave them their bearings. Their very inexperience faced them, more often than other men, with the choice of being a hero or a traitor. They were far more often heroes than traitors.

Trepper was now at the crossroads.

However much he might dazzle the Kommando with his technical virtuosity, the fact remained that he was in their power. Should he bargain? Come to terms? Embark on a long and intricate strategic game? But he was the Big Chief, and his opponents would hardly be content with a few pawns when he had the power to deliver the knights and castles of his network—indeed the whole game!

Would he prove a traitor or a hero?

———◆———

Next day, November 25, 1942, Madame Alfred Corbin was arrested, together with her daughter Denise and her brother-in-law Robert Corbin. Giering had given the two women advance notice that he wished to bring them face to face with Alfred Corbin, and it had been arranged that a Kommando car would call for them at the Rue Cernuschi at three in the afternoon. The Gestapo was on time. Madame Corbin asked whether she should take some blankets along. "What for?" said the Germans, "You'll be coming right back." Despite these reassurances, the thought of the ordeal ahead distressed her so that Robert Corbin was persuaded by his wife, who happened to be present, to accompany the two women to the Rue des Saussaies. But in fact the Gestapo car drove the trio straight to Fresnes

———

* *Ibid.*, p. 544.

prison. Robert Corbin was thrust into an empty cell, with his wrists handcuffed behind his back. A square of black cloth had been nailed in front of the window to keep out the daylight, but an electric-light bulb hung from the ceiling; it could not be switched off from inside the cell. Later, the prisoners who brought his supper whispered to him that the Red Card had been affixed to the door, meaning that his was an especially serious case. "I just couldn't make sense of what was happening," he says. "It was as if the sky had fallen in on me."

One thing is certain, however: the catastrophe was none of Trepper's doing.

On that very same day, the people in charge of Simexco were arrested in Belgium. Robert Christen, the forceful proprietor of the Florida, still quivers with indignation when he recalls the event. "I give you my word of honor that never, not for a single moment, had the thought of working for the Resistance crossed my mind! The Gestapo should have been ashamed of themselves for not recognizing my good faith!" He was taken to St.-Gilles prison, where he found himself in the company of Henri de Ryck, publisher; Jean Passelecq and Charles Drailly, businessmen; the lawyer Beublet, legal adviser to the firm; Louis Thévenet, owner of a cigarette factory. Henri Seghers was thrown into a cell in Breendonck fort for playing bridge with Margarete Barcza and letting himself be talked into joining the board of Simexco. Nazarin Drailly, the company's managing director, escaped the roundup. He took refuge in the house of a woman friend, Mademoiselle Ponsaint, who made thorough preparations for his escape to a safe hideout. But Drailly's wife had been caught, and he refused to go into concealment until Mademoiselle Ponsaint delivered a parcel to her. Mademoiselle Ponsaint agreed, and was promptly arrested; the Gestapo went and picked up Nazarin Drailly.

He had joined the network through Grossvogel, who had been a close friend for years; indeed, Madame Drailly had at one time managed one of the branches of Le Roi du Caoutchouc. Like Alfred Corbin, his counterpart at Simex, Nazarin had been warned of the coming storm; Trepper had arranged for him to slip across the border into Switzerland. But like Corbin, with whom he seems to have had more than one point in common, including thought for other people's sufferings, Drailly was well aware that he could not vanish from the scene without compromising his associates. He had simply warned the Big Chief that he did not think he would be able to stand up to torture. His sacrifice had not prevented the capture of his wife or his brother Charles, who owned stock in Simexco.

And Madame Grossvogel was another of those arrested on November 25. She was collected from the hospital where she had just given birth to the child for which she had longed for so many years. She had feared that she might be sterile, but a course of treatment at Salies-de-Béarn had at last worked the miracle: she was a mother. Her husband, forewarned of the threat hanging over the network, had begged her to leave the hospital immediately and get to the hiding place he had prepared for her. She had refused, so that the baby would not be deprived of medical care too soon. The Gestapo placed her in a cell at St.-Gilles prison; she was allowed to keep her infant with her.

Bill Hoorickx was captured a few days later. He had spent the night in the cabaret where Django Reinhard was playing. At dawn he was arrested at a friend's home by an SS officer and a squad of German police armed with submachine guns. The Gestapo already knew Rauch's address. They instructed Hoorickx to telephone him and lure him into a trap. As soon as he had his friend on the line, Hoorickx shouted: "Get out! I'm arrested!" His guards hurled themselves upon him and knocked him cold. All the same, Rauch was arrested the following day. By now he was playing only an episodic role in the network's activities, but his son had become an important source of information. This young Czech, an engineering student had been forcibly conscripted into the Wehrmacht and assigned to construction work on the Atlantic Wall. Whenever he came to Brussels on leave, he would hand his father a thick bundle of papers.

Thus the last vestiges of life were drained from the Belgian network. But Trepper had no hand in this final killing.

The Gestapo also visited the Rue du Dragon, in Marseilles, where Simex had established its branch office. They arrested Jules Jaspar, together with his wife and a young secretary named Marguerite Marivet. Monsieur Jaspar, patrician, former member of the Belgian consular service and managing director of the Foreign Excellent Trench Coat Company, was informed by the Germans that he was a member of a Soviet spy network. He turned bright red and cried, "Ah, the dirty dogs! And there I was, thinking I was working for British Intelligence!"

Trepper may have misled him about whether he was furthering the interests of Moscow or London, but it was certainly not his fault that poor Monsieur Jaspar was now debarred from further work for what he had always imagined to be His Britannic Majesty's Service: the Gestapo had found the address of the Marseilles branch in the files of the parent company, back in Paris.

After that, the Lyons group fell. Operating under the leadership of the zealous and resourceful Romeo Springer, it had established useful contacts with such prominent figures as the former Belgian minister, Balthazar, and the United States consul. It had acquired its own transmitter and was preparing to transmit information straight to Moscow when the Gestapo struck. Among those arrested was Otto Schumacher, the man who had housed and fed Wenzel in Brussels. Germaine Schneider, the 'Professor's' mistress, managed to escape, but not for long; she was picked up by the Kommando in Paris. Romeo Springer defended himself gun in hand, and it took a regular siege to overpower him. When finally caught, he was taken to Paris with the others and imprisoned in Fresnes prison. There, he climbed over the safety rail on the third gallery and jumped to his death with his secrets. He had always been courageous.

So ended the short-lived Lyons network. It was Raichman, not Trepper, who had precipitated its collapse.

However, the German documents do credit the Big Chief with the arrests of Katz, Grossvogel, Vasili Maximovich and Robinson. He began by betraying Katz, the stanchest of his lieutenants, his old companion of the Palestine days. On Giering's orders, he telephoned and arranged to meet him at the Madeleine Métro station. Little Katz was arrested on one of the platforms, driven to the Rue des Saussaies and brought face to face with Trepper. "Katz," said the Big Chief, "we must cooperate with these gentlemen. The game is over." For in the jargon of the Soviet secret service, spying was known as "the game." Next he betrayed Vasili, and then came the turn of Leo Grossvogel, the network's chief of staff. That indefatigable organizer had prepared a whole series of lifelines which would enable the survivors to stay out of harm's way until things quieted down. There was only one thing he had not allowed for: the disloyalty of his chief.

A traitor.

Fortner says: "I did not attend the early interrogations of the Maximoviches, but I know Giering's men were extremely harsh with them—especially Rolf Richter, who was dealing with Anna. They used every available means of softening them up. You see, a man like Trepper, an officer in the Red Army, couldn't be blamed for working against us. He was merely doing his duty. But Maximovich, the son of a Tsarist general! I said to him, 'How could you, a White Russian, have agreed to help the Communists?' 'My sympathies were with the Germans,' he replied, 'until the day I read in the newspapers that they intended giving the Ukraine its independence. I am a Russian first and last. No Russian can sit back and watch his country being dismembered.' Well, I couldn't argue with that.

"It wouldn't be fair to say the Maximoviches broke down. That would be going too far. Still, they did talk. And that, of course, made an enormous scandal. Almost every staff officer in Paris was implicated. *And* the embassy! *And* the Reich Ministry of Labor! The mind boggles at the thought of all the contacts they had.

"Giering left me to handle the investigation, for anything relating to the Abwehr and the military administration was for the Abwehr to deal with; the SS had no right to poke its nose in. So I took over from his men. Maximovich put us onto a hard-core member of the network, Käthe Voelkner. We knew that Raichman used to receive blank official forms from Paris. Maximovich admitted that they were supplied by a woman working for the Sauckel Organization, and it didn't take me long to discover that this was Voelkner. She happened to be away from Paris at the time, on vacation in Königsberg with her boss. As soon as she got back, I called at her office and found her on her knees, opening a safe. 'Are you Mademoiselle Voelkner?' I asked. 'Yes,' she said, 'and I know why you're here. You've come to arrest me.' 'Exactly. Hand over that key and follow me.' She was fair and rather small, very strong and wiry.

"I may add that when her boss returned to the office next day he nearly exploded. 'Why, you must be insane!' he said to me. 'That girl is irreproachable. . . .' And so on and so forth. 'Calm down, calm down,' I said, 'Just consider yourself lucky you aren't being arrested yourself. Your friend Voelkner is a spy.' He was absolutely staggered. It was from him that I obtained the address where the girl was living with an Italian named Podsialdo. We rushed straight there, but there was no sign of him; and when we questioned Käthe about him, she wouldn't talk. We went back there and made inquiries of the neighbors. One woman said, 'The Italian? Why, he works for the Germans too!' And that was how we came to find him working in one of the offices of the Sauckel Organization; he and Voelkner were attached to different departments.

"She was of the same breed as Sophie Poznanska, the cipher expert at the Rue des Atrébates. She wouldn't reveal anything—anything at all! But Podsialdo told us the whole story: how they had traveled all over Europe and been stranded in Leningrad and so on. He was a poor fish, that Podsialdo, spineless as they come. He told us that his girl friend often typed secret reports on a typewriter hidden in their flat, and that we would even find copies of some of them. We took her around there with us, and when we found her typewriter she got quite worked up. We had to handcuff her wrists behind her back. 'That doesn't bother me!' she cried, and quick as a flash she twisted herself and brought her hands in front of her. She was an acrobat all right! We all laughed. And then we took the handcuffs off her.

"Podsialdo also confessed that he was in touch with a Frenchman working for the Wehrmacht's Central Billeting Office in Paris. Soon afterwards, we shot the Frenchman; but I can't begin to tell you the harm he must have done us. He used to work in the *Jeip-Fahrer* Department. '*Jeip*' was a word made up from the first letters of the phrase '*Jeder einmal in Paris*' ["Everyone to Paris once"]. In other words, the department's job was to see that every German soldier had a visit to the French capital. A form of propaganda: it was good for morale. Mind you, the invitations were sent to individual men; there could be no question of pulling entire units out of the front line. The Paris office would be informed that Private A, serving with Unit B, was due to arrive from Point C for a spell of leave in Paris. You grasp what this meant? It meant that, thanks to this piffling little Frenchman, Trepper was able to build up a more or less complete picture of how our forces were deployed. Ah, that's what I call espionage! And the Frenchman wasn't really supposed to refer to the lists at all. But he had wormed into the confidence of the two NCOs in charge, and they left him alone. The pair of them were sentenced to eight years' hard labor.

"They weren't the only ones. Margarete Hoffman-Scholtz, Maximovich's fiancée, got six years. And a good many senior officers who were mixed up with the Maximovich affair received stiff sentences. What a rumpus! I went to see General Schaumberg, the man in charge of security matters at Paris H.Q. When he heard what I had to tell him, he was beside himself with fury. 'I'm going to prune this place with an ax!' he shouted. But alas, by that time the damage was done. Anyway by then there was a sort of intuitive decision to close ranks. Had Berlin learned the full truth, there would have been hell to pay! We agreed among ourselves that our official reports would contain only a considerably watered-down version of events. As a result, they never found out how deeply implicated Paris H.Q. really was."

Fortner found a parakeet in Käthe Voelkner's flat. He entrusted it to a neighbor, saying with a laugh: "It's yours. You can keep it, for the other bird won't be coming back." Käthe's fourteen-year-old son, however, was sent to a "Nazi Party Reception Center" in Berlin. There was no reason why, after a suitable "reeducation," he should not become a stanch servant of those who were about to kill his mother.

———————◆———————

Kent cracked.

They let Margarete linger in her cell at the Alexanderplatz for four whole days before taking her to Gestapo headquarters. "He was there. Poor darling, it came as a terrible shock to him: it was the first time he had ever seen me looking messy, with no makeup on and my hair all over the place. The Gestapo man who was with us saw how upset he was and said to him, 'I'll make you a deal; we'll leave you alone with her all day, but you'll talk to us at night.' Vincent agreed. And so I was able to see him every day. But the Germans remained suspicious. Imagine, every time we separated they used to look inside my mouth to make sure Vincent hadn't slipped me a message while he was kissing me! Even at the prison, they began to treat me more kindly. Willy Berg often used to come and see me. Oh, he was repulsive-looking, that one, with Gestapo written all over him; but when you got to know him you felt sorry for him. He had already lost two children, poor thing, both of them carried off by diphtheria. And one day he came to my cell absolutely overcome with grief. 'I've just buried the last of my children,' he said. A little girl ten years old. Diabetes. Afterward his wife tried to commit suicide. Poor thing, it was impossible not to feel for him."

Each parting kiss was like the kiss of Judas. Having devoted his days to love, Kent devoted his nights to betrayal. He confirmed the Gestapo's belief that he had conspired with Schulze-Boysen and Harnack—it was for this purpose he had been brought to Berlin. He disclosed Alfred Corbin's activities in Leipzig. He revealed detail after detail about the Brussels network. These admissions told the Gestapo little they did not know, but they were welcome evidence of Kent's servility.

In these closing weeks of 1942 which had seen the Kommando's conclusive victory over the Red Orchestra, the Gestapo chiefs were already beginning to think of the future. Upon the ruins of the stricken network they aimed to build a masterpiece of offensive counterespionage. On the evening of November 24, Giering had sent word to Hitler (whom he knew personally) of the Big Chief's capture; the Führer had been so gracious as to voice his congratulations. Himmler too had found it hard to contain his joy when Giering telephoned him to announce the marvelous news; he had concluded the conversation with the following almost medieval entreaty: ". . . And now throw him into the deepest cellar in Paris and load him with chains. Whatever happens, he must not escape!" But these were just words, of course. The Reichsführer and his deputies had devised an altogether different role for their captive, fully commensurate with his rank and gifts. They had not captured the head of Soviet espionage in western Europe to let him rot in the depths of a dungeon.

Late in December, 1942, Kent was informed that he was going to be moved to Paris. There Big Chief and Little Chief, working together again, were to be the instruments of the most extraordinary *Funkspiel* that had ever been known.

Kent agreed. Trepper had already given his assent.

25. Last Echoes in Berlin

The members of the Berlin network reacted with greater individual strength.

In that roundup of early September, 1942, one hundred and eighteen people were packed off to the city's jails, the most important of them to Gestapo headquarters in Prinz-Albrechtstrasse. They were a strange hodgepodge drawn from every class and clique: young and old, factory hands and society women, army officers and students, Communists and reactionaries. It was rather like one of those great dawn roundups before the war, when the police net closed indiscriminately on early-shift workers and on the last of the night's revelers, still clad in their tailcoats and evening dresses. Nothing could have been further removed from the methodical demolition of the associate networks. In Brussels and Paris, every stone loosened by the Gestapo had brought about the collapse of a particular stretch of wall, without undermining the rest of the structure. But here, barely had the two main pillars of the network been knocked away when the whole edifice came crashing down. The Gestapo spent all its time sorting out the debris.

One hundred and eighteen people, not one hundred and eighteen agents. How many of them knew of the transmitters' existence, of the links with Trepper and Kent, and of the hundreds of messages which made German troops a sitting target for the Soviet artillery? Five at least, fifteen at most. Also to be counted among the agents were Erna Eifler and Wilhelm Fellendorf, who had been dropped over East Prussia the previous month but had never got farther than Hamburg; there they had just been arrested, together with fifteen Communist dockers. And two other agents were Albert Hössler and Robert Barth; they had been parachuted into the country, with a transmitter, a few days before Schulze-Boysen's arrest, but were caught before they could do more than establish preliminary contact with Moscow.

But is it possible to assert that Colonel Gehrts, for instance, was consciously a spy? Politically he belonged to the right, if not the extreme right. After serving as a flying officer in the First World War, he tried his hand at journalism and became editor of the conservative publication *Tägliche Rundschau*. In 1935 he returned to the colors, worked his way up the ladder and, in 1942, was put in command of the Special Missions branch of the Luftwaffe. The nature of his duties gave him access to a wide variety of top-secret information. Among other things, he received advance notice of airborne operations on the eastern front. Officially, his job was to arrange transport for the paratroops; but his unofficial activities guaranteed them a quick death as soon as they leaped from the aircraft. Despite his anti-Communist beliefs, Gehrts had taken the view, from the very first, that the war against Russia was a piece of criminal lunacy. Many of his colleagues thought so too, but did not see it as an adequate reason to betray their country. Schulze-Boysen, however, had an extraordinary talent for winning men over to his cause; he would have made a brilliant recruiting sergeant. Gehrts was profoundly superstitious, with a strong interest in the occult; he was forever reading cards and tea leaves. He was brought into contact with Anna Krause, a fortune-teller. For here was a network that had its own fortuneteller. Among her patrons were many senior officers, civil servants and businessmen. While unveiling the future to them, she would encourage them to talk about the present. Promises of meetings with women dark or fair were interspersed with inquiries about the patron's working life (she supplied with a list of questions especially adapted to each individual). Once Gehrts was under her thumb, was he a spy or a dupe?

Most of the prisoners were members of the underground Resistance.

There had been that memorable night in 1941 when sixty of them had spread through the streets of Berlin to paste anti-Nazi posters on the walls; they had been protected by uniformed officers with drawn pistols. The operation had been directed by Harro Schulze-Boysen. He had staged it in response to Goebbels's "Soviet Paradise" exhibition, which had presented the German public with startling evidence concerning the poverty of the Russian people. The next morning the citizens of Berlin had been stunned to read Schulze-Boysen's reply: "The Nazi Paradise: War—Hunger—Lies—Gestapo. How much longer?"

There were those young men who used to stride the streets of Berlin after dark, like exhausted travelers returning from a long journey. Their suitcases were so heavy that they had to stop and set them down at frequent intervals, while they caught their breath. Each time one of these cases was set down, the pavement was stamped with an anti-Nazi slogan.

There were the editors, printers and distributors of the fortnightly newspaper *The Inner Front*, a propaganda sheet aimed principally at the mass of foreign workers employed in Germany; besides the German edition, there were others in Russian, Italian, Polish, Czech and French.

There were the anti-Nazi leaflets placed in telephone boxes or under seats in public vehicles, or slipped into letterboxes late at night.

There were the carefully thought-out, illegally printed pamphlets which were sent to people who served the Nazi system without always sharing its ideology and were considered amenable to reason. They had titles like: "The Birth of the Nazi Party," "Who Made War Inevitable?" "Summons to Resist" and "Why the War Is Lost." The best of these pamphlets, "Napoleon Bonaparte," described the ordeals of the Wehrmacht in Russia and foretold the fate in store for it, with supporting quotations from histories dealing with the defeat of the Grand Armée.

In addition, there were escape routes to Switzerland and Sweden for Jews, fugitives from concentration camps, and all who were persecuted by the regime.

Finally there was the plan for a nationwide sabotage campaign. This was in the final stages of preparation when the Gestapo struck.

How brave and enterprising it all was, but at the same time how insane! Harro Schulze-Boysen was one of Moscow's three or four most valuable sources of information. Yet here he was, in his fine uniform, brandishing a pistol while his little friends pasted up notices which would be torn down in a few short hours! Here he was, drafting leaflets and correcting proofs of *The Inner Front!* A man whose value to the Russian war effort was equivalent to that of several divisions in the field, he deliberately put himself at the mercy of any casual police patrol, of confessions of some petty distributor of leaflets, or betrayal by any of the foreign workers—after all, a good many of them were toiling for the Reich of their own free will. He was cautioned on several occasions. The wary and secretive Harnack begged him to desist, but he would not listen. And Hugo Buschmann, though he could not claim to be a professional, showed considerable common sense:

I used to tell Harro that propaganda must be kept in a separate compartment from the all-important work of secret transmissions. Experience proved that such propaganda was always discovered in the end. It would be terrible if far more vital tasks were jeopardized in this way. Harro would make promises, but he was never able to keep them. He persevered with both activities until the very end.*

Was it his all-consuming need for action that impelled him to engage in any enterprise, however trivial? Or did the rocklike

* H. Buschmann, "De la résistance au défaitisme," p. 274.

Schulze-Boysen possess a few human faults after all? Perhaps he felt
he could perform his awesome task only if he was surrounded by the
generosity and enthusiasm of pure-heartedness of those who risked
their lives for very modest results. Or perhaps, as he hammered
away mercilessly at what seemed to him the monstrous features of his
own country, he welcomed these paltry scraps of evidence—a leaflet
here, a pamphlet there—as proof that he too was helping to fashion a
new face for Germany.

Caught in the net with the real agents and the real members of
the Resistance were the people who used to perplex and infuriate
Ernst von Salomon's friend Ille—"There they stand, leaning against
the mantelpiece, with a cup of tea in their hand, quite casually discussing things . . . things—well, any of the things they discussed
could cost them their heads!" Some were now in cells. Others, four
or five hundred, were being harried and cross-examined by the police:
they sat on hard wooden stools, without a teacup in sight, giving
little away beyond the fact that Schulze-Boysen had been blurting
out his hatred of the Nazis at every dinner party in town—information already shared by one or two thousand Berliners.

Buschmann writes:

I longed to teach Harro discretion. He was terribly indiscreet. At
that time it was smart, in fashionable quarters of Berlin, to tell what were
known as political stories. Harro couldn't refrain from joining in. He
would sit there in his Luftwaffe uniform, sporting his Iron Cross, and
cause an absolute sensation by making wild disclosures about the ministry,
about the various theaters of operations, about prisoners being executed,
and so on. Those elegant ladies and talkative gentlemen used to prattle
away until dawn; but afterward the women never forgot to mention this
radiant officer who was a god to every one of them. They did not know
how dangerous it was to have dealings with him.*

But what was the Gestapo doing all this time? One can understand why Schulze-Boysen, despite his rebellious views, was admitted to the "Institute of Research"; he had been recommended by
Reichsmarschall Goering. Moreover, it would be quite wrong to suppose that terror was the only weapon by which the Nazis achieved
and clung to power; they were so convinced that they were right, so
aware of their own dynamism and enthusiasm, that they never

* *Ibid.*, p. 272.

doubted that sooner or later they would convert even their fiercest critics. And events proved them right, for if a few thousand unyielding opponents were eventually packed off to concentration camps, how many tens of thousands renounced their own party insignia in favor of the Swastika? Finally, according to Dr. Meyer, a senior administrator under the Third Reich, due allowance must be made for a specifically German trust in other people, an inherent inability to foresee treachery. "From the moment Schulze-Boysen donned the uniform of a Luftwaffe officer, he was beyond suspicion. Who would dream of suspecting a German officer? Being a traitor and wearing a German uniform simply do not go together."

One can even accept that the wild words spoken by Harro and his friends were dismissed by the Gestapo as being of no account. Every country and every regime has its dinner-table satirists. Their existence was no more to be wondered at in Berlin than anywhere else. Besides, as Meyer says:

There is a general tendency today to exaggerate the totalitarian nature of the regime and the efficiency of the Gestapo. This is understandable enough, for it is in everybody's interest, especially in Germany, to claim that he or she suffered under the Nazis. They all like to make out that for twelve whole years they lived in constant fear of the Gestapo pounding on their doors. It simply isn't true. In Berlin especially, there was quite a broad measure of tolerance. Jibes against the regime, unbridled conversations, and entertainments after the style of the famous "fourteen-point" parties—all these were commonplace whims among the ruling circles.

Even so, surely the behavior of a man like Schulze-Boysen, whose "jaw quivered whenever the Nazis were mentioned," went far beyond the norm. (The norm was represented by remarks like: "My dear, did you know that Ley, the Minister of Labor, used to have a *v* in his name, between the *e* and the *y?*")

But what about the sixty men who had put up posters in the streets of Berlin, the six-language edition of *The Inner Front*, and the ceaseless production and distribution of leaflets and pamphlets? A great many people were in on the secret. It only needed one of them to break down and confess, and the network itself would be wide open to attack—including the central nucleus of agents in touch with Moscow.

There is no point in mincing words: it is staggering, breathtaking, that the Gestapo could have remained so blind. Quite inexplicable. Their failure is so irrational that there is a temptation to invoke the supernatural. Rémy, whose network was a technical miracle in comparison with Schulze-Boysen's, but who was well aware that by all known laws he *should* have been caught, observes:

Why was I protected, when so many others succumbed? Doubtless the mission which had been entrusted to me, and which far exceeded my modest personal capacity, *had* to be brought to fruition. I can see no other reason. Alone, unarmed, inexperienced, I was afraid, constantly afraid. If I held out, if I was aided, it was because I prayed, putting all my trust in Her who has never ceased to lavish her blessings upon me and to whose care I now proposed entrusting the network.*

It is doubtful that Schulze-Boysen and Harnack would have accorded the Virgin Mary a place in their security arrangements. But one thing is certain: their long period of impunity—like Rémy's survival against all odds—suggests that intelligence is not an exact science, and that the fate of the best agent, or the worst, ultimately rests in the lap of the gods.

What, then, was the use of training?

What use was it, for instance, in preventing the downfall of the German network, toppled through the fault of some official at the Moscow Center who didn't know his job? If the man on the spot was a tightrope walker like Schulze-Boysen, all the more reason for his high wire to be securely fastened. And such things can be learned. It was really outrageous for the Director of Soviet Intelligence so calmly to have committed those three addresses to a single telegram, and for Schulze-Boysen and his men, who had led charmed lives for so long, to have been undone by the incompetence of their own superiors in Moscow. For the Gestapo had not spotted them until the Center pointed them out.

"Stalin was to blame; Stalin was solely to blame!" writes Marshal Yeremenko, of the first wave of Russian military disasters. The Director might reasonably have said the same about the catastrophe in Berlin. Stalin's political blindness had prevented Soviet Intelligence from establishing cohesive organization in Germany. And after the launching of Barbarossa, the Center had fallen victim to the panic and con-

* Rémy, *Mémoires d'un agent secret* . . . , Vol. 1, p. 329.

fusion which afflicts any country at a time of headlong retreat. The fateful telegram to Kent with those three addresses had been dispatched on October 10, 1941. A few days later, on October 19, all radio contact was severed between the Moscow base and the scores of Soviet transmitters scattered about the globe; indeed, some pianists receiving instructions from Moscow that night were cut off in the middle of a cipher group; they were left in the dark for six weeks—and then the Moscow radioman calmly picked up his cipher group exactly where he had abandoned it. The explanation was that the German Panzer divisions were racing toward Moscow, and the base had been ordered to fall back to Kuibyshev. Senior officers received only twelve hours' notice, and lower ranks received none at all. With the brain center in such disarray, is it surprising that the limbs lost all coordination?

But Kent had already established preliminary contact with the Berlin group in April, 1941, on the occasion of his trip to Leipzig. That was before Barbarossa, and the Director had had plenty of time to organize a proper rendezvous, complete with passwords, signs of identification, and all the other trappings of strict security procedure. This would have been an ideal chance to establish a sound communications system between the Brussels experts and the amateurs in Berlin. Why had this not been done? That was the great mistake! True, there were obvious risks: if the networks were linked, the discovery of one might lead to the other. But there was no shortage of technical tricks to enable agents to keep their distance—"letterboxes" (living or dead), "cutouts," and so on. A careful staggering of their transmissions would have guaranteed security.

Afterward, of course, there was no time. All the intelligence technicians to whom I have spoken defend the Director for having sent that telegram. How could he adhere rigidly to the rules when German tanks were within sight of the Kremlin? What did the death of the Berlin network matter, if its sacrifice helped save Moscow? Moreover, the extraordinary wealth and size of Soviet espionage justified him in this calculated slaughter; Schulze-Boysen and his companions would soon be replaced.

So they had been sacrificed—just like the rear guard a general may sacrifice to save the main body of his army. It was rational, and they themselves would probably have accepted it as such. Yet their fate continues to shock and offend us, while the fate of the sacrificed infantryman merely touches our hearts. This is because a soldier jeopardizes his life, and nothing else; everyone knows—including the soldier himself—that he becomes cannon fodder as soon as he steps into uniform. The agent risks worse than death; he risks torture and, with it, the possibility of betraying his comrades, his wife and even his children. So that ultimately he risks losing what one may term, for simplicity, his soul.

———◆———

They withstood the ordeal well.

Koppkow and Panzinger meted out degrees of suffering commensurate with their victims' standing in the network. At the lower end of the scale came the "drawing-room revolutionaries." These, in accordance with their usual practice, talked unrestrainedly. Yes, they had occasionally listened to the BBC; yes, they had been known to make fun of Dr. Ley and his drinking habits, of little Goebbels and his mistresses, and even—yes, even of the Führer. But they had never belonged to a spy ring. They hadn't imagined such a thing could exist in Berlin. They swore they weren't agents. And it was true; they were only sources. How could they have suspected that the secrets they had given away, simply in order to shine at social gatherings, were collated and sent to Moscow? In due course they would be punished for their careless talk, just as the superiors and colleagues of Harnack and Schulze-Boysen would be punished for having let them pry into affairs outside their own sphere. But should they, then, have suspected a protégé of Goering? Or suspected Harnack, that seemingly irreproachable civil servant, the very embodiment of conscientiousness? The whole affair was bewildering.

The captured members of the Resistance had to endure the blinding glare of lamps in offices which felt terribly overheated after the freezing cells; their handcuffs tightened until they tore the skin; the interminable interrogations interspersed with beatings. A few broke down, but most held firm and fought savagely for their lives. Among the latter was Gunther Weisenborn, the well-known dramatist. On Schulze-Boysen's instructions he had joined the German broadcasting service, where he had attended secret conferences. It was through his efforts that the speeches of Stalin, Churchill and Roosevelt, obviously censored by the Nazis, had been distributed in leaflets to the German public. He denied every allegation. Then he learned that a woman had denounced him to Panzinger. He kept up hope: under German law, two prosecution witnesses are needed to obtain a conviction. Soon afterward, however, the sculptor Kurt Schumacher also incriminated him, as Weisenborn learned in the course of an interrogation. When he got back to his cell, Weisenborn tore a strip off his bed sheet and concealed it in case he should need to commit suicide. Kurt Schumacher was placed in the next cell. Between them was a wall four feet thick. Weisenborn took a pencil and tapped on the wall—one tap for *a*, two taps for *b*, three taps for *c*, and so on. The sculptor replied with an incoherent hammering. He had failed to grasp the simple code. Weisenborn kept at the task all night long, with an eye on the peephole, in constant fear that a guard might burst in. At dawn he threw himself onto his bunk, exhausted and in despair: he had still not succeeded in making Schumacher understand. Next night he returned to the attack. Suddenly the taps from the other cell acquired a distinct pattern and rhythm. Weisenborn made out the word "understood."

With enormous relief, he sent back the following message: "Essential you retract your statement. Second deposition against me. Will mean death sentence."

"Did not know," came the reply. "Will retract."

Weisenborn had no idea whether this would really save him, whether the law would be respected; but he believed that a man must always fight to the end.*

———◆———

Agents belonging to the spy ring qualified for torture—real torture. Pain drove Hans Heinrich Kummerow to such distraction that he deliberately smashed his spectacles and swallowed the glass; but this didn't do the trick. He slashed his wrists, but was saved in time. Then, using a length of thread, he cut deeply into the flesh between his toes and did his best to infect the wounds; but he was saved from gangrene. He had been one of the ablest engineers at Loewe-Opta-Radio, the company whose direction finders had been so ingeniously sabotaged. Among the vital informations passed on by Kummerow were plans for a night-fighter guidance system and for a new iconoscopic bomb.

Walter Husemann, a fitter by trade, tried to jump out of an open window and carry Panzinger to his death with him; they were caught just in time. Husemann had been given two minutes to disclose two names.

---

* The episode is described by Eric H. Boehm in his book *We Survived* (New Haven, Conn.: Yale University Press, 1949).

Johann Sieg and Herbert Grasse succeeded in killing themselves. Frieda Wesolek had to watch the barrel of a revolver being held to the back of her small son's head.

Though their bodies were savagely burnt with ultraviolet rays, Schulze-Boysen and Harnack would not talk. Science having failed, the Gestapo turned to the medieval repertoire of tortures. The Littré Dictionary gives the following definition of the Boot: "Name of a form of torture in which the criminal's legs were crushed between pieces of wood, which were tightened by striking wedges between them." The Gestapo brought the method up to date, substituting screws for wedges; they also boosted efficiency by applying the equipment to the forearms as well as to the legs. The two prisoners must have screamed with pain, but they did not talk.

Libertas Schulze-Boysen was assured that her life would be spared if she confessed. She told all she knew, and she knew almost everything. What little she forgot to tell Koppkow she confided to her fellow prisoner, Gertrud Breiter, who was in fact a Gestapo spy. Libertas even went so far as to hand her some letters compromising a great many other people. Breiter had claimed she had some means of smuggling them out of prison; of course she handed them straight to the authorities. Beautiful, reckless and even a little crazy, Libertas was all too clearly born to enjoy life; instead, it destroyed her. Subsequently Pastor Poelchau, the prison chaplain, wrote of her: "She was a person without much will power, highly irresponsible, devoid of critical sense and very easily led." * She had always had a presentiment that she would emerge unscathed; when the ordeal came, she took measures to see that she did.

In fact, of course, Panzinger and Koppkow had no real need for confessions. There was nothing hieroglyphical about the network's debris. Despite occasional touches of ingenuity (the recruiting of a man like Gollnow, for instance, and the use of small newspaper ads reminiscent of the technique Trepper had employed in Brussels to bring Alamo and Grossvogel together), the Berlin network acted with astonishing naïveté. Harnack, one of its two leaders, even used his own Christian name as an alias. He used to sign his telegrams "Arvid," just as in Rémy's network Monsieur Louis cheerfully called himself "Joe"; Monsieur Petit, "Poucet"; Monsieur Colas, "Nick"; and Monsieur Bernard, "the Hermit." Harro Schulze-Boysen remained

---

* Harald Poelchau, *Die letzten Stunden* (Magdeburg: 1949).

silent under torture; but he had been extremely talkative on the telephone before his arrest, and his line had been tapped.

◆

Alexander Kraell, German magistrate says: "The discovery of a spy ring on such an unprecedented scale, and in which a predominant role was played by officials attached to various ministries, came as a bombshell. Hitler called for swift, severe punishment." *

The Führer also called for absolute secrecy. The affair was classified as a "state secret." Merely talking about it made anyone liable to the death sentence. According to one of the Gestapo chiefs: "We could not allow such a story to be made public. The accused were neither Jews nor persons of low mentality nor social failures. On the contrary, they were members of the elite." † There was no reference to the spy ring on the radio or in the newspapers. Schulze-Boysen's colleagues imagined he had been sent on a mission abroad. The Economics Ministry continued to send Harnack his salary, and it was not until the very last moment that the Minister himself—Herr Funk —learned that his deputy had been guilty of treason. But Funk can hardly have had his ear to the ground; for, of course the news finally leaked out and was discreetly circulated by word of mouth.

Even Ulrich von Hassell, a prominent member of the Resistance, recorded in his journal: "A vast Communist conspiracy has been discovered at the Air Ministry and in other departments. Fanatics, it would seem (impelled by hatred of the regime); they claim their purpose was to set up a standby organization to meet the possibility of a Bolshevik victory." ‡

At social gatherings, in the anterooms of ministries and along the corridors of service headquarters, there was talk of this evil-smelling abscess suddenly discovered at the heart of the Third Reich. Everyone claimed to know the whole story; what people did not know, they invented; a myth took shape and the wildest suspicions flourished—the inevitable price of secrecy, unless that secrecy is absolute. Berlin shivered with dismay, and even apprehension, for there was an obvious temptation to see a link between these events and the fatal paralysis that seized the Wehrmacht along the banks of

---

* Taken from Herr Kraell's statement at the official inquiry, in 1948, into Manfred Roeder's activities.

† G. Weisenborn, Der lautlose Aufstand, Hamburg, 1953.

‡ Ulrich von Hassell, D'une autre Allemagne, Éditions de la Baconnière, 1948, p. 263.

the Volga. A certain currency was gained by Admiral Canaris's bitter estimate, "This spy network has cost Germany the lives of two hundred thousand soldiers." To say nothing of the strategic consequences.

Swift, severe punishment: that was what Hitler wanted, and doubtless the ordinary people would have wanted it too, had they known.

But the Nazi beasts of prey were less impatient, if not less harsh. They prowled around the captive flock, seeking out any black sheep of a rival service, at the same time making every effort to whitewash their own associates. Goering was the most seriously compromised: several Luftwaffe officers belonged to the network; Schulze-Boysen was its leader. Sensing the peril, the Reichsmarschall reacted forcefully. Later, when Ribbentrop would write his memoirs in his cell at Nuremberg, he would choose this episode to set the tone of his relationship with Goering:

> Whenever I was with the Führer and Goering, the latter would monopolize Hitler's attention and I did not exist; I used to suffer as a result of the repercussions which this had in the field of foreign policy. Goering knew just how to exert his influence on Hitler. I remember a characteristic scene which was enacted at Klesheim Castle; in his anxiety to give Hitler a touched-up picture of the espionage affair known as the "Red Orchestra," in which several Luftwaffe officers had been implicated, Goering threw the blame onto an innocent official at the Ministry for Foreign Affairs. Hitler, who disliked the staff at the Wilhelmstrasse, took Goering's side as usual; it was only by protesting vehemently that I reestablished the truth.*

Hitler doubted that he could obtain swift punishment through normal channels, which would entail a court-martial composed of senior officers. A public tribunal, on the other hand, would soon dispose of the accused. To the Führer, every additional hour of life accorded the prisoners seemed a personal insult. He wanted to get the whole thing over and done with.

The Gestapo were alarmed by this haste. They were reluctant to see a dangerous precedent established. If the Führer fell into the habit of depriving them of their prisoners before they had been fully exploited, their job would become impossible. And not all spy and

---

* Joachim von Ribbentrop, *De Londres à Moscou* (Paris: Grasset, 1953), p. 41.

Resistance networks were likely to prove as easy to dismantle as the Berlin branch of the Red Orchestra. Himmler, for his part, would feel happier if he could lead a few more black sheep to the slaughter—if possible, those bearing the brand of the Ministry of Foreign Affairs. This would mean that he and Martin Bormann were the only two heads of the Nazi Party to escape embroilment. He conferred with Goering, whose word still carried considerable weight with Hitler. The Marshal was so deep in the mire that he had more to gain than anyone else from splashing his colleagues. Himmler outlined the advantages that would accrue to him from the Ilse Stöbe affair. Goering was won over and began to press his views on the Führer. His perseverance reaped results: the defendants of the Red Orchestra were to be tried by a Luftwaffe court-martial, and not by a public tribunal. This would give the Gestapo a few months' grace and enable them to follow up the Stöbe lead.

———◆———

Ilse Stöbe, alias "Alte," * was a functionary in the information office at the Ministry of Foreign Affairs and guardian angel—on behalf of Moscow—of Rudolf von Scheliha, embassy counselor. Ilse was a perfectly straightforward, deeply committed young Communist. From the aesthetic point of view this spoils the picture, for Scheliha ought ideally to have been paired with a Mata Hari; he himself was a thoroughly crude figure. But still, after those Berliners whose motives and attitudes defy analysis, how refreshing to find a spy committing treason purely from love of women, horses and gambling.

Scheliha's salary and his wife's dowry would, at a pinch, have covered the upkeep of harem and stable, but baccarat brought him to the edge of ruin. In 1937 he was toying, as the expression goes, with the idea of blowing his brains out, the only fitting solution for the noble scion of an old Silesian family, when the good-natured souls of British Intelligence and the Moscow Center miraculously intervened, settling his gambling debts and plucking him from the abyss. We do not know the exact nature of the work he subsequently undertook for London. In Moscow, the Director permitting himself a touch of humor, saddled him with the cover name "the Aryan," which soon became notorious among the Center's cashiers for the enormous amounts of money assigned to it. As a rule, Soviet Intelligence was frugal, and much happier dealing with idealists than with mercenaries;

* German for "old."

but at that time Scheliha was serving on the embassy staff in Warsaw, where a vital diplomatic game was being played out. He reported on Germany's efforts to bring Poland into the anti-Soviet coalition. His reports earned him six thousand five hundred dollars, transferred by the Chase National Bank of New York, via Crédit Lyonnais, to his account with the Julius Bär Bank, Zurich.

On the eve of the war Scheliha was recalled to Berlin, but continued to amaze the Moscow cashiers. In February, 1941, they sent him the sum of thirty thousand marks. The Soviet embassy delivered the cash to Ilse Stöbe, who in return handed over Scheliha's reports. Four months later, Barbarossa sent the Russian diplomats scurrying home and compelled the Director to find some other system of communication. He turned to Kent. On August 28, 1941, six weeks before the notorious telegram with the three addresses, Kent received a message instructing him to establish contact with "Alte," living at 37 Wielandstrasse, Berlin, and to set up a radio link for her, independent of the Schulze-Boysen group. When the Director drafted this order, German Panzer divisions were not at the gates of Moscow; they were still three hundred miles away, and sweeping southward toward the plains of the Ukraine. All the same, Ilse Stöbe's name and address were clearly spelled out in the telegram. So that although the Director may have been the anguished figure earlier described, distressed at having to sacrifice a handful of agents in order to save his country, it is equally possible that he was a stolid bureaucrat pinning his simple faith on the uncrackability of his codes. In which case the Berliners, instead of being sacrificed to invincible higher necessities, would have been victims of his arrogant self-assurance—which would be even more galling.

One man solved all Kent's problems in Berlin. It will be recalled how he introduced Schulze-Boysen's amateur pianist to an expert in radio work, and how the amateur received a number of profitable lessons. The expert in question was Kurt Schulze, formerly a radioman in the navy. Kent entrusted him with a code and introduced him to Ilse Stöbe, with instructions to transmit all Scheliha's subsequent reports.

Moscow's radio message giving "Alte's" address was decoded like the others. On September 12, 1942, Ilse Stöbe was jailed, together with her companions. She refused to admit anything, despite the incriminating document. The interrogations continued. But Himmler and Goering's desire to gain time was not impelled solely by the prospect of wringing a confession out of her; they were hoping for a good deal more, thanks to the interception of another message. For the Director must really have believed he had found that marvel of marvels, the unbreakable code. All of them believe it at some time or other, which alone would earn them a place in hell if they were not bound there anyway. Perfectly cynical, they would not be shocked to learn that they had been betrayed by their own parents and that their favorite child was an agent manipulated by the enemy; totally naïve as well, they gape in wonderment at the masterpieces produced by their coding departments, however grieved they may feel when experience confirms, for the nth time, that other mathematicians are capable of unmaking what their own mathematicians have made.

Early in September, 1942, the German monitoring station at Prague intercepted and decoded the following message from the Director to a Czech Resistance network: "Notify Alte Berlin-Charlottenburg 37 Wielandstrasse imminent arrival Köster."

A woman member of the Gestapo moved into Ilse Stöbe's apartment. Two policemen lurked in ambush in the building opposite. The trap was set for "Köster," who might, perhaps, cause the Ministry for Foreign Affairs to be dragged into the Red Orchestra scandal.

But a clap of thunder suddenly petrified the Nazi beasts of prey, uniting their previously divided interests—this was the affair of the Stockholm documents.

26. Silence

On September 30, 1942, a naval captain named Eric Schulze, who had just arrived from Holland, walked into Gestapo headquarters in the Prinz-Albrechtstrasse. He was there to see his son, Harro Schulze-Boysen. Relatives of the other prisoners had begged leave to do the same, but their applications had been remorselessly rejected—and continued to be rejected until the very end. The accused were being kept in solitary confinement. Except for their leader, who was about to receive a visit from his father. According to the dark legend which still has currency, even today, among Abwehr and Gestapo veterans, Eric Schulze, an ardent patriot, drew his pistol and attempted to kill his son on sight; he had to be forcibly restrained from doing so.

Here is his own account:

Superintendent Koppkow, Panzinger's colleague, conducted me to a
first-floor room, which was apparently not ordinarily occupied. There
was a bare desk in a corner and a sofa against a wall, two armchairs and a
small table. I waited alone for a minute or two. Then a concealed door
opened and Harro came in, accompanied by Koppkow and another officer. He lumbered forward as though he were no longer used to walking;
but he held himself very erect, with his hands behind his back, so that I
thought they must be tied, which wasn't the case. His face was colorless
and terribly thin, with rings under his eyes. Apart from this, he looked
almost well-groomed, as if he had prepared himself for this meeting. He
was wearing a gray suit and a blue shirt. I took his hand, drew him to one
of the chairs and sat down in the second, drawing it close to his. I took
both his hands and kept them in mine throughout our conversation. This
pressure of our hands was like a long, intimate dialogue between us.

The two officers sat down at the desk and kept an eye on us. One of
them seemed to be taking down what we were saying.

I told Harro that I had come to him full of fatherly feelings, to help
and fight for him, to hear from his lips how I could help him and why he
had been arrested. At the same time I gave him the affectionate wishes of
his mother, who was also in Berlin, and of his brother. They had not been
allowed to come and see him. He replied calmly but firmly: it was impossible to help him; any fight would be hopeless. For years he had been
knowingly betraying his country. In other words, he had been fighting
the present regime in every possible way and on every possible occasion.
He was perfectly aware of the consequences and fully prepared to bear
them.

One of the officers—they had remained silent until then—asked a
question concerning a matter which Panzinger had already mentioned to
me and which seemed to be worrying the Gestapo. Certain clues had led
them to suppose that prior to his arrest Harro might have smuggled some
vitally important secret documents out of the country—very likely containing revelations about Nazi crimes—with the probable, or even certain,
aim of providing himself and his friends with a form of security in case
they were discovered. Until now, Harro had refused to breathe a word
about this; but perhaps now he would be prepared to discuss it.*

This was the trap. Ever since Schulze-Boysen had hinted that he
had forwarded a number of highly compromising top-secret files to
friends in Stockholm, the Nazi leaders had been in a real state of panic.
Over their heads hung, not a sword of Damocles, but an obscene
bucket full of mire, blood and excrement; their own crimes—the

* This statement was published in June, 1951, by the German weekly *Der Stern*
as part of the series *"Rote Agenten mitten unter uns."*

torturings, the mass executions, the death camps. It was entirely up to Schulze-Boysen whether this filth would be poured over them, sullying faces which, though hardly angelic, were not yet, in 1942, appreciated in their full horror. They themselves knew the truth, and they were afraid. "All I have to do is press a button," Harro had threatened. The documents would be forwarded to London or Moscow, no one knew which. Even their contents were a mystery, which left open all sorts of possibilities.

As usual, the first method resorted to was physical terror. Goering instructed the Gestapo to employ "all available means to force Schulze-Boysen to disclose the facts." Himmler signed an official permit for a "reinforced interrogation." This meant, in Nazi legal jargon, that the prisoner could be flogged. The flogging administered to Schulze-Boysen was duly set down in the official records. A farce, if ever there was one, for what were a few lashes to a man who endured the Boot without weakening?

Unable to break Schulze-Boysen, the Gestapo attempted to soften him by authorizing a visit from his father.

"He firmly rejected their demand," his father continues. "The rest of our conversation was of a personal and intimate nature, but, in view of the presence of the two officers, Harro and I refrained from expressing our feelings outwardly. However, at the end, grief got the better of me, and I stood up, saying, 'The road before you is a hard one. I don't wish to make it even more painful. I'm going now.' Harro stood up too. He drew himself very erect and looked at me proudly, but, for the first time, tears came to our eyes. I only managed to say to him: 'I have always loved you.' He answered softly, 'I know.' I held out my hands to him, and at the door I turned around, looked at him once more, and nodded.

"We both felt that we were seeing each other for the last time."

———◆———

Ilse Stöbe's doorbell rang. The Gestapo woman rushed to see who it was and found a young man on the doorstep.

"I'm looking for an old acquaintance," he said quietly.

"Looking for whom?"

"An *old* acquaintance."

"Come in," she said. "It's me."

But the young man handed her an envelope and vanished before the two policemen hiding in the building opposite had time to intervene. No one ever found out who the messenger was, where he came from, or who had sent him.

Inside the envelope was a sheet of paper, stating simply: "Köster probably arriving 20 October. Arrange contact Köster-Scheliha."

The Gestapo raced to the Ministry of Foreign Affairs, only to learn that Rudolf von Scheliha was in Switzerland, near Lake Constance. He had fled—of this, there was no doubt. The arrest of Ilse Stöbe must have sent him scurrying. He was placed under surveillance by German agents operating in Switzerland. Panzinger himself set out for Lake Constance. But how could Scheliha be brought back by force?

There were no callers at Ilse Stöbe's apartment on the next two days, October 21 and 22. On the night of October 22–23, the Luftwaffe reported a Russian bomber flying over East Prussia; it went away without dropping any bombs. Köster had arrived.

At this point, Gestapo headquarters received an astonishing piece of news from one of its agents in Switzerland: Scheliha was packing and preparing to return to Germany. Did this mean that his journey abroad had not been an attempt to escape? Could it have been mere coincidence, despite the letter from the mysterious messenger? Was Soviet Intelligence—having learned of Alte's arrest—trying to put the Gestapo on the wrong track? Or was the report from the agent in Switzerland simply incorrect? Panzinger stationed himself at the frontier post at Konstanz and, without any great confidence, kept watch for the diplomat's arrival.

At about 5 P.M. on October 26, the two Gestapo men opposite Ilse Stöbe's house saw a man enter who was of medium height, wearing a raincoat and carrying a suitcase. They left their hideout and concealed themselves in the street. The Gestapo woman had a pistol, but her two male colleagues held themselves in readiness to rush to her assistance; for if Köster knew Alte personally, there was no telling his reaction when he discovered that a switch had been made. Five minutes went by. The man emerged from the building. He was no longer carrying the suitcase. He walked away serenely. One of the police officers followed. His companion raced to Ilse Stöbe's apartment. The woman beamed at him and made her report. Yes, it had been Köster. His suitcase contained a transmitter. He had asked to see Scheliha, and she had suggested a rendezvous that same evening at the Café Adler in the Wittenbergplatz. He had muttered some threats against Scheliha: if he didn't do what he was paid to do, he would suffer the consequences. Köster had shown the woman a receipt for six thousand five hundred dollars, signed by the diplomat in 1938. Köster went to the rendezvous. He was really Heinz Köhnen, son of a former Communist deputy at the Reichstag. The father was in London, taking part in the celebrated Operation Black Radio, an attempt to demoralize the Wehrmacht through propaganda broadcasts; day after day, anti-Nazi Germans incited their compatriots to rebellion, giving them the news censored by Goebbels. Meanwhile the son had withdrawn to Moscow. The Center enrolled him in Operation Parachute, aimed at reviving the German network. After Erna Eifler, Wilhelm Fellendorf, Albert Hössler and Robert Barth had been dropped without success, Heinz Köhnen bailed out from a Russian bomber and landed near Osterode, in East Prussia. His chief mission was to establish contact with Scheliha and reawaken his zeal. For some time past, the latter's reports had been infrequent and of poor quality, although his post at the Ministry of Foreign Affairs gave him access to the secrets of German diplomacy. Doubtless he had developed cold feet. The atmosphere of Berlin in 1942 was very different from that of gay Warsaw in the thirties. Scheliha would probably have preferred to back out of this private game in which a man gambled his life, not just his fortune; but renouncing a commitment to the Director was not as easy as getting up and leaving the baccarat table. Heinz Köhnen had been sent from Moscow to remind him of this fact. With him he had eight thousand marks and the old 1938 receipt. The carrot and the stick. If the sight of riches was not sufficient to revive Scheliha's enthusiasm, the threat of handing the receipt to the Gestapo would certainly goad him to action.

Köhnen was arrested at the Café Adler. Impossible to say whether he was tortured or whether he talked without physical coercion, totally disheartened by the obvious fact that the Gestapo knew all about him from the confessions of his four predecessors—"We told him to his face, for instance, where he had lived in Moscow, the number of the streetcar he took to go to his intelligence school, what kind of doors the school had, the names of students and teachers of the school, the names of his friends, etc.; he felt exposed and betrayed." *

Köhnen talked; Ilse Stöbe talked, convinced that her silence was of no further avail; Rudolf von Scheliha talked as soon as he was

---

* Testimony of a Gestapo agent, quoted by David J. Dallin in *Soviet Espionage*, p. 254.

arrested at the frontier post at Konstanz. Goering had succeeeded in compromising Ribbentrop. As for Himmler, he had completed his probings: apart from the SS and Bormann's chancellery, every branch of government would be represented in the dock.

But the trial could not open until the matter of the Stockholm documents had been settled.

No one can say what thoughts passed through Schulze-Boysen's head as he lay in his cell, and it is hard to fathom the strategy of a man who had only one trump card left—and who knew that his life depended on it. Harro had been magnificent until the very end; even from the depths of jail, he managed to strike terror into the hearts of the Nazi leaders. And he was disconcerting until the very end. Another man would have clung desperately to this final lifeline: he would have warned Panzinger and Koppkow that the Stockholm documents would be published if a single member of the network were executed, and then sat back and waited to see if the gamble paid off. Harro did not sit back and wait. He was quite open with the Gestapo. He informed Panzinger that he was prepared to disclose where the papers were hidden in return for a guarantee that no executions would take place before December 31, 1943. (He was convinced that Hitler would have lost the war by then.) The Gestapo referred the matter to the highest authorities in the land: Himmler, Goering, the Führer himself. The deal was concluded. Schulze-Boysen insisted that his father be present when the facts were revealed, and that the Gestapo must reiterate its promise in front of him.

"Harro came into the room with a confident smile," Eric Schulz relates. "Panzinger formally confirmed that the agreement would take effect as soon as he told the truth about the hiding place of the documents—whatever the nature of that hiding place. After a brief pause for effect, Harro declared: 'The documents have not stirred from the Air Ministry files. I deliberately awakened the Gestapo's suspicions so that I should have a means of bringing pressure to bear.' The officials were absolutely dumbfounded. After a moment, Panzinger declared that the conditions of the contract had been fulfilled, and that the agreement was therefore valid."

As a password, Harro Schulze-Boysen used often to choose the following quotation from the poet Stefan George: "A frank eye and a firm hand are more eloquent than words."

On the day the trial opened, a team of workmen were already busy in the building at Plötzensee prison, where decapitations were carried out. They were affixing to the ceiling a steel rail fitted with sliding hooks. The prison staff did not know what to make of this hurried installation (the task was classified as "important and urgent"), for the penal code stated categorically that anyone sentenced to death was to be either shot or guillotined; there was no hanging in Germany.

The court-martial was made up of senior officers. The case for the prosecution was to be made by Manfred Roeder, *Oberstgerichtsrat* to the Luftwaffe, whose fanatical zeal had earned him the nickname "Hitler's bloodhound." The defense lawyers, appointed by the court, had not had time to study the case; and indeed, it appeared that some of them had no wish to do so.

In the dock were thirteen members of the Red Orchestra. The Schulze-Boysens and the Harnacks, naturally, were included in this first batch. So were Horst Heilmann, of Kludow's team of code breakers; Herbert Gollnow, the ambitious young man who had supervised the training of the Caucasian deserters; Kurt Schulze, Scheliha's radio operator; and his pupil Hans Coppi, Schulze-Boysen's amateur pianist. Also present was Johann Graudenz, former United Press correspondent in Moscow and *The New York Times* correspondent in Berlin; he had been liaison man between armament factories and the Luftwaffe, and he had passed German aircraft production figures on to Schulze-Boysen, together with full details of individual bombers and fighters. The sculptor Kurt Schumacher was there too; he was the prisoner who had taken so long to understand the SOS Günther Weisenborn had tapped out on the wall between their cells. Now he sat in the dock with his wife, Elisabeth. Kent had admitted meeting them at the time of his visit to Berlin. And next to the Communist Schumacher was the reactionary Colonel Erwin Gehrts, dabbler in spiritualism and patron of the fortuneteller Anna Krause.

Lastly there was a very beautiful young woman with a radiant smile and an aura of tremendous vitality, Countess Erika von Brockdorf. Like Elisabeth Schumacher, she had been working at the Ministry of Labor since the outbreak of war. Her husband was an officer. She had kept Coppi's transmitter concealed in her home and sheltered some of the agents dropped by parachute. Roeder, the prosecutor, was so stung to see her coming to her trial as though to a party that he snarled at her: "You'll soon lose that smile!" "Not as long as I'm looking at you," she retorted.

The thirteen accused knew that they were liable to the death penalty. Harro Schulze-Boysen was doubtless hoping that the death sentence, if pronounced, would not be carried out within the next twelve months. As for Libertas, she was convinced that only a light penalty was in store for her—she thought she might even be released at the end of the trial. The prosecution's case rested almost entirely on her statements. The gentlemen of the Gestapo had explained to her the position of what the British call a "Crown witness": his statements and testimony against his accomplices gain him immunity from punishment. Libertas had been told that if she agreed to appear as "Gestapo witness," she would enjoy the same privilege. Admittedly, the German legal system provided for nothing of the kind; but it had been a long time, under the Third Reich, since the law code had been taken very seriously. Libertas felt sure she would get out of it. As for the others, we don't know what they may have felt as they sat in the dock. Fear, no doubt, and probably hope as well—for hope is tenacious. But Arvid Harnack's features expressed nothing but a profound melancholy, while the Countess von Brockdorf's smile was beyond fear and hope.

The trial was held behind closed doors, but there were a few spectators in the courtroom: Gestapo officials and representatives of the various ministries implicated in the scandal. For them there was not the slightest doubt that the thirteen accused were doomed to torture as soon as these sham proceedings were over. They were wrong. The court returned from its deliberations to pronounce eleven death sentences.

Roeder lived up to his reputation. To send the accused to their deaths, he had only to prove that they had engaged in spying; and that proof was already written into his brief. But by this stage the lives of the thirteen were of no further interest to him—he had already disposed of them in his mind. It was their names he was now bent on destroying. He accused Schulze-Boysen of embezzling the organization's funds. He spoke at length about the "fourteen-points" parties; and instead of drawing a graph of the network's activities, he subjected the judges to highly detailed sketches of the sex lives enjoyed by individual agents. Obviously the aim was to smear the accused. But for whose benefit? The general public knew nothing of the trial, and Roeder and the judges firmly believed they would never know. The Gestapo chiefs and Nazi officials present in the courtroom were not likely to be shocked by a few sexual pranks; in any case, they already knew all about those in the dock. So it must have been for posterity that the prosecutor was projecting these pornographic pictures, forgetting that posterity does not take orders from courts-martial and that its verdict is often different from theirs.

Arvid Harnack, speaking in a tired, subdued voice, was content to offer the court a statement of principle concluding with the words: "I acted in the conviction that the ideals of the Soviet Union are paving the way for the world's salvation. My aim was the destruction of the Hitler regime by every available means." Schulze-Boysen fought like a lion, denying every detail that was not positively proved. He turned himself from accused into accuser and pilloried his opponents with a whole series of proud and fiery interjections; he had to be called to order. The others measured up to the same high standards. One of the officials who attended the hearing told me, "The fact is, they all conducted themselves splendidly. Except Libertas."

Eleven death sentences. Two of the women received prison terms; Mildred Harnack got six years; Erika von Brockdorf ten.

"When the verdict was pronounced," recalls Herr Behse, one of the defense lawyers, "Libertas screamed and fainted. Although I had begged her more than once to wake up to her situation and prepare herself for the worst, she had remained confident and optimistic until then. And now she explained to me that, as a reward for her confessions, the Gestapo had promised her a light sentence or even freedom."

Theoretically, the sentence was subject to confirmation by the president of the court-martial; he had the right to ratify or reject it. But in this particular instance, Hitler had reserved the privilege for himself, in exchange for renouncing a public tribunal. The fate of all thirteen therefore lay in his hands.

A messenger went to report the findings to Goering, as soon as they were announced. According to Generaloberstabrichter Lehmann, he reacted violently—"He exploded at the words 'prison sentences' and said the Führer would never give his consent." * A few hours later, Hitler himself was informed by his aide-de-camp, Admiral Puttkamer. He confirmed the death sentences, annulled the prison sentences and ordered new trials for Mildred Harnack and Erika von Brockdorf.

* From Herr Lehmann's statement to the court of inquiry into the Manfred Roeder case.

Eleven people went to their death three days later, on December 22, 1942. The executions of Herbert Gollnow and Colonel Gehrts had been postponed, for they were needed for the second trial of Mildred Harnack; but Rudolf von Scheliha and Ilse Stöbe took their places, they too having been sentenced to death in the meantime.

December 22 was cold and dismal; an icy east wind battered Berlin, and darkness fell even earlier than usual. Yet the tradition of Christmas is so deeply rooted in German hearts that even on such a day as this, in spite of the war, in spite of the harsh winds and the harsh news from the east, in spite of difficulties and poverty—even on such a day as this, the streets of Berlin must have carried an echo of the Christmases of old.

The women were decapitated, in accordance with the law. To cap all her other tribulations, Libertas was informed that her cellmate and confidante, Gertrud Breiter, was a member of the Gestapo. She wrote to her mother, a few hours before the end:

> I have had to drain the cup of bitterness to the dregs, for now I learn that a person in whom I had complete trust, Gertrud Breiter, has betrayed us, you and me:
>
> *Now harvest what you have sown*
> *For whosoever betrays shall himself be betrayed.*
>
> Through selfishness, I betrayed my friends. I wanted to be free and come back to you—but, believe me, I would have suffered immensely from the knowledge of my crime.

According to a macabre legend circulating among the Gestapo, Libertas had seduced a young SS guard at Gestapo headquarters. A blind eye was turned to their hasty amours. Having requested and obtained permission for her lover to be with her until the very end, she got him to make love to her one last time in the vehicle which drove her to her execution.

Next day, December 23, her mother, the beautiful Countess Thora Eulenburg, a well-known pianist, hurried about Berlin in the freezing cold, knocking on the door of every prison, begging that her daughter be given the Christmas parcel that she had prepared for her. She was turned away time after time, but no one told her that Libertas had been executed a few hours earlier. Finally, exhausted and beside herself with anguish, the poor woman went and rang the doorbell of her friend Reichsmarschall Goering; he often used to ask her to play the piano for his guests. Goering feigned ignorance. But he probably knew that Libertas's decapitated body was at that very moment being subjected to an autopsy. For immediately after sentence was carried out, Roeder had learned of a rumor that Libertas had been pregnant by her SS friend; knowing that under German law a pregnant woman was not to be executed until after she had given birth, she had tried to use this as a means of gaining a reprieve. The implacable Roeder ordered an autopsy; the results proved negative.

The eight men had been transferred from Prinz-Albrechtstrasse to Plötzensee prison in the course of the afternoon. Before leaving his cell, Harro carefully folded a poem which he had just written and concealed it in a chink in the wall. He disclosed the fact to one of the other prisoners, who, when the time came for his own execution, passed it on to a third. The latter survived and returned after the war to search among the ruins of the building. Miraculously, the poem was intact. The closing stanza runs as follows:

> *The final arguments*
> *Are not the rope or the knife,*
> *And those who judge us today*
> *Will not preside at the Last Judgment.*

They were placed in eight cells of Third Division. The doors were left open, to make it easier for the guard to keep an eye on them. Each condemned man was allowed to write one letter of farewell. Arvid Harnack wrote to his family:

ALL MY DEAR ONES,

I shall be departing this life within the next few hours. I would like to thank you once again for all the love you have given me, especially in these last days. The thought of that love has lightened my burden. I am also thinking of the wonders of nature, to which I feel so close. This morning I recited aloud:

> *The sun, in accordance with ancient rite,*
> *Mingles its voice with the harmonious choir of the spheres*
> *And runs its prescribed course*
> *With thunderous step.*

But above all I think of humanity in its evolution. These are the three foundations of my strength.

I was especially happy to learn that there is soon to be an engagement in the family. I should very much like my signet ring, which was once my father's, to be given to F. This would mean that L. could wear his own. My ring will be sent to you with my effects.

This evening I shall give myself a small Christmas celebration by reading the story of the Nativity. And after that it will be time for me to be on my way. I would have loved to see you all once more. Alas, it is not possible. My thoughts go out to you, and I shall not forget anyone—you must each know that, especially Mother.

For the last time, I embrace you all.

Your Arvid

PS. You must celebrate Christmas as usual. This is my last wish. And be sure to sing "I Invoke the Power of Love."

Harro Schulze-Boysen wrote:

Dear Parents,

So the time has come; another few hours and I shall be parting company with my "self." I am perfectly calm, and I beg you to be so too and to accept the news unperturbed. Such important things are now at stake on this earth that the extinction of a single human life is of small account.

I do not wish to say anything further about what is past and what I have done. Everything I have done, I have done with the full knowledge of my head and heart, and by conviction. That is the light in which you, my parents, must accept them. I beg you to do so.

This way of dying suits me. Somehow, I always knew it would be like this. It is, in Rilke's phrase, my "personal way of dying."

It is only when I think of you that I feel heavyhearted, my dear ones. Libertas is close to me and will be sharing my fate at the same hour. You two are now suffering both a loss and a feeling of shame, and this you have not deserved. Time will soften your sorrow—not only do I hope it, but I am convinced of it. I am only a pioneer, with my impetuous impulses and my sometimes rather confused intentions. Try to believe, as I do, that time, which is just, will bring all things to ripeness.

I shall be thinking until the very end of the last look my father gave me—I shall be thinking of my darling Mama's tears at Christmas. It has taken these last months to bring me so close to you—I, your prodigal son, now completely returned to the fold. After so much impulsiveness and passion, after following so many paths which seemed so strange to you, I have finally found my way home.

I am thinking of dear H. and am glad he is better. My thoughts take me back to Freiburg, where I saw Helga and her family for the first and last time. Yes, I conjure up the memory of so many other people, the memory of a full and beautiful life, for which I owe you so much—so much that was never returned.

If you were here—you *are* here, even if invisible—you would see me laughing in the face of death. I conquered my fear of it long ago. In Europe, blood usually has to nourish ideas. It is possible that we were only a pack of fools. But when death is so close, one is surely entitled to a little self-delusion.

Yes, and now I reach out my hand to you all, and in a little while I shall deposit a tear here (just one) as a seal and as a token of my love.

Your Harro

———◆———

Pastor Poelchau, the prison chaplain, had learned only by chance that a party of prisoners under sentence of death had arrived at Plötzensee. He went there quickly and visited every cell, one by one. Schumacher, the sculptor, made a profound impression on him. Only a few hours before death, he radiated a sense of joy. Harro, on the other hand, seemed to shy at the prospect. Not that he was afraid; he was absolutely calm. But it pained him to think of all the opportunities for action he would be losing; just as a vanquished soldier suffers at having to surrender his weapons, so Harro Schulze-Boysen was having difficulty in accepting the fact that the fight was over and that he must now deliver his courage and strength into the hands of death. The poem which he had hidden in his cell contained the following outburst:

> *With death at your throat,*
> *How you love life . . .*
> *And your mind is brimming over*
> *With all that used to propel it.*

The lights in the cells had to be switched on very early; outside, it was almost dark. The guards paced up and down the corridor. They were inhuman, like robots, treating their charges with silent hostility. In prisons all over the world, guards will display a degree of friendliness in the last moments of a condemned man, even if he has committed the most abominable crimes. Were the guards at Plötzensee always so implacable, or did they become so only to the members of the Red Orchestra?

One official arrived before the rest and stationed himself close to Scheliha. Ribbentrop had requested a stay of execution for the diplomat, on the grounds that he had not yet completed a list of informations he had been passing to the Russians since 1937. No reply to this petition had been received as yet. In case a favorable answer should arrive at the last moment, the Minister of Foreign Affairs had sent one of his officials, Karl Hofman,* to Plötzensee.

Hofman knew Scheliha. He considered him charming and hoped he would obtain his reprieve. Perhaps Scheliha was a traitor, but Hofman felt there would have been a good chance of his life being spared if he had not been caught in the same net with the Red Orchestra people.

Pastor Poelchau found Harnack calm and serene. He was ready to die for his convictions, although he knew that such a sacrifice would not save Germany. He told the chaplain of his anguish for the German people, whose souls had been corrupted by Hitler. Then he asked him to recite the lines from Goethe's *Orpheus*. When the chaplain had finished, Harnack requested him to read the account of the Nativity given in the Gospel.

Hans Coppi, Schulze-Boysen's amateur radio operator, was no doubt thinking of his baby son, born on November 27 in the prison where his wife, Hilde, was being held. As soon as the news of the child's birth had reached him, Hans had written Hilde a letter, begging her not to worry about the future but to enjoy the great happiness which the present had bestowed on them. For him, this happiness had lasted twenty-six days.

Scheliha's reprieve did not arrive. Hofman, greatly distressed by the cruelty of these endless hours of waiting, at last saw the guards go into the cells and start preparing the prisoners for death. Their hair was cropped and they were given a change of clothes. Then the officials arrived. The chaplain complained to Roeder about not having been officially informed of the execution. "The participation of a clergyman was not provided for," replied the prosecutor. †

---

* Pseudonym chosen by the author.
† Harald Poechau, *Die letzten Stunden*.

The guards brought the condemned men out of their cells and lined them up in the corridor. The roll was called, and then the eight prisoners were ordered to march toward the door at the end of the corridor. They left with a firm step, holding their heads high—all except Scheliha, who rolled about on the concrete floor, crying that he did not want to be killed. He found it harder to accept his fate than the others, for he was dying only for a few thousand dollars.

The door at the end of the corridor opened on to a courtyard. A few yards farther on was the place where they would be killed. A large curtain concealed the execution chamber. The procession halted, then one corner of the curtain was raised, and the executioners appeared. There were three of them, all attired in tailcoats, white gloves and top hats. They took delivery of the prisoners and led them to the other side of the curtain, followed by the officials. The chaplain was not allowed to go with them.

Inside, there was another halt near the door. The president of the court-martial read out the eight sentences a few yards from the guillotine that rose in the middle of the room. After this, the party moved on again, past the guillotine; through an open door on their right they could see their coffins lined up in a shed. At the far end of the room the workmen had fashioned four cubicles from huge sheets of black paper; attached to a steel rod above them was a length of rope hanging down into each cubicle. Each prisoner had to stand on a stool; one of the executioners would slip the noose around the victim's neck, while the other pulled the stool away. This form of death, chosen by Hitler, had appealed to him for two reasons: for its degrading character and the suffering it entailed. Guillotining took a total of eleven seconds, whereas the executioners at Plötzensee had been warned by the prison doctor that the bodies must not be cut down for at least twenty minutes, before which time he could not be certain of their death.

As Roeder, the prosecutor, came away from the execution chamber, he remarked: "That Schulze-Boysen died like a man."

"Afterwards," writes Pastor Poelchau, "there was silence. The guards dispersed, and the officials went away. The guard on duty walked along the corridor jangling his bunch of keys; he closed the doors of the now empty cells and turned off the lights one after the other.

"There was darkness everywhere."

27. The Great Radio Game

Franz Fortner was quite positive when he told me: "I wasn't present at all his interrogations—far from it—for after his arrest I went back to my work in Brussels. But I can guarantee one thing: if the Big Chief talked, it wasn't from fear of torture or to save his skin. That man was not afraid. There was nothing of Raichman or Wenzel about him. Even under torture, I'm convinced, he wouldn't have talked if he had decided not to. Mind you, it was only much later that I understood his attitude—after the war, when we knew the methods of Russian espionage a little better. Oh, he had been very clever! He took us in all right! The Russians always had three networks lined up —one at work, one in reserve, and the other 'sleeping.' When the active network was captured, they didn't waste time trying to save the bits and pieces. They wrote it off, and the reserve network went into action, complete with its chief and staff, its liaison agents and radio operators. The 'sleeping' network moved into reserve, ready to take over when the next blow fell. You see the cunning of it? Trepper threw us a few scraps, and while we were gobbling them up and wasting time cleaning up the remains of his network, the one in reserve was quietly taking its place! Trepper had talked, it's true, but he had orders to do so. It was his duty. Odd though it may seem, he would have been a traitor to Moscow by remaining silent."

Three networks maneuvered like battalions of toy soldiers? The reservists mobilized on receipt of a telegram from the Director and took over prepared positions, while the "sleepers" roused themselves and stretched their limbs? Fortner must have got his dates mixed, and confused the Red Orchestra with the networks that the Center set up after the war. For if Moscow had had such a three-echelon espionage organization in France, Trepper would not have been so worried about radio communications; a few radio operators would probably have been called up from the reserve, instead of deciding to pierce the partition separating the Communist Party from the Intelligence organizations. Three networks? But they would already have been thrown into the battle! At Waterloo, even the Imperial Guard was sent forward. And there were many Waterloos on Russian territory between 1941 and the date of the Big Chief's arrest.

Suppose we accept this story of three networks. Agents can be enlisted and radio operators trained, but what about the sources? They can't be multiplied at will. A source of information isn't trained; it is discovered, usually by chance, and then tapped. Fortner's theory was applicable to Grossvogel or Katz; Trepper could betray those old comrades, for they had their replacements in the reserve network. But who could replace Maximovich or take over the work of Käthe Voelkner? The Director's detailed planning could hardly provide—certainly not in 1942—for reserve sources and "sleeping" sources.

The weakness of Fortner's explanation mattered little. The essential was that he should have felt it necessary to find a logical justification. He had arrested the Big Chief and had spent a number of hours with him, and was quite sure that neither fear of physical pain nor of death could have made him talk. And yet Trepper *had* talked—as reports in the Gestapo files bear witness. So there must have been a reason. What was it?

French specialists are unanimous on one point: when Trepper was captured, his one thought was to protect the Communists and their subsidiary organizations. The Gestapo did everything in its power, until the last day of the German occupation of France, to track down the Central Committee; and the Gestapo archives show how close it came to succeeding. Known Communist leaders were left at liberty in the hope that they would lead the Gestapo to the holy of holies. But the Central Committee was extremely prudent. After making contact with it, even Rémy felt some annoyance: "this phantom Committee surrounds itself with so many safeguards that it takes at least a fortnight to reply to my slightest question." But he acknowledged that "the Communists can give us lessons on the subject of prudence." * The reasons for that prudence and the Gestapo's persistence are obvious: the capture of the Committee would have been a deadly blow to the whole Communist Resistance movement. And through Trepper, the Gestapo had a chance of reaching the Committee.

Trepper's dilemma was, therefore, cruel but simple. He could choose to remain silent. Torture would follow; and no one can be certain of his own stoicism under torture. On the other hand, Trepper could give the names of his agents who were still free, convince the

---

* Rémy, *Mémoires d'un agent secret* . . . , Vol. 2, p. 121.

Gestapo of his willingness to cooperate, and by telling enough, make them believe he was telling everything, and so avoid being asked for the rest. Placed on this awful balance, Katz and Grossvogel were bound to be considered lightweights. Even Maximovich and Käthe Voelkner would not carry much weight. What good were sources if there was no longer a network to exploit them?

Such was the reasoning of specialists, and their arguments had some force. However, the plausibility of the supposition did not necessarily mean that it was correct. Had Trepper's attitude been really determined in that way? I went to Stuttgart to ask Heinrich Reiser.

He was an elephantine man with close-cropped white hair, and his blue eyes were like two oases in a Sahara of pink flesh. There was certainly no tenderness shining from them. He sank into a chair as though he would sit there forever, folded his arms and talked for five hours on end, in French, and without a single gesture or change of expression. One could almost hear him thinking. Each word seemed to weigh a ton. His slender, trim little wife listened adoringly. She knew no French, but that didn't matter; the oracle was speaking. He had never told her about his work; she knew only that he had spent most of the war in Paris. She was as little interested in the nature of his occupations there as in the meaning of the phrases to which she now listened as though to a divine melody. Whatever he had done had naturally been done well. Her domain was the home: she had been cleaning and polishing it for thirty or forty years. There was not a speck of dust to be seen in the apartment; everything shone with unrelenting cleanness.

Reiser had held the rank of *Hauptsturmführer* in the SS and, like Giering and Berg, had been an old cop before being raked in by Himmler. A specialist in counterespionage even before the Nazis came to power, he was posted to Paris in the early days of the German occupation. Giering was in command, but was always coming and going between Berlin, Brussels and Paris. Elephant Reiser never budged. Giering supervised everything at the international level, and it was Reiser, his deputy, who commanded in France.

Reiser said: "I battled against the Red Orchestra even before the Kommando was formed. It was I who arrested the Sokols. We didn't know they were working for the Russians. We thought it was just an ordinary Resistance network taking orders from London. Berlin claimed them at once. If they were tortured, it was in Berlin, not Paris. . . .

He said: "What a tragedy war is! And how stupid! I've always been fond of France. Even now I go to lectures at the French Institute here in Stuttgart every week. My favorite authors are Henri Bordeaux and René Bazin, but I read that existentialist woman writer too—what's her name—Simone de Beauvoir. . . .

He said: "When I arrived in France I told my men that they were not to beat up prisoners. Torture was never used in my department. Besides, at the end of the war we were captured by the French and kept in prison for a long time, but they finally found that there was no case against us. They wouldn't have released us like that if we had used torture. There was a special section, quite independent of us, that dealt with difficult customers, those who wouldn't talk. It was called the 'service for intensified interrogations.' Some very unpleasant things went on there. . . .

"It was I who arrested Katz. We got onto him through Raichman, the 'shoemaker' from Brussels. He knew the addresses of a few people in contact with Katz. I had a watch kept on all of them, with no result. Not until the Big Chief was arrested. Then Katz seemed to lose his head. He kept changing his hideout. One night he took refuge at the home of a woman friend, a Communist, whom Raichman had told us about. The men on watch alerted me, and I went there and arrested him."

Was everything about him like an elephant, except his memory?

I said to him, "Herr Reiser, there's some mistake. Katz was betrayed to you by Trepper himself."

"No, you're wrong. The Big Chief didn't give away any of his agents, for the good reason that he wasn't asked. If he had, I'd have known. I was there all the time."

I said, "Yet the Gestapo report is quite explicit. Trepper telephoned Katz and arranged to meet him at the Madeleine Métro station. When Katz was taken to Gestapo headquarters, Trepper said to him, 'We must work with these gentlemen. The game's up.' "

Reiser was huddled on his chair, his hands clenched so that the veins stood out, and his steely eyes were no more than two blue dots. "Now listen to me, sir. If you want to understand something of that affair you must not believe a word of what the Gestapo reports say about the Big Chief. Not a word!"

At the moment, that seemed to put a very different light on the affair. On reflection, however, nothing was changed.

As we know, a *Funkspiel* is a delicate, nerve-racking game that is intended to dupe the enemy. But before the game can be won, one must first obtain permission to play it. The powers-that-be are cautious; it may pay big dividends, but if it fails, the enemy will have been fed true information all to no purpose. So they require guarantees, first and foremost that the agent who has been "turned" can be counted on in his new role.

The Gestapo decided to use Trepper to launch a *Funkspiel* of greater proportions than ever before attempted. It was a right decision. Giskes had done marvels with his radio game against London, using only a few minor pianists. How much more could be hoped for, using one of the chiefs of Russian espionage against Moscow! But first, the powers in Berlin had to be convinced.

Since Trepper's arrest, Berlin had showered Paris with telegrams, all demanding much the same thing: "What has the Big Chief told you?" The Big Chief was recounting his life history and making fascinating revelations on the uses of a telephone directory. If Berlin were informed of this fine achievement, Himmler would choke with rage and cancel the *Funkspiel* outright. And he would be right. In order to get the OKW (German Supreme Headquarters), the Foreign Ministry and others to supply him with the necessary "feed" he would have to guarantee the prisoner's reliability.

So what was to be done with Trepper? They could hand him over to the "service for intensified interrogation" and drag the names of his agents from him. That would be one solution. Of course, his network was of little further interest to the Gestapo. However well organized, once the foundations had collapsed the structure and partitions would come tumbling down with the rest. The survivors would be picked up one by one. Even if a few escaped, they would be helpless to act. But by breaking Trepper and making him talk, by forcing him to betray his men, Berlin would be reassured.

However, torturing Trepper until he talked was one thing; getting him to cooperate in a *Funkspiel* for several months was quite another. He was not easy to handle. He was refusing to talk, but he was chatting away over coffee and cigarettes. He might close up like a clam if pressure were put on; and his collaboration was essential. Only he could give messages the manner and style that would satisfy Moscow.

So the ingenious solution was reached: they would create a "legend," appeasing Himmler with the touched-up portrait of an utter traitor. Schellenberg has revealed how the Gestapo faked reports in order to claim the credit due to others. In Trepper's case, the duplicity had some justification. As Giering explained to the Big Chief, "The military must not be told everything, because they understand nothing of politics; and the politicians mustn't be told everything either, because they understand nothing about Intelligence work." "Who ought to know everything, then?" Trepper asked. "The leader of the game. And it's up to him to distribute the rations to each of them."

Himmler received a good measure. Giering's reports left no doubt about the prisoner's treachery. Fortner, like everyone else who read them, believed that Trepper really had betrayed Katz, Grossvogel, Robinson, Maximovich. In some reports the date of the Big Chief's arrest was brought forward from November 24 to November 16, 1942, so that the end of the Simex and Simexco, the roundup in Belgium and the capture of the Lyons group could all be imputed to him.

Giering's actions can be easily understood. But Trepper? Surely he must have realized what was at stake in this game in which he would be the Gestapo's trump card.

The stake was enormous. Many German leaders, civilian as well as military, thought that their country was heading for disaster. Germany had never won a war fought on two fronts. It was time to negotiate with the West or with the East. But to suggest such a thing was equivalent to committing suicide; one would be accused of defeatism, in other words, of treachery. Better to march steadily toward the precipice, everyone in step.

Himmler was not everyone. He was not affected by the general terror, for he was the source and instrument of that terror. Neither was he frightened of the Gestapo: he was the Gestapo. No one was better placed than he to find a remedy for the situation.

The winter of 1941–42 had brought disillusionment to the German people. Instead of a quick victory over the Russians, the campaign would be long and hard. In the spring, when the Wehrmacht's offensive toward the Caucasus roused general enthusiasm—for all of Germany believed it would end the war on the eastern front—Himmler could still see matters clearly. Ciano, the Italian foreign minister, noted in his diary on May 19, 1942, that Himmler thought the offensive was going to be splendid but not decisive, with the prospect of a difficult winter to follow, from the point of view of morale and supply. Himmler's forecast proved correct. And so, in December, 1942, he authorized a lawyer friend of his, a man named Langbehn, to open conversations with British and American officials in Zurich and in Stockholm, and to sound them out on the chances of a separate peace with the Western powers, on condition of a change of regime in Germany. Nothing definite emerged from these contacts. Himmler began to turn to the anti-Nazi conspirators for contact with the West.

Historians have related in detail how Himmler endeavored to make use of every group of plotters for his own political ends. From 1942 until July 20, 1944, the date of the assassination attempt on Hitler, the plotters in contact with the West benefited from extraordinary benevolence on Himmler's part. When discovered, they were not arrested until the very last; and when arrested, the majority were not executed until after July 20, 1944, when it was no longer possible to save them.

The German Resistance became aware of Himmler's game and of the anxieties felt by SS leaders as to the final outcome of the war. At the same time, the plotters despaired of getting the timid generals to join them in a putsch against Hitler. These things combined gave birth to an idea that was frightening but rational—to enrol Himmler in the Resistance movement. It was risky, but the leading plotters thought the game was worth the candle. If Himmler and his SS went along with them, the army chiefs could hardly refuse to take action.

The go-between was Langbehn, the man who had already made tentative contacts with the West. He arranged a meeting between Himmler and Popitz, the finance minister of Prussia, who was in the Resistance. It took place at the Ministry of the Interior on August 26, 1943. Popitz suggested that attempts should be made to negotiate with the West even without Hitler's consent. Himmler ("faithful Heinrich," as the Führer was pleased to call him) said very little, but enough for Popitz to have the impression that "he was not against it in principle." * That was already enormous! Langbehn dashed off to Switzerland to give the good news to his Western contacts there. Unfortunately, the Gestapo picked up a radio message emanating from Switzerland which gave Allied Intelligence a résumé of the information conveyed by Langbehn. Hitler was informed before Himmler was able to intervene; the latter, obliged to cover himself, had Lang-

* J. W. Wheeler-Bennett, *The Nemesis of Power* (London: Macmillan, 1953), p. 578.

behn arrested but left Popitz at liberty for the moment.* The operation had come to naught because of an unforeseen incident, but it was nevertheless indicative of Himmler's political policy.

Himmler had his head in the clouds, but his feet were firmly on the ground. It seemed only sensible to him to put an end to the war on two fronts. There could be no question of a deal with the Soviets; Himmler fiercely believed in the Anti-Bolshevik Crusade. His efforts, therefore, tended toward opening negotiations with the West. Obviously, it was mad to think that Churchill or Roosevelt would enter into talks with him and place their hand in his, stained as it was with the blood of millions of victims. However, Himmler's illusions—which he kept right to the end—were his affair. Here we are concerned with his policy.

There may seem little connection between Himmler's political game on an international scale and the acts of the prisoner Trepper. But, to conclude a separate peace with the West, the first need was to create a rupture between Russia and the Western Allies. History abounds in instances of coalitions that dissolved before bearing fruit. To be allies is to look in the same direction as one's neighbor while keeping an eye on him; to march forward in step while taking care not to be tripped up; to issue joint statements in which no sign appears of the reservations and doubts that haunt each partner. And so, the best of alliances is never very far from separation or even divorce. A perfect illustration of this is provided by Stalin, Churchill and Roosevelt. At the beginning, when Russia was reeling under the German blows, Churchill and Roosevelt feared that Stalin might come to terms with Hitler. When the Russian armies went over to the offensive, at a cost of ten thousand casualties a day, Stalin was wrathful to see the Western Allies delaying the opening of the second front, then he came to suspect them of wishing to negotiate with the Reich in order to block the Red Army's sweep into Central Europe.

The Nazis' game, therefore, consisted of exasperating the antagonisms between East and West, of inflaming their mutual suspicions so as to cause the alliance to disrupt. The manner in which this was done has been clearly explained in Schellenberg's *Memoirs;* it was by making each side believe that Germany was about to enter into negotiations with the other. "It was, therefore, very important," he wrote (and this thought occurred to him in the summer of 1942),

---

* The two were not executed until after the July assassination plot.

"to make contact with the Russians at the same time we were opening negotiations with the West. The growing rivalry between the
Allied powers would strengthen our hand." * But he adds that the
chief difficulty was to start talks with the Russians.†

The Western powers were easily accessible. Stockholm, Madrid,
Geneva, Lisbon and Ankara were all swarming with envoys and representatives, official and otherwise. The cautious Himmler tried to get
in touch with some of them through the German Resistance, in order
to conceal his overtures from his Nazi colleagues. But if he had really
decided to open negotiations, he could easily make contact with the
Western powers through any neutral country.

The Russians were much more difficult to reach, as we have seen.
Yet Himmler's game depended on reaching them. The solution was
to "play back" the Red Orchestra's captured transmitters, though it
is not known who first suggested this. Moscow had obviously to be
kept in the dark about their seizure and had to be convinced of the
operators' continuing good faith—which was why the information
they sent had to be so good. The Red Orchestra started up again
without a suspiciously long interval, but this time it was playing on
behalf of Berlin. The soloists of the new symphony were Yefremov,
Wenzel and Winterink. The main objective, however, was still to
bring back the accredited conductor, the Big Chief, who alone possessed the power and breadth of vision needed to dupe Moscow in
matters of international politics.

---

* *The Schellenberg Memoirs*, p. 378.
† Historians of the Second World War have so far noted only one direct contact between German and Russian representatives. In December, 1942, and
again in June, 1943, Peter Kleist, a German diplomat, while on a mission to
Stockholm, was approached by Edgar Clauss, a Soviet agent, who proposed a
meeting with Alexandrov, the head of the European department at the Soviet
Foreign Ministry. According to Clauss, the Kremlin was prepared to come to
a compromise peace agreement with Germany. A blunder committed by
Clauss (who also contacted the Stockholm representative of the Abwehr,
whose chief, Admiral Canaris, was intensely anti-Communist) resulted in
Hitler hearing of the affair. The Führer exploded with rage over this "insolent
Jewish provocation" (Clauss being presumed a Jew), and ordered an investigation to be made into Alexandrov's racial antecedents. "This mission was
carried out with special care," wrote Peter Kleist. "But it had no result, for
there was no chance of questioning the 'Soviet Central Office for the determination of race and origins' about the family tree of Comrade Alexandrov." (Kleist, *Entre Hitler et Staline*—Paris: Plon, 1953.)
    The sole attempt to establish a link between Berlin and Moscow thus ended
in typical Nazi ridicule.

Stone by stone, the Germans built up the wall of suspicion behind which they hoped to isolate Stalin from the West. Three of these stones are described below, as examples.

The SS chiefs received a ten-page report drawn up by Goebbels's Propaganda Services. It contained, in condensed form, the results of a public-opinion poll on the outcome of the war. Two conclusions emerged: the German people still believed in victory; but in case of a Wehrmacht defeat, the man in the street thought that Germany should make terms with the West at any price that would keep the Russians from crossing the eastern frontiers. The report was top-secret, but after much argument the SS obtained permission to transmit the gist of it to Moscow under cover of the Big Chief. It provided Stalin with proof that the Nazis were prepared to make terms with the West in order to throw all the weight of the Wehrmacht against the Red Army.

British and American air crews shot down over the Paris area were sent to the hospital at Clichy if wounded. The Rote Kapelle Kommando sent, over the Red Orchestra transmitters, some statements made by a number of these airmen, whom a member of the network was supposed to have succeeded in meeting. They said they were fed up with the war, and had strong doubts about its justification. Most of them appeared to be more anti-Communist than anti-Nazi. They thought that by crushing Germany they might not be destroying the real enemy. Stalin was thus informed of the true sentiments of Allied fighters toward their Russian ally. He already suspected there was dirty work afoot between the Nazi leaders and Churchill and Roosevelt. The Goebbels report and the interviews with Allied airmen at Clichy would show him that the intrigues at the summit were unlikely to meet with disapproval from the mass of people.[*]

Moscow asked one of the "turned" pianists to send information about the defenses of Calais. The Rote Kapelle Kommando replied with a few details, but the Center wanted more. It was told of the difficulties involved, that Calais was swarming with German police armed with Sten guns. The Center swallowed the bait—how had the Germans come to be in possession of so many Stens? It was urgent to find out! The Rote Kapelle Kommando reported back that the Stens had been bought in a neutral country, that the British knew

_____
[*] The author has no proof of the authenticity of the interviews. The airmen's "statements" were probably fabricated for the good of the cause.

they had been purchased on behalf of the Wehrmacht, but had agreed to the sale on condition that the Stens were not used on the eastern front.

This was a fine piece of deceit: from it Stalin would probably draw two mistaken conclusions, either of which could have serious consequences. First, that the British were supplying arms to the Wehrmacht, and if they forbade their use in the East, it was obviously to prevent this betrayal of the Alliance from becoming known through the capture of some of the Stens. And their use on the western front freed other weapons for the German armies on the eastern front. Moreover, if the British increased the fire-power behind the Atlantic Wall so obligingly, it could only mean that they had no intention of opening the second front for a long time to come. So the Western Allies were calmly waiting for "the last Russian soldier to kill the last German soldier," in the words of the famous saying. Unless they were thinking of coming to terms with Germany so that it would be the last German soldier who killed the last Russian.

———◆———

Later on January 17, 1944, *Pravda* was to print the following item under the heading "Rumors in Cairo":

Cairo, January 12, (from our special correspondent).

According to well-informed Greek and Yugoslav sources, a secret meeting between Ribbentrop and two important British personalities took place recently at a coastal town in Spain. The object of the meeting was to determine the conditions of a separate peace with Germany. It is presumed that the talks were not without some result.

In Berlin, Goebbels was dumbfounded when this item was brought to his notice.

"It had the effect of a powerful drug on the Minister," one of his chief assistants, Wilfred von Oven, wrote later. "When he called me in for the conference on the material to be distributed to the press, among which was the *Pravda* news item, he seemed very excited. The item was on top of a pile of telegrams and he had used his green pencil to put brackets round it—a sign of its great importance—and there were also several exclamation points in the margin. The Minister gave me a significant look and, tapping the piece of paper with the back of his hand, said: "This is the most important item of news possible

at the present moment. Evidently—and, I must say, unfortuna
it's an invention from beginning to end. The question that aris
this: what is Stalin—for that cunning old fox and no one else is (
tainly behind it—what is Stalin up to with this hoax?" *

The same question was being asked in London and Washington.
There was of course no truth whatever in the *Pravda* news item, but
if Stalin liked to believe it—and *Pravda* printed nothing that he had
not approved—the Alliance could be compromised. The Foreign Office issued a denial of the story; inquiries revealed that *Pravda* had no
correspondent in Egypt. The Russian news agency *Tass* put out the
Foreign Office denial, and at the same time made insinuating refer-
ences to the shady activities of the German ambassador in Turkey,
Franz von Papen. Confusion was general.

In Berlin, Goebbels said to Wilfred von Oven: "We must follow
this business very closely. In any case, it confirms what I've been
saying for a long time—the Allies are threatening each other with
coming to terms with us. Of course, the public must know nothing of
this business. And we must not let it be known abroad how interested
we are. So clamp down on the story at home and with the foreign
press. I'm making you responsible for seeing there are no leaks." †

But there were leaks. Ulrich von Hassell noted in his diary on
February 7: "Significant pointer to the situation—the 'stink bomb'
that *Pravda* dropped on the Allies, reporting that Ribbentrop was
believed to have had talks with Hoare in Spain. Result in Germany:
increased mistrust on the part of the leaders who, while not suspecting Ribbentrop, think that other groups are in contact with the British. Schwerin ‡ told me that a watch is being kept on a group of young
men in the Foreign Ministry." §

London and Washington had no idea what could be behind the
news item. Neutral capitals were puzzled by it too. In Berlin, Goebbels, Schwerin von Krosigk, the Finance Minister, and practically all
the Nazi leaders were equally uncertain. Even historians of the Third
Reich have stumbled over the story, believing it to be just a fake.

The story had been fabricated by the authors of the *Funkspiel*,
sent by the Gestapo to Paris and transmitted to Moscow on Kent's

---

* Wilfred von Oven, *Mit Goebbels bis zum Ende*, 2 vols. (Buenos Aires:
Dürer Verlag, 1949–50), Vol. 1, p. 180.
† *Ibid.*
‡ Schwerin von Krosigk, the Reich's Finance Minister.
§ Hassell, *D'une autre Allemagne*, p. 315.

radio transmitter. A much earlier message transmitted on the same set had informed Moscow that the Little Chief was in contact with an important official in the German Foreign Ministry. The Director had at once asked for his name, and the Rote Kapelle Kommando gave that of an actual German diplomat who had been stationed in Lisbon before the war and whose anti-Nazi sentiments were well known. The sudden abundance of important diplomatic information in Kent's messages was thus justified. The information concerning the talks between Ribbentrop and the British representatives was supposed to have come from this source. The agent supplying Kent was said to have had access to a report made by a neutral diplomat while in London, the report having been intercepted by the German special services. And it was true that the diplomat in question was in London at that time—his presence could easily be checked by the Russians—and that he had sent a report to his government which had been intercepted by the Germans. The *Funkspiel* directors had only to alter a few sentences to change the sense entirely—so that it announced a meeting on neutral territory between British and German representatives, motivated by the anxiety caused in London by the great territorial gains of the Red Army.

The aim was to convince Stalin, after having carefully played on his doubts about the loyalty of his allies, that they were preparing to negotiate peace terms with Germany—so that he would try to get in first. A breach might thus be made in the combined front against Germany.

Such was the great radio game to which, at the end of 1942, Trepper had to give his support if he were to save his life.

28. The Prisoners' Fate

So far it was not a bad life. After his capture in Dr. Maleplate's office, Trepper had been taken to Gestapo headquarters in the Rue des Saussaies. There he was welcomed by SS Sturmbannführer Boemelburg, who a fortnight earlier had arrested Kent in Marseilles. "Ah, so we've got the Russian bear after all!" cried Boemelburg. The good news was at once telephoned to Berlin, then the prisoner was bundled into a car and taken to Fresnes prison, escorted by several other cars full of armed police.

Trepper spent only one night in Fresnes. He probably had some difficulty in sleeping, for he was handcuffed behind the back in accordance with Giering's instructions for all prisoners from the Red Orchestra.

The next morning he was taken back to the Rue des Saussaies and put in an improvised cell on the ground floor. There he was to remain for two and a half months. No one ever laid a hand on him. He was well fed and supplied with cigarettes. As he had heart trouble, an army doctor saw him twice a week. Reiser has said that the Big Chief was even allowed to have a bath two or three times a week, up on the top floor of the building. He complained of boredom, of having nothing to do, and he was given a dictionary, paper and pencil, so that he could occupy his leisure in improving his knowledge of German.

His interrogations went on in the most informal manner. They took place after lunch, for the members of the Rote Kapelle Kommando were not at their best in the mornings, when they were suffering from hangovers. They were a jolly band, who set off on a drinking bout—all except the strict Reiser—as soon as the offices closed, ready to relax after a tiring day. Their favorite haunt had been a Russian bar; but then they met the singer Suzy Solidor there, and she charmed them into transferring their custom to her nightclub in the Rue St.-Anne. Every evening, Giering and his men went with their mistresses (who were in the Wehrmacht auxiliary forces) and drank steadily while listening to Suzy Solidor singing "Lily Marlene" and other melancholy tunes in her husky voice. They had many a good joke, too. When Suzy once returned from a trip to Berlin she described the flags flying at the railway station, all bearing the letters SS (in honor of Himmler). But, said Suzy with a sigh, "There was really no need to put out flags with my initials." Fortner still laughs over this.

And so, nearly every day after lunch Giering and Trepper sat down with a bottle of brandy and a huge coffeepot. They chatted away the afternoon like two old comrades exchanging reminiscences, and only rarely did a turn in the conversation remind them that they were not on the same side of the fence. For instance, one afternoon Giering announced that the Russians had crossed the Dnieper, and added: "In Berlin, people are beginning to count the rivers between

them and the front." This reminded Trepper of the celebrated anecdote about the Kaiser telling his aide-de-camp in 1918 that he wished
to visit the front; and the aide-de-camp replied, "Be patient, Your
Majesty. It won't be long before the front reaches you." Giering
went livid. Trepper realized that he had gone too far, and he added
philosophically, "Oh, rivers—first they flow one way and then the
other." The phrase was meaningless, but with the help of the brandy
it soothed Giering down.

Giering was wasting away, and his voice had become hollow; his
cancer was progressing even faster than the Red Army. Trepper
sympathized with him and encouraged him to increase his consump-
tion of alcohol—the only way, according to Trepper, of reducing a
malignant tumor. Oddly enough, the Big Chief became a kind of medical adviser to the Rote Kapelle Kommando, recommending treat-
ments and freely giving advice. His most regular client was Giering's
chief assistant, Willy Berg, whose hangovers were monumental. The
Big Chief would comfort him, saying, "I know a pharmacy here in
Paris that makes a marvelous remedy; we'll go there together, one of
these days."

And indeed, Trepper was soon being taken on outings. The
first times he went out for a drive, two Gestapo cars preceded and
followed his; but before long this escort was halved and then withdrawn altogether. Trepper was driven around Paris with just two
policemen beside the chauffeur. Even this precaution was reduced,
and Trepper was allowed out with only one watchdog, who was usually Willy Berg. The latter often wanted Trepper to take him to the
pharmacy with the marvelous remedy, but Trepper always pleaded
some excuse, and the suffering Berg ended by thinking that he had
invented the whole story.

———◆———

The pianists of the Belgian and Dutch networks who had "turned"
were also being treated gently. Yefremov and Wenzel had been given
a requisitioned apartment in Brussels, at 68 Rue de l'Aurore. Winterink
was in Amsterdam. The Rote Kapelle Kommando used them only to
prepare the messages at first, fearing they might have a sudden fit of
conscience and return to their old allegiance. Their places at the
transmitters were taken by German radio experts who tried to renew
the dialogue with Moscow. But the Center was suspicious and refused to reply. There was nothing surprising about this. Every

pianist had his own style, his personal touch and rhythm on the Morse key—his "signature" as individual as his voice or fingerprints—which enabled him to be identified at the receiving end.

After a few weeks of this silence, the Kommando realized there was no remedy but to use the three prisoners for sending messages. But first they took the precaution of having them transmit "into the void"—in other words, without letting them make contact with Moscow. These messages were recorded and examined by experts, who tried hard to detect any anomaly that might have warned the Russians. There was nothing suspicious, so the three pianists were allowed to make contact with the Center. "What's been happening?" they were asked. The Kommando had them send the reply: "There has been some confusion due to arrests; everything now all right." And the quality of their information soon calmed Moscow's suspicions.

From then on, everything went splendidly. A former member of the Funkabwehr has said: "The prisoners' love for their work became a real passion. They were treated reasonably well, they had a certain amount of freedom, and their relations with the German officers supervising them improved as time went on."

These relations, which had begun in mutual distrust, grew into warm comradeship. They were all specialists greatly interested in the same subject, they talked shop all the time, and their days were spent together, sharing the same meals, smoking the same cigarettes, exchanging jokes that soon became customary. The outside world ceased to exist; there was just the roomful of men intent on a fascinating task. After a few weeks, a visitor would have found difficulty at first sight in telling prisoners from their guards.

The officers in charge of the Funkspiel were aware of this phenomenon, but despite all efforts, they were unable to put a stop to the fraternization.

One day in January, 1943, Wenzel and his supervisor arrived in the transmission room. The stove was almost out and it was cold. The German bent down to build the fire, Wenzel fell on him and knocked him out. The key was still in the door; Wenzel locked it behind him, dashed down the stairs and out to the street. He was free. And despite intensive search, the Kommando never found him.

His guardian angel took his place at the transmitter. He had had ample opportunity to study Wenzel's "signature," and the Center did not notice the substitution.

Yefremov and Winterink paid for Wenzel's escape by being sent to Breendonck concentration camp, near Brussels, for greater security. They were brought from their cells when needed to continue the *Funkspiel*.

———◆———

In Paris, the Big Chief's comfortable life was sometimes marred by brief sights of the Kommando's other prisoners. Katz had had his glasses smashed on his face by a blow from Jung's fist, and his face was all cut up. And they had also torn out his fingernails. But as he showed his bloody fingers to Trepper he whispered, "I didn't tell them a thing!" Grossvogel too had been tortured, and he too had refused to talk, even after being told that his silence would mean the death of his wife and child. It was through love of them that he had been caught. The Kommando had his wife in their power and threatened to kill her child before her eyes if she did not help them set a trap for her husband. The poor woman agreed. Grossvogel responded to her call, despite his suspicion, and was arrested. This had happened a week after the capture of the Big Chief.

Robinson was caught a few weeks later by Reiser and Fortner. According to Reiser, the Kommando had got a lead on him while tracking down some of the Comintern spy rings. He was given a rendezvous at the Palais de Chaillot, which he kept. Trepper watched his capture from the back seat of a Gestapo car. When Reiser had told the Big Chief that he would be taken to the scene in order to identify Robinson, he had replied: "You can arrest that one if you like. He's been nothing but a nuisance to me, and it'll be no loss to anyone!"

Robinson, who posed as a journalist, lived in a small hotel room, in a state of disorder typical of the Comintern. Books and papers were overflowing the drawers and piled on chairs. In the midst of this jumble the Kommando discovered five passports, three of which were in the name of Henri Robinson. All three had been recently used for journeys to Switzerland, as was shown by the date stamps of the frontier control. Yet the name of Henri Robinson had been appearing in the "Wanted Persons" lists of the German police since 1930! It was incredible that a secret agent should have used such incriminating documents. The number of passports was understandable: by alternating them when crossing the frontier, he did not arouse suspicion by the frequency of his journeys, as shown by the tell-tale date stamps in any one passport. But for them to be in Robinson's own name was incomprehensible to the Kommando. Trepper, however, saw it as typical of the amateurism of the Comintern in general and of Robinson in particular.*

Reiser and Fortner took their dazed prisoner to the Kommando offices and Fortner started to interrogate him in his usual amiable way, so that after a time Robinson exclaimed: "But why are you being so nice to me?" Fortner was taken by surprise, and all he could think to say was: "Because I like you." Then Willy Berg joined them, having just finished examining the contents of Robinson's briefcase. He listened to the questions and answers for a while, but seemed dissatisfied with the tone of the interrogation, for he suddenly struck Robinson hard across the face. Robinson got up, shouting, "What do you want from me? I'm just a journalist!"

Fortner, very upset, exclaimed to Giering: "If you start knocking him around, I'm leaving!"

Giering sent Berg away; but, from that day on, Fortner was out of favor with the Kommando. He knew that for quite a while the others had been annoyed by his insistence on the proprieties. The first time he had seen a prisoner whose face showed marks of a beating he had said to Giering, "Look here, you're a professional policeman and you know that such methods are illegal." Giering had replied, "What do you mean? This fellow just bumped into a door, that's all." The Kommando's prisoners seemed to have a positive mania for bumping into doors. But all this made Fortner quite content to be kept out of things, and he eventually went back to Brussels and stayed there. He could hardly have imagined how delighted Giering was to see him leave; the Kommando had no desire for a member of the Abwehr to know about the great radio game started by the SS. Fortner's squeamishness had served to get him out of the way.

Gentle Mildred Harnack was beheaded in Berlin on February 16, 1942. When Hitler had annulled her original sentence, her defense counsel had expressed to her family his astonishment at such an un-

---

* The Kommando's perplexity is shared by the secret services of the Western powers. Their astonishment is increased by the chance discovery in West Germany in 1947 of a number of passports prepared before the war and all bearing a photo of Robinson. Investigations led to a Basel policeman named Max Habijanic. When arrested in 1948, he admitted having supplied the Comintern with forged passports for twenty years. (Dallin, *Soviet Espionage*, p. 203.) This makes it even more puzzling that Robinson, having the services of such an expert "shoemaker," should run the risk of using passports in his own name.

precedented retrial. Arvid's cousin Axel von Harnack decided to appeal to the public prosecutor, Manfred Roeder, of whom he wrote later, "I have never felt such an impression of brutality in a man. He surrounded himself with an atmosphere of terror." *

Roeder replied to the petition: "I warn the Harnack family against any approaches in favor of this woman. You must act as though she has nothing to do with you. She no longer belongs to your family." And he ended with undisguised threats as to the consequences of any further intervention.

Mildred Harnack and Countess Erika von Brockdorf were brought to trial again. No fresh evidence was submitted by the prosecution, no new witnesses were called. But the judges, in compliance with their Führer's wishes, this time sentenced the two women to death.

Mildred had grown very weak; in five months, her lovely blond hair had turned white. The prison chaplain, Poelchau, later wrote to one of her relatives:

> She was very brave, well aware of all that was happening, but she had obviously already finished with this world. She had erected a wall round herself to shut out painful thoughts and to exclude all sentimental feelings. Only her mother's photograph brought her out of this state for a few moments. She would hold silent but passionate dialogues with her mother, while her eyes filled with tears. Then she covered the photograph with kisses, and calmed down.†

On February 15, she translated some lines of Goethe into English:

> *Song of the Traveller in the Night*
>
> *Thou who comest from on high*
> *To calm suffering and grief,*
> *Thou who doubly soothes,*
> *Who doubly knows unhappiness,*
> *I am tired of all this woe!*
> *What good is sorrow and happiness?*
> *Gentle peace come,*
> *Come to my heart!*

---

* A. von Harnack, "Axel und Mildred Harnack."
† Günther Weisenborn, *Der lautlose Aufstand.*

When they came for her the following morning—this young American who had married a German student fifteen years earlier, leaving her Midwestern university at his insistence—she only said: "And I loved Germany so much!"

She walked to the scaffold with a firm step, between two jailers.

Six days earlier, Colonel Erwin Gehrts, the client of the fortuneteller Anna Krause, had been beheaded. And eight days earlier, Wilhelm Thews. This onetime officer in the International Brigade had escaped from a French internment camp to return to Germany and continue the fight.

On February 23, which was a Red Army holiday, the Kommando transferred its Russian bear to a more suitable den, a private house at the corner of the Boulevard Victor Hugo and the Rue du Rouvray at Neuilly. It was a charming house, surrounded by a garden, and with a façade of white columns that gave it the air of a Greek temple. The Gestapo had requisitioned it for persons of note, and it already held the Spanish Republican leader Largo Caballero, Colonel de la Roque,* and several French politicians. The house was guarded by a dozen Slovak volunteers. Conditions for the inmates were by no means rigorous. Each had a comfortable room with plenty of books, and his meals were brought to him from outside. He was kept locked in his room, but had only to knock for a guard to appear, ready to accede to any reasonable request. Two women came in to do the cleaning. Daily exercise could be taken in the garden, around the front lawn or the vegetable patch at the back, which was lovingly tended by the caretaker, Prodhomme, and his daughters. The high railings surrounding the garden had been covered over with black galvanized sheeting to block the view, but there were a few chinks here and there. As the prisoners strolled about, they could hear traffic noises, conversations of passers-by, and even the sweet murmurings of courting couples who leaned trustingly against the railings, for there was no sentry on guard outside. The Gestapo relied more on secrecy than on a display of force to guard against attacks by the Resistance; and events proved them right.

There too the host was Boemelburg. He welcomed Trepper, showing him his dog, "Stalin." Trepper answered, making a face,

---

* The chief of the prewar right-wing organization Croix de Feu. (TRANS-LATOR)

"Yes, I know, many Communists call their dog 'Hitler'; I've always found that sort of thing very silly." Boemelburg looked sulky. He was not a bad fellow at heart, but he was drunk from the moment he got up in the morning and started the day with pistol practice; his targets were large photographs of Communist leaders and important Jews wanted by the Gestapo.

There were some peculiar prisons run by the Gestapo in Occupied Europe, but probably none as odd as the one at Neuilly, with its respectful Slovak guards, its caretaker and family tending the vegetables, its distinguished inmates strolling gravely round the garden, heads bent in thought, as though still treading the corridors of power. The place certainly intrigued that eminent ambassador François-Poncet, when he was taken there in company of Albert Lebrun, former President of the Third French Republic, in August, 1943. They were kept there only six days before being deported to Germany.

Monsieur François-Poncet wrote in his "Carnets d'un captif": *

"The house in which we're staying greatly puzzles us. It is most mysterious; a small town house that must have been very comfortable and which still has a certain elegance. But to what use is it now put? There are ten numbered bedrooms. Have they all been turned into prison cells? And who occupies them?

"I can see a church steeple above the railings. Horse carriages go past with seedy-looking drivers and even seedier horses, and cyclists too; but no one even glances at this strange house.

"But who occupies the ten bedrooms? What is this house, which holds Gestapo officials who appear to be having a rest and also German and French prisoners? We can't make it out.

"Walking round the lawn, we see a bald man of about fifty, wearing a sports jacket; also a younger man, more gaunt than the other, who seems very thoughtful; and a third, holding himself erect and throwing out his chest, chatting familiarly with the guards."

That well-set man was Trepper—all the survivors of the network are agreed on the point. ("He held himself just like Léon Zitrone," † said one of them.)

Monsieur François-Poncet continues: "From the window of my attic room I can see a woman outrageously blond, middle-aged, in woolen pajamas. She is sitting in a deck chair and reading, but looks up now and again to reply to a woman speaking to her from the

---

* *Historia*, August, 1951.
† A well-known French lecturer and TV personality. (TRANSLATOR)

house. I can hear a mixture of German and French passing between the two." That was obviously Margarete Barcza. However, it was August, 1943, when Monsieur François-Poncet saw her at the house in Neuilly, and we are still in the month of February.

In February, 1943, Kent and his mistress had not yet become guests of Boemelburg; Kent was still being held at Gestapo headquarters in the Rue des Saussaies, and she was in Fresnes prison. Earlier, on January 4, 1943, in Berlin, Margarete had been told by the Gestapo: "You're being set free. You'll be taken back to Paris. Kent is going to Paris too, but we shall still need him." They had been taken by train, handcuffed. A kindly policeman had put her hat over Margarete's hands, to keep the other passengers from seeing the handcuffs. But when they reached Paris, instead of the freedom promised her, Margarete had been put in a cell at Fresnes. This sent her into hysterics. Five or six days later, two members of the Kommando had taken Kent to see her.

Margarete says: "I was looking awful. I had no makeup, and I was mad with worry. He broke down."

The two SS were dumbfounded to see Kent burst into tears; he threw himself to his knees, crying: "I'll do anything you like, only leave her alone! Set her free!"

Margarete was kept in Fresnes prison, but the lovers were allowed to meet once a week. After each meeting, a woman guard made Margarete take off all her clothes and examined her in most intimate detail. By producing fits of hysterics, Margarete obtained additional meetings with Kent. Her worn-out jailers would say, "All right, just stop and we'll take you to see him." And she would be driven to the Rue des Saussaies.

———

The Simex people were in Fresnes prison too. Only Alfred Corbin and Suzanne Cointe knew why.

While waiting for the torture specialist to arrive from Berlin, the Kommando had tried to break Alfred Corbin by their favorite method—threatening to kill loved ones. On November 30 his wife and daughter had been put into the same cell; they were told to stand with their faces to the wall. They heard steps approaching and two or three people come into the cell. Someone with a German accent advised another person to make a full confession if he did not want a particular threat to be carried out. The two women then heard Alfred Corbin replying that he had nothing to say. The German advised Madame Corbin to beg her husband to tell what he knew. She uttered a few words, but he remained silent. The three prisoners were taken back to their cells. On the way, Denise stumbled and fell down some steps. The jailers rushed to pick her up—not from solicitude, but because they were always worried about suicide attempts. But Denise was far from such dark thoughts; she was studying hard to pass her school examinations. On several occasions she had been taken to the Rue des Saussaies to be interrogated by Reiser. There, one of the Kommando interpreters, SS Oberscharführer Siegfried Schneider, very young, very well-mannered, had shown her an active sympathy, even to the extent of going and collecting her schoolbooks from her home. Oberscharführer Schneider will appear again later in these pages.

The torture specialist arrived with his equipment on December 3. Alfred Corbin was handed over to him at six-thirty, and three hours later was taken away unconscious. The session had started with a beating on the thighs and back, then on the soles of the feet; the boot torture had been applied next, perhaps with the same apparatus used on Schulze-Boysen and Harnack. Corbin underwent three sessions of that kind during December, then the specialist went back to Berlin. Corbin still had not talked.

Suzanne Cointe's arrest was being kept secret and her family had no news of her. She had once said to her sister, "If I'm ever arrested, go and ask Jean-Paul [Le Chanois] what's to be done." So on the evening of November 19, her sister climbed the stairs to Le Chanois's top-floor apartment and told him of her disappearance. His reaction was to swear and to start emptying the drawers. He gave no advice (and what advice could he have given?) except to destroy all the addresses to be found among Suzanne's papers. A few days later, Madame Cointe mysteriously received a message from the prisoner: "We're starving, send some food." Not knowing which prison her daughter was in, Madame Cointe entrusted some food parcels to various charity organizations (such as the Quakers, the Red Cross), but all were refused by the prison authorities. Finally, one evening Madame Cointe received a telephone call from a friend, Madame Malavoix, whose daughter Odette ("Dolores" in the Resistance) was in Fresnes but not held *incommunicado*. Odette had sent her mother a slip embroidered with a red cross and the word "Yaya," and Madame Malavoix knew this was the name by which Suzanne's family called her. Madame Cointe thus learned where her daughter was imprisoned, but all attempts to get food parcels to her failed.

All the other Simex prisoners were dumbfounded or horror-stricken when they learned the real reason for their arrest. Robert Breyer, a dentist, was probably the most astounded. A friend of the Corbins and godfather to their daughter, he had become a Simex stockholder in the same way as the Belgian civil servant Seghers had agreed to join Simexco—as a friendly gesture. And now he risked losing his life!

Robert Corbin too was aghast at the situation. Three days after his arrest, four German soldiers and a corporal, all armed, had entered his cell and told him to undress. They left him in his shirt, handcuffed, like the others, behind his back. A black cloth was nailed over the window; the electric light remained on day and night. The prison barber and the "trusties" who brought the meals around whispered to him that the fateful "red card" was on his cell door. On Christmas Eve he was taken from his cell, the handcuffs were removed, and he was driven in a splendid American car to the Rue des Saussaies. On the way he thought of trying to escape, but decided against it—after all, what could he be accused of? At Gestapo headquarters, it was found to be a mistake. Alfred was wanted for interrogation, not Robert. And he was taken back to Fresnes.

In March, however, he was given a very gentle interrogation by Jung. Some astonishing questions were put to him, such as, "Are you related to the ambassador Corbin?" (The latter was with the Free French in London. The presence of Scheliha and Baron Jaspar in the organization had caused the Kommando to suspect the Red Orchestra of having set up cells in European embassies.) Jung ended by reassuring Robert Corbin, telling him that he would soon be set free, along with his niece. Back in Fresnes, the handcuffs were removed, and he began to feel hopeful.

Keller had twice been interrogated by Jung, each time with interludes for blows and kicks and the application of the tourniquet —but without noticeable unpleasantness for the victim. Then, like Robert Corbin, he was taken to Gestapo headquarters by mistake. He was kept there waiting for the police van that took prisoners back to Fresnes in the evening. During the afternoon he had to go to the lavatory. The soldier guarding him went with him. At a certain moment Keller needed more freedom of movement, but the soldier refused to take off the handcuffs; instead he did for Keller what Keller was unable to do for himself—so great was the fear of prisoners committing suicide. Keller was greatly impressed by the incident; it convinced him that the Gestapo thought he was important. He would have much preferred to be of minor interest.

When he was taken from his cell for the fourth time he thought it was the end for him. A young soldier came in with a cloth and said, "I'm sorry, but I have orders to put this over your head." It was a hood, and prevented him from seeing anything. The soldier led him out to a car and helped him to get in. Keller could feel another man sitting next to him. On the way, someone asked a question in German, and the man sitting beside Keller replied; it was Grossvogel.

In the course of this third interrogation, Keller received the shattering revelation that Simex was the cover for a spy ring. His astonishment was as great as his previous blindness. "Oh, my God! Oh, my God!" he exclaimed, slumping back in his chair. A quarter of a century later he was honest enough not to gloss over this immediate reaction. "If I had known, I wouldn't have gone there," he admitted. As a Swiss national he had no need to go to war; but the war had sneaked up and taken him.

Of all the Simex prisoners, Keller was most adaptable to prison life. He had found it hard to sleep with the handcuffs on, but his mechanical skill soon enabled him to get them off at night and to handcuff himself again at dawn. Besides, his jailer often came in and took them off during the day. He was a young German about twenty-two years old, tall, fair and handsome; in civilian life he was a forest warden. On Christmas Eve he shared his food parcel with Keller. Later, Keller heard that he had been executed by a German firing squad for the crime of passing a letter to a prisoner.*

Keller became very popular with the jailers at Fresnes. The fact that he spoke their language perfectly would not have been enough, but in addition he had that exceptional warmth of human sympathy. Never a week passed without a procession of jailers coming to his cell to say goodbye. They had been posted to units on the eastern front, and tearfully poured out their distress to Keller. He comforted them as best he could.

He was given the envied job of "mess orderly," of taking the food, such as it was, to the prisoners in their cells, and was thus able

---

* The staff at French prisons taken over by the Germans was provided by the Wehrmacht throughout the Occupation. The Gestapo never succeeded in gaining control over the administration of the prisons.

to exchange a few words with his Simex friends. They stood in great need of his sympathy and encouragement. Fresnes prison was very different from the house at Neuilly; they were on a starvation diet.

29. The Condemned and Their Judges

On the morning of March 8, 1943, Jung went to Fresnes prison in a Simca and collected Alfred Corbin and Keller. It was the first time the two prisoners had seen each other since their arrest on November 19. Keller found Corbin "much thinner, very pale, and with hardly any voice left." He seemed to be completely broken in spirit. This impression was all the more striking as Corbin bore no outward mark of any torture.

The Simca took them through the heart of Paris. As it crossed the Place de la Concorde, Alfred Corbin murmured, "Ah, I'll never see this place again." The car stopped opposite the Élysée, and Jung took his two prisoners into the office building belonging to the Coty Perfume Company. It had been requisitioned and in it were held the "courts-martial of accelerated procedure of the G.O.C. Third Air Force Region." The operative words, as will shortly be seen, were "accelerated procedure."

The entrance hall was full of German officers. Jung took one of them by the arm as he was about to enter the elevator, pointed to the two prisoners and said, "Priority! Candidates for death." The officer stood aside.

The three went up to the sixth floor and to a small room with benches around the walls and a table at one end. Above the table was an ebony bust of Hitler flanked by swastika flags; and in each corner of the room stood a potted palm tree.

An officer went up to Keller and said, "I am your lawyer. Tell me your story." Keller explained how he had joined Simex and insisted on his complete ignorance of the firm's undercover activities.

"All right, I'll try to get you off," said the other. "But, whatever sentence they give you, I advise you not to protest. Does your friend Corbin speak German?"

Corbin did not know the language, so Keller acted as interpreter. The dialogue was brief:

"Herr Corbin, do you realize the seriousness of the charge against you?"

"I do."

"You understand that as a German officer there's little I can say in your defense. You must expect the worst."

"I know."

Rarely can a defending counsel have dealt with his client so cavalierly. But Corbin showed no surprise; he seemed resigned to his fate.

The room gradually filled with officers who sat on the benches. Then the Court entered, headed by its president. This was Manfred Roeder, who had been prosecutor at the trial of the Berlin network. After obtaining death sentences for sixty members of the network—and boasting of it—he had gone to Brussels to send another tumbril-load to the executioner. He was now in Paris dealing with the French network. Wherever "Hitler's bloodhound" went, he left fallen heads behind him.

Jung stood up and gave the Nazi salute, then read out the charges against the two. Of Keller he said: "This one was not directly concerned, but he showed himself sympathetic to the others. Moreover, after his arrest he was reserved in his statements."

Anyone used to court procedure would have found the manner of passing sentence very strange. Roeder told Keller to stand up and then read out the sentence: "Five years' hard labor." Despite the advice of his counsel—who had made no move on his behalf—Keller cried out, with tears in his eyes: "Five years for having done nothing, that's paying dearly!" At which the defending counsel plucked up courage to address the court and mutter: "What happened to this man could happen to anyone of us. I ask the court to reconsider the sentence."

Roeder hesitated, then withdrew to consult with his assessors, who were all senior Luftwaffe officers. When they returned, Roeder read out the revised sentence: "Three years' hard labor."

Alfred Corbin's trial was very swift.

"Do you realize the seriousness of your activities?"

"Yes."

His sentence was read out immediately: "Sentenced to death by beheading."

The defense counsel had not said a word.

Roeder added sarcastically: "You see, you lose your head even for economic espionage!"

Corbin looked at him and said in a quiet voice, hardly more than a whisper, "That's of no importance. You will lose your war."

Roeder grew scarlet and left the room, banging the door behind him.

Corbin and Keller were taken back to Fresnes. Corbin said nothing during the journey. In the evening, when Keller took around the soup to the prisoners, he whispered to Robert Corbin: "Your brother has just been sentenced. He got the maximum."

Nearly all the Red Orchestra prisoners got the maximum. They were kept in Fresnes while waiting for their sentences to be carried out. A rumor went through the prison that the German practice was to carry out the execution of condemned prisoners exactly one hundred days after sentence had been passed.

———◆———

On April 15, however, there was much upheaval in the prison. The jailers took the Red Orchestra prisoners from their cells and assembled them in the courtyard. We do not know just how many there were, nor their names. Neither Trepper nor Kent was included, of course, nor were Grossvogel, Katz, Robinson and the two Maximoviches. Those present certainly included Alfred Corbin, his wife and brother, the Jaspar couple, Robert Breyer, Keller, Suzanne Cointe, Germaine Schneider (Wenzel's ex-mistress) and her husband, and the Todt engineer, Ludwig Kainz. Also the Griotto couple, members of Robinson's Comintern spy ring, Medardo Griotto, a professional engraver who, like Raichman, had been the expert in forged documents and identity papers.

Käthe Voelkner was not among them. She had been brought before Roeder, who had sentenced her to death. She had given the Communist salute, saying with a smile: "I am happy to have been able to do a few small things for Communism." She had been executed with the shortest possible delay.

Denise Corbin was still in her cell. The evening before the fifteenth she had heard a bustle of activity in the next cell; Suzanne Cointe was being put there for a few hours. The two prisoners managed to communicate, and Suzanne informed Denise that they were all going to be transferred elsewhere. But the jailers had taken Suzanne away and not Denise. She was most alarmed at being left, at not being treated like the others, and a few days later she sent a note to the Rue des Saussaies: "Everyone has gone except me. Why? What's going to happen to me?" She was kept in suspense for a few more weeks, then released in June, just in time to pass her exams.

Of those assembled in the courtyard on that fifteenth of April, most had been condemned to death, a few had been sentenced to hard labor, and others, like Robert Corbin, had not had a trial at all. But none of that seemed to matter. An army officer announced to the amazed prisoners that they had all been pardoned and were being sent to work in Germany, where there was an industrial-manpower shortage. The prisoners were given back their identity papers, which had been taken from them after their arrest. Then they were driven under escort to the Gare du Nord and put on a train, six or eight to a compartment. The doors and windows were locked, and armed SS guards strolled the corridor. The prisoners had been grouped according to length or severity of sentence, so that although Robert Corbin caught sight of his brother he was unable to speak to him. Alfred was with the others who had been condemned to death, among them Baron Jaspar, whose joviality was proof against everything, despite his advanced age, and who had a fund of bawdy stories. Also in that compartment was Ludwig Kainz, who had concealed his spying activities from the Gestapo, but had been sentenced to death for corruption and black-market dealings.

The train stopped at Lille just before midday. It was stifling in the locked compartments, and the prisoners begged for something to drink. The guards selected Keller as "trusty" because of his comparatively light sentence, gave him a large jug and told him to have it filled with coffee at the army canteen. A soldier went with him. While the jug was being filled, Keller asked permission to go and wash his filthy hands. His guard agreed, and let him go alone to the toilets. There was a door at the other end leading to the street. Keller hesitated, then decided against making a break for freedom. After all, he had only three years to go; it would be stupid to escape only to be caught again and probably sentenced to death. He went back to the train with the jug of coffee.

The next stop was at Brussels, where the prisoners were horrified to see a group of wretched men and women, little more than skin and bones, being led by guards toward the train; some of them with large, festering sores on their legs. These unhappy creatures were members

of the Dutch and Belgian networks, who had been brought from
Breendonck concentration camp.

◆

Breendonck was in some respects even worse than Dachau,
Mauthausen or Buchenwald, because it held comparatively few prisoners and they were known personally to their guards, who had an eye
on each one of them from morn to night. There was no possibility of
being lost to view among an anonymous mass of prisoners as at
Dachau or Buchenwald.

Near Brussels, the camp consisted of a series of connecting huts
surrounded by a wide ditch full of stagnant water. Access was by a
drawbridge, and once inside, prisoners were in the hands of SS
guards with power of life and death over them. The low scale of
rations very soon caused prisoners to waste away. Every morning,
those who could still stand were formed into work gangs and went
off singing to their exhausting tasks. Their watchdogs wielded clubs
like maniacs; death was always just around the corner.

After the tortures of Berlin and five months of Fresnes prison,
Hersch and Myra Sokol were cast into this hell on earth. Their sufferings have been related by Madame Betty Depelsenaire, a Brussels
lawyer, who was a prisoner in Breendonck from September to December 1942. Myra's cell was unheated, she was kept handcuffed
behind the back and so tightly that she fainted with the pain. Daily
exercise was taken with a hood over her head, and the SS guard
amused himself by making her stumble and then punishing her with a
flurry of blows. And always the stabbing pain and hallucinations
brought on by starvation.

Myra's only distraction was to see through her window the work
gangs being assembled in the morning and returning in the evening.
Once she caught sight of a familiar figure—her brother-in-law, Jack
Sokol. He had been captured while working for a Resistance network (not the Red Orchestra). Every morning, he and the others
were marched off to work, spades over their shoulders, and as they
went they sang:

> *Before the day is awake,*
> *Before the sun is smiling,*
> *The columns are marching*
> *In the grayness of the dawn*

Toward the toils of the day,
And the woods are dark
And the sky is red,
And we have a crust of bread in our sack
And in our hearts, in our hearts, our distress.

A dark and narrow passage led to the torture chamber. "There was no window to this room, and it was never aired. A smell of burnt flesh and mold caught you by the throat and made the stomach turn. There was a table, a stool, a thick rope attached to a pulley in the ceiling, and a telephone with a direct line to the police in Brussels."*

Myra was taken there, and made to kneel, bending over the stool. They whipped her, but she still refused to talk. So then they tied the rope to her handcuffs annd hoisted her up so that only her toes touched the floor. The handcuffs cut into her wrists, while the effort to support herself on her toes brought on an excruciating cramp. They whipped her, beat her with a club, and then with a stick. She screamed, but did not talk. The cramp had bent her legs so that she dangled and swayed with the blows, and one of them held her still for them to have full effect. But she could no longer talk: she had fainted. They lowered her down and unfastened her. When she came to, they hoisted her up again and went on with the beating. She fainted a second time. At that point the camp commander left the room with his dog, a ferocious animal that had been trained to attack prisoners.

After that session, Myra was put in the "tortured prisoners" hut. Hersch was already there, and they were able to communicate, though without seeing one another. The hut was divided into a number of cells, but the partitions ended about eighteen inches from the ceiling. Myra and Hersch were separated by the whole length of the hut and had to shout. If a guard heard, a beating inevitably followed. Each cell had a drop bench for the prisoner to sleep on. They were forbidden to sit down during the day, which exhausted their little remaining strength. Hersch was given a medical examination, and afterward Myra was aghast when he told her how little he weighed—eighty-two pounds.

In the cell opposite Myra's was the "Russian diplomat"—Danilov. He was the official at the Soviet consulate in Paris who had been sent to Brussels to join the Belgian net, and who was earlier dismissed

---

*Betty Depelsenaire, *Symphonie Fraternelle* (Brussels: Éditions Lumen, n.d.), p. 28.

in these pages as a poor drudge.* He deserves an apology. At Breendonck writes Madame Depelsenaire, "Dan was loved by all of us. He
had a very gentle voice and chose his words like a real diplomat, and
he was always quite calm. He never gave an opinion without having
considered the pros and cons, and his whole attitude gave the impression of a sound and balanced mind. In many discussions he proved to
be our guide and counselor." †

Another person who deserved to be mentioned earlier was Hermann Isbutsky, known as Bob, the odd-job man of the Belgian network. He was a thin, seedy-looking individual, with the appearance
of a traitor in some melodrama, but of whom the Big Chief used to
say, "he's one of those who pull the plow." He had been betrayed by
Yefremov, arrested and tortured—for the Gestapo knew he was in
touch with Grossvogel—but he had not talked. He had the cell next
to the door in the "tortured prisoners" hut. The lieutenant particularly
disliked him, and for every slightest misdemeanor it was Bob who got
the kicks and blows. It was he who kept a lookout and shouted
"Twenty-two," or "Twenty-three," according to whether the guard
was approaching or moving away. This system enabled the prisoners to
talk to one another, which was a great help in keeping up their spirits.
And it was he who said with a laugh one day: "I wonder if we'll leave
here on our feet or feet first." He realized at once that the thought
might depress some of them, and tried to pretend that he had
been joking, adding that they must all consider themselves as soldiers
voluntarily sacrificing their lives. "We're at war," he said, "and it's
better to die this way than under the bombs." ‡

The Gestapo came now and then and took some of them away as
hostages. More often it was the camp torturer who came, a huge
sergeant with the face of a bruiser and a fixed smile, who took a
prisoner to the torture chamber after putting a hood over his head.
Hersch Sokol was frequently taken. Then one morning he was
attacked by terrible stomach pains and writhed in agony for hours,
unable to restrain his groans, which were heard by Myra, so close
and yet so far. The guard refused to take him to the infirmary. He
was merely put in another hut at the far end of the camp, where his
groans would not inconvenience anyone. Myra was taken before
the camp commandant, who told her that her husband was very ill
and would be given medical treatment if she agreed to talk. She re-

---

* See pages 152–53.
† B. Depelsenaire, *op. cit.*, p. 37.
‡ Ibid., p. 35.

fused. Hersch's pains were better on the following day, and he was taken back to his cell. But he was wasting away, unable to keep down any food. He became so deaf that he could no longer hear his wife when she called across to him. Being a doctor, he knew he had not long to live. The camp doctor knew it too, and was even surprised that he was lasting so long. "Not dead yet!" he would exclaim after visiting Hersch; "He's tough, that one. It's amazing how long the human organism can hold out. I must make a note of this case in my statistics book. I'll prescribe some yeast; that may keep him alive a little longer." * But he refused to the end to admit the dying man to the infirmary.

Hersch Sokol's long martyrdom did not end in his cell but in the torture chamber. This specter of a man was taken there for a last interrogation; he was suspended from the ceiling and the camp commandant set the dog on him. †

He died. A few days later, Myra was transferred to St.-Gilles prison.

———◆———

The members of Simexco who had been in St.-Gilles were also put on that train to Berlin. There were Charles Drailly, Mademoiselle Ponsaint, Robert Christen, Henri de Ryck, the publisher, and Jean Passelecq.‡ The cigarette manufacturer, Louis Thévenet, was missing;

---

* B. Depelsenaire, *op. cit.*, p. 59.
† Hersch Sokol's grave is in the former Army Firing Range just outside Brussels—the place where Edith Cavell was shot by the Germans in the First World War. Three hundred Resistance members executed by the Germans have their graves there.
‡ A cousin of Passelecq, arrested at about the same time, was still in St.-Gilles. The cousin had not belonged to Simexco or any other network. He had escaped to England and joined the British secret service. After being parachuted into Belgium he had telephoned to Jean Passelecq who, himself in danger of arrest by the Gestapo, had intimated that a meeting between them was impossible. Later, they both found themselves in St.-Gilles, where they were able to exchange a few words from their respective cells. The cousin was eventually deported to Germany and beheaded. After the war, Jean Passelecq received the diary his cousin had kept while in England. It contained a few details about his mission in Belgium, and great was Passelecq's surprise to read that it consisted chiefly of making contact with Simexco. British Intelligence seemed to have been well informed about the firm and its undercover activities, for the pseudonyms of several of the members were given, including those of Nazarin Drailly ("shopkeeper"), Mademoiselle Ponsaint, and Jean Passelecq himself. I suggested that the information had been given to London by Rauch, but Jean Passelecq thought this was improbable. Is one to conclude that British Intelligence had a second agent within the network?

he had died in prison. But Rauch, the British Intelligence agent, was there; also Bill Hoorickx, the painter; Madame Grossvogel; and Augustin Sesée, the police inspector from Ostend, who had been betrayed by Yefremov. Myra Sokol was probably among them, but there is no proof of this.

The group from Breendonck certainly included Henri Seghers and Simexco's lawyer, Beublet; Simexco's managing director, Nazarin Drailly; Camille, the pianist captured in the Atrébates raid; Bob Isbutsky; and Alamo. The most pitiful were Nazarin Drailly, Beublet, Camille and Alamo; they, like Sokol, had been "interrogated by the dog" and were hardly able to walk. Alamo had been so badly hurt that he was taken to the camp infirmary. As for Nazarin Drailly, he was so changed that his wife did not recognize him among the others on the platform.

The guards distributed the Brussels contingent among the others according to their sentences. Then the train left for Berlin with most of the Red Orchestra on board.

Two or three Belgians clutching Red Cross parcels had been put into Robert Corbin's compartment, and they generously shared their treasures with the famished prisoners from Fresnes. Robert Corbin ate so much chocolate that he suffered a violent attack of indigestion.

The train suddenly halted; there was an air-raid warning. The guards locked the carriageload of prisoners and disappeared. Bill Hoorickx left his compartment and went into the one with Alamo, Camille and Beublet, all three in a pitiful state. Hoorickx, deeply moved, embraced Alamo. Alamo said, "Forgive me for having drawn you into this business." Beublet, his haggard features tearful ("he was a broken man, exhausted"), then said, "It's my fault, I'm the cause of it all. They forced me to give them names. But there are some things impossible to bear."

The all-clear sounded, and the train moved on again.

It reached Berlin on the morning of April 17, forty-eight hours after leaving Paris. The exhausted prisoners had the impression of setting foot on another planet. It was a Sunday, and the railway station was crowded with Berliners gaily going off to picnic in the woods outside the capital.

The Gestapo sorted out their herd. Suzanne Cointe and Madame Robert Corbin were taken to Moabit prison, while Keller, Alfred Corbin, Robert Breyer, Medardo Griotto and Ludwig Kainz went to the Lehrterstrasse prison—and probably Makarov, Danilov, Camille and Isbutsky too, but the survivors are not sure.*

Keller well remembers arriving at the Lehrterstrasse prison. It was like a fairground, full of German soldiers, most of them very young, joyfully singing and swapping jokes. They were deserters expecting to be shot. Keller, completely nonplused, said to some of them: "I don't understand; after all, you've been condemned to death . . ." They replied: "But it's a paradise here! The rations are almost the same as on active service. And we only have to stand against a wall to die, whereas in Russia you have all kinds of suffering before finally getting killed."

The Belgians were first taken to Gestapo headquarters at Alexanderplatz, then sent to Mauthausen concentration camp. Their arrival has been described in simple, undramatic terms by Robert Christen, the Brussels cabaret singer, one of the few survivors. The camp first appeared as a long, walled fortress on the horizon, then they passed an immense, deep quarry swarming with thousands of human ants in striped uniforms. It was like a lunar landscape. "Who can they be, working there?" the new arrivals asked one another. "Where are we?" That evening, they saw for the first time a man murdered before their eyes. The Kapos had pounced on him and beaten him almost to death; he lay there, unconscious but still living. The Kapos called for the camp executioner to give the traditional *coup de grâce*, and his name rang through the camp from one hut to the next. The terrified Belgians did not sleep that night, wondering what would happen to them next.

---

* Each prisoner in his cell was in a little world of his own, where everything was most familiar to him—the times when the jailers made their rounds, the noises from neighboring cells, et cetera—and each small incident, each unusual happening, was noted and considered. When plucked away from this little world of his, the prisoner was overwhelmed by new impressions, especially since any transfer was a cause of great anxiety. (Where was he being taken? What would happen to him?) So that each prisoner on arriving in Berlin was full of his own anxieties and almost indifferent to the fate of others. If we lose track, at least for a time, of some men and women who have played prominent parts in this story, the confusion is even greater for those in minor roles. And not all of these, by any means, have been mentioned. For instance, Winterink's capture has been described, but little has been said about the destruction of his network. However, to have included all the rank and file of the networks in Brussels, Amsterdam, Paris, Lyons, Marseilles—several scores of men and women—would have made this book even more complicated than it is. And although they may not have done as much as their leaders, at this moment they were about to make a greater sacrifice.

There had been sixty-eight of them on the train to Berlin. Only nine survived to see the end of the war.

On May 13, thirteen members of the Berlin group were executed.* Countess von Brockdorf went to her death as though to a fete, smiling even before the scaffold. The officials present were astounded, even scandalized. The Nazis often knew how to die, but seem never to have understood that people can die joyfully.

A condemned man's last letter is usually calm and serene, as if he were already detached from the troubles of this world and thinking only of his near and dear ones. Even Harro Schulze-Boysen sealed his last letter with a tear. Here is the letter from Walter Husemann † to his father just before his execution.

MY DEAR FATHER,

Be strong, I shall die as I have lived, as a fighter for the working classes. It is easy to call oneself a Communist when one is not called upon to shed blood. It's only at the testing time that one proves one is really a Communist. Father, I am a Communist. I am not suffering, Father, you must believe that. No one will see me weaken. To die well is my final duty. Be proud of your son, overcome your grief—you still have a task to perform. You must do it doubly, even trebly, since your sons are no more. Poor Father, happy Father, you have had to sacrifice to your ideals all that has been most dear to you. But the war won't last forever and your time will come. Think of all those who have already taken this road and of those who still will. And remember this about the Nazis: every sign of weakness they see will cost pools of blood. That is why you must remain strong. I regret nothing in life, except perhaps not having done enough with it. But my death will reconcile those who have not always agreed with me. Oh Father, my dear, good Father, if only I knew that you wouldn't break down because of my death. Be tough, tough, tough! Now is the time to prove that you have always, from the bottom of your heart, been a fighter for the working classes. Help him, Friede, stand by him, sustain him! He must not let it

---

* These were: Fritz Thiel, Walter Husemann, Karl Behrens, Wilhelm Guddorf, John Rittmeister, Thomfor, Heinz Strelow, Walter Küchenmeister, Fritz Rehmer, Philippe Schaeffer, Hans-Helmuth Himpel, Richard Wüsstensteiner, Erika von Brockdorf.

† Walter Husemann is the man who tried to throw himself out of the window at Gestapo Headquarters, and to take Inspector Panzinger with him. (See page 277.)

overwhelm him. His life no longer belongs to him, but to the Party. Now a thousand times more than ever before. This is the time for him to prove that his convictions are based not on some romantic ideal but on an inexorable necessity.

Look at Marthe, she is your daughter. She will help you to bear my disappearance. Remember me to all my friends, to all those whose names I don't want to mention. To each of them I give my hand with deep gratitude for the love he has shown me.

I shall die easily, for I know the reason. Those who are about to murder me will soon meet with a painful death, I'm convinced of it. Be tough, Father, be tough! Don't give way! At each moment of weakness, think of the last wish of your son Walter.

"Those who are about to murder me will soon meet with a painful death, I'm convinced of it." A fortnight after interviewing Dr. Darquier at St.-Tropez, I was listening to "Hitler's bloodhound," Manfred Roeder, at his house at Glashütten, on the slopes of the Taunus.

If he is to be believed, he very soon knew that he would escape death, painful or otherwise, after the collapse of Germany. (But is he to be believed? Anti-Semites of his kind would like everyone to share their vice, and have no hesitation in twisting the truth to suit themselves.) In any case, according to Roeder, he was arrested by the Americans at the end of the war and placed in charge of a Major Vale. Roeder's history was known to the Americans, but apparently was not held against him. The major's junior officers showed him a ring they all wore, and told him: "That's a West Point ring. When you see an officer wearing one of these you'll know he has nothing in common with the three million American Jews." When Roeder was being taken to Nuremberg for interrogation, Major Vale is supposed to have said to him, "Forgive me for sending a sergeant with you, but the Jews you'll meet at Nuremberg are not worth my sending a lieutenant." And he advised him, "Above all, don't tell them anything. We suspect all those Jews at Nuremberg are working with the Communists." *

---

* Many of the interrogators for the American military tribunals at Nuremberg were German Jews who had emigrated to the United States before the war. As naturalized American citizens they had enlisted or been drafted into the Army, and during the occupation of Germany they were given tasks in connection with denazification because of their wide knowledge of the country.

No grounds were found for prosecution, and Roeder was re-leased. However, at many public meetings organized by a neo-Nazi movement, he dragged the names of those "Red Orchestra swine" through the mud, attacking in particular one of the survivors of the Berlin group, Adolf Grimme, who had become head of Hamburg Radio.*

Roeder's usual attack was on the theme "A traitor is contaminat-ing our air waves." Grimme retorted over Radio Hamburg: "How is it that such a man has the right today to address public meetings in Germany?" The survivors of the Berlin group protested vigorously and frequently against Roeder's political activity, and he prudently quitted the scene. A man who knew him well and who, like him, had served the Third Reich, admitted to me: "After all, he only did his job. If he had been sentenced, all the public prosecutors would have had to be sentenced. But Roeder was so hard, so implacable, so un-pleasant, that I can quite understand the survivors' wanting to get him jailed."

He had disappeared, and I heard that for two years he had been living in South America, where his elder daughter had settled. But I found him at Glashütten, a pretty little town in a woodland setting where well-off Frankfurters have weekend cottages. Roeder is now deputy mayor, with an active law practice, leading a happy and pros-perous life with his wife—who must have been a very pretty woman —and his younger daughter. The elder is now in the United States, having married an American. Roeder readily brings out phrases such as: "In 1965, when I was invited by the former Governor of Michi-gan . . ." and "The last time a C.I.A. chief came to see me . . ." He has a magnificent house, built in pure Californian style as though in

---

* Adolf Grimme, a former Prussian minister, is one of the twenty Berlin prisoners who escaped a death sentence. The tribunal found him guilty of subversive talks with Arvid Harnack and Adam Kuckhoff ("who had ninety per cent convinced him") and of hiding five thousand marks entrusted to him by Harnack in a radiator pipe at his house. But they found no proof that Grimme knew of the espionage activities of Harnack and Kuckhoff, or of the origin of the five thousand marks and the use for which they were intended. He was sentenced to three years' imprisonment for not having denounced the subversive activities of Harnack and Kuckhoff.

Günther Weisenborn, who was much more compromised than Grimme, also got a three-year sentence. It appears that members of the Berlin network had a fair trial if they did not have the misfortune to appear before the court with a "bad" group of prisoners. The Gestapo sent its prisoners for trial in small groups, and endeavored to include a few of the most compromised each time, so that the others would be tainted by them.

tribute to his friends. A big Opel and a small Fiat stand in the garage.

Roeder is a tall man, a little bent now, with white hair, a blotchy complexion and a large purple nose. His mouth is hideously deformed by protruding teeth. Only the large brown pupils with their pitiless stare are visible behind the thick lenses of his spectacles.

As a relief from gazing at that face, I looked out through the wide window now and again at the great plain stretching to the horizon. And I thought, not even of his dead victims, but of the Mignon couple still stuck in their slum apartment near the Seine, while the Roeders and the Darquiers of this world lord it over their beautiful surroundings. And it seemed to me that the war had upset everything while changing nothing.

◆

Inspector Koppkow was not so fortunate with the British. According to Roeder, they inflicted on him not a painful death, but a vaudevillian one. When arrested, he was sent to Edinburgh, where he was interrogated for four years, telling all he knew—and he knew plenty. When he had finished, British Intelligence feared that if they set such a valuable witness free, other hands would seize him—Russian hands. So they sent a false death certificate in Koppkow's name to his wife in Germany, and then he was allowed to return there. He went under the name Cordes, and with the stipulation that under no circumstances was he to contact his wife and family. He scrupulously obeyed these instructions, for he knew he would find Moscow much less pleasant than Edinburgh. A job had been found for him with a textile firm, and for five years he lived alone under his false name. In 1954 the Cold War became lukewarm and the British decided that Koppkow could be resurrected. He was allowed to add his real name to that of Cordes, and his astonished widow fell into the arms of a phantom who was very much alive.

The two now live at Gelsenkirchen in the Ruhr. I spent two days trying to see the ex-inspector, but he preferred to leave town. His wife is a strange person with a subdued manner and an expressionless voice. She seems to be fearing some imminent disaster. According to her, the threat is now German, not Russian; her husband is at the mercy of any zealous public prosecutor.

This was precisely the case with Inspector Panzinger. At the end of the war he avoided capture by hiding away in a monastery.

When he thought all danger was over he went and settled in Munich. But in 1961 the Bonn public prosecutor opened a file on him and began investigations. And Panzinger, realizing that his whereabouts were known, committed suicide.

30. To the Scaffold

Alfred Corbin shared a cell with two other prisoners, neither of whom had belonged to the Red Orchestra—a young Dutchman and a Belgian schoolmaster. As there were only two drop benches, Corbin slept on the floor. The lack of space for movement made the cold even harder to bear, but the food was better than in Fresnes. The prisoners' ration was three quarters of that in the army, so they had more than German civilians and twice as much as prisoners in Fresnes. Moreover, Ludwig Kainz had been sent to work in the prison kitchens, and he did all he could for his fellow members of the network. Right until the end, he was their secret provider of wonderful feasts, and he even obtained German newspapers for them.

The prisoners in the Lehrterstrasse jail were allowed paper and pencil. Alfred Corbin kept a diary, or rather, three times a day he wrote to his wife, Marie (who was in the Moabit prison), as though talking to her face to face. His words, in a microscopic handwriting, which got even tinier as time passed, seem to be the transcription of an unending conversation between husband and wife, as though they were unseparated by prison walls and armed guards, and without constant risk of being interrupted by the executioner.

On May 12, 1943, he wrote: "Should we be glad to have been transferred to Berlin? In any case, we lose nothing by it! I don't believe we've been brought here especially to be shot one hundred days after being sentenced, as is the rule here—or rather, *was*, since the young Dutchman and many others sentenced to death six months ago have been left undisturbed. Will we be given a retrial, as everyone says? Perhaps. Anyway, we shall see; morale is good, and I want to return with you, as you asked. I returned from Belgium, from the war in France—why not from this trip to Germany?

"My intention is to hand over the Simex business to my brother, if he still wants to leave Creed's, and I'll just look in now and then to keep an eye on things. I've made a good many foreign contacts, and I think there'll be plenty to do in import and export after the war. In any case, I'll change the name of the firm."

On May 19: "I keep figuring when the war will end—some say in three months, others not before the end of the year. It's enough to drive one crazy! Especially as my own fate depends on it. I have no illusions as to the sentence that will be given here, so it's all a question of gaining enough time to escape being executed before the war ends."

On May 20: "I've just made a little friendly sign to Keller, who's in the exercise yard. But Breyer, who is in the same group, never looks toward my window. He seems to be plunged in deep thought—probably also calculating when the war will end!"

On June 4: "What an awful morning! Our Dutch cellmate has been executed, together with all his group of forty. We were roused at half past three this morning, and I thought they had come to take me for my last walk. All three of us were told to dress, and when we were ready they took away this young man of twenty-three who has been awaiting his fate since October 2, 1942! What a filthy business! I've been on edge for some days and felt there was something brewing. Of course, I don't know what's in store for me, but I'm still hopeful! Which is probably idiotic. But if I am wakened like that one morning, you can be quite sure, dearest, that I shall be very, very calm. I am even a little surprised at being so serene."

On June 6: "The fellow who's become a little crazy stayed in our cell for a couple of hours on Friday morning, and proved to us by adding two and two together that the war would not end before 1945! That was a comfort!"

On June 12, Alfred Corbin received a book from the prison library for the first time, a French book entitled *Le Monde où l'on s'ennuie* (*This Boring World*). But Corbin was not bored. He had for long been a contributor to *Rustica,* a gardening magazine, writing under the pen name of "Bellême," and soon after his arrival in Lehrterstrasse prison he had begun to write a book intended for his faithful *Rustica* readers.

His foreword was as follows:

> To my cellmates, Gérard Biront of Louvain (Belgium)
> and Jean Vrolyk of Zwyndrecht (Holland).

Lehrterstrasse 3,
Berlin, April 1943.

I must first of all apologize to the readers of *Rustica* for having left them so suddenly, but they can be quite sure that it was not my fault! And I think of them often.

Five months in prison in Fresnes, followed by a death sentence, have apparently not been considered sufficient by the German police, who have brought me here to this prison in Berlin.

What better can one do, while awaiting one's Fate, than to think of friends and work for them? I have therefore settled down to a subject that has always interested me—the running of poultry farms. I hope that this little book will serve as a guide for all my friends who are or may become poultry breeders. I cannot say when it will be published, if ever, but during my lonely hours here I was reminded of those words of William of Orange: "It is not necessary to hope in order to begin, nor is it necessary to succeed in order to persevere." And so I began, with the means available—that is to say simply, with my knowledge of the subject and my memory.

I trust the reader will therefore forgive me if he does not find *all* the details he would like to find. I have no reference library to consult, and therefore no means of compiling material. Besides, present figures will probably be of no use for the future, and so I must keep to the generalities and basic principles.

The French poultry and game industry will soon recover from its present ruined state. I hope this little book will help that recovery: such is my dearest wish.

A. Corbin-Bellême

All admiration goes to the man who wrote those lines in a condemned cell. They bear witness, in their naïve way, to man's greatness.

———◆———

On July 21, Margarete Barcza left Fresnes prison accompanied by a Gestapo policewoman and took the train to Marseilles. For some days, she had been rehearsed in the part she was to play, which consisted in pretending that she and Kent were still free. The members of the Marseilles spy ring—if it still existed—would thus be reassured about the fate of their chief and his mistress. The idea was to allay their suspicions, so they would not warn Moscow about the messages sent over Kent's transmitter.

It all went off very well, and Margarete received her reward on

her return to Paris. They put her with Kent in the house at Neuilly.
Her Fresnes jailers "fêted her like a film star" when she left, and
presented her with a bouquet as a sign of reconciliation.

At Neuilly she was given room number 7, next to Kent's. At
first they were allowed to be together only on Sundays, but Margarete set about changing this harsh ruling. She went on a hunger
strike on August 12. When they asked her why, she burst out:
"What? You dare ask me that? I'm without my husband and I have
no cigarettes, and yet you know perfectly well, from all my documents, that today's my birthday!"

They quickly brought Kent and a package of Gauloises. Besides,
an unexpected though foreseeable event soon decided Boemelburg
to put the lovers in the same bedroom. Margarete was pregnant, and
the coming months would be terrible for everyone if Kent was not
by her side to help her through this difficult period.

So their life recovered some of the delights of earlier times in
Brussels and Marseilles. They passed their days monotonously but
happily, sunbathing in the garden, playing cards with the guards, and
love making. Kent had still not explained to Margarete the reason
for the upheaval in their lives, and she still thought it had something
to do with his Uruguayan nationality. A chance incident opened her
eyes a little. She heard one of the guards shouting for "Kent's Russian
typewriter." * Did this mean that he knew Russian, that he really was
a Russian? She asked Willy Berg, who regretfully confirmed Kent's
Russian nationality, adding: "But don't let him know that you know.
It would upset him terribly. When he was arrested he begged me to
hide his nationality from you, as he knows you detest Russians and
he's afraid he'll lose you because of it." Margarete promised to keep
quiet, and did so. It was true that she disliked Russia. But why did
Kent also insist he was not Jewish, when she herself was, and so
could hardly hold it against him? But Margarete gave little thought
to these matters, just as she was indifferent to changes of fortune so
long as she and Kent remained together. Her only hell was to be
separated from him; so that Neuilly, despite its inconveniences, was
a paradise.

One does not run away from paradise, especially when one's
beloved would be left behind as a hostage. A few weeks after arriving
at Neuilly, Margarete was allowed to return to Marseilles to get her

---

* In fact, the guard called it "Fritz's Russian typewriter," for the Kommando
had nicknamed Kent "Fritz Frisch."

son, René. Jung accompanied her—which meant that he left her in her hotel room with the door unlocked while he went to all the bars. But Margarete never once thought of escaping. She put her son, then eleven years old, into a Paris boarding school and went once a week to spend the afternoon with him. The rest of the week she spent her time much as Monsieur François-Poncet has described. Trepper would stop to chat with her as she sat in her deck chair, as did Katz and Schumacher, who had been arrested in Lyons. In fact five of the ten rooms of the Neuilly prison deluxe were occupied by members of the Red Orchestra.

On July 1, 1943, Alfred Corbin wrote in his diary: "We're starting a new month and the second half of the year. Will they bring us our freedom?"

On July 20: "I've just been asked whether I'm Belgian or French. The object might be to put me in another cell, or something much worse! I don't particularly like this interest in my humble self!"

On July 21: "I forgot to tell you that I was asked this morning whether I'm a civilian or a soldier! I'm afraid there will be some changing of cells."

A wave of optimism was sweeping through the prison just then. Like prisoners of war all over Germany, those in the Lehrterstrasse prison seized on any rumor to build up the highest hopes. Their information was restricted to the official communiqués appearing in the Berlin newspapers, but they read into them the collapse of Germany in the very near future. Corbin took no part in these fantasies, but confined his own doubts to his diary. Not that he thought the war would last until 1945—an opinion he deemed as silly and pessimistic as the other was overly optimistic—but he felt certain that only an Allied invasion of France could bring the Wehrmacht to its knees. Even the invasion of Sicily, on July 10, 1943, did not make him change his opinion, whereas this news caused his companions to think their liberation was imminent. Even the fall of Mussolini on July 25—which made the others wild with hope—did not obscure his clear-sightedness. He studied the reported speeches of the king of Italy and of Marshal Badoglio, and concluded, "It's not over yet."

However, a few days later, on July 27, he was carried away by the general optimism. "I feel sure it will all be over by the end of the year," he wrote.

The following morning: "Good morning, dearest. I slept fairly well, in spite of the noise from the railway station and a plane that kept circling overhead. I thought I was the only one to be on edge and to feel like giving way at times, but Biront has been terribly upset. It's hard on the nerves. Italy must collapse before Germany does, but when will that be? Dearest, dearest, I think of you so much—of both of us."

Shortly after writing those lines, he was taken from his cell and told to leave his personal belongings behind. He knew what that meant.

Six members of the Red Orchestra, among them Benjamin Breyer and Medardo Griotto, were beheaded with Alfred Corbin, in the building at Plötzensee prison, where Schulze-Boysen and Harnack had been hanged. According to the prison chaplain Kreuzberg, all of them died bravely.

Eight days later, on August 5, fifteen members of the Berlin group met their death on the scaffold.*

Twelve of them were women: Oda Schottmüller, a dancer, who had hidden a transmitter at her home, as had Rose Schlesinger; the fortuneteller Anna Krause; Cato Bontjes van Beek, a pottery worker; Eva Maria Buch, who had translated into German an article written by a French workman for the Communist paper *The Inner Front* and who saved the life of her unknown comrade by declaring that she was the author; Klara Schabbel, who had acted as courier between Berlin and Brussels; Ingeborg Kummerow, the wife of Hans Heinrich Kummerow, an engineer with the Loewe-Opta Radio; Rose-Marie Terwiel, Schulze-Boysen's secretary; Ursula Goetze, a student; Frieda Wesolek, who had sheltered parachutists, and whose father and husband were executed at the same time; Liane Berkowitz, aged twenty, who had given birth while in prison and whose baby was taken from her—to die in an SS hospital before she was executed; and Hilde Coppi, who had also had a baby while in prison, and who wrote shortly before being executed: "I'm very calm, even content, and happy for each day I can spend with my son. And he laughs so much, he is so gay—why should I cry?"

---

* These were: Rose-Marie Terwiel, Hilde Coppi, Emil Hubner, Frieda Wesolek, Stanislas Wesolek, Adam Kuckhoff, Oda Schottmüller, Ursula Goetze, Liane Berkowitz, Eva Maria Buch, Anna Krause, Cato Bontjes van Beek, Rose Schlesinger, Klara Schabbel and Ingeborg Kummerow.

Of the three men, Adam Kuckhoff was the most remarkable. A well-known author and playwright, he had been one of the pillars of the Berlin group, organizing its finances and writing numerous anti-Nazi articles and tracts. His address had been one of those in that disastrous message sent to Kent by Moscow. His last play, *Till Eulenspiegel,* had been used as the key for encoding the network's messages. He was a small, thickset man with a round head and strong features. When sentenced to death, his chief concern had been for his son, Ule, aged five, who would be left fatherless. Just before being taken to the scaffold he scribbled these verses on a piece of paper:

> *For Ule,*
> *My beloved son, my great and final happiness,*
> *I am going away and leaving you fatherless.*
> *No! A whole people—no, that's not enough—*
> *The whole of humanity will be a father to you.*

A few weeks later, Wilhelm Schürmann-Horster, Wolfgang Thiess and Eugen Neutert were executed, and the Berlin group was no more. Two of its members had succeeded in committing suicide, eight had been hanged, and forty-one had been beheaded.

———

In Paris, Giering, the Kommando chief, was admitted to Landsberg hospital in August, 1943, and died of cancer at the end of the year. He had the consolation of having won his race against time, for he had lived to see the Red Orchestra destroyed, and the Big Chief and Little Chief his obedient servants. Giering had shown himself to be cruel and violent, but also cunning and intelligent. He had inflicted torture without flinching, and had borne the torture of cancer without flinching. The survivors of the Red Orchestra hate him, and they also respect him.

Reiser ought to have succeeded him as the head of the Kommando, but unlike Giering he proved incapable of rising above the level of routine police work. He had a bureaucratic mind, intent on avoiding responsibility and refusing to take the initiative. He had not even been told of the great radio game; he merely knew that a *Funkspiel* was in progress, but had no idea of its importance. Moreover, he was so timid that six months after the Big Chief's capture he was still convinced that he was duping the entire Kommando. Giering had his suspicions too, but that had not prevented him from going ahead. And each time Reiser went to Berlin he poured out his doubts to the Gestapo chiefs, without any proof, of course, but basing his suspicions on his flair as an old police hand. His chiefs got tired of hearing him, and ended by saying, "Enough of your everlasting suspicions! It's obvious that the man is working with us!"

Reiser was removed from the Kommando and sent back to Germany, to Karlsruhe, on the pretext that he had been in Paris so long that the enemy was bound to have found out all about him.

And so Giering's successor was Kriminalrat Heinz Pannwitz—a typical example of the type that William L. Shirer has called "the intellectual gangsters of the Third Reich." When Hitler came to power in 1933, Pannwitz was twenty-two and had very little interest in politics; he was studying for the Church. But he never completed his theological studies; instead, he entered the Nazi police. When war came, Pannwitz put up the plan of assassinating Winston Churchill by parachuting into England two mental patients obsessed with the idea of killing the British Prime Minister. This was at a time when Walter Schellenberg was in Lisbon with the intention of kidnaping the Duke and Duchess of Windsor, and Heydrich had set up a deluxe brothel in Berlin which was to be patronized by foreign diplomats whose conversations would be recorded by hidden microphones. Pannwitz's idea was accepted by his chiefs, who were certainly not lacking in imagination themselves, and for several weeks psychiatrists endeavored to inculcate a hatred of Churchill into the minds of a couple of poor devils—but in vain.

All quite amusing. But later activities of Heydrich and Pannwitz were not so funny. On September 29, 1941, Heydrich arrived in Prague as "Vice-Protector of Bohemia and Moravia." Hitler had given him full powers to quell Czechoslovakia—which the appointed "Protector," Baron von Neurath, had failed to do. Heinz Pannwitz was one of those who accompanied Heydrich to Prague; with the latter's support he had risen rapidly in the Gestapo, and now held the rank of *Kriminalrat* (equivalent to Chief Detective). In Prague, he was Heydrich's right-hand man in carrying out a policy which can be described as "the whip and the sugar."

The whip was applied first—deportations and mass executions at the slightest sign of trouble. A fortnight after Heydrich's arrival, Himmler received the following report from him:

"All the Waffen SS battalions will be brought in turn to the

Protectorate of Bohemia-Moravia to carry out executions by shooting and to keep order at hangings. To date, ninety-nine people have been shot and twenty-one hanged in Prague, and fifty-four shot and seventeen hanged in Brünn, making a total of one hundred and ninety-one executions including sixteen of Jews."

That was only a beginning. But while any SS brute could have wielded the whip, the "sugar policy" called for intelligence and skill. Heydrich had both. He devised a scheme through which every Czech workman who worked overtime was paid in ration tickets (for extra meat or fats) instead of money, which had no real value. Heydrich had aimed low but had hit the target. Industrial production soared— as it would have in any German-occupied country, given such an incentive. Heydrich broadened his scheme (holidays at first-class hotels for the best workers, and so on) and then introduced a propaganda campaign on the theme of German-Czech reconciliation. The third stage was designed to give the Czechs a certain autonomy in exchange for taking part in the great anti-Soviet crusade. But this was too much for the Czech government-in-exile. Two secret agents were parachuted into Czechoslovakia with the mission to kill Heydrich, the "Angel of Evil." On May 27, 1942, they attacked the open Mercedes in which Heydrich was traveling and mortally wounded him, and then fled. Heydrich died a week later.

At this point the career of Heinz Pannwitz reached its zenith. A few days before the attack he had implored Heydrich not to travel without an escort, but the Vice-Protector had refused to change his habits. He was everything except a coward. Pannwitz, as Gestapo chief in Prague and so responsible for Heydrich's safety, now risked his life for his chief's temerity. On the very evening after the attack, Schellenberg and Gestapo-Müller arrived in Prague, demanding massive reprisals. Goebbels had already had five hundred Jews arrested in Berlin (of whom 252 were later executed), while another three hundred were seized from the Theresienstadt ghetto. Baldur von Schirach, the Gauleiter of Vienna, wanted to destroy an English town of cultural value as a reprisal. But obviously it was the Czechs who would pay with their blood.

More than three thousand people were arrested in Prague and the large towns, and 1,331 Czechs—201 of them women—were summarily executed. In the country, five thousand villages were searched and 657 people shot. Heydrich's death on June 4 gave fresh impetus to the massacres, and firing squads operated in the courtyards of prisons, shooting seventeen hundred Czechs in Prague and thirteen hundred in Brünn. Then, on June 10, came the wiping-out of the village of Lidice—the male population massacred; the women and girls sent to Ravensbrück; the babies and young children slaughtered on the spot.

Heinz Pannwitz had not been the instigator of these bloody measures, but by his very functions he was one of the people in charge of them. And it was he who directed the hunt for Heydrich's assassins. This began in the torture chambers of the Gestapo and ended on June 18 in the crypt of a church where the parachuted agents and their comrades had taken refuge. Pannwitz directed the assault of a whole SS battalion, which the seven heroic Czechs held off for several hours; in the end, the crypt had to be flooded.

Heydrich was given a state funeral. Hitler came from his headquarters to deliver the eulogy; the Berlin Philharmonic played the funeral march from *Die Götterdämmerung;* the coffin was lowered into the grave, and the Nazi leaders returned to their desks, gorged with blood, and having had their fill of fine music and flags flying in the wind. It had been a magnificent spectacle.

Heydrich's death had also been a good thing for most of the Nazi leaders, as Pannwitz was well aware. He knew their physical terror of his late chief and their jealousy at his rapid rise to power. Pannwitz also realized that the end of Heydrich meant the end of the hopes of his protégés—there would be no more promotions for Kriminalrat Pannwitz. This was probably why he worded his report on the assassination in such an unusual manner. The first part was a bald statement of the facts; but the remainder, while ostensibly examining the assassins' motives, was an accumulation of critical remarks attacking Heydrich's policies in Czechoslovakia—a real accusation of incredible violence against the dead man.

Pannwitz was playing for high stakes. If Heydrich's enemies welcomed the turncoat into their ranks, his career would again be promising. But if they rejected him, the worst might happen; for those who remained loyal to Heydrich would never forgive him.

Pannwitz lost this, his first, gamble. He was summoned to Berlin, where his report had scandalized the SS chiefs, was given a cool reception and then ordered to return to Prague. His welcome might have been different if he had betrayed Heydrich when alive, but he had only betrayed the corpse.

Pannwitz lost his head. Rightly or wrongly, he thought his life was in danger. He had friends in the High Command of the Wehrmacht, and implored them to save him. The best they could do was to draft him into the army and post him secretly to a unit stationed on Lake Ladoga on the Russo-Finnish frontier. It belonged to the notorious Brandenburg Division, a special task force directly under orders of the Abwehr. The SS would not come looking here for Pannwitz.

He was at the front for four months, until the end of 1942. In January, 1943, having made his peace with his old chiefs, he was back in Berlin and working under Gestapo-Müller. Six months later, he was given the command left vacant by Giering. It was a flattering appointment. He owed it to the fact that Giering's reports had passed through his office and he was in close touch with the Kommando's work. But he owed it also to the novel ideas he had advanced, during his time in Prague, for breaking up the Resistance. The traditional way was to wipe out a group entirely once it was discovered; but no sooner was one group destroyed than another rose from its ashes. There was no end to it. Pannwitz proposed leaving the rank and file in peace, and concentrating their efforts on capturing the leaders. These would be "turned" and made "policy advisers" to the Germans; and thanks to them the Resistance setup—still intact—would itself be used to destroy the Resistance. It was astute and audacious—too audacious for the time. But it was just the kind of thinking needed to make a success of the great radio game, and the shrewd Pannwitz was obviously the man to take over from Giering—especially as the radio game was about to enter its vital phase. Six months had been spent in gaining Moscow's trust, in getting the red fish to bite; the time had come to land it.

Pannwitz arrived in Paris just before Reiser's departure. "Until now you've only been tinkering," Pannwitz told him. "Me, I'm going into big-time politics."

Reiser replied that he himself was just a policeman wanting to do a policeman's job, and so was only too willing to hand over to him.

Pannwitz was then thirty-two, and—according to one of his colleagues—he was "chubby, pink and fresh as a little pig."

31. A Battle of Wits

On September 13, 1943, Willy Berg woke up with terrible stomach pains. The previous evening he had drunk even more than usual to drown his sorrows—it was the anniversary of the death of one of his children. He arrived at the house in Neuilly at about eleven-thirty in a state of complete prostration. Trepper sympathized and offered to take him to the pharmacy that sold that wonderful remedy that did wonders. Berg thanked him warmly, and they set off in one of the Gestapo cars. Trepper told the driver to go to the Gare St.-Lazare, to the Pharmacie Bailly in the Rue de Rome, on the west side of the station. It was no small pharmacy, but a huge establishment with a dozen counters on the ground floor and offices and laboratories on the floors above. There was an entrance in the Rue de Rome and another around the corner in the Rue du Rocher.

The car stopped opposite the main entrance. Trepper got out and held the door open for Berg, who struggled up.

"But there are several doors into this pharmacy," he said, frowning.

"Of course, but you're coming with me, aren't you?"

Berg hesitated, then fell back on the seat. "What an idea! I can trust you. Go ahead."

The Big Chief went into the pharmacy by the Rue de Rome and out again by the Rue du Rocher, disappearing into the crowd.

It was just midday.

When the Big Chief had left Dr. Maleplate's office between Giering and Fortner his impatience was even greater than his anxiety. For months past he had been racking his brains for an explanation of the strange workings of the Kommando and of Moscow's astonishing credulity in face of the *Funkspiel*. He would soon know the answer.

He was taken from Fresnes prison to Gestapo headquarters the day after his arrest, as we know. In the evening he was brought before a whole array of Gestapo chiefs, some of whom had arrived from Berlin the same day. One of them was named Müller and was treated with considerable deference; he may have been Gestapo-Müller in person.

Giering did the talking. He said: "You've lost, that's certain. And you've lost not only against us, but with Moscow too. They stopped believing in you a long time ago. After the Atrébates arrests, they blamed you for getting in a panic over nothing. After Yefremov's arrest, you tried to warn the Center in Moscow and you got it in the neck again. It is we, the Gestapo, who have the Center's confidence, not you. But you knew all that already, of course. When a man of your quality sees his agents fall one after the other, whatever he does, he's bound to realize that the enemy is in contact with his own chiefs. And that's what has happened. Look, here are a few of the messages we've exchanged with Moscow. They'll show you to what extent we're masters of the situation."

The Big Chief looked through the messages and then handed them back to Giering.

"And now, what are we going to do with you?" Giering continued. "Obtain from you the names of your last few agents? That's of no interest to us. Your network was a fine thing, I grant you, but it's finished. If you want proof, here it is."

And Giering read out the list of Red Orchestra agents who had been arrested. He went on to mention all those whose whereabouts were known and who could be picked up at any time, and he even gave the names of men and women who were merely suspected of working for the network.

"So, you see, we don't need you in order to wipe out your organization. But, again, that doesn't interest us. We have a much more important objective, one that goes far beyond all of us, you included. It's a matter of reaching a peace agreement between Russia and Germany to put an end to this absurd war. It benefits only those capitalist plutocrats who are just waiting till we've finished cutting each other's throat before stepping in to pick up the booty. That would be idiotic, and we want to prevent it.

"Obviously you may refuse to help us. Frankly, that wouldn't worry us much. As you know, we're 'playing back' some transmitters, and you saw the messages proving that it's working well. We are in contact with Moscow and can start talking even without your help. Simply, it would be better to do it with you.

"If you refuse, you will die twice, so to speak. Here, we'd shoot you as a spy. And then we'd make Moscow believe that you'd turned traitor and gone over to us. You know we can do that. Moscow swallows everything we send.

"I'm waiting for your answer."

Trepper had carefully noted the contents of the messages Giering had shown him, as well as the names of the agents he had so obligingly recited. And he told himself: Their only hold over you is that you're sitting handcuffed in their office. But you're in a stronger position than they are, and you'll win.

He replied: "To be shot is something I expected. As for being thought a traitor by Moscow, you can guess how much I care. But your story of a peace agreement, yes indeed, that's not without interest.

"But your scheme won't work, I'm warning you at once. You admit that my organization had a certain worth; but the Russian Intelligence system is as nothing beside the system Moscow has set up to protect and keep an eye on it. We call that 'counterespionage.' It is everywhere, and all-powerful. It will quickly learn of my capture and warn Moscow. When they know that I've fallen, it will be the end of your plans."

Giering pointed out that the arrests and the "turnings" in Brussels had not been discovered by Russian counterespionage. To which Trepper replied by giving many details about the Kommando's activities in Belgium, pretending that his information had come from counterespionage. In fact, he had it from the control group he himself had set up after the Atrébates raid.

"Until now," Trepper went on, "you've succeeded in hiding from the Center that a few pianists and underlings such as Yefremov have been 'turned.' That's obvious, and I'm bound to acknowledge it. But let me tell you that things will be different in my case. I'm not Yefremov or someone like that. No one can whisk me away without repercussions."

The battle of wits continued until dawn. Trepper did not refuse to collaborate; he contented himself with pointing out the practical difficulties of doing so. And Giering did not insist on a definite answer; it would have belied his assertion, sincere or otherwise, that he could do without the Big Chief's help. During this first confrontation, the two had sized each other up. When it ended, Trepper knew that Giering was a formidable adversary.

Trepper was put into a small room on the ground floor, in order to have him at hand while keeping his arrest secret. Giering was anxious about the French police, who still had a few offices there. Yet a notice was hung outside Trepper's cell, saying, "Special prisoner. Keep out"—which immediately aroused the curiosity of everyone in the building.

Trepper was not so very astonished by what he had learned from Giering about the radio game. He already knew, from Maximovich's earlier reports about General von Pfeffer's group,* that some elements in the Wehrmacht were hoping to negotiate with the West in order to settle their accounts with the East. But for them it was little more than wishful thinking; whereas for the SS Intelligence chiefs to embark on the same course could have infinitely more serious consequences. Trepper was persuaded that Giering's talk about a peace agreement with Russia was merely designed to facilitate his own betrayal, and the purpose of the *Funkspiel* must be to open the way to a compromise peace between Germany and the Anglo-Americans—or at least to create tension and suspicion among the Allies. In either case, the outcome of the war might be changed.

The Big Chief had always been careful with the lives of his agents, even when upbraided by the Center in no uncertain terms. But there in his small cell at Gestapo headquarters he came to the conclusion that the SS plan had to be sabotaged at all costs. There were two possibilities: to warn Moscow, or to upset things at the Kommando end. In either case, he had to improve his situation, and quickly. He needed more freedom of movement.

He had guessed what Giering was getting at. Thanks to Kent, who had been arrested two weeks earlier, Giering knew that the Big Chief's most important messages were sent over the Communist Party's transmitters. If Giering could put his hands on these, his messages to Moscow would be stamped with undeniable authenticity. And in addition he would learn whether the Big Chief's capture had been reported by counterespionage.

Two men could lead the Kommando to the Party—Trepper and the Director.

At the end of November, 1942, a few days after Trepper's arrest, Giering gleefully showed him a message received from the Center over Kent's radio. In it, the Director ordered a meeting between Trepper and Michel, his contact with the Party and fixed the date, time and meeting place.

Giering had no intention of arresting Michel, but had him shadowed in the hope that he would lead them to the Party. But Michel did not turn up. He had a standing agreement with Trepper not to go to any rendezvous arranged by the Center until two days plus two hours after the given date and time.

---

* See page 179.

The second round had gone to Trepper. But the final result of the contest was still in doubt. Giering kept his prisoner in his cell. And Trepper could do nothing unless he could get out.

◆

Leaving his cell for some questioning or confrontation was hardly getting out. The most dramatic confrontation was with Vasili Maximovich. The baron had not killed himself before his arrest; he had obeyed the Big Chief, and done his best to drag with him into the next world "as many of those scum" as he could.

At present they were grilling him about General Pfeffer's circle of officers, whose fate depended on the words "negotiate with or without the Führer." Giering asked Trepper whether Maximovich's original report had definitely stated that those words had been uttered by Pfeffer. The Big Chief emphatically confirmed that they had—and he saw "a great joy light up Maximovich's martyred face." For good measure, Trepper added that all the officers close to Pfeffer favored negotiating with the West, "with or without the Führer." This was true about the negotiating but guesswork as regarding the Führer. Trepper, however, saw no reason for haggling over words; he wanted to strike down the greatest possible number of supporters of a separate peace, whether SS or not.

Trepper was also questioned about the curare, for Anna Maximovich had insisted she had supplied him with enough of it to poison a thousand people—a statement that had engendered a most heartening panic. That was one of Trepper's good moments.

He was interrogated many times about his German sources by the army judge-advocate preparing the case against him. Even in his cell, he had caught faint echoes of the scandal which had shaken *Gross Paris*, and which continued to grow as they discovered the extent to which the Red Orchestra had penetrated the German General Staff. It was a fine tribute to his past work. And his appearances before the judge-advocate gave him the opportunity to add to that work, for they put into his hands the lives of many German officers. Undisturbed this time by considerations of high policy, he distributed death, hard labor or reduction in rank, just as he felt inclined, sparing the "good" ones, accusing the "bad."

His first thought, naturally, was to save Ludwig Kainz. This he did by maintaining that Kainz had only done black-market deals with Simex, and he said: "If you punish him for that, then you ought to punish every official of the Todt, from the deputy director down."

He also saved the good Austrian colonel in the Wehrmacht Supply Corps from whom he had learned of the imminence of Operation Barbarossa. On the other hand, he implicated all the SS officers he knew, as well as some particularly fanatical Wehrmacht officers. He said that he had bought them; in fact they had only been a bit too talkative. To the execution post with them! That was another of Trepper's good moments.

He dispensed death, and he was also badly hit by it. The Kommando had found a passport with Trepper's name and photograph at the home of Madame Grossvogel. Giering showed it to him. "Bravo! That's my real passport," he exclaimed. "Trepper is in fact my name." Giering was suspicious at this readiness to admit his real identity. But Giering could not know how anxious the Big Chief was to keep them from discovering his old pseudonym, "Domb," under which he had been known in Communist circles. A member of the Kommando was sent to Neumarkt, in Poland, to find any early traces of Leopold Trepper. His report reached Berg just as he was interrogating the Big Chief. Berg read it out: "Neumarkt is *judenrein*.* The records have all been burned. The cemetery has been destroyed and plowed up, so that it is impossible to search the tombstones for the name of Trepper."

And so it was that the Big Chief learned that all of his family had been exterminated. In the few moments it took to read the message, he had lost his mother, his brothers and sisters, his aunts and uncles and cousins—forty-eight people in all. The adults had been sent to the gas chambers. The children and old people had been massacred.

The Big Chief shrugged and said to Berg, with a smile: "You ought to search the police records here in Paris. It would be surprising if you found nothing under the name of Trepper."

———◆———

Giering had let him have a dictionary, paper and pencil, and during the day he scribbled away under the unconcerned eye of the guard on duty in the cell itself. The guards were forbidden to speak to the prisoner, but at night the rule was frequently broken. The guard would remain silent until about one in the morning, but when the whole building was asleep he and the prisoner would chat away for an hour or two. Then the guard settled down on his cot and fell

---

* "Cleaned of Jews." In the Nazi vocabulary, this meant that the entire Jewish population of a town had been shot or deported.

asleep too. Trepper would wait another half hour before getting up and retrieving a roll of paper hidden in one of the hollow legs of his bed.

This was his report to Moscow, and it began with a mass of detail. For months Trepper had been sending them warnings, which had not been heeded. This time, they must believe him. It was the last chance. So he minutely described his arrest—the date, time and place —and his imprisonment in Fresnes; his present detention and each interrogation—by whom, when and where. All of that could be verified, even if the famous counterespionage was just a bluff. Feeling almost certain that the Center would be convinced he really was a prisoner of the Kommando, he went on to give the names of agents already arrested, and, above all, the names of those Giering suspected of belonging to the network. The most important of the latter was Fernand Pauriol, the Party's radio operator. Trepper emphasized that he must go into hiding as quickly as possible.

Then he exposed the great radio game—its aims and the means employed. As proof of what could be achieved with a few "turned" pianists, he quoted the messages Giering had obligingly let him read and gave the latter's comments. He ended the report by warning that he would attempt to escape, and setting forth several plans. He thought the best opportunity would be afforded by a café with two exits at the lower end of the Boulevard St.-Michel.

Many nights were needed to complete the report. Trepper could work at it only between three and six in the morning, always with an eye on the sleeping guard. The most helpful of them was Berg, whose drinking sent him into a sound sleep. The most vexatious was a priest who had been drafted into the army and who spent his guard-duty nights praying for the prisoner's soul.

Trepper drafted the report in Hebrew, Yiddish and Polish, mixing the three languages as tightly as possible. If the roll of paper were discovered, they would need three translators to sort out the text, which would give at least a few hours' respite. It was a minor precaution, but typical of the Big Chief. Tied to the execution post, he would be considering a plan of action in case all twelve bullets missed their mark.

His report completed, he decided that it was time to take his chance with Giering. Of all the risks he had run in his life, this was the greatest.

Giering knew that the first link in the chain leading to the Party was a certain Juliette, a long-time militant Communist. She worked in a wholesale confectioner's near the Châtelet. But instead of sending Trepper to see her, as Trepper had been hoping, Giering decided to use Raichman, the Brussels forger, who had been in contact with Juliette a year previously.

"You're wasting your time," Trepper told Giering. "She'll pretend she doesn't know Raichman, you'll see."

She did pretend not to know Raichman. Some months earlier, Trepper had instructed Juliette not to recognize any messenger or contact man, other than himself or Katz, unless the person showed her a small red button as a recognition sign. Neither Giering nor Raichman knew this.

The third round had gone to the Big Chief.

Giering and Willy Berg went to Berlin, and on their return Berg urged Trepper to collaborate. He replied that he asked for nothing better, but he was being prevented by his confinement. He had been prepared to go to see Juliette; it was not his fault if Giering had preferred to send Raichman. He was quite ready to assist the Kommando, but they must at least enable him to dupe the counterespionage by going to his usual places; and he had to be able to contact certain agents again. Berg said that he himself would gladly agree, but that Giering would never give his consent—not so much from distrust of the Big Chief as from fear of an attack on him. Giering was convinced that all the Communist Resistance groups in Paris had received orders either to rescue Trepper or to kill him and so shut his mouth.

It was then the Big Chief suggested sending Hillel Katz to see Juliette.

———◆———

Trepper had felt both despair and relief on learning of the arrest of his faithful lieutenant. The sorrow was only natural; the relief was due to Katz's exceptional qualities and the fact that with his assistance the game became a little less difficult.

Katz had been tortured but had refused to talk. He kept repeating: "Trepper is my chief, and will remain so to the end. I'll do what he asks me to do, and nothing else." It was certain that he would not go to see Juliette unless ordered by the Big Chief. Berg managed to persuade Giering to bring the two together, and so they saw each

other again for the first time since November 23. Katz was disfigured
by the blows he had received.

The meeting had been carefully arranged by the two Germans
and Trepper. The great difficulty was that Katz, unlike Trepper, did
not speak German; and neither Giering nor Berg knew French. There
was no question of using the Kommando's interpreter, Oberscharführer Schneider; if Reiser was being kept out of it, a simple noncom
could hardly be brought in. On the other hand, Giering and Berg
could not allow the two prisoners to talk together without being able
to understand what they were saying.

It was the Big Chief who had found the solution. He said to Berg,
"You understand Yiddish well enough; I'll talk to Katz in Yiddish,
and so you'll be able to check that I'm not deceiving you." Yiddish,
which is derived from old German, is understandable to a German.
But it also contains many Hebrew words whose meaning is obviously
lost to anyone not knowing Hebrew.

The Big Chief made a long speech to Katz, urging him to do as
the Kommando wished, and then instructed him to go to see Juliette,
giving much advice on how to be accepted by her—all quite unnecessary, as she would in any case accept Katz. And the Big Chief
sprinkled his speech with various words in Hebrew. These words,
when detached from the rest, conveyed the message: "She must reply
that she will try to make the contact, but can make no promise."

Reiser still has a vivid memory of Katz's meeting with Juliette. It
was on a rainy afternoon in December. A force of plainclothes policemen had surrounded the Châtelet area, and the Kommando had taken
up positions in the streets near the confectioner's. But they let Katz
go in alone to see Juliette. Trepper had warned that the counterespionage was probably keeping a watch on her; and if Katz's
guards kept close to him, they would be seen and the whole thing
would fall through.

Katz came back with the reply as instructed by the Big Chief.

A week later, Giering sent Katz to the confectioner's again. And
in accordance with Trepper's instructions, Katz reported that Juliette
had said to him: "I've got the contact, but the chief has to come himself."

Giering was tormented by the thought that some trap was concealed in all this, but Trepper reassured him. "Of course not! It's
simply that they're worried about my sudden disappearance. I'm tired
of telling you that if I'm not seen around, they'll be sure I've been

arrested and your whole affair will fall through. They're already beginning to suspect something."

It was too late for Giering to draw back. By arresting the Big Chief he had in fact risked everything. If he succeeded in laying hands on the Party's transmitters he would be able to reinforce the *Funkspiel* and make the messages seem perfectly genuine. But if the Big Chief's arrest became known to Moscow, the Center would probably realize that his earlier fears had been justified. Then they would reexamine the network's situation, which would certainly unmask the "turned" pianists. It would be the end of the radio game.

So Giering decided to let Trepper go to see Juliette. Even greater security precautions were taken this time. Groups of *Feldgendarmes* in plain clothes were on duty at all the crossroads leading to the Place du Châtelet, while the Gestapo and its French auxiliaries were responsible for inner protection.

Giering had given Trepper a message which Juliette was to pass on to her chiefs for transmission to Moscow. It was supposedly from the Big Chief, explaining that the network had received some hard knocks but had not been destroyed, and suggesting that radio communications be closed down for a month, to let the storm die down. The Center itself would give the signal for reopening communications by sending the Big Chief the usual congratulatory message on the occasion of the Red Army's fête day.

The month's break was Trepper's idea. He had told Giering that the Center, being used to his prudent ways, would expect some such proposal. Actually he wanted to give Moscow time to check his report, and in the meantime to block any further action by the Kommando.

The coding of the message had set a problem. Giering knew through Kent that a top-secret code was used for messages sent over the Party's transmitters, but when Trepper was asked to supply it he burst out laughing and said: "What? You don't think a top man like me wastes his time coding and decoding?" Kent had revealed that Grossvogel knew the code; but, as we know, all efforts to break Grossvogel were in vain. In the end, the message was put into one of the codes used by Brussels.

———◆———

Willy Berg accompanied Trepper into the confectioner's, but then pretended to be interested in the display counter. Trepper went

358 THE BIG CHIEF

up to Juliette and gave her some papers—Giering's message, his own trilingual report, and a letter that began: "Dear Comrade Duclos, I implore you to do everything possible to get this document to Dimitrov and the Central Committee of the Communist Party in the Soviet Union. There's something wrong in Moscow. It's even possible that a traitor has slipped in among us."

Juliette took the papers without saying a word. But Trepper murmured to her: "Disappear immediately after passing these on, and don't come back." Then he went out again, followed by Berg.

So far as Trepper was concerned, he had won the battle of wits. He had succeeded in communicating with Moscow under the very eyes of his jailers and from the very heart of the Gestapo. Thanks to him, the Center would receive more than enough trump cards to beat the Kommando's game. Nevertheless, he was still haunted by a vague fear, for the final decision was in the hands of the Director—and if he refused to put faith in Trepper's report, the Kommando would win after all.

———◆———

Giering became impatient long before the month's break was over. Only three days after the message had been handed to Juliette he sent a French policeman to the confectioner's to ask, on Trepper's behalf, whether it had been successfully passed on to the higher ranks. But Juliette was not there. Her employer said that she had taken a few days off. A week later, she was still absent. At the end of the following week, the employer told the policeman that Juliette had been called to take care of a sick aunt and no one knew when she would return to work.

Giering demanded an explanation from Trepper. "I've told you often enough," he said ruefully, "by keeping me confined here, you're bound to arouse suspicions."

He was allowed out, one car preceding and another following the car he was in. He thus took his Gestapo guards to various shops where, he said, he had agents. His guards let him go in alone, but kept close watch outside. Obviously they made no arrests—that would have caused alarm, and the object of the exercise was to promote reassurance. But even if they had made arrests, they would only have roped in the Big Chief's tailor, his bookseller, tobacconist, and so on—all good people who knew nothing whatever about their client's activities.

On February 23, the Red Army's fête day, Giering received the congratulatory message sent to the Big Chief by the Director. It was the green light for resuming communications with Moscow—and especially for the great radio game. The plan to make use of the Party's transmitter would have to be temporarily abandoned, as all trace of Juliette had been lost, but the Center's message proved to Giering that it was unaware of Trepper's arrest. The *Funkspiel* could go out under his name.

That day was probably a celebration for the Kommando too; many bottles of brandy must have been drunk at Suzy Solidor's. Trepper benefited from the general euphoria: that same evening he was moved to the house at Neuilly. Kent, however, was kept at Gestapo headquarters. He had been in a room next to Trepper's, and the two had been able to exchange a few words. Kent had said, "I'm sure you're not really working for them. You're just trying to fool them." Trepper had replied: "But of course I am! What else is there to do? You can see it's all up!"

Trepper's transfer was not purely a reward. Giering was becoming increasingly suspicious of the French police who still shared the building in the Rue des Saussaies. He grumbled to his men: "Every time we work with them, something goes wrong." His distrust was further increased by some remarks Trepper had made about the sympathy the French police had for the Resistance. And Giering was inclined to listen when his prisoner made a suggestion. Trepper pointed out that he had neither identity papers nor money in his possession. The members of the Kommando carried false papers instead of their German documents—pretending to be Dutch, Flemish or Swedish businessmen resident in the French capital—and they produced these papers whenever they were stopped by a French police check. But what would happen if Trepper's car was stopped by French police during one of his outings? They would inevitably want to arrest a man without identity papers or money. The matter would probably go no further, but its consequences might be far reaching. There was the likelihood of the Resistance being informed of a mysterious prisoner whom the Germans were driving around Paris. Trepper's description would be circulated. . . .

Giering took the point and had the Big Chief supplied with papers and some money.

———◆———

The next six months were a matter of walking round and round the lawn at Neuilly. The Kommando consulted the Big Chief only about the general lines to follow; the practical work of the *Funkspiel* was done by Kent, who wrote out and coded the messages—his own in French, and Trepper's in Russian.

Katz had nothing to do and was at loose ends. He had been moved to Neuilly at the Big Chief's insistence, as similarly Grossvogel's life had been spared through the Big Chief's maintaining that he might be indispensable for the *Funkspiel*. Otto Schumacher—at whose home Wenzel had been captured, and who had been arrested in Lyons—was looked at askance by his companions in detention. Probably acting as a stool pigeon, he kept asking Katz: "But can it be true that the Big Chief is working for them? Don't you think he's playing a double game? I can't believe he's turned traitor!" Katz would raise his eyebrows and say with astonishment: "Are you dreaming? What else is there to do but make the best of it and go along with them?"

A strange thing was that Kent, who had completely gone along with them since his capture, now appeared to be retracing his steps. After being brought to Neuilly in his turn, he had told Trepper repeatedly that he did not believe he was really working for the Germans; and some of Kent's remarks gave the impression that he regretted having done so himself. A little longer, and it was not impossible that the Little Chief would again be of use.

With Berg, conditions were ideal. He had produced his favorite saying for Trepper's benefit: "I've been a cop under the Kaiser, a cop under the Weimar Republic, I'm a cop under Hitler, and I'll still be a cop if Thaelmann comes to power." The two men understood one another. Berg, who had lost three children through illness, went to Berlin on leave and came back a broken man; his wife had gone mad during an air raid. Thereafter, his one desire was for the war to end; and Trepper often thought that here at least was one German who sincerely wished for a compromise peace, of whatever kind. Berg became an unexpected "source" for the Big Chief, informing him daily, in great detail, of the Kommando's activities, so that he knew of Giering's plans even before they were put into operation. There was no question of Berg having been "turned," or of any tacit complicity. Trepper had the impression that Berg's mind worked thus: "If the Big Chief is really working for a separate peace and for us, there's no harm in talking to him. If he's playing a double game, well, who knows how the war will end, and I'll talk to him just the same."

It was a very different matter with Giering. Until the last day,

Trepper knew that on no account must he lower his guard. He learned of Giering's departure with relief, and of the arrival of Pannwitz with satisfaction, convinced that the change could only be to his advantage. He was right, for various reasons, notably that Giering thought Jews were worth no more than anybody else, whereas Pannwitz absolutely believed they were worth less.

Twenty-three years after these events, Pannwitz described the Big Chief to me in these terms: "A great actor! When he thought he wasn't being watched, his eyes were very hard, very wary, and his bearing was quite calm and serene. But as soon as anyone turned their attention to him, he started to put on an act. If you pressed him with questions, he'd put a hand to his chest to remind you that he had a weak heart. But he was first and foremost a Jew. The Russians made a great mistake in putting so many Jews into that network—just think, the Red Orchestra was ninety per cent Jewish!—for a Jew is much too shrewd to die for a lost cause." *

Before coming to Paris from Berlin, Pannwitz had read the reports describing Trepper's betrayal of his masters, so he was little inclined to believe in Trepper's heroic virtues. It was significant of the lack of mutual trust within the Gestapo that no one explained to Pannwitz, when he took up his new post, that the "Trepper legend" was a piece of fiction. They let Pannwitz take over the Kommando with a completely false idea of his chief prisoner—and so he trusted him entirely. Trepper was told that he would soon be leaving Neuilly and would be given an apartment in Paris, where he could come and go as he liked, under discreet surveillance. But first he was to help initiate Pannwitz's "high policy."

Pannwitz had the impatience of youth and wanted to rush ahead. He considered that the radio game had attained its objective of gaining Moscow's confidence. But to talk politics at the highest level, they needed a more direct approach than the exchange of coded messages by radio, and he advocated sending Moscow an envoy accredited by the Big Chief. Before leaving Berlin, Pannwitz had submitted this idea to Himmler, who had not appreciated its boldness. Himmler had said in his sententious way, "No. The Bolshevist ideology is so attractive that no one must be sent there, the risk of contamination is too great."

However, Pannwitz clung to his idea; but instead of sending an

---

* Manfred Roeder, who saw Trepper after his arrest, described him in these terms: "An intelligent and adaptable businessman, a most amiable, well-mannered person." Fortner's impression of him was "an officer type."

envoy to Moscow he would persuade Moscow to send someone to
him. He asked Trepper whether it was customary for the Soviets
to delegate a high official to discuss matters of exceptional interest on
the spot. Trepper thought it was. But when Kent was asked the same
question, he said the opposite. Pannwitz was worried, and asked
Trepper to explain this contradiction. "But how do you expect Kent
to know what happens at that high level?" Trepper exclaimed, raising
his arms in astonishment.

Pannwitz saw his point. So the Center received a long message
from the Big Chief explaining that he was in contact with a powerful
group of anti-Nazis very favorable to the Soviet Union. As he himself had no authority to deal with political affairs, he asked if the
Director would send someone with power to open negotiations? The
rendezvous was fixed for successive dates at Katz's old apartment in
the Rue Edmond Roger.

Trepper was taken there on the first date, and was surprised to
find Raichman, who now lived there. The two had a short chat. Like
Kent and Schumacher, Raichman said to his former chief: "I can't
really believe that you're working for them." And as with Kent and
Schumacher, the Big Chief gave a despairing answer.

The man from Moscow did not turn up that time, but Pannwitz
was still hopeful. However, before the last date arrived, the Kommando was shaken by a time bomb left by Giering.

◆

It was Giering's last success, but he probably never knew of it,
for he was nearing his end in his hospital bed at Landsberg.

The Juliette affair had made him uneasy. Why had the woman
disappeared so suddenly and without trace? It was possible that the
"counterespionage" had been anxious about the Big Chief and told
her to go into hiding. But she should have reappeared after Trepper
was allowed out, and in any case after the message of congratulations
on February 23. If that message had been "sincere," it meant that
the Center did not suspect anything and Juliette should therefore have
returned to her job. As she had not, was Moscow's message sent to
dupe the Kommando?

The only way to get to the bottom of the business was to arrest
the next link in the chain leading to the Party. That link was Fernand
Pauriol.

Giering knew of his existence from Raichman; and from Kent

he learned of his role in the Party setup, and that he had been the Red Orchestra's courier between Juliette and the Central Committee. His arrest might throw some light on the Juliette affair, and reveal if Moscow was really being taken in by the *Funkspiel*.

The Gestapo all over France had orders to bring in Pauriol, but no trace of him could be found. Months went by, but Giering did not forget him. He wanted Pauriol badly, and he laid a Machiavellian trap —he would make the Center deliver up the man whom the Gestapo had been unable to capture.

The transmitter used to send the Big Chief's messages had broken down. Instead of calling on German technicians, Giering had a message sent over Kent's set informing the Center of the breakdown and urgently requesting them to send one of the Party's radio experts. It was a clever move. If the Center had not tumbled to the *Funkspiel*, they would send Trepper the expert requested. But even if Trepper's report had reached Moscow and been acted upon, *even if the Director knew that Giering was setting a trap*, he would have to pretend to be taken in and so arrange contact with a radio repairman. If it meant sacrificing him, one man more or less made little difference to the Center—or to Giering, for that matter, and he might not even bother to rope in an agent of such minor importance. The message announcing the breakdown could have only one aim: to give verisimilitude— a network without its troubles did not exist, or existed no longer.

The Director informed Trepper about a Communist radio technician known as "Jojo." His parents kept a café in the St.-Denis quarter, and he had a workshop where he built and repaired radio transmitters.

There was no certainty that Jojo would lead to Pauriol, and it would probably be a long haul (in fact Giering left Paris before the end of it was reached), but the Kommando butchers got to work. It was the old story of a man gasping out a name or two when his body could no longer support the pain, when his mind reeled and his spirit was broken. Jojo gave away Auguste, who gave away Marc, who gave away Michel. Michel gave a lead to Francis—or François—who was in hiding near Bordeaux. Fernand Pauriol, alias Duval, was at Bordeaux. He was lured to Paris, where he was trapped on August 13, 1943. As he remained absolutely silent, it was three weeks before the Gestapo discovered his real identity.

One day in early September, Berg burst into Trepper's room shouting joyfully, "This is it! We've got Duval!"

It came like a bolt from the blue to the Big Chief, and for the first time, he thought the end of his long battle had come, that at any moment he would be taken out and shot. All that remained was to make a good death. In his usual methodical way, he prepared the fine phrase he would throw into the faces of his executioners.

But Fernand Pauriol did not talk. Atrociously tortured, he did not talk. Threatened with seeing his wife shot before his eyes, he did not talk.

His calvary was to last exactly one year, but Pauriol never talked.

The Big Chief had hardly surmounted these fears when a fresh blow fell. On September 12, Berg told him that he was being taken under escort to the south of France. The Funkabwehr had discovered a Communist transmitter down there and had seized copies of messages sent and received. Kludow, the famous code breaker, was on his way to France to tackle the messages, but the Kommando was already convinced that this was the transmitter that had sent Moscow the message Trepper had given Juliette. So they would soon know how the Center had replied and any questions it had put to the Party. Trepper's presence might well be needed.

A catastrophe appeared to be imminent. If this set had transmitted the Gestapo's message, it probably had also transmitted Trepper's trilingual report; and once this was found, Kludow would not take long to decipher it. This reasoning was logical enough, but it was based on a false premise: the set had not been used for the message; and as for Trepper's report, Jacques Duclos had sent it by courier to London, to be forwarded to Moscow. But Trepper could know nothing of that, and he believed it would soon be all up with him. He had a short respite—they were not leaving for the south for two days.

Trepper had had plenty of time to note the security measures at Neuilly during his six months' residence, and to evaluate his chances of escape. There was a risk of being shot by the Slovak guards, but it had to be taken. He spoke of his intention to Katz that same evening, but Katz refused to follow him. Katz's wife and children were being held as hostages at the Maximovich château at Billeron, and he had been told they would be shot if he did not play straight. He had risked their lives in the Juliette affair, because of what was at stake; but he could not do it to save his own skin. He would stay at Neuilly, but wished his old friend good luck.

Trepper changed his plan. He had thought of breaking out of the house in order not to leave Katz behind. Alone, there was a better way; he had identity papers and some money, and could take advantage of Berg and his hangovers. The following morning, he offered to take Berg to the Pharmacie Bailly.

The Big Chief had not reckoned on Berg remaining in the car. He had planned to knock him down in the pharmacy and make a dash for it. There were always plenty of people there, and if Berg drew his revolver they would prevent him from taking aim. It was even likely that someone would try to disarm him.

In the event, his escape was simplicity itself. He had only to go in at one door and out by another.

Two years earlier, on September 13, 1941, the Big Chief had escaped from the trap set by Fortner in the Rue des Atrébates. Ever since his childhood he had taken thirteen as his lucky number.

32. On the Run

More dead than alive, Willy Berg telephoned headquarters, where his words caused panic. Pannwitz at once had the area round St.-Lazare cordoned off by police; dozens of people had their papers checked or were arrested, the Bailly building was searched from roof to cellar, but no trace of Trepper was found. At the end of the afternoon Pannwitz withdrew the police cordon, which was no longer serving any useful purpose. It was then that Trepper walked into the Gare St.-Lazare from the Rue d'Amsterdam and jumped into a train for St.-Germain-en-Laye.

He had expected the Gestapo to concentrate on the St.-Lazare area, so had rushed from the pharmacy to the nearest Métro, got into the first train that came along and stayed in it until the terminus. Then he had gradually made his way back to the center, finally taking a bus to St.-Lazare.

His train stopped at Le Vésinet, but he did not get out. He did not know if Georgie de Winter still lived in their chalet at 22 Rue de la Borde. She might not have had money to pay the rent; besides,

the lease was running out, if it hadn't already expired. So he got off
the train at St.-Germain-en-Laye, and went to that boardinghouse
run by the two sisters, where Georgie's son, Patrick, had briefly
stayed. They welcomed Trepper, and he at once telephoned Le Vésinet. But there was no reply.

Katz, they thought, was sure to have known of his chief's escape
plan, and probably knew his hiding place. Katz was taken to the Rue
des Saussaies and put to torture, but did not talk. He was brought
back to Neuilly in a pitiful state. Horrified, the caretaker, Prodhomme, bent over him as he lay prostrate on the floor. Katz whispered
to him: "The man who escaped will come back here. Tell him that
even if they torture me to death, I'll die happy. And ask him to take
care of my children for me."

That evening, Pannwitz sat and stared at his telephone for some
time. He finally mustered up courage and asked to be put through to
Gestapo-Müller's office in Berlin. When he had Müller on the line he
said: "Now don't faint. Trepper has escaped." There was silence.

"Hello, hello," cried Pannwitz. "Have you fainted?"

A burst of oaths and curses assailed his ear. When Müller tired
of swearing he muttered in a hopeless sort of voice: "And how do
you expect me to announce that to Reichsführer Himmler when he
ordered us to throw the prisoner into a deep cellar and load him with
chains?"

"There's one way out," said Pannwitz.

"Oh yes? What?"

"Not to tell him anything at all!"

Müller was dumbfounded for a moment, then agreed that it
was the only way to escape Himmler's wrath. The two agreed to
keep silent. (And Himmler never knew of the Big Chief's escape.)

Pannwitz had avoided the worst and was still head of the Kommando. But he knew it was only a respite. If he did not soon recapture the Big Chief, the radio game would be over before it had really
begun.

Georgie, in the chalet at Le Vésinet, was having a dream: she
was with her lover on the platform at Rueil railway station, their
last rendezvous, where she had waited for him in vain.

The ringing of the telephone roused her from sleep—she had been late returning home—and when she lifted the receiver she recognized the voice of one of the sisters at the boardinghouse at St.-Germain.

"Madame, come at once."

"Me? But why? What's the matter?"

"I can't tell you anything over the phone. But you must come at once."

She dressed quickly, took a train to St.-Germain, rang the bell at the boardinghouse. Trepper opened the door. They fell into each other's arms. She had always known that they would meet again— "People like us overcome everything."

He talked to her for a long time. He told her he was not working for British Intelligence; he held the rank of general in the Red Army and directed a great Russian Intelligence network. She was surprised, having believed that he really was in the British service. But such matters of allegiance were of no great interest; what was important to her was his last sentence: "You must help me."

They decided to hide temporarily at Le Vésinet. Trepper wrote a letter to Pannwitz. In it, he explained that his disappearance was not an escape, but was due to an unexpected circumstance. He had entered the pharmacy only intending to get the medicine for Berg, but he had been approached by a member of the counterespionage who had given the password and told Trepper he was in grave danger and must go into hiding at once. Trepper had been obliged to go with him, for a refusal would have aroused suspicions and the radio game would have been jeopardized. The counterespionage agent would not have understood his ignoring the warning. Besides, it was an order and had to be obeyed. He had been taken away in a car by several members of the counterespionage; then they had all taken the train. He thought he was being taken to safety in Switzerland, and was mailing the letter while the train stopped at Besançon. Trepper ended with a plea for Willy Berg—it was no fault of his, and he ought not to be punished.

One of the sisters agreed to leave at once for Besançon to mail the letter there.

Like Pannwitz, the Big Chief was doing all he could to save the radio game, but for a very different reason. He was convinced that Moscow would draw the greatest advantage from it.

———◆———

In the next few days, Georgie de Winter went all over Paris trying to find a contact with the Party. She succeeded on September 17. The Big Chief left his hideout and met an envoy with full powers.

From him, Trepper learned that his report had been relayed to Moscow, and not by that transmitter in the south of France that later fell into German hands. So the Kommando would not find proof that Trepper had duped them, and the radio game could continue. Trepper asked the Party to inform the Center of his escape, to explain the reasons for it and to say that it was unlikely to cause any change in the Kommando's plans. The envoy gave him the cyanide pill he had asked for; he did not intend to be recaptured alive and risk ruining everything by talking under torture.

Very early on their fourth morning at Le Vésinet, the lovers were wakened by a knocking on the front door. Trepper rushed to the window and saw a cluster of men on the sidewalk. At the same time there was more knocking, and someone called out. Then Trepper heard a key being turned in the lock, and the door being opened. He took his cyanide pill and went into a room overlooking the back. Georgie had followed him, but he told her to go and hold off the intruders for a moment or two. When the men entered, he would swallow the pill and throw himself out of the window. Then he heard the voice of the landlord apologizing to Georgie. Georgie had given him notice, and he was trying to show the place to prospective tenants. He said he had tried the previous day but found no one home, so had returned very early this morning hoping to catch her in.

Trepper put away his pill. Another moment or two, and he would have swallowed it for nothing.

But he had to find another hideout.

◆

The Queyrie family lived at Suresnes, a western suburb of Paris. They had a house like thousands of others—a kitchen that was the hub of activities, a living room that was hardly used, and two bedrooms, all kept spotlessly clean by Madame Queyrie. He was a municipal gardener, and they had one child, Annie, aged ten at that time.

Patrick had been in Madame Queyrie's care for almost a year, since October, 1942. When he arrived from the St.-Germain boardinghouse, he had been in a terrible state—thin, dirty, covered with scabies and his head full of lice. She had scrubbed him as clean as her kitchen and set to work to "save him, feed him well and see that he benefited." Through her loving care—she loved the child as though he were her own—Patrick soon recovered. He was lively and intelligent, with fair hair, clear eyes and a determined little chin. The Queyries had just celebrated his fourth birthday. He called Madame Queyrie "Mamma Annie"—for "Annie's Mother." But why he called Trepper "Papa Nano" remains a mystery—though of all the Big Chief's pseudonyms it was undoubtedly the most charming.

The Queyries had never met Trepper, they merely knew through Georgie that he was "fighting against Germany." She had also told them of his arrest, and they had thought he was done for, though they dared not say so to Georgie.

Then suddenly, on September 18, Madame Queyrie remembers, "Georgie came here looking almost wild. She said to me, 'Papa Nano has escaped! You must hide him here!' I was deeply affected, of course; my head was in a whirl, and Georgie kept saying 'He's here, at Suresnes, and we've nowhere to go! Mamma Annie, you're the only one who can save him!' "

Madame Queyrie considered for a moment or two—not about the principle, but about the means. Her own house was already full; but her mother had a tiny flat at Suresnes, and she was away at the moment. Trepper could go there. She told Georgie to get him, and she would take him there.

"But he had a head on him, that Papa Nano! He had it all worked out already! Georgie told me what I had to do. I had to go to the Place de la Paix, walk across it and then walk right to the hideout without taking notice of anyone. Trepper had my description from Georgie, and would follow me without a word passing between us. So I went to the Place de la Paix, where I saw a man waiting, holding a suitcase and looking very calm. He followed me, and I led him to the flat."

It was while staying there that Trepper received Moscow's reply to the message announcing his escape. Its curtness made him go cold all over: "We are very happy for you. You must now sever all contacts and disappear." It was true that his disappearance was necessary for the radio game to continue. But why was the message worded so coldly? Could the Director still have doubts about him?

Trepper remembered something that Giering had once said to him: "If you ever escape and then warn Moscow, you'll be considered a traitor all the same. They'll say you couldn't have known at the start if you'd be able to warn them, so they'll accuse you of having bargained with us simply to save your own skin."

Kent had heard about the boardinghouse at St.-Germain, though how he came to do so is something of a mystery. Perhaps it was through Trepper himself, for he had often advised Kent and Margarete, when he had visited them in Marseilles, to board out young René for the child's safety; and he may well have mentioned young Patrick as an example. But in any case Kent did not know the address of the boardinghouse.

Trepper's escape had upset the peaceful life at Neuilly. The inmates met with scowls instead of smiles from the Kommando, and the house echoed with curses and dire threats. Kent caved in, as he had done before, and told Pannwitz that one of Trepper's possible hideouts was a boardinghouse at St.-Germain.

The Kommando took a week to discover the address, then they sent Kent to question the two sisters. They said they had no idea what he was talking about. The Kommando sent Katz there, under close watch; the sisters gave him the same reply.

Pannwitz saw he had no choice but to arrest them. Trepper heard almost at once. Now the Kommando could get a lead to Suresnes through the two sisters—they knew that Patrick had been taken from them to be placed with Madame Queyrie.

Once more, he had to flee.

◆

Claude Spaak says: "Toward the end of September, 1943, a very pretty woman called at my apartment in the Rue de Beaujolais, and said she had been sent by Trepper. She said to me, 'He would like your wife to go and see him at once. He's in an apartment house at Suresnes, and he can't go out because the Gestapo is looking for him.' There was obviously some danger, so I preferred to go myself. He opened the door for me and threw himself into my arms. Then he said, 'The Gestapo is on my tail. Can you help me?' "

The Big Chief was faced with two problems: how to reassure Pannwitz, and how to make contact with the Party again. The Spaak couple might be able to help him with the latter, but no one could help him with the former. The arrest of the two sisters at St.-Germain had done more than oblige him to leave Suresnes; it also threatened to compromise the radio game, for if Pannwitz discovered that his Besançon letter had been mailed by one of the sisters, he would know that Trepper had lied to him at least once—which would make him suspicious of the letter altogether.

Trepper wrote him a second letter. As it would be mailed in Paris, he explained that counterespionage had decided at the last moment to bring him back there instead of taking him into Switzerland. Then he expressed indignation at the arrests made by the Kommando after his flight. (Pannwitz had pulled in the managers and employees of the shops Trepper had visited during his captivity, under pretense that he had to be seen by certain agents. All of Trepper's suppliers were in custody; altogether, more than one hundred people had been arrested.) Trepper sharply reproached Pannwitz for such imprudence —by creating such a stir, he would only warn the counterespionage. He must release the prisoners, and the sooner the better.

This letter would obviously not remove the effect of any confession made by the sisters. The best Trepper could hope to do was to confuse matters. He knew that Pannwitz's great desire was to believe that his *Funkspiel* had not been compromised; and this second letter might provide him with reasons for thinking he was not being fooled.

But for Trepper there could be no question of disappearing and breaking all contact. Moscow had ordered this in the interests of the radio game. But the arrest of the two sisters threatened to change the situation completely; it was not even certain that the radio game could go on. Trepper had to be able to inform the Center of future developments. He had lost contact for the moment, but Suzanne Spaak would help him to reestablish communications.

———◆———

"When the deportations began," Claude Spaak told me, "she devoted herself to saving Jewish children. As you may know, the Germans proceeded by stages. They arrested the men first, then the women, and finally the children, who were sent temporarily to centers run by French people. The children there were a kind of reserve into which the Gestapo dipped when there was still room left on trains taking deportees to Germany.

"But there was often a period of time between the arrest of the parents and the children, during which these were all alone, more or less abandoned. It was then that my wife and her friends tried to save them, but the great problem was finding shelter and feeding them. Someone had the bright idea of introducing them unofficially into the centers where they would be fed and looked after without the Germans knowing. So each center had two lists of children, an official and an unofficial one.

"Then one day we heard that the Germans were going to empty

them and deport all the children to Germany. We were aghast, as you can imagine. What about the children there unofficially—how could we save them? The minister of the Protestant church by the Louvre agreed to take them in, but that was only a temporary solution, as he obviously couldn't feed a hundred children, nor even shelter them for long. Suzanne dashed around to all the people she knew who could take in one or more children, and she found homes for all of them. We hid half a dozen of them ourselves, in our house at Choisel.

"Suzanne dedicated herself to this with complete disregard for the danger. She was warned several times, but took no notice. On one occasion, for instance, a priest came to tell her to be careful, as she had been reported to the local police. But it had no effect. She went on as before."

By September, 1943, Suzanne Spaak had become one of the "turntables" of the Resistance. She was in touch with the most diverse underground organizations—networks that reported to the Free French, and others under British Intelligence, antiracist movements, Communist Resistance groups, and so on. Her activities in aid of Jewish children had brought her into contact with Dr. Chertok, a young and active member of the National Movement against Racism, and with Charles Lederman, a lawyer who was one of the organizers of Jewish Resistance in France. Lederman was in touch with Kovalsky, the great Communist Resistance leader.* As head of the M.O.I. (Main d'Oeuvre Immigrée—Immigrant Workers' Resistance), Kovalsky reported to the leaders of the Communist Francs-Tireurs et Partisans, who were in constant touch with the Central Committee of the French Communist Party.

Such was the long chain by which Trepper would attempt to resume contact with Moscow. But while waiting for results from Suzanne Spaak, he and Georgie still had to find a new refuge. The Queyrie couple, though well aware of the risk involved in harboring Trepper, were sorry to see him leave. His simplicity and humanity had won their hearts, and his affection for Patrick had greatly touched Madame Queyrie—she had taken the boy to see him several times. And she and her husband would miss their interesting conversations —"Tell me, Papa Nano, as you know about politics—do you think the war will last much longer?" "In my opinion, Mamma Annie, the end is not far off now."

---

* See page 153.

Many years later, after having endured much anguish and imprisonment because of Trepper, after having been questioned at length about him, during the Cold War, by French security police, Madame Queyrie still maintains her opinion of him—an opinion shared by all the French people concerned in his story and by the author of this book today—"We're not exactly used to spies and all that, but we really felt he was working for France."

Now Georgie found them a refuge through her friend Denise, whom she had first met at the dancing school in the Place Clichy. Denise was a fearless girl, twenty-two years old, who had lost count of the number of times she had deceived her husband, a prisoner of war in Germany. Georgie did not have a very high opinion of her, but was amused by her cheeky Parisian ways. They used to spend hours together listening to records and dancing.

Denise lent Georgie her little room in the Rue du Chabanais, and Georgie and Trepper moved into it on September 24. The strain of being hunted was beginning to tell. They were afraid; Trepper never went out.

———◆———

The two sisters from St.-Germain gave nothing away, and it was most unlikely that Pannwitz suspected they could put him on the track of the fugitive. To him, they were probably just two of the hundred-odd people arrested since September 13. The Kommando lost several days and nights in questioning them all; instead of holding agents of the Big Chief, the Kommando found themselves with a crowd of shopkeepers all protesting their innocence. Willy Berg, eager to recover his reputation, almost went crazy with them.

Pannwitz put his hopes elsewhere. He had inquiries made about Georgie de Winter, whose existence had long been known, but about whom no one had bothered until now. In less than twenty-four hours, her Belgian connections were discovered; her mother and several of her friends were arrested in Belgium and held for a time. In Paris, the Kommando tried to discover her earlier activities, her friends and the places she frequented. Pannwitz had asked for and obtained reinforcements from Berlin.

———◆———

Every day, Georgie went from the Rue du Chabanais to the Spaaks' apartment in the Rue de Beaujolais to get news from them for Trepper. Suzanne arranged a preliminary rendezvous between

Georgie and a Party emissary in the Luxembourg Gardens. The password was "*Leben.*" But Georgie, disguised and wearing glasses, waited in vain. Another rendezvous was arranged, this time outside the church at Auteuil. Georgie had to be carrying a newspaper under her arm and a crucifix in her hand; the emissary would say, "Is the vicar here?" and she had to reply, "No, but you'll find him at the neighboring church." Georgie stood in the church doorway, but again no one came.

The person she was to have met would have fitted perfectly into that picture, judging by his appearance today: pink complexion, plump cheeks, a halo of curly hair, and a gentle voice—a canon of the Church, one might say. But Charles Lederman is a Paris lawyer whose talents and courtesy are much respected by his colleagues, though they may not care for his Communist affiliations. At the time, he knew practically nothing about Trepper and his network.

Lederman told me: "I was aware of the existence of a very secret organization engaged in military intelligence work, and that there was a very important person at its head. And I suspected this or that man of belonging or having something to do with it. But we never mentioned it among ourselves. The subject was taboo."

No one seems to know why the rendezvous was not kept. A misunderstanding over the time, probably.

After staying in for three days, Trepper wanted to change. Georgie had come and gone so many times to the Spaaks' apartment and her various rendezvous, that there was a risk that she had been followed. Until they found a really safe hideout their best chance was to keep on the move. They spent the night of September 28 as guests of the minister of the Protestant church by the Louvre, having been sent to him by Suzanne Spaak. He gave them separate rooms and they stayed there until four in the morning, then had to leave. Trepper still had his air of unshakable calm, but Georgie knew he was terribly worried.

The following evening they were at the Spaaks' apartment.

Claude Spaak says: "We talked for a long time—listening to Trepper was like reading a novel—and he told his extraordinary story in detail, beginning with his arrest at the dentist's. (Incidentally—how small the world is!—just recently, I was at my doctor's and he said to me: 'One of my patients, a dentist, told me an odd story the other day. It appears that the chief of Russian espionage during the Occupation was arrested in his office, practically under the drill.') So Trepper described his arrest, and his appearance before a supreme commission of the Gestapo. He also told me how and why he had decided to pretend to work for the Germans. It was a very serious decision, involving enormous risks, but he saw no other way of saving his men, those who had been arrested and the others as well.

"So he had made a bargain with the Gestapo: he would work for them, but they would spare the prisoners, and not touch his agents who were still free. That was a matter of course, for from the Germans' point of view Moscow had to be kept in ignorance of his arrest at all costs. The object of the operation was to send false information to Moscow.

"He was allowed to move around Paris. They kept close watch on him at first, though his guards followed at a distance so as not to excite suspicion. He amused himself by pretending he had an agent in that big store, Au Printemps, and as his guards couldn't follow him inside they had to watch all the exits and entrances—and there are quite a few!

"Of course, he had already made contact with one of his agents, a woman employed at the Bailly pharmacy. Through her, he'd been able to warn Moscow of the game the Gestapo was playing.

"I remember him telling me, as an example, that Moscow asked him for the number of German troops stationed in the south of France, and the names of their units. The Gestapo chiefs said they could certainly not give such important information—Moscow obviously wanted to know whether an Allied landing there would meet with much opposition. But Trepper pointed out that they had every interest in revealing the true facts to Moscow. By reporting how few German troops were stationed in the south they would add to the Russians' grievances over the Western Allies' delay in opening a second front. The Gestapo chiefs saw his point and answered Moscow's question.

"I was particularly struck by the high standard of his information. Do you know, he told me about the V.1 rockets—he knew how they worked and where the launching ramps were. And that was in October, 1943!" *

Trepper talked because he was more or less obliged to. It was not unknown for the Gestapo to organize the "escape" of a "turned"

---

* The first V.1s did not fall on London until July, 1944, almost a year later.

agent with the object of penetrating a Resistance group. If Spaak suspected him, he would not help him to make contact with the Party. But Spaak had no doubts about him. He says: "I didn't ask him for all those explanations, and he had no need to give them to me. I always felt he had all his cards on the table, and his frankness never gave me cause for the slightest doubt."

But Trepper still kept a few cards up his sleeve. Not because he distrusted Spaak in any way, but because Spaak could be arrested and tortured to tell what he knew. Trepper did not give the real reason for his "collaboration" with the Kommando, nor did he reveal what was really behind the *Funkspiel*. He said nothing about Juliette, but pretended that his agent was an employee at the Bailly pharmacy. This was designed to reassure Pannwitz in case he ever arrested Spaak and got him to talk. Pannwitz would know from Berg that the Big Chief had *never* been to the pharmacy while in the hands of the Kommando. Pannwitz would therefore conclude that what Trepper told Spaak was just a lot of boasting, to make himself appear a hero.

Now they had to find a refuge for Trepper and Georgie. The Spaaks' apartment was not safe, since the Gestapo might descend on the "turntable" at any moment from half a dozen different directions. Suzanne Spaak obtained from a friend the address of a boardinghouse at Bourg-la-Reine (just outside Paris) where several Jewish children were being cared for. Georgie went and saw the owner, and he agreed to take her and Trepper. But Trepper did not feel that the house was very safe, with a group of clandestine little guests already living in it. There was another boardinghouse in the same street, La Maison Blanche, kept by two elderly ladies. Trepper got a room there, but decided to send Georgie out of reach of the Kommando. When she protested, he said: "Listen to me, I must stay to reestablish contact with the Party, for I'm completely cut off. And after that, I'll probably be sent far away, to another country, and we won't see each other for a long time." Did he really believe that they would ever meet again? He had never concealed from her that his bond with his wife, Luba, was indissoluble. His liaison with Georgie had begun with the war and would end with it.

The Spaaks had two English friends, cousins, Ruth Peters and Antonia Lyon-Smith, who had been stranded in Paris by the German advance in 1940 and had been living in hiding ever since. The younger of the two, Antonia, knew a Dr. de Joncker who lived near the Swiss frontier, at St.-Pierre-de-Chartreuse, and who helped people in danger to cross the frontier illegally. Antonia agreed to write and ask him to help Georgie de Winter.

Trepper feared for his mistress; every minute she was with him, she risked falling into the merciless hands of the Gestapo. So, while waiting for Dr. de Joncker's reply, he sent Georgie into hiding in a village near Chartres, with some peasants to whom she had been recommended by one of her friends (not Denise) at dancing school. Trepper gave her one hundred thousand francs, which would keep her going for a good while; and she had a letter of introduction from Antonia Lyon-Smith to Dr. de Joncker.

There remained the problem of someone to act as courier for Trepper in Georgie's place. She suggested Madame May, an elderly lady whom she had met through her dressmaker. Madame May was the widow of a singer and composer who had been well known before the war, and whose royalties now produced enough for her to live on. She was a gay and lively old lady, and she and Georgie had taken to each other. She readily agreed to help a man being sought by the Gestapo. Madame May went to stay at the boardinghouse as "nurse" to Trepper, thus providing an explanation of his remaining indoors while she went out and around on his behalf.

The Spaak couple had asked Dr. Chertok if he could put Trepper in touch with a Communist Resistance group. He had listened while they described Trepper's odyssey, then burst out laughing and said: "My poor friends, you've been taken in by a first-class storyteller! That can't be anything but a tissue of lies!" However, on their insistence, he agreed to try and find a contact. When he saw the Spaaks a few days later, his attitude was very different. "You were right," he said. "It's a serious business." A rendezvous with a Party emissary had been fixed for October 22, in a street at Bourg-la-Reine. The time would be given by Chertok in a day or two; he would telephone Spaak, who would contact Trepper.

◆

Pannwitz learned that Georgie de Winter had taken dancing lessons, tracked down the address of the school and arrested Denise. In keeping with her character, she took the easiest way out and told what she knew. She had been to the house at Le Vésinet, she knew about the Queyrie couple (it was she who had recommended them to Georgie, a year previously), and she knew of Madame May. (Georgie had introduced her to the lady.)

At Le Vésinet, the Kommando found only signs that the two fugitives had stayed there recently.

At Suresnes, the Queyrie house was taken by storm. Two Gestapo cars raced up, screeched to a stop, and the Kommando at full strength broke into the house brandishing their pistols. Pannwitz felt certain that Trepper was there, but he found only the grandmother. Monsieur Queyrie was at work; his wife, taking Trepper's advice, had gone off with Patrick to Corrèze, to the home of a sister-in-law where her daughter, Annie, had been staying for the past few months.

Corrèze is a small town in the middle of the *département* of the same name. In 1943 the surrounding uplands were the haunt of the maquis (who later attacked the *Das Reich* division in June, 1944, and kept them from reinforcing the Germans fighting in Normandy). The Kommando members were of one mind, without a word passing between them—rather than go to Corrèze, they would try to persuade Madame Queyrie to return to Paris. She received a telephone call from Paris; a strange voice told her that her husband had broken his leg and was asking for her. Madame Queyrie was suspicious and remained where she was.

So the Kommando had to go to Corrèze. Pannwitz felt it all the more necessary as he was convinced that Trepper was Patrick's father, and so the boy's capture would be an excellent blackmail device. Pannwitz and his men set off in two cars, armed to the teeth. To hear Pannwitz describe the expedition, it was another Stalingrad. The SS suicide squad sped southward, reached Corrèze, seized Madame Queyrie and Patrick. ("You should have seen them," she says; "they were like madmen.") They headed back to Paris without waiting a moment longer in that unhospitable area. It was one in the morning when they arrived back in the Rue des Saussaies. Madame Queyrie heard the heavy gates close behind her, and her heart sank. Patrick was asleep on her lap. She took him in her arms and was led upstairs to a smoke-filled room. A young woman was sitting on the edge of the table, her skirt hitched up and a cigarette dangling from her lips, chatting familiarly with the Germans—it was Denise.

Madame Queyrie and the child were put in a room with a couch. They remained on that couch for three days and nights, clinging to it like shipwrecked people on a raft, bewildered by all the tramping to and fro, and terrified by the incomprehensible shouts and yells. A bright light appeared in the gloom—the Kommando's interpreter, Siegfried Schneider. He was as helpful to Madame Queyrie and the child as he had been to Denise Corbin. "He was a tall, handsome boy," says Madame Queyrie, "always in civilian clothes and wearing suede shoes. To my mind, he must have been the son of a good family placed in the Gestapo to keep him safe. He was much too nice to be really in the police." She learned from him that her mother and husband were both in Fresnes prison, but were well.

The Kommando held a meeting to decide what was to be done with Madame Queyrie and the child. It was a stormy session, and at the end Pannwitz informed Madame Queyrie: "You'll both be taken to one of our centers, at St.-Germain. If you try to escape, your mother and your husband will pay for it." Schneider added on the sly: "They thought of sending Patrick away to Germany, somewhere in the Black Forest. He's being left with you because he's so obviously attached to you." And indeed, ever since their arrival at the Rue des Saussaies, Patrick had clung to Madame Queyrie and screamed if anyone tried to separate them.

They were taken to the Legion of Honor building at St.-Germain, requisitioned by the Wehrmacht as a convalescent home. Two of the "gray mice," as the French called the German army nurses, fell in love with the little boy at once and put him and Madame Queyrie in the best bedroom. And when their first meal was brought to them, Madame Queyrie was amazed to see a slice of white bread. Papa Nano's adopted son was still in luck.

At Madame May's, the Kommando suffered another setback— the apartment was empty. But Pannwitz left a few of his French auxiliaries there, in case anyone arrived. These were members of the notorious Lafont gang. Its leader, Henri Chamberlain, alias Lafont, a well-known figure in the Paris underworld, had placed his gang at the Gestapo's service and did much of their dirty work for them, including the torturing of prisoners.

In the course of searching the apartment, Pannwitz had discovered from Madame May's papers that the anniversary of her husband's death was approaching, and this gave him an idea for a clever trap. When the day came, Pannwitz headed a delegation to the cemetery carrying a superb wreath with a band inscribed: "From the Friends of Song." They waited for hours in the chilly wind sweeping between the tombstones, but Madame May did not come to visit her

husband's grave. Twilight fell; the cemetery watchmen announced
that it was closing time. The sad members of the Kommando laid
their wreath on Monsieur May's grave and gloomily returned to the
Rue des Saussaies.

The manhunt had been under way for a month; and the Big
Chief was still running free.

33. Every Man for Himself

Georgie de Winter was bored. On October 14, 1943, unable to
stand it any longer, she left the village and returned to Bourg-la-
Reine. Trepper scolded her for this imprudence, but could not conceal his delight at having her with him again. Their reunion lasted
only one night. The following morning he sent her back to the
village in the Beauce. As she was leaving, Madame May said to her,
"You'd better give me your address, so I can at least let you know
if anything happens." Georgie gave it to her.

That same day, October 15, Trepper sent Madame May on a
mission to Paris. Before his arrest, the Center had arranged a system
of routine rendezvous for him. On the first and fifteenth of each
month a contact man would post himself in front of a certain church
in the Buttes Chaumont district of Paris, for the Big Chief to meet
him if necessary. Georgie had gone to the rendezvous on October 1,
but found no one there. Trepper was hoping that Madame May would
be more fortunate. The Spaaks had informed him of the meeting
arranged for October 22 at Bourg-la-Reine, but Trepper did not
want to neglect any chance of resuming contact. Besides, the Center's
agent could arrange a new liaison with the Director much more
quickly than the Party.

Madame May said that she would take the opportunity to go
to her apartment—which was also on the Buttes Chaumont—and collect a few things. Trepper strongly advised against it, but she was
an obstinate old lady and he could see there was nothing to be done.

Pannwitz says: "I jumped into a car as soon as Lafont's men
telephoned me, and drove to Madame May's place. The old lady was
furious, because the gang had rifled the apartment and turned every-

thing upside down as usual. When she saw me come in, she rushed
at me, screaming insults, and gave me a hard kick on the right shin.
It hurt like anything. I cried out with pain and instinctively bent
to rub my leg, whereupon she began hitting me with her umbrella
and I fell to my knees. Lafont's men managed to drag her away. I
left them to interrogate her, for I was absolutely beside myself and
it would have gone badly with her."

Madame May had a son. Threatened with seeing him shot before
her eyes, she gave the addresses where Trepper and Georgie could
be found.

Trepper had said to her: "If you're arrested, all I ask is that
you hold out for two hours. I'll know something has happened to
you, and I'll act accordingly."

The rendezvous up at the Buttes Chaumont was for noon. At
two o'clock, Trepper began to get alarmed. At three, he left La
Maison Blanche, saying to the proprietress, Madame Parrend: "Listen,
I have the idea that you have a few guests whose situation is . . .
irregular. If so, they had better make themselves scarce at once."
And he added: "Someone may come to see me or call me on the
telephone. Kindly say that I've gone out for a walk and will be back
at seven o'clock."

Although he was unaware of Georgie's indiscretion, he knew
that Madame May had the Spaaks' address, for he had sent her there
several times. He had to warn them without delay. And by pinning
the Kommando to Bourg-la-Reine, he hoped to be able to make his
visit in the Rue de Beaujolais.

At the moment that a police operation began in Bourg-la-Reine,
Trepper walked unhindered up to Claude Spaak's apartment and
told him to clear out right away. But, Spaak told him, his wife had
gone to Orléans and would not be back until the evening. And what
about the children—a boy of twelve and a girl of thirteen? Trepper
begged him to face up to realities—at any minute the Gestapo might
ring at his door! He had to get away! And they also had to warn
the friend who had given the address of the first boardinghouse at
Bourg-la Reine; by questioning the two ladies of La Maison Blanche,
the Gestapo would soon get a lead to them all.

Claude Spaak was finally convinced. "And where are you
going?" he said, as he accompanied Trepper to the door.

"I have no idea."

Suzanne returned home at nine o'clock. Her husband told her the bad news, and she went at once to warn the friend who had supplied the address. Then she and her husband and the two children went to stay for the night with Ruth Peters, who was hiding away in an apartment on the Avenue Matignon.

As for the Big Chief, he spent the night in the open, shivering with cold on a bench in a square, at the mercy of any police patrol.

The following morning, Claude Spaak went to the Belgian consulate and obtained a permit for his wife and children to go to Belgium.

The day after, October 17, he went with them to the Gare du Nord to put them on the train. Suzanne said very little; in her usual way, she thought it was a lot of fuss over nothing. But her husband had pointed out that they had no right to take chances with the lives of their children.

On the platform, Claude said to her: "We don't know what may happen. If I get a letter from you beginning 'My dear Claude' instead of the usual 'My darling,' and signed 'Suzanne' instead of 'Suzette,' I'll know I mustn't believe what it says." (He always called his wife "Suzette"; he used "Suzanne" only when they quarreled.)

A similar arrangement was agreed upon for Claude's letters to her.

The train began to move. "I'm sure you're exaggerating," she said. "I'll be back in a week, you'll see!"

He was never to see her again.

At about that time, the Big Chief was walking toward the church at Auteuil where Georgie had once waited vainly, a newspaper under her arm and a crucifix in her hand. His rendezvous was not with Charles Lederman, but with an agent sent by the printer Grou-Radenez, who belonged to a Resistance group taking orders from London. The contact had been arranged by the unflagging Suzanne Spaak in case Chertok's efforts failed. Trepper intended to ask the agent to put him in touch with the Soviet embassy in London. At this point, every possibility had to be tried.

When he came within sight of the church, he saw a black Citroën—the car used by the Gestapo—standing in front of it.

Trepper turned on his heel. A few minutes later he was in a

telephone booth and dialing La Maison Blanche. A strange voice answered and tried to prolong the conversation. Trepper hung up. The Gestapo was at Bourg-la-Reine too.

Claude Spaak left the Gare du Nord feeling easier in his mind now that his family was safely out of the way, and better prepared to meet whatever the future held. He had to return home to the Rue de Beaujolais, although the Gestapo might have laid a trap there, as Dr. Chertok was going to telephone him at noon to tell him the hour of the rendezvous at Bourg-la-Reine. Now, of course, there was no question of Trepper and the Party's emissary keeping their rendezvous; other arrangements would have to be made.

The apartment was empty. Spaak sat down and waited. At twelve o'clock precisely the telephone rang and startled him. He snatched up the receiver and said quickly, "We've been spotted! No one is to move!" There was silence at the other end, then came the click of a receiver being replaced. Puzzled, he hung up in turn. Why had Chertok not spoken? Had it really been he? Spaak left his apartment and went back to the Avenue Matignon. In four days he was to meet Trepper outside Trinity Church to tell him the hour given by Chertok. But he wondered if Trepper was still free, and if so, would he still be free on October 21? Would it be Trepper waiting at La Trinité, or the Gestapo?

Spaak had four days of suspense ahead of him. After the silence from the other end of the telephone he feared the worst.

As for Chertok, he had been startled by the other's hurried warning and had hung up automatically. He had no means of contacting the Party's emissary—who was in fact Kovalsky—before October 22. Kovalsky, the chief of the Immigrant Workers' Resistance, would walk straight into the arms of the Gestapo! And his capture would be a disaster for the Resistance as a whole.

What was Chertok to do?

———◆———

On the afternoon of October 17, Georgie had gone for a long walk along the lanes of the Beauce to kill time. She returned to the farmhouse to find the kitchen table set for the evening meal, and sat down between the farmer and his wife.

Pannwitz was lying in wait just outside. His men, armed to the teeth, were hiding in the farmyard and waiting for his signal. The

place was surrounded by *Feldgendarmen*—Pannwitz had brought
fifty men with him, to be on the safe side.

He peered in at the kitchen window, hoping to see a fourth
person join the others at table. When Georgie began to eat her soup
he realized that the Big Chief was not there, and he gave the signal.

"The kitchen was suddenly invaded by a rush of men," says
Georgie de Winter. "There were nine of them, headed by Pannwitz
and Berg. 'Your papers! What's your name?' I showed them my false
identity papers and they sneered. The farmer and his wife were trembling like leaves. 'Maud? Your name is Maud? And where do you
come from?' It was an avalanche of questions! I tried to hold firm.
To gain time, I made them repeat every question, saying, 'What?
What do you mean?' Pannwitz got furious, and shouted, 'That's
enough of your little tricks! Anyhow, we know who you are. Go
get your things!'

"I'd been having my meals at the farm, like that, but I slept at a
neighbor's. A funny little room, you know, with a wreath of orange
blossom on the mantel and a bed so high you needed a stepladder
to get into it. Well, a couple of them went there with me, and the
woman there called me every name under the sun when she saw
me between two policemen. She was frightened, obviously. She kept
moaning, 'Ah, if I'd only known I was renting my room to someone
like that!'

"Then they took me out to a Citroën. There was one holding
my left arm and another my right. I was trembling, and I didn't
want them to notice it. But they did, and one said, 'You must be a
little cold.' So I wouldn't feel ashamed, you know. Pannwitz sat next
to me in the car. He started a conversation right away. 'So Otto
[as he called Trepper] has escaped and left us holding the bag,' he
said. Eddy [Trepper] had told me what to say in case I was arrested,
so I replied, 'No, far from it! He went to arrange the whole business.'
And it was then that I got in the thing about Bismarck. Eddy had
rehearsed me—'You'll tell them: "He's gone to prepare the way for
the negotiated peace, for he absolutely agrees with Bismarck in everything concerning relations between Germany and Russia."' Bismarck
was always for an agreement with Russia, you know. Well, Pannwitz beamed at that! He became as gay as a lark, and we just chatted
away for the rest of the journey.

"But I was terribly afraid that they'd find the letter to Dr. de
Joncker I had on me."

They stopped at Chartres, at the house where the local Gestapo had its offices. Georgie asked to be allowed to go to the toilet.

Pannwitz says: "If she hadn't been so cheerful and relaxed, I'd probably have let her go alone. But her cheerfulness had made me suspicious, and I asked one of the women auxiliaries to search her thoroughly."

The woman found Trepper's hundred thousand francs and, concealed on Georgie's lovely body, the letter from Antonia Lyon-Smith to Dr. de Joncker. Most imprudently, his name and address appeared on it.

"After that," says Georgie, "we all went and had dinner at a restaurant in Chartres. The owner put us in a private room. You'd have thought it was a real party, we were so merry. I was at the place of honor, on Pannwitz's right. He admitted to me, laughing: 'In the three weeks we've been chasing you, we haven't even taken the time to eat and sleep.' The others were very nice to me, too, almost paternal. They called me *Mädchen*."

There was only one false note: when Georgie again wanted to go to the toilet, Pannwitz ordered one of his men to accompany her. She pointed out to the man that she had already been searched, but he replied with a shrug, "We're upstairs, and you could try to commit suicide by jumping out of the window."

After dinner, they drove on to Paris. Georgie spent her first night as a prisoner on a couch at Gestapo headquarters—perhaps the same one on which her son had slept with Madame Queyrie.

Pannwitz rejoiced—he felt at last that he had retrieved the situation. Trepper might still be at liberty, but what did that matter if he was working to organize negotiations between Berlin and Moscow? It was quite obvious that Georgie had no head for politics. She was incapable of inventing what the Big Chief had said. That reference to Bismarck was especially significant.

Thinking it over, Pannwitz was not so surprised that his late prisoner should be continuing the work begun while in custody. Trepper was obliged to continue, even after escaping, for the Gestapo had on file the proof of his many betrayals (Maximovich, Katz, Robinson—all given away by him). If he did not want Moscow to know of it, he had to fall in with the Kommando's wishes. He was probably putting all his hopes for rehabilitation into a successful conclusion of the radio game, thinking that Moscow would not hold

his past against him if he were instrumental in bringing about peace
with Germany.

But why was the idiot leaving Pannwitz without news? Why
didn't he keep him informed, instead of wearing him out with an
interminable manhunt? However, now that Georgie was in custody,
things would be different.

———◆———

On October 21, the date fixed for Trepper and Spaak to meet
outside La Trinité, Trepper had been wandering about Paris for almost a week, eating very little and sleeping where he could. The
Todt officials would certainly not have recognized in him the well-
dressed, well-fed businessman who had given them millions of francs
worth of contracts, and invited them to drink champagne in nightclubs.

The rendezvous was for nine in the evening. But Trepper had
had no news of Spaak since October 15. Would he be there—or
would it be the Gestapo instead?

Paris Soir went on sale in the afternoon. The front page carried
three headlines:

PARISIANS, YOUR MEAT RATION IS ASSURED
UNTIL THE END OF THE MONTH,
SAYS PRIME MINISTER LAVAL.

THE BOLSHEVIKS BRING UP MORE RESERVES.

M. DE BRINON HAS MIRACULOUS ESCAPE
FROM TERRORIST ATTACK.

Also on the front page was a long article headed: "Chocolate-
flavored chestnut flour and rose hip jam are the latest official products
from the gathering of wild fruits." The article ended on a jovial note:
"When crushed, pounded, sweetened and cooked until thick, these
cynorrhodons (the scientific name) give us a delectable jam extremely
rich in vitamin C."

The small "public notices" on page two were also in keeping
with the times:

Wagonette for one or two horses, convertible, Griffaut make, almost new, and several sets of light harness for sale. Outstanding bargain.

I have four oxen to collect from Lieux (Haute-Vienne) and need truck with haulage permit to return to Rambouillet. Write Tavel, 146 Champs Élysées, Paris. Tel: Ely. 3134.

But there were at least two items which must have puzzled careful readers. They were identical; both were on page two, one under the Crosswords and the other under a philatelist's announcement:

EDGAR! Why don't you telephone?—Georgie.

It was the distress call that Pannwitz had thought up to urge the Big Chief to emerge from the shadows.

Claude Spaak says: "On the evening of the twenty-first I left my hideout in the Avenue Matignon, filled with the darkest forebodings. I had decided to leave a little early, to reconnoiter the meeting place. It was about a quarter to nine when I got to La Trinité. You could hardly see anything in the blackout; there were just a few shaded blue lights here and there. But in all that darkness there shone a round, yellow moon—the church clock, still strangely lighted up.

"I walked round the church square. Behind the church, in the Rue de la Trinité was a building occupied by Germans; there seemed to be a lot of activity going on inside, which made me more anxious than ever. I kept wondering whether he'd been arrested, and if so, whether he had talked. I had the feeling I was walking into a trap. On the other hand, he absolutely had to be warned that the rendezvous at Bourg-la-Reine was off. Let's admit: I was in a cold sweat!

"The church clock struck nine. Convulsed with fear, I went and stood in front of the church door, right in the little circle of light from the clock. And I saw Trepper emerge from the darkness and come toward me. We fell into each other's arms. And it was when I felt how he was trembling that I realized I was in the same state. We went up the Rue de Clichy, clinging to each other like two drowning men."

They parted again in the Place Clichy, Spaak having told him about the Bourg-la-Reine rendezvous, and sending his family to Belgium; and Trepper having described his wanderings during the past week. Trepper ended by saying: "It's all right now—I've found somewhere to go."

This was not true, but Trepper probably thought that Spaak had done enough for him, and did not wish to burden him further. After their farewells, he watched Spaak hurrying away and wondered once again where he himself could spend the night. He hailed a passing bicycle-taxi and asked to be taken to the Gare Montparnasse. He had no reason for going there; he just wanted to sit and rest for a few minutes. Like Spaak, he had had to overcome an appalling fear to keep the appointment outside the church. His weak physical condition and the nervous strain had brought him to the breaking point. While being bumped and jolted on the way to Montparnasse, one question kept stabbing his mind: where could he spend the night?

He arrived at the destination, extricated himself from the little box and gave a bill to the cyclist. The latter, an elderly, tired man, was touched by his client's wretched appearance. Trepper confessed that he had nowhere to go. The man hesitated, then murmured, "I would ask you to my place, but I have to have one more fare to complete my day's work."

"If you wish, I'll pay you that last fare, and you can take me home with you."

Trepper left there at four in the morning, a little rested, but still faced with the problem of finding a night's shelter at the end of a long day treading the Paris pavements.

As that day dawned, Dr. Chertok and Charles Lederman each woke with the same anxiety that had possessed Trepper and Spaak the previous evening. They too sensed that they would be walking into a trap. As they had been unable to warn Kovalsky, they intended to try to catch him in time at Bourg-la-Reine.

It was a mad thing to do, as the Gestapo would probably have men on watch and the two would walk straight into them, and their false identity papers would hardly stand up to close examination. Moreover, Chertok had heard nothing further from Spaak and so was without news of Trepper. If either of them had been arrested and disclosed the rendezvous under torture, then Chertok and his companion were indeed taking an enormous risk.

In the morning, Trepper telephoned Spaak's apartment in the Rue de Beaujolais. Just from curiosity. A woman's voice answered: "Monsieur Spaak's secretary speaking. . . ." Trepper knew that Spaak had no secretary. "Will you tell him, please, that his friend will call to see him at two o'clock this afternoon?" he said. Just for amusement.

Pannwitz, on being informed, sent his men to Spaak's apartment.

Chertok had lunch at a restaurant in the Rue Laromiguière with a fellow Resistance worker, Charlotte. At the dessert, he gave her his bunch of keys and a briefcase bulging with documents.

"Take care of these for me," he said. "I'll be back in three hours or not at all. In the latter case, make yourself scarce."

Then he went to meet Lederman, and they took the Métro from the Luxembourg station. A study of a map of Bourg-la-Reine had shown that Kovalsky could reach the rendezvous by any of several routes, so the only sure way of intercepting him was to go to the immediate neighborhood of the rendezvous—which added greatly to the risk.

They got out at Bourg-la-Reine, and saw no one in the station. They reached the main road to Paris and separated, Lederman going south and Chertok north. There were no signs of any police check, but every passing car made their hearts sink—would it screech to a stop and disgorge a load of German police? Suddenly Chertok caught sight of Kovalsky walking ahead. He quickened his pace, caught up with him and as he passed him ground between his teeth: "Get out! Get out of here!"

One behind the other, silent and tense, they walked on to the next Métro station.

That afternoon's edition of *Paris Soir* carried three public notices, all saying: "EDGAR! Why don't you telephone?—Georgie."

That day, October 22, was Claude Spaak's birthday. Full of euphoria about his family's removal to safety and his successful rendezvous with Trepper, he told Ruth Peters he was going home to get a bottle of good wine. She implored him not to be so foolish, but he insisted on celebrating his birthday in a proper manner. However, she just managed to persuade him to telephone his apartment first. He had already arranged a warning system with his maid, Madame Mélandes. If she answered addressing him as "Cher Monsieur," it meant that it was safe to come and collect his mail. But if she called him "Monsieur," it meant danger.

When he telephoned, she said "Monsieur" several times, and he was really alarmed when she said, "Is that all I should say to him?" Then he was cut off.

His birthday was celebrated with plain water.

Madame Mélandes was surrounded by fourteen Germans armed with machine pistols. They had snatched the telephone from her and began threatening her for having warned Spaak.

She answered: "But you are idiots! He only thought I was speaking to the concierge!"

And they admitted having got excited too soon.

When night fell, Trepper was so weary that he resigned himself to a rash act. During his time with Simex—it seemed a century ago—his doctor had prescribed a series of injections for him. Alfred Corbin had given him the address of a nurse, Lucie—a kindly, helpful woman, she had seemed. Why not go and ask her for shelter?

For three good reasons.

First, the Corbins might have given her name along with the dentist's, and the Kommando was certainly keeping watch on all suspects. Second, Lucie lived in the house in which the notorious collaborator Marcel Déat had installed the offices of his pro-Nazi party, the Rassemblement National Populaire; and there was always an armed guard in the entrance. Third, the address was in the Rue de Surène, a street leading into the Rue des Saussaies.

But the Big Chief had reached the point of seeking refuge within a hundred yards of the Kommando's offices. He reached the house safely, went through the entrance without being stopped, and rang at Lucie's door.

She opened and let him in. "Look, you didn't know it, but I'm a Jew," he said. "The Germans arrested me and put me in a concentration camp, but I've just escaped. Can you hide me for a few days, despite the risks you'll be running?"

To his great surprise and even greater annoyance, she burst into tears. But through her sobs she said, "How can you say such a thing? Of course I'll hide you!"

Trepper breathed again. Now that he was inside, two of the

arguments against it had turned to his advantage. The Kommando would not look for him so close to home, and certainly not in a building guarded by Déat's men.

A short time later, the bell rang and Lucie went to the door. She came back at once to reassure Trepper. "Don't worry, it's a Resistance leader. He's going to spend the night here."

Trepper jumped up. "No, that won't do! I assure you, we can't both stay here; one of us must leave."

Lucie introduced him to the Resistance leader, and they consulted briefly. Then the other left, as he had another safe place to go to.

From the windows of Lucie's apartment, Trepper watched the comings and goings of the Kommando's black Citroëns whose numbers he had carefully noted during his months as a prisoner.

The day after her arrest, Georgie de Winter was taken to Neuilly, but not directly; the car was driven around Paris and the suburbs for a long time before heading toward the house at Neuilly, probably to prevent her from knowing its locality. She was greeted on arrival by "a great big fellow, just like Erich von Stroheim." It was Boemelburg, with a black band across one eye; he had scratched his cornea with a sheet of paper. Trying to act gallantly, he said to Georgie, "Will you be my guest?" But his natural character returned at once, and he growled at her: "Be careful what you do! There are other prisoners here, and if you try to talk to them it'll be Fresnes for you!"

Katz was no longer one of the "guests." The Kommando had lost all interest in him after the Big Chief's escape. Perhaps he was in Fresnes, or in Germany, unless he had already been executed—it is not known what happened to him.

Georgie was given the room her lover had occupied six weeks earlier. Each day she was driven to the Rue des Saussaies for interrogation.

"They made me tell my life story," she says, "but what they really wanted to know was where Eddy might be hiding. Pannwitz showed me a large album full of photos of members of the network. As Eddy had told me which ones had been arrested, I identified those and said that I didn't know the others. There was one photo they were greatly interested in. They asked me: 'Do you know who this is?' 'Oh yes, of course,' I said, and they jumped for joy! 'Who is it?'

'Why it's François Périer, of course!" It was a photo of Claude Spaak and the film star, side by side.

"They kept asking me about Eddy's friends, so I invented one for them. Paul, I called him. Every day I told them something more about him, but it was tiresome, because I had to be careful not to contradict myself. They had him looked for all over France. Berg got most excited about it. He was always shouting 'Aber wo ist Paul?' *

"They kept talking about, that story of a separate peace. There was even a Gestapo chief who questioned me for hours, after telling me he'd come specially from Berlin. It seemed very important to them.

"Oh, I've forgotten something. Eddy had asked me to tell them a story—that after his escape he'd arrived at Le Vésinet with several men who'd taken him away with them, and then brought him back again two days later. So I told that to Pannwitz, though I had no idea what it was all about." †

Her interrogations took place in the most agreeable manner. They still called her *Mädchen*, she was offered tea, and a bag of candy was slipped into her pocket when she was returned to Neuilly. Clearly, Pannwitz and his aides thought the Big Chief's consort was just a pretty, empty-headed girl, and quite harmless.

For her part, Georgie says: "I always felt I had the better of them. They swallowed everything I said. The famous Paul, for instance—they'd have sworn he really existed. It was the same thing with that separate peace business. I told Pannwitz that Eddy meant to come back as soon as he'd organized things. That made Pannwitz very happy, and he waited for him like the Messiah. It was just that it was taking so long. . . ."

Very long. So that Pannwitz ran those public notices in *Paris Soir*. He doubted that they would be answered, for it was not the first time his voice had cried in the wilderness. After his raid on Corrèze to arrest Madame Queyrie, he had put an ad in the Paris papers: *Georgie! Why don't you come? Patrick is with his uncles.* And nothing had come of that invitation.

If the Big Chief did not telephone, at least he continued to write. Pannwitz received a third letter from him (written at Lucie's), expressing his previous reproaches even more sharply:

---

* "But where is Paul?"
† Obviously intended to counter any admissions by the sisters from St.-Germain and to give some kind of confirmation to the Big Chief's pretense that he had mailed his first letter to Pannwitz at Besançon.

"You have not released anyone. On the contrary, you persist in making arrests. It all goes to prove you're not serious and it's impossible to work properly with you. You must understand that on no account must the counterespionage be alerted. Besides, the people you've arrested have nothing to do with the affair, as you know very well. If you don't release them, I'll break up your radio game myself."

Pannwitz would willingly have released the prisoners if, instead of threatening him, the Big Chief had sent him a report on his approaches to Moscow. But Pannwitz was not going to release them without being sure of Trepper's good faith. They were his hostages, Georgie especially. And he still had hopes—though increasingly faint —of catching Trepper. The hunt was still on.

Charles Spaak, Claude's brother, was arrested in Paris. Other members of the family were pulled in by the Gestapo in Belgium. And the usual pressure was applied—if Suzanne's whereabouts were not revealed, they would all be shot. Someone weakened and gave Suzanne's address, and she was arrested on November 8.

Pannwitz was unaware that in Suzanne Spaak he held the key to half a dozen underground organizations. He thought he had arrested a distinguished woman with little sense of reality, who had let herself be implicated in the Big Chief's affairs, just like the sisters from St.-Germain, and the Bourg-la-Reine couple, and Madame May, and Madame Queyrie.

Many years later, when Pannwitz learned from me of the great part Suzanne Spaak had played in the Resistance movement, he said grumpily, "Ah, she fooled me, all right, with her respectable airs! And to think she never stopped telling me about her charities! . . ."

Yet if Pannwitz had known, at the time, of his prisoner's importance, it is by no means certain that he would have had her tortured to make her speak. The third Spaak brother, Paul-Henri, was foreign minister in the Belgian government-in-exile, in London. This fact, coupled with the way the war was going, led Pannwitz to deal very carefully with Suzanne. He asked two friends, both of them German war correspondents, to observe all the interrogations, so that they could eventually testify to his correct behavior. This was a flagrant violation of the Kommando's secrecy, but Pannwitz thought it advisable to look to the future.

Evidently, Pannwitz had changed considerably since his Prague days.

His patience was finally rewarded: Trepper telephoned. Georgie heard the news from Pannwitz himself, during an interrogation. But Pannwitz seemed disappointed, even bitter.

"What did he say?" she asked.

"Oh, he was very evasive," Pannwitz muttered in a tired voice.

———◆———

On November 17, 1943, the French police all over the country received this message:

"Bring in Jean Gilbert. Has penetrated police organization on behalf of Resistance. Has stolen documents. Use every means to effect arrest. Report to Lafont."

This was followed by a description, and later a photograph, of Trepper, alias Jean Gilbert. A reward was offered for his capture, and increased three times during the next few months.

The wording of the message had been carefully thought out. There was no mention of the Gestapo, and the recipients were led to believe it was a French police matter. The reference to Lafont was designed to increase their zeal, for Lafont had been associated with Inspector Bony, one of the big names at the French Sûreté before the war. The Kommando was banking on the friendships he still must have among his old colleagues. (But in fact Bony's pro-German activities had earned him the scorn of the whole police force; so it was a very poor psychological maneuver.)

At the same time, a poster bearing Trepper's police photograph and the words "Very dangerous spy. Escaped." was sent out to all Gestapo and Abwehr offices and all German army and civil headquarters in France and Belgium.

Two months after Trepper's escape, Pannwitz was thus setting the whole of the French and the German police on his trail. After having played a subtle game for two months, alternately using force and persuasion, torture for Katz and tea and candy for Georgie, setting traps and inserting appeals in the papers—after having spent weeks spreading his web, Pannwitz now swept it away with one stroke. He despaired of ever discovering the Big Chief's real intentions, of knowing whether he was betraying the Kommando, or betraying Moscow. And the uncertainty would remain as long as Trepper confined himself to vaguely worded letters and "evasive" telephone calls. He alone was in a position to give fresh impetus to the radio game or to hold it up. He held the initiative, and that was something Pannwitz could not permit. His plans could not depend on the whims of an escaped prisoner, even if he was the Big Chief. And Pannwitz was thirty-two years old—an age when a man is more inclined to cut the Gordian knot than to try to unravel it.

Those thousands of posters displayed in offices and those "Wanted" notices sent all over France were bound to alert the enemy, even if the vaunted counterespionage was just a myth. Pannwitz knew that. He wanted to recapture Trepper, but this alone would not have allowed him to take such a serious step. He had a better plan in mind.

Kent's transmitter was still in the south of France (in the villa of the couturière Chanel), and it had to remain there for the *Funkspiel*, so that Moscow could check its position when messages were being transmitted. Pannwitz naturally believed that the Center also thought Kent was still there with his set. Banking on this, Pannwitz sent a message to Moscow, signed by Kent, and asking permission to go to Paris, as something appeared to be wrong with the network and he wanted to investigate. Permission was received. Then Pannwitz sent a message expressing Kent's bewilderment: "What has happened to Trepper? I see 'Wanted' notices for him posted everywhere. He must have escaped from a German prison."

Back came a reply from the Center: "Avoid Trepper. The Party must not give him a crust of bread. To us he is a traitor."

Pannwitz had attained his aim: the initiative was no longer in Trepper's hands. The Big Chief could no longer threaten to break up the radio game. Whatever he did or said, Moscow would not believe him. Pannwitz's audacious coup had purely and simply eliminated him from the game. He was neutralized.

It was an interesting operation, and with immense consequences. For *Kent's message revealed to Moscow that Trepper had been in the Gestapo's hands for months, and that all his radio messages for those months were part of a German attempt to dupe Moscow!*

The very basis of the *Funkspiel* had been undermined, and the indispensable trust of the Center, so patiently acquired by Giering, had been destroyed by his successor. On what foundations did Pannwitz now expect to build? Did he really hope that after such a commotion Moscow would continue to have confidence in the messages from France? Did he not see that his bold stroke was really a fit of madness—and that by trying at all costs to eliminate Trepper, he had destroyed the radio game along with him?

PART III

MOSCOW

34. Prison Deluxe

The year 1943 was drawing to an end. The approach of Christmas was enough to cause excitement among the nurses at St.-Germain, but the sudden announcement of a visit by Field Marshal Goering sent them all into a real flurry. They frantically polished every square inch of the huge building. "You couldn't find fault," says Madame Queyrie. "You could have eaten off the floors." Goering carried out his inspection, bestowed a friendly smile on Patrick, and proceeded to other pleasures. He would probably have been much surprised to learn that the bright-eyed, fair-haired little boy was the adopted son of the leader of the Red Orchestra.

Christmas feasting and celebrating had started with Advent, as is the German custom. Madame Queyrie, well fed and rested, was not too worried about her mother and husband. Schneider regularly gave her satisfactory news about them. On Christmas Eve there was a magnificent party, with champagne for everyone. At dinner, Madame Queyrie sat on the commanding officer's right. Like everybody else, this officer was fond of Patrick. He kept putting his cap on the little boy's head, lifting him up, shouting "Now you're a soldier!" But on January 8, to everyone's consternation, he received orders to release Madame Queyrie and the boy.

A sad surprise awaited Madame Queyrie when she arrived at Suresnes; her house was in a filthy state. Pannwitz had left some of Lafont's hoodlums there to catch any callers, and they had indulged in their usual jokes—excrement in the drawers, and so on. Before leaving, they had opened all the taps, and water was now streaming out as far as the street. She set to work.

All the other suspects arrested by the Kommando were also set free. They took up too much room. And Pannwitz could afford to satisfy the Big Chief on that point, now that he had recovered the initiative. Even if Trepper had lost the Center's ear, it would be better if he kept quiet about the radio game. After Patrick had been freed with Madame Queyrie, Pannwitz published this notice in the Paris papers: "The child is well. He is back home."

A fourth letter from Trepper proved to Pannwitz that he had judged correctly. Its tone was weary and disillusioned: "I am tired, I've had enough and I'm giving up. You can continue with the radio game without misgivings, provided you don't start arresting people again. On that condition, I promise not to interfere."

The Big Chief had left Lucie's and had rented a room in the Avenue du Maine, from a bachelor who thought his lodger was a refugee from the north who had lost his family in an air raid.

At heart, Trepper's letter told the truth: he was at the end of his rope. He had finally managed to meet Kovalsky and warn Moscow that the radio game was continuing. But it would go on without him. Not surprisingly, the months to follow would be harder for him than the nerve-racking years preceding his arrest and the months of anxiety that had followed it. The sudden release of tension left him depressed and at a loss. An elementary prudence forbade the Party to give him any other work to do, for he was being hunted by all the police forces in France. All the Party could do was to keep paying him—in banknotes that were far too new. The Big Chief filled in the hours by crumpling them.

Very occasionally, an incident ruffled the boredom of his days. Once, while strolling along the Rue de Vaugirard, he saw Willy Berg. The German did not recognize him; he had lost a lot of weight and had grown a fine upturned mustache. Another time, he risked going to recover a suitcase of clothes that he had left with a school-teacher who lived near the Place Pigalle. The woman was very frightened to see him; only a few days earlier, Kent had come to ask if she had seen him, and had shown her a letter from Marshal Pétain naming Trepper a "bad Frenchman," whom all good Frenchmen should denounce to the police.* Kent had told her to detain Trepper as long as possible, if he showed up, and to call a certain telephone number. Well, said Trepper, why not? It was Sunday, the Kommando would be out drinking as usual, and there would only be a guard left as the Rue des Saussaies. "Go on! Call them right now! They'll take their time, you'll see!"

Three hours later, two black Citroëns drew up in front of the building.

---

* This was obviously forged by the Kommando.

One day at the end of January, two black Citroëns stopped outside Madame Queyrie's house. Pannwitz and some of his men pushed
their way in and searched every room. Whatever it was they were
looking for, they did not find it. As they left, one of them said to
Madame Queyrie, "The chief's compliments. Your house is one of
the cleanest in France."

Schneider, the interpreter, did not give compliments, but was
much more helpful. He came regularly with news of the prisoners
in Fresnes, and he always brought a present for Patrick—fresh eggs
or fruit. He also agreed to take parcels to the two prisoners. ("So
that they would knew the parcels came from me," explains Madame
Queyrie, "I wrapped them in paper they'd recognize.") Finally,
Schneider agreed to take letters to them.

Unlike these irregular practices, the visits to Georgie were quite
official. Madame Queyrie and Patrick would go to the Rue des
Saussaies, and from there Schneider took them to Neuilly by car.
He was always present at their meetings with Georgie, and as she
hardly knew him she chose to talk to Madame Queyrie in Parisian
argot. This precaution seemed unnecessary to Madame Queyrie, especially as there was nothing startling about the atmosphere of the
house. "I assure you, she had never looked better. And well treated,
too. Just think, she had her own room and servants to wait on her."

———◆———

But Georgie's room was kept locked, and the servants were
Slovak guards. Nevertheless, the detention would not have been unpleasant had it not been for the boredom which weighed on her. She
prevailed upon them to get her tutu and ballet shoes from Le Vésinet,
and she practiced toe dancing for hours, to the great pleasure of the
Slovaks, who had their eyes glued to the keyhole. But she could not
dance all day long. One day, Pannwitz went to her room and found
that the table had been dragged into the middle, a chair placed on it,
another chair on that, and then a stool, and balancing on the stool
and touching the ceiling was Georgie. She poked her tongue out at
him. But she could not poke her tongue at Pannwitz all day long
either.

Suddenly, everything changed.

"I spent hours at my window, on the first floor. It gave on the
back of the house, and I could see the other prisoners strolling around

Prodhomme's vegetable patch. We used to wave to each other, and smile, you know. Then one of them—a man wearing puttees—took advantage of my open window to throw me a letter, weighted with a candy. The letter began: 'To a young captive,' just like Chénier's poem, you know. It was really nice, very sweet. I don't know how to describe the style—it was very poetic and very military at the same time. Anyway, it was signed 'General Dumazel.' He ended by saying, 'I hope you will answer me. Put your letter into the aspirin tube hidden at the foot of the bush.' I did answer, naturally, and we started quite a correspondence.

"After that, there was another soldier, General Delmotte. We wrote each other, too. He was much bolder, Delmotte, while General Dumazel always remained very discreet, very poetic, in the Chénier style. But Delmotte, he said he had fallen in love with me.

"But the most persistent was Dungler. Oh, he stopped at nothing! He had noticed that the lavatory transom was next to my dressing room window. One day, I heard someone knocking on my window. It was Dungler. He passed me a long letter, which began by telling me that he was one of the Resistance chiefs in Alsace.

"After that, he never stopped asking to go to the lavatory. It was quite a business, you know. You had to ring for a guard to come and let you out; then he took you right to the door and waited outside. We passed our letters through the transom. But Dungler did better than that: he got around one of the guards—Hans was his name, a dark little German, very nice. Dungler sent him to the Brasserie Alsacienne in the Faubourg Montmartre, whose owner was one of his friends, and Hans brought him back food and bottles of wine. I got all of this through the transom. The bottle had to be returned the next day, so, you see, I drank it all the same evening, and as it was Burgundy I was pretty gay when I'd finished. Later on, he persuaded Hans to get him a duplicate key to his room. So he could get out at night, when everybody was asleep except the guards on the ground floor, and he came and took the imprint of my lock with some bread. Hans had another duplicate key made. That's how we got to see each other. But what scares we had! There was a thick carpet in the hall, and you couldn't hear footsteps, so we were always afraid someone might suddenly enter the room. That did happen once, and Dungler just had time to hide in my dressing room. I thought of using the key to escape. One night I went as far as the stairs, my heart in my mouth, but I didn't dare go any further and hurried back to my room. There were the guards down below. And besides, they'd told me that if I tried to escape, Patrick would suffer.

"My three lovers occupied almost all my time, and I spent hours writing to them and reading their letters. When we had no paper, we tore out the flyleaves of the books they loaned us—there was a complete set of the Pléiade classics. I even read all of Balzac."

◆

It was very pretty, Georgie's old prison, the day I first went to see it. All around were tall new apartments, and the old private house was a welcome relief to their geometric severity. But it was looking rather shabby and quite deserted, as though no one had entered since the Slovak guards had left. The trees were covered with creepers, there were weeds even on the stone steps to the front door, and moss was growing everywhere. That house with its closed shutters and cracked walls reminded me of the strange old manor in *Le Grand Meaulnes*. The doors were bolted, and the bell was out of order. None of the neighbors could tell me anything. So, unable to enter that place from which so many had longed to escape, I stayed an hour— or perhaps two—standing at the rusty gate and visualizing the Big Chief walking around the lawn, Boemelburg stumbling up the stone steps; Dungler passing a bottle of Burgundy to Georgie through the transom and Georgie handing him back a letter; Pannwitz strutting about; Margarete sunbathing and Kent watching her from a window. Yes, that day I could see all of them.

A year later, I went back to Neuilly to take some photographs. But there was only a huge crater where the house had been, and a notice announcing the construction of a luxury apartment house. I was as upset as if someone had torn down a building that had been part of my own life, and disappointed for more practical reasons: the photographs.

◆

Early in May, 1944, Georgie was taken to the building where Alfred Corbin, Keller and others had been tried and sentenced the previous year. She was told to sit down in the small waiting room. A man suddenly came in, his face ghastly pale. He looked at Georgie, appeared to recognize her and rasped out, "I have just been condemned to death!" She cried out: "But that's frightful!" A guard forbade further exchanges. Georgie tried to remember where she had

seen that man. Yes, there had been a photograph of him in the album
Pannwitz had shown her. She was certain it was Dr. de Joncker, who
had been going to help her cross into Switzerland.*

Then came her turn, and she was taken into the courtroom.
Boemelburg was one of the judges. Pannwitz and Berg were also
present, but they adopted a cold and reserved attitude to their
Mädchen in front of the judges. She appeared not as an accused, but
as a witness; she was submitted to close questioning, especially about
Grossvogel, and tried to say as little as possible. She began to droop
with fatigue, and Berg spoke sharply to her: "Stand up straight!" She
was completely exhausted when they took her back to Neuilly. This
session, at which any one of her phrases might have sent a man to his
death, remained one of her most terrible memories.

One morning later the same month, Madame Queyrie was pulled
out of bed by an early visit from a member of the Kommando. He
told her to leave Patrick with some neighbors and to go with him.
It was seven-thirty in the morning when she entered the court waiting room. Two women came up to her and introduced themselves as
the ladies from Bourg-la-Reine. "Do you know why we are here?"
Madame Queyrie asked them.

"But Madame, it's our trial!" They were waiting with perfect
serenity, convinced that their innocence would be established.

They were mistaken. Madame Parrend, the director of La Maison
Blanche, was sentenced to be deported; she returned home after the
war only to die a few years later as a result of illnesses contracted in
the camp. The fate of her assistant is not known. The two sisters
from St.-Germain were both deported; only one was to return.
Antonia Lyon-Smith escaped a death sentence, helped perhaps by the
fact that one of the Kommando had fallen madly in love with her.
Madame May was condemned to death, but was reprieved by Reichsmarschall Goering. Suzanne Spaak was also condemned to death. A
little later, her mother-in-law received a long letter from her, written
in Fresnes. Suzanne described her life in prison (she had knitted a tie
for her son, using two toothpicks; she had managed to grow a little
flower in the groove of her window and had slipped it into the envelope for her daughter), but her main news was that she had been
condemned to death, and she asked Madame Spaak to give Claude a
proposition from the Gestapo: if he would give himself up, his wife

---

* But she was mistaken. Although Dr. de Joncker was questioned by the Gestapo he succeeded in clearing himself, despite the incriminating letter.

would be reprieved and set free. He himself would only have to answer a few questions, then he would be allowed to live at home, merely having to report to the local police at regular intervals. Suzanne ended by begging her husband to give himself up, for her sake and for the children.

It was late afternoon before Madame Queyrie was taken into the courtroom. She saw her husband, his face pale and swollen. She also had some conversation with her counsel, a sympathetic German officer who spoke fluent French. Before the Court, she repeated that it was true she was taking care of the Big Chief's son (the Gestapo had no doubt of the relationship. Much later, Pannwitz still held to his conviction: "I tell you, the boy is his son! There's no mistaking the resemblance!"). Madame Queyrie also admitted that she had harbored Trepper for a week, but knew nothing of his activities.

She was acquitted. Outside on the pavement, she discovered that she had left home without any money. Her counsel came out of the building just then, saw her distress and gave her some Métro and bus tickets. She was worried about how to repay him, and he said with a smile, "Oh, let it go! And I hope it will bring you luck."

At the end of the month, her mother was released from Fresnes, having been held for eight months, without even a trial. She spoke of an extraordinary woman who had kept up the prisoners' morale—it was Suzanne Spaak. In June, Monsieur Queyrie returned home to Suresnes, having served an eight-month sentence. A friendly prisoner had given him a pair of slippers—it was Leon Grossvogel, who was executed soon afterward.*

———◆———

Margarete Barcza's labor pains began on April 21. Pannwitz had her sent to a private hospital in Neuilly, without even specifying that she was his prisoner. She gave birth to a son, whom she and Kent decided to call Michel. Her lover visited her every day, always accompanied by three of the Kommando. On May 2 a car was sent to collect mother and child. But instead of taking them "home," it took them to the Rue de Courcelles in Paris, to a larger and much more sumptuous house than the one at Neuilly. It had belonged to Monsieur Veil-Picard, a millionaire and well-known art collector. The Wehrmacht had requisitioned the servants' quarters in 1940; they were occupied by a few elderly soldiers employed in repairing and

---

* Probably at the same time as Vasili and Anna Maximovich.

painting army vehicles. Then Goering's expert looters had descended
on the house and taken away the paintings and furniture. Finally, in
April, 1944, Pannwitz decided to install his Kommando there.

The son of Monsieur Veil-Picard says: "We weren't quite considered Jews and not quite Aryans. It was a somewhat ambiguous
situation. We had left the house, but my father passed by once or
twice a week. When these new ones moved in, he sent me to explain
that they had no right to, as we were not quite Jews, and so on. I
was shown into a room . . . I can still see those big Germans—there
were two of them—with their cold gray eyes and raincoats coming
down to their ankles. I started telling them my story, but one of them
raised his fist at me, and I realized I had better not insist. I got out of
there fast."

Pannwitz was still haunted by the idea of an attack by the Resistance, and he took extraordinary precautions. He spread the rumor
that his Kommando came under the military police and not the Gestapo. Then he put the house in condition to withstand a siege. The
side door which opened electrically from the concierge's lodge was
left alone, but the main door was barricaded with two huge beams
(the bolts that held them in place can still be seen today). A machine
gun was mounted on the stone steps to the house and commanded the
inner court. A whole arsenal was on hand in the entrance hall.

To the left of the house was an empty space used as an army
parking lot. Pannwitz had an opening made in the dividing wall, so
the comings and goings of his black Citroëns would not attract attention—people would think the vehicles were just going in to park.
Prisoners were taken from the car, through the opening in the wall, to
the side door leading down to the cellar. This had been converted into
two cells, each with drop benches. A heavy steel door with two large
bolts made escape impossible. Finally, on the second floor a maid's
room had been turned into a "luxury cell," with bars at the window
and bolts outside the door.

The furniture was looted from various places. Pannwitz had the
Spaaks' country house at Choisel cleared out, and he also helped
himself to some pieces from their apartment in the Rue de Beaujolais.

Margarete says: "They gave a splendid dinner party for my return. 'It's to celebrate your marriage to Kent,' they said. And really
it was like a wedding party. Afterward they gave me presents: a
cradle and an absolutely magnificent carriage for Michel. Pannwitz
told me that he wanted to be godfather, and he gave me bits of ad-

vice: 'If he cries at night, above all, don't pick him up; you'll only give him bad habits. And don't worry if he wakes us; it doesn't matter.' And from that day on, they all called me 'Mammy.' "

Pannwitz had two rooms made into a little apartment for the couple and their baby, with a dressing room installed in a large closet. Members of the Kommando often went up to visit and unburden themselves to "Mammy." Karl Ball, for instance, came up and cried there the whole night, after having killed a man during an arrest—it was his first killing. And her visitors often referred to Eric Jung's cruel fate.

"He was fed up," says Margarete. "You can see he was fed up. And he drank a lot. He was bound to end badly." One night Jung returned home dead drunk—and he had a room on the third floor of a requisitioned house. An officer who knew him took him up in the elevator and gently pushed him out at the third floor, despite Jung's shouts that he wanted to go higher. Absolutely furious, he rushed up two flights of stairs and as the officer stepped from the elevator Jung emptied his pistol into him. Jung was sentenced to ten years' hard labor; he appealed, only to be given a death sentence. He was finally sent to a punishment battalion on the Russian front, and nothing more was heard of him.

The doors of her apartment remained bolted, but every afternoon at the same time Margarete was allowed to take Michel down into the garden. They followed the prisoner from the "luxury cell"—none other than the Ukrainian Yefremov. Margarete also had permission to go out on Thursday afternoons to see her son René, and she even attended his First Communion with Kent and three of the Germans. After church, the Germans left her while she had lunch with René, then brought her back to the Rue de Courcelles to feed Michel; she put the baby in his carriage and went off to meet René again at six o'clock, and they spent the evening together. "I could have escaped a hundred times, but I knew they'd kill Kent."

That was not too sure; Kent had become much too useful. In addition to his collaboration in the radio game, he was well on the way to effecting the penetration of an important Resistance network.

———◆———

It had all begun with a message from the Director:

Previously worked for us Ozols Waldemar alias Solja stop I repeat Ozols Waldemar former Latvian general stop fought with

Spanish Republican Army stop gave information on German troop movements stop had a network stop we have provided transmitter stop Solja lived in Paris address unknown stop lived at a dentist's stop also has a family stop inform us if you know whereabouts Solja and present activity stop be careful stop the Greens * interested very early by Solja activities.

This message had been sent to Kent on March 14, 1943, four months after Trepper's arrest. Giering—then still head of the Kommando—saw the possibility of laying hands on yet another Russian network, and ordered the Kommando to find Ozols. It was July before they discovered his hideout in Paris, at 24 Villa Molitor. Kent immediately informed the Center that he had tracked down Ozols. The Director instructed him to contact him by sending him a letter signed "Z." Kent wrote to suggest a meeting on August 1, 1943, at the Café Dupont, in the Place des Ternes.

The general kept the appointment, having no reason to suspect the writer of the letter, as it had been signed "Z,"—the recognition sign arranged by the Center in case of any future contact. Besides, he was reassured after exchanging a few words with Kent, who, like all of his generation, spoke "modern" Russian. Because of the population movements in Russia since 1918, and the influence of the radio, there is as much difference between the Russian spoken before the Revolution and "modern" Russian as between English and American. Ozols was therefore quite convinced that he was dealing with a young Soviet Officer and not with an emigrant's son working for the Germans.

He told his story to Kent. He had fought with the International Brigade and taken refuge in France after the defeat of the Spanish Republicans. In 1940, the air attaché of the Soviet embassy in Paris had ordered him to set up an intelligence network. Ozols had recruited a dozen agents and had begun to send in reports. When the Soviet diplomats had left Paris, the air attaché had given him a transmitter, but Ozols had not been able to find an experienced pianist, and his attempts to contact Moscow had failed. Soon afterward, realizing that the Gestapo was on his track (two of his agents had been arrested), he went into hiding in Normandy. In 1943 he returned to Paris and was now available for further work.

It is unlikely that Ozols mentioned to Kent that he had been in

---

* The Director's favorite name for the Germans.

touch with the Big Chief in 1940, for the matter probably seemed of no interest to him. One important factor was certainly unknown to Kent: the Center had advised Trepper to be very careful in his dealings with Ozols, as he was suspected of working for Moscow, for the French Deuxième Bureau and for the Gestapo—all at the same time!

Kent instructed him to revive his network and to enlarge it by recruiting technicians and French officers who could supply political, economic, and military information. Kent gave him an advance of ten thousand francs and told him he would be paid twelve thousand francs a month.

In December, 1943, a mutual friend put Ozols in touch with Paul Legendre, a sixty-five-year-old reserve officer. For three years, Legendre had been head of the Marseilles group of the Mithridate network, one of the biggest in the French Resistance. In the spring of 1943, when the Gestapo was hot on his trail, he had fled to Paris. He had lost contact with his chiefs, and he too was available for other work. Ozols revealed that he belonged to the Russian service, and asked Legendre to join him. Legendre replied: "Certainly, so long as the principal objective is the fight against the Germans." The Latvian general then pompously informed him that he would be enrolled as number 305 in the B network of Russian Intelligence. He would be paid six thousand francs a month.

In January, 1944, Ozols arranged a meeting between Legendre and Kent, who was chief of the B network. In the course of conversation, Legendre mentioned that his wife had been arrested and deported. Kent expressed his sympathy and promised to see what he could do about it. Legendre probably thought this was just a tasteless boast, but a few weeks later his wife was released and rejoined him. Overcome with admiration for the power of the Russian services, Captain Legendre was henceforth Kent's man.

He gave Kent the complete list of his old agents at Marseilles, thus enabling the Gestapo to penetrate the Mithridate network and get a lead on its chiefs. But Legendre was mainly engaged in setting up a new underground organization in agreement with Kent. France was to be divided into eight military regions; Legendre would be in charge of the Marseilles and Paris regions. His pay was increased to twelve thousand francs a month, plus fifty thousand a month for his agents. His men were already at their posts in the south, and he energetically continued his recruiting in the Paris region. One of his notable recruits was Maurice Viollette, who had been a minister in one of the prewar governments and mayor of Dreux. Viollette thus unwittingly embarked on a Gestapo galley while believing that he was rowing for the Allies.

At the start it was only a classic operation to penetrate and manipulate the Resistance. But in the spring of 1944, with the increasing rumors of the imminence of Allied landings, a bold plan formed in the inventive mind of Kriminalrat Pannwitz. He would make use of Legendre's groups *after* the landings, to have them send information to the Gestapo from behind the Allied lines—information that would help the German High Command to mount its counteroffensive.

Such was the fine work in which Kent was engaged after the birth of his son. It called for tact and cunning, as the men of B network might well be surprised at being asked to continue their work *after* the landings. Kent made Legendre bring each of his radio operators to see him, and to each he made this speech:

"London and Washington do not keep Moscow informed of their military plans, which is a great pity, because it prevents the forming of a combined strategy. Moscow doesn't even know whether the coming landings will be only a raid like Dieppe, or a major operation. By keeping us informed of the strength and nature of the forces landed, you will enable the Soviet High Command to form a clearer idea of the operation and so bring its own strategy into line, thus hastening the defeat of Germany."

Some of the pianists considered this a very tall story, but others accepted Kent's reasoning and agreed with his suggestion.

◆

The black Citroëns came and went, Margarete took her walks, Kent often went out, prisoners were transferred, Pannwitz and his men went about their business—all of which was observed and noted by Trepper's hidden watchers. The Big Chief had only needed a new incentive to emerge from the despondency into which his isolation had plunged him; no sooner had he assigned himself the task of spying on the Kommando than all his old vitality returned. He had organized a surveillance group with the help of an old comrade, Alex Lesovoy, who became his "chief of staff," as Grossvogel had been in the past. His men photographed every car, every pedestrian who entered or left the house in the Rue de Courcelles. Like Prodhomme at Neuilly, the concierge and his wife had been allowed to stay—and they gossiped. One of the conscripted laborers employed by Pannwitz was a Jew, and he kept an eye on the Kommando's activities.

This observation work was merely preparation for action. Pannwitz was not the only one to sense that the Allied invasion of Europe was imminent. The Big Chief too had formed a bold plan.

35. A Belgian Woman and a Frenchman

At Neuilly, where Georgie still remained, everyone was getting nervous—the Germans, the Slovaks, and even the prisoners. One night, the inmates were rudely awakened by the yelling of the guards and the rattle of a submachine gun. Someone was trying to escape. The man managed to get away, but traces of blood near the gate showed that he had been wounded.

It was wonderful weather, that month of May, 1944, and the Paris sky was streaked almost daily by the white trails left by American Flying Fortresses. When the sirens wailed, the prisoners were hastily taken down to the cellar. Georgie was thus able to talk to her three friends, Dumazel, Delmotte and Dungler. And she was also surprised to find Prince Michael of Montenegro, to whom she had been presented as a girl, when he had been living in exile in Brussels.*

She had a very old radio in her room, and the only station she could get on it was the BBC. She listened to the news bulletins, her ear glued to the set, ready to turn it off if a guard appeared. She missed the news one morning. A little later she was watching General Delmotte walking around the vegetable patch when she saw him gesturing wildly, a thing he was not in the habit of doing. By signs, he conveyed to her that the Allies had landed in France at dawn that morning, June 6, 1944.

This tremendous event had its effect on the Kommando. When Georgie was taken to the Rue des Saussaies for an interrogation, she

---

* Mussolini had offered to restore Prince Michael to the throne of his ancestors, but he had refused, being little inclined to assume the role of a Quisling, even a royal one. He had then been arrested by the Gestapo. Like Monsieur François-Poncet, the Prince wrote about his detention at Neuilly in his book, *Souvenirs d'un roi sans couronne.*

was told gloomily: "*Ach, Mädchen,* your head is not very safe on your shoulders today." This could not help but dampen her spirits and make her very anxious about her future. One day she was taken to the Avenue de la Grande Armée and told to walk along the right-hand pavement toward the Étoile. Two of the Kommando followed her from a distance, one behind her and the other on her left. She was so frightened that when she came to the corner of the Rue Pergolèse, she had an almost irresistible urge to make a dash for it; only the thought of Patrick restrained her. She never knew why she was made to take that walk.

At the end of June, she was told that she was to be transferred to Fresnes prison, under the pretext that they could no longer assure her safety. She felt relieved at this news, oddly enough. Her status of "special prisoner" now seemed to her more dangerous than enviable, and she preferred to be one of a crowd.

She was put by herself in a cell on the ground floor, but soon adapted to this new situation. She managed to exchange messages with the prisoners on the floor above, and one of the women even passed a piece of material to her through the transom, to make a blouse. Georgie was very good at dressmaking and did it well. Then she was caught exchanging messages and put in a punishment cell, a dungeon with only a drop bench to sleep on. She learned that Suzanne Spaak was in Fresnes, and on her release from the dungeon she sent her an oral message, receiving in return an affectionate and comforting reply. A few days later, Georgie happened to find herself next to Suzanne during the exercise hour. Georgie said to her: "I'm terribly sorry, it's because of us that you've been arrested." Suzanne replied, smiling: "Never mind: it's of no importance." With her generosity and optimism, Suzanne was a ray of sunshine in the prison and a great support to the other women. She later sent another message to Georgie to tell her that all was well and to be confident.

Georgie had one peculiarity that set her apart even in the singular world of Fresnes, and that was her American nationality. As time passed, the German wardress in charge of Georgie's block of cells began to unbend and became almost deferential. She brought Georgie books to read and even gave her a sweater, saying, "When your compatriots arrive, I count on you to tell them I treated you well."

On the Normandy front, the British were pushing back the main German forces in the east and the Americans had just broken through in the west.

On August 9, Pannwitz requested the pleasure of Margarete's company in a game of ping-pong, and while they played he told her that the Allied advance obliged him to take certain security measures. Kent and young René were to remain in Paris with him, but Margarete and Michel were being sent to Germany. She reacted in her usual dramatic manner when her love life was affected: she said that if she and Kent were to be separated, Pannwitz might as well have them both shot at once. He tried to calm her down and finally got her to agree. An attentive, if unofficial, godfather, Pannwitz sent out for armloads of toys and various things difficult to get in Germany, such as feeding bottles and baby clothes.

On August 10, Georgie was taken from her cell to the registrar's office. One of the Kommando was waiting for her. "*Ach, Mädchen,* you're leaving Fresnes!" he said. Her handbag and jewels were returned to her. The German burst out laughing when he saw Georgie draw from inside her blouse a ring that she had succeeded in concealing while being searched on arrival. He took her out to a car. "Where are we going?" she asked. "It's a lovely day, *Mädchen,*" he replied. "Just right for a drive!" The weather was indeed glorious, but instead of going out into the country she found herself being driven across Paris. The car stopped at the Gare de l'Est, and the German led her to the platform, where she found Pannwitz with some of his men. All around them were invalid soldiers and nurses encumbered with children, scrambling to get on the train standing at the platform.

The Allies were speeding toward Paris and there was nothing to stop them.

Pannwitz drew Georgie to one side. "You're going to Germany," he said, "for you'd be in danger here. I'll soon be joining you, and we'll probably have news of Trepper there."

"And Patrick? What are you doing about him?"

"If you escape, I'll send him to the Black Forest and you'll never see him again. If you don't try to get away, I promise that everything will be all right."

Georgie was very anxious, despite this promise. What would happen to her son? She remembered his first visit to her at Neuilly. Patrick had been upset by the guards and the strange atmosphere of the place. "I don't want to stay here!" he had cried, clinging to Madame Queyrie. "Take me away!" The following morning, Georgie had found her first gray hair.

She caught sight of Kent at the end of the platform and ran toward him. "I know you're in the same situation as I am; you have a small child, too. I implore you to watch over Patrick, to see that no harm comes to him."

Kent looked at her with indifference and turned away.

Georgie was told to get on the train. Margarete and her baby soon joined Georgie in the compartment, followed by the two secretaries of the Kommando, Ella Kempka and a younger woman.

The train started. Margarete got out some knitting, while Georgie took care of the baby. The two German women chatted. The train stopped among fields several times, because of air-raid warnings. It would have been easy for Georgie to get away—but what would have happened to Patrick? They reached Metz in the evening; the four women and the baby passed the night at the local Gestapo headquarters. They continued the journey in the morning. Two days after leaving Paris the train arrived at Karlsruhe, where Ella Kempka lived. She had little room for the four of them, but they managed fairly well. Margarete was treated as a friend, and even Georgie was able to go out almost as she liked, accompanied only by the younger secretary. The latter took her to the hairdresser's, left her there and returned two hours later, then they went and had tea together.

But a few days after her arrival in Karlsruhe Georgie was summoned to the Gestapo offices. There she was taken before a burly, hard-faced man—it was Reiser, formerly Giering's deputy, who had been posted to Karlsruhe the year before. He asked her if she thought that Trepper would decide to get in touch with the Kommando. When she replied in the affirmative, he growled in a threatening way, "It'll be better for you if he does, otherwise things may go badly with you."

Georgie began to feel anxious again. She thought it was extremely perilous to be mixed up in this affair of a separate peace.

Trepper felt certain that the end of the radio game was in sight. The defeat of the German armies in Normandy meant that the Allies would soon be at the very gates of Germany. And nothing would prevent him from carrying out his plan—to attack the Kommando before it fled from Paris. Nothing would be more pleasant than to capture the men who had been hunting him for years and who had taken so many of his agents.

He had appealed to Kovalsky for help, and the latter had placed thirty well-armed Resistance fighters at his disposal. The attack on the Kommando had been planned by Alex Lesovoy, who was quite sure of success. "The only way they can escape us is by committing suicide!" he said. The Big Chief replied, laughing, "You can trust them not to do that, never fear!"

Moscow had to be informed, of course, and a message had been sent asking for the green light. The reply was slow in coming.

Meanwhile, General Leclerc and his Free French Armored Division were advancing on Paris; the leading elements had already reached the southern suburbs. Pannwitz and his men packed their bags and prepared to leave. They were doubtless feeling very melancholy. They had worked hard, suffered disappointments and defeats, worn themselves out tracking down agents and torturing some of them —but on the whole, the past three years had been good. None of them had been killed in Paris; they had been much safer there than in Stalingrad, Warsaw, or even Bengasi. Even Willy Berg, who should have been court-martialed and shot for letting the Big Chief escape —even old Berg was there with the others, packing up his souvenirs. Berlin had known nothing of it. Berlin had never known more than they had been pleased to report. And the German authorities in France had had no powers over the Kommando. For the past three years they had been a band of old pals waging their own little war. From being unimportant cops they had become all-powerful police barons with no overlord within reach, with one of the finest cities in the world as their territory. They had lived in style, eaten well and drunk even better, and women had been easily come by. Money had never been lacking, especially after Pannwitz had founded his own Simex—the Helvetia Company, with head offices at Monte Carlo to avoid taxation, and branches in Paris and Madrid; it dealt in goods in short supply, particularly quinine and wolfram.

And now they had to leave all that. The Kommando moved out on August 26, through a Paris in a state of insurrection. The laden convoy, bristling with weapons, had to make several detours because of street barricades, but eventually reached the suburbs and joined the stream of German army units hurriedly retreating toward the Rhine.

Trepper had still not received any reply from Moscow by August 26. He dropped his plan of attack, sent the thirty Resistance fighters back to Kovalsky, and set out with Alex Lesovoy to try to reach the Rue de Courcelles. They were held up by the street fighting here and there, and even took a hand in the battle going on round the Majestic Hotel, seat of the German military headquarters, where Vasili Maximovich had so often gone. When Trepper and Lesovoy finally reached the Rue de Courcelles, it was to learn that the Kommando had left two hours earlier. The concierge and his wife were still trembling with fear over Kent's last words to them. Just before getting into his car he had shouted, "Take care! Don't think it's all over: we'll be back!"

———◆———

At two o'clock that afternoon, Claude Spaak and Ruth Peters reached his apartment in the Rue de Beaujolais. They found it looted of everything but the heavy furniture, the library and pictures. A heap of papers and books on the floor of his study proved the thoroughness of the search. While the two were wandering through the emptied rooms, there came a knock at the door. It was Pauline, the maid of the writer Colette. Colette, who was unable to move, had sent her to express her sympathy and to ask Claude Spaak to come and see her. "Do you need any money?" she asked him in her practical way as soon as he stepped inside. He thanked her, and declined her generous offer; he did, however, accept a piece of soap.

A little later, a man called to tell him: "I'm a furniture mover, and in March the Germans sent me here to collect a whole vanload of things. I took them to a house in the Rue de Courcelles."

Spaak went there and was shown into a large room with beautiful wood paneling but furnished with nothing more than a table, two chairs and a stove. Sitting close to the stove, huddled in his overcoat and with his hat on, was an old gentleman, Monsieur Veil-Picard. His housekeeper took Spaak up to the second floor, which was filled with stacks of furniture. "Help yourself," she said with a large gesture. "Take whatever you like. The owners are dead."

Spaak claimed a few pieces that had been looted from his apartment and his house at Choisel, but to the housekeeper's astonishment, he refused to take away a splendid Persian carpet that had never belonged to him.

In the cellar he discovered the bathtub from Choisel, but would not take it until he was satisfied that it had never been used for torturing prisoners.

The housekeeper also took him to the gallery covered with a skylight, which had held a magnificent collection of eighteenth-century paintings before the war. The walls and parquet floor were splattered with blood. It had been the Kommando's torture chamber.

Claude Spaak still had no news of his wife.

———◆———

It was at this point in his story that Claude Spaak was overcome by his emotions. We were sitting in his study at Choisel, where everything was in perfect order and harmony, and I had been listening to him for hours with the greatest interest and also with professional admiration for his mastery of facts and sure choice of evocative detail. But when he came to those weeks following the liberation of Paris he lost control, his face trembled, and his eyes filled with tears. He looked away, and I felt that his words were addressed more to himself than to me:

"I had heard rumors about shootings at Fresnes a few days before the Liberation, but nothing definite. It was said that there had been a revolt among the common-law prisoners. That would not have concerned Suzanne. There was still hope. But then I received a letter. Her last letter. She had just been told that she was about to die. The letter ended with the words, 'I'm thinking again of Myra.' There was also a note for the children. Suzanne had given the letters to the prison chaplain. I don't know to whom he handed them; they reached me from the Ministry of Foreign Affairs. In the envelope there was also a certificate of burial in Bagneux cemetery.

"We found two fresh graves there, but no names on the simple wooden crosses, just the words, 'a Belgian woman' and 'a Frenchman.'

"We weren't certain that it was Suzanne, so the body had to be exhumed. I didn't want to go to the mortuary. Dr. Chertok went, taking Suzanne's dental chart. It was she. We left her buried at Bagneux. I'm a freethinker, and I have no devotion to cemeteries. The true cemetery is in the heart. But one day, all the same, I wanted to see her grave. Ah, it's terrible . . . an immense necropolis where three thousand soldiers are buried . . . there are flowers everywhere. And among all those men, just two women—Suzanne and one other. . . .

"Some time after the Liberation, a woman who had been in Fresnes came to see me. She told me how wonderful my wife had been there, and how admirable, and she said that Suzanne had expressed the wish that I go and see her cell, in case she didn't return.

"So I went to Fresnes—this was in January, 1945. I asked the prison governor for permission to see the cell—I had the number from my visitor. His reply was positively bureaucratic: 'It's not worth the trouble. All the inscriptions made on the walls by Resistance prisoners have been copied into a register.' I went through the register, but there was nothing. Not a single sentence was attributed to Suzanne. I insisted, despite everything, on being allowed to see the cell. The governor replied that it might not be easy—at that time, the prison was packed with collaborators—but he'd see what could be done. And he came back to say that I could visit it: it was only being used as a storeroom for blankets.

"On the walls there were more than three hundred inscriptions in Suzanne's hand.

"I don't remember how long I stayed there. Weeping, I went from one wall to the other, copying all these writings on office paper the governor had given me. There were her thoughts, and poems, and a kind of diary she had kept during the last days. She had noted hopefully that American tanks were reported at Chartres. She was also amazed at being still at Fresnes, when nearly all her fellow prisoners had been evacuated. But read for yourself . . ."

He was weeping, and handed me some sheets of paper he took from a drawer. I looked through them and gave them back quickly— too quickly. But I was oppressed by knowing I was the cause of his suffering. My eye had caught a few phrases: "Alone with my thoughts, I am still free." And those words of Socrates, "My enemies can kill me, but they cannot harm me."

Then he showed me the letter his wife had written after being sentenced to death. It had been sent to Claude Spaak's mother in Belgium, but she had been unable to give it to him until after the Liberation. It was the letter in which Suzanne had given her husband the Gestapo's offer—that she would be reprieved and set free if he gave himself up. And she had signed it in huge letters, "Suzanne."

"There you are, she was thirty-nine when she died, and I don't know how. It's certain she was given warning of her execution, as she had time to write her last letters. But then I found that there were no shootings in Fresnes nor at Mont Valérien after mid-August. So I don't know . . . But there's something that I can't forget—that large brown stain I saw on the floor of her cell . . ."

He stood up, tears running down his face. As he showed me out, he stopped in the drawing room in front of a Magritte painting. It depicted an open book, whose right-hand page showed white clouds in a blue sky; the other page had a portrait of Suzanne Spaak—a bold nose, straight brown hair, and a lively look.

"The family didn't like that portrait when it was painted," he said. "We thought it made Suzanne look older than she was. But now it is we who are growing old, while she remains young."

At the door we shook hands, unable to say a word. He was overcome with emotion. I could see him as I drove away, still standing there, shattered. Then a curve in the road hid him from sight, and I was alone with the memory of Suzanne Spaak, a woman of whom I had known nothing a few hours earlier, and whom I can now never forget. And as I drove along the valley of the Chevreuse, I was thinking that to live fully was perhaps to die like Suzanne Spaak.

"A Belgian woman" and "a Frenchman." The man was Fernand Pauriol, alias Duval, who had remained silent to the very end. The two had been executed at the same time. He came from Marseilles, she from Brussels; different paths had led them to Fresnes, to die and be buried there, side by side. She came from a rich middle-class family, he was a Communist; the same fight had united them until death. Such was the Red Orchestra.

36. The Hero's Return

In October, 1944, two months after the liberation of Paris, a Soviet military mission arrived in the French capital and took up its quarters at the former Lithuanian embassy, but soon moved to the former Esthonian embassy in the Boulevard Lannes. The mission was headed by Lieutenant Colonel Novikov.

The Big Chief at once got into contact with him, and it was agreed that Trepper would be sent to Moscow by the first available means. The wait promised to be long. The Allied advance had come almost to a halt on the Rhine, dashing hopes of the war being over before the end of the year. Direct comunications between Paris and Moscow seemed unlikely to be reestablished for some time.

Trepper used the delay to seek out the survivors of his network and to try to discover the fate of those who had been captured. He found Katz's wife and children at the Maximovich château at Billeron.

Raichman had been to see them, and so had Willy Berg, but the Kommando had decided it would be better to leave them as bait rather than be hampered with them. Trepper took Madame Katz with him to visit the Queyrie family on September 29, Patrick's birthday, and in the afternoon they took the boy to the Médrano Circus. Trepper often went to see Claude Spaak and helped him in his sad quest. Quite by accident, he also found Emmanuel Mignon, crossing the Place St.-Michel; they had a drink together, recalling the good old days with the Simex firm. Trepper had no news of Georgie, of course. He left two trunks full of new clothes and presents with Madame Queyrie, and asked her to give them to Georgie if she turned up again.

At the end of November, Novikov informed Trepper that Stalin's personal plane had arrived at Le Bourget—it had brought back Maurice Thorez, the leader of the French Communist Party, who had spent the previous four years in Moscow—and a seat was reserved for Trepper for the return journey. He therefore packed his things and waited to be summoned. His wait lasted for more than a month. The plane's crew—three colonels—were not insensible to the pleasures of Paris, and a series of mechanical difficulties kept the plane grounded. Finally, a sharply worded order from the Kremlin set the engines turning again, and the plane took off for Moscow at nine o'clock in the morning of January 6, 1945, with the Big Chief on board. The plane was supposed to be taking back Russian prisoners of war, but only one of the eight passengers came into that category; the rest were either diplomats or the Center's agents returning to the fold, though there was an old Russian revolutionary who had been living in exile for twenty years and whom Stalin had just pardoned.*

The plane had to take a roundabout route, landing at Marseilles, Castel Benito, Cairo, Teheran and Baku before finally putting down at a small airfield near Moscow at four in the afternoon of January 14, 1945.

It was six years since the Big Chief had left Russia. They had been years of joy and anguish, of mourning and of triumph. Six years of combat. He was returning feeling proud of his accomplishments, but without arrogance.

---

* One of the passengers later described him as follows: "Repatriation certificate No. 4 was held by a man called Ivanovsky, a Soviet agent of unknown nationality. He spoke Russian and French fluently and could get along in English. I heard that he had spent much of the war in hiding. He was a delightful traveling companion, but I know nothing more about him."

A car was waiting to take him to the Center in Znamensky Street. On arrival he was shown into the Director's office. Their dialogue was brief:

"What are your plans for the future?" the Director asked him.

"Before talking about the future, we might have a word about the past! Why didn't you believe me from the beginning? How were you able to mess things up so badly? I sent you enough warnings, didn't I?"

"Have you returned to settle accounts?"

"And why not?"

"In that case, they won't be settled in my office."

The Big Chief was immediately sent to Lubianka prison. He was to remain there for ten years.

37. The Fate of the Others

Soon after the liberation of Paris, Reiser sent for Georgie again. "The situation is getting worse," he told her. "It's not unlikely that they'll attempt to set you free. So you'll understand that I'm obliged to put you in prison." She did not know whether some unknown friends were preparing to help her, but she herself was thinking of escaping (the Kommando could no longer take reprisals against Patrick). And now Reiser was dashing these hopes. But she was under no illusion as to the difficulty of crossing enemy territory, with her small knowledge of German, and reaching the French frontier. Nor was she too downcast at being put back into a prison cell; as at Neuilly, she preferred prison to the equivocal status of a privileged detainee.

She returned to Ella Kempka's place to collect her things, then went not unwillingly to become an inmate of Karlsruhe prison. So began the hard road that took her to Frankfurt-am-Main, Leipzig, Ravensbrück, Frankfurt-an-der-Oder, Orianenburg, Sachsenhausen. She confronted the successive dangers and terrors protected by her beauty, her vitality and her nationality, but she owed her survival to a deeper quality, one difficult to define. Like everyone else, she must have endured humiliations and sometimes touched the depths of despair, yet she speaks only of the sufferings and despair of her companions. This quality of hers can be seen as self-abnegation or as thoughtfulness of others, but that would be examining the effects and not the quality itself. Listening to her talking of her experiences, one has the impression that she remained impervious to everything, that she came through unscathed ("without being bitten," as she said). She would not die, she would not be degraded, she would not lose her good looks. *People like us overcome everything*—she believed it; it was her talisman.

In Karlsruhe there were terrifying air raids that shook her cell door, which was always locked. But her chief memory of Karlsruhe is the Frenchman, a very young boy, almost a child, who broke the silence in the prison one night with a single cry: "I'm going to be shot tomorrow!" She had not known that the human voice could express such heartrending distress. Then Reiser came to tell her that she was going to be transferred, as he still feared a rescue attempt.

The next stage was Frankfurt-am-Main. The prison was terribly overcrowded; there was a revolt among the prisoners, which was put down.

Leipzig was next. Her prison was a small hut already crowded with a score of Russian women. They had to sleep huddled together on the floor, and woke up each morning amidst the excrement that had overflowed from the sanitary can. But there was a bench, and the Russians insisted that Georgie sleep on it. When she first arrived, they had admiringly stroked her face and fingered her rich clothes.

The Leipzig prison was evacuated, and SS men escorted the wretched band to the railway station. People in the streets shouted insults, and children threw stones. The prisoners were packed into freight cars, and the train set off. They nearly died of suffocation, and the sanitary can constantly overflowed; the torturous journey ended at last—at Ravensbrück. Georgie's hair was not shaved off; the badge she wore—it said "American"—was stared at with curiosity; she was beaten only during general punishments. She made friends with a Mademoiselle de Fourcroy and her sister-in-law Nicole, both from Brussels. For the first time in her life she saw a human being killed—a German woman guard rushed at the prisoner who was digging close to Georgie and split her head open with a spade. Georgie says that there was a moment when "things weren't going well" (she had a very high fever and was delirious). But her outstanding memory of Ravensbrück is of the Gypsy woman standing in line outside the death-selection hut and hugging in her arms her baby, hardly a fort-night old, and naked in the bitter cold.

Then Ravensbrück was evacuated, and Georgie was sent to a camp near Berlin. The prisoners worked in a synthetic-rubber factory making wires for field telephones. There was much sabotage. Then she helped to dig antitank ditches outside Frankfurt-an-der-Oder; the picks bounced off the frozen ground. Finally, as the Russians were still advancing, the horde of prisoners was made to begin the sadly famous "death march," during which thousands of bewildered women were kept plodding around in the ever-narrowing gap between the eastern and western fronts, driven along by the cudgels of SS whose hatred was exacerbated by fear. Stragglers were shot on the spot. Many a time a woman stepped out of the long column—stepped out of life—and passively waited for the bullet in the nape of her neck which would put an end to her sufferings. The only food they had was a ration of soup gulped down by the roadside. One evening, there was some jostling in the line at the field kitchen. The woman in front of Georgie stumbled against the soup pot. An SS man was supervising the distribution:

"He pulled out his pistol as one pulls out a handkerchief and shot her, without the slightest expression, as though it was the most ordi-nary thing to do. I was so hungry that I stepped forward and held out my mess tin while she, poor thing, was dying at my feet, clawing at the earth with fingers that moved slower and slower."

They slept in barns which were too small to take all of them, and the women fought savagely for a place inside; those who were un-successful were found frozen to death at dawn. "I used to climb up to the beams of the barn, and I slept on the highest one, up above everybody."

They were kept moving more and more quickly, and given less and less to eat; the death roll was mounting, and Georgie realized that she was near breaking point. She and her two friends from Brus-sels decided it would be better to die while escaping than to be shot in cold blood. The most opportune moment was at nightfall, when the starving column stumbled on blindly to the rattle of mess tins and spoons dangling from their tattered clothing—a sinister clatter heralding misery and death, like the lepers' bells of olden times.

The first of the three women chose a bend in the road, where she darted from the column and plunged into a hedge. Georgie and the other waited for the next village. They saw an open gate into a

garden, rushed through it and hid behind the wall. A dog started to
bark furiously, but the SS guards took no notice. The two trembling
women listened to the tinny sound of the column becoming fainter,
then they left the garden and went back to find their companion,
still hidden in the hedge.

They spent the night in a shack on the edge of a duck pond, and
woke to the sound of guns rumbling in the distance. A Russian
deportee passed by and left them three matches. So they were able
to light a fire and cook a few roots. "Afterward we got completely
nude and bathed—ah, it was marvelous!"

The roots had not appeased their hunger, and the bath made them
ravenous. It was decided that Georgie would go and look for some
food. She made her way across the fields, with the gunfire becoming
louder and shaking the earth like a ceaseless rumbling of thunder. She
arrived at a farmhouse; in the big kitchen some peasants were sitting
at a table which held the remains of a great feast. Dressed in their
Sunday best, they were sitting there in somber silence and waiting
for the arrival of the Russians. Georgie asked if she could have something to eat. The master of the house nodded permission. She was stuff-
ing herself while they looked on indifferently, when a Cossack wearing a fur cap burst in and demanded some schnapps. The master said
he had none. Whereupon the Cossack calmly told them that if he was
not given some schnapps he would shoot them all. And he loaded his
machine-pistol. That was the moment when Georgie felt the greatest
fear of her life. The Cossack was given his schnapps, gulped it down
and went away satisfied.

Georgie was sent back to France with some repatriated prisoners
of war and arrived in Paris on May 15, 1945. When she rang the bell at
the house in Suresnes, Madame Queyrie and Patrick were at the neighbor's opposite. Patrick recognized his mother's back, went pale and
began to weep for joy. Madame Queyrie sheltered her for the next
eighteen months, and under her care Georgie soon recovered. Madame
Queyrie did not tell Georgie what she confessed to me years later:
"Obviously, it's not a nice thing to say, but I loved that child so
much that I sometimes hoped deep down that Georgie would not
come back; for then I could adopt him and keep him with me always."
Patrick was indeed a lucky boy. After so many vicissitudes he had
reached peaceful shores at last, thanks to the loving care of kind
Madame Queyrie.

Eighteen months later, in Brussels, Georgie met old Baron Jaspar again; he had survived Mauthausen. His fellow prisoners had been charmed by his picturesque appearance, for he had been given the blue jacket and red trousers of a Yugoslav cavalryman—and his morale matched those colors. Everything, even Mauthausen, seemed to make him younger. But his wife was dead. The camp commandant had announced one day that he was setting up a special center for old and sick prisoners. Madame Jaspar volunteered to help, despite the warnings and pleadings of other prisoners. The special center turned out to be Auschwitz and the gas chambers.

The two lonely people, Georgie and the widower, lived together in the Cévennes until he died. Two years after his death, she married a Polish colonel who had been second in command to General Bor during the Warsaw insurrection, and who had also chosen to end an adventurous life in the bleak Cévennes. He died on May 18, 1966, leaving Georgie alone in the old fortified farmhouse set on the mountain slopes. Strange indeed had been the destiny of this woman, so little suited for secret warfare, prison life, and loneliness, and who lived through all of that because, on a certain day in 1939, she happened to drop her gloves in a Brussels pastry shop.

———◆———

Mauthausen concentration camp was freed too late to save Henri de Ryck, stockholder in Simexco; Rauch of British Intelligence; and Charles Drailly of Simexco (whose brother Nazarin had died in Dachau of bubonic plague).

Robert Christen, former owner of the Florida, says: "I survived thanks to my funny faces." Every Sunday there was a "recreation matinee"—a supreme mockery—at which prisoners who had been acrobats or jugglers performed before an audience of living specters. Christen sent in his name for an audition. He could neither jump nor juggle, and to sing his comic songs was quite out of the question, even in Esperanto. When asked what he could do, he said, "Make funny faces." They had the gift of making the SS laugh, and he was taken on. He had no more to eat than the others, but he tired less as he was excused from hard labor. His privileged position lasted until his transfer to Gouzen 1, an annex of Mauthausen and an extermination camp. There were no "recreation matinees" there—only an accordion and an oven. The man in charge of the crematory possessed an accordion but could not play it, and he asked Christen to give him lessons. Moreover, some of the prisoners in Gouzen 1 were not *Nacht und Nebel*,* and they received food parcels. They used to give their mess tins to Christen for him to heat up the food, paying him with a portion. So every evening, Christen put the tins on the glowing bones in the crematory, then took up the accordion and played waltzes for the man in charge while the food cooked.

Robert Corbin had been put in the camp's tailor shop. The rags he was given to patch up had little in common with the Harris tweed he had once sold at Creed's in the Rue Royale, but the work was not very tiring, he was out of the bitter cold, and this enabled him to survive.

The hardest fate befell Jean Passelecq; fortunately, with his broad shoulders and extraordinary vitality he was best equipped to support hardships that would soon have crushed others. The whims of German bureaucracy threw him into a sort of tour of concentration camps. In two years he passed through *ten* different camps, probably a record. Each transfer was catastrophic, as before leaving he was stripped of the poor little treasures he had been able to collect and was given the oldest and thinnest rags to wear; and on arrival at the new camp he was invariably given the most grueling work, put in the worst hut, under orders of the cruelest Kapo. No sooner had he adapted himself to the new conditions, made a few friends—absolutely necessary for survival—he would be moved on again and had to start from scratch in another hell. These tribulations had left him with a face of some old sea dog who had rounded the Horn ten times in Nazi galleys; but he had not let them break him.

When the surviving members of Simex and Simexco were freed and repatriated they were loud in their praises of Bill Hoorickx, who had remained behind in Mauthausen. Fate plays strange tricks; it needed deportation for him to show his true worth as a man. He rose to great heights of devotion and boldness at Mauthausen. Through some bureaucratic error, his record showed him to be a doctor. He did not contradict this, although his medical knowledge consisted only of what he remembered from a crash course in colonial medicine he had once taken when he was thinking of becoming a missionary. At most, he would have made a good medical orderly; the camp commandant appointed him head doctor and placed several prisoners who were qualified doctors under his orders. They never

---

* Literally "night and fog," the Nazi expression for prisoners whose fate was not to be divulged to their families.

discovered the truth about him—it is true that medical care in concentration camps was necessarily limited in scope. Hoorickx, lacking
drugs and medical equipment, was not able to care for prisoners'
bodies as he would have liked, but he had enough generosity and
selflessness to comfort men's hearts and give them courage to fight
the contagion of despair. He saved many of his companions from
the gas chamber by smuggling them into the isolation hut for contagious diseases which the camp guards never entered. Then, when
the camp was liberated, he remained behind with the sick. He was
the last to leave Mauthausen; the only souvenir he took with him
was a bundle of letters in which the doctors who had served under
him extolled his good work for the prisoners, and almost concealed
their embarrassment at not having discovered that he was hardly their
"eminent colleague." If they could have, they probably would have
made him doctor *honoris causa* of the Mauthausen Faculty of Medicine.

Two months after Alfred Corbin's execution, Vladimir Keller
had been transferred from the Lehrterstrasse prison to the civilian
prison at Tegel, where he was put to work on a printing press.
His production included six thousand visiting cards for Himmler, and he was very impressed by the number of honorary ranks held
by the Reichsführer. His next stage was a Czechoslovak jail, where
he suffered cruelly from cold and hunger. He thought many times
of the street door in the lavatories at Lille railway station, which
would have saved him from so much suffering. Eventually, on May
8, 1945, the liberating Red Army appeared in the shape of a single
officer on horseback. His toes were poking through his boots; Keller,
a true Swiss, remarked on this peculiarity. "Never mind that," the
Russian answered, laughing, "What mattered was to win the war!"

Ludwig Kainz was among the survivors, as were Mademoiselle
Ponsaint and Henri Seghers, of the Belgian network. But all the others
who had been taken to Germany on that sad convoy in April, 1943,
remained there forever, having been executed or having died from
exhausion and starvation.

———————◆———————

An exception may have been Lieutenant Makarov, alias Carlos
Alamo. In February, 1943, the court-martial presided over by Man-

fred Roeder, "Hitler's bloodhound," had sentenced him to death. He had been on the train to Berlin with the others, and Hoorickx had exchanged a few words with him. But after arrival in Berlin all trace of him was lost. Not one of the survivors of the network ever saw him again.

But, when Roeder was in the hands of the Americans after the war, he told his judges a strange story, which he later recounted to me. According to him, he was looking through the file on Makarov and discovered that he was a nephew of Molotov, then the Soviet Foreign Minister.* This relationship obviously gave a new significance to the condemned man; his execution would have a political reper- cussion. The sentences of a court-martial were subject to confirma- tion by Hitler, but in Makarov's case, as in one or two others, the Führer had delegated his powers to Goering. When Roeder sub- mitted to him the sentence passed on Makarov, he mentioned that the condemned man was related to Molotov and suggested that it might be expedient to keep him alive—either to serve for an exchange with the Russians or to prevent a hitch in eventual negotiations with Mos- cow; in other words, with his uncle Molotov. Still according to Roeder, Goering approved his suggestion and ordered Makarov to be sent to concentration camp. There he was entered under the name of Kokorine. He was freed by the Americans and returned to Russia.

It is a fact that *The New York Times* reported in May, 1945, that a group of "important prisoners" had been liberated, and men- tioned among them one named Kokorine. However, I do not feel that this could have been Makarov.

Captain Payne-Best, one of the two British Intelligence officers kidnaped at Venlo early in the war, knew Kokorine well. Payne- Best had been sent to Sachsenhausen and put in the special bunker with other important prisoners. Early in 1943, Kokorine joined them. He came from the war-prisoner section of the camp, where one of his fellow prisoners had been Stalin's son, who was an Air Force officer and had been shot down behind the German lines. The two had attempted to escape but had failed.

Kokorine told Payne-Best that he had been dropped behind the German lines to take command of a group of partisans. He was tracked down by the Germans and obliged to give himself up be- cause his feet were frostbitten. When Payne-Best saw him, he was

* The Big Chief's wife, Luba, knew the Molotov family, and she confirms that Makarov was a member of it.

still wearing his Red Army uniform and his toes had been amputated, which gave credibility to his story. He was then twenty-two years old, which was also much younger than our Makarov. Moreover, unlike Makarov, he wore glasses—and after his escape attempt he had tried to commit suicide by cutting his veins with one of the lenses. Also, Makarov spoke English, and Kokorine did not, for his conversations with Payne-Best were carried on in very poor German and included such remarks as: "Stalin very fine man . . . he loves my mother enormously . . . she goes to see him every day after dinner . . . Stalin very lazy, hates work . . . likes good food, good wine and pretty girls . . . Stalin magnificent fellow . . . never worries and likes to laugh a lot." * Makarov may have been a simple soul, but not as simple as that.

There is another inaccuracy in Roeder's story: Kokorine did not return to Russia. The group of "important prisoners" had been transferred to the Prags Wildbad Hotel near Niederdorf, a small town in the Tirol. They were liberated by an American patrol. A few days later, Kokorine disappeared into the mountains; the cold brought back his frostbite, his old wounds opened, gangrene set in and he died of it. He had told Payne-Best he had made up his mind never to be repatriated, as he was sure that an unpleasant fate awaited him in Russia.†

So Kokorine was not Makarov. The question remains whether Roeder was mistaken or whether he was lying. There seems no reason for him to have lied—unless it was to pose as the savior of Molotov's nephew, which seems unlikely. In any case, it would have been a useless lie, as it could easily be checked and exposed. So he was probably mistaken. But to what extent? It can be taken for granted that he did suggest that Goering spare Makarov's life, and that Goering decided to send Makarov to a concentration camp—Roeder wrote out his suggestion himself, and he received Goering's answer. But Roeder would not have known what subsequently happened to the prisoner. It can be presumed that, on hearing after the war of the existence of a nephew of Molotov's named Kokorine, Roeder mistakenly concluded that the man was Makarov. If this theory is correct, Alamo may have been *another* of Molotov's nephews; he

---

* Payne-Best, *The Venlo Incident* (London: Hutchinson, 1950).
† It is known that repatriated Russian prisoners had a very cool reception; they were blamed for having let themselves be captured. Ten years after the end of the war, ex-POWs still felt the stigma and were discriminated against.

may in fact have been imprisoned in circumstances which gave him a real chance of survival.

A strange coincidence gives support to Roeder's belief that Makarov is still alive—or in any case, that he was alive in 1948. At that time, Roeder was being held in Nuremberg prison. In October, the American counterespionage service in Germany arrested Frantisek Klecka, a Czech agent working for the Russians and who, during the war, had belonged to the Czechoslovak network of the Red Orchestra. By a strange chance, this Red Orchestra veteran shared a cell with the man who had sent so many of its members to the scaffold or the firing squad. Boredom soon broke down the coldness between them, and they talked about the old days. Roeder later said that Klecka gave him greetings from Makarov and suggested that he go and see him in Berlin.

I have proof that a Captain Makarov was posted to East Berlin in 1948. He was in charge of Group I of the M.G.B.—the Soviet secret service. So it is possible that our Alamo continued with the work he had found so boring in Brussels, and that the Center retained his services despite his unfortunate beginnings. But the name Makarov is so common in Russia that the M.G.B. captain may only coincidentally have shared the surname of the Red Orchestra agent.

◆

Soon after Georgie had been taken to Karlsruhe prison, Margarete was joined by Kent and her son René, who arrived with most of the Kommando.* Kent, with Pannwitz, left again almost at once for Hornberg, in the Black Forest, to which the western department of the SS intelligence service had retreated. Pannwitz was informed by Reiser that Berlin had ordered them to destroy all the Kommando's files without delay. They had been sent to a place near Würzburg, in the Tauber valley. Pannwitz and Reiser proceeded to burn them all.

Karlsruhe was being subjected to constant air raids, and in mid-September Pannwitz sent Margarete and her two children to a guest-house in Friedrichroda, where various harmless notabilities were already interned, among them the Italian Princess Ruspoli and the family of General Giraud. There was no guard on the house, as it

---

* Yefremov was among them. According to some accounts, which I have been unable to verify, he escaped to South America at the end of the war, having been supplied with false identity papers by the Kommando.

was unlikely that mothers encumbered with children would go far. Michel fell ill with double pneumonia in October; Kent came to see him on October 22, and stayed for a few days. He returned on December 13, without any future instructions, and Margarete thought their separations were at an end, that they would await the end of the war together, and then settle down after five years of wandering to a peaceful life of love. But Pannwitz suddenly arrived on the scene in mid-February and, despite Margarete's hysterical cries, took Kent away with him.

Friedrichroda was captured by the Americans, then handed over to the Red Army, as it was in the Russian occupation zone. Margarete, delighted with this transfer of power, went to the local Russian headquarters and introduced herself to the duty officer as the wife of a Soviet agent whose code name was Kent.

"Kent?" exclaimed the officer. "But we're looking everywhere for that traitor!" Then, seeing how upset Margarete was, he added, "Of course, you're not responsible for what your husband did."

In June, 1945, while she was still at Friedrichroda, the mails began to function again; and one day she almost fainted when the mailman gave her an envelope on which she recognized Kent's writing. He had written the letter in April and had mailed it in Stuttgart. It was brief and to the point: "When you read this, I shall be a corpse. Open our little box. If necessary, break it open." He had left the box with her when he went off with Pannwitz. She forced open the lid and found a typewritten letter which began: "I have betrayed my country." Kent then went on to confess to his mistress—for the first time—that he was a Russian secret agent; and unexplicably, as if it were the one important thing, he insisted that he was not a Jew. He mentioned that his official date of birth, July 3, 1911, was inaccurate, as he was born in 1912; and he ended by giving much advice for herself and the children. A doctor, a fellow detainee of Margarete's, very sensibly suggested that she would be wise to destroy the letter. So she burnt it.

The formalities for her repatriation were finally completed in September, 1945, and she was able to leave Friedrichroda; there was no point in her staying, since Kent had vanished. She had decided to go back to France. At the frontier, she and her children were taken off the train by French security police; she was questioned about Kent for a long time, though she could not make out whether they were interested in him as a Russian agent or as a willing collaborator of the Kommando. They got very excited when they found a pipe in her pocket—they were convinced that Kent had been on the train with her but had left it before reaching the frontier. Actually, the resourceful Margarete had supplemented her few cigarettes by smoking the stubs in one of Kent's old pipes.

After many long interrogations, she and the two children were sent to an internment camp which already held some hundreds of people suspected of collaboration with the Germans. Conditions there were hard, very different from Neuilly, the Rue de Courcelles and Friedrichroda. She was cold and hungry, and depressed above all by her continuing misfortunes. The Germans had kept her prisoner for over two years, and now the French had interned her. She seemed fated to end her days behind barbed wire, never knowing what crime she had committed. If it had been her love for Kent, the light of her life, why continue to torment her now that he was dead?

The order for her release came through at the end of the year, but Michel was not yet well enough to be moved. She finally left the camp six months later, on May 18, 1946. The police had made her sign a pledge to notify them if she had news of Kent.

She had the responsibility of two children—one fourteen and the other three years old. She had no money and no training, and her health was seriously impaired. While others were slowly returning to the pleasures of normal life, ten years of illness and poverty stretched before Margarete Barcza.

◆

Pannwitz, Kent and a few of the Kommando had fled to a lonely chalet at Bludenz, about eight miles from the Swiss frontier. To reach this southern corner of Germany they had to travel two hundred miles, threading their way through retreating German units, past roadblocks manned by police or SS quick to shoot troops turning their backs to the enemy. But Pannwitz had a document signed by both Himmler and General Jodl, empowering him to go anywhere and to requisition from civilians and the military.

Huddled in their chalet, they listened to the rumblings of war becoming louder. Some tanks of the French First Army were the first to reach Bludenz. Pannwitz and the others burned all their real identity papers, then tensely waited for the arrival of the enemy. They went on waiting. They had envisaged everything except this —that no one would come for them. Two or three weeks passed, and they were still kicking their heels in the chalet amidst meadows full of spring flowers and singing birds. Every evening, Kent made radio contact with Moscow. Down in the valley, at Bludenz, the French were settling in for a tranquil occupation. It was disconcerting.

The French took notice of them only after they were denounced by one of their own countrymen, a refugee from Berlin. One morning they saw soldiers taking up positions around the chalet and mounting a machine gun. They were being given an opportunity to make a gallant end. But Pannwitz was too shrewd to die for a lost cause. He waved a white handkerchief, and his men put up their hands. A young French lieutenant entered, pistol in hand, and without even glancing at them went across to a photograph of Hitler, pulled it down and tore it up, while the Gestapo men scowled at the Iron Cross hanging from the back of his belt.

Pannwitz looked at Kent, who stepped forward and said: "I belong to the Russian Intelligence service, and I hold the rank of major in the Red Army. These gentlemen belong to a German Resistance movement and have been working with me for a long time." The lieutenant was taken aback and seemed little inclined to believe this story, so Kent showed him the latest messages he had received from the Center. He added: "These gentlemen are, of course, under my protection. I need them. As for this equipment"—he indicated the transmitter and the Kommando's side arms— "it is the property of the Red Army and I must ask you not to touch it."

The lieutenant was apparently convinced by the messages from the Center. He saluted and left, the Iron Cross still bouncing against his backside. But a week later, his unit was relieved, and another was brought in. The officer who took over went up to the chalet, raised his eyebrows at Kent's story, but sensed the possibility of a diplomatic incident and deemed it prudent to get rid of this Red Army major and those gentlemen of the German Resistance. He had them conducted to headquarters at Lindau, where Pannwitz and Kent were received by an overworked colonel. Between two telephone calls, the colonel asked them if they had heard of a Gestapo unit with the odd name of "Rote Kapelle Kommando." Pannwitz fidgeted in his chair and asked for more definite information. The colonel showed him a message from the nearest American H.Q. warning of the presence in the region of the Kommando headed by a certain Heinz Pannwitz and requesting its capture—according to reports, its mission was to assassinate General Patton.

Kent hastened to change the conversation. He gave his name and rank, and details supporting his claim to be a Russian Intelligence agent. Pannwitz produced his false identity papers and vehemently professed his anti-Nazi sentiments. The colonel was probably impressed, although not entirely convinced, and decided that a drink could do no harm; so they all cheerfully drank to the Allied victory. The colonel then hastened to write a report for General de Lattre de Tassigny. The Kommando men and Kent spent the night in a billet with several French soldiers, who took little notice of them. At the usual time for contacting Moscow, Pannwitz was astounded to see Kent unobtrusively hand his radio receiver to one of the Kommando. The set had been taken from a captured British agent and was a great technical achievement for its time; the two batteries could fit into a matchbox and the earphone was minute. When the transmission started, the French soldiers hardly noticed the Kommando leaning his head on his hand, his eyes shut, and seemingly murmuring in his sleep. Actually, he was an experienced radioman; the earphone was hidden in his palm, and he was repeating the message as it came through. Kent was writing it down in the margin of his book, to all appearances making notes on the text. It was a useless feat, but it served at least to calm their nerves.

The following morning, Pannwitz and Kent learned that they were being sent to Paris, as General de Lattre had decided to pass them on to the War Ministry. And so, ten months after having fled from General Leclerc's men, Pannwitz and Kent were conducted back to Paris by one of de Lattre's officers. They had ten suitcases containing their personal belongings, and Pannwitz still had his pistol; no one had asked him to open the briefcase bulging with documents that he carried around with him.

The War Ministry, at a loss, contacted the Soviet mission headed by Lieutenant Colonel Novikov. He said he would gladly see the Red Army major, as the chief object of his mission was to arrange the repatriation of Russian nationals; and he would also see what could be done about the gentlemen of the German Resistance.

On June 6, 1945, Pannwitz and Kent were taken by car to Le Bourget and put aboard a waiting plane. They took off for Moscow with their ten suitcases and the bulging briefcase. Novikov had kept only Pannwitz's pistol.

———◆———

The two had had plenty of opportunity to escape. They had been only two hours away from the Swiss frontier, although it was well guarded, and almost impossible to slip across. The nearby Austrian Tirol was a much easier matter, with its dense forests and hidden valleys. All the Nazi escape routes went that way and continued to Genoa, the gateway to South America. While Pannwitz slept in his chalet, dozens of prominent Nazis were panting up mountain paths behind their guides.

Perhaps he knew nothing of the escape routes, though that is difficult to believe of a *Kriminalrat* and Kommando chief. Even so, in the spring of 1945 millions of refugees and displaced persons were swarming across Germany; war prisoners of all nationalities were making their own way home, hundreds of thousands of German families from the east were fleeing before the Red Army, a million Sudeten Germans were thronging the roads to escape Czech reprisals, and the Wehrmacht had disintegrated into long columns of prisoners. With the Allies not yet firmly in control, disorder reigned. It was a state of chaos such as Europe had probably never known since the barbarian invasions.

Pannwitz had false identity papers, plenty of money, an unremarkable appearance. Yet he made no move. He did not plunge into the seething mass and disappear. He waited at the chalet for someone to come for him.

It would have been even simpler for Kent, as he was Russian. He had only to walk into Bludenz, a mere four hundred yards, and to pose as a Russian war prisoner or deportee. The French would have repatriated him, of course, but with less zeal than for a Russian secret service officer; he probably would have been kept waiting for months —with ample opportunity to disappear altogether.

In any case, it would have seemed imperative to avoid being caught in company with the Gestapo; Kent should have put as much distance as possible between them and himself. But he did not budge. Like Pannwitz, he just waited for someone to come for him.

Someone did come, and the two were lucky enough to fall into the hands of the Western Allies—the great desire of millions of Germans just then. The merest German corporal, whose only crime was to have fought for his country, would have crossed Germany on hands and knees to escape the Russians and become a prisoner of the Western Allies. But not Pannwitz. On the contrary, he did everything to get to Russia—for from the moment Kent revealed himself as a Russian officer, it was obvious that their final destination would be Moscow. For a Gestapo *Kriminalrat* and SS *Hauptsturmführer* to set course for Moscow was strange enough. But for the director of the radio game to rush headlong toward those he had been trying so hard to dupe is nothing less than astonishing. Pannwitz was better placed than anyone to know of the tensions existing between the Allies; he and his Kommando had even been inclined to exaggerate their importance. It should have been obvious to him that the Western powers would not have been heartbroken to learn that he had duped their Russian ally; their secret services might even have taken a guarded interest in the matter. Yet instead of taking refuge in their reassuring arms, Pannwitz threw himself into those of his worst enemy—the Director of the Moscow Center.

As for Kent, he was heading straight for the firing squad. Between Bludenz and Lindau and Paris he could have escaped a dozen times; he and Pannwitz were not guarded, only accompanied, and he had but to walk away. Instead, he continued on, toward his death.

38. A Little Game

First, Gestapo-Müller. "A very decent little man," was how Captain Payne-Best described him. Schellenberg wrote of him: "He was short and thickset, square-headed like a peasant, and with a prominent forehead; he had thin lips and piercing brown eyes, and his drooping eyelids had a nervous twitch. He had large hands with blunt fingers." * Heinrich Müller had joined the Bavarian police long before Hitler appeared on the scene. As a servant of the Weimar Republic, he fought the Nazis in their rise to power and dealt some telling blows, then worked for them when they became the masters. He was not a turncoat; his livery was that of the state, whatever it might be. A loyal servant of the Weimar Republic, he was no less loyal to the Third Reich, and would have loyally served the King of Prussia if he had come to the throne. Müller was the same type as Giering and Berg. But while those two changed color as casually as a chameleon, each change of political power gratified Müller's passion for order and authority—for the state. Wilhelm Hoettl, an *Obersturmführer* in the SS Intelligence service, observed: "The only law he recognized was the overriding power of the state, and any person

---

* Schellenberg, *Memoirs*.

suspected of mere intellectual resistance to it was considered an enemy. He took the Russian secret police as his model, and he certainly succeeded in creating an organization worthy of that ideal." * Reitlinger wrote: "For ten years he was the personification of a cold, dispassionate chief of police, always on the job." † And Edward Crankshaw: "He was the perfect prototype of a public servant without political opinions, bent on personal power and devoted to the service of authority, of the State." ‡

So little was he a Nazi, and so unacceptable his past record, that the Party persistently turned down his applications for membership. Not that Müller was itching for a membership card, but his chief, Heydrich, thought it undesirable for the Gestapo head not to be a Party member when the lowest civil servant was eager to join. Müller was admitted in the end, through Heydrich's influence, but this was not until 1939, just before the outbreak of war.

Rudolf Hess had been at the head of the Nazi Chancellery ever since its creation. One of Hitler's earliest supporters, he was second in line of succession (after Goering). When he flew off to Scotland in May, 1941, with the senseless of idea of concluding a separate peace between Germany and Great Britain, he left the Chancellery under control of his deputy, Martin Bormann.

Bormann was another early Party member. Once an overseer on an estate in Mecklenburg, he had carried out sabotage in the Ruhr in 1923, during the French occupation, been sentenced by a German court for a political murder in 1924 and released a year later. "He was a thickset man with square shoulders and a bull neck. He held his head forward and slightly to one side. His eyes were like those of a boxer advancing on his opponent. His fingers were short and thick, and covered with dark hairs." § Even before Hess's departure, Bormann had attained key positions on the road to power. He became Hitler's privy counselor and financial administrator—posts that opened the way to intimacy with the Führer. || By May, 1941, Bormann was

---

* Wilhelm Hoettl, *The Secret Front* (London: Weidenfeld and Nicolson, 1953), p. 58.
† Gerald Reitlinger, *The SS* (London: Heinemann, 1956), p. 39.
‡ Edward Crankshaw, *Gestapo: Instrument of Tyranny* (New York: Putnam, 1956), p. 96.
§ Schellenberg, *op. cit.*, p. 396.
|| It was Bormann who built the Berghof, the mountain chalet where Hitler liked to relax. Bormann also selected and bought the pictures and other furnishings. (See Trevor-Roper, *The Last Days of Hitler*.)

strongly enough entrenched not to fear the consequences of Hess's action. Hess's chief assistants were arrested or dismissed, but not Bormann, who continued to strengthen his position.

One of Hitler's secretaries wrote of him: "A fiend for organizing and paper work, Bormann relieved Hitler of all the tedious business." * Rosenberg, the Minister for the Eastern Territories, said of Bormann: "When the conversation at table turned to some event or other, he made a note of it. If the Führer was annoyed by something or other, Bormann noted it down. When a matter seemed obscure, Bormann left the table and went out to give orders to his office to look into the matter at once, to telephone, send telegrams, write and make inquiries. . . . So that sometimes Bormann was able to throw light on the matter before we reached the end of the meal." † Trevor-Roper's conclusion was that Bormann became the sole depository of Hitler's secrets and the sole go-between for his ministers.

Müller had known Bormann for a long time, but his first real contact with him was after the Hess affair, when Müller was ordered to clean up the Chancellery—which in Hitler's eyes had become the Augean stables of the Third Reich. For Bormann this was an opportunity to work off some old grudges and especially to eliminate eventual rivals. Müller fell in with his proposals, having decided to hitch his wagon to this rising star; and even high officials innocent of any complicity with Hess found themselves unjustly punished. "Müller had realized that Bormann would succeed Hess and that he was a much more dynamic personality. So, while pretending to Himmler and Heydrich to be against Bormann, he began to form a close relationship with him." ‡

They had too much in common for Müller not to succeed in this. They were both beasts of prey, using the same means to reach identical ends; each had a thirst for power as an end in itself, aside from questions of ideology or politics. The spotlights were on Goering, Ribbentrop, Goebbels, until the end, but it was Bormann who controlled the projectors and adjusted the lighting from the shadows. As for Müller, "his great ambition was to have a central index containing a card for every living German, on which would

---

* Albert Zoller, *Douze ans auprès de Hitler*, p. 51.
† Serge Lang and Ernst von Schenck, *Testament nazi: Mémoires d'Alfred Rosenberg*, p. 191.
‡ Schellenberg, *op. cit.*, p. 217.

be entered every 'suspicious incident,' however trivial." * That was where real power lay.

It is significant that historians of the Third Reich have used almost similar images in writing of these two. Trevor-Roper describes Bormann as having the nature of a mole, carefully avoiding light and publicity; and he stresses the fact that very few photographs of him exist.

"Martin Bormann was the invisible power . . . his name rarely appeared in the German press during the five war years, his photograph was hardly ever published, and his activities were referred to by Goebbels's propaganda machine in the most discreet · manner. . . . There is scarcely a German alive today who can say whether this man was short or tall, thin or fat." †

Edward Crankshaw wrote of Müller that he left hardly any trace behind him, that nothing is known of him—neither where he came from nor where he disappeared to. ‡

The two men were born to understand each other.

As head of the Gestapo, Heinrich Müller was technically responsible for the radio game from start to finish, but the political side changed hands. Himmler had started it with the secret aim already described—to reach a compromise peace with the West—but in order to "feed" a *Funkspiel* of such amplitude he needed information of a high order from various ministries, the Foreign Ministry in particular. In the conflicts that followed, Hitler had given Bormann the task of arbitrating between the various parties. From that moment, the initiative had slipped from Himmler's grasp. Bormann had taken over the radio game and, on Hitler's orders, attended to it personally and without help even of a secretary. The only people in the know, apart from the Gestapo chiefs, were Ribbentrop and a small group of handpicked experts. The files were kept locked in a large safe; they were labeled "Operation Bear."

◆

In the spring of 1943, a routine matter brought Schellenberg and Müller together. Schellenberg relates in his memoirs how their meeting developed:

---

* W. Hoettl, *op. cit.*, p. 58.
† Lang and Schenck, *op. cit.*, p. 190.
‡ E. Crankshaw, *op. cit.*, p. 96.

Müller, with whom I was becoming increasingly friendly, had been particularly civil and courteous that evening. I thought he was tipsy when he expressed the wish to have a talk with me, for it was already very late. He began by referring to the Red Orchestra. He had been looking into the cases of some traitors, examining their motives and their intellectual background.

"I think that your own experiences," he said, "have led you to conclude, like me, that the Soviet influence in western Europe has spread to the educated classes. In my opinion, that is an inevitable development and in the nature of these times, especially if one considers the spiritual 'anarchy' of our Western culture—including the ideology of the Third Reich. National Socialism is no more than a sort of dung heap in this spiritual desert! Against that, everyone can see that a spiritual and living force is developing in Russia. The spiritual and material revolution to which Communism is leading presents a kind of positive electric current to the negative current of the West."

I was sitting opposite Müller, lost in thought. This was the man who had directed the most merciless and brutal attacks on Communism, the man who, in the course of his investigations into the Red Orchestra affair, had explored every inch of ground in the hope of discovering the slightest signs of a conspiracy. What a *volte-face!* He went on talking: "You know, Schellenberg, it's stupid for us to be at loggerheads all the time. I thought we'd get on well together, but it hasn't turned out that way. You have certain advantages over me. My parents were poor, and I've had to make my own way up. But you're an educated man, you've studied law and you've traveled . . . look at the members of the Red Orchestra whom you knew—Schulze-Boysen, Harnack—they were intellectuals too, but of a different kind, progressives seeking a definite solution . . . and they died still believing it possible. National Socialism is too tainted with compromise to induce such faith, but spiritual Communism could do so. I must say that I see Stalin in a different light now. He's greatly superior to all the leaders of the Western nations and, if you want my opinion, I think we should come to terms with him as quickly as possible. . . . You always know where you are with the Russians, at least; they either cut your head off or embrace you. Whereas the Western powers talk about God and a lot of vague things. . . . Germany would be on top if the Führer had gone about things the right way. But with us a start is made at everything and nothing is ever finished, and if we're not careful it'll be the end of us! Himmler is energetic, but only when he has the Führer behind him. . . . Bormann knows his own mind, but he hasn't got what it takes. . . ."

I was astounded as I listened to all this. I had always heard Müller call Bormann a criminal. What a sudden change of attitude! I felt increasingly nervous—what was he getting at? He kept emptying his glass of

spirits as he went on spouting abuse against the decadent West and all
our leaders—Goering, Goebbels, Ribbentrop and Ley, whose ears must
have been burning. As Müller was a walking card index, and knew the
most intimate details about people, it became quite amusing. Still, I was
uneasy. What was he after? Müller had never been so talkative before.
Finally, I tried to give a light touch to the conversation by saying:
"That's fine, comrade Müller—let's all shout 'Heil Stalin!' And gaffer
Müller will become cock of the walk at the N.K.V.D."

He looked at me with a nasty glint in his eye. "That'd be fine," he
said scornfully, in his thick Bavarian accent. "And you'd be for the high
jump, you and your blasted bourgeois friends!"

I came away from that odd meeting still not knowing just what
Müller had been getting at . . . but I understood some months later.*

———◆———

At the time that decidedly odd meeting took place, German
Resistance leaders were trying to bring Himmler into their ranks.
His interview with one of them, and Langbehn's mission to Switzerland, has been described at length.† The whole thing fell through,
it will be remembered, following the interception of a message from
an Allied agent in Switzerland, reporting developments to his chiefs.

It has never been discovered which branch of German Intelligence intercepted the message, but certainly Himmler was not informed. Müller showed it to Bormann, to make the best use he could
of this discovery. Himmler further compromised himself by seeing
Langbehn on his return from Switzerland and hearing his report. In
1943, Himmler was still powerful enough to ride the storm, but he
was obliged to cover himself by arresting Langbehn and cutting off
this contact with the West. ‡

Bormann and Müller thus blocked this attempt to open negotiations with the West, thereby rendering Stalin a great service. Since
the Teheran Conference, Stalin had been haunted by the thought of
his allies making a separate peace with Germany.

---

* Schellenberg, op. cit., p. 397.
† See pages 304–305.
‡ Müller and Bormann acted with such determination that the whole operation
may well have been a put-up job. Allen Dulles, head of American Intelligence
in Switzerland at the time, has categorically denied that the message was sent
by any Allied agent. A possible explanation of this mysterious "intercepted
message" is that Müller heard of Langbehn's mission from one of his informers
(the German Resistance was the most talkative of any Resistance movement),
and that Müller decided to bring the matter to Hitler's notice in the form of
an "intercepted" message—which was a forgery.

Paul Leverkuehn, one of Admiral Canaris's assistants, has told how his chief disliked Nazism but hated Communism, and that the only redeeming quality he saw in the former was its implacable opposition to the latter. But the secret leanings of some prominent Nazis seemed to be weakening this antagonism. Leverkuehn writes: "He was extremely worried about the situation revealed by the discovery of the Red Orchestra, being convinced that the network stretched into Hitler's own H.Q. and possibly to his deputy, Martin Bormann." * And the head of the Abwehr called Bormann the "brown Bolshevik." †

Schellenberg writes: "In 1945, having a very clear idea of the general situation and being quite aware of the danger he [Bormann] was running, he was one of the first to try to go over to the East." ‡

And again: "This conversation [with Müller, reproduced above] took place at the time Müller had just made his intellectual *volte-face*. He no longer believed in a German victory and thought the best way out was to make peace with Russia, a solution which was in keeping with his methods. Judging by his actions, his idea of the relationship between State and the individual had never been a German conception, nor National Socialist, but purely Communist. How many converts had he made and pushed into the camp of the Eastern powers?"

And Schellenberg concludes: "His animosity toward me cost me dearly in worry and energy . . . *especially when, toward the end of 1943, I discovered that he was in communication with the Russian secret service.*" §

With a slight variation in the date, Wilhelm Hoettl of the SS Intelligence service renewed and extended the accusation: "Early in 1944, Schellenberg had suspected that Müller was using 'turned' radio operators to make real and sincere contact with the Russians. He stated that he had obtained proof of this after having several of the radio operators watched. In any case, he told Kaltenbrunner, Heydrich's successor, that he was prepared to supply proof of his allegations. Kaltenbrunner did not take the matter seriously and put Schellenberg's accusation down to professional jealousy. However, Schellenberg persisted and said that if Kaltenbrunner did nothing he would

---

* Paul Leverkuehn, *German Military Intelligence*, p. 197.
† "Brown Eminence," "Brown Bolshevik"—from the brown shirt of the Nazi uniform.
‡ Schellenberg, *op. cit.*, p. 397.
§ Schellenberg, *op. cit.*, p. 400. Italics by the author.

keep his proof for a later date, so that people should know that the head of the Gestapo had worked for the Russians." *

In April, 1945, when Berlin was encircled by the Red Army, most of the Nazi leaders had already left the threatened capital—but not Bormann or Müller. Wild scenes were taking place in the Chancellery bunker.† Loyal followers were committing suicide; Goebbels died with his wife and five children; Hitler and Eva Braun put an end to themselves. But, Trevor-Roper wrote, "there was at least one man in the bunker who thought only of living—Martin Bormann." He seemed immune from the general hysteria; calm and undismayed in the midst of madmen, as though this "twilight of the gods" was no affair of his, as though the sun would always rise for him, and intriguing up to the last.‡

Then he disappeared from the scene.

Müller had not taken up his quarters in the Chancellery bunker. He went there regularly to report, but returned at once to the Kurfürstenstrasse building to which Gestapo headquarters had moved after being bombed out of the Prinz Albrecht-Strasse. Its underground shelter was as safe as Hitler's and it had some not inconsiderable ad-

---

* W. Hoettl, *op. cit.*, p. 302.
† One scene was indicative of how far Müller had become separated from the SS hierarchy. Hitler had just been told that Himmler had opened negotiations with Count Bernadotte to bring about an armistice with the Western powers. His fury was as great as his amazement—"faithful Heinrich" had betrayed him! A witness later stated that he raged like a madman. His face went brick-red and he was almost unrecognizable. The whole of the SS was suspected of treachery, bribery and corruption. But Himmler and his crew were out of reach of Hitler's fury. Luckily, there was a scapegoat at hand—Fegelein, an ex-jockey risen to become an SS general and Himmler's representative with the Führer. He had married Eva Braun's sister, so was more or less Hitler's brother-in-law. But such family considerations weighed little with Hitler. And whom did he charge with interrogating Fegelein and making him confess his betrayal? Heinrich Müller, an SS general himself and Himmler's colleague! This choice shows that Hitler did not consider Müller as belonging to the SS, and that the gulf between him and Himmler was well known.
‡ He was even capable of black humor, as appears in his words to some young staff officers in the bunker—"He started to talk about Wenck's troops and the imminent relief of Berlin. Then, in his usual emphatic way, he added: 'As for you who have been loyal to our Führer and have lived through the darkest days with him, you will be rewarded with high posts in the state when we have won the war, and be given large estates for your loyal service.' Then he smiled graciously at us and went off with the utmost assurance." That was on April 27, three days before Hitler's suicide. (See Gerhard Boldt, *La Fin de Hitler*, Éditions J'ai Lu, p. 141.)

vantages. Secret little rooms—accessible only through ingeniously disguised doors—were well equipped for a long stay. There was
electricity and water, stocks of food and medical supplies. Several
tunnels, one a mile long, led to emergency exits. Adolf Eichmann had
called this underground lair "the foxhole." Müller had made it his
residence when Berlin was encircled. With him was his loyal lieutenant, Scholtz, who was responsible for the technical side of the radio
game.

"Schellenberg stated that Müller was still in radio communication
with the Russians after going to ground in his 'foxhole.' If this was
really so, it would give great support to Schellenberg's allegations.
For what man with any sense—and Müller had plenty—would continue trying to dupe the enemy by a complicated procedure when
that enemy was victorious and no more than a mile or two away?
So, if Müller really did use his transmitter as Schellenberg affirms, it
is extremely likely that he was in sincere contact with the Russian
secret service." *

The supposition that Müller went on transmitting almost under
the tracks of Russian tanks cannot be dismissed as fanciful or merely
a shot in the dark; for we have already seen Pannwitz, Müller's
subordinate, transmitting within four hundred yards of French tanks.†
And if Müller's determination bears out the truth of Schellenberg's
allegations, what can be said of Pannwitz's obduracy in keeping in
contact with the Center *several weeks after the end of the war?*

Bormann's fate after he left the Chancellery bunker has been
much discussed. Organizations specializing in the hunt for Nazi
criminals are now certain that he is alive and in South America.‡ As
for Müller, who disappeared with his faithful lieutenant Scholtz, a
grave in his name was found in the ruins of Berlin and he was officially
reported dead. But when it was decided to exhume the body to
establish its identity, the grave was found to contain the remains of
three men, all younger than Müller at the time of their death. Schellenberg wrote: "He went over to the Communists in 1945, and I was
told in 1950 by a German officer who had been a prisoner in Russia
that he had seen Müller in Moscow in 1948, and that he had died soon
afterward." § But Jacques Delarue, member of an international or-

---

* W. Hoettl, *op. cit.*, p. 303.
† See page 434.
‡ Eichmann confirmed this after his capture by Israeli agents.
§ Schellenberg, *op. cit.*, p. 401.

ganization engaged in tracking down fugitive Nazis, wrote: "A much later report speaks of Müller being with Bormann in Chile." *

Had Bormann and Müller really used the Red Orchestra transmitters to enter into genuine contact with the Center? The answer is to be found in the hundreds of messages exchanged with Moscow; but they are not available. Instead, let us examine what evidence there is.

Canaris's accusation that Bormann had connections with the Red Orchestra can be dismissed as mere gossip—at most, as a statement without proof. As for the conversation between Schellenberg and Müller, it is highly suspect, like the whole of Schellenberg's memoirs, which were put together with the help of journalists. Schellenberg was writing several years after the events described, and could hardly have remembered every remark made by Müller. Besides, it seems very odd that a man like Müller, so careful and secretive, should have made such confidences to a rival. It would be asking for trouble, almost inviting Schellenberg to set a watch on the "turned" radio operators. And after the war Schellenberg never did publish his proof —as he threatened Kaltenbrunner he would—which does not necessarily mean that he never possessed it. As a prisoner of the British, Schellenberg saved his neck by telling all he knew to Intelligence officers.† His proof perhaps lies in a safe in London.‡ As for Hoettl, he only repeats and enlarges upon the allegations of Schellenberg, his chief; and in any case he does not claim to prove anything. He is interesting insofar as he shows that there was indeed a "Müller affair," and that Schellenberg's condemnation of Müller after the war was not just an invention to give spice to his memoirs.

Müller and Bormann made a skillful move over the Langbehn affair, but their aim is not clear. Was it to nip in the bud any negotiation with the West, or simply to enable Bormann to score off Himmler—or perhaps both? We shall probably never know. And as long as there exists the possibility that they acted merely out of self-interest—and the sabotage of the Langbehn mission was a result and not the aim—it cannot be deduced that the two associates were playing a double game.

It is true that they reduced the radio game to a mere thorn in the side of the Allies, whereas Himmler had conceived it as the lever for

---

* Delarue, *Histoire de la Gestapo* (Paris: Fayard, 1962), p. 444.
† Schellenberg was released in 1951, and died the following year.
‡ If so, it will probably stay there for a very long time.

a new diplomacy. The radio game could produce results only if used on a grand scale; as Schellenberg pointed out, contact had to be made with Moscow at the same time as negotiations were opened with the West, to hasten the split between the Allies. But the fact remains that it was Hitler who overestimated the tensions in the enemy camp, and felt sure that the alliance would finally break up of itself. Hence the disillusioned comment of a former official in the Foreign Ministry who had been connected with Operation Bear: "Either Hitler did not want to turn the radio game into a diplomatic reality, or he was not capable of doing so. And there was no Talleyrand in Berlin to take the matter in hand."

Another theory is that Bormann and/or Müller used the radio game to secure their future by sending authentic information to the Center. Perhaps they played their own little game within the big radio game. It is declared that Bormann very liberally fed the radio game, to the horror of the ministers concerned, as they saw such important information transmitted to the enemy. But this cannot be accepted as proof. It is also said that the attempt on Hitler's life on July 20, 1944, left Müller with a free hand. Hitler put an end to Operation Bear; the group of experts was disbanded. But the Gestapo continued the radio game on its own account, and with no further obligation to submit to higher authority the messages sent to Moscow. And this gave Müller the opportunity to enter into sincere contact with the Center at very little risk to himself. But the fact that the opportunity existed is no proof that he took it.

In fact, every smallest detail is full of contradictions and varying interpretations. This is hardly surprising. If Bormann and Müller succeeded in betraying their country without being discovered by any of their compatriots, except perhaps Schellenberg, historians will be very lucky to find proof of this betrayal. Those two, so clever at undercover work, were well able to cover their own traces.

Perhaps they should be given the benefit of the doubt.

Only they, of all the Nazi leaders, were ever suspected of working for Russia, and by two such utterly different men as Canaris and Schellenberg, each of whom had his information from a different source. They were placed high enough to see the signs of inevitable defeat; they were clear-sighted enough to accept that defeat, as, unlike many others, they were not blinded by fanaticism. Heaven knows they had much to fear from that defeat, but they happened to possess a means of making early contact with the most realistic of their enemies. They chose to stay in encircled Berlin, although the Führer had allowed his entourage to flee and all the necessary false papers and escape routes were available to them. They clung to the condemned capital together with the last handful of fanatics and romantics, and they were neither fanatical nor romantic. Then, at the last hour, they disappeared—and have never been found. *All* the other leaders of the Third Reich were captured or their bodies were found. It is not perhaps just by chance that the only Nazi leaders to escape retribution had been so closely associated with the radio game.

However, let us see what Heinz Pannwitz, the former *Kriminalrat*, now living in Stuttgart, has to say.

39. The Hunter's Last Gamble

The youthfulness of Pannwitz's appearance is altogether remarkable. True, he was only thirty-two when he was put in charge of the Kommando, but one might have expected his features to show signs of all he had been through; in fact, they are quite unmarked. His face is round and smooth, with no visible bone structure, and despite the iron-gray hair, he has the complexion of a young girl. The eyes behind his glasses are alert. He is short, rather thin and full of restless energy. He smiles a good deal and chatters tirelessly, hopping from subject to subject. His joviality is of a somewhat peculiar kind: he will embark on an anecdote and laugh until he nearly chokes—nothing could be more infectious. And then gradually, his temper begins to rise; his eyes harden, and soon he is bawling with rage and hammering the table with his fist.

Twenty years ago, his wife must have been a magnificent specimen of the Master Race: tall and erect, with the ringing voice and flaxen hair of a Valkyrie. She has never got over having to leave the splendors of Prague in 1945; she and her children were put aboard an open truck, with no possessions, not even a suitcase. She speaks of the Czechs as if they were some obscure primitive tribe, but lavishes love and attention on her two dogs.

They have three children, including a boy who plans to be a gardener and a girl training to be a welfare worker. Pannwitz receives a pension from the Bonn government. He works in a bank specializing in building loans, but a recent thrombosis has made him take things easier. He owns a rather ancient Mercedes. Their apartment is small, well-furnished, pleasant. Obviously they are not rolling in money, but they lead a comfortable, middle-class existence.

He began by asking which intelligence service had sent me; he couldn't decide whether it was the American C.I.A. or the French S.D.E.C.E. My reply did not seem to carry much weight. "If it's true," he growled, "you really get the palm—you're the first person ever to approach me on his own initiative." When the Russians finally released him, after more than ten years, he fell afoul of German, American and British Intelligence, all of whom tried to make him confess his true reasons for going to Moscow. He was subjected to the lie detector, but emerged victorious.* For years afterward, he received visits from former colleagues, brimming with sympathy and clapping him on the back. "Listen," they would say, "strictly between ourselves, what exactly was behind that trip to Moscow?" One of the most persistent was Reiser, who also lives in Stuttgart. He invariably came armed with a handsome present for Frau Pannwitz. "Far *too* handsome," Pannwitz comments with a smile. "I realized he couldn't possibly be paying for such gifts out of his own pocket, so I stopped seeing him." Various emissaries from the Western intelligence services still persevere in attempts to get the truth out of him. He maintains that his telephone is tapped, his mail opened, his visitors spied on by the German secret-services of General Gehlen. And his tone, when he tells of these things, is certainly not that of a compulsive liar, but rather of a man complaining that his concierge doesn't like him.

The fact is that I had traced him without help of any intelligence service, through someone who, like Pannwitz himself, had held high office under the Third Reich. It was through this third party that I had opened what proved to be delicate negotiations with Pannwitz. He did not rule out the possibility of an interview, but hinted at certain conditions. And it took several months before he admitted that these would be of a financial nature. I told the go-between to offer him five hundred marks—a modern equivalent of thirty pieces of silver. Even then he would not commit himself. But he asked me to

---

* According to Pannwitz, the lie-detector technique leaves much to be desired. For instance, the suspect is asked the most brazen questions about his sexual fantasies. If sufficiently shrewd and uninhibited, he will react with the utmost calm; whereas the ordinary, decent human being who never dreamed of such eccentricities is terribly shaken. His palms begin to sweat, and his heartbeats quicken. His interrogators infer that he is lying, even though that is not the case.

come and see him, and I interpreted the invitation as a veiled acceptance.

Under the circumstances, he answered my questions with a surprising reticence. He deliberately sidestepped, treating me to one rambling anecdote after another, never providing a coherent picture of events. I even had the impression that he was annoyed to see me taking notes. Why should that be? What was he after?

There was one topic on which he was willing to speak fully: the death of Madame Spaak. Whenever he spoke her name, a flicker of anxiety came into his eyes. Nervous enough at best, at these moments he was like a hunted man rehearsing the justifications he would have to give a jury. Haunted by the dead woman's ghost, he invoked it again and again, perhaps in an attempt to exorcise it; and all the time he spoke, he mechanically went through the motions of washing his hands. He protested, he shouted, he swore to his innocence. He repeated tirelessly: "In Moscow, the Big Chief accused me of being responsible for her death. But if the Russians had seriously believed that, if they had the slightest proof of it, I would never have come back alive." And again: "The mere fact of my going to Moscow shows I had a clear conscience. The Red Orchestra agents executed under my command had been sentenced to death before I appeared on the scene. *I could go before the Russians with clean hands.*" And again: "I took the precaution of having two war correspondents attend her interrogations. Would a man who thus assures his retreat then commit the folly of covering himself with blood?" Finally he asked: "Anyway, why would I have wanted her killed?"

Trepper has his own answer to that question: "Because he could not afford to leave behind someone who knew all about the great radio game. Pauriol and Madame Spaak would have been able to tell their rescuers that the Kommando was engaged in a *Funkspiel* at Moscow's expense." The argument does not lack force. It is quite true that Pannwitz could not risk having the Americans or the French informed of his *Funkspiel*, for they would have warned the Center at once. But if Pannwitz's contacts were authentic—"sincere," as Hoettl calls them—what need was there for concealment? Besides, Pannwitz could have silenced Suzanne Spaak and Fernand Pauriol without killing them: he could have taken them to Germany with Kent and Yefremov. One would have expected Pannwitz to spare their lives, if only out of prudence. It would not have been surprising if he had ordered the killing of Pauriol, a militant Communist. But Suzanne

Spaak was the sister-in-law of a prominent politician on the winning side.

Pannwitz was so deeply conscious of this fact that he wrote a letter from Germany to Paul-Henri Spaak, the Belgian foreign minister. "Your sister-in-law is well," the letter stated. "We have been obliged to take her with us, but you may rest assured no harm will come to her." The minister was in London when he received this news and immediately set out for Paris to tell his brother Claude; but by this time the latter was already certain of Suzanne's death.

The Big Chief sees this letter as a final and damning piece of evidence in the case against Pannwitz. In his view, it is a monumental piece of hypocrisy, for Pannwitz knew he had not taken his prisoner with him; its sole purpose, therefore, was to confuse the issue permanently. Even before that letter, the names of the two martyrs had been omitted from their graves to make identification impossible. The message was to make the Spaaks believe Suzanne was still alive, so that Pannwitz could later claim she had disappeared in the chaos of the defeat, and entirely without his knowledge.

This is possible. It is equally possible that Pannwitz sincerely believed that Suzanne Spaak had been transported to Germany with the other prisoners from Fresnes. The absence of names on the crosses is open to various interpretations. But if the authorities were bent on concealing all trace of the executions, they would hardly have marked the graves with the words "a Belgian woman," and "a Frenchman," which pointed to the identity of the bodies. Last, and above all, why was Suzanne Spaak allowed to write that final letter telling her husband she was about to be executed? The existence of this letter, plus the fact that Pannwitz was unaware of it (or he would not have bothered to write to Paul-Henri Spaak), strongly suggests that he had no hand in the tragedy at Fresnes. I have already remarked that Pannwitz in Paris was a very different man from Pannwitz in Prague.

After January, 1944, French prisons were opening their gates to certain grim visitors who always came in threes, armed with French and German documents giving them free disposition of the inmates. These were the executioners of the French militia. Sometimes they gave a semblance of formality to the proceedings, for a Vichy law enabled them to set up as court-martial and pass sentences without appeal, executed on the spot. On these occasions, they would arrive with a firing squad and a supply of coffins. Jacques Delarue, the Resistance worker who spent some time in the Santé Prison, did not actually see these courts-martial in operation (those who did never lived to tell the tale); but from the depths of his cell he often heard the macabre sounds which accompanied them—from the arrival of the trucks laden with empty coffins, to the hammering of the lids over the dead bodies.* On other occasions, the executioners would turn up without a firing squad and do their own killing. Dominique Ponchardier, who killed some of these butchers, recalls how they "would drive from town to town, flourishing papers, genuine or forged, [and] commandeering batches of captured Resistance workers, selected purely at random. They would take them out into the countryside and, unbeknownst to Vichy or even to the German authorities, line them up by some quiet lane and calmly machine-gun them." †

This may well have been how Suzanne Spaak and Fernand Pauriol met their deaths—at the hands of Frenchmen.‡

———

I kept trying to elicit Pannwitz's true reason for going to Moscow. Each time he countered my question with one of his own, which never varied: "Which intelligence service sent you here?" In three days of almost uninterrupted talks, I managed to get past his guard only three times. Once I congratulated him on his courage in having bearded the lion—or rather, the bear—in his own den. "Don't be a fool!" he said derisively. "The British and Americans never stopped broadcasting the fate they had in store for people like me. I had no illusions on that score. In leaving for Moscow I went directly into hell, it's true. But there, at least, I'd be able to help heat up the fires!" He also told me his decision had been long and carefully considered: by 1945 he had a foolproof escape route into Spain, but in the end he had chosen Moscow. How had he known he wouldn't be shot within an hour of arriving there?

"Listen, a car was waiting for me at the airport and took me straight to the Ministry of Security. Abakumov, the minister, received me at once, and we talked for two hours. That alone ought to show you that various steps had been taken before my departure, and I wasn't blundering around in the dark." Vague as they were, these three items of information confirmed the statement a Kommando member, Otto Schwab, made to the French police at the Cherche-Midi prison in 1947: "Kriminalrat Pannwitz told me confidentially that if Germany lost the war he would not remain with the Ameri-

---

* Jacques Delarue, *Histoire de la Gestapo* (Paris: Fayard, 1962), p. 397.
† Dominique Ponchardier, *Les Pavés de l'Enfer*, p. 225.
‡ Madame Pauriol, however, is convinced that her husband was executed by the Germans.

cans. On the contrary, he would take refuge with the Russians and place himself at their service."

On the third day, he suddenly asked me, "Well now, on what basis are we going to work, and how will we organize that work?" Flabbergasted, I replied: "But we already are working, aren't we?"

He scowled, appeared to hesitate, then took the plunge: "Your offer of five hundred marks was obviously not serious—why, that's chicken feed! Let me tell you that an American movie company once offered me a hundred thousand dollars for my memoirs. At that, it wasn't even my memoirs: all I had to do was guarantee the movie's authenticity. There was to be a credit saying something like. 'Ex-Kriminalrat Pannwitz guarantees that the story we are presenting to you is fully in accordance with the historical facts.' But the Americans reserved the right to put whatever they liked in the script. I went into the matter with a few friends. We decided that by the time I paid the tax, there wouldn't be enough money left to buy the desert island I'd need to escape the wrath of my former colleagues! So I turned it down. For the past ten years, German publishers have been hounding me for my memoirs. I've refused them, too. Present political conditions aren't right for it. I *may* decide to come to some arrangement with you, but certainly not for five hundred marks!"

I replied that if I were in a position to spend a hundred thousand dollars on research, I probably wouldn't bother: I'd retire to a desert island of my own. Five hundred marks was as high as I could go. If it wasn't enough, we'd have to part company.

And I really thought that would be the end of it. But he immediately came up with a proposition he felt would settle the whole thing: we would share the author's royalties, and in return he would tell me all he could remember about his Kommando days; he would even allow me to preface my book with the celebrated seal of authenticity: "Ex-Kriminalrat Pannwitz guarantees . . ."

It was hard to control my astonishment. When I had agreed to paying him thirty pieces of silver, it had never occurred to me that he might suggest going into partnership, thus making me his literary collaborator—the "ghost," in short, of SS Hauptsturmführer Pannwitz, ex-Kriminalrat, et cetera. I finally told him that all I wanted from him was a candid statement of his motives for going to Moscow. But he remained as evasive as ever and suggested a compromise formula: "There are two hypotheses: I may have gone there because I felt I could be of use to Germany one last time. Equally, I may have gone because I had been in touch with them, quite genuinely, for a long time past. In my view, it's better to leave the issue undecided; simply lay the alternatives before the reader and let him form his own conclusions. That would be quite effective, don't you think? It would introduce an element of mystery, it would add suspense. . . ."

I agreed, but pointed out that the whole purpose of my visit to Stuttgart had been to reduce suspense. He begged me to consider the potentially explosive nature of his revelations and the grave consequences they might entail for him. Finally, he told me that our three days of talks had been merely exploratory: he had wanted to find out with whom he was dealing. He was reasonably well satisfied and had now asked one of his friends, Thomas Lieven, to come and join us. Lieven was his unofficial adviser in this matter, and Lieven's verdict would clinch things one way or the other.

Pannwitz found it hard to believe that I did not know of Lieven. He pointed out that the German writer Mario Simmel had written an international best-seller based on Lieven's reminiscences, *Es muss nicht immer Kaviar sein.* There had been two movie versions of the book, which had sold a million copies in Germany and many more in the rest of the world. When I subsequently came to read it, I soon realized it was clear that its success was due to the outstanding qualities of its hero. Lieven emerged as a miraculous blend of Batman, Robin Hood, Rothschild, Casanova and Lucullus. With his astonishing good looks, good humor and wealth, he had gone through the Second World War running rings round every intelligence service in the field and showing an appropriately amused commiseration for their puny attempts to trap him. Only the Gestapo had roused him to anger. Thomas Lieven did not like the Gestapo and had made his dislike painfully clear.

I told Pannwitz that I was delighted by the prospect of meeting Thomas Lieven.

While we were waiting for him, we talked about General Ozols and Paul Legendre and the services they had rendered the Kommando. Pannwitz assured me that the two men had been convinced, from start to finish, that they were working for Soviet Intelligence. On August 16 Kent had taken leave of Ozols, informing him that he was setting out on a "very dangerous mission," giving him thirty thousand francs, and urging him to carry on the good work. According to Pannwitz, that gigantic hoax of the transmitters installed in Normandy —proved a stunning success; several weeks after D-Day, they were still sending them information from behind the Allied lines.

Pannwitz did not know what had later become of his two un-suspecting victims. As it happens, I did know of their subsequent fate, and found it perplexing. On November 17, 1944, Ozols and Legendre were arrested by the French authorities on charges of col-laborating with the enemy. The Germans had managed to plant sev-eral German agents in the Mithridate network, and these had informed on Legendre; by giving the enemy a list of the organization's members, he had, they insisted, exposed it to infiltration and partial dismantle-ment. It would probably have been very hard for Legendre to explain his conduct to a French court and to convince his judges that he had sincerely believed he was furthering the Allied cause. Similarly, Ozols would have had the greatest difficulty proving that he had been un-aware that Kent was a Gestapo agent. But the two men were never brought to trial. *Lieutenant Colonel Novikov, head of the Soviet mission in Paris, went to the French authorities and intervened on their behalf.* He vouched for them, and as a result they were released. Legendre was not questioned further—much to the amazement of his former colleagues in Mithridate. Ozols was repatriated to Russia.

Novikov's intervention is thought-provoking enough; but the affair of the Normandy transmitters is, perhaps, even more significant. It was imperative for the German High Command to ascertain, at a very early stage, whether the Anglo-American landings represented a full-scale invasion or were simply a raid. Stalin was equally anxious for information; angered by the continual delays in opening the sec-ond front, he suspected his allies of wishing to limit themselves to a repeat performance of the Dieppe raid. As early as July, 1942, when talk of a second front had just begun, the Center flashed the follow-ing message to the Big Chief: "Make every effort to install a trans-mitter at each strategic point at which an Anglo-American landing may occur and arrange for us to receive accurate and detailed reports every two days on the disembarked forces and their objective."

It may well be that two years later, instead of Trepper it was Heinz Pannwitz who carried out the Center's instructions, while re-maining, to all outward appearances, a loyal servant of his own coun-try.

We also talked about the Swiss network. For the Russians had also established a spy ring on that distant planet, as Switzerland seemed in relation to the rest of wartime Europe. Its members were engaged in the same work, as Trepper, Schulze-Boysen, Harnack, and all the others, but their distance makes it hard for us to see their activities as forming part of the same pattern. What comparison can there be between Agent A's life in a small, peaceful country and Agent B's life in a continent gripped by war and ruthlessly patrolled by the Gestapo? Agent B knew that capture meant almost certain death by hanging or shooting; he also ran the risk of being savagely tortured. But the Swiss police were internationally renowned for their correctness and restraint—any agent caught in Switzerland would probably be let off with a severe reprimand from the Swiss magistrates; at worst, he might be jailed for a few months.*

The decision to exclude the Swiss network from this narrative was not prompted by these dissimilarities, nor by an erroneous belief that the network's achievements were in any way paltry. On the contrary, I was well aware that it had brought off the most astonishing coups. However undramatic its history may have been, in terms of effectiveness it was a match for the entire Red Orchestra. The American historian Dallin observes that its "contribution to the Soviet victory was of paramount importance." † One of its members, the Englishman Alexander Foote, goes even further: "In fact, in the end Moscow very largely fought their war on messages from 'Lucy' [one of the network's informants], as, indeed, would any High Command which had access to genuine information emanating in a steady flow from the High Command of their enemies." ‡ Finally, two French authors go so far as to claim that "the war was won in Switzerland." § This may be an overstatement, but it is not entirely without foundation.

My reason for neglecting the Swiss network is that it formed a separate entity, operating independently at the heart of the Swiss enclave, whereas the Nazi hegemony united the Red Orchestra's German, Belgian, Dutch and French networks into a single body: they were battling, in identical conditions, against the same pursuer. And indeed, that pursuer never included the Swiss network under the generic title "Red Orchestra"; they gave it an individual code name, "the Three Reds," because it employed three transmitters.

The code name showed a proper appreciation of the facts, for the importance of the Swiss group lay primarily in those transmitters.

---

* The stiffest sentence imposed on a member of the Swiss network was ten months' imprisonment. There were a number of acquittals. Some prisoners were released without being brought to trial.
† David J. Dallin, *Soviet Espionage*, p. 182.
‡ Alexander Foote, *Handbook for Spies*, p. 76.
§ Pierre Accoce and Pierre Quet, *La Guerre a été gagnée en Suisse* (Paris: Presses de la Cité, 1966).

It was not so much a network, in the customary sense of the word, as a relay station—a kind of "letterbox" into which information was slipped for immediate transmission to Moscow. Normally the quest for "sources" (the network's task, of course, was to spy on Germany, not on neutral Switzerland) takes up most of a network's efforts; but in this case it was no problem at all—the informants volunteered their services. The majority were refugees, and militantly anti-Nazi. The most valuable of these was Rudolf Rössler, alias Lucy, who was able to draw on the services of agents working in the key departments of the Third Reich, notably the High Command. Alexander Rado, the head of the network, never knew who Rössler's sources were. In vain did the Center seek to establish their identity. They remain unknown to this day, whatever may have been written or said, and the Western intelligence services are still making every effort to unmask them.*

---

* It has sometimes been suggested that Schulze-Boysen and his friends were among Rössler's sources. No evidence has ever been advanced in support of this theory; indeed, it is belied by all the facts which have so far come to light. The reports furnished by the Berlin network on one hand, and by Rössler's agents on the other, were not of the same category. Schulze-Boysen had access to sectors—e.g., the economic sector—which remained closed to Rössler; whereas the latter seems to have been far better informed about purely military matters. Moreover, had Schulze-Boysen been in a position to send his reports via the Three Reds, the inexperience of his own pianists would not have been such a stumbling block; nor would the Center have dispatched Kent to Berlin in such hazardous circumstances.

It is significant that the disappearance of the Berlin network during the summer of 1942 in no way affected the quantity or quality of the messages Rössler passed to the Three Reds—as it certainly would have done, had he previously been supplied with information by Schulze-Boysen's network. (Besides, the Abwehr's listening posts reported that after the Berlin transmitter went off the air in November, 1941, there was a directly proportionate increase in the volume handled by the Brussels "PTX" transmitter.)

Finally, it is clear from one particular incident that Schulze-Boysen did not have an organized method of piping information to Switzerland. In 1942, Horst Heilmann informed him that the Abwehr had broken a British code. Schulze-Boysen realized that the British must be informed at once and cast about for some way of reaching London's representatives in Switzerland. He contacted a certain Marcel Melliand, who was known to be in sympathy with the network's activities and was fairly confident of being able to get to Basel. He agreed to warn the British embassy about the code and, at the same time, reveal the Luftwaffe's plans to attack an Allied convoy sailing from Iceland to Murmansk. In the end, however, he was unable to obtain his visa, and there the matter rested. Obviously, if Schulze-Boysen had been in constant touch with the Swiss network, he would have lost no time in sending these two items to Rössler. The latter would certainly have passed them on to the British, for in addition to working for Soviet Intelligence he was employed by the secret services of Switzerland and the Western Allies.

The fact that these investigations still continue so long after the end of the war indicates how desperate and ruthless they must have been in the days when every message from the Three Reds was a stab in the back for the Wehrmacht. Rado's pianists were subjected to the same technological warfare as Trepper's—at first long-range detectors, then short-range detectors. It did not take the Germans long to discover that one transmitter was in Lausanne and the other two in Geneva. Their telegrams were duly recorded and passed on to Kludow's team of code breakers. As with the Red Orchestra, a few messages were successfully deciphered. And there was the same feeling of terror and bewilderment when these revealed that really vital secrets were being passed to the enemy in a steady flow. Unlike the Red Orchestra's pianists, however, those of the Three Reds were reasonably safe from the Abwehr and the Gestapo: the Swiss frontier was an effective safety curtain. Force was out of the question; the German security services had to resort to guile. Their aim was to infiltrate the Swiss network, discover its sources, and destroy it from within.

The captured members of the Red Orchestra could well lead to the Three Reds. For although the two groups operated independently, they obviously never quite lost touch with each other. Malvina Gruber, mistress of the Brussels "shoemaker" Abraham Raichman, announced that she had crossed the Franco-Swiss frontier a good many times between 1940 and 1942. Kent acknowledged that he had gone to Switzerland on two occasions, in March and in December, 1940; while there, he had met the head of the network. Several passports found in the possession of Robinson, the former Comintern leader, bore entries proving that he had crossed the Swiss border time and time again.

These, then, were the cards Giering held in his hand. Which one should he play? Malvina Gruber, like her friend Raichman, had been employed so extensively by the Kommando in Paris and Lyons, that her credibility as a loyal member of the Orchestra was now exhausted; there could be no question of sending her to Switzerland. Kent had been out of touch since 1940. Robinson, on the other hand, had two things strongly in his favor: he was an important agent and he had had recent contacts with the Swiss network.

Giering decided to use Robinson as his trump card. But first he had to be broken and turned into a tractable tool. He was subjected to worse torture than almost any other member of the Red Orchestra, but even the most savage treatment failed to make him talk about his previous contacts with the Swiss network. Whereupon the Kommando, predictably, resorted to blackmail. Franz Schneider—the husband of Wenzel's mistress—had disclosed the name and address of a German woman serving as courier between Berlin and Brussels. The woman was Klara Schabbel; she lived in Hennigsdorf. According to Schneider, Klara was Robinson's wife. In fact, she had lived with him in 1920, when Robinson was a young man engaged in an armed struggle to establish Communist rule in Germany. They had had a son. The Gestapo arrested Klara Schabbel and discovered that the son was in the Wehrmacht; he had been wounded on the Russian front and was now recovering in a Berlin hospital. Heinz Köhnen, who had parachuted into East Prussia on October 22, 1942, admitted that his mission had been to contact the wounded man with orders not to let himself be invalided out, but to try to get himself posted to an important military headquarters, where he could obtain information.

The Gestapo staged a confrontation between father and son.

Robinson was overcome. He had been unaware that his son had recently joined the Berlin network; he now realized that the young man had been influenced by his own militant politics. It was partly on his account that the poor boy (he was only twenty-one) had stumbled into the clutches of the Gestapo. The latter proposed the usual deal: the son's life in exchange for the father's revelations. Robinson would not talk. He was subjected to further torture, but still he would not talk. He was then tried before Manfred Roeder, who sentenced him to death.*

Giering realized that he would have to fall back on Kent. The latter suggested using Vera Ackermann, alias the Black Woman. Vera was a beautiful, charming Belgian, a veteran of the Spanish Civil War;

---

* Klara Schabbel went to the scaffold on August 5, 1943, with fourteen members of the Berlin network. But was Robinson himself executed? Roeder, Reiser, Fortner and Pannwitz all maintain that they were officially informed of his execution. No record of any such execution is to be found in the German archives, however. And there is more to it than that: whereas the Gestapo's reports and the statements of Reiser, Fortner and Pannwitz unite in lauding his heroism, discordant voices are raised in the opposite camp. "When he was caught, that one did plenty to save his skin," asserts the Big Chief. "The Gestapo found a mass of documents in his hotel room, together with duplicates of all his reports. Why had he broken the rule against preserving papers? To whom had he been planning to sell them?" Thus an enormous question mark hangs over the life, and even the death, of this elusive, rather romantic figure. Yet, whatever doubts may be entertained about him, one thing is clear: he did not put Giering on the track of the Swiss network.

Incidentally, Robinson's son was not executed.

her husband had been killed while fighting in the International Brigades. Trepper had recruited her in Brussels, where she had been working as an artist's model. After 1940 he had summoned her to Paris. Her primary function there had been liaison with Robinson and Maximovich, but on occasion he also sent her to Switzerland on urgent business.

Giering was jubilant, for here was the ideal *agent provocateur*—but where, in fact, *was* the Black Woman? Kent had no idea, but claimed that Trepper knew her address. Trepper denied this indignantly. A brief, fruitless search was made for her. "It makes no odds," said Giering. "I don't need your Black Woman. I can easily send someone else who will pass for her." And he asked the Big Chief to draw up a message informing the Director that he was transferring the Black Woman to the Swiss network. "To the Swiss network?" exclaimed Trepper. "Oh, that's awkward! I can't tell you exactly where she is hiding, but it's very possibly in Switzerland. If you send a fake Vera Ackermann there, she may get a chilly welcome—and you'll have put them on guard for nothing." Giering conceded that the risk was not worth taking. He dismissed the plan from his mind.*

But he did not give up his efforts to penetrate the Swiss network. How could he, when this last bastion of Soviet espionage was the primary objective of Germany's combined security forces? He knew he must leave no stone unturned in the attempt to reduce the Three Reds to silence.

Kent proposed an alternative course of action. Alexander Foote, one of the heads of the Swiss network, recalls:

Early in June [1943] I received instructions from the Center to meet a courier from France and hand over some money to him for the French network. I was given four different days and two places as rendezvous. . . . It was only at the last rendezvous . . . that an individual came up to me and we exchanged the correct passwords and I handed over the money.

The Director had ordered me to have no conversation with the courier, but merely to hand over the cash and go away. However, the courier handed over to me, in his turn, a large book done up in a bright-orange paper, and told me that between two of the pages I should find three ciphered messages which must be sent off urgently by radio to the Center. He also said that he had valuable information which he wanted

---

* Trepper had sent the Black Woman into hiding at the time of the first wave of arrests in Belgium, where she was known to several members of the network. She continued to lie low, in the vicinity of Clermont-Ferrand, until the end of the war.

to get over, and suggested a further meeting as soon as possible and named a place near Geneva which was also very near the German-controlled French frontier.

All this made me very suspicious, as such loquacity against strict orders was unusual in a Soviet agent. I began to suspect that perhaps the original courier had been arrested and his place taken by an Abwehr agent. The orange paper would serve as a convenient beacon light for anyone who was trailing me home, and the meeting place near the frontier would serve admirably for an abduction in the best Gestapo traditions.* As for the cipher messages, if these were also phony, then they would serve as admirable pointers toward identifying my transmitter. I had no doubt that the Germans had long been monitoring the network, and, if on one of the services that they were listening to they suddenly found the three messages that they had planted, it would at once identify that transmitter as mine.

I tried to dissemble my suspicions as much as I could and said that I could not attend a meeting for that week, as I had business elsewhere, and so fixed on a meeting in a week's time.†

Foote's intuition was sound: the emissary was one of Giering's agents. At Kent's suggestion, the head of the Kommando had calmly asked the Center to organize the rendezvous—and the Director had walked straight into the trap. The conception was masterly, even if the execution suffered through undue haste (the orange paper, the talkativeness, the fake messages, the rendezvous at the frontier—all this was more than enough to arouse the suspicions of an experienced agent). Foote did not turn up at the second rendezvous. Giering recognized his own blunder. Nevertheless, he had effected a sizable breach in the Swiss bastion. He had only to show a little patience, let a few weeks or months go by, and the Center would probably be quite prepared to arrange another meeting. By then, Foote's suspicions would have been allayed by the lack of unpleasant repercussions from the earlier encounter. He would have no reason to stay away.

But at this point cancer put Giering out of action. What steps did his successor, Pannwitz, take?

None whatever.

"As soon as I arrived in Paris," Pannwitz told me, "Kent disclosed that it was he who had furnished the Swiss network with its transmission code. I believe this happened around 1940. The code was based on a technical book published in Kiev; only a very few copies

---

* Presumably a reference to the "Venlo incident."
† A. Foote, *op. cit.*

had been printed. But I had no intention of following it up. I was not in the least interested in working against the Swiss network, and I took care not to organize a second rendezvous. Why? For two reasons. In the first place, I already had enough to do. And if Berlin had known I was in a position to act against the Swiss network, they wouldn't have given me a moment's peace. Besides, I was anxious not to turn Kent into a complete traitor. It was important to preserve his image, you see; to leave him something he hadn't given away."

At those astonishing words, I wondered if there was any point in waiting for Thomas Lieven; Pannwitz had told me quite enough! His failure to employ every available means of destroying the Swiss network was high treason in itself. He knew the role of the Three Reds and their terrifying efficiency, and that every one of their messages cost innumerable German lives on the eastern front. He was not so overworked that he hadn't found time for highly profitable business trips to Spain on behalf of Helvetia, his private company. His observations about Kent were even more revealing, however. If he was "anxious not to turn him into a complete traitor," it was because he was clear-sighted enough to realize that Germany had lost the war, and that Kent would have to account to Moscow for his actions. Against this day, Pannwitz was "preserving his image" so that Kent might return the compliment. Kent would emerge as the man who had not betrayed the Swiss network, and Pannwitz would emerge as the man who had not asked him to do so.*

◆

Thomas Lieven was a disappointment. He was a tall, thin man about sixty-five years old, with a weak mouth and rather tough look. There was something soft and evasive about his manner, which showed the cynicism of a man well-acquainted with the seamy side of life. He said· "I've worked for everyone, and I've betrayed everyone, but I've never ratted on a friend." In addition to financial security, Simmel's bestseller has also assured him a happy old age—he has begun to believe that he really is as the book describes him, a man of many parts, all of them exceptional.

---

* This may be pure coincidence, but veterans of the Funkabwehr accuse Gestapo-Müller of sabotaging their work against the Swiss network. (The charge is leveled, for instance, in W. F. Flicke's *Agenten Funken nach Moskau*, published by Verlag Welsermühl Wels.) He used to hide their reports in the drawers of his desk, never showing them to his superiors and never taking the steps they advocated. When General Fellgiebel, head of the Wehrmacht's Transmissions Corps, personally undertook to look into the matter, the files relating to the Swiss network mysteriously disappeared.

He leaned toward me and said: "Listen, I'll let you into a secret. Thomas Lieven isn't my real name. Take a look at this book." The book was *The Secret War of Josephine Baker*, written by a Commandant Abtey, late of the Deuxième Bureau. He devotes a chapter to Lieven, whom he describes as "the most extraordinary human being I have ever met." He does not call him Lieven, but Mussig.

With an absurd, pedantic pride, I cried: "Ah! Hans Mussig, alias Jean Varon! You had a woman friend named Georgette Dubois, alias Patricia Delage, alias Anne-Marie Rendière!"

The room went very quiet. Eventually Mussig said: "All right. Well, there's no further point in pretending you aren't a secret service man: only a well-informed agent could possibly know the facts you have just given." I told them of my long years of research, the nights spent poring over faded documents, and the obsession that enabled me to remember the birthdays of minor agents and pursuers even though I had difficulty in recalling those of my own family. They condescended to believe me. Feelings simmered down. Lieven recovered his serenity.

Hans Mussig! He joined the Nazi Party in its early days and held office in the Hitler Youth. After a time he slipped into France, for undetermined reasons,* and placed himself at the disposal of the Deuxième Bureau. After the fall of France, he retreated south and became a black-marketeer, which resulted in his arrest by the Gestapo in 1943. He was sent to Fresnes prison. Pannwitz released him from his cell to make him his interpreter (he spoke fluent French). So from 1943 until the end of the Occupation, Mussig belonged to the Kommando—whereas the biographical novel built around him never tires of harping on Lieven's bitter hatred of the Gestapo. It is quite true that he did not betray his superiors in the Deuxième Bureau (hence Abtey's glowing words of praise); but how could he have denounced them without denouncing himself?

He obviously knew all about Pannwitz's project for our "literary collaboration." I explained that Pannwitz's evasiveness kept the plan from being very tempting. "Oh come, come," he said airily, "if he doesn't tell you the whole story, I'll tell you myself." Pannwitz pleaded an engagement in town and left us alone. Mussig folded his

---

* According to a recent work by Commandant Abtey, Mussig helped himself to the funds of the local branch of the Hitler Youth in revenge for his political disappointments! (J. Abtey, *Deuxième Bureau contre Abwehr*—Paris, La Table Ronde, 1967—p. 147.)

hands over his belly, stretched his legs, and examined me with a calculating eye.

"Now look here," he said softly, "are you an idiot or are you
playing a game?"

"What game?"

"Pretending you don't know what happened. His dealings with
the Russians. Surely the truth is plain enough?"

"Not enough for me."

"You are funny. Can you really picture him walking into the
lion's den, in 1945, without first taking careful precautions? If so,
you don't know him very well! Believe me, there weren't many ordinary Germans who would have gone to Moscow in those days, let
alone members of the Gestapo! I can't claim I caught on at the very
beginning; it wasn't possible. Oh, we got on well together from the
moment he got me out of Fresnes. He was surrounded by tired, boring
cops, and it gave him pleasure to have someone to talk to, someone
who was up to scratch, as you might say. But at the same time our
difference in rank kept him from really confiding in me. I certainly
smelt something fishy; I was convinced he was hatching something—
but what? He didn't tell me. On the other hand, he did tell me,
and he made no bones about it, that Germany was finished! You can
take my word for it: by the time he arrived in Paris, Pannwitz was
convinced the war was lost. And that's the kind of little detail that
makes all the difference. As I say, I didn't catch on at the time, but he
told me the whole story when he came back from Russia. It turned
out to be perfectly simple, perfectly logical, as you'll see.

"Put yourself in his place. Here was a man up to his neck in
trouble as a result of his activities in Prague. I take it that you know
all about the Heydrich assassination? And about the repression which
followed? Then I don't have to tell you they didn't do things by
halves: it was a real bloodbath! So our friend Pannwitz was in the
soup. And believe me, he was under no illusions; the BBC branded
him as a war criminal, promising that he'd be hanged, and so on.
Afterwards, in Berlin, he saw his superiors secretly insuring themselves against the future. Most of them were fishing for guarantees
from the West. But Pannwitz found himself moved to Paris, with
orders to carry on a *Funkspiel* with the Russians, and he decided that
they were the people to come to terms with. It wasn't only because
it gave him technical facilities for conversing: he told himself that the
Russians were realists and wouldn't shed crocodile tears over the poor

Czechs, and that they were only interested in practical results.
Whereas with the Western countries, it was something else! You only
had to hear the BBC to know that! Pannwitz was convinced they
would hand him over to the Czechs without any shilly shallying, and
I think he was right.

"The funniest part of all—or the saddest, if you prefer—was that
in the end he was convinced he had done far more than save his own
skin. He felt sure he'd get a hero's welcome from the Russians! Just
think: before flying off, he put one final present for them into his
briefcase—a complete record of the diplomatic telegrams exchanged
between London, Washington and Paris for several months past. They
had been intercepted by our monitoring units. Quite an offering, no?
He knew they'd interest Moscow tremendously. He genuinely anticipated making his home in Russia, sending for his wife and children
and carving out a nice, cozy little life there. It didn't exactly turn out
like that, as you know. The Russians were really rotten to him. They
kept him in jail for nearly ten years and then threw him out as though
he had some disease. Back here, in Germany, Gehlen's men and the
Americans thought he had defected and come back as a spy, and they
gave him the lie-detector test! You see the irony of it: he who had
fondly imagined he was shrewder than the rest, was now being put
through the hoop by former colleagues who were now back in business with Gehlen or the Americans. He felt he had got the worst of all
worlds.

"And now? Now he thinks he can rake in a fortune if he tells
his story, but he doesn't dare take the plunge. He's afraid. Haven't
you noticed he is a frightened man? You see, his main source of in-
come is his pension as a *Kriminalrat*. Oh yes, it's quite normal for him
to receive it: the Federal Republic is legal heir to the Third Reich and
has to pay pensions. But suppose he describes his past acts of treason,
what will happen then? The Republic will say, 'Look here, we don't
have to pay good money to a man who betrayed the Reich! The Reich
would have stood him up against a wall and shot him; therefore we,
as legal heir, are under no obligation to support him! It is my duty to
pay a pension to a *Kriminalrat*, but not to a *Kriminalrat* who has been
a traitor.' So you see, he'd be kissing his pension goodbye. And he's in
bad health, he has his children to consider. But what bothers him even
more than the pension is the possibility that the whole thing may
backfire. A story like this could easily set the sparks flying. And that's
why he has turned down every offer until now. And then suddenly
you appear on the scene, looking like the answer to all his problems.

In the first place, you're young—which means you're not personally embroiled in the events of the last war. In the second place, you're French, which is a big point in your favor. He doesn't want a German to do the story—that would be out of the question. But it's easy enough to repudiate anything a foreigner may say or write. Anyway, if things get too hot, he can always take his newfound wealth to Switzerland and stay there, out of harm's way.

"Well, that's the whole story. Are you happy?"

Afterward, everything happened very quickly. Pannwitz came back with the contrite but relieved look of a penitent who has bared his soul through a third party. I asked him whether he was hoping to go down in history as the most extraordinary double agent of the Second World War. "That wouldn't be true," he replied. "I never ran the show. It wasn't on my initiative that we began to make sincere contact with the Russians. What was I, when all is said and done? Just a link between Moscow and a group of people in Berlin. I would never have got involved if I hadn't received backing and protection. Indeed, once you know how the *Funkspiel* was organized you'll realize that it would have been impossible for me to perform as a lone operator." He also expressed the wish that his treason should be invested with a certain ideological hue. Some of the July 20th conspirators had taken a pro-Moscow line, he said, and it would be nice if his name could be linked with theirs.

To find out more, to obtain an elucidation of the part played by Bormann and Müller, to secure answers to all my queries, I would have to accept a deal which could obviously never be honored, and play a double game with this master of the double game. But I was unable to go through with it. This man filled me with an almost physical revulsion. As the Big Chief remarked, "Giering was a rough, thorny customer to deal with, but at least you knew where you were with him. Pannwitz was slimy. In his presence, you felt dirty."

A few weeks later, I received a letter inviting me to a meeting with a Swiss publisher. I did not reply.

Perhaps one day we shall know the full truth about the great radio game; but we may wait a long time, and it probably will not come from Moscow. The Kremlin will keep quiet for political reasons. The East German authorities hide the true nature of the work carried out by Schulze-Boysen and his friends, for fear of reviving the legend of the "stab-in-the-back" with which German nationalists sought to explain their defeat in 1918. Any publicity given to the treasonable activities of people like Bormann and Müller would enable the neo-Nazis to launch a similar campaign, and claim that, but for this accursed pair, the "pure" Nazis would have led the Reich to victory. But the important point is not whether Bormann and Müller were guilty of treason, nor even whether their treachery contributed to Germany's defeat. The important point is that the Nazi regime was of a kind that allowed creatures like Bormann and Müller to rise to key positions.

Those two may still be wrapped in mystery, but Pannwitz's game seems to be clear. After the death of Heydrich, he attempted to switch sides; this, his first maneuver, ended in defeat and cost him a few hard months on the banks of Lake Ladoga. Subsequently, he doubled his stakes and pinned all his hopes on Moscow; the loss of this second round led to his spending ten years in the Lubianka prison and at Vorkuta camp. The deal which he offered me represented a third round: he was hoping to cash in on his past treason, whatever storms it might unleash. There will be other rounds. Kriminalrat Pannwitz is too much of a gambler to stop there.

40. The Long Wait

On May 8, 1945, VE-Day, investigations into the Red Orchestra embarked on a new phase. German counterespionage had dealt some severe but rather haphazard blows to the organization's structure. Now the British, the Americans, the French, the Belgians and the Dutch took over. Their resources were greater. Above all, they were able to carry on the quest with patience and continuity—for, unlike the Germans, they had the time. Their preliminary aim was perfectly reasonable and self-protective: they were anxious to find out how many Red Orchestra agents had survived and whether they were still in business. This is why Claude Spaak, Georgie de Winter, and all persons connected with Simex or Simexco were placed under surveillance. The advent of the Cold War did more than perpetuate this attitude of suspicion; it exacerbated it to such a degree that some of the network's veterans began to wonder whether their past activities were not being held against them, quite as much as any present ones.

They even began to wonder whether it had become a crime to have helped the Russians win the Battle of Stalingrad. Most of them had only a slender understanding of the vast events in which they had been involved (it is the hallmark of a well-constructed network that only the people in charge are allowed a comprehensive view), and this sudden wild distortion of the facts finally convinced them of the world's insanity. (They were already aware of its ingratitude, having been refused recognition as members of the Resistance.)

There is no finer example of this general intellectual confusion than the trial of Abraham Raichman. In June, 1944, having squeezed the last ounce of usefulness from him, the Kommando characteristically expressed its gratitude by throwing him into a Brussels jail. On September 2, just before the Allied troops reached the city, he and the other inmates were put aboard a train bound for Germany. This was known forever after as the "Lucky Train," for the Belgian Resistance prevented it from leaving and set the prisoners free. Raichman was tried by a court-martial convened in Brussels shortly after the end of the war. He was indicted on three counts. The prosecution charged him with working for Soviet Intelligence prior to May 10, 1940 (this was going back a long time!) and with cooperating with the Gestapo after his arrest (the court appears to have been less concerned over this than over the rest of it); it further arraigned him for his espionage activities between May 10, 1940, the day Belgium came into the war and June 22, 1941, the day when Barbarossa was launched and when Russia became the ally of the Belgian government-in-exile. The prosecution conceded that the existence of this alliance legitimatized Raichman's *subsequent* work at the expense of the German invader, but nobody questioned the need to punish him for his activities before the alliance came into effect. Thus, at the very time when the Communists were being hotly accused of keeping out of the fray until after Barbarossa, Raichman's sentence was extended because he had started fighting the Germans in 1940. It really seemed as if membership in the Red Orchestra was sufficient to expose a man or woman to a paradoxical fate.*

---

* The court-martial sentenced Raichman to twelve years' imprisonment; his mistress, Malvina Gruber, was jailed for four. In 1948, while they were both serving their terms, United States counterintelligence in West Germany arrested Malvina's son, Eugene Gruber, on charges of forging passports for the use of Soviet Intelligence. Gruber had been too young, at the time, to work for the Big Chief. It was not until after the war that he followed the family tradition and set up as a "shoemaker." Frantisek Klecka, Manfred Roeder's cellmate (see page 430), is the only member of the Red Orchestra who is known to have carried on espionage activities after May 8, 1945.

The Western intelligence services displayed an immediate practical interest in the Red Orchestra, but lost some of their enthusiasm when successive investigations showed that the survivors were quite harmless. Theoretical interest, on the other hand, sharpened as time went by (nowadays a study of the network has a firm place in the curriculum of every spy school). The West was anxious to find out all it could about an organization which, in size and effectiveness, surpassed all previously known networks, somehow combining supreme professionalism with the fervor and idealism of a Resistance group—a blend which had given rise to a masterpiece of intelligence organization.

Since the leading members of the Red Orchestra were not available for questioning, every attempt was made to elicit information from their opponents. The hunt for members of the Kommando began long before hostilities were over, and the Allied authorities did their best to round up all Abwehr or Gestapo agents known to have worked against the network. The French grabbed the lion's share, seizing Reiser, Schwab, Ball, Richter and many others. The Belgians hung on to Fortner and the Brussels Gestapo team. The British took Koppkow to Edinburgh. The Americans had to be content with Roeder, but this was of no real consequence, for the time was not far distant when the intelligence services of western Europe would have no further secrets for their American big brother.*

So the Red Orchestra was discussed for years afterward, in prisons all over Europe. Nowhere was it discussed at quite such

* The interpreter Siegfried Schneider slipped through the net, and no one knows what has become of him. If he should ever chance to read these lines, he can rest assured that his memory is still alive in the hearts of the men and women to whom he behaved so charitably. Their gratitude does not stem solely from the small material services which he rendered them: he has a beam of light among the shadows, living proof that humanity and kindness were capable of flourishing even in the grim world of the Gestapo.

According to some reports, Willy Berg was loyal to his profession of faith: after the war he joined the East German police. If these reports are true, then he has—as he foretold—served under the Kaiser, under the Weimar Republic, under Hitler and under Ulbricht (successor to Thaelmann, who perished in a Nazi concentration camp). In the eyes of Berg's former colleagues, this final transformation is proof that he deliberately allowed the Big Chief to escape. Yet surely, if this were so, Trepper would be aware of it. According to a psychoanalyst, Berg's behavior is a perfect example of what is known as an "abortive act." Unconsciously, he was anxious to help Trepper and wanted him to escape, but this latent desire remained blocked at the conscious level, so that Berg was able to claim in perfect good faith that he had not been a party to the deed: he had made the escape possible without even realizing the fact.

length as in the Lubianka jail, where the richest haul was gathered: Trepper, Pannwitz, Kent, Wenzel and Ozols.

What exactly did the Director wish to learn from them?

———◆———

It would be intellectually, if not emotionally, satisfying, and in keeping with certain current trends,* to believe that the Center had seen through the great radio game from the very beginning and that this clairvoyance had been the cause of its implacable treatment of the members of the Red Orchestra.

If we accept that theory, the rest is quite straightforward. The Director—realizing from the outset that the pianists Wenzel, Yefremov and Winterink had defected—fully anticipated the explanation that Giering subsequently gave Trepper: the destruction of the network and the capture of its leaders were no longer ends but means. What, then, were the Germans really after? The Director did not know, but was itching to find out. It must be something extraordinary, of really crucial importance, or the enemy would never have hatched so costly a scheme. He bided his time. And naturally he pooh-poohed Trepper's warnings, simulating an unshakable sense of security: his telegrams might be intercepted (many of them were), or the Big Chief might be arrested (as he eventually was), and the Germans must not be allowed to gather, from the telegrams or from the Big Chief, that Moscow had seen through their game—for this would undermine a conspiracy which the Director felt sure would turn out in his favor, *since he knew the conspiracy was afoot.* His implacable attitude was a nightmare to Trepper and the members of his Old Guard, making them feel that their sacrifices were in vain and that they would soon be dying to no purpose; yet that attitude was fully justified by higher considerations. Or so the argument runs.

There is a fairly common tendency, at present, to devise brilliant and impressive justifications for out-and-out blunders on the part of secret services. Secret agents themselves are all in favor of this: they would far rather be thought unfeeling than slow-witted. If a general botches an attack, the wholesale slaughter of his troops is enough to convict him of total incompetence. But a secret-service chief is a very different matter. Point out to him that his networks have fallen, like ripe fruit, into the enemy's hands, and he will wink at you and

---

* Consider *The Spy Who Came in from the Cold*, and other novels of the same school.

whisper complacently, "Ah, yes; I had to sacrifice them to keep on fooling the enemy!"

Just occasionally, espionage lives up to its reputation for high drama. More often it is a tragicomedy, the tragic element being supplied by the enemy and the comic by the people back at headquarters. Take, for instance, the security checks devised by Britain's Special Operations Executive. These security checks took the form of prearranged errors which radio operators had to incorporate in all their messages; the absence of such errors would reveal that they were transmitting under duress. The importance of the measure cannot be overstated: this was the only way in which agents could warn London of their "defection." Every S.O.E. radio operator was told: "If you are caught, collaborate in the *Funkspiel*—but, remember about the security check!" One of these pianists fell into the hands of German counterespionage, which of course insisted on his transmitting under their control. He feigned acceptance, but carefully omitted the security check from his message. He had now discharged his duty to the full. Imagine the poor man's bewilderment when, in full view of the Germans, he received the following reply from London: "Watch it, old boy, your mind must be wandering: you left out your security check." The story is authentic, and I could quote a dozen like it. Indeed, it would be possible to compile an endless list of the monumental oversights and irreparable blunders perpetrated by the secret services of every nation.*

Admittedly, the task is not simple. A secret-service chief is like a man living on another planet. He has little knowledge of the battlefield or of the enemy's numerical strength and technical resources. It took London months to discover that the Germans were systematically recording all the messages exchanged with its networks—a slow, painstaking process which enabled them, once the code was broken, to trace the history of each individual network and ascertain all its ins and outs. The Director's insistence that Red Orchestra pianists must transmit for hours at a stretch was partly due to his ignorance of the Funkabwehr's advances in radio detection; he did not believe that

---

* Strictly *technical* oversights and blunders. Secret services can hardly be blamed for the incredible bungling which so often attends the exploitation of agents' reports. It was Stalin's fault, not the Center's, that the urgent warnings given by Sorge, Trepper, Rado and others were simply not heeded. Likewise it was the French High Command's fault, not the Deuxième Bureau's, that no notice was taken of reports clearly indicating where the Wehrmacht planned to launch its offensive in May, 1940.

transmitters could now be located so easily and swiftly. (His disbelief persisted as late as 1945 and cost Kriminalrat Pannwitz a painful beating.) A few months of war and the twenty miles of water between Dover and Calais were enough to turn France into a land of mystery in which even British Intelligence had difficulty in finding its bearings. So it is easy to imagine the confusion of the young bureaucrats who staffed the Center after the purges. Most of them had never set foot outside Russia. The countries of Europe were as remote from them as Patagonia. While Pannwitz was being interrogated by one of them, he happened to say: "So I caught a train from Hamburg to Munich—" The Russian immediately pulled him up. "Be more precise," he objected pedantically. "First you had your domestic passport stamped by the police . . ." Pannwitz goggled. He thought this must be a joke. Finally he realized that the interrogator imagined that Germans, like Russians, needed police permission to travel from one city to another.

Yet even the handicaps of geographical distance are as nothing compared with the misunderstandings caused by the psychological gulf between the home base and its troops. Sooner or later, the loneliness of his work induces the head of a network to imagine that he is the hub of the universe. He treats his parent unit as if it were a firm of suppliers and bitterly resents being treated, in turn, like an expendable pawn in a game of chess. His comrades in the field are his flesh and blood: he would move mountains to save them; but to the men at headquarters, the network's members are so many faceless troops. The deaths of Katz and Grossvogel, deeply upsetting to Trepper, were seen by the Director in the light of over-all Soviet casualty figures: an average of five or six thousand men a day. This fundamental incompatibility of outlook, continually reinforcing the practical misunderstandings described earlier, quickly makes the head of a network feel that he has been forsaken, if not betrayed. And his reticences and accusations prompt the head of the service to entertain doubts about his diligence, perhaps even his loyalty. Neither is really to blame for the decline in their relationship. On the one hand there is a hunted spy, too close to events to see them in perspective; on the other, a staff officer living in an isolated, bureaucratic world.

This, I believe, is how things were between the Director and Trepper.

◆

In the eyes of the Big Chief, Fortner's raid on the house in the Rue des Atrébates constituted a serious defeat and was the harbinger of even greater disasters; he ordered his agents in Brussels to lie low for six months. The Director found it hard to understand why a minor setback should entail such stringent security measures at a time when Russia was struggling for her existence. Red Army generals did not grant spells of leave to their buffeted troops: on the contrary, they at once hurled them into the attack. Trepper replied that as the man on the spot he was the better judge of what ought to be done. It is true that the Director was not on the spot—and he had no more reason for being on the spot than a commander in chief has for being in the front line: his duties require him to hold aloof and preserve a broad strategic view of the battle. But these tactical disputes were of little account. There was a basic clash of principle between the Director, who for various reasons had cheerfully sacrificed the Berlin group, and the Big Chief, for whom no security measure was superfluous if it would save the lives of his men. His extreme caution was termed chicken-hearted at the Center. Could it be that Trepper was beginning to lose his nerve?

It certainly seemed so when he announced that the pianists had been arrested and were now working for the other side. We must remember that the idea of a *Funkspiel*, though familiar today, was a novelty in 1941. The *Funkspiel* was the outstanding innovation in the field of espionage in the Second World War. The Director might have caught on to it had the allegedly renegade pianists sent him a series of colossal lies; but they did nothing of the kind. Was he really expected to believe that the Gestapo would destroy a network only to carry on its activities? Trepper stuck to his guns, gloomily prophesying the worst, while the pianists in Belgium made everything seem fine. Next, Trepper resorted to protests and threats; he committed an act of disloyalty, indeed of positive treason, against the Center by entrusting his most important messages to the French Communist Party's transmitters. These messages went straight to Dimitrov's office instead of to the Director's; and they were patently designed to sow panic and foster suspicion. Via Dimitrov, Trepper was telling the all-powerful Central Committee of the Soviet Communist Party: "It is possible that traitors have crept into our secret service."

Ah, this was more than enough to make the Director succumb to the congenital vice of Soviet Intelligence: distrust. At the Center, people are constantly being suspected of one thing or another—of leftist deviationism, rightist deviationism, being too partial to women, not altogether indifferent to men, having a weakness for money, being a Trotskyite, working for the British. . . . If a network is doing badly, the man in charge is assumed to be guilty of sabotage; if it is doing well, then he must be a double agent, otherwise things could never be going so smoothly. As for Trepper, ever since the start of the war he had done nothing but criticize and complain. He had shown the wariness of a snake when the situation called for the audacity of a lion. He was always moaning about not having enough transmitters. Was he a traitor? Perhaps not, although it had been unwise to put him in touch with people like Robinson (probably in the pay of the Deuxième Bureau) or Ozols (possibly in the pay of the Gestapo). No, perhaps not an out-and-out traitor, but a man who wasn't up to his job. The Director kept a sharp eye on him.

He lost track of him in November, 1942. Was he even aware that the Big Chief had been arrested? Impossible to say for certain. Three months later, the trilingual message reached the Center. The Director couldn't believe his eyes! What was he to make of it, and how had Trepper managed to send it? There was surely no chance of its being a genuine report drafted and transmitted under the Gestapo's nose. The Director did not believe in fairy tales. In Moscow—as in London and Washington—everyone had formed a clear mental picture of the Gestapo. There was no room in that picture for Giering soothing his cancer with brandy, for old Berg drunk by midday, and for nightly binges at Suzy Solidor's. The Gestapo was seen as a harsh and infallible police machine. As if it would allow prisoners to write messages as and when they chose! As if it would take them on joy rides through the streets of Paris!

The following theory presented itself: Trepper, an enemy agent, had failed to shake the Director's confidence in the Brussels pianists; the trilingual message might be another step in the same direction, a further attempt to discredit the Brussels group—the only part of the network still loyal to Moscow. On the other hand, transmission via Jacques Duclos was in itself a guarantee of authenticity. Duclos would never have accepted a document of doubtful origin. He had made his inquiries and acted in full knowledge of the facts. Besides, there was this "great radio game" Trepper kept talking about. . . . It was confusing!

According to Reiser, the Director's confusion lasted three months: in May, 1943, the messages received by the Kommando became distinctly guarded and suspicious; the Russians displayed a newfound appetite for specific details. According to the Big Chief, it took the Center four months to verify his report: by June, 1943, Moscow was convinced of its truthfulness. My own belief is that this conviction dates from the second week of June. It will be recalled that at the beginning of June he had ordered one of the heads of the Swiss network, Alexander Foote, to meet an emissary of the French network. He had made it clear that Foote was to "have no conversation with the courier." Was this a mere precautionary measure dictated by Trepper's warning? It is supposable that the Director had decided to use the meeting as a test: if the messenger broke the rule of silence, it would mean that an attempt was being made to infiltrate the Swiss network—and this, in turn, would confirm the Big Chief's report. As we have seen, the results were conclusive: the loquacity, the book wrapped in orange paper, the coded messages handed over for transmission, the insistence on a second rendezvous. Foote himself writes:

> On leaving the rendezvous I hid the book as well as I could under my coat and returned home by a roundabout route, taking evasive action. In my next transmission I reported this fully to the Director, and he agreed that I should not attend the meeting. As regards the cipher messages, which were there as the courier had said, gummed between two pages and in a cipher that I did not know, the Director asked me to send them over, but so to disguise them with dummy groups and then by re-enciphering in my own cipher that they would neither be recognizable as the original messages to the monitors nor serve as a guide to our cipher to the crytographers.
>
> A fortnight later the Center informed me that my suspicions were correct and that the courier had been a German agent.*

---

* A. Foote, *Handbook for Spies*, p. 112. I have already described the meetings which took place in Stockholm between the German Paul Kleist and the Soviet agent Clauss (see p. 306). The second of these meetings, and the most important, took place on June 18, 1943—i.e. at about the time when the Center, finally pinning its faith on the trilingual report, informed Foote that the French emissary was an enemy agent. It is possible that the unexpected turn taken by the negotiations in Stockholm can be explained in the light of the great radio game. On his return to Berlin, Kleist—who had acted on his own initiative and in the greatest secrecy—had the unpleasant surprise of being arrested as soon as he stepped off the plane. Later, he found out the reasons for this black welcome: "Clauss, wondering whether I really would transmit Alexandrov's offer, had sought out the German military attaché in Stockholm and delivered a message to him. The military attaché had telegraphed his superior, Admiral Canaris, and the latter had informed Hitler. His telegram said: 'The Jew Clauss states that the Jew Alexandrov is in Stockholm awaiting the arrival of a German negotiator. Unless the latter presents himself within four days,

Thus the Foote episode marked the end of the Director's uncertainties, *but it had taken him a year to come to believe in the defections which the Big Chief had announced time and time again.* Was this a sign of stupidity? Yes and no. It had been the Center's bad luck, at a time when such procedures were not yet part of the normal pattern of espionage, to play guinea pig to a most amazing *Funkspiel*—miles in advance of the standard methods of interservice duplicity, since its aim was not technical but political, and since the importance of the stake had prompted its authors to send only authentic information at first, thus preventing the Director from seeing that he was being duped by the Kommando.

The revelation afforded by the trilingual message enabled the Center to indulge in a few pranks, all the more remarkable in that Soviet Intelligence generally displays a sad lack of humor. As we have seen, the object of Foote's rendezvous had been to hand over funds for the French network. There were no perquisites for Giering and his gang. Like all intelligence people, nothing delighted them more than the chance of pocketing money belonging to the enemy.

Alexandrov will fly on to London and set the seal on the Kremlin's collaboration with the Western powers.' (P. Kleist, *Entre Hitler et Staline,* p. 213.) Obviously, such a summons could only rouse the Führer's ire; he saw it as an 'impudent Jewish provocation.' The ill-considered visit to the German embassy was a surprising act on the part of Clauss, who seems to have been a top-flight agent, shrewd, cautious, experienced and, furthermore, operating under the supervision of Madame Kollontay, the celebrated Soviet ambassadress to Sweden. That he should have allowed himself so spectacular a gesture, even going so far as to hand the German military attaché an invitation in the shape of an ultimatum, may stem from the fact that the Kremlin, finally alerted to the existence of the great radio game, had logically deduced that Berlin was eager to negotiate and that the matter could therefore be conducted in the most blunt and open manner.

It should be added that German historians take the view that Stalin entered into the Stockholm talks for the sole purpose of putting pressure on the West by dangling the threat of a separate peace settlement between Russia and Germany; according to this view, the talks were really no more than a great radio game *a la Russe.* (See *Die Sowjetische Deutschland Politik,* by Boris Meissner, Europ Archiv, 1951.)

Further, it must be emphasized that Moscow's publication of an article accusing the British of meeting Ribbentrop in Spain (*Pravda,* January 17, 1944) does not contradict the fact that the Russians had known about the great radio game for the preceding six months. Stalin's obsessive fear of being betrayed by his allies probably made him see Kent's message as the first move in a major German diplomatic offensive; the article in *Pravda,* which was bound to receive worldwide publicity, seemed an excellent way of nipping any such offensive in the bud.

Thus, while reserving Paris for the *Funkspiel* proper, they were only too willing to use the three Belgian and Dutch transmitters for fundraising purposes.

Prior to Wenzel's escape in January, 1943, they had made him ask Moscow for some "expenses." A mysterious can of beans had arrived from Bulgaria; hidden among the beans were a hundred pounds sterling—chicken feed! After the trilingual message reached Moscow, the Kommando demanded further "expenses." The Center replied as follows: "Apply to Bodhen Cervinka, engineer, living in the Rue Edison, Brussels: he will give you five thousand dollars." An agent promptly called to see Cervinka, who threw him out with the utmost brutality. His sincerity was so obvious that the Kommando did not trouble him further. But the Germans did not lose hope of getting money out of the Center. A further attempt was made on Winterink's transmitter. After some evasiveness, Moscow asked where the money should be sent. The Kommando supplied the address of an ex-member of the Dutch Communist Party. At this, the Center slyly observed: "Are amazed. This man's connections with the Gestapo are well-known to us." A third attempt was made, this time using Yefremov's transmitter. Center: "Go and see X, a tombstone dealer in Charleroi: he has a debit account of fifty thousand Belgian francs in Moscow." When questioned about the fifty thousand francs, the tombstone dealer explained contentedly that the matter had now been settled; an Italian insurance company had reimbursed him. Reimbursed? So he was a creditor, not a debtor? Quite so: Moscow owed him fifty thousand francs! This little joke put an end to the Kommando's cadging, thus doubly rejoicing the Center, which was extremely tight-fisted with its rubles.*

But if the trilingual message enabled the Kremlin to see through the great radio game, and allowed the Center some fun at the Kommando's expense, it did not long succeed in maintaining cordial relations between its author and the Director.

---

* It is worth noting that eleven months after Wenzel's escape in January, 1943, Jojo and Michel—the two captured French radio operators who had apparently defected (see p. 363)—succeeded in making their getaway. Finally, in March, 1944, Winterink broke loose and vanished, after Moscow had instructed him, *on his German-controlled transmitter*, to link up with a Communist shock group. A real epidemic, which can be seen as the outcome of fraternization between prison guards and seemingly renegade pianists. It is also permissible to wonder whether Pannwitz may not have had a hand in this series of escapes, as an additional way of showing Moscow that he was in earnest.

Five months after the Foote episode, Trepper escaped. The Center was appalled by the news. By fleeing, he had jeopardized the great radio game and the advantages which Moscow was hoping to wrest from it; for the Kommando surely knew that the fugitive's first thought would be to expose the fraud to his superiors. And it also prompted fresh doubts concerning the Big Chief's loyalty. Escapes always made the Center terribly suspicious—with a distrust dating from prerevolutionary days, when the Tsarist police had attempted to plant *agents provocateurs* among the conspirators by passing them off as escaped prisoners. A Communist does not escape until he has sought and obtained permission from his superiors.* Otherwise he is treated with considerable doubt. Now, Trepper wasn't just any Communist and the Gestapo wasn't just any police force—could anyone seriously believe it would be so foolish as to let such a prisoner escape? True, the trilingual message gave evidence of the Big Chief's loyalty; but it was now eight months old. What had happened in the meantime? Perhaps Trepper was now a broken man, a defector in the fullest sense?

Then came a misunderstanding which merely served to intensify the Center's suspicions. As soon as he reestablished contact, Trepper suggested that the Director send an emissary to Paris to check his statements and generally examine the position at first hand. And whom did he suggest for the job? His wife Luba! In the Big Chief's eyes, there could be no clearer evidence of sincerity than this proposal which would put his wife in a position of great danger. But, as we know, the Director took a very different view. He saw it as an attempt by Trepper to retrieve Luba and "take a dive," as they say in Soviet Intelligence jargon—in other words, give up his work and break with the Center, either because he had betrayed, or simply because he was tired and disheartened by the Director's persistent failure to understand and trust him.

Either his escape was genuine, in which case it would bring the great radio game to an abrupt and unsatisfactory end, or it had been rigged by the Gestapo for purposes that remained a mystery. The Center must have been torn between these two hypotheses. A few weeks later came the grotesque message by which Pannwitz hoped to see the great radio game in motion again ("What news of Trepper? Everywhere I look, I see Wanted notices about him"). This threw the Director into a state of total confusion. He thought it unlikely

---

* In several instances, prisoners who had escaped without prior permission were ordered to give themselves up and go back to jail. And they did.

that Pannwitz held him in such low esteem as to hope to fool him with this crude trick. For to proclaim the Big Chief's escape was to admit that all his telegrams of the past six months had been sent under German supervision, was to disclose the existence of the *Funkspiel,* was to create such distrust at the Center that any future dissimulation would be a wasted effort. The Director could not make head or tail of it; nevertheless, he came up with the answer Pannwitz was expecting: "In our view, Trepper is a traitor. Let the Party not give him even a morsel of bread." And the Director waited. And it was not long before he realized, from subsequent messages, that Pannwitz didn't care about being consistent: his overriding aim was to maintain contact with Moscow, in the hope that the highly individual and "sincere" twist he proposed to give that contact would be sufficient to allay the Center's concern. The Director, who had expected to have to play a really subtle game, suddenly saw his adversary rushing straight into his outstretched arms: all's well that ends well.

Except where the Big Chief was concerned. For Pannwitz's sudden change of tack, though easy to explain in the light of Germany's approaching defeat and his desire to have his own skin, did not make the previous enigmas any more intelligible. And at this point Trepper made things worse for himself by proposing to kidnap the Kommando as it drove out of Paris! What was his motive? What incriminating documents or damning witnesses was he trying to get rid of? There could be no question of permitting it. The Director had just heard from Kent, who wanted to know whether to stay in Paris, where the Allies were expected at any moment. The Director's reply is worth quoting word for word: "Withdraw with your German friends. Do not desert these influential figures with whom you are on such good terms, and who supply you with such valuable information. They may be very useful to us later." It would be a fine thing if Trepper seized the whole outfit and was then obliged to hand them over to the French authorities! Pannwitz and Kent must be allowed to continue their work until the end of the war. Besides, men who knew so much must not be exposed to the risk of a stray, or a carefully directed, bullet.

How the Director must have relished the sight of the star performers arriving in Moscow one after another! First Trepper, then Kent and Pannwitz, then Ozols, then Wenzel. He held them all in the palm of his hand. Now at last he could get to the bottom of the affair.

Did it really take ten years for the French Communist Party and Kovalsky's M.O.I. to confirm the circumstances in which the trilingual message was conveyed to Juliette? Ten years to make sure that the escape was genuine? (After all, Willy Berg was available for questioning in Pankow.) Ten years to acknowledge that the Big Chief had been clearheaded in the midst of chaos, courageous in peril, ingenious in adversity—and quite unshakable, despite the relentless lack of understanding displayed by his superiors? It is not as if the Center had a reputation for slowness in conducting important inquiries. Six months had elapsed between the liberation of Paris and the Big Chief's flight to Moscow—insufficient time to clear up all the enigmas surrounding the Red Orchestra, but long enough for the Director to have had Trepper's statements checked in France. When the Big Chief eventually reported to Znamensky Street, many questions still remained to be put to him, but his basic loyalty was already beyond dispute.

And indeed the Director's opening remark was significant: "What are your plans for the future?" The inference was that Trepper had not forfeited the right to a future. But the remark also contained a veiled warning: the past was never to be alluded to—not at any price! By the nature of his answer, Trepper determined his own fate. He was in no mood to draw a discreet veil over the past four years. On the contrary, he was seething with indignation, brimming over with invective, hell-bent on squaring accounts. Such an attitude plainly marked him for Lubianka. *For the Director could not possibly allow an embittered man to roam free in Moscow, telling all and sundry that he had thrice warned Stalin of the coming German attack and had afterward spent years racking his brains in an attempt to right the Center's errors.* Had the Japanese not hanged him, Sorge too would have finished up in Lubianka, if he had returned to Moscow in the same frame of mind as Trepper.

Nor, surely, did it take ten years to calm the Big Chief's anger and teach him the merits of resignation. But as he had been sent to Lubianka for that purpose, he was kept there for other reasons. He was like a castaway swamped by successive ocean waves.

The first wave consisted of his colleagues—agents and network chiefs who, like himself, were back in Moscow after five years of working abroad. The Director did not recognize them. They were not the same men. War had made them fall back on their own devices and work out rules to fit an unforeseen situation; they had been governed not by the Center, but by changing circumstances. Scattered throughout the countries of Europe as spies, they had in a sense been naturalized by the struggle against the Nazi invader; they had teamed up with the national Resistance movements; men of completely opposite political opinions had become their brother in arms, fighting shoulder to shoulder.

Trepper said: "I knew Ozols had kept in touch with ex-members of the Deuxième Bureau. It didn't bother me in the least, for weren't we waging the same war?" Similarly, Rémy—a man of right-wing views—afterward wrote of the support he had given the Communist partisans: "In 1942, we thought only in terms of men and women engaged in the common fight to drive out the invader; we did not bother our heads about the political allegiance of this or that group." * Even Schulze-Boysen had attempted to warn London that one of its codes had been cracked by the Funkabwehr. The Center would have reprimanded him, had it known. In 1942, Alexander Rado, head of the Swiss network, came into possession of documents of enormous value to the British. He informed the Director and proposed that the documents be handed over by a reliable courier who had access to the British embassy in Bern. The Director turned this down and ordered the documents to be burned. In 1943, at a time when the Swiss police were fast dismembering his organization, Rado told the Center that there was only one way out: he must retire to an embassy and carry on his work under cover of diplomatic immunity. Since the Soviet Union had no embassy in Bern,† he suggested seeking asylum from the British, who as allies would surely be willing to help. The Director erupted at the idea. Rather than agree to this, he would watch the destruction of the entire Swiss network, even though its contribution was irreplaceable. Rado was under suspicion of working for British Intelligence; even so, he proceeded to Paris after the Liberation and reported to the Novikov mission. On January 6, 1945, he boarded the plane for Moscow, along with the Big Chief. But when the plane touched down at Cairo, his nerves got the better of him and he fled; the plane flew on without him. Moscow contacted the British authorities and denounced him as a deserter. Eventually he was picked up and handed over to the Russians. His artless belief that the fight against Nazi Germany took precedence over the old war against British Intelligence cost him ten years in jail.

---

* Rémy, *Mémoires d'un agent secret* . . . , Vol. 2, p. 53.
† Switzerland did not establish diplomatic relations with the Soviet Union until after the Second World War.

His colleagues returning from abroad shared his views, even if they had never revealed them to the Center. They had known the magic of international and interparty cooperation, and they would never forget the experience. In their absence, a new generation of young officials had taken over the controls at the Center. These cold bureaucrats gazed with hostile contempt at the old revolutionaries now returning to the fold: seasoned Party members who had miraculously survived the purges ("security risks"); veterans of the Spanish Civil War ("security risks"); men who had fought side by side with Resistance groups of every political complexion ("security risks"). They called them "romantics" and "cosmopolitans"; they damned them as "incurable."

"The worst of it is, they were right," I was told by one of these incurables. "We had become 'objectively' unemployable. Especially by a normal, peacetime secret service resorting to blackmail and all sorts of other low tricks. That was out of the question, after what we had experienced. And they were right, too, to call us 'cosmopolitans.' We had met too many people, sampled too many environments, spent five years fraternizing with people who were about to become our enemies again. You know, since then I've often thought that being gunned down by the Germans would have been better than being rejected by one's own people, knowing that they had good grounds for it and that they were right."

The Big Chief's status as an incurable would probably not have been sufficient reason to put him in prison, but it was a powerful motive for letting him rot there. The man now thought of as unfit for service had been one of the pillars of Soviet Intelligence. The Director, knowing what Trepper knew, preferred to keep him locked up rather than let him run loose, at the mercy of fate, or of temptation.

The second wave drowned the Director. It came from Canada, in September, 1945, with the discovery by the local police of a Soviet spy network directed by a colonel of the Center, and with the subsequent arrest of the "atom spy," Allan Nunn May, among others. This was a serious defeat. The Center's old rival, the K.G.B., took the occasion to settle a few scores. The Director and his deputies were retired from office. A further purge decimated Red Army Intelligence and brought disgrace on all its members, old and new alike. It was after the Canadian scandal that Abakumov, Minister of Security and a loyal follower of Beria, remarked to Trepper: "Just think, if you had been working for us instead of for those bastards at the High Command, you would have rows and rows of ribbons on your chest by now!" And, pointing out of the window at Red Square, he added with a smile: "Look, that's where you would have been proclaimed a Hero of the Soviet Union!"

The first two waves had been almost concurrent. The third broke three years later, in 1948, and it was a wave of anti-Semitism. It is too notorious for there to be any need to recall how strong it was and how long it lasted. Once more, Trepper was taken from his cell, through the underground passage connecting Lubianka with the Ministry of Security, and deposited in Abakumov's office. "Why did you surround yourself with traitors?" the minister asked. "Explain your purpose in giving all the key positions in your network to traitors!" "Traitors? What traitors?" asked Trepper. The minister reeled off a list of names: "Katz, Grossvogel, Springer, Raichman, Schneider—all of them Jews, and therefore traitors!"

In Moscow, the heads of the "Jewish Anti-Fascist Committee" were arrested. Among them were some of Trepper's oldest colleagues, dating back to the long-ago period (1935) when he had contributed to the Jewish newspaper *Truth*. Nearly all of them "confessed" and were executed.

A cosmopolitan, an incurable, a veteran of the Center, a Jew: in Stalin's Russia, this was more than enough to keep a man locked in Lubianka. But, even in Stalin's Russia, injustice was given the trappings of legality. An administrative "troika" tried the man who had created and managed the largest network in Europe, an organization the Western intelligence services were poring over, even at that moment, with a mixture of fear and admiration. The only charge that could be brought against him, after a thorough sifting of his five years' activity as head of the Red Orchestra, was that he had agreed to enter the great radio game without the prior consent of the Director. The Big Chief could not help remembering Giering's warning: "You'll be considered a traitor all the same. They'll say you couldn't have known at the start if you'd be able to warn them, so they'll accuse you of having bargained with us simply to save your own skin."

It was true: he had not known for certain that he'd have the chance to tip off the Center. But would it have been better to do nothing—just sit there and watch the disaster occur? He flung at his judges: "In short, I was in a burning house, and you reproach me for playing the fireman." He was well aware, however, that his protest was futile. Stalin's "troika" confirmed Giering's prophecy: Trepper was sentenced to fifteen years in prison.

———◆———

For Pannwitz, and even more for Kent, the Big Chief's presence in Moscow had come as a terrifying surprise. After Trepper's escape, the Director had continually pressed Kent for news of him: "Do you know where he is? Why doesn't he get in touch?" And later, following their withdrawal to Germany, the two confederates were informed: "Trepper has taken a dive. He has refused to return to Moscow." The implication was that nobody would be able to deny Kent's story, and that he could return to the fold without qualms: not only would he be credited with Pannwitz's "defection," but it would be quite easy for him to impute his own earlier acts of treason to the Big Chief. Kent had swallowed the bait whole. With Pannwitz's willing assistance, he had compiled a carefully edited dossier from which he emerged pure as the driven snow, while Trepper figured as an out-and-out renegade. With Trepper himself in Moscow, this caricature was obviously difficult to sustain, and Kent's bid failed. But the authorities were grateful to him for leading Pannwitz along the path to treason, and this gratitude saved his life.

Meanwhile, the Center could certainly not be accused of half measures in interrogating Pannwitz. He was questioned for a year and a half, then given four months' rest, then questioned for another year and a half. According to Pannwitz, the atmosphere was reasonably relaxed. He soon picked up enough Russian to understand questions as they were asked, which thus gave him time to prepare his answers while the interpreter was translating. On the other hand, the Russians' ignorance of living conditions in the West made for slow going. At the mention of even the smallest detail which differed from Soviet practice, the interrogator would frown, and it took a wealth of patience and eloquence to allay his suspicions. Pannwitz felt like an explorer holding forth on the customs of some savage tribe, for the benefit of a stunned and faintly incredulous audience. It would have been amusing, had the lecture not lasted three whole years.

The atmosphere deteriorated as a result of the "M complex" (M for Moscow). It was a basic tenet of Soviet Intelligence that there were no spies in Moscow. If a doubt was ever expressed, if the sacred, inviolable nature of the Russian capital was ever disputed, then the Center would fall prey to the M complex and frantically seek out the culprit. Now, the Director was convinced that the radio-direction finders could not, by themselves, have led the Germans to the Red Orchestra's transmitters with such devastating speed. He reasoned that a traitor must have put them on the track and he did not exclude the possibility of this traitor's being in Moscow. When questioned, Pannwitz dismissed the idea, but was unable to convince his interrogators of his sincerity. One day (it happened to be Pannwitz's wedding anniversary) a colonel working for the Center informed him in a pained voice that he had received written orders to have him beaten if he did not talk. Pannwitz insisted on seeing these orders, and the colonel handed him a document, signed by Abakumov, authorizing an "exceptional procedure." The colonel opened a drawer and took out a rubber truncheon. He showed it to Pannwitz, inviting him to notice that it was of German, not Russian, manufacture. Then the prisoner's trousers were taken down and he was laid flat on his stomach. The colonel began to beat him, ten strokes at a time. A doctor examined Pannwitz after each series of strokes, to see if it was safe to continue. Pannwitz fainted. He was revived, and the beating went on. Finally the doctor said: "You must stop now." The colonel immediately put the truncheon away and, with an expression of extreme distaste, grumbled: "You see, we are a democratic police force. Here in Russia, it's the colonels who have to do the dirty work." Pannwitz concedes that the beating was administered in a correct manner. "All the blows were aimed at my buttocks and thighs. Had they landed anywhere else, they might have caused lasting injuries." That he knew from experience.

That session brought an end to talk of traitors in the Soviet capital. Pannwitz was informed that he was an extremely lucky man, for it was most unusual for a prisoner to escape with his life once the M complex came into play.*

---

* Even today, the Big Chief believes that the Atrébates transmitter was discovered as the result of a denunciation. In his view, it had not been transmitting long enough for the Funkabwehr to locate it by December 13, 1941, whatever the quality of its equipment or the skill of Fortner's self-assured sergeant. After the raid, Trepper learned from his counterespionage group that the house in the Rue des Atrébates had been reported to the police by a Flemish family living in the neighborhood. The family had no inkling that the premises were being used for espionage; they were merely indignant at the number of male callers received by Rita Arnould and Sophie Poznanska. Fortner maintains that the discovery of the "music box" was due entirely to the excellence of the Funkabwehr's technical resources. Yet he himself acknowledges that in 1941 it took about three weeks to pinpoint a transmitter—and the one in the Rue des Atrébates had been operating for less than a week.

Meals in Lubianka remained frugal: heavy black bread, sauerkraut, salt fish. Pannwitz complained to the prison doctor, a woman. "Sir," she retorted, "we have three hundred years' experience of feeding convicts. You need have no worries: none of our prisoners has ever fallen ill through malnutrition." The truth of this sweeping pronouncement was borne in upon him when he found that inmates who had arrived with ulcers or other stomach complaints were continually being cured by the prison diet. He himself remained in very good physical shape.* Prison regulations were strictly observed. He was weighed at regular intervals, and if ever he lost a few pounds his rations were immediately increased.

He never saw Trepper and Kent again. Occasionally their statements were read out to him, but the Center did not stage any confrontations. In Lubianka, movements were so regulated that prisoners associated with the same case never came into contact, or even caught sight of one another. Still, he knew they were there, and he reflected more than once that it really was an amusing paradox that the head of the Kommando and the head of the Red Orchestra should be cooped up in identical cells, in the same Moscow prison, only a few yards apart.

When the questioning was finally over, he was sent to Vorkuta camp, in Siberia, near the Kara Sea. He says: "It was a harsh place, and you can imagine the cold, but the decency of the guards made up for it. The Communist regime is the Communist regime, but one can't overpraise the kindness and humanity of the individual Russian. Hearts of gold! Mind you, that didn't stop them from keeping to the rules. If a guard had been ordered to shoot a prisoner dead, he would have done it without hesitation—but with tears in his eyes. And it was the same at Lubianka." †

The possibility cannot be ruled out that Fortner is trying to protect his informants, even after all these years. It would be quite characteristic of him—and very much to his credit.

* Paradoxically, it was after he went back to Germany that his health suffered a sharp decline. He had great difficulty in readjusting to "good living."

† The reader will probably be surprised by the almost idyllic account Pannwitz gives of his life as a prisoner. His impressions sound disturbingly like advertisements extolling the delights of the "Kara Sea Club" and its "friendly members." Admittedly, life at Vorkuta must have seemed pleasantly mild to a member of the SS, whose colleagues had Treblinka, Auschwitz and Buchenwald to their credit. And people who have served sentences in Soviet camps invariably remark on the humanity displayed by the guards, even while painting a black picture of the general conditions. Concentration camps are infamous institutions, at all times and in all places. But there can be a difference between the

Finally, in 1955, the camp's loudspeakers announced the signing of the "Adenauer Agreement" in Moscow. The old Chancellor had secured the repatriation of all his fellow countrymen. The guards immediately scrambled down from their watchtowers, hurried over to the German prisoners and threw their arms round them. "It's all over!" they cried. "There's nothing to keep us apart any more! We're all brothers again!" Ten years had gone by since Pannwitz had arrived in Moscow, bursting with self-importance, clutching a briefcase full of diplomatic secrets, utterly certain that a golden future lay as his feet. His dreams had not been realized, but at least he had saved his life: that was the main thing. He was overjoyed at the thought of going home and set off in a mood of confidence, blissfully unaware of the lie detectors and other little things awaiting him in the West.

———◆———

On his very first night at Lubianka, the Big Chief had set himself a goal: he was determined to outlive "that gang," if only by one hour. This aim was his salvation. Month followed month, year followed year, in a seemingly endless pattern, but he remained buoyed up by his obsessive urge to outlive "them." It was the rock to which he clung; no wave was powerful enough to dislodge him. All around him, he saw companions in misfortune giving way to despair and refusing their food; he forced himself to eat. He saw some who were literally consumed with the injustice meted out to them; he rejected anger, knowing that it tired a man; he needed his strength to survive. Others escaped the rigors of the present by retreating into the past, losing all notion of time and place; he, on the other hand, ached for the future in every limb. In forty years of adventurous living he had fought and won many battles, but this was the hardest—the battle against his own side.

He was not ill-treated. Only once, as a warning, a prisoner was flung into his cell after undergoing the "exceptional procedure." He also learned from hearsay that Wenzel was being tortured. But, like Pannwitz, he never once saw Kent or Ozols or Wenzel, or any of his old subordinates who might have been in Lubianka without his knowledge.

Among his fellow captives were the aircraft designer, Tupolev,

---

system and the human beings who operate it. In Germany, the system—already far, far worse than in Russia—was further aggravated by the individual atrocities of sadistic guards. The inmates of the Soviet camps were at least spared this final ounce of suffering (for a man finds it easier to be crushed by a system than to be martyrized and humiliated by a fellow human being).

several famous Party leaders and a whole collection of generals, many of whom had served on Marshal Zhukov's staff. It was as though the nation's elite were assembled in Lubianka.

From time to time, Abakumov would send for Trepper and use him as a butt for his cynical humor. When the Soviet spy ring in Canada was uncovered, he showed him some Western press clippings which insinuated that the chief of the Red Orchestra had probably had a hand in the affair. And Abakumov burst out laughing: "Now let's hear you complain! Every police force in the world hunting for you and you're right here in Moscow, nice and snug with us, out of harm's way! Isn't that perfect?"

The only man who sensed what he really felt was the examining magistrate in charge of his case. He was friendly, and kept offering cigarettes, which Trepper always declined. One evening, after a long, taxing interrogation, he said to him: "You've made up your mind to survive us, haven't you? That is what gives you the strength to hold out?" Trepper did not answer. "I have something to tell you," continued the magistrate. "I'm giving up the case. There is no case. I'm convinced you are being held for other reasons which have nothing to do with all this. I don't know what the consequences will be for me, but I refuse to continue. I cannot be party to such a thing." Trepper leaned forward, picked up the package of cigarettes on the desk and took one. The magistrate smiled as he gave him a light. "Now I know you will win," he said. "A smoker capable of refusing a cigarette is a man to reckon with!" *

His wife Luba did not know that he was in Moscow. The Director had notified her that he had "taken a dive," and that she must not expect to see him again. Alone and without resources, she earned a living for herself and her children as a traveling photographer. She would probably have been jailed or sent to Siberia but for the fact that visitors from France—notably Jacques Duclos—never failed to inquire after the Big Chief. They were told he was abroad on a special mission; but the authorities thought it wise to keep his wife and children on hand, in case they were needed for display purposes. Thus she eked out a wretched existence, living in a hovel and trudging from village to village with her old, heavy camera on her back. Meanwhile her husband paced his cell, as prisoners do all over the world.

And this went on for ten years.

---

* After he came out of prison, Trepper happened to meet the magistrate on a Moscow street corner. His decision to give up the case had led to his dismissal, but he had been reinstated after Stalin's death.

On March 5, 1953, Lubianka prison was gripped by a sudden panic. Guards hurried along the corridors. The prisoners were subjected to especially stringent security measures; their exercise period was cancelled. They imagined the Third World War had broken out and were filled with a mounting panic. But it was a false alarm. The prison soon returned to its calm old routine, and in the end the inmates grew weary of wondering what could have caused that sudden bout of fever.

A few months later, the Big Chief was once again escorted along the underground passage to the Ministry of Security. Instead of being taken to Abakumov's office, however, he was shown into a room containing an elderly, mustachioed general who was a strange contrast to the young bureaucrats of the Center; he might have stepped out of some engraving of the October Revolution. He gazed at the prisoner and asked: "How are you?" Trepper was so taken aback that he was unable to reply: it was nearly ten years since anyone had inquired how he was. The general opened a desk drawer, took out a copy of *Pravda* and handed it to the prisoner. It was by no means a recent issue. The front-page story described how a handful of Jewish doctors had tried to kill Stalin. "What do you think of that?" asked the general. Trepper read the story twice before he answered: "It's nonsense," he said. "It just doesn't make sense. If someone wanted to get rid of Stalin, they wouldn't bother with doctors. There are trained experts available." "So you think we dabble in nonsense?" "It has happened," said Trepper. The general nodded reflectively and produced another issue of *Pravda*. "Here," he said, "read this." The doctors had been rehabilitated. Trepper read the story without comment. The old gentleman handed him a third newspaper; this one had an enormous headline announcing Stalin's death on the previous March 5. The Big Chief said nothing. He thought: Stalin is dead, but his gang is still running the army and the police. They're still in command. But the general had a fourth issue of *Pravda* in his drawer. It was dated December, 1953. He handed it to the prisoner, who read the news of Beria's liquidation.

And then the Big Chief smiled. He had won. He had outlasted them.

He smiled and began: "Comrade—" At once he broke off and apologized. Inmates of Lubianka were not allowed to use the word "comrade." If ever they employed it inadvertently, the guards would shout: "Your comrades are roaming the steppes!" (In other words: "Your comrades are the wolves!") The general gestured impatiently and said: "Listen to me: I worked with Dzerzhinsky in the old days.* We of the old Cheka made some mistakes, no doubt, but our intentions were pure. It's more than twenty years since I gave up this job. Today I've been asked to return and clear up a few important cases. I'm starting with you, for I regard your case as one of the most important of all."

After this, Lubianka became "a sort of luxury hotel." Then came a steady stream of releases. In 1955, Trepper was reunited with his wife and children after fifteen years of separation. They were given a fine apartment while awaiting repatriation to Poland. Ozols and Rado were likewise freed; we do not know what became of Wenzel. Even Kent was set at liberty.† But he was merely pardoned, whereas the Big Chief's conviction was reversed by the highest Soviet court as being "wholly without foundation." Trepper was awarded a formal certificate of rehabilitation.

41. "Trains Run Late at Times..."

On October 15, 1965, the weather in Warsaw was beautiful. I walked along Nowy Swiat, the city's main thoroughfare, until I came to Nowogrodska Street. This is a small side street curiously reminiscent of Greenwich Village; add fire escapes to the walls of the buildings, and the illusion would be complete. Beside the door of number 5, the headquarters of the Jewish Cultural Union, were half a dozen name plates inscribed in Polish and Yiddish, or possibly in Hebrew. There were a few people waiting in the entrance hall. I

---

* Founder of the Cheka, following the October Revolution. The Cheka was both an internal police force and an intelligence service.
† Like Pannwitz, he had been transported to Vorkuta. In 1956, Pannwitz read a book entitled *Slave 1E-241* (New York: Devin-Adair, 1956), in which the author, John Noble, himself a former prisoner at Vorkuta, describes the famous revolt which broke out at the camp in July 1953. One of the leaders of the uprising was called Gurevich—Kent's real name. His description and characteristics (he was a pipe smoker, for instance) led Pannwitz to believe, beyond all doubt, that it was Kent. According to Noble, Gurevich showed amazing courage and coolheadedness at the time of the revolt. It has not been possible to verify that this Gurevich was really Kent. All I know is that the latter is today living in Leningrad.

*asked the man at the reception desk if I might see Mr. Leiba Domb.
He asked me to follow him and showed me to one of the offices. My
heart was pounding, much as the Big Chief's heart must have pounded
twenty-two years earlier, when he had reached out to open the door
of Bailly's pharmacy.*

*Manfred Roeder says: "The Americans had a very high opinion
of him. They were itching to get their hands on him. But in 1948 a
department head at the C.I.A. informed me that he had just been
shot by the Russians." I was aware that the report had never been
confirmed. Indeed, nobody knew what had become of the Big Chief,
and everybody—the intelligence services of Britain, the United States,
France and Belgium—would have given a great deal to find out. He
was like the Scarlet Pimpernel—forever being talked about, but never
seen. Occasionally there were rumors that he had turned up here or
there; but although careful checks were made at once, he was never
located, let alone caught. Knowing all this from the outset, I need
hardly say that I had never had the faintest hope of ever coming
face to face with this man to whom I had devoted several thousand
hours of my existence—even assuming that he was still alive. I should
have been vain indeed to imagine I might succeed where such powerful organizations had failed. Luck was on my side, however, and it
proved relatively simple to find Leiba Domb, who—unbeknownst to
the C.I.A., the Abwehr, British Intelligence, the D.S.T. and the
Gestapo—was also Leopold Trepper.*

*Claude Spaak had told me on April 28, 1965: "After the war, I
received no further news of him. But four or five years ago when
I dined with my friend Dr. Chertok, he told me he had picked up
some information about Trepper: it seems he is now living in Warsaw."*

*Dr. Chertok, whose entirely fortuitous role in this story has been
described earlier, is a psychiatrist of worldwide reputation. Five days
after Claude Spaak mentioned him to me, the French newspapers
reported on a paper he had read at the international conference on
medical hypnosis then going on in Paris. I was expecting to see an old
gentleman with a beard, but he turned out to be an energetic figure
with a sparkling eye and a hearty laugh.*

*He told me: "I often think back to my chance involvement in
that venture. After all, it was one of the most frightening experiences
of my life. And I have frequently wondered what became of the
principal character. Well, a few years ago I attended a scientific conference in Warsaw and met up with a few old comrades of the Re-*

sistance. Naturally we started reminiscing. One of them mentioned the Big Chief. I got quite a shock when I realized that the person in question was none other than 'the man at Bourg-la-Reine' (as I had continued to think of him). I was told that he was living in Warsaw in perfect liberty, but rather seriously ill. His real name is Leiba Domb. He is President of the Jewish Cultural Union of Poland."

It took several months to decide what to do. If I wrote and asked for an interview, he might turn me down flat. On the other hand, if I knocked on his door without warning, I might jeopardize the small chance that he might receive me. In the end, I decided to pin my faith on an unannounced visit. Even if he threw me out, I should at least have caught a glimpse of the Big Chief. And that in itself would make my journey worthwhile.

———◆———

He had aged, of course, but I recognized him at once from his expression, which his former colleagues had so often described. Those pale-gray eyes focus on one with extraordinary intensity. The wavy hair, which used to be blond, is now almost white. When I entered the room, he was sitting at a small desk strewn with papers and booklets. He rose and came toward me with outstretched hand. He wore a brown tweedlike jacket, dark flannels and a light-gray pullover. His movements were rather heavy. I saw the well-known posture—the arched back. His very soft, modulated, musical voice was in striking contrast to the inflexible look in his eyes and that experience-scarred face.

I said nervously that I had come from Paris to talk to him about the past. He nodded. His features remained impassive. In his left hand he held a miniature pipe like that of President Tito; a cigarette was wedged in the bowl. The hand was trembling. I attributed this to his heart condition; yet there was no sign of a tremor during any of our subsequent meetings.

"For the past two years," I said, "I've been more or less living with you—living, that is, with the Trepper of twenty years ago."

"Ah, really?"

"I want to write a book about your network."

"Why not, if you have nothing better to do?"

"I take it you've read what has previously been written about you?"

"Very little. I'm just not interested."

"Are you willing to talk to me?"

"Talk? Oh, we can always talk . . ."

"And what will you tell me?"

When he laughs he sheds twenty or thirty years, and his face instantly loses its implacable look. He is just like a student describing a prank.

He roared with laugher and said: "Why, everything you already know, of course!"

———◆———

Trepper had entered Lubianka while the Second World War was still being fought. When he came out, the Cold War was over. The last time he had seen his two children, they had been nine and four years old, respectively; now he was confronted by a man of twenty-three and a youth of eighteen—he had been robbed of their childhood and adolescence. Luba had been treated in the same way as Frau Koppkow, wife of the high-ranking Gestapo official; each was suddenly brought face to face with a husband she had believed lost forever. Indeed, Luba had suffered even more, for Frau Koppkow had simply been told that her husband was dead, whereas Luba had been told that Trepper had deserted her and betrayed his country. The head of the Red Orchestra had been humiliated by being held in the same prison as Pannwitz. He had been deprived of ten years of his existence which no certificate could ever restore. He had known the living death suffered by those who have sacrificed everything, only to be repaid by ingratitude and injustice. Who would wish to change places with him? It is with awed respect that one thinks of Trepper emerging from the Lubianka. He would not want to leave us like this, walking away from prison with his bundle under his arm, a tired, aging victim of Stalinist excesses.

He says: "Stalinism? It was a disease. All one had to do was wait for it to pass." And he says: "The journey from Paris to Warsaw took me eleven years—but trains run late at times." He left Lubianka, as he had entered it, a Communist. And this should be a cause for rejoicing; for when a man discards his convictions in the face of vicissitudes, however appalling they may be, it is a defeat for all of us.

After all, what picture are we to retain of him?

The rebel of Dombrova? The ardent activist in Palestine? Doubtless they are dear to his heart, but those distant precursors of the Big Chief are little more than strangers to us. The young spy serving his

apprenticeship with the Fatômas network? Or the man who thwarted
the great radio game? Even if the historians show that he prevented
the Kremlin from being fatally duped and misled between June,
1943, and the Teheran Conference, this is still not the image of Trepper I should like to preserve. The great radio game consisted of ruses,
guile, duplicity, misrepresentation. He proved more than a match for
his opponents; but I admire him for quite different qualities.

The leader of the Red Orchestra? Yes, it would be tempting to
choose that picture. For it was partly through the Orchestra's achievements that the war was finally won. But such a statement would offend him. He says: "No battles and no wars have ever been won by
an intelligence network. They are won by men dying in battle. The
people who saved Stalingrad were the troops willing to die among
its ruins. They and no one else."

He would probably prefer us to think of him as he is today:
"Leiba Domb - Publisher." Jewish classical literature has been his life-
long passion; and now, after repeated postponements, it has become
his profession. We spent a number of evenings together in Warsaw.
The weather was already turning cool. He would walk along with his
hands in his raincoat pockets, and with a rather faded Basque beret
pulled down to his ears. It was no longer the Big Chief who walked
beside me, it was Leiba Domb, publisher of Jewish classics. And as I
listened to him talking animatedly about texts whose glories were beyond my reach, I would ask myself if this could be the same man who
had once made the Gestapo tremble.

Occasionally a random phrase had the power to carry him back
to the past. ("What a good idea that was, disguising yourself as a
rabbit vendor when you went to the Rue des Atrébates!" "Me? A
rabbit vendor? Who told you that?" "Fortner." "Oh, he would! No,
no. I talked them into believing I had an appointment at a requisitioned garage near the house. It was my Todt Organization pass that
did the trick.") I was seldom so lucky. As a rule, I had to work hard
to conjure up the ghost of the Big Chief. But when I succeeded, he
was exactly as he must have been in the days when he kept his
perilous appointments on the pavements of Paris and Brussels. He
would stop in his tracks, lean back and say softly: "Let us examine
the various hypotheses stemming from this situation . . ." Then
would come a dazzling display of reasoning and speculation, with occasional asides about "those poor wretches" (the Gestapo). When the
moment had passed, the Big Chief would once again surrender the

stage to Leiba Domb, publisher—a man who does not belong to us, but to Luba, to his sons, and to his authors.

The picture I shall retain of him is a recent one. It is dated April 11, 1965, ten years after his rehabilitation, twenty years after his return to Moscow. Delegations from every land had assembled at Auschwitz to celebrate the twentieth anniversary of its liberation. The Polish prime minister was there. Also present was the Soviet general who had opened the gates of Auschwitz in 1945. Sitting before him was Leiba Domb, president of the Jewish community in Poland. He stood up to address the eighty thousand people gathered in front of the platform. Listen to him: he is speaking, on behalf of the Red Orchestra's dead, to the dead of Auschwitz and the living throughout the world; speaking for Adam Kuckhoff of Germany, Pauriol of France, Suzanne Spaak of Belgium, Kruyt of Holland, Danilov of Russia, Mildred Harnack of the United States; speaking for those who had the courage to stay silent and those who, through frailty, talked; speaking for the hanged and the shot and the beheaded. Listen to him: it is fitting for him to speak on their behalf—not because he was their leader, but because he paid the heaviest price of all; they died at the hands of the enemy, but he had to endure the wounds inflicted by his own countrymen. It is fitting for his voice to ring out over Auschwitz, for it was precisely to prevent the unspeakable crime committed there that the members of the Red Orchestra had fought and died; they were of every nationality, every race, every religion, every outlook, but their abhorrence of Nazism had united them during the battle and forever after. It is fitting that a place which had witnessed the slaughter of so many defenseless women and children, of so many Jewish men unable to fight back, should reecho with the voice of the Jew who must surely have dealt the Third Reich its deadliest blows.

A Note on Sources

Among a number of general works dealing with the Second World War and the activities of intelligence organizations, I have drawn more particularly on the books mentioned in the bibliography below. [Translator's note: Where an American or English edition exists, which would be more accessible to the English-speaking reader, that edition has been given here. The editions cited in footnotes to the text, however, are those used by the author.]

I was able to refer to Gestapo and Abwehr reports concerning the Red Orchestra, and to the texts of several judgments delivered by the German military court. I was fortunate enough to have access to certain other documents, but I am not free to say what they were or where they came from. I must ask the reader to bear with me.

I also conducted a number of personal interviews. There is no point in listing these here, for the reader has already had sight of them. But I should like to convey my thanks to all the people whom I besieged so frequently and at such length, and who always received me so kindly, even though my ceaseless questioning must have reopened many painful wounds.

Finally I wish to acknowledge my special gratitude to Constantin Melnik, without whom this book, of which he disapproves in many respects, would never have been written.

Bibliography

Accoce, Pierre, and Quet, Pierre, *The Lucy Ring*. London: W. H. Allen, 1967.
Boehm, Eric, *We Survived*. New Haven: Yale University Press, 1949.
Boldt, Gerhard, *In the Shelter with Hitler*. New York: Citadel Press, 1948.
Boveri, Margaret, *Treason in the Twentieth Century*. London: Macdonald, 1961.
Burgess, Alan, 7 *Men at Daybreak*. London: Evans Brothers, 1960.
Buschmann, Hugo, *"De la Résistance au defaitism,"* Les Temps modernes, 1949.
Carell, Paul, *Hitler's War on Russia*. London: George G. Harrap, 1964.
Chatel, Nicole, and Guérin, Alain, *Camarade Sorge*. Paris: Julliard, 1965.
Crankshaw, Edward, *Gestapo*. New York: Putnam, 1956.
Dallin, David J., *Soviet Espionage*. New Haven: Yale University Press, 1955.

Delarue, Jacques, *History of the Gestapo*. London: Macdonald, 1964.
Depelsenaire, Betty, *Symphonie fraternelle*. Brussels: Éditions Lumen, n.d.
Dourlein, Pieter, *Inside North Pole*. London: William Kimber, 1953.
Dulles, Allen Welsh, *Germany's Underground*. New York: Collier-Macmillan, 1947.
Flicke, W. F., *Spionagegruppe Rote Kapelle*. Verlag Welsermühl Wels, 1957.
Foote, Alexander, *Handbook for Spies*. London: Museum Press, 1964.
Ganier-Raymond, Philippe, *Le Réseau étranglé*. Paris: Fayard, 1967.
Giskes, H. J., *London Calling North Pole*. London: William Kimber, 1953.
Harnack, Axel von, "Arvid und Mildred Harnack," *Die Gegenwart* 31 January, 1947.
Hassell, Ulrich von, *Diaries*. London: Hamish Hamilton, 1948.
Hitler, Adolf, *Hitler's Table Talk, 1941–1944*. London: Weidenfeld & Nicolson, 1953.
Hoettl, Wilhelm, *The Secret Front*. London: Weidenfeld & Nicolson, 1953.
Kleist, Peter, *Entre Hitler et Staline*. Paris: Plon, 1953.
Lang, Serge, and von Schenck, Ernst, *Testament nazi. Mémoires d'Alfred Rosenberg*. Les Trois Collines, 1948.
Lehman, Klaus, *Widerstand im Dritten Reich*. V.V.N. Verlag, 1948.
Leverkuehn, Paul, *German Military Intelligence*. London: Weidenfeld & Nicolson, 1954.
Manvell, Roger, and Fraenkel, Heinrich, *Heinrich Himmler*. London: Heinemann, 1965.
Orlov, Alexander, *Handbook of Intelligence and Guerrilla Warfare*. Ann Arbor: University of Michigan Press, 1963.
Oven, Wilfred von, *Mit Goebbels bis zum Ende*, 2 vols. Buenos Aires: Dürer Verlag, 1949–50.
Payne-Best, S., *The Venlo Incident*. London: Hutchinson, 1950.
Poelchau, Harald, *Die letzten Stunden*. Magdeburg: 1949.
Ponchardier, Dominique, *Les Pavés de l'enfer*. Paris.: Gallimard, 1950.
Reitlinger, Gerald, *The SS*. London: Heinemann, 1956.
Rémy (pseud., i.e. G. L. E. T. Renault-Roulier), *Mémoires d'un agent secret de la France Libre*. France-Empire, 1960.
Ribbentrop, Joachim von, *Memoirs*. London: Weidenfeld & Nicolson, 1954.
Salomon, Ernst von, *The Answers of Ernst von Salomon*. New York: Putnam, 1954.
Schellenberg, Walter, *Memoirs*. London: Andre Deutsch, 1956.
Tillon, Charles, *Les FTP*. Paris: Julliard, 1962.
Trevor-Roper, H. R., *The Last Days of Hitler*. London: Macmillan, 1956.
Weisenborn, Günther, *Der lautlose Aufstand*. Hamburg: 1953.
Wheeler-Bennett, John W., *The Nemesis of Power*. London: Macmillan, 1953.
Zoller, Albert, *Douze ans auprès de Hitler*. Paris: Fayard, 1949.